CW01024495

The Roman Mass

This volume offers a new, synthetic overview of the structure and ritual shape of the Roman Mass from its formative period in late antiquity to its post-Tridentine standardisation. Starting with the Last Supper and the origins of the Eucharist, Uwe Michael Lang constructs a narrative that explores the intense religious, social, and cultural transformations that shaped the Roman Mass. Lang unites classical liturgical history with insights from a variety of other disciplines that have drawn attention to the ritual performance and reception of the mass. He also presents liturgical developments within the broader historical and theological contexts that affected the celebration and experience of the sacramental rite that is still at the heart of Catholic Christianity. Aimed at scholars from a broad swathe of subjects, including religious studies, history, art history, literature and music, Lang's volume serves as a comprehensive history of the Roman Mass over the course of a millennium.

Uwe Michael Lang is an adjunct faculty member at the Institute of Theology and Liberal Arts at St Mary's University, Twickenham and Allen Hall Seminary. A priest of the Oratory of St Philip Neri in London, he is the author of *Turning towards the Lord: Orientation in Liturgical Prayer* (Ignatius Press, 2005) and *Signs of the Holy One: Liturgy, Ritual and Expression of the Sacred* (Ignatius Press, 2015). He is the editor of *Antiphon: A Journal for Liturgical Renewal*.

The Roman Mass

From Early Christian Origins to Tridentine Reform

UWE MICHAEL LANG

St Mary's University, Twickenham

CAMBRIDGE
UNIVERSITY PRESS

Shaftesbury Road, Cambridge CB2 8EA, United Kingdom

One Liberty Plaza, 20th Floor, New York, NY 10006, USA

477 Williamstown Road, Port Melbourne, VIC 3207, Australia

314–321, 3rd Floor, Plot 3, Splendor Forum, Jasola District Centre, New Delhi – 110025, India

103 Penang Road, #05–06/07, Visioncrest Commercial, Singapore 238467

Cambridge University Press is part of Cambridge University Press & Assessment, a department of the University of Cambridge.

We share the University's mission to contribute to society through the pursuit of education, learning and research at the highest international levels of excellence.

www.cambridge.org
Information on this title: www.cambridge.org/9781108832458

DOI: 10.1017/9781108957908

First published 2022

A catalogue record for this publication is available from the British Library

Library of Congress Cataloging-in-Publication data
NAMES: Lang, Uwe Michael, 1972– author.
TITLE: The Roman mass: from early Christian origins to Tridentine reform / Uwe Michael Lang.
DESCRIPTION: First edition. | Cambridge; New York, NY: Cambridge University Press, 2022. | Includes bibliographical references and index.
IDENTIFIERS: LCCN 2021061952 (print) | LCCN 2021061953 (ebook) | ISBN 9781108832458 (hardback) | ISBN 9781108958455 (paperback) | ISBN 9781108957908 (epub)
SUBJECTS: LCSH: Mass–History. | Lord's Supper–Catholic Church–History. | Catholic Church–Liturgy. | BISAC: RELIGION / Christian Church / History
CLASSIFICATION: LCC BX2230.5 .L36 2022 (print) | LCC BX2230.5 (ebook) | DDC 234/.163–dc23/eng/20220316
LC record available at https://lccn.loc.gov/2021061952
LC ebook record available at https://lccn.loc.gov/2021061953

ISBN 978-1-108-83245-8 Hardback

Additional resources for this publication at www.cambridge.org/RomanMass23

Contents

Figures

Acknowledgements

The plan for this work goes back to a liturgy coursebook I wrote for the Maryvale Institute, Birmingham, in 2013. My thoughts progressed especially when I had the welcome opportunity to teach a course on the history of the Eucharist at two summer sessions of the Liturgical Institute at Mundelein, Illinois, in 2014 and 2019. The material on the first eight centuries also developed as I was teaching a module on early Christian worship at Heythrop College, University of London, in 2017. At various conferences and seminars, I had the occasion to test my ideas before sympathetic and critical audiences.

Most of the writing was in fact done during the COVID-19 pandemic in 2020 and 2021. Being given the opportunity to concentrate on this was the proverbial silver lining to this dark period. Without the wealth of online resources that are now available to scholars, I could not have completed this book. Among the libraries and other institutions whose services I gratefully used, special thanks are due to the Bodleian Libraries, Oxford, for their electronic document delivery. I also relied on the efficient assistance of the British Library and of Heythrop Library at the London Jesuit Centre.

There are many debts to friends and colleagues for their support, advice and constructive criticism. In a list that is far from complete, I should like to mention Helmut Hoping, Mgr Stefan Heid, Fr Innocent Smith OP, Hans-Jürgen Feulner, Fr Daniel Cardó, Fr Gabriel Diaz Patri, Fr Sven Conrad FSSP, Nigel Morgan, Tessa Webber, Gabriela Signori, Jörg Bölling, Aden Kumler and Matthias Simperl. I am particularly grateful to those who have helped me in preparing the manuscript for publication, Fr Martin Stamnestrø and especially Br Joseph Rodrigues whose assistance has been invaluable.

Last but not least, I would like to thank the editorial team at Cambridge University Press, especially Beatrice Rehl, for their support and professionalism in seeing this project through.

Abbreviations

CCL   Corpus Christianorum, Series Latina (Turnhout, 1953–)

CCM   Corpus Christianorum, Continuatio Mediaevalis (Turnhout, 1966–)

CSCO   Corpus Scriptorum Christianorum Orientalium (Paris; Louvain, 1903–)

CSEL   Corpus Scriptorum Ecclesiasticorum Latinorum (Vienna, 1866–)

GCS   Die griechischen christlichen Schriftsteller der ersten drei Jahrhunderte (Leipzig; Berlin, 1897–)

MGH   Monumenta Germaniae Historica (Hanover; Berlin; Munich, 1826–)

PG   Patrologiae Cursus Completus, ed. Jacques-Paul Migne, Series Graeca (Paris, 1857–1866)

PL   Patrologiae Cursus Completus, ed. Jacques-Paul Migne, Series Latina, 221 vols. (Paris, 1844–1855)

PTS   Patristische Texte und Studien (Berlin; New York, 1964–)

SC   Sources Chrétiennes (Paris, 1942–)

Introduction

In an age of ever-greater academic specialisation, it may appear outdated for a single author to offer a history of the basic structure and ritual shape of the Roman Mass, which aspires to begin with the Last Supper and the origins of the Eucharist and constructs a narrative through centuries of intense religious, social and cultural transformations to conclude with the aftermath of the Council of Trent. My chosen topic is vast and intricate, and its manifold aspects have been treated in depth by a plethora of scholars in the last few decades. Such a broad subject may, it might be argued, be better considered in a companion or handbook, which would incorporate chapters from a range of contributors with well-defined expertise.

In view of such legitimate questions a reader may raise, it will be important to acknowledge the legacies of earlier scholarship and to state what this book is not. It is not meant to compete with the classical work of Josef Andreas Jungmann, *Missarum sollemnia*, which is still indispensable for its command of primary sources. Nevertheless, Jungmann's narrative of decline from the original and pure idea of *eucharistia*, which is a key assumption in his work, has rightly been criticised.[1]

---

[1] Josef A. Jungmann, *The Mass of the Roman Rite: Its Origins and Development (Missarum Sollemnia)*, trans. Francis A. Brunner, 2 vols. (New York: Benziger, 1951–1955). This translation is based on the first German edition of 1949. In this book, I mostly use the last revised edition *Missarum sollemnia: Eine genetische Erklärung der römischen Messe*, 2 vols., 5th ed. (Wien: Herder, 1962). For a critique of Jungmann's approach, see Eamon Duffy, 'Worship', in *Fields of Faith: Theology and Religious Studies for the Twenty-First Century*, ed. David F. Ford, Ben Quash and Janet Martin Soskice (Cambridge: Cambridge University Press, 2005), 119–134.

While I cannot match the detail of Jungmann's scholarship, I propose to offer a new overview of key developments in the Roman Mass from its formative period in late antiquity to its post-Tridentine standardisation, based on a wide range of specialist contributions. This broader perspective will open up insights that can advance scholarly research and debate.

The topic and character of this work will make it of immediate interest to students of liturgy and theology, both in an academic and in a pastoral setting. When I first conceived the idea for this book, I also had in mind students of history in general and, in particular, students of the history of architecture, art, music and literature, who are in need of a compact guide to the Roman Mass, since it has been such a powerful social and cultural force in Western civilisation. In this regard, I seek to follow in the footsteps of Theodor Klauser's short introduction to Western liturgy, which is still cited as a point of reference in studies from related historical disciplines.[2] Much of Klauser's historical scholarship needs to be updated and its theological hermeneutic calls for a critical examination. Marcel Metzger's outline of liturgical history is useful but short and does not give an adequate account of the Roman Mass in the central and later medieval period.[3] There are reference works that introduce the reader to liturgical sources, above all by Cyrille Vogel but also by Éric Palazzo,[4] and I have made ample use of them, but they do not give us the richer picture of a liturgy celebrated and lived.

Two more recent publications need to be mentioned, since they cover some of the same ground as this book but have a different scope and focus. Firstly, I have drawn on the erudition of Bryan Spinks' historical account of the Eucharistic liturgy in the early Christian period. The medieval development of the Roman Mass is given limited attention in Spinks' book, since he also deals with Eastern liturgical traditions and Protestant communion rites and takes his narrative up to the current period.[5] Secondly, I have profited much from Helmut Hoping's study of

---

[2] Theodor Klauser, *A Short History of the Western Liturgy: An Account and Some Reflections*, trans. John Halliburton, 2nd ed. (Oxford: Oxford University Press, 1979).

[3] Marcel Metzger, *History of the Liturgy: The Major Stages*, trans. Madeleine Beaumont (Collegeville: Liturgical Press, 1997).

[4] Cyrille Vogel, *Medieval Liturgy: An Introduction to the Sources*, rev. and trans. William G. Storey and Niels Krogh Rasmussen (Washington, DC: The Pastoral Press, 1981); Éric Palazzo, *A History of Liturgical Books from the Beginning to the Thirteenth Century*, trans. Madeleine Beaumont (Collegeville: Liturgical Press, 1993).

[5] Bryan D. Spinks, *Do This in Remembrance of Me: The Eucharist from the Early Church to the Present Day*, SCM Studies in Worship and Liturgy (London: SCM Press, 2013).

the history and theology of the Eucharist, which concentrates on the Roman Mass up to the present day.[6] My approach is less specifically theological than Hoping's, and I intend to explore to a greater extent the social and cultural contexts that shaped the celebration of the Eucharist in the Roman tradition.

With this initial apologia, I hope to have convinced the reader that this is a propitious moment for a new, synthetic approach to my chosen topic. The last two decades or so have in fact seen seminal contributions to the study and practice of Christian liturgy. In the Roman Catholic context, the impact of the liturgical writings of Joseph Ratzinger (Pope Benedict XVI) was nothing short of a game-changer.[7] Ratzinger inspired a new generation of scholars to question the prevailing narrative that the Roman liturgy moved from early dynamic development through medieval decline to early modern stagnation. He also encouraged scholars and practitioners alike to reflect critically about twentieth-century liturgical reforms and to articulate their unease about the present state of Catholic worship.

Classical liturgical scholarship in the twentieth century was largely occupied with texts, especially those that have survived in written documents from the late ancient and early medieval periods. Archaeological research furnished additional data for understanding the history of Christian worship, even though the interpretation of its findings is beset with difficulties and hence often contested. More recently, this useful and necessary study has been beneficially supplemented by a renewed focus on the actual celebration or, in terms of social anthropology, the ritual performance of the liturgy, especially the Eucharist. Multidisciplinary approaches to the history of the Mass include musical, artistic, literary, social and, more generally, religious perspectives. In the light of such contributions, I propose to present liturgical development within the broader historical and theological context that shaped the celebration and experience of the sacramental rite that is still at the heart of Catholic Christianity.

In the Roman tradition, the Mass is firmly rooted in the words and actions of Jesus 'on the day before he was betrayed' (*pridie quam*

---

[6] Helmut Hoping, *My Body Given for You: History and Theology of the Eucharist*, trans. Michael J. Miller (San Francisco: Ignatius Press, 2019).

[7] I am thinking especially of Joseph Ratzinger's monograph *The Spirit of the Liturgy* (*Der Geist der Liturgie*) of 2000, which has been re-published as part of *Theology of the Liturgy: The Sacramental Foundation of Christian Existence*, ed. Michael J. Miller, trans. John Saward, et al., Joseph Ratzinger Collected Works 11 (San Francisco: Ignatius Press, 2014).

pateretur), as the Canon of the Mass introduces the words of consecration. Hence, I have found it necessary to begin this book with a critical discussion of the Last Supper tradition and its relation to early Christian Eucharistic practice. These initial two chapters were the most challenging to write and will likely prove the most contentious. Recent scholarship has presented a highly diverse picture of early Christianity, and the origins of the Eucharist have been subjected to radical questioning. On the other hand, it will be seen in Chapter 1 that New Testament exegetes now appear more confident than liturgical historians about the central importance of the Last Supper tradition in shaping the early Christian Eucharist. In the light of this biblical evidence, I find theories untenable that regard the words of institution within Eucharistic prayers as interpolations dating from as late as the fourth century.

Chapter 2 offers a necessarily incomplete discussion of the Eucharist in the first three centuries of the Church. Extant sources are few and far between, and while they offer some answers, they leave us with even more questions. At the same time, I hope to highlight a common thread that runs through them and has its origins in the 'Temple piety' that forms the background to primitive Christianity. There is a broad stream of early Christian tradition that saw in the Eucharist the fulfilment of the prophecy of Malachi 1:11 that a pure sacrifice would be offered to God in every place. Thus, the sacred meal that emerged as the heart of Christian worship came to be celebrated as a memorial in which the sacrifice of Christ became present and its saving effects were communicated to those who partook of it. This sacrificial understanding is reflected in the common elements of the earliest Eucharistic prayers that have come down to us. Thus, Chapter 3 continues the narrative with an examination of the earliest available anaphoras that most likely have pre-Nicene origins, and this is followed by a condensed survey of key developments in Eastern liturgical traditions after the Constantinian settlement, especially the formation of the anaphoras of the Antiochene and of the Alexandrian type.

The wider scope of the first three chapters is, I believe, essential for providing the foundation on which the Latin liturgical tradition builds. In Chapter 4, I analyse essential prayer texts that document the formation of Latin as the liturgical language of the Roman Rite from the fourth century onwards. The substantial Chapter 5 examines the ritual structure and shape of the papal stational Mass, which was to become a pattern for subsequent liturgical development in the West. Between the fifth and the early eighth century, an impressive corpus of books was produced that codified the texts to be used (sacramentaries, lectionaries, antiphoners) and the performance of the rites (*ordines*). The *Ordines Romani* are invaluable and engaging sources for understanding the liturgical shape of the Mass.

This richer flow of liturgical sources must not make us oblivious to the fact that the picture they offer is at best partial and often fragmentary. Victor Leroquais, whose catalogues of liturgical manuscripts are still indispensable for historians, has put this elegantly: 'Liturgists are a bit like archaeologists: they reconstruct the past with debris and their constructions are necessarily affected by the insufficiency, sometimes even the scarcity, of materials.'[8] Moreover, the task of interpreting the sources that have come down to us is far from straightforward, as Helen Gittos reminds us: 'Given the oral nature of the transmission of liturgy in the Middle Ages it is even more important than ever to ask: Why were texts written down?'[9] Documents we now consider epochal for the history of the Roman Mass, such as *Ordo Romanus I*, may have been produced in the first place as an aide-mémoire for practical purposes, or as an instrument to correct real and perceived abuses or to reflect order and authority in the papal curia – or indeed for all of these reasons. As the history of the Western liturgy progresses in the long Middle Ages, we can discern a transition from oral to written culture.

Recent contributions from a variety of historical disciplines offer us a better understanding of the multifaceted process of exchange and transformation of Roman and Franco-German traditions in the Carolingian period, which is the topic of Chapter 6. Gallican patrimony was not simply replaced but was to some degree integrated into the Roman Rite. The chapter shows the slow pace and gradual implementation of the Carolingian reforms, their dependence on local initiative, and their focus on education, first of the clergy and, through them, of the people.

At the beginning of the second millennium, the mixed Roman-Frankish rite of Mass was adopted in the city of Rome itself. Chapter 7 examines the genesis of the *Ordo Missae* as a distinctive set of prayers and rubrics, which would come to exert significant impact upon the ritual shape of the

---

[8] Victor Leroquais, 'L'ordo missae du sacramentaire d'Amiens, B.N. lat. 9432', in *Ephemerides Liturgicae* 41 (1927), 435–445, at 437: 'Les liturgistes sont un peu comme les archéologues: ils reconstruisent le passé avec des débris et leurs constructions se ressentent forcément de l'insuffisance, parfois même de la pénurie des matériaux.'

[9] Helen Gittos, 'Researching the History of Rites', in *Understanding Medieval Liturgy: Essays in Interpretation*, ed. Helen Gittos and Sarah Hamilton (London; New York: Routledge, 2018), 13–37, at 20.

Mass, especially with the spread of what has come to be known as 'private Mass'. This chapter also traces the increasing liturgical standardisation that was envisaged in the Gregorian reform movement and effected by the rapidly expanding Franciscan order. Moreover, the profound veneration of the Eucharist at the time brought new elements to the rite of Mass that proved to be very popular, such as the elevation of the consecrated species, and led to the institution of the feast of Corpus Christi.

Medieval liturgical sources are generally prescriptive and convey an idea of how a rite *should* be celebrated. They do not tell us how the rite actually was carried out on specific occasions. While they claim to have normative force, this does not necessarily mean that their instructions were always followed to the letter. Moreover, in most historical periods, liturgical books are concerned with those who officiated, and this means above all clerics and monks. There is a difference between the rite as performed by liturgical actors and the rite as experienced by the people attending.

The increasing level of literacy in the high Middle Ages initiated a flourishing of historical, pastoral and devotional literature, not only for the clergy but also for the educated laity, which offer us glimpses of ordinary Catholics at worship beyond the prescriptive liturgical sources. These resources will assist us in taking a fresh look at later medieval developments in Chapter 8. In standard textbooks, the period is often seen as marked by decline and corruption. By taking into account various aspects of liturgical life at the time, I intend to show that the overall picture is more complex and that elements of decay and vitality existed side by side. Chapter 9 concludes my narrative with an assessment of the liturgical reforms that followed the Council of Trent (1545–1563). With the *Missale Romanum* of 1570, a process of codification and standardisation that had been underway for centuries reached its culmination. The four hundred years that followed are rightly called 'Tridentine', since they brought only peripheral developments in the structure and shape of the Roman Mass.

The Last Supper

For the Christian tradition, the historical connection and continuity of the Eucharist with the Last Supper is essential. As Joseph Ratzinger (Benedict XVI) wrote: 'If Jesus did *not* give his disciples bread and wine as his body and blood, then the church's eucharistic celebration is empty – a pious fiction and not a reality at the foundation of communion with God and among men.'[1] As theologian and pope, Ratzinger made this bold statement fully aware of the strong tendency in recent scholarship to emphasise the diversity of primitive Christianity and to question received positions on the origins of the Eucharist. In this chapter, I propose to approach this vast and challenging field of research by selecting key contributions from New Testament scholars that will help us to reassess the central importance of the Last Supper tradition. This will include a consideration of the date and character of the event itself and of the words of institution and their possible earliest liturgical use.

THE SEARCH FOR EUCHARISTIC ORIGINS

A conventional history of the Eucharist would begin with the Last Supper and its foundational and formative role in early liturgical practice. Thus, Josef Andreas Jungmann asserted with confidence in his classical work on the history of the Roman Rite of Mass: 'The first Holy Mass was said on

---

[1] Joseph Ratzinger – Benedict XVI, *Jesus of Nazareth. Part Two: Holy Week. From the Entrance into Jerusalem to the Resurrection*, trans. Philip J. Whitmore (San Francisco: Ignatius Press, 2011), 104.

"the same night in which he was betrayed" (1. Cor. 11:23).'[2] Contemporary historians are averse to constructing grand narratives, but even a critical scholar, such as Bryan Spinks, is positive about the formative impact of the Last Supper tradition upon the Christian liturgy, at least from the fourth century onwards:

> What does seem safe to say is that by the fourth century there emerged from the different geographical areas of Christianity, rites which, by osmosis and because of the emergence of a canon of Scripture, used bread and wine mixed with water, and related these in prayer in some way or other to a sacrifice fulfilled by Jesus in his death, and linking the bread and wine to his body and blood.[3]

When it comes to the first three centuries, however, liturgical scholars have become increasingly sceptical as to what extent early Christian practice was shaped by the Last Supper tradition. Such doubts are strengthened by the observation that not all the community gatherings often described as Eucharistic contained a remembrance (*anamnesis*) of the Passion and death of Jesus, nor did they all explicitly evoke the Last Supper through repetition of the words of institution or through the use of bread and wine mixed with water.

The question of early liturgical development is inseparable from the question of the historical authenticity of the biblical testimony. Applying the exegetical methods of form criticism and redaction criticism, Rudolf Bultmann considered the Last Supper narrative in Mark (with Matthew and Luke dependent on it) to be not a historically reliable memory but rather an etiological cult legend. While Jesus did hold a farewell meal with his disciples before his death, what is recorded in the Synoptic Gospels should be considered, in Bultmann's view, a creation of early Christian communities seeking to explain and legitimise their practice of celebrating the Lord's Supper, which had been formed under the impact of Hellenistic meal practice and to which Paul (1 Cor 11) is the oldest witness.[4] Among biblical scholars today, Bultmann's radical scepticism is represented prominently by John D. Crossan and the 'Jesus Seminar'.[5]

---

[2] Josef A. Jungmann, *The Mass of the Roman Rite: Its Origins and Development (Missarum Sollemnia)*, trans. Francis A. Brunner, 2 vols. (New York: Benziger, 1951–1955), vol. I, 7.

[3] Bryan D. Spinks, *Do This in Remembrance of Me: The Eucharist from the Early Church to the Present Day*, SCM Studies in Worship and Liturgy (London: SCM Press, 2013), 2.

[4] See Rudolf Bultmann, *Theology of the New Testament*, trans. Kendrick Grobel, 2 vols. (New York: Scribner, 1951–1955), 144–152.

[5] See John D. Crossan, *The Historical Jesus: The Life of a Mediterranean Jewish Peasant* (San Francisco: Harper, 1991), 360–367.

In his influential study entitled *Mass and the Lord's Supper*, Hans Lietzmann argued for the origins of the Eucharist in a Hellenistic-Jewish context. He identified two types of sacred meal: first, the 'breaking of the bread' (see Acts 2:46) in Jerusalem, which was a post-Easter continuation of the table-fellowship begun by Jesus among his disciples during his public ministry, now oriented in joyful expectation of his Second Coming; secondly, the 'Lord's Supper' in remembrance of the death of the Christ, as attested in 1 Corinthians 11, developed in the Hellenists' community of Antioch and shaped by the Apostle Paul. The subsequent history of the Eucharistic liturgy, according to Lietzmann, shows the reception and adaptation of these two types of sacred meals.[6]

Constructing a similar hypothesis, the leading liturgical scholar Paul Bradshaw sees the Eucharist as a sacramental celebration emerging at a later stage (even as late as the third century) from the common meal practice of Christians, in which they would experience an eschatological anticipation of the kingdom in remembering the words and deeds of Jesus.[7] According to Bradshaw, it was Paul who associated the sayings of Jesus about being fed with his body and his blood – as well as their sacrificial interpretation – with the Last Supper. The words of institution as recorded in the Synoptic Gospels represent a tradition superimposed on the original account of a simple meal.[8] This would have been a source of consolation for those who suffered persecution, above all in Rome. It was in that city that the author of Mark would have grafted these words onto an already existing narrative of the Last Supper.

On the other side, exegetes indebted to the Scandinavian school of Harald Riesenfeld and Birger Gerhardsson have argued for the essential

---

[6] Hans Lietzmann, *Messe und Herrenmahl: Eine Studie zur Geschichte der Liturgie*, Arbeiten zur Kirchengeschichte 8 (Bonn: A. Marcus und E. Weber, 1926). In the Anglophone world, Lietzmann's study has received considerable attention since the publication of the English version: *Mass and the Lord's Supper: A Study in the History of the Liturgy*, trans. Dorothea H. G. Reeve (Leiden: Brill, 1979). See also Reinhard Meßner, 'Grundlinien der Entwicklung des eucharistischen Gebets in der frühen Kirche', in *Prex eucharistica. Volumen III: Studia. Pars prima: Ecclesia antiqua et occidentalis*, ed. Albert Gerhards, Heinzgerd Brakmann and Martin Klöckener, Spicilegium Friburgense 42 (Fribourg: Academic Press, 2005), 3–41.

[7] See Paul F. Bradshaw, 'Did Jesus Institute the Eucharist at the Last Supper?', in *Issues in Eucharistic Praying in East and West: Essays in Liturgical and Theological Analysis*, ed. Maxwell E. Johnson (Collegeville: Liturgical Press, 2010), 1–19. See also Paul F. Bradshaw and Maxwell E. Johnson, *The Eucharistic Liturgies: Their Evolution and Interpretation*, Alcuin Club Collection 87 (London: SPCK, 2012), 1–24.

[8] See Paul F. Bradshaw, *Reconstructing Early Christian Worship* (Collegeville: Liturgical Press, 2009), 3–19.

reliability of the canonical Gospels as sources for the historical Jesus. Following rabbinic models, the transmission of religious teachings was guided by well-established methods and techniques, above all memorisation.[9] According to Riesenfeld, one of the privileged loci wherein the Christ-tradition was handed on was its recitation and proclamation in worship.[10] After strong initial criticism, there now seems to be a growing trend in biblical scholarship towards recognising the validity of the approach of the Scandinavian school, though not of all its claims.[11] Among New Testament exegetes, arguments for the substantial historicity of the Last Supper tradition are viewed more favourably, despite considerable differences as to what exactly this historical nucleus consists of.[12]

In recent decades, both New Testament exegetes and historians of early Christian liturgy have sought to understand the Last Supper in the wider context of the meals Jesus held during his public ministry, which are set against the backdrop of contemporary Jewish meal practice as well as the broader framework of table customs in Greco-Roman culture. Thus, Gordon Jeanes claims: 'If we are to make sense of what the Eucharist is, we need to start with those meals recounted in the New Testament.'[13] The daily meals of Jesus with 'tax collectors and sinners' (Mt 11:19; Lk 7:34)

---

[9] In his preface to the republication of two works that originated in the 1960s, Gerhardsson enumerates some of these principles: 'memorization; the principle "first learn, then understand"; terseness; abridgment of material into short, pregnant texts; poetic artifices; rhythm; cantillation; mnemonic devices; use of written notes; diligent repetition'; Birger Gerhardsson, *Memory & Manuscript: Oral Tradition and Written Transmission in Rabbinic Judaism and Early Christianity, with Tradition & Transmission in Early Christianity*, with a Foreword by Jacob Neusner, The Biblical Resource Series (Grand Rapids: Eerdmans; Livonia: Dove Booksellers, 1998), xii.

[10] See Harald Riesenfeld, 'The Gospel Tradition and Its Beginnings', in *The Gospels Reconsidered: A Selection of Papers Read at the International Congress on the Four Gospels in 1957* (Oxford: Blackwell, 1960), 131–153; also in Harald Riesenfeld, *The Gospels Tradition: Essays* (Oxford: Blackwell, 1970), 1–30.

[11] See the discussion of Eric Eve, *Behind the Gospels: Understanding the Oral Tradition* (London: SPCK, 2013), 33–46.

[12] Above all, Brant Pitre, *Jesus and the Last Supper* (Grand Rapids: Eerdmans, 2015); also Craig Blomberg, *Contagious Holiness: Jesus' Meals with Sinners* (Downer's Grove: InterVarsity Press, 2005); and Richard Bauckham, *Jesus and the Eyewitnesses: The Gospels as Eyewitness Testimony*, 2nd ed. (Grand Rapids: Eerdmans, 2017).

[13] Gordon Jeanes, 'Eucharist', in *The Study of Liturgy and Worship: An Alcuin Guide*, ed. Juliette Day and Benjamin Gordon-Taylor (Collegeville: Liturgical Press, 2013), 135. See also *The Eucharist – Its Origins and Contexts: Sacred Meal, Communal Meal, Table Fellowship in Late Antiquity, Early Judaism, and Early Christianity. Vol. III: Near Eastern and Graeco-Roman Traditions, Archaeology*, ed. David Hellholm and Dieter Sänger, Wissenschaftliche Untersuchungen zum Neuen Testament 376 (Tübingen: Mohr Siebeck, 2017); *T&T Clark Handbook to Early Christian Meals in the Greco-Roman*

serve as images of the coming kingdom of God (see, for instance, Mk 2:16; Mt 22:1–14), and they are often linked with significant words (parables) and deeds (miracles). Customary Jewish concerns, such as ritual purity and ceremonial observances, are deliberately disregarded and challenged. Jesus' feeding miracles are presented as symbolic anticipations of the messianic banquet in the age to come (Mt 14:13–21; 15:33–39; Mk 6:31–44; 8:1–9; Lk 9:10–17; Jn 6:5–15). Notably, the Risen Christ is recognised by his disciples in connection with eating, and he makes himself known in the 'breaking of the bread' (Lk 24:13–35; Jn 21:1–14).[14] Eugene LaVerdiere identifies in the Gospel of Luke a substructure of ten meal narratives, with the Last Supper standing at a critical juncture: it marks the climax of the earthly Jesus' meal practice and at the same time anticipates the table fellowship of the risen Christ.[15]

Philippe Rouillard[16] has observed that the general human dimension of meals, with its aspects of hunger, nourishment, life and order, provide a hermeneutical key for the Eucharist. Meals are human activities that are held not simply for the purpose of feeding but which are expressions of fellowship and are experienced as pleasing. Most religions in fact have a kind of sacred meal as part of their ritual. The Old and the New Testament conform to this pattern, as they are filled with meal symbolism.

While these perspectives of more recent scholarship enrich our understanding of the early Eucharist, they tend to underestimate the singular character of the Last Supper, which is attested both in the Synoptics and in Paul, and hence would seem to be intrinsically linked with the core of the New Testament canon emerging in the second century. The Last Supper is presented as unique in that it is in immediate proximity to the Passion and death of Jesus. N. T. Wright sees in the Last Supper 'the central symbolic action which provides the key of Jesus' implicit story about his own death'.[17] Unlike other meals in the public ministry of the Lord, this one is limited to the Twelve, his closest circle of disciples. The

World, ed. Soham Al-Suadi and Peter-Ben Smit (London; New York: Bloomsbury T&T Clark, 2019).

[14] See Jeanes, 'Eucharist', 135–136.

[15] See Eugene LaVerdiere, *Dining in the Kingdom of God: The Origin of the Eucharist according to Luke* (Chicago: Liturgical Training Publications, 1994).

[16] Philippe Rouillard, 'From Human Meal to Christian Eucharist', in *Living Bread, Saving Cup: Readings on the Eucharist*, ed. R. Kevin Seasoltz (Collegeville: Liturgical Press, 1987), 126–157.

[17] N. T. Wright, *Jesus and the Victory of God* (Minneapolis: Fortress Press, 1996), 554.

setting is not that of open table-fellowship but a private room that would have been provided by a wealthy patron. While the words and actions of Jesus are embedded in this meal, they stand out and transform it into a new reality.

Any historical argument in favour of Jesus' institution of the Eucharist as a sacred meal in remembrance of his sacrificial death needs to account for the evident differences in the four narratives of institution in the New Testament (Mt 26:26–29; Mk 14:22–25; Lk 22:14–20; 1 Cor 11:23–26) and for the absence of the narrative in the Gospel of John. In particular, such an investigation needs to include the questions: when did the Last Supper take place, what character did the meal have, what were the words used by Jesus over the bread and wine and how are they to be interpreted?

THE DATE AND CHARACTER OF THE LAST SUPPER

The Synoptic Gospels seem to present a clear picture: Jesus celebrated the Last Supper with his disciples on the first day of unleavened bread, in the evening (Mt 26:17, 20; Mk 14:12, 17; Lk 22:7, 14). Since Jews reckoned the day from sunset to sunset, this evening meal was held at the start of the fourteenth day of the Jewish month of Nisan, the date of the Passover feast, after the lambs had been sacrificed in the Temple in the afternoon. This day would be a Thursday, with the crucifixion taking place on Friday, 'the day before the sabbath' (Mk 15:42; also Mt 27:62; Lk 23:54). The Synoptic narratives present the Last Supper as a Passover meal, most clearly perhaps Luke, where Christ tells his disciples, 'I have earnestly desired to eat this Passover with you before I suffer' (Lk 22:15).[18]

At the same time, typical elements of the Passover, above all the lamb, but also the unleavened bread and the bitter herbs, are not mentioned in the description of the meal itself in the Synoptic Gospels. Only bread and wine are mentioned, which were characteristic of every kind of festive Jewish meal at the time. Another relevant detail may be the fact that the Greek word for bread used in the Synoptic accounts (ἄρτος) usually indicates (ordinary) leavened bread and not the unleavened bread required for the Passover.[19]

---

[18] Unless otherwise noted, biblical citations are taken from *Revised Standard Version Catholic Bible* (New York: Oxford University Press, 2006).

[19] However, according to some Jewish scholars, before the destruction of the Temple (and hence the rabbinic attempt to systematise religious observances) the Passover meal would

The Fourth Gospel presents a different chronology: while it agrees regarding the days of the week, it clearly implies that Jesus was crucified as the day of preparation for the Passover (13th Nisan) was drawing to its close (Jn 18:28; 39; 19:14). Significantly, Jesus dies on the cross at the time when the lambs were slaughtered for the celebration of the Passover. At the time, this could be done only in the Temple. Since outside Jerusalem the Passover had to be celebrated without a lamb, thousands of Jews went on pilgrimage to the holy city for the high feast. According to this timeline, therefore, the Last Supper was held on the evening before Passover, and it could not have been a Passover meal. Still, it would have been in close proximity to it, as explicitly stated in John 13:1, and thus takes on many of the marks and meanings of the Passover. Unlike the Synoptics, John does not describe the meal itself but focusses on Jesus washing the feet of his disciples (13:2–11).

How can the apparent discrepancy between the Synoptic Gospels and the Fourth Gospel be reconciled?[20] There have been theories about the use of two different calendars, notably by Annie Jaubert, who argued that John followed the official lunar calendar of the Jerusalem Temple, whereas the Synoptics adopted a solar calendar attested in the *Book of*

---

mainly have consisted in eating the sacrificed roast lamb and may not necessarily have included the eating of unleavened bread (*matzah*), bitter herbs or perhaps even the drinking of wine. See Joshua Kulp, 'The Origins of the Seder and Haggadah', in *Currents in Biblical Research* 4 (2005), 109–134, esp. 112–113.

[20] The question is not a new one. The Alexandrian philosopher and theologian John Philoponus (d. c. 575) relies on the Johannine chronology to support his argument that the Last Supper was not a Passover meal in his treatise *De paschate*: ed. Karl Walter, Commentationes philologae Ienenses 6,2 (Leipzig: Teubner, 1899), 197–229. Philoponus seems intent on refuting the use of unleavened bread in the Eucharist, for which there is some evidence from the Christian East in the late sixth century. See Jean Michel Hanssens, *Institutiones liturgicae de ritibus orientalibus, Tomus II: De missa rituum orientalium, Pars prima* (Rome: Apud Aedes Pont. Universitatis Gregorianae, 1930), 133–141. In the Armenian church, this practice is confirmed by the synod of Dvin in 719 and may go back to the seventh century but is doubtful for the sixth century, *pace* Leslie B. MacCoull, 'John Philoponus, *On the Pasch* (CPG 7267): The Egyptian Eucharist and the Armenian Connection', *Jahrbuch der Österreichischen Byzantistik* 49 (1999) 1–12 (reprinted in Leslie B. MacCoull, *Documenting Christianity in Egypt: Sixth to Fourteenth Centuries*, Variorum Collected Studies 981 [Farnham: Ashgate, 2011], no. XII). St Thomas Aquinas (1225–1274) seeks to show that John agrees with the Synoptics, with the aim of defending the Latin practice of unleavened bread against criticism from the Greeks; see John P. Joy, 'Ratzinger and Aquinas on the Dating of the Last Supper: In Defense of the Synoptic Chronology', in *New Blackfriars* 94 (2013), 324–339.

Jubilees (mid-second century BC) and in some of the Dead Sea Scrolls.[21] In this view, the Last Supper would have been an anticipated Passover meal held on a Tuesday evening.[22] While Jaubert's theory continues to attract considerable scholarly interest, there are strong arguments against it, especially the improbability that Jesus would have concrete links with the Qumran community, let alone follow their calendar. Moreover, placing the Last Supper on the Tuesday before the crucifixion on Friday cannot be reconciled with either the Synoptic or the Johannine chronology of Jesus' Passion.[23]

Joachim Jeremias presented the case for the Last Supper as a Passover meal in a widely received study.[24] More recently, Martin Hengel and Anna Maria Schwemer have cogently resumed this argument. They observe that a night meal, as described by the Synoptics, was not normal among the common people at the time and would therefore suggest an extraordinary occasion. Moreover, the fact that the participants were reclining on couches marks the meal as a truly festive banquet. The meal itself had a ritual structure, as shown by the formal words spoken as its constituent parts. At the conclusion of the meal, the Hallel psalms (Ps 113–118) were chanted, which were presumably part of the Passover liturgy by then.[25]

Any reading of the Last Supper as a Passover meal needs to recognise that our knowledge about Jewish meal practice at the time of Jesus is more limited than often assumed. Jewish sources detailing the observance of the Passover and other ritual celebrations are considerably later than the New Testament material and cannot simply be used as such to shed light on the Last Supper (or the earliest Christian Eucharist, for that matter). In particular, the Haggadah (literally, 'telling') that prescribes

[21] Annie Jaubert, *The Date of the Last Supper*, trans. Isaac Rafferty (New York: Alba House, 1965); translation of *La date de la Cène: Calendrier biblique et liturgie chrétienne*, Études bibliques 27 (Paris: Gabalda, 1957).

[22] This particular dating is supported by the unique testimony of the third/fourth-century Syriac *Didascalia apostolorum*; see Jaubert, *The Date of the Last Supper*, 69–76.

[23] See the detailed discussions in John R. Meier, *A Marginal Jew: Rethinking the Historical Jesus. Volume One: The Roots of the Problem and the Person*, The Anchor Bible Reference Library (New York: Doubleday, 1991), 390–395; and Pitre, *Jesus and the Last Supper*, 260–280.

[24] Joachim Jeremias, *The Eucharistic Words of Jesus*, trans. Norman Perrin, The New Testament Library (London: SCM Press, 1966); translation of *Die Abendmahlsworte Jesu*, 3rd ed. (Göttingen: Vandenhoeck & Ruprecht, 1964).

[25] Martin Hengel and Anna Maria Schwemer, *Jesus und das Judentum*, Geschichte des frühen Christentums 1 (Tübingen: Mohr Siebeck, 2007), 583–584.

the Passover Seder, as contained in the Mishnah, the systematic collection of rabbinic rulings about religious practices, stems from the late second century and cannot simply be projected into the time of Jesus. The destruction of the Second Temple had a definitive impact on the celebration of the Passover, since it made the sacrificial offering of lambs impossible and shifted the emphasis entirely on the meal. Moreover, as the Israeli scholar Israel Jacob Yuval has argued, the codification of Passover Seder happened under the impression of the early Christian Eucharist and in conscious opposition to it.[26]

From the historian's perspective, perhaps the strongest arguments against the Passover character of the Last Supper are the difficulties this would create for the chronology and sequence of the events of Christ's Passion. If the Last Supper really took place as a Seder meal in the evening that marked the beginning of 14th Nisan, this would mean that in the night and in the early morning of the Passover feast, Jesus was arrested for a capital crime, formally tried with witnesses before the Sanhedrin (specially convened for this case) and sentenced and handed over to the Roman authorities to be executed on the same day.[27] All this would go against the stated intention of the high priests and scribes who were looking for a possibility to have Jesus executed, but 'not during the feast' (Mt 26:5; Mk 14:2) to avoid a tumult among the people.

There are further problems with the Synoptic chronology, which have been discussed at length by biblical exegetes. To name just two examples: first, the custom of releasing a prisoner at the feast (Mt 27:15; Mk 15:6; Jn 18:39) was precisely to enable him to take part in the Passover meal in the evening. Second, Simon of Cyrene reportedly came from the field (Mt 27:32; Mk 15:21). This would imply that he had previously worked, which would be prohibited on the solemn feast. Moreover, those attending the Passover in Jerusalem were not allowed to leave or enter the city.

These considerations speak in favour of the Johannine chronology, which places the crucifixion of Jesus on the day of preparation for the Passover. There is no lack of scholarly proposals to reconcile the

---

[26] See Israel Jacob Yuval, *Two Nations in Your Womb: Perceptions of Jews and Christians in Late Antiquity and the Middle Ages*, trans. Barbara Harshav and Jonathan Chipman (Berkeley: University of California Press, 2006), 31–91; and 'Easter and Passover As Early Jewish-Christian Dialogue', in *Passover and Easter: Origin and History to Modern Times*, ed. Paul F. Bradshaw and Lawrence A. Hoffman (Notre Dame: University of Notre Dame Press, 2000), 98–124.
[27] See Meier, *A Marginal Jew*, 395–396.

discrepancy between the Synoptics and John. Challenging a wide consensus of contemporary New Testament exegetes, Brant Pitre, by drawing on the semantic range of the term 'Passover', makes a strong case that the Gospel of John *does* present the Last Supper as a Passover meal.[28] There is also renewed interest in the question of whether the apparent discrepancy would reflect calendrical variations in the complex reality of first-century Judaism, and Jaubert's theory has been restated and refined.[29]

In favour of the Johannine chronology, John P. Meier offers the intriguing proposal that,

> if Mark's Passion Narrative is shorn of two passages that probably come from either a secondary level of the tradition or from Mark's own redactional activity, the remaining Passion Narrative contains no clear indication that the Last Supper was a Passover meal or that Jesus died on Passover Day.[30]

Meier refers here to the half verse 14:1a, which introduces the Markan Passion Narrative: 'Now it was the Passover and [the feast] of the unleavened bread after two days.' This is a vague indication, which could imply lack of familiarity with Jewish customs, and its reading depends on whether or not 'after two days' supposes inclusive counting. The time frame becomes clearer when connected with the narrative of the preparation of the Last Supper, especially v. 12, which gives a clear date: 'And on the first day of the unleavened bread, when they were accustomed to sacrifice the Passover lamb, his disciples say to him.'[31] It could be argued that only Mark 14:12–16 presents the Last Supper unambiguously as a Passover meal. Some exegetes consider these verses a stratum of tradition different to the rest of the Markan Passion narrative and possibly a later addition.[32]

---

[28] Pitre, *Jesus and the Last Supper*, 331–373; see also the thorough but inconclusive study by Barry D. Smith, 'The Chronology of the Last Supper', in *Westminster Theological Journal* 53 (1991), 29–45.

[29] See Stéphane Saulnier, *Calendrical Variations in Second Temple Judaism: New Perspectives on the 'Date of the Last Supper' Debate*, Supplements to the Journal for the Study of Judaism 159 (Leiden: Brill, 2012). The scientist Colin J. Humphreys, *The Mystery of the Last Supper: Reconstructing the Final Days of Jesus* (Cambridge: Cambridge University Press, 2011), drawing on astronomical research, argues for the use of a pre-exilic solar calendar along the official Jewish lunar calendar to explain the discrepancies between the Synoptics and John. He places the Last Supper on the Wednesday night before the crucifixion on Friday.

[30] Meier, *A Marginal Jew*, 396.

[31] The translation of Mk 14:1 and 12 is by Meier, *A Marginal Jew*, 396–397.

[32] See Jeremias, *Eucharistic Words*, 92–96; and Meier, *A Marginal Jew*, 425–426, n. 94, with further references.

Even if the Last Supper was not a Passover meal, it was not simply an ordinary meal in continuity with the table-fellowship of Jesus' public ministry. Meier proposes the following scenario:

sensing or suspecting that his enemies were closing in for an imminent, final attack, and therefore taking into account that he might not be able to celebrate the coming Passover meal with his disciples, Jesus instead arranged a solemn farewell meal with his inner circle of disciples just before Passover. Wanting privacy, and having his days taken up with teaching in the Jerusalem temple, Jesus chose to have an evening meal with his closest followers in the house of some affluent Jerusalem supporter on a Thursday around sunset . . . . The supper, though not a Passover meal and not celebrated as a substitute Passover meal, was nevertheless anything but an ordinary meal. With Jesus bidding farewell to his closest disciples as he prepared himself for the possibility of an imminent and violent death, the tone of the meal would naturally be both solemn and religious, accompanied by all the formalities (reclining at table, drinking wine, singing hymns etc.) that Jeremias uses to prove the Passover nature of the supper.[33]

What would have been the 'formalities', or ritual elements, of such a 'solemn and religious' meal? While attempts to postulate Jewish antecedents remain somewhat conjectural, near-contemporary sources, such as the Qumran documents or *Joseph and Aseneth*, an apocryphal expansion on the Joseph narrative in Genesis, variously dated between the first century BC and the second century AD, give a broad context that can to some degree illuminate the Last Supper.[34] In *Joseph and Aseneth*, there are several places where a meal is described with the use of bread and of a cup of wine. These passages speak of 'blessed bread of life' or 'bread of life' and of a 'cup of blessing' or 'blessed cup of immortality'. While there is little to suggest that there is any mutual influence, there are parallels

---

[33] Meier, *A Marginal Jew*, 399.
[34] See Spinks, *Do This in Remembrance of Me*, 5–11. As for the wider Hellenistic cultural setting, Spinks concludes his brief overview (ibid., 2–5) with the observation that 'it is not what the New Testament meals might have in common with Greco-Roman Symposia that are of particular importance, but rather, their *differences* and their *theological significance*' (ibid., 5; italics in the original). See also the general assessment of Walter Burkert, *Klassisches Altertum und antikes Christentum. Probleme einer übergreifenden Religionswissenschaft*, Hans-Lietzmann-Vorlesungen 1 (Berlin: Walter de Gruyter, 1996), 43: 'Für die konkrete Situation der frühen Kaiserzeit wird man das Jüdische und das darauf aufbauende Christliche in seiner Besonderheit, in seiner Originalität anerkennen müssen.' On *Joseph and Aseneth*, see Christoph Burchard, 'The Importance of Joseph and Aseneth for the Study of the New Testament: A General Survey and a Fresh Look at the Last Supper', in *New Testament Studies* 33 (1987), 102–134; and John C. O'Neill, 'Bread and Wine', in *Scottish Journal of Theology* 48 (1995), 169–184.

with the 'bread of life' of John 6:48 and with the 'cup of blessing' of
1 Corinthians 10:16.[35] In the words of Christoph Burchard, the key idea
of this narrative is that benedictions 'will somehow imbue food, drink,
and ointment with the spirit of life .... The spirit will in turn permeate a
person as he or she consumes blessed food and drink'.[36] There is thus a
sacramental quality to the ordinary elements of human subsistence when
blessings are pronounced over them before they are taken.

At any formal Jewish meal, such as the weekly supper on the eve of the
Sabbath, nothing was to be eaten without God having first being thanked
for it. The Mishnah contains short blessings for use with various types of
food, the *berakot*.[37] As already indicated, the systematic collection of
ritual practices in the Mishnah, dating from the end of the second century,
cannot simply be projected back into the time of Jesus. However, it can be
safely assumed that at the beginning of a festive meal, such as the Last
Supper, some form of blessing (*berakah*) would be used. This practice is
attested by the Qumran community and in the Jewish author Josephus.[38]

In the fully-fledged rabbinic tradition, the meal is concluded by a
standard grace, the *birkat-ha-mazon*. According to the Mishnah, this
consisted of three different blessings.[39] While the Mishnah does not
specify the words of this tripartite blessing, the Hebrew *Book of
Jubilees* has Abraham offer this type of grace, firstly blessing God for
the creation of heaven and earth and for the gift of food and drink,
secondly giving thanks for his own longevity and thirdly asking for
God's mercy and peace.[40] It is often argued that a type of *birkat ha-
mazon* was used at the Last Supper and would have followed this pattern:
firstly, blessing God the Creator for the food he provides; secondly, giving
thanks to God the giver of the land and of the covenant and thirdly,
praying for his eschatological intervention in favour of the people of the
covenant.[41] To be sure, some form of this blessing at the end of the meal
was likely to have been established in Palestinian Judaism at the time of

---

[35] Some scholars have argued for a Christian background to *Joseph and Aseneth*; see the
discussion by Angela Standhartinger, 'Meals in *Joseph and Aseneth*', in *T&T Clark
Handbook to Early Christian Meals in the Greco-Roman World*, 211–224.
[36] Burchard, 'The Importance of Joseph and Aseneth for the Study of the New
Testament', 117.
[37] Mishnah, Tractate *Berakot* 6.1–3.
[38] See Bradshaw and Johnson, *The Eucharistic Liturgies*, 5–6.
[39] Mishnah, Tractate *Berakot* 6.8.   [40] Jubilees 22:6–9.
[41] See Louis Finkelstein, 'The Birkat-Ha-Mazon', in *Jewish Quarterly Review* 19 (1928/29),
211–262.

Jesus, but it is unlikely that these prayers would already have reached a fixed form, as in the later rabbinic tradition.[42] For these reasons, attempts to derive early Eucharistic prayers from Jewish meal blessings, especially the *birkat ha-mazon*, should be met with great caution.

For the Last Supper, we can expect the ritual use of bread and wine, the latter being a particular sign of a festive occasion. However, according to the institution narratives in the New Testament (Mt, Mk, Lk, 1 Cor), what Jesus said and did on the occasion was unprecedented and cannot simply be derived from any Jewish ritual context.[43] The actual words he spoke over the bread and over the cup of wine make them signs anticipating his redemptive Passion and death. While I consider it more likely that the Last Supper was not a Passover meal in the proper sense, the vicinity of the Passover is significant and provides a theological context for understanding the new reality instituted by Jesus.[44]

Joseph Ratzinger follows to a large extent John P. Meier's interpretation of the Last Supper narratives (without, however, accepting Meier's argument for different strata of redaction in Mk 14):[45] Jesus was fully aware that he was about to die and he anticipated that he would not be able to celebrate the coming Passover according to the established Jewish custom. Therefore, he gathered the Twelve, his innermost circle of disciples, for a special meal of farewell that followed no specific Jewish ritual, though it would include the customary meal blessing. In the course

---

[42] For increasing scepticism among Jewish scholars regarding first-century practice, see Stefan C. Reif, 'The Second Temple Period, Qumran Research, and Rabbinic Liturgy: Some Contextual and Linguistic Comparisons', in *Liturgical Perspectives: Prayer and Poetry in Light of the Dead Sea Scrolls*, ed. Esther G. Chazon (Leiden: Brill, 2003), 133–149; and Richard S. Sarason, 'Communal Prayer at Qumran and Among the Rabbis: Certainties and Uncertainties', in ibid., 151–172.

[43] Meier, *A Marginal Jew*, 399, notes that 'if we should allow the basic historicity of the eucharistic narrative (Mark 14:22–25 parr.), we would have to admit that Jesus did and said some astounding things at the Last Supper, things that cannot be explained simply by positing the context of some Jewish ritual meal, Passover or otherwise. Given the unique circumstances of this unusual person, it is not surprising that what he did at his last meal with his inner circle of disciples does not fit neatly under any conventional religious rubric of the time'.

[44] See Gerard Deighan, 'Continuity in Sacrifice: From Old Testament to New', in *Celebrating the Eucharist: Sacrifice and Communion. Proceedings of the Fifth Fota International Liturgical Conference, 2012*, ed. Gerard Deighan, Fota Liturgy Series 5 (Wells: Smenos, 2014), 87–107, at 93: 'It is enough to agree, as is generally done, that the Last Supper was conducted in the *atmosphere* of the Passover' (italics in the original).

[45] See Ratzinger, *Jesus of Nazareth*, 112–115; Meier, *A Marginal Jew*, 398–399; also Helmut Hoping, *My Body Given for You: History and Theology of the Eucharist*, trans. Michael J. Miller (San Francisco: Ignatius Press, 2019), 45–50.

of this meal, he gave himself as the true Lamb and so instituted his own Passover. This would be the import of the somewhat ambiguous saying in Lk 22:15–16, 'I have earnestly desired to eat this Passover with you before I suffer; for I tell you I shall not eat it until it is fulfilled in the kingdom of God'. While the reference to the Passover could mean *this meal* Jesus was holding with the Twelve, it could also point to the new reality he was about to institute in anticipation of his Passion and death. The decisive moment of this Last Supper meal was not the customary consumption of the Passover lamb (which even the Synoptics do not mention in their description of the actual meal) but Jesus instituting the new Passover and giving himself as the true Lamb. This is implied in John 19:36, where the sacrificial rubric of Exodus 12:46 (also Num 9:12) is applied to the crucified Jesus: 'You shall not break any of its [the lamb's] bones.' The new Passover is Jesus' sacrificial death, which fulfils and exceeds the meaning of the old Passover. This would also be in harmony with 1 Corinthians 5:7: 'Christ, our Passover lamb, has been sacrificed.' The content of this new Passover is signified in the Last Supper when Jesus shares with his disciples bread and wine, which he identifies with his body and his blood.

THE WORDS OF INSTITUTION

If we follow the standard assignment of the Synoptic Gospels to the Flavian period (AD 69–96),[46] then the earliest witness to the Last Supper narrative would be 1 Corinthians 11:23–26. Scott Hahn has noted the singular character of this text in the Pauline corpus:

The *only* significant narrative overlap between the Gospels and the letters attributed to Saint Paul is the institution narrative. Though Paul was Jesus's most prolific interpreter, he rarely quoted the Master. Yet here he carefully narrated the scene and reported Jesus's words at length. It is by far the longest quotation of Jesus's teaching found in the Pauline corpus. The Apostle emphasized that he himself is not the origin of the tradition. He is simply passing on what has already been well established in the Church. 'For I received from the Lord what I also

---

[46] The case for an earlier dating has been advanced, for instance, by John A. T. Robinson, *Redating the New Testament* (London: SCM Press, 1986); and Hans-Joachim Schulz, *Die apostolische Herkunft der Evangelien: Zum Ursprung der Evangelienform in der urgemeindlichen Paschafeier*, Quaestiones Disputatae 145, 3rd ed. (Freiburg: Herder, 1997). However, such proposals remain a minority position.

delivered to you, that the Lord Jesus on the night when he was betrayed took bread ...' (1 Corinthians 11:23).[47]

Hahn's observation is important: the institution narrative in 1 Corinthians is by far the most substantial verbatim quotation the apostle ever makes of Christ's teachings. Moreover, Paul presents it as having been handed down to him from the Lord himself. The letter's date (AD 53/54) means that we are less than a generation away from the reported events.

The institution narratives in the Synoptic Gospels fall into two distinct groups: Mark 14:22–25 is close to Matthew 26:26–29, both referring to the blood of the covenant of Mount Sinai (Ex 24:8), whereas Luke 22:14–20, which has an affinity to 1 Corinthians 11:23–26, takes up the announcement of a new covenant in Jeremiah 31:31. While the Fourth Gospel does not contain the words of institution, it would appear that John 6 (especially verses 51–58) presupposes them, as shall be argued below.

The dominical words of institution thus exemplify one of the 'primary criteria' for sayings or deeds attributed to the historical Jesus, as developed in New Testament scholarship and presented in synthesis by John P. Meier, namely that of 'multiple attestation'.[48] It is noteworthy that this criterion is usually applied to 'general motifs and phrases', such as 'kingdom of God', but here we are confronted with 'precise sayings and deeds', where 'one cannot usually expect such a broad range of attestation'.[49] Hence, the fact that Jesus' very words over the bread and wine at the Last Supper are found in independent sources speaks in favour of their historicity. Moreover, a case can be made that the words of institution fulfil all five 'primary criteria' listed by Meier: (1) embarrassment (the difficult idea of eating the body and drinking the blood of Christ); (2) discontinuity (the originality of Jesus' 'new Passover'); (3) multiple attestation (as we have seen); (4) coherence (with the mission of Jesus and in particular with his Passion); (5) Jesus' rejection and execution (the alienation caused by the difficulty and novelty of the words).[50]

These criteria, proposed in what is known as the quest for the historical Jesus, have recently sustained vigorous criticism from New Testament

---

[47] Scott Hahn, *Consuming the Word: The New Testament and the Eucharist in the Early Church* (New York: Image, 2013), 43.

[48] See Meier, *A Marginal Jew*, 174–175.   [49] Ibid., 175.   [50] See ibid., 168–177.

scholars.[51] However, they serve to establish a strong plausibility that the dominical words at the Last Supper, as transmitted by Paul and the Synoptic Gospels, represent the *ipsissima vox* of Jesus (the 'kind of thing' he would have said), even though the multiplicity of their attestation raises the question of the *ipsissima verba* (what exactly he said). This question may in the end be impossible to answer, but the path of historical inquiry will help us to attain a better understanding of the biblical testimony and of the Last Supper tradition.

First Corinthians 11 is generally held to be the oldest *literary* account of the dominical words (c. AD 53/54). Paul introduces the narrative with the affirmation that he 'received (παρέλαβον) from the Lord' what he 'handed on (παρέδωκα)' to the church at Corinth. The same expressions are used in 1 Corinthians 15:3, where Paul presents the eyewitnesses of Jesus' resurrection. These terms correspond to the technical rabbinic vocabulary for transmitting sacred tradition faithfully and accurately, namely *qibbêl* and *mâsar*.[52] Thus Paul does not simply offer his own teaching here but relates what he himself was taught and what at least the churches he ministered to accepted as an 'official version of events', as Eric Eve puts it.[53] In other words, Paul is 'constrained' by the tradition, which he considers authoritative, and 'expects his audience to be so [constrained] also'.[54]

While Paul must have received some instruction between his conversion experience outside Damascus in c. 34 and his visit to Jerusalem in c. 37, his account of the 'Lord's Supper (δεῖπνον κυριακόν)' (1 Cor 11:20; the expression is found only here in the New Testament)[55] is held to reflect liturgical practice at Antioch, where he stayed in the early 40s. The Syrian metropolis had become a centre of the Hellenist followers of Jesus after the martyrdom of Stephen (Acts 11:19).[56] In Corinth, the Lord's Supper was combined with the (evening) meal, though the ritual action

---

[51] See the contributions in *Jesus, Criteria, and the Demise of Authenticity*, ed. Chris Keith and Anthony Le Donne (London; New York: T&T Clark, 2012).

[52] See Gerhardsson, *Memory & Manuscript*, 290; William D. Davies, *Paul and Rabbinic Judaism: Some Rabbinic Elements in Pauline Theology*, 3rd ed. (London: SPCK, 1970), 246.

[53] Eve, *Behind the Gospels*, 166.   [54] Ibid., 167.

[55] As Bradshaw and Johnson, *The Eucharistic Liturgies*, 10, note, it is rare in early Christian writings; they list *Apostolic Tradition*, 27,1 and Tertullian, *Ad uxorem*, 2,4.

[56] See Jerome Kodell, *The Eucharist in the New Testament* (Wilmington: Michael Glazier, 1988), 71; Ulrich Wilckens, *Theologie des Neuen Testaments. Band 1: Geschichte der urchristlichen Theologie, Teilband 2: Jesu Tod und Auferstehung und die Entstehung der Kirche aus Juden und Heiden* (Neukirchen-Vluyn: Neukirchener Verlag, 2003), 77.

with bread and wine was clearly distinct from it. While Paul does not indicate the frequency of the celebration, it must have happened with some regularity, perhaps weekly. Repetition is implied in the double command included in the dominical words to observe the ritual action 'in remembrance of me' (1 Cor 11: 24, 25). In fact, to partake in the bread and the cup 'proclaim[s] the Lord's death' in hope of eschatological fulfilment – 'until he comes' (1 Cor 11:26). The formulaic way in which Paul presents Jesus' sayings at the Last Supper suggests their liturgical use, which would have been familiar to his addressees.

Following the seminal work of Ferdinand Christian Baur (1792–1860), biblical exegesis tended to see Petrine (Jewish) and Pauline (Gentile) Christianity in antithesis. Paul was regarded as generally standing apart and often in conflict with other apostles. The liturgical practice of the Pauline communities would thus only offer a partial picture of primitive Christianity. For instance, Hans Lietzmann argued that the Hellenist 'Lord's Supper' in 1 Corinthians differed in many respects from the Hebrew 'breaking of the bread' of the Jerusalem church (see above, p. 9). More recently, however, New Testament scholars have localised Paul within the context of Second Temple Judaism.[57] Paul's declarations that he intended on working with the other apostles – despite the tensions that existed – need to be taken seriously (see esp. Gal 2:1–10).[58] Daniel Cardó notes that Paul 'was not disinterested in individual churches' conformity with the beliefs and practices of others (see 1 Cor 4:17; 7:17; 11:16; 14:33b; 16:1)'.[59] The fact that Paul only refers to the Last Supper tradition in one of his letters does not imply that it was observed only at Corinth. Baptism occupies an important place in the apostle's theology and practice but is not mentioned in every letter.[60] The apostle writes to settle particular questions and not to offer general instruction.

The narrative beginning with 'on the night when he was betrayed …' (1 Cor 11:23) presupposes a fuller description of the Passion of Jesus that

---

[57] See Magnus Zetterholm, *Approaches to Paul: A Student's Guide to Recent Scholarship* (Minneapolis: Fortress, 2009); and Paula Fredriksen, *Paul, the Pagans' Apostle* (New Haven: Yale University Press, 2017).

[58] See Eve, *Behind the Gospels*, 167–168.

[59] Daniel Cardó, 'The Eucharist in the First Three Centuries', in *The Cambridge History of Ancient Christianity*, ed. Bruce Longenecker and David Wilhite (Cambridge: Cambridge University Press), forthcoming.

[60] See ibid., with reference to Everett Ferguson, *Baptism in the Early Church: History, Theology, and Liturgy in the First Five Centuries* (Grand Rapids: Eerdmans, 2009), 146–155.

is known to the Corinthians, but Paul sees no need to recall it at this point. According to the pre-Pauline tradition, Jesus took bread (v. 23), said a prayer of thanksgiving (εὐχαριστήσας), broke the bread and said: 'This is my body (τοῦτό μοῦ ἐστιν τὸ σῶμα), which is for you (τὸ ὑπὲρ ὑμῶν).' By comparison with the bread saying in the Synoptic Gospels, there are two distinct features: the highlighted position of the possessive pronoun (μου) after the demonstrative pronoun 'this' and the added phrase 'which is for you', which cannot easily be rendered into Aramaic, the language Jesus presumably used at the Last Supper. This specific wording would thus point to a Greek-speaking tradition.[61] In fact, the explanatory addition 'for you' suggests an existing liturgical use, possibly in the Antiochene (Hellenist) church. Following right after, the dominical command 'Do this in remembrance of me' is recorded for the first time (v. 24).

The rite over the cup follows 'after supper (μετὰ τὸ δειπνῆσαι)'. From this terse description, it does not seem clear whether the two ritual actions provided the frame of the common meal (as in normal Jewish practice) or whether they are both held at the end of it; the same question is raised by the description in Luke.[62] The action over the cup unfolds 'in the same way (ὡσαύτως)' as the action over the bread. The cup saying, 'This cup is the new covenant in my blood', relates to the proclamation of a new and eschatological covenant in Jeremiah 31:31, which is, however, not connected with sacrifice or shedding of blood. Then follows the second command to repeat the action in the Lord's memory: 'Do this, as often as you drink it, in remembrance of me' (v. 26). While the first command after the bread saying has a parallel in Luke 22:19, the second one is recorded only in 1 Corinthians. This parallel structure might originate from an already existing use of the words of institution in worship. The term ἀνάμνησις (memory or remembrance) has been subjected to much scholarly scrutiny, and it has been interpreted against the backdrop of Hellenistic memorial or funeral meals. However, parallels between such meals and the early Christian Eucharist remain very generic: communal

---

[61] See Spinks, *Do This in Remembrance of Me*, 17, with reference to Panayotis Coutsoumpos, *Paul and the Lord's Supper: A Socio-Historical Investigation*, Studies in Biblical Literature 84 (Frankfurt am Main: Peter Lang, 2005), 46–51.

[62] The fact that 1 Corinthians 10:16–17 speaks first of 'the cup of blessing which we bless' and then of 'the bread which we break' is sometimes taken as an indication of diverse Eucharistic patterns at Corinth; see Spinks, *Do This in Remembrance of Me*, 15. However, these verses form part of moral exhortation with a careful rhetorical structure. The reading that sees in chapter 10 the reflection of a specific meal practice that would be different from chapter 11 seems overstretched.

eating and drinking, and the use of bread and wine. Anamnesis as an act of remembrance rather takes up the Hebrew understanding of remembering God's salvific deeds, especially the events of the Exodus and the entry into the Promised Land (*zikkaron*; e.g., Ex 12:14). Bryan Spinks also notes that *zikkaron*

recalls Jewish cultic celebrations such as the Passover, which is often linked with a sacrifice, and serves as a proclamation. This latter is made explicit in the Pauline narrative, for the Lord's Supper is to be celebrated to proclaim the Lord's death until he comes.[63]

The (pre-)Pauline narrative concludes on this strongly eschatological note and sees in the repeated enactment of the ritual meal an anticipation of the Lord's Second Coming and of the messianic banquet in the kingdom of God.

In the Synoptic Gospels, the accounts of the Last Supper form part of the Passion narrative. According to Mark 14, it was during the meal that Jesus took bread, said the blessing (εὐλογήσας), broke the bread, gave it to his disciples and said: 'Take, this is my body' (v. 22). He then took the cup and said the prayer of thanksgiving (εὐχαριστήσας), gave the cup to his disciples, who drank of it (v. 23), and said: 'This is my blood of the covenant, which is shed for many' (v. 24). The prayer of blessing over the bread may be identified with the Jewish *berakah* at the beginning of the meal, while the prayer of thanksgiving may be a form of *birkat ha-mazon* at the end of the meal (see above, pp. 18–19). However, despite the use of two different terms, there is no significant difference between the two kinds of prayer, as both would include the elements of blessing and thanksgiving.

While the words over the bread are the same as in 1 Corinthians (with a very minor grammatical variation), the words over the cup are distinct: they refer to the narrative of the covenant made on mount Sinai (Ex 24:1–18; see also Heb 9:20). After having made the animal sacrifice, Moses sprinkled half of the blood on the altar and read the Book of the Covenant, to which the people gave their obedience. Then Moses 'took the blood, sprinkled it on the people and said, "This is the blood of the covenant that the Lord has made with you in accordance with all these words"' (v. 8). Together with the leaders of the Israelites, Moses went up the mountain 'and saw the God of Israel .... But God did not raise his

---

[63] Spinks, *Do This in Remembrance of Me*, 17.

hand against these leaders of the Israelites; they saw God, and they ate and drank' (vv. 10–11).

The reference to the Mosaic covenant is also evident in the phrase 'shed for many (τὸ ἐκχυννόμενον ὑπὲρ πολλῶν)', which highlights the sacrificial character of the action, that is, the offering of blood. The present-tense, passive-voice participle of the verb ἐκχύν(ν)ειν[64] can refer to the present 'pouring out' of the cup at the Last Supper or to the future 'shedding' of Jesus' blood on the cross. While the former reading is preferred by most modern exegetes, Lynne C. Boughton makes a lexical and grammatical argument in favour of the latter: the verb denotes the forceful shedding of a liquid, as in an act of sacrifice, rather than the orderly pouring, as during a meal; the aspect of the Greek verb points to completion and fulfilment in the future. This is the understanding of most patristic commentators, including Jerome in his Vulgate translation, and it is worth noting that almost the entire Latin liturgical tradition of the words of institution renders the participle in the future tense ('will be shed' – *effundetur*).[65] Even if we keep the future reference to the blood shed on the cross in mind, the words relate to the cup that Jesus has just given to the Twelve to drink from.[66] At the same time, the Markan narrative, like 1 Corinthians, opens the perspective of eschatological fulfilment, with Jesus saying: 'Truly, I say to you, I shall not drink again of the fruit of the vine until that day when I drink it new in the kingdom of God' (Mk 14:25).

The Last Supper account in Matthew would seem to be a literary (and probably liturgical) redaction of the account in Mark, from which it is distinguished by only a few additions. The most noteworthy differences are as follows: adding the exhortation 'eat (φάγετε)' after 'take' (Mt 26:26). In the rite over the cup, in place of the description 'and they all drank of it' there is the Lord's exhortation 'drink of it, all of you' (v. 27). Finally, the cup saying includes 'for the forgiveness of sins' after 'for many', emphasising the propitiatory effect of the sacrificial action

---

[64] This is a Hellenistic variant of ἐκχεῖν; see Walter Bauer, *A Greek-English Lexicon of the New Testament and Other Early Christian Literature*, rev. and ed. Frederick William Danker, 3rd ed. (Chicago; London: University of Chicago Press, 2000), s.v. ἐκχέω.

[65] See Lynne C. Boughton, '"Being Shed for You/Many": Time-Sense and Consequences in the Synoptic Cup Citations', in *Tyndale Bulletin* 48 (1997), 249–270; and 'Transubstantiation and the Latin Text of the Bible: A Problem in the *Nova Vulgata Bibliorum*', in *Gregorianum* 83 (2002), 209–224.

[66] Deighan, 'Continuity in Sacrifice: From Old Testament to New', 91, speaks of 'the possibility … of an intentional ambivalence'.

(v. 28). The eschatological conclusion of the dominical words substitutes 'kingdom of God' with 'my Father's kingdom' (v. 29).

How are we to understand Jesus' statement that his blood of the covenant is shed 'for many' (ὑπὲρ πολλῶν in Mk 14:24; περὶ πολλῶν in Mt 26:28)? Catholic theologians and liturgists have discussed this question extensively during the recent process of revising the translations of the *Missale Romanum* into modern languages. After the Second Vatican Council (1962–1965), most vernacular editions of the missal rendered the Latin expression *pro multis* with an equivalent of 'for all'. This decision was based largely on the argument of the noted Lutheran exegete Joachim Jeremias that the Aramaic underlying the Greek of the Gospels has no proper expression for indicating a totality and hence the phrase 'for many' is to be taken inclusively. Moreover, he posits that the Hebrew *rabim*, in contrast to the Greek πολλοί, refers to an immeasurable number and is tantamount to 'for all'.[67] These philological arguments are now generally rejected, since it has been shown that, just as in Indo-European languages, both Hebrew and Aramaic are capable of distinguishing between 'all' (*kol/kūl*) and 'many' (*rabim/sagī*).[68] Jeremias was right, however, in connecting the words over the cup in Matthew and Mark with the prophecy of the suffering servant in Isaiah 52–53: 'the righteous one, my servant, [shall] make many to be accounted righteous; and he shall bear their iniquities … he poured out his soul to death, and was numbered with the transgressors; yet he bore the sin of many, and made intercession for the transgressors' (Is 53:11–12). Leaving aside the disputed question of whether Jesus identified himself with the suffering servant of Isaiah, it seems clear that by alluding to Isaiah 53 in the words of institution, Jesus presents his own death as sacrificial and redemptive (see also Mt 20:28; Mk 10:45, where he refers to himself as the Son of Man who came 'to give his life as a ransom for many'). In Matthew, this link is even clearer since Jesus pours out his blood 'for many for the forgiveness of sins' (Mt 26:28). Moreover, in Isaiah the suffering servant is offered 'as a covenant to the people' (Is 42:6, 49:8); and in all four

---

[67] See Jeremias, *Eucharistic Words*, 179–182; and 'polloi', in *Theological Dictionary of the New Testament*, ed. Gerhard Kittel and Gerhard Friedrich, trans. Geoffrey W. Bromiley, 10 vols. (Grand Rapids: Eerdmans, 1964–1976) vol. VI, 536–545 at 536.

[68] See the thorough study of Franz Prosinger, *Das Blut des Bundes – vergossen für viele? Zur Übersetzung und Interpretation des hyper pollôn in Mk 14,24*, Quaestiones non disputatae 12 (Siegburg: Franz Schmitt, 2007); for a summary of the discussion, see Manfred Hauke, 'Shed for Many: An Accurate Rendering of the Pro Multis in the Formula of Consecration', in *Antiphon* 14 (2010), 169–229, at 173–175.

narratives of institution; Jesus explicitly associates the offering of his blood with the (new) covenant (Mt 26:28; Mk 14:24; Lk 22:20; 1 Cor 11:25).[69] Against this background, Jeremias argued that the 'many' in the Eucharistic words of Jesus stand for the Gentiles.[70] While this reading was widely accepted by exegetes, more recently the position has gained ground that the 'many' should rather be identified with the people of Israel. In favour of this interpretation, Rudolf Pesch recalls that the Last Supper, unlike other meals of Jesus, is specifically held with the twelve apostles who represent the twelve tribes of Israel (most of which had disappeared since the Assyrian invasion and the loss of the northern kingdom in the eighth century BC). Hence, it is a covenant for the eschatological restoration of Israel that is established by Jesus' offering of the cup to the Twelve. However, as Helmut Hoping notes, 'indirectly the Gentiles are being considered too, since Israel's election consists precisely in the vocation to be a sign for the nations (cf. Is 56:7; Mk 11:17), so that we can say that Jesus dies not only for Israel but [also] for the Gentiles'.[71] This context makes clear that here 'Jesus was not talking about the question of whether "many" or "all" will be saved'.[72] Jesus' description of the eschatological banquet in the kingdom of God 'with Abraham, Isaac, and Jacob' (Mt 8:11; also Lk 13:28) clearly states that not all will share in it.[73] Such and other biblical evidence inform the discussion in systematic theology on the universal offer of salvation and its particular realisation;[74] however, it has no immediate bearing on understanding (and translating) the words of institution.

The Last Supper narrative in Luke shows a number of particular features. The dominical words of institution are preceded by a section that accentuates the eschatological horizon of the entire meal (which in Matthew and Mark forms the conclusion of the narrative):

---

[69] See Pitre, *Jesus and the Last Supper*, 100–104, with further literature.

[70] See Jeremias, *Eucharistic Words*, 225–231.

[71] Hoping, *My Body Given for You*, 370. See Rudolf Pesch, *Das Abendmahl und Jesu Todesverständnis*, Quaestiones disputatae 80 (Freiburg: Herder, 1978), 95–96.

[72] Hoping, *My Body Given for You*, 368, with reference to Gerhard Lohfink, *Gegen die Verharmlosung Jesu* (Freiburg: Herder, 2013), 131–132.

[73] For the disputed question of identifying those who are gathered for the banquet, see Pitre, *Jesus and the Last Supper*, 460–481. Pitre makes plausible that 'those who are excluded from the banquet are simply those who reject Jesus' proclamation of the kingdom', both Israelites and Gentiles (ibid., 466).

[74] See Hoping, *My Body Given for You*, 370–372; and esp. Hauke, 'Shed for Many'.

And when the hour came, he sat at table, and the apostles with him. And he said to them, 'I have earnestly desired to eat this passover with you before I suffer; for I tell you I shall not eat it until it is fulfilled in the kingdom of God.' And he took a cup, and when he had given thanks he said, 'Take this, and divide it among yourselves; for I tell you that from now on I shall not drink of the fruit of the vine until the kingdom of God comes.' (Lk 22:14–18)

After this initial cup, the two ritual actions over the bread and the cup are described. The account is very similar to Mark and Matthew, with some differences: Luke records that Jesus 'gave thanks (εὐχαριστήσας)' (v. 19), as he had done with the initial cup (v. 17). The bread saying has the addition 'which is given for you (τὸ ὑπὲρ ὑμῶν διδόμενον)', followed immediately by the command 'Do this in memory of me' (v. 19), which suggests an already existing liturgical practice. The subsequent ritual action over the cup 'after supper' is introduced pithily with 'likewise (ὡσαύτως)', with the dominical words being given as: 'This cup is the new covenant in my blood, which is shed for you' (v. 20). The parallels between Luke and the pre-Pauline tradition in 1 Corinthians 11 are evident. Apart from some stylistic modifications, there are two significant explanatory additions: the body is 'given (διδόμενον)' and the blood is 'shed (ἐκχυννόμενον)'. While the latter is also found in Mark and Matthew, the former is unique to Luke. In the context of the Passion narrative, both additions point to the sacrificial character and the salvific benefit of the bread and wine offered by Jesus to his disciples.

New Testament scholarship distinguishes between the 'longer reading' of Luke 22:17–20 and the 'shorter reading', which omits the (second) cup in vv. 19b–20. The shorter reading is attested in an important Greek New Testament manuscript, the fifth-century Codex Bezae (D), and in a few Old Latin manuscripts. Some Syriac witnesses present different modifications of the text, with the Peshitta omitting vv. 17–18. This is not the place to discuss such an intricate question of New Testament textual criticism and it may suffice here to note that today biblical exegetes tend to support the originality of the longer reading.[75] The early manuscript variations would seem to reflect attempts to resolve the difficulty created by the sequence cup-bread-cup in the longer reading. Some exegetes, notably Heinz Schürmann, saw in Lk 22:15–18 the record of an

---

[75] See Meier, *A Marginal Jew*, 427, n. 99, with reference to Bruce Metzger, *A Textual Commentary on the Greek New Testament: A Companion Volume to the United Bible Societies' Greek New Testament (Fourth Revised Edition)*, 2nd ed. (London; New York: United Bible Societies, 1994), 173–177.

independent tradition,[76] while others argue for a redactional expansion, and indeed inversion, of the narrative in Mark. John P. Meier identifies 'a neat pattern of two words about not eating and not drinking any ordinary food, followed by the two words of institution over the bread and the wine' and regards the Lukan redaction as 'early Christian reflection on the Last Supper'.[77]

Like Eugene LaVerdiere (see above, p. 11), Scott Hahn sees in the narrative of the Last Supper the key juncture of the Lukan accounts of Jesus' table-fellowship, which are saturated with images of the coming kingdom of God. While Eucharistic themes are present in the feeding of the five thousand (Lk 9:10–17) and in the breaking of bread at Emmaus (Lk 24:13–35), the Last Supper occupies the central place in this concatenation of events. In Mark and Matthew, Jesus' prophecy about not drinking again of the fruit of the vine 'until that day when I drink it new in the kingdom of God' (Mk 14:25; see Mt 26:29) follows the ritual with bread and wine. Luke, on the other hand, places the prophecy at the beginning of the meal (Lk 22:18) and adds a similar one about not eating the Passover 'until it is fulfilled in the kingdom of God' (Lk 22:16). Thus, the Last Supper is closely related to the imminent arrival of the kingdom, which in turn is linked with eating and drinking. The prophecy is fulfilled when the Risen Christ eats with his disciples, notably at Emmaus. There he physically disappears after having broken and distributed the bread, which, in the light of the institution narrative, is identified with his body.[78] The institution narrative is of key importance for the Lukan history of the nascent church:

The 'breaking of the bread' ... in Acts 2:42, as well as 20:11 and 27:35, is no simple eating but eucharistic celebration and proleptic participation in the messianic banquet. In the continuing practice of 'the breaking of bread' the Apostles experience the fulfillment of the promise 'to eat and drink at my table in my

---

[76] See Heinz Schürmann, *Eine quellenkritische Untersuchung des lukanischen Abendmahlsberichtes, Lk 22, 7–38. Bd.1: Der Paschamahlbericht, Lk 22, (7–14) 15–18*, Neutestamentliche Abhandlungen 19/5, 2nd ed. (Münster: Aschendorff, 1968), 1–74.

[77] Meier, *A Marginal Jew*, 398. See Marion L. Soards, *The Passion According to Luke: The Special Material of Luke 22*, Journal for the Study of the New Testament. Supplement Series 14 (Sheffield: JSOT Press, 1987), 45, 50, 116.

[78] See Scott Hahn, *Kinship by Covenant: A Canonical Approach to the Fulfillment of God's Saving Promises*, The Anchor Yale Bible Reference Library (New Haven; London: Yale University Press, 2009), 222–226.

kingdom' (Luke 22:30) and the whole eschatological community shares in the fulfillment with them.[79]

Having reviewed the biblical data, we are now in a better position to assess the historicity of Jesus' words and actions at the Last Supper. In the first place, we should take stock of the similarities between these four accounts. Even an extremely sceptical scholar, such as Gerd Lüdemann, concedes that, 'all in all, the difference between the words of institution in Mark and Paul is not all that great'.[80] The limited variances between the four accounts are representative of a tradition that is stable but not fixed.[81] Recently theories of 'social memory' that offer a context for the transmission of the Jesus tradition reach similar conclusions: memory can be malleable, but at the same time it mediates the basic data of tradition.[82] The study of memory thus fills a lacuna that was left by the form-critical method Bultmann applied to the study of the Gospels.[83]

With such caveats in mind, there is a strong plausibility for the words and acts of Jesus at the Last Supper, as transmitted by Paul and the Synoptic Gospels. Allowance needs to be made for limited variability in the process of oral tradition and the work of a final redactor. There would seem to be a wide consensus among biblical scholars that Jesus indeed broke bread, gave it to his disciples and said 'This is my body'. Neither the Hebrew nor the Aramaic language use the copula 'is', but it can be safely assumed that Jesus identified the broken and shared bread with his body and hence with his voluntary self-offering in the violent death he was about to suffer.

The words over the cup are often considered to have undergone some post-Easter editing from distinctive theological perspectives. Both

---

[79] Ibid., 234.

[80] Gerd Lüdemann, *Jesus After 2000 Years: What He Really Said and Did*, trans. John Bowden (London: SCM Press 2000), 96. Boughton, 'Transubstantiation and the Latin Text of the Bible', 209, observes: 'Yet in transmitting his words at the Last Supper, these evangelists [Mt, Mk, Lk] exceed their usual degree of concurrence by using almost identical vocabulary and syntax.'

[81] Eve, *Behind the Gospels*, 169, lists other examples of constrained variability: 'when Paul explicitly cites Jesus' sayings elsewhere ... the wording never corresponds all that closely to anything we find in the Gospels .... Moreover, although Paul, Mark and the other Evangelists agree in the fact of the resurrection, they are quite at odds over the details'.

[82] See Dale C. Allison Jr., *Constructing Jesus: Memory, Imagination, and History* (Grand Rapids: Baker Academic, 2010); and *Jesus, Criteria, and the Demise of Authenticity*, ed. Keith and Le Donne.

[83] See Alan Kirk, *Memory and the Jesus Tradition*, The Reception of Jesus in the First Three Centuries 2 (London: Bloomsbury T&T Clark, 2018), who also offers a critical appreciation of Gerhardsson, *Memory & Manuscript*.

versions (1 Cor/Lk and Mt/Mk) agree that Jesus identified the cup of wine as his blood and offered it to his disciples in order to establish a (new) covenant. Many exegetes tend to prefer the pre-Pauline and Lukan version, because it mitigates the scandal to Jewish ears to some degree by designating the cup as the 'new covenant' in Jesus' blood, which is a reference to Jeremiah 31:31. This raises the difficulty that the announcement of an eschatological covenant in Jeremiah has no connection with sacrifice or the offering of blood. On the other hand, some exegetes have argued that there is an implicit allusion to the covenant sacrifice of Exodus 24:8 in Paul and Luke.[84] The statement that the blood is shed 'for you' (Lk 22:20) could reflect a liturgical formula already in use by early Christian communities.

The version of Matthew and Mark makes explicit reference to Exodus 24:8, where covenant, blood (sacrifice) and meal are already connected. However, Jeremiah 31:31 is present in the background. Seyoon Kim comments: 'Although the word "new" does not appear before "covenant" in Mk 14.24, a covenant established by Jesus' blood can only be a "new covenant", different from the Mosaic one.'[85] There is considerable originality in the words of Jesus linking the expectation of the messianic age to come with the suffering servant of Isaiah 53, who lays down his life 'for many'.[86] Because of the difficulties that Jesus' direct identification of the cup of wine with 'my blood' would raise in a Jewish context, it is not likely to be a creation of the post-Easter community. Helmut Hoping raises the pertinent question: 'Why should the more difficult version of the words over the chalice be secondary and not the easier version instead?'[87] At any rate, it would become clear from a post-Easter perspective that this

---

[84] See Pitre, *Jesus and the Last Supper*, 94, with n. 105, where he cites Joseph A. Fitzmeyer, *The Gospel According to Luke*, Anchor Bible 28–28A, 2 vols. (New York: Doubleday, 1983–1985), vol. II, 1391.

[85] Seyoon Kim, *The 'Son of Man' as the Son of God*, Wissenschaftliche Untersuchungen zum Neuen Testament 30 (Tübingen: Mohr Siebeck, 1983), 98.

[86] See Pitre, *Jesus and the Last Supper*, 120; Hoping, *My Body Given for You*, 42–43.

[87] Hoping, *My Body Given for You*, 42; see also Deighan, 'Continuity in Sacrifice: From Old Testament to New', 89–91: 'the starkness of the formula ... recommends itself'. I am not convinced by Pitre's argument that Jesus' telling his disciples to drink his blood is contextually plausible because it would not break any positive precept of the Law, as the Torah only prohibited the consumption of animal blood, not of human blood (Gen 9:3–4; Lev 17:10–12; Deut 12:16; see Pitre, *Jesus and the Last Supper*, 108–109 and 429–430). Surely, the idea of drinking of human blood in worship would have been abhorrent to Jews, as it was to most Greeks and Romans (which is noted by Pitre, ibid., 430, n. 138).

is not about drinking the human blood of Jesus but rather a sacramental participation in his redemptive self-offering.

THE BREAD OF LIFE DISCOURSE OF JOHN 6

The account of the Last Supper in the Fourth Gospel does not contain words of institution as in the Synoptic Gospels. The focus of John's narrative rests instead on Jesus washing of feet (Jn 13:2–11), by which he gives an 'example' (Jn 13:15) to his disciples of the 'new commandment' to love one another as he has loved them (Jn 13:34). The washing of feet is not only an act of humble service but also a sign of Jesus 'loving his own who were in the world ... to the end' (Jn 13:1) by laying down his life. There are baptismal resonances in the act of washing, which is interpreted in the dialogue between Jesus and Peter as an act of symbolic cleansing (Jn 13:6–11).[88] Sandra M. Schneiders interprets the washing of feet as a prophetic action that is fulfilled on Calvary, when Jesus sheds his blood and 'washes' away the sins of the world, without which no one may have 'part' with him (Jn 13:8).[89]

The absence of an institution narrative in John does not mean, however, that the Eucharist was unknown to Johannine communities. Strong evidence to the contrary is offered by the 'bread of life' discourse (John 6:22–59), which Jesus gives in the synagogue of Capernaum shortly before the Passover (Jn 6:4), after the feeding of the five thousand (Jn 6:1–15) and walking on the water of the Sea of Galilee (Jn 6:16–21).[90] Having witnessed the miracle of the multiplication of the loaves, those listening to Jesus in the synagogue bring up the manna, the bread God gave every day to nourish the Israelites during the exodus from Egypt (Ex 16:4, 31), referring in v. 31 to Ps 78:24: 'He rained down upon them manna to eat, and gave them the bread of heaven.' In response, Jesus speaks of himself as the new manna that nourishes for eternal life (esp. vv. 48–51). When Jesus identifies himself as the 'bread of life' or 'the

---

[88] George R. Beasley-Murray, *John*, Word Biblical Commentary 36, 2nd ed. (Nashville: Thomas Nelson, 1999), 234–235, discusses baptismal readings, while disagreeing with them. The washing of feet formed part of the baptismal liturgy in Ambrose of Milan and the later Gallican tradition.

[89] See Sandra M. Schneiders, 'The Foot Washing (John 13:1–20): An Experiment in Hermeneutics', in *Catholic Biblical Quarterly* 43 (1981), 76–92, at 81 and 84; see also Jan van der Watt, 'The Meaning of Jesus Washing the Feet of His Disciples (John 13)', in *Neotestamentica* 51 (2017), 25–39.

[90] For a comprehensive discussion of the teaching in the synagogue of Capernaum, see Pitre, *Jesus and the Last Supper*, 193–250.

living bread which comes down from heaven' (vv. 35, 51), this can be taken in a personal sense, and eating of this bread can be understood as fellowship with Jesus through faith in him. The following section, however, is pervaded by a startling Eucharistic realism:

'I am the living bread which came down from heaven; if any one eats of this bread, he will live for ever; and the bread which I shall give for the life of the world is my flesh.' The Jews then disputed among themselves, saying, 'How can this man give us his flesh to eat?' So Jesus said to them, 'Truly, truly, I say to you, unless you eat the flesh of the Son of man and drink his blood, you have no life in you; he who eats my flesh and drinks my blood has eternal life, and I will raise him up at the last day. For my flesh is food indeed, and my blood is drink indeed. He who eats my flesh and drinks my blood abides in me, and I in him. As the living Father sent me, and I live because of the Father, so he who eats me will live because of me. This is the bread which came down from heaven, not such as the fathers ate and died; he who eats this bread will live for ever.' (Jn 6:51–58)

Here the bread of life discourse moves away from the earlier figurative sense of eating. This shift is enforced when Jesus replaces the common verb for eating (φαγεῖν) with the more palpable 'chewing' (τρώγειν, vv. 54, 56, 57, 58). He presents his flesh and blood as 'real' food and drink (ἀληθής, v. 55) in a literal sense.[91] At the same time, by identifying himself with the messianic 'Son of man', Jesus makes clear that he is not inviting cannibalism but a sharing in his risen and glorified flesh and blood, which is a supernatural reality. This heavenly food is linked with an eschatological promise: those who receive it will enter into eternal life and be raised on the last day.

A purely metaphorical reading appears difficult to sustain at this point. Raymond Brown observes:

'To eat someone's flesh' appears in the Bible as a metaphor for hostile action . . . . Thus, if Jesus' words in 6:53 are to have a favorable meaning, they must refer to the Eucharist. They simply reproduce the words we hear in the Synoptic account of the institution of the Eucharist (Matt xxvi 26–28): 'Take, eat; this is my body . . . drink . . . this is my blood'.[92]

The lexical parallels between John 6 and the Last Supper tradition in the Synoptics are unmistakable. One significant difference consists in the

---

[91] See Pitre, *Jesus and the Last Supper*, 209–210, with further references to modern commentators.

[92] Raymond E. Brown, *The Gospel According to John*, Anchor Bible 29–29A, 2 vols. (New York: Doubleday, 1966–1970), vol. I, 284–285. However, the case for a metaphorical reading of John 6:52–58 has been restated by Jens Schröter, *Nehmt – esst und trinkt: Das Abendmahl verstehen und feiern* (Stuttgart: Katholisches Bibelwerk, 2010), 54–59.

Johannine use of 'flesh' (σάρξ) rather than 'body' (σῶμα). Helmut Hoping argues that this preference derives from the Fourth Gospel's Christology that presents Jesus as the Word made flesh (Jn 1:14). Moreover, Johannine Christology has a strong anti-Gnostic and anti-docetist emphasis.[93] In a similar way, Ignatius of Antioch (early second century) and Justin Martyr's *Apology* (c. 150) develop an anti-docetist Christology and employ the same Eucharistic terminology as John.[94]

At first sight, Jesus' response to the disciples who remained with him may call the realism of the previous teaching in question:

'Do you take offense at this? Then what if you were to see the Son of man ascending where he was before? It is the spirit that gives life, the flesh is of no avail; the words that I have spoken to you are spirit and life. But there are some of you that do not believe.' (Jn 6:61–64)

Brant Pitre argues that the key to understanding this passage is the statement about the Son of man ascending into heaven. When Jesus declares that 'the flesh' on its own is 'of no avail', he reiterates that eating 'his flesh' is not an act of cannibalism but means 'consuming his resurrected and spirit-filled body in the form of food and drink'.[95] Jesus also makes clear that such sacramental eating does not work automatically but offers union with Christ and the pledge of eternal life through faith.[96]

Thus, the full meaning of Jesus' bread of life discourse is accessible only from the perspective of his cross and resurrection, and this raises the question of its historicity. Most modern exegetes would see in John 6 a reflection of the faith of the Johannine community or school. Pitre, on the other hand, makes a bold case that 'the substance of the Capernaum teaching' (Jn 6:48–66) is historically plausible in the context of Second Temple Judaism and derives 'from Jesus during his public ministry in Galilee'.[97] Moreover, he also argues that the coherence of this teaching with the words of institution in the Synoptic Gospels and in 1 Corinthians counts in favour of its historical plausibility, rather than against, as many scholars hold. At the same time, Pitre rejects the idea that the Eucharistic

---

[93] See Hoping, *My Body Given for You*, 55.

[94] See Ignatius of Antioch, *Romans*, 7,3: *The Apostolic Fathers: Greek Texts and English Translations*, ed. and trans. Michael W. Holmes after the earlier work of J. B. Lightfoot and J. R. Harmer, 3rd ed. (Grand Rapids: Baker Academic, 2007), 232 and 233; *Philadelphians*, 4: ibid., 238 and 239; *Smyrneans*, 6,2: ibid., 254 and 255. Justin Martyr, *First Apology*, 66: PTS 38,127–128.

[95] Pitre, *Jesus and the Last Supper*, 220.   [96] See Hoping, *My Body Given for You*, 55.

[97] Pitre, *Jesus and the Last Supper*, 250; see the full discussion, ibid., 220–250.

elements of John 6 constitute 'the Johannine forms of the words of institution',[98] precisely because they do not institute a rite, as in the Synoptic
and Pauline account.[99] Would this fact allow for the conclusion that the
first Johannine communities did not have a Eucharistic celebration? It
would appear very unlikely that the strong sacramental realism of John 6,
set against the background of the Last Supper tradition, did not find an
expression in these communities' practice of worship.

CONCLUSION

The review of recent New Testament scholarship on the Last Supper in
this chapter has found considerable support for the thesis that Jesus, in
proximity of his arrest, trial and execution, was preparing for his death,
which he understood as a redemptive sacrifice. In the atmosphere of the
Passover, he assembled the twelve apostles for a meal in which he anticipated his self-offering on the cross by identifying the broken bread as his
body and the poured cup of wine as the blood of the covenant. Acting as a
new Moses, he inaugurated a new covenant to gather the twelve tribes of
Israel, and through them the Gentiles, into an eschatological kingdom. By
giving himself as the true Lamb, Jesus instituted a new Passover that
fulfilled and exceeded the meaning of the old Passover. This new
Passover was a 'cultic' or liturgical act: by repeating the rite Jesus instituted over bread and wine, the disciples would not only remember his
saving death but also receive a share in its saving effects and a foretaste of
the messianic banquet in the heavenly kingdom. There seems to be a
broad agreement among New Testament scholars that the substance of
the Eucharistic words of institution originate with Jesus himself. While
the practice of the early Church has often been taken as an argument
against the historicity of the gospel data,[100] it is most implausible that the
celebration of the Eucharist, which developed within a short time of Jesus'
departure, could simply be the creation of the post-Easter communities
without a firm point of reference in his Passion. In Chapter 2, I shall
discuss how the sacrificial character of the words of institution offered
early Christians the hermeneutical key for understanding the cultic meal
that came to be the heart of their worship.

---

[98] Brown, *The Gospel According to John*, vol. I, 285.
[99] See Pitre, *Jesus and the Last Supper*, 241–245.
[100] For a critique of this methodology, see Pitre, *Jesus and the Last Supper*, 21–28 and
passim; also Wright, *Jesus and the Victory of God*, 109–112.

2

The Eucharist in the Early Church

In the twentieth century, some prominent German-speaking Catholic theologians, including Romano Guardini, Josef Andreas Jungmann, Joseph Ratzinger and Walter Kasper, engaged in a discussion on the 'basic structure' or 'basic form' (*Grundgestalt*) of the Mass. The backdrop to this theological debate was formed by the movements for liturgical renewal both before and after the Second Vatican Council.[1] Responding to attempts to derive the Eucharistic liturgy from the Last Supper, Joseph Ratzinger formulated two key hypotheses: first, 'the Last Supper is the foundation of the dogmatic content of the Christian Eucharist, not of its liturgical form. The latter does not yet exist';[2] second, the dominical command 'Do this in remembrance of me' (1 Cor 11: 24, 25; Luke 22:19) 'does not refer to the Last Supper as a whole ... but to the specifically eucharistic action'.[3] I consider these two insights crucial for investigating the nascent liturgical forms of the Eucharist.

The celebration of the Eucharist in early Christian communities was shaped by apostolic tradition, which was initially handed down not by

---

[1] See the helpful overview of this debate by Manfred Hauke, 'The "Basic Structure" (*Grundgestalt*) of the Eucharistic Celebration According to Joseph Ratzinger', in *Benedict XVI and the Roman Missal: Proceedings of the Fourth Fota International Liturgical Conference, 2011*, ed. Janet E. Rutherford and James O'Brien, Fota Liturgy Series (Dublin; New York: Four Courts Press; Scepter, 2013), 70–106.

[2] Joseph Ratzinger, 'Form and Content of the Eucharistic Celebration', in *Theology of the Liturgy: The Sacramental Foundation of Christian Existence*, ed. Michael J. Miller, trans. John Saward, et al., Joseph Ratzinger Collected Works 11 (San Francisco: Ignatius Press, 2014), 299–318, at 305 (originally published in 1978).

[3] Ibid., 306.

reference to written texts (except for the emerging canon of biblical books) but in fidelity to oral teaching, with a special role for social memory.[4] The Apostle Paul offers an example of this process: he had already instructed the church in Corinth about the Lord's Supper during his long stay in the city. In writing, he addresses only the specific problems that have arisen and does not repeat his entire teaching. In fact, he prefers to resolve matters in person (see 1 Cor 11:34). Later Christian authors, such as Tertullian (d. after 220), Cyprian of Carthage (d. 258) and Basil of Caesarea (d. 379) confirm the importance of unwritten liturgical and devotional practice.[5] The very nature of oral tradition frustrates the historian's effort at reconstruction; our knowledge of liturgical practice in the earliest period is very limited and much scholarship in this field is hypothetical.

With due caution, therefore, I propose first to contextualise the developing forms of the Eucharist within the religious culture of Second Temple Judaism, with particular attention to the early Christian reading of Malachi 1:10–12. The following discussion of key sources (*Didache*, Ignatius of Antioch, Justin Martyr) will be prefaced by a methodological section about the problems posed by ancient liturgical sources. A consideration of material settings of the early Christian Eucharist will complete this chapter.

THE TEMPLE CONTEXT OF THE EARLY CHRISTIAN EUCHARIST

New Testament scholars have increasingly drawn attention to the Temple context of the Last Supper: According to the Synoptic Gospels, Jesus was staying in Bethany on the Mount of Olives (Mt 26:18; Mk 14:13; Lk 22:10), and it would have been safer for him to remain there. However, he went to Jerusalem just before the Passover, because the feast could be properly celebrated only in the city, with the eating of the lamb that was sacrificed in the Temple (see Deut 16:5–7). The Synoptics also highlight the preparations the disciples were to make for the Passover meal at their

---

[4] 'Christian institutions were formed in milieus of oral culture at a time when books, rare as well as expensive, were available only to the educated elites. With the Scriptures as their basic text, Christian communities preserved, developed, and transmitted their essential traditions through memory.' Marcel Metzger, *History of the Liturgy: The Major Stages*, trans. Madeleine Beaumont (Collegeville: Liturgical Press, 1997), 9.

[5] Tertullian, *De corona*, 3–4: CCL 2,1042–1045; Cyprian of Carthage, *Ep. 63*, 1 and 11: CSEL 3/2,701 and 709–710; Basil of Caesarea, *On the Holy Spirit*, 27, 66: SC 17bis,478–486. See Metzger, *History of the Liturgy*, 9–10, 18.

Master's behest.[6] Jesus had a complex relationship with the Jerusalem Temple: like any faithful Jew, he participated in Temple worship, but he also criticised its priestly establishment for systemic corruption and contamination of the sacred space. This critique found a dramatic climax in the prophetic sign known as the cleansing of the Temple (Mt 21:12–15; Mk 11:15–18; Lk 19:45–48; also Jn 2:13–16).[7] Several exegetes have proposed a link between the symbolic actions in the Temple and at the Last Supper. Gerd Theißen and Annette Merz argue that 'Jesus offers the disciples a replacement for the official cult in which they could either no longer take part, or which could not bring them salvation – until a new temple came'.[8] Note that Theißen and Merz also support the sacrificial or cultic character of the words of institution, for which Brant Pitre has made a strong argument (see Chapter 1). As for the temporary nature of this new cult, Pitre shows that it was to last until the eschatological fulfilment of the kingdom of God.[9]

The Letter to the Hebrews and the Book of Revelation

Two writings of the New Testament canon in particular contain allusions to early Christian worship against the background of the Jewish Temple: the Letter to the Hebrews and the Book of Revelation. In both cases, the identification of such liturgical material is far from straightforward and is contested in contemporary exegesis. Nonetheless, these biblical books confirm the Temple as a point of reference for Eucharistic celebrations in the churches of the first century.

First, Temple worship offers the hermeneutical key for understanding the saving work of Jesus Christ in the Letter to the Hebrews, which is likely to have been written in Italy (Heb 13:24) – possibly Rome – before the destruction of the Temple in AD 70, although some scholars have

---

[6] See Brant Pitre, *Jesus and the Last Supper* (Grand Rapids: Eerdmans, 2015), 389–403, with further literature.

[7] Among the extensive literature on this prophetic sign, see esp. Nicholas Perrin, *Jesus the Temple* (Grand Rapids: Baker Academic, 2010), 80–109; see also Pitre, *Jesus and the Last Supper*, 436–437.

[8] Gerd Theißen and Annette Merz, *The Historical Jesus: A Comprehensive Guide*, trans. John Bowden (Minneapolis: Fortress Press, 1998), 434. The authors note that this argument is strengthened if the Last Supper was indeed a Passover meal but does not depend on it. See also Jacob Neusner, 'Money-Changers in the Temple: The Mishnah's Explanation', in *New Testament Studies* 35 (1989), 287–290

[9] See Pitre, *Jesus and the Last Supper*, 444–512.

dated it after this cataclysmic event.[10] Hebrews presents Christ as the high priest 'who is seated at the right hand of the throne of the Majesty in heaven, a minister in the sanctuary and the true tent which is set up not by man but by the Lord' (Heb 8:1–2). He has entered this heavenly sanctuary 'with his own blood, thus securing eternal redemption' (Heb 9:12) and became 'the mediator of a new covenant' (Heb 9:15) for the effective remission of sins. Jesus was of course not a Levitical priest but fulfils the biblical type of Melchizedek, the mysterious figure introduced in Genesis 14:18 as 'priest of God Most High'. In particular, Hebrews applies Psalm 110:4, 'You are a priest for ever after the order of Melchizedek', to Jesus Christ (the verse is cited in Heb 5:6 and 7:17).[11] Hebrews does not comment on the narrative in Genesis that Melchizedek, on meeting Abraham, offered bread and wine (Gen 14:18) – later Christian tradition saw in this sacrifice a type of the Eucharist (see Chapter 4). Rather, the author of the letter identifies the priestly sacrifice of Jesus Christ with his self-offering on the cross.

This raises the difficulty that the death of Jesus could not be understood as a sacrifice in the context of Second Temple worship. Jesus was executed as a common criminal by the Roman authorities outside the boundaries of the holy city, and his death did not involve any priestly rite. Hence, Albert Vanhoye proposes that the source for a sacrificial understanding of the death of Jesus is found in the words of institution at the Last Supper, especially in the reference to the Mosaic 'blood of the covenant' in Exodus 24:8.[12] This particular verse is cited in the letter's description of the sealing of the Sinai covenant in Hebrews 9:20; significantly, it is not cited in the common Greek wording 'Behold the blood of the covenant . . .' (ἰδοὺ τὸ αἷμα τῆς διαθήκης; Ex 24:8 LXX) but in the form 'This is the blood of the covenant . . .' (τοῦτο τὸ αἷμα τῆς διαθήκης), which echoes Jesus' words over the cup in Matthew 26:28 and Mark 14:24. An allusion to the Eucharist can also be recognised in Hebrews 13:10: 'We have an altar (θυσιαστήριον) from which those who serve the tent have no

[10] See David L. Allen, *Hebrews*, The New American Commentary 35 (Nashville: B&H, 2010), 74–79.
[11] See Knut Backhaus, *Der Hebräerbrief*, Regensburger Neues Testament (Regensburg: Friedrich Pustet, 2009), 256–275.
[12] See Scott Hahn, *Kinship by Covenant: A Canonical Approach to the Fulfillment of God's Saving Promises*, The Anchor Yale Bible Reference Library (New Haven; London: Yale University Press, 2009), 327–331, with reference to Albert Vanhoye, *Old Testament Priests and the New Priest: According to the New Testament*, trans. J. Bernard Orchard (Petersham: St Bede's, 1986), 50 and 53–54.

right to eat (φαγεῖν).' Stefan Heid argues that this 'altar' corresponds to the 'table of the Lord' of 1 Corinthians 10:21 and indicates the sacred table that was dedicated for use at the Eucharist.[13]

There is no consensus among New Testament exegetes in accepting these passages from Hebrews as Eucharistic references. Thus, it has been argued that, for the author of the letter, the sacrifice of Christ brings all material worship to an end. In response, Scott Hahn points to Hebrews 6, which affirms the importance of 'outward, material rites even in the new covenant order', such as ablutions and the laying on of hands, because they are in fact *'foundational* for the Christian faith'.[14] As Hahn argues, for Hebrews the difference between the Old Covenant and the New Covenant mediated by Christ is not ritual worship as such but its effectiveness. When the letter claims that the 'gifts and sacrifices [of the Old Covenant] cannot perfect the conscience of the worshipper' (Heb 9:9), the implication is that 'the New Covenant rites *can* and *do*'.[15]

Second, it is evident that the Book of Revelation incorporates liturgical language, but the actual use of these scattered texts in worship can barely be identified.[16] In the letters to the seven churches, the promises that those who conquer will eat 'from the tree of life' (Rev 2:7) will be fed with the 'hidden manna' (Rev 2:17) and will eat with Christ himself (Rev 3:19) have Eucharistic overtones and may relate to the ritual meals held by Christians. Also in these letters, the ascetic nature of these meals is contrasted with the excesses of pagan cultic meals that include the eating of meat sacrificed to idols and sexual immorality (see Rev 2:14–15, 20).[17] Christian meal celebrations culminate in the 'marriage supper of the Lamb' (Rev 19:9), which is a participation in the heavenly liturgy (see

---

[13] See Stefan Heid, *Altar und Kirche: Prinzipien christlicher Liturgie* (Regensburg: Schnell & Steiner, 2019), 32–42.

[14] Hahn, *Kinship by Covenant*, 330 (italics in the original).

[15] Ibid., 331 (italics in the original); see also Helmut Hoping, *My Body Given for You: History and Theology of the Eucharist*, trans. Michael J. Miller (San Francisco: Ignatius Press, 2019), 70–72.

[16] This discussion is indebted to Hoping, *My Body Given for You*, 68–70. For liturgical readings of Revelation, see Carlo Manunza, *L'Apocalisse come 'actio liturgica' cristiana: Studio esegetico-teologico di Ap 1,9–16; 3,14–22; 13,9–10; 19,1–8*, Analecta Biblica 199 (Rome: Gregorian & Biblical Press, 2012); and Ian Coleman, 'The Rubrics of Revelation: A Liturgical Reading', in *Antiphon* 21 (2017), 290–318.

[17] See also 1 Corinthians 8:1–13. It must remain uncertain, however, whether at the Christian meals envisaged by Revelation water would have replaced wine, as practised later by Ebionites, Encratites and others. See Andrew B. McGowan, *Ascetic Eucharists: Food and Drink in Early Christian Ritual Meals*, Oxford Early Christian Studies (Oxford: Clarendon Press, 1999), 143–174.

Rev 19:1–10). The hymns sung at this occasion – the only occurrence of the word 'alleluia' in the New Testament (Rev 19:1, 3, 4, 6) – and in the heavenly 'liturgy of the scrolls' (Rev 4–5) might have been used in Christian worship. Of particular interest is the variation on the *Sanctus* from Isaiah 6:3, 'Holy, holy, holy, is the Lord God Almighty, who was and is and is to come' (Rev 4:8). In Isaiah, the prophet's vision of the hymn of praise by the six-winged seraphim surrounding the throne of God is set in the Temple. In Revelation, the *Sanctus* is sung in heavenly worship, and the description of the scene draws on the visions of the four living creatures and the chariot-throne (*merkavah*) from Ezekiel 1 and 10. Such themes are common in the apocalyptic literature of Second Temple Judaism, where the angelic hymn (*quedusha*) is conceived as an expression of the union of earthly and heavenly liturgy. The idea of heaven and earth joined in the praise of God inspired the insertion of the *Sanctus* into Christian Eucharistic prayers in the fourth (and possibly as early as the third) century.[18]

Temple imagery features prominently in the visions of the Seer (e.g., Rev 7:15, 11:1 and 14:15). In the final vision of the heavenly Jerusalem, the measuring of the holy city (Rev 21:15–21) is reminiscent of the measuring of the Temple in Ezekiel 40–42. This holy city has no need of a temple building, because 'its temple is the Lord God the Almighty and the Lamb' (Rev 21:22). The Lamb is a Christological image: the fact that it was 'slain' (Rev 5:12; 13:8, among others) and that its blood has saving power (Rev 7:14) refers to the death of Jesus on the cross and carries allusions of the sacrificed Passover lamb. At the same time, the Lamb is standing (Rev 5:6) and is 'in the midst of the throne' of God (Rev 7:17), by which the resurrection and glorification of Christ are indicated.

The epilogue of Revelation offers a spiritual interpretation of Christian worship but gives us hardly any clues how this might have related to liturgical practice. The nuptial symbolism of the marriage supper of the

---

[18] The *Sanctus* is quoted in the late first century by *First Clement*, 34,6: SC 167,158. This may reflect liturgical use but not necessarily in the Eucharist. See Bryan D. Spinks, *Do This in Remembrance of Me: The Eucharist from the Early Church to the Present Day*, SCM Studies in Worship and Liturgy (London: SCM Press, 2013), 55–57; also Albert Gerhards, 'Crossing Borders. The Kedusha and the Sanctus: A Case Study of the convergence of Jewish and Christian Liturgy', in *Jewish and Christian Liturgy and Worship: New Insights into its History and Interaction*, ed. Albert Gerhards and Clemens Leonhard, Jewish and Christian Perspectives Series 15 (Leiden: Brill, 2007), 27–40.

Lamb shows the Church as bride in loving expectation of her bridegroom, Jesus Christ: 'The Spirit and the Bride say, "Come". And let him who hears say, "Come". And let him who is thirsty come, let him who desires take the water of life without price' (Rev 22:17). The desire for communion with Christ culminates in the prayerful invocation 'Come, Lord Jesus!' (Rev 22:20), which the Apostle Paul quotes in the Aramaic form *maranatha* (1 Cor 16:22). In the eschatological vision of the heavenly Jerusalem, there is no temple, since the whole city of the redeemed is formed by the adoration of God and the Lamb (Rev 22:3). However, this will come to pass only when heaven and earth are renewed and, at the very least, the empirical conditions of the present life still demand a suitable place (and time) for worship. Therefore, Helmut Hoping concludes, 'The Christian meal celebration in the Book of Revelation would ... certainly have been familiar with an altar table.'[19]

The importance of the imagery of temple and sacrifice in early Christianity can be understood in the context of what scholars have called the 'templization' of Jewish religious life in the late Second Temple period.[20] Robert Hayward argues that evidence from the Dead Sea Scrolls, from the writings of Josephus and Philo of Alexandria and possibly from early rabbinical sources '[allow] us to describe a distinctive type of piety, found both in the Jewish homeland and in the diaspora, which sought to replicate in some measure the holiness and purity of the Temple and its service outside the Temple courts'.[21] In other words, forms of Temple worship were imitated in religious practice outside Jerusalem. This found concrete expression in ritual washings with clean water and in meals that were held in common and had a distinctly cultic character. Hayward concludes: 'For this type of piety, common meals consumed in purity, and in societies characterised by order and hierarchical structure, could be described in sacrificial terms.'[22] Such practice provides a historical context for the development of baptism and the Eucharist (as well as the ordained ministry) in early Christianity. This is not meant to suggest an unbroken continuity between Jewish temple culture and early Christian liturgy. As already mentioned, Jesus' own relationship to the Jerusalem Temple was complex, and it combined reverence for its rituals

---

[19] Hoping, *My Body Given for You*, 70.
[20] See Robert Hayward, 'The Jewish Roots of Christian Liturgy', in *T&T Clark Companion to Liturgy*, ed. Alcuin Reid (London: Bloomsbury T&T Clark, 2016), 23–42; see also Jonathan Klawans, *Purity, Sacrifice, and the Temple: Symbolism and Supersessionism in the Study of Ancient Judaism* (Oxford: Oxford University Press, 2006).
[21] Hayward, 'The Jewish Roots of Christian Liturgy', 29.   [22] Ibid., 29–30.

with a critique of its present condition. Moreover, Jesus and his followers consciously overturned food laws related to purity (see Mk 7:1–16 and Acts 10:9–16), but their observance was tolerated (see Rom 14:1–8). At the same time, norms of sexual purity were considered binding in early Christianity (see 1 Cor 5:1–15; 6:12–16). The Qumran sect offers an instructive example of how a highly critical attitude towards the current state of the Jerusalem Temple and its priesthood went hand in hand with an *imitatio templi*, which Jonathan Klawans defines as 'the effort of channelling the sanctity that pertains to the temple (and its sacrificial cult) to other forms of worship'.[23]

The idea of *imitatio templi* also shaped the development of contemporary synagogue worship. Stefan C. Reif argues that in Palestine the synagogue's 'original functions were social, educational, and even recreational, rather than purely liturgical'.[24] These activities were framed by personal prayer, but a 'synagogue liturgy', that is, formalised communal worship, emerged only gradually in the Second Temple period and was standardised by leading rabbis after the calamitous events of AD 70. At the same time, the synagogue came to be seen as a 'holy place'; it was increasingly understood in categories derived from the Jerusalem Temple and integrated temple motifs in its decorative programme.[25]

The Importance of Malachi 1:11 in Early Christianity

A key biblical text for the early Christian understanding of the Eucharist is Malachi 1:11:

> For from the rising of the sun to its setting my name is great among the nations, and in every place incense is offered to my name, and a pure offering; for my name is great among the nations, says the Lord of hosts.

This verse forms part of God's diatribe – through his prophet Malachi – against the priests of the Jerusalem Temple for dishonouring the altar by

---

[23] Klawans, *Purity, Sacrifice, and the Temple*, 172; see ibid., 168–174.

[24] Stefan C. Reif, 'Prayer and Liturgy', in *The Oxford Handbook of Jewish Daily Life in Roman Palestine*, ed. Catherine Hezser (Oxford: Oxford University Press, 2010), 545–565, at 548. The term used for synagogues in the Diaspora, προσευχή, indicates that prayer was probably their primary purpose. See Peter von der Osten-Sacken, 'Von den jüdischen Wurzeln des christlichen Gottesdienstes', in *Liturgie als Theologie*, ed. Walter Homolka (Berlin: Frank & Timme, 2005), 130–153.

[25] See Steven Fine, *This Holy Place: On the Sanctity of the Synagogue during the Greco-Roman Period*, Christianity and Judaism in Antiquity Series 11 (Notre Dame: University of Notre Dame Press, 1997).

defective offerings. In response to the failings of the Temple priesthood, God announces that a 'pure offering' (LXX: θυσία καθαρά) will be made to his name, and this offering will be made 'in every place' (LXX: ἐν παντὶ τόπῳ) – not just in Jerusalem, but 'among the nations'. The Hebrew word employed for this pure and universal offering is *minhah*, which designates the bloodless meal offering, usually a baked loaf and wine libation that accompanied the burnt offering in the Temple (see Num 15:4–5).[26]

The earliest allusion to the prophecy from Malachi can be found in the Apostle Paul's First Letter to the Corinthians. In his initial greeting, Paul includes the Corinthians among those who 'in every place call on the name of our Lord Jesus Christ' (1 Cor 1:2). This particular phrase, 'to call on/invoke the name of the Lord', is used in the Old Testament in the context of cultic worship, which typically involves a sacrifice (e.g., Gen 12:8, 13:4 and 26:25).[27] The addition 'in every place' (ἐν παντὶ τόπῳ) would seem to echo the altar law of Exodus 20:24 ('An altar of earth you shall make for me and sacrifice on it ... in every place where I cause my name to be remembered I will come to you and bless you') and extend it to the Gentiles by associating it specifically with Malachi 1:11.

Malachi's prophecy features more prominently in 1 Corinthians 10, where Paul addresses the question of whether it is legitimate for Christians to eat meat that had been sacrificed to idols. The meat that was left over from pagan sacrificial worship was sold at the market (see 1 Cor 10:25) or could be eaten in temple restaurants (see 1 Cor 8:10). On high festivals, large quantities of high-quality meat became available cheaply. This was tempting for Christians at Corinth, especially since most people would eat meat only rarely. Paul emphasises that the gods of the heathen are mere idols but at the same time sees in their cult the work of demons. Eating from the victim is an essential part of sacrificial worship. Paul issues a warning to 'shun the worship of idols' (v. 14), which he connects with a teaching on the Eucharist:

The cup of blessing which we bless, is it not a participation in the blood of Christ? The bread which we break, is it not a participation in the body of Christ? Because

---

[26] After the destruction of the Temple, *minhah* came to designate the Jewish afternoon prayer service.

[27] See Dieter Böhler, 'The Church's Eucharist, the Lord's Supper, Israel's Sacrifice: Reflections on Pope Benedict's Axiom "Without Its Coherence with Its Old Testament Heritage, Christian Liturgy Simply Cannot Be Understood"', in *Benedict XVI and the Roman Missal*, 107–123, at 110–111; also Joseph A. Fitzmyer, *First Corinthians: A New Translation with Introduction and Commentary*, The Anchor Yale Bible 32 (New Haven; London: Yale University Press, 2008), 127.

there is one bread, we who are many are one body, for we all partake of the one bread. (vv. 16–17).

This sharing in the body and blood of Christ is explained in analogy with the sacrifices of Israel and in contrast with pagan sacrifices to idols. In the case of Israel, eating from the sacrifices establishes communion at the altar (v. 18), just as sharing in the one bread establishes the Church as one body. In like manner, those who sacrifice to demons enter into communion with them (v. 20). Hence, Paul admonishes the Christians at Corinth: 'You cannot drink the cup of the Lord and the cup of demons. You cannot partake of the table of the Lord (τραπέζης κυρίου) and the table of demons' (v. 21). Paul here constructs a dense argument with complex biblical allusions that probably eluded most of his Gentile addressees at Corinth.[28] The word τραπέζα is used in the Greek versions of the Hebrew Scriptures for the table carrying the bread of the Presence in the Tabernacle of the desert (e.g., Ex 25:23–30) and in the Temple of Jerusalem; as such, this table is identified as an 'altar' (Ezek 41:21–22; Mal 1:7).[29] This is confirmed by Malachi's invective against the priests' negligence in preparing the sacrificial offerings, which frames the above-quoted prophecy. Through his prophet the Lord accuses the priests of despising his name by

offering polluted food (ἄρτους, literally 'loaves') upon my altar (τὸ θυσιαστήριόν μου). And you say, 'How have we polluted it?" By thinking that the Lord's table (τράπεζα κυρίου) may be despised .... But you profane [my name] when you say that the Lord's table (τράπεζα κυρίου) is polluted, and the food for it may be despised. (Mal 1:7, 12)

While Malachi uses 'altar' and 'table of the Lord' interchangeably, Paul stops short of calling the table of the Lord's Supper an altar. However, this is clearly implied, as Joseph Fitzmyer notes: 'Paul is arguing primarily from the function of the altar in the cult of Israel and the relation of worshippers who offered sacrifices at it. What he says is predicated by implication of the table of the Lord in the Christian cult."[30] Consequently, the Lord's Supper is understood as the sacrificial meal of Christians that stands in sharp contrast to pagan sacrificial meals. The liturgical practice of the church at Corinth exemplifies the fulfilment of

---

[28] See E. P. Sanders, *Paul: The Apostle's Life, Letters, and Thought* (Minneapolis: Fortress, 2015), 327–328.

[29] On the bread of the Presence and its relation to the Eucharist, see esp. Pitre, *Jesus and the Last Supper*, 121–147.

[30] Fitzmyer, *First Corinthians*, 392.

Malachi's prophecy: the 'name' of the God of Israel is glorified 'among the nations' and 'in every place' a 'pure offering' is offered to him in the form of bread and wine. Whatever form the Eucharistic table may have taken in the domestic setting of the celebration at the time, it is recognised as an altar, and by calling it 'the table of the Lord', Paul 'explicitly puts it on a par with the Jerusalem altar, and sees it too in rivalry with pagan altars'.[31] While Paul's use of the prophetic text is somewhat coded, a broad stream of early Christian tradition from the late first century onwards cites Malachi 1:11 and identifies the 'pure offering' among the nations with the Eucharist.[32]

To conclude this section, any discussion of the early Eucharist needs to be mindful that in the ancient world the sacrifice of animals and of the produce of the land was at the very heart of religious worship, whether Greco-Roman or Jewish (before the destruction of the Temple in AD 70). One of the most momentous religious transformations of late antiquity was the interiorisation and spiritualisation of sacrifice, which was achieved in early Christianity through Christ's once-for-all sacrifice of the cross, and in rabbinical Judaism as a consequence of the destruction of the Jerusalem Temple.[33] It was still taken for granted that some kind of offering had to be made to God and that this sacrifice had to be carried out in an external, ritual form of worship. In the Christian Eucharist, Jewish concepts of sacrifice are not simply superseded but transformed.

SOURCES FOR EARLY CHRISTIAN LITURGY

In one of his letters, Erasmus of Rotterdam (d. 1536) buttressed the great project of Renaissance Humanism to return to the sources (*ad fontes*) with the claim: 'It is at the very sources that one extracts pure doctrine.'[34]

[31] Böhler, 'The Church's Eucharist, the Lord's Supper, Israel's Sacrifice', 114.
[32] The earliest references are as follows: *Didache*, 14: Anton Hänggi – Irmgard Pahl, *Prex eucharistica. Volumen I: Textus e variis liturgiis antiquioribus selecti*, Spicilegium Friburgense 12, 3rd ed. (Freiburg; Schweiz: Universitätsverlag, 1998), 68; Justin Martyr, *Dialogue with Trypho*, 41,2–3 and 117,1: PTS 47,138 and 271; Irenaeus of Lyon, *Against Heresies*, 4,17,5–18,1: SC 100,590–596; see Karl Suso Frank, 'Maleachi 1,10ff. in der frühen Väterdeutung: Ein Beitrag zu Opferterminologie und Opferverständnis in der alten Kirche', in *Theologie und Philosophie* 53 (1978), 70–79.
[33] See Guy G. Stroumsa, *The End of Sacrifice: Religious Transformations in Late Antiquity*, trans. Susan Emanuel (Chicago: University of Chicago Press, 2009).
[34] *Opus Epistolarum Des. Erasmi Roterodami*, ed. Percy Stafford Allen, Hellen Mary Allen and Heathcote William Garrod, 12 vols. (Oxford: Clarendon Press, 1906–1958), vol. II, 284.

In the history-conscious nineteenth century, John Henry Newman (d. 1890) illustrated his theory of the development of doctrine (and worship) with a strikingly different image:

It is indeed sometimes said that the stream is clearest near the spring. Whatever use may fairly be made of this image, it does not apply to the history of a philosophy or belief, which on the contrary is more equable, and purer, and stronger, when its bed has become deep, and broad, and full.[35]

The search for the origins of the Christian liturgy certainly vindicates Newman over Erasmus. The sources that have come down to us are few and far between, and there are good reasons to question whether the snippet view they grant us suffices to reconstruct the history of Christian worship in the first two centuries. Hence, the leading liturgical scholars of the twentieth century, such as Gregory Dix and Josef Andreas Jungmann, have sustained much criticism for their approach to develop a mono-linear narrative from an original structure or shape.[36] The comparative method of Anton Baumstark has greatly broadened the horizon of liturgical studies and has alerted us to the variety of early Christian worship, even though Baumstark's 'laws' of liturgical development, which are adapted from evolutionary biology and propose an 'organic' model, cannot be applied absolutely and need to be used with circumspection.[37] In his highly influential work on liturgical methodology, Paul Bradshaw affirms the irreducible pluriformity of early Christian worship;[38] and in his historical studies (many of which were the fruit of collaboration with Maxwell Johnson), he consistently implements this premise. Moreover, Bradshaw applies the hermeneutic of suspicion that has dominated modern biblical exegesis to liturgical sources and insists how little we really know about early Christian worship. While this methodology has yielded impressive results, for instance, in the re-evaluation of the

---

[35] John Henry Newman, *An Essay on the Development of Christian Doctrine*, 14th impression (London: Longmans, Green, and Co., 1909), 40.

[36] See Gregory Dix, *The Shape of the Liturgy* (London: Dacre Press, 1945); and Josef A. Jungmann, *Missarum sollemnia: Eine genetische Erklärung der römischen Messe*, 2 vols., 5th ed. (Wien: Herder, 1962). At the same time, we can still profit from Jungmann's extensive knowledge of sources.

[37] See Anton Baumstark, *Liturgie comparée: Principes et méthodes pour l'étude historique des liturgies chrétiennes*, Collection Irénikon, 3rd ed. (Chevetogne: Éditions de Chevetogne, 1954).

[38] See Paul F. Bradshaw, *The Search for the Origins of Christian Worship: Sources and Methods for the Study of the Early Liturgy*, 2nd ed. (Oxford: Oxford University Press, 2002), esp. 1–20.

problematic document known as *Apostolic Tradition* (see below, pp. 80–82), it tends 'towards deconstruction and fragmentation', as Daniel Van Slyke notes in his recent overview of theories and methods in the study of early Christian worship.[39]

This radical shift is of course part of a sea-change that has affected early Christian studies in their entirety. The New Testament scholar Bart Ehrman coined the term 'proto-orthodoxy' to describe a Christian group that is most visible in second- and third-century sources but was just one sect among others. After the group had gained ascendancy by the late third century, it established itself as 'orthodoxy' at the Council of Nicaea in 325 and its aftermath and created a narrative in which its rivals were branded as 'heretics'.[40] The pillars of the emerging proto-orthodox consensus were (1) monepiscopacy (the government of the local church by a single bishop) and apostolic succession, (2) baptismal creed and rule of faith and (3) the canon of scripture.[41] Critics of Ehrman's theory have noted that the idea of 'normative Christianity' (a term given currency in early Christian studies by Arland Hultgren)[42] is already evident in the first century. As Larry Hurtado argues,

to a remarkable extent early-second-century proto-orthodox devotion to Jesus represents a concern to preserve, respect, promote, and develop what were by then becoming traditional expressions of belief and reverence, and that had originated in earlier years of the Christian movement. That is, proto-orthodox faith tended to affirm and develop devotional and confessional tradition.[43]

The 'proto-orthodox' bishops and theologians who engaged with rival interpretations of Christianity (above all, those gathered under the

---

[39] Daniel G. Van Slyke, 'The Study of Early Christian Worship', in *T&T Clark Companion to Liturgy*, ed. Alcuin Reid (London: Bloomsbury T&T Clark, 2016), 43–71, at 63.

[40] See Bart D. Ehrman, *The New Testament: A Historical Introduction to the Early Christian Writings* (New York: Oxford University Press, 1997), 7–8. Ehrman builds on the work of Walter Bauer, *Rechtgläubigkeit und Ketzerei im ältesten Christentum*, Beiträge zur historischen Theologie 10 (Tübingen: Mohr, 1934), which was widely received in English-speaking scholarship after the publication of the second German edition and of the translation: *Orthodoxy and Heresy in Earliest Christianity* (Philadelphia: Fortress Press, 1971).

[41] See the useful overviews of Joseph H. Lynch, *Early Christianity: A Brief History* (Oxford; New York: Oxford University Press, 2010), 62–78; and Everett Ferguson, *Church History. Volume One: From Christ to Pre-Reformation* (Grand Rapids: Zondervan, 2005), 106–122.

[42] See Arland J. Hultgren, *The Rise of Normative Christianity* (Minneapolis: Fortress Press, 1994).

[43] Larry W. Hurtado, *Lord Jesus Christ: Devotion to Jesus in Earliest Christianity* (Grand Rapids: Eerdmans, 2005), 495.

heading 'Gnostic') understood themselves as defenders of a tradition that was handed down from the apostles and certainly not as innovators. The emerging biblical canon is a case in point: it is not determined but recognised by third-century authors. A critical scholar is inclined to question the veracity of such self-awareness, but the claim has very early roots.

Mark Edwards, who proposes a sophisticated theory of how 'heresy' actually played a constructive role in the development of orthodox doctrine, at the same time observes that '[t]here is scarcely any book of our New Testament which does not contain an invective against false teaching'.[44] According to Edwards, 'while there was evidently some difference of belief and much diversity in the expression of belief, there was no unregulated ferment of opinion such as is posited by those who speak of different and competing Christianities'.[45] In fact, the teaching office of bishops appears more united before Nicaea than after, when the Arian controversy caused deep divisions especially in the Christian East.[46]

Robert Taft insists that there is some truth in mono-linear narratives, because 'there existed an original apostolic kerygma to which everything Christian can be ultimately traced'.[47] Taft offers a linguistic simile that may help to elucidate the liturgical diversification of early Christianity:

in phase one the original kerygma, implanted in different areas, gave rise to a plethora of local liturgical usages. In a given region these usages were all of the same 'type', just as Proto-Indoeuropean evolved into a multitude of eastern and western subfamilies, each with its many dialects or spoken varieties even within the same limited geographical area. But in a later phase, the many *dialects* of each of these subgroups became unified into, or gave way before newer literary *languages*.[48]

Taft points to the variety of languages and dialects in Italy today, which differ from the 'standard Italian' that results from the literary dominance of the Tuscan dialect. Given the increasing cultural homogeneity of Italy and the effects of mass communication (radio, television etc.), local dialects will increasingly vanish and be replaced by standard Italian. In

---

[44] Mark Edwards, *Catholicity and Heresy in the Early Church* (Farnham; Burlington: Ashgate, 2009), 3. Edwards also refers to Newman's 'notes' or 'tests' for authentic development and argues that Newman should have made more of the 'power of assimilation' as a 'note' of catholicity (ibid.).

[45] Ibid., 1.   [46] See ibid., 5–6.

[47] Robert F. Taft, *The Byzantine Rite: A Short History*, American Essays in Liturgy (Collegeville, MN: Liturgical Press, 1992), 24.

[48] Ibid, 25.

the post-Constantinian period, a similar process affected Christian worship:

a multitude of related but different liturgical "dialects" within a given zone of ecclesiastical politico-cultural influence gave way to the growing predominance of the "standard" language or rite – usually that of the metropolis. The result was greater unity, not greater diversity.[49]

The above-mentioned three pillars of normative Christianity in the first two centuries had a direct impact on liturgical practice, but it may be opportune to add a distinct fourth pillar: the Last Supper tradition and the institution of the Eucharist, which came to shape the central ritual of the Christian faith. This is not to deny the insights of recent scholarship into the diversity of early Christian meal gatherings, not all of which were a 'Eucharistic Christ-anamnesis' (Reinhard Meßner) in ritual shape and interpreting word.[50] However, in analogy to the other three elements, the Last Supper tradition can be recognised as a regulative force of the Eucharist in the variety of its liturgical forms.

Discipline of Secrecy?

Historians coined the term *disciplina arcani* or 'discipline of secrecy' for the practice of keeping the most important rituals and formulas of Christianity hidden from those who were not full members of the Church. The concept has come under criticism, because it suggests that Christians were obliged to keep strict silence especially about the baptismal and Eucharistic liturgies in analogy to Greco-Roman mystery cults, where the sacred rites were only known to the initiates. The Christian sacraments were never *arcana* in a strict sense, neither were the creed and the Lord's Prayer, about which early theologians published written

---

[49] Ibid.
[50] Reinhard Meßner, *Einführung in die Liturgiewissenschaft* (Paderborn: Schöningh, 2009), 164, speaks of 'eucharistische Christusanamnese'. On the diversity of early Christian meals, see *The Eucharist – Its Origins and Contexts: Sacred Meal, Communal Meal, Table Fellowship in Late Antiquity, Early Judaism, and Early Christianity. Vol. III Near Eastern and Graeco-Roman Traditions, Archaeology*, ed. David Hellholm and Dieter Sänger, Wissenschaftliche Untersuchungen zum Neuen Testament 376, (Tübingen: Mohr Siebeck, 2017); Andrew B. McGowan, *Ancient Christian Worship: Early Church Practices in Social, Historical and Theological Perspective* (Grand Rapids: Baker Academic, 2014), 20–33; *T&T Clark Handbook to Early Christian Meals in the Greco-Roman World*, ed. Soham Al-Suadi and Peter-Ben Smit (London; New York: Bloomsbury T&T Clark, 2019).

works.[51] Christoph Jacob interprets the rhetoric of secrecy in Christian authors as a merely pedagogical or, rather, mystagogical device for initiating catechumens into the faith and the sacraments.[52] While there is no evidence for a *disciplina arcani* in the strict sense, a variety of early sources do suggest reticence among Christians to disclose their beliefs and practices to outsiders. In its embryonic form, this idea is already implied in Matthew 7:6: 'Do not give what is holy to the dogs, or throw your pearls before swine.' Joachim Jeremias has claimed somewhat implausibly that the absence of the words of institution from the Gospel of John can be explained with the desire to hide the sacred formula from profanation. There may be more probability in his argument that desire to protect the Eucharist accounts for the reticence in speaking about it in the Acts of the Apostles (pseudonyms for the Eucharist), the Letter to the Hebrews (reservation of Eucharistic teaching for the 'mature') and the *Didache* (silence about the Eucharistic ritual).[53]

Tertullian uses the term *arcanum* when referring to non-Christian worship and when speaking about the 'secret' doctrines and practices of heretics. At one point, he mocks the obscurantism of the Valentinians. There are also *arcana* of the Christian faith, such as the teaching on the fall or the Eucharist, which are not accessible to pagans, but this does not prevent Tertullian from writing about them. Nonetheless, he attests that there was some secrecy about Christian liturgical assemblies, particularly in a hostile environment that could burst into occasional persecution. Non-believers and catechumens were excluded from the celebration of the Eucharist.[54] Origen (d. 253) elaborates in his *Homilies on Numbers* that there are ecclesiastical customs that are not understood by many, such as the ceremonies of baptism and the Eucharist. They are veiled like the holy things of the tent of meeting, which are covered by Aaron and his

---

[51] For a critical account of the 'discipline of secrecy' theory, see Douglas Powell, 'Arkandisziplin', in *Theologische Realenzyklopädie* 4 (1979), 1–8; also Edward J. Yarnold, *The Awe-Inspiring Rites of Initiation: The Origins of the R.C.I.A.*, 2nd ed. (Collegeville: Liturgical Press, 1994), 55–56.

[52] See Christoph Jacob, *'Arkandisziplin', Allegorese, Mystagogie: Ein neuer Zugang zur Theologie des Ambrosius von Mailand*, Theophaneia 32 (Frankfurt am Main: Anton Hain, 1990).

[53] See Joachim Jeremias, *The Eucharistic Words of Jesus*, trans. Norman Perrin, The New Testament Library (London: SCM Press, 1966), 125–137.

[54] On secrecy in Tertullian, see Jörg C. Salzmann, *Lehren und Ermahnen: zur Geschichte des christlichen Wortgottesdienstes in den ersten drei Jahrhunderten*, Wissenschaftliche Untersuchungen zum Neuen Testament II/59 (Tübingen: Mohr Siebeck, 1994), 396–399 and 427–429.

sons (Num 4). While this passage shows Origen's reserve in speaking on Christian worship, elsewhere he does comment on it more openly.[55] The appeal to an, albeit mitigated, discipline of secrecy is an argument from silence that may not carry much weight. At the same time, it cannot be discarded entirely and serves as a reminder that the extant sources of early Christian worship – for a variety of reasons – grant us no more than a partial view. The best we can do is to keep close to the sources and be circumspect when constructing hypotheses.

Didache

The *Didache* is the earliest representative of the genre of texts known as Church order, which is a collection of catechetical teachings and liturgical instructions that regulate the life of a particular community. The work was known in Christian antiquity, but its text was discovered only in 1873 in a manuscript that lists the title first as 'The Teaching of the Twelve Apostles' and then in a fuller version as 'The Lord's Teaching to the Gentiles through the Twelve Apostles'.[56] The *Didache* is a composite document from Syria or Palestine that is usually dated between 80 and 100 but relies on earlier material. The work's claim to apostolic authority led to the book occasionally being numbered among the canonical Scriptures, and several later Church orders show its influence.

The *Didache*'s Jewish-Christian background is reflected in its concern for how to receive and integrate Gentile converts and is prominent in the catechesis of chapters 1 to 6, which are considered the oldest part of the document. Chapters 7 to 10 contain instructions for baptism, fasting and meal celebrations. The meal prayers in chapters 9 and 10, which most likely precede the final redaction of the *Didache*, have received different readings and the questions they raise are still being discussed controversially in historical scholarship.[57] Both sets of prayers present themselves as prayers of thanksgiving, and chapter 9 is properly introduced as

---

[55] Origen, *Hom. in Num.*, V, 1: GCS Orig. VII, 26–27.
[56] For an introduction to the extensive scholarship on the *Didache*, see Kurt Niederwimmer, *Die Didache*, Kommentar zu den Apostolischen Vätern 1, 2nd ed. (Göttingen: Vandenhoeck & Ruprecht, 1993); and *The Didache in Modern Research*, ed. Jonathan A. Draper, Arbeiten zur Geschichte des antiken Judentums und des Urchristentums 37 (Leiden; New York: Brill, 1996).
[57] This discussion is indebted to Spinks, *Do This in Remembrance of Me*, 22–27; and Hoping, *My Body Given for You*, 73–80.

'thanksgiving' (εὐχαριστία) – the earliest known use of the term for a Christian meal celebration:

> [1] Regarding the Eucharist (εὐχαριστίας), give thanks (εὐχαριστήσατε) as follows.
> [2] First for the cup:
> 'We give you thanks, our Father,
> for the holy vine of David, your servant,
> whom you have revealed to us through Jesus, your servant.
> Glory be to you forever.'
> [3] Then for the broken bread:
> 'We give you thanks, our Father,
> for the life and the knowledge
> which you have given us through Jesus, your servant.
> Glory be to you forever.
> [4] As this broken bread, scattered over the mountains,
> was gathered together to be one,
> so may your Church be gathered together in the same manner
> from the ends of the earth into your kingdom;
> for to you are the glory and the power
> through Jesus Christ forever.'
> [5] Let no one eat or drink of your Eucharist except those who
> have been baptized in the name of the Lord; for it was in regard to
> this that the Lord said, 'Do not give what is holy to the dogs.'[58]

The thanksgiving for the cup precedes the thanksgiving for the broken bread, which is linked with a prayer for the gathering of the Church, spread throughout the world, into God's kingdom. After the final doxology is appended an exhortation to share the Eucharist only with the baptised, which is reinforced by the stark dominical saying also found in Matthew 7:6.

The prayers of chapter 10 are placed after a regular meal and begin by offering thanks and praise for the graces and blessings God grants through Jesus:

> [1] After you have been filled, give thanks (εὐχαριστήσατε) as follows:
> [2] 'We give you thanks, holy Father,
> for your holy name
> which you have made to dwell
> in our hearts,

---

[58] *Didache*, 9: The Greek text is available in Hänggi–Pahl, *Prex eucharistica*, I, 66. The English translation is taken from Lawrence J. Johnson, *Worship in the Early Church: An Anthology of Historical Sources*, 4 vols. (Collegeville: Liturgical Press, 2009), vol. I, 37–38 (no. 187).

and for the knowledge, the faith, and the immortality
which you revealed to us
through your servant Jesus.
Glory be to you forever.
[3] 'Almighty Lord, you have created all things
for the sake of your name.
You have given all food and drink for refreshment
so that they may give you thanks.
But to us you have given spiritual food and drink and eternal life
through [Jesus] your servant.
[4] 'For everything we thank you
because you are powerful.
Glory be to you forever.
[5] 'Lord, remember your Church; deliver it from all evil
and perfect it in your love.
Gather this sanctified Church from the four winds
into the kingdom you have prepared for it.
For to you belong the power and the glory forever.
[6] 'May grace come, and may this world pass away.
Hosanna to the God of David.
If anyone is holy, let him come;
if anyone is not, let him do penance.
Maranatha.'
[7] Allow the prophets to give thanks as they wish.[59]

The thanksgiving for 'spiritual food and drink and eternal life' seems to imply that it is precisely this spiritual eating and drinking that bestows eternal life. As in chapter 9, the prayers include a petition for the gathering of the Church into God's kingdom and a doxology. There is also an exhortation that grants access to those who are holy and imposes penance on those who are not. Unlike in chapter 10, however, this exhortation is framed by an eschatological supplication for the passing of this world and by the Aramaic invocation *maranatha* ('Come, our Lord'; 1 Cor 16:22, see also Rev 22:20).

The parallels in language and content between the prayers in chapters 9 and 10 offer some support for the hypothesis of Alan Garrow that they originally belonged to two separate meal rituals that have been combined into one.[60] In particular, the exhortation 'If anyone is holy, let him come' can be interpreted as an invitation to join in the spiritual food and drink

---

[59] *Didache*, 10: *Prex eucharistica*, I, 66–68; trans. *Worship in the Early Church*, 38 (no. 187).
[60] See Alan J. P. Garrow, *The Gospel of Matthew's Dependence on the Didache* (London: T&T Clark, 2003), 28.

mentioned just before. On the other hand, the eschatological context might suggest that the invitation refers to sharing in the fulfilment of God's kingdom when the Lord will come again.[61]

Alternatively, in the order in which the texts have come down to us, chapter 10 can be understood in analogy to a post-communion prayer. Scholars have often noted similarities with the Jewish *birkat ha-mazon*, the tripartite blessing said at the end of a meal. However, the difficulty with this comparison lies in the fact that there was no fixed text of this prayer at the time the *Didache* was composed. The form of the *birkat ha-mazon* that is known to us results from the rabbinical standardisation of Jewish ritual and prayer in the Mishnah from the late second century onwards (see Chapter 1). Hence the idea that the post-prandial prayers of the *Didache* represent a specific reworking of the *birkat ha-mazon* has drawn considerable criticism. At the same time, there is no doubt that these prayers follow Jewish models that were already used at the time, even if their formal codification post-dates the *Didache* itself.[62] For instance, the petitions for the gathering of the Church in chapters 9 and 10 recall prayers for the gathering of Israel in the *Amidah* (which is to be recited three times a day) and in the *Musaf* service of the Day of Atonement (Yom Kippur).[63]

There has been much debate about the Eucharistic nature of the prayers in *Didache* 9 and 10. The memorial (*anamnesis*) of the Lord's death and resurrection, which is at the heart of later Eucharistic prayers, is at best implicit: addressing Jesus as 'servant' (παῖς) of God (9,2–3) might evoke the suffering servant of Isaiah 42; giving thanks for the 'immortality' (10,2) and 'eternal life' (10,3) gained through Jesus might allude to his resurrection.[64] Moreover, the prayers do not include the words of

---

[61] See Hoping, *My Body Given for You*, 78, with reference to Reinhard Meßner, 'Grundlinien der Entwicklung des eucharistischen Gebets in der frühen Kirche', in *Prex eucharistica. Volumen III: Studia. Pars prima: Ecclesia antiqua et occidentalis*, ed. Albert Gerhards, Heinzgerd Brakmann and Martin Klöckener, Spicilegium Friburgense 42 (Fribourg: Academic Press, 2005), 3–41, at 12.

[62] See Spinks, *Do This in Remembrance of Me*, 23–25, with reference to Jonathan Schwiebert, *Knowledge and the Coming Kingdom: The Didache's Meal Ritual and Its Place in Early Christianity* (London: T&T Clark, 2008), 118–119.

[63] See Hoping, *My Body Given for You*, 77 and 78, with reference to Gerard Rouwhorst, 'Didache 9–10: A Litmus Test for the Research on Early Christian Eucharist', in *Matthew and the Didache: Two Documents from the Same Jewish Christian Milieu?*, ed. Huub van de Sandt (Assen; Minneapolis: Royal Van Gorcum and Fortress Press, 2005), 143–156, at 149.

[64] An explicit *anamnesis* is added in the reworking of *Didache*, 9 in *Apostolic Constitutions*, VII, 25, 4: SC 336,54.

institution that would connect the Eucharist with the Last Supper. Hence, many scholars, including Josef Andreas Jungmann, Kurt Niederwimmer and Willy Rordorf, have argued that the meal described in these texts is not Eucharistic in the proper sense but resembles an *agape* celebration of the local church. More recently, however, the common opinion emphasises the diversity of early Christian meal practice. Thus, Bryan Spinks concludes:

if it is accepted that the term 'Eucharist' had a much wider meaning in the first three centuries, and was not always associated with the Institution Narratives of the New Testament, then there is no need to conclude that this was not a Eucharist. Equally, though, it is the Eucharist of *this particular community*, and not necessarily representative of all other Christian communities at this time.[65]

Spinks also observes that the particularities of the meal prayers are consistent with the primitive Jewish-Christian character of the *Didache*:

Given that this community preached what Jesus preached, but did not preach Jesus, we should not be surprised that the meal, like the whole document, has no reference to the death of Jesus, and thus no association of the bread and wine with his body and blood.[66]

Another question that needs to be considered is the relationship of the meal ritual of chapters 9 and 10 with the gathering on the Lord's Day in chapter 14:

[1] And on the Lord's Day gather to break bread and to give thanks (κλάσατε ἄρτον καὶ εὐχαριστήσατε), after having confessed your offenses so that your sacrifice (θυσία) may be pure. [2] But let no one who has a difference with a companion join you till they are reconciled so that your sacrifice (θυσία) not be defiled. [3] For this is what the Lord said, 'In every place and time let there be offered to me a pure sacrifice for I am a great king, says the Lord, and my name is revered among the nations.'[67]

The liturgical assembly on the Lord's Day is described as a breaking of bread (an expression used in Luke 24:30, 35, Acts 2:42, 20:7, 11 and 27:35) and as a Eucharist. This may well be the earliest reference to a liturgical celebration on Sunday, the first day of the Jewish week, outside the New Testament writings. The relationship of the community Eucharist in chapter 14 to the meal prayers of chapters 9 and 10 raises a number of questions that can hardly be resolved: Were these prayers

[65] Spinks, *Do This in Remembrance of Me*, 23.   [66] Ibid., 27.
[67] *Didache*, 14: *Prex eucharistica*, I, 68; trans. Johnson, vol. I, 40 (no. 191), slightly modified.

meant to be used at the assembly on the Lord's Day? Do they instead apply to a distinct meal celebration in a domestic setting? Or should we rather consider the whole section comprising chapters 11 to 15 to represent a separate stage in the evolution in the *Didache* community?

Three times in the short chapter 14, the Eucharistic breaking of the bread on the Lord's Day is referred to as the 'sacrifice' (θυσία) of those who share in it. Participation in this sacrifice calls for confession of sins and reconciliation with one another, and this demand is reinforced with a quotation of Malachi 1:11. Huub van de Sandt locates the *Didache* within the broader stream of Jewish temple piety, which has been discussed above. The sanctity of the Jerusalem Temple is channelled into the community meal, which is understood as a sacrifice:

> The meal was conceived in terms of holiness because the sanctuary and its sacrificial ritual were well known to signify God's presence among His people .... The framework of the blessings in Did 9 and 10, the stereotyped form of expression in Did 9:5d, the emphasis on purity in Did 14 and the explicit mention of 'sacrifice' in the same section suggest that the Eucharist table is compared to the temple altar.[68]

While the sacrifice of Christ is not mentioned in chapter 14, I suggest that it is precisely the 'missing link' that enables the community of the *Didache*, which identifies as Christian, to conceive of the breaking of the bread on Sunday in sacrificial terms and see in it the fulfilment of Malachi's prophecy.

Ignatius of Antioch

Ignatius of Antioch was brought as a prisoner to Rome, where he was executed in the games during the reign of the Emperor Trajan, around the year 110.[69] On the way to his martyrdom, he wrote seven letters that are generally considered authentic. These letters are an important source for the early development of monepiscopacy. This type of Church order was adopted throughout Christianity in the course of the second century.

---

[68] Huub van de Sandt, 'Why Does the Didache Conceive of the Eucharist as a Holy Meal?', in *Vigiliae Christianae* 65 (2011), 1–20, at 20; see also Schwiebert, *Knowledge and the Coming Kingdom*, 167.

[69] Transporting a condemned criminal from the provinces to Rome for the games was not entirely unusual at the time. See Allen Brent, *Ignatius of Antioch: A Martyr Bishop and the Origin of Episcopacy* (London: T&T Clark Continuum, 2007), 15–17.

Ignatius regularly speaks of the Eucharist, which is celebrated by the bishop (or his delegate), as an effective sign of the unity of the church:

Take care, therefore, to participate in one Eucharist (for there is one flesh of our Lord Jesus Christ, and one cup that leads to unity through his blood; there is one altar, just as there is one bishop, together with the council of presbyters and the deacons, my fellow servants), in order that whatever you do, you do in the name of God.[70]

The regular use of θυσιαστήριον (translated 'altar' or 'sanctuary') in connection with the Eucharist indicates that its character is understood as cultic and sacrificial.[71] Ignatius' observation that 'disciples of Jesus Christ' no longer observe the sabbath, but live 'in accordance with the Lord's day, on which our life also arose through him and his death' could suggest a weekly celebration of the Eucharist.[72]

The letters testify to a strong belief in the Eucharistic presence of Christ, which is rooted in a distinctly Johannine Christology. Ignatius calls the Eucharist 'the flesh (σάρξ) of our savior Jesus Christ, which suffered for our sins and which the Father by his goodness raised up'.[73] The use of 'flesh' (σάρξ) rather than 'body' (σῶμα) for the Eucharist points to Jesus' 'bread of life' discourse. Ignatius develops the language of John 6 when he speaks of 'breaking one bread, which is the medicine of immortality, the antidote we take in order not to die but to live forever in Jesus Christ'.[74]

In a remarkable passage from his letter to the Roman church, Ignatius expresses his ardent desire for martyrdom and describes it in Eucharistic terms: 'I am God's wheat, and I am being ground by the teeth of the wild

[70] Ignatius of Antioch, *Philadelphians*, 4: *The Apostolic Fathers: Greek Texts and English Translations*, edited and translated by Michael W. Holmes after the earlier work of J. B. Lightfoot and J. R. Harmer, 3rd ed. (Grand Rapids: Baker Academic, 2007), 238 and 239; see also *Smyrneans*, 8,1: ibid., 254 and 255.

[71] See Ignatius of Antioch, *Ephesians*, 5,2: ed. and trans. Holmes, 186 and 187; *Magnesians* 7,2: ibid., 206 and 207; *Trallians* 7,2: ibid., 218 and 219. On the importance of cultic imagery in Ignatius, see Jonathon Lookadoo, *The High Priest and the Temple: Metaphorical Depictions of Jesus in the Letters of Ignatius of Antioch*, Wissenschaftliche Untersuchungen zum Neuen Testament II/473 (Tübingen: Mohr Siebeck 2018).

[72] Ignatius of Antioch, *Magnesians*, 9,1: ed. and trans. Holmes, 208 and 209.

[73] Ignatius of Antioch, *Smyrneans*, 6,2: ed. and trans. Holmes, 254 and 255; see also *Romans*, 7,3: ibid., 232 and 233.

[74] Ignatius of Antioch, *Ephesians*, 20,2: ed. and trans. Holmes, 198 and 199. See Pitre, *Jesus and the Last Supper*, 246–248; also Lothar Wehr, *Arznei der Unsterblichkeit: Die Eucharistie bei Ignatius von Antiochen und im Johannesevangelium*, Neutestamentliche Abhandlungen, N.F. 18 (Münster: Aschendorff, 1987).

beasts, so that I may prove to be pure bread.'[75] The association of martyrdom with the Eucharist is also found in the *Martyrdom of Polycarp* (usually dated between 155 and 160) and in the *Passion of Perpetua and Felicity* (203/204),[76] and it becomes an important factor in liturgical development from the fourth century onwards (see Chapter 4).

The letters of Ignatius offer valuable insight into the doctrinal content of the Eucharist but contain little information about its liturgical form. Whether the references to the 'one altar' can tell us something about the actual setting of the Eucharist will be discussed below.

Justin Martyr

The earliest description of a Eucharistic celebration hails from mid-second-century Rome and forms part of the *First Apology* of Justin Martyr. Born in Flavia Neapolis (modern Nablus) in Palestine c. 100, Justin frequented various schools of philosophy until he found in Christianity the 'true philosophy'. In the reign of the Emperor Antoninus Pius (138–161), Justin settled in Rome and founded a philo-sophical school. In c. 165, he suffered martyrdom, and the acts of his trial and execution are generally considered authentic.

The *First Apology*, written in Rome between 150 and 155, is an explanation and defence of Christian faith and practice, written in Greek and addressed to Emperor Antoninus Pius and his sons. Justin's depiction of the worship of Christians includes an account of a post-baptismal Eucharist, which is followed by a brief doctrinal exposition and a description of a typical Sunday Eucharist. The *First Apology* is written for a presumed non-Christian readership and therefore only the essential structure of the liturgical celebrations is given in language intelli-gible to outsiders; no detailed information is provided about its ritual shape or the contents of prayers.

---

[75] Ignatius of Antioch, *Romans*, 4,1: ed. and trans. Holmes, 228 and 229. Some manuscripts read 'bread of Christ' and others 'bread of God'.

[76] On Polycarp, see Boudewijn Dehandschutter, *Polycarpiana: Studies on Martyrdom and Persecution in Early Christianity: Collected Essays*, ed. Johan Leemans, Bibliotheca Ephemeridum theologicarum Lovaniensium 205 (Leuven: Leuven University Press, 2007). On Perpetua and Felicity, see Elizabeth Klein, 'Perpetua, Cheese, and Martyrdom as Public Liturgy in the Passion of Perpetua and Felicity', in *Journal of Early Christian Studies* 28 (2020), 175–202.

Justin was born in the Eastern Mediterranean and travelled through different parts of the Roman world before settling in the capital. Hence, it is not clear whether his account of the Sunday Eucharist is specific to Rome or follows a common pattern he experienced in various local churches. It is noteworthy that the basic liturgical structure he describes has remained the same throughout the centuries:

And on the day that is called Sunday all who live in the cities or in rural areas gather together in one place, and the memoirs of the apostles and the writings of the prophets are read for as long as time allows. Then after the lector concludes, the president verbally instructs and exhorts us to imitate all these excellent things. Then all stand up together and offer prayers; as I said before, when we have concluded our prayer, bread is brought forward together with the wine and water. And the presider in like manner offers prayers and thanksgivings according to his ability. The people give their consent, saying 'Amen'; there is a distribution, and all share in the Eucharist. To those who are absent a portion is brought by the deacons. And those who are well-to-do and willing give as they choose, as each one so desires. The collection is then deposited with the presider who uses it on behalf of orphans, widows, those who are needy due to sickness or any other cause, prisoners, strangers who are traveling; in short, he assists all who are in need. But Sunday is the day on which we hold our common assembly since this day is the first day on which God, changing darkness and matter, created the world; it was on this very day that Jesus Christ our Savior rose from the dead.[77]

Justin is the oldest available source to confirm that readings from Scripture – 'memoirs of the apostles' and 'writings of the prophets' – formed part of the Eucharistic liturgy. In the first half of the twentieth century, Anton Baumstark and Gregory Dix held that the 'Liturgy of the Word' – as it is widely known today – derived from the synagogue. Scholars are less confident about this theory today, since the rabbinical standardisation of synagogue worship does not necessarily reflect first-century practice, at least not in detail. Important witness comes from the New Testament: The visit of Jesus to the synagogue in Nazareth on the Sabbath included a reading from the prophet Isaiah (Lk 4:16–30). Similarly, when Paul went to the synagogue in Antioch of Pisidia on the Sabbath, there were readings from the Law and the Prophets (Acts 13:15). It would seem likely that even the primitive Christian Eucharist included some form of scriptural reading and religious instruction.[78]

---

[77] Justin Martyr, *First Apology*, 67,3–8: PTS 38,129–130; trans. Johnson, vol. I, 68–69 (no. 246).
[78] See Hans Georg Thümmel, 'Versammlungsraum, Kirche, Tempel', in *Gemeinde ohne Tempel/Community Without Temple: Zur Substituierung und Transformation des Jerusalemer Tempels und seines Kults im Alten Testament, antiken Judentum und*

The expression 'memoirs of the apostles' is frequently found in the *Dialogue with Trypho*, which Justin wrote a few years after the *First Apology*. This particular use and variations in gospel citations has often been taken to indicate that Justin relied on a gospel harmony similar to the *Diatessaron* that was produced by his disciple Tatian in c. 170.[79] On the other hand, Justin himself identifies the 'memoirs' (ἀπομνημονεύματα) composed by the apostles with the 'gospels' (εὐαγγέλια) in the section of the *First Apology* that precedes his account of the Sunday Eucharist.[80] Helmut Koester suggests that 'memoirs' was a term associated with the faithful transmission of oral tradition about Jesus and it may have been preferred by Justin to set himself apart from Marcion, who appears to have been the first to speak of 'gospels' as written documents and disputed their reliability.[81] Marcion also rejected the Hebrew Scriptures as the manifestations of an unjust and jealous demiurge. Justin's choice of words in the *First Apology* can be understood against the background of the Marcionite controversy, as Koester notes: 'In direct antithesis to Marcion's use of the written gospel, Justin binds these gospels to the prophetic revelation in the Old Testament scriptures.'[82] At a crucial time for the formation of the New Testament canon, 'memoirs of the apostles' in Justin most likely stand for the Synoptic Gospels and quite possibly include John as well.[83]

Another particularity in Justin's *First Apology* is the generic phrase 'he who presides' (ὁ προεστώς), by which he avoids any technical terminology for office-holders in Church (he does, however, mention deacons later). In all probability, it is the bishop or presbyter who preaches after the scriptural readings and leads the Eucharistic prayer. The homily is followed by prayers that are specified in the post-baptismal Eucharist as

---

frühen Christentum, ed. Beate Ego, Armin Lange and Peter Pilhofer, Wissenschaftliche Untersuchungen zum Neuen Testament 118 (Tübingen: Mohr Siebeck, 1999), 489–504, at 489–490.

[79] See, for instance, Eric F. Osborn, *Justin Martyr*, Beiträge zur historischen Theologie 47 (Tübingen: Mohr Siebeck, 1973), 120–138, who reviews earlier debates.

[80] Justin Martyr, *First Apology*, 66,2: PTS 38,127; trans. Johnson, vol. I, 68 (no. 245).

[81] See Helmut Koester, *Ancient Christian Gospels: Their History and Development* (London: SCM Press, 1990), 36–43.

[82] Ibid., 43.

[83] See Everett Ferguson, 'Factors Leading to the Selection and Closure of the New Testament Canon: A Survey of Some Recent Studies', in *The Early Church at Work and Worship. Volume 1: Ministry, Ordination, Covenant, and Canon* (Eugene: Cascade Books, 2013), 247–279, at 256–257. The paper was first published in *The Canon Debate*, ed. Lee Martin McDonald and James A. Sanders (Peabody: Hendrickson, 2002), 295–320.

intercessions 'both for ourselves and for those who have received illumination and for people everywhere'. It is only in the post-baptismal celebration that Justin mentions a kiss of peace after the intercessory prayers.[84] Then bread and wine mixed with water are prepared and 'he who presides' offers 'prayers and thanksgivings' (εὐχὰς ... καὶ εὐχαριστίας). The comment that this is done according to the presider's ability indicates that the wording of the Eucharistic prayer was not fixed but allowed for some variation (see Chapter 3). In the post-baptismal Eucharist, Justin appears to distinguish between two parts of this prayer: The first part is marked by 'praise and glory to the Father of all things through the name of his Son and of the Holy Spirit' and might correspond to what is known as the preface in the later Roman tradition. The second part focuses on offering 'thanks at considerable length for our being counted worthy to receive these things at his hands'.[85] The people's response, 'Amen', is given particular significance in both accounts of the Eucharist, since it expresses the people's consent. The distribution of communion follows, and deacons bring some of it to those who (for reasons that are not specified) do not take part in the assembly. In the post-baptismal Eucharist, it is noted that those who are absent receive a portion of the Eucharistic bread and wine. It is likely that this not only refers to those who are sick or imprisoned but includes taking the Eucharist to Christian homes, where it was reserved reverently so that the faithful could partake of it even daily. Tertullian and Cyprian confirm this practice for North Africa in the early and mid-third century.[86] It is difficult to ascertain how widespread the private reception of communion was. The custom is often associated with the precarious situation of Christians before Constantine, but there is evidence that it continued in some places in the fourth and possibly even the fifth century.[87] Going back to Justin's account, he emphasises the final collection for those in need as part of the Sunday Eucharist. He concludes by explaining that this 'common assembly' is held on Sunday, because it is the first day of God's creation and the day of Christ's resurrection.

In the section between the two descriptions of a liturgical celebration, the *First Apology* offers doctrinal teaching on the food called 'Eucharist'.

---

[84] Justin Martyr, *First Apology*, 65,1–2: PTS 38,125; trans. Johnson, vol. I, 67 (no. 244).

[85] Ibid., 65,3; PTS 38,126; trans. Johnson, vol. I, 67 (no. 244).

[86] Tertullian, *De oratione*, 19: CCL 1,267–268; *Ad uxorem*, 2,5,2: CCL 1,389; Cyprian, *De lapsis*, 26: CSEL 3/1,256.

[87] See Daniel Callam, 'The Frequency of Mass in the Latin Church ca. 400', in *Theological Studies* 45 (1984), 613–650, at 614–615.

Similar to the *Didache*, Justin emphasises that sharing in it is not uncon-ditional but requires faith, baptism and moral conduct. He also under-lines that the Eucharist is not 'ordinary bread and ordinary drink' and elaborates on the Eucharistic presence of Christ in analogy with the Incarnation:

> just as Jesus Christ our Saviour, having been made flesh by the Word of God, assumed flesh and blood for our salvation, so also we have been taught that the food over which thanks have been given through a word of prayer that is from him (δι'εὐχῆς λόγου τοῦ παρ' αὐτοῦ εὐχαριστηθεῖσαν), from which our blood and flesh are nourished by transformation, is the flesh and blood of that Jesus made flesh.[88]

This dense passage clearly affirms the reality of Christ's presence in the Eucharistic offerings. Like Ignatius of Antioch before him, Justin prefers the Johannine terminology of 'flesh' (σάρξ) to 'body' (σῶμα), and he does so for Christological reasons. Bread and wine are literally 'eucharistized' and thus become the flesh and blood of the Incarnate Jesus. The ambigu-ous phrase δι'εὐχῆς λόγου τοῦ παρ' αὐτοῦ, which indicates the agency of this change, has been interpreted differently: as a Logos-epiclesis, invok-ing the transformative power of the divine Word, or as a reference to the Eucharistic prayer as a whole. There has been some controversy whether or not the Eucharistic prayer known to Justin contained the biblical words of institution, as might be implied whether we take the phrase to mean 'through a word of prayer' or 'through the prayer of a word' – that comes from Christ.[89] The precise words of institution are subsequently cited in the *First Apology* – not to explain the historical origins of the Eucharist but to authorise present ritual practice:

> For the apostles, in the memoirs composed by them, which are called Gospels, thus handed down what they were commanded: Jesus took bread and, giving thanks, said, 'Do this in remembrance of me, this is my Body.' Likewise taking the cup and giving thanks, he said, 'This is my blood', and gave it to [the apostles] alone.[90]

The way the citation merges the dominical command of Luke 22:19 with the words over the cup from Matthew 26:28 and Mark 14:24 would

---

[88] Ibid., 66,2: PTS 38,127; my own translation.
[89] See Hoping, *My Body Given for You*, 85–86l and Spinks, *Do This in Remembrance of Me*, 32–33.
[90] Justin Martyr, *First Apology*, 66,3: PTS 38,128; trans. Johnson, vol. I, 68 (no. 245), modified.

point to actual liturgical use, at the very least in the post-baptismal Eucharist. This hypothesis is supported by the fact that Justin goes on to compare the Christian rite with the cult of Mithras for the benefit of his non-Christian audience:

Which also the wicked demons have imitated in the mysteries of Mithras and handed down to be done. For that bread and a cup of water are placed with certain sentences (μετ' ἐπιλόγων τινῶν) in the rites of initiation, you either know or can learn.[91]

The point of comparison with the cult of Mithras is not only the sacred meal but also the repetition of ritual formulas (the word used by Justin here, ἐπίλογοι, is sometimes translated as 'incantations'), and this would not apply to the Eucharistic prayer as a whole, but to the words of institution, as noted by Gerd Theißen.[92]

Reference has already been made to the *Dialogue with Trypho*, a literary conversation set in Ephesus with a possible factual basis, in which Justin attempts to convince the Jew Trypho of the truth of Christianity. In chapter 41 of the dialogue, Justin presents the cereal offering that accompanied the animal sacrifice for the cleansing of lepers (Lev 14:10) as 'a type of the bread of the Eucharist (τοῦ ἄρτου τῆς εὐχαριστίας), which our Lord Jesus Christ has handed down for us to observe (παρέδωκεν ποιεῖν) in remembrance (εἰς τὴν ἀνάμνησιν) of the Passion he endured for those whose souls are cleansed from all sin'.[93] There are several important points here: first, Justin conceives of the offering of the Eucharistic bread as the full reality of the offering or oblation (προσφορά) that was foreshadowed in the sacrifices under the Old Law. Second, this offering was handed down by Jesus to be ritually enacted. Third, the offering is made in remembrance (*anamnesis*) of the Passion of Jesus, and this memorial is ordered towards an action of thanksgiving to God for his creation and redemption from sin. Justin corroborates his teaching with a citation of Malachi 1:10–12 and then challenges his Jewish interlocutor by commenting on the passage: 'By speaking of the sacrifices that are offered to him in every place by us

---

[91] Ibid., 66,3; PTS 38,128; my own translation.

[92] Gerd Theißen, "Sakralmahl und sakramentales Geschehen: Abstufungen in der Ritualdynamik des Abendmahls", in *Herrenmahl und Gruppenidentität*, ed. Martin Ebner, Quaestiones disputatae 221 (Freiburg: Herder, 2007), 166–186, at 176–177, fn. 18.

[93] Justin Martyr, *Dialogue with Trypho*, 41,1: PTS 47,137; my translation.

Gentiles, namely, the bread of the Eucharist and the cup of the Eucharist, he [Malachi] prophesies that we glorify his name, but that you profane it.'[94]

In chapter 70 of the *Dialogue with Trypho*, the priests of the cult of Mithras are accused of misusing Old Testament prophecies for their own purposes. This is followed by a quotation of the entire passage of Isaiah 33:13–19, which includes the promise that to him who walks righteously 'his bread will be given him, his water will be sure' (Is 33:16) – a prophecy that Justin takes to allude to the Eucharist, which is offered in remembrance of Christ's Incarnation and redemptive Passion.[95]

In chapter 117 of the dialogue, Justin returns to the prophecy of Malachi 1:10–12, which he sees fulfilled in 'the Eucharist of the bread and of the cup', which is offered by Christians 'in every place'.[96] Prayers and thanksgivings are sacrifices acceptable to God only if they are offered by those who are worthy. In the Old Covenant, only the priests offered sacrifices, but they have profaned these sacrifices, as Malachi reveals. By virtue of their baptism, Christians share in the high priesthood of Jesus Christ and are now 'the true high priestly family of God'.[97] As such, they are worthy to offer a perfect and acceptable sacrifice to God in their celebration of the Eucharist, which is done in remembrance of the Passion of Christ. Thus, Justin confirms that he understands the Eucharist as a priestly and sacrificial action. The fact that he speaks here of the common priesthood of all the baptised and not of an ordained ministerial priesthood could be understood as a reflection of his own role as a lay member of the Church.

The works of Christian authors from different regions in the late second and early third century, including Irenaeus of Lyon (d. 202), who was born in Asia Minor, Clement (d. c. 215) and Origen of Alexandria, Tertullian and Cyprian of Carthage, offer rich contributions to a theology of the Eucharist. Their varied lines of thought converge in a clear understanding of the sacrificial character of the Eucharist and a realistic sense of the presence of Christ in the consecrated offerings and of the salvific effects they bestow on those who receive them in faith. They also testify to the great reverence in which Christians held the body and

---

[94] Ibid., 41,3; PTS 47,138; my translation.   [95] See ibid., 70,1–4: PTS 47,191–192.
[96] Ibid., 117,1: PTS 47,271; my translation.
[97] Ibid., 116,3: PTS 47,270; my translation.

blood of Christ.[98] However, their writings contain little concrete information about the ritual shape and wording of the liturgical celebration. Of particular interest is Cyprian's very influential *Letter 63*, wherein he contends with groups who use water in place of wine for the Eucharist – a practice that is known from the Syrian *Acts of Thomas* and other New Testament apocrypha from the late second or early third century.[99] Cyprian elaborates a theology of the Eucharist as the offering of an unbloody sacrifice in remembrance of the Passion of Christ. In the sacrifice of the Church, Christ, the high priest of the New Covenant offers himself, and the ordained priest acts in the person of Christ by imitating what he did at the Last Supper.[100] Cyprian comments on the sacrificial connotation of wine in Old Testament prophecies and argues that its use is inseparable from the liturgical memorial of Christ's Passion. Moreover, to reject its consumption in the Eucharist is unfaithful to the Last Supper tradition. To underscore his argument, Cyprian cites the words of institution from Matthew 26 and 1 Corinthians 11.[101]

MATERIAL SETTINGS

When the Apostle Paul wrote to the church in Corinth around the year 53/54, the Lord's Supper was held in conjunction with a filling community meal in the evening. A conflict had arisen because apparently the wealthier members of the congregation started eating before the poorer members arrived after a long working day, so that nothing was left for the latter. Hence Paul's reproach: 'Do you not have houses to eat and drink in?' (1 Cor 11:22). In the *Didache*, the Eucharist is likewise combined with an ordinary (evening) meal. The growth of Christian communities (and possibly the recurrence of problems such as those experienced in

---

[98] See Hoping, *My Body Given for You*, 92–99 and 104–108; and Daniel Cardó, 'The Eucharist in the First Three Centuries', in *The Cambridge History of Ancient Christianity*, ed. Bruce Longenecker and David Wilhite (Cambridge: Cambridge University Press), forthcoming.

[99] See Spinks, *Do This in Remembrance of Me*, 39–45; and Harald Buchinger, 'Liturgy and Early Christian Apocrypha', in *The Oxford Handbook of Early Christian Apocrypha*, ed. Andrew Gregory and Christopher Tuckett (Oxford: Oxford University Press, 2015), 361–377, at 366–369. On apocryphal writings in general, see Richard Bauckham, 'Imaginative Literature', in *The Early Christian World*, ed. Philip F. Esler, vol. 2 (London: Routledge, 2000), 791–812. Bauckham notes the radical asceticism of apocryphal texts (ibid., 808–809).

[100] Cyprian of Carthage, *Ep.* 63, 14 and 17: CSEL 3/2,712–713 and 714–715.

[101] Ibid., 9–10: CSEL 3/2,707–709.

Corinth) facilitated the eventual separation of the Eucharist from the common meal. New Testament evidence points to an initially domestic setting of the Eucharist, which could have been a house belonging to a member of the community, with a spacious enough dining room.[102] This has given rise to the widely accepted idea that in the earliest phase of Christian expansion in the Mediterranean world, congregations generally met in 'house churches', for which the town house of the upper classes (*domus*) with its formal dining room (*triclinium*) served as a model. Linked with this idea is the conception of a familiar character of the Eucharist, with the male head of the household (*paterfamilias*) presiding. More recently, however, the theory of early 'house churches' has been challenged, especially since the seminal study by Edward Adams, who does not dispute that houses of believers served as Christian meeting places but shows that the evidence for them is not as extensive and exclusive as is usually thought.[103] Christians assembled for worship, instruction and fellowship also in a variety of commercial and leisure spaces that could be rented, such as shops, workshops, warehouses or inns, as well as outdoors where this was possible.

At a second stage, existing buildings were acquired and adapted in a more enduring fashion for the purposes of the Christian community, including liturgical use. Scholars have called these buildings *domus ecclesiae*, with the implication that a residential house has been turned into a church. However, the term is problematic, since it only appears in post-Constantinian sources and simply indicates a church building.[104] One of the very few surviving examples is the Christian building of Dura-Europos, a Roman frontier city on the river Euphrates. The city was almost completely destroyed by the Sassanians in 256 and was not rebuilt afterwards. Owing to these circumstances, the structure of a house that had been adapted for Christian use has been preserved from the first half of the third century. The building includes a baptistery and an oriented assembly hall, presumably for the Eucharist.[105]

---

[102] An example would be the upper chamber at the house in Troas (Acts 20:7–12), the house of Prisca and Aquila in Rome (Rom 16:3–5) and of the house of Gaius in Corinth (Rom 16:23).

[103] See Edward Adams, *The Earliest Christian Meeting Places: Almost Exclusively Houses?* (London: Bloomsbury, 2013).

[104] See Kristina Sessa, '*Domus Ecclesiae*: Rethinking a Category of *Ante-Pacem* Christian Space', in *Journal of Theological Studies* N.S. 60 (2009), 90–108.

[105] See Carl H. Kraeling, *The Christian Building*, Excavations at Dura Europos: Final Report VIII,2 (New Haven: Dura-Europos, 1967).

At a third stage, dedicated church buildings appear in the second half of the third century, when Christian communities in the Roman Empire enjoyed a period of peaceful growth. The Neoplatonic philosopher Porphyry notes in his work *Against the Christians*, written in the last quarter of the third century, that they imitate the construction of temples and build very large houses (μεγίστους οἴκους) in which they come together and pray.[106] This information is confirmed by Eusebius of Caesarea, who speaks about the building of large churches (ἐκκλησίαι) on the foundations of older buildings that had become too small for the growing congregations of believers.[107] Eusebius also presents the destruction of churches as a characteristic of the Diocletianic persecution, which started in 303.[108] These pre-Constantinian churches could be well provided with precious objects for worship, as emerges from the report of a confiscation in the church of Cirta in North Africa dated 19 May 303.[109]

The Temple background to early Christian worship questions the conventional narrative that the early Church identified itself exclusively as an eschatological body of believers that rejected ideas of sacred space and saw no need for places dedicated specifically to ritual and worship. Jenn Cianca argues that 'despite a lack of materially articulated or physically separate space, the house-church Christians were indeed meeting in sacred space'.[110] This sacred space was, by practical necessity, temporal not permanent, and it was constituted through and in ritual performed by the body of believers, especially the Eucharist. In her analysis of the scarce evidence of how early Christians embodied their liturgical worship, Cianca draws on insights from social anthropology and ritual studies, including the contributions of Arnold van Gennep, Jonathan Z. Smith and Catherine Bell. Van Gennep considered the sacred a relative entity or quality 'that readily shifts in different situations and at different ritual stages'. By speaking about the 'pivoting of the sacred', van Gennep

---

[106] Porphyry, *Adversus Christianos*, fragment 76, ed. Adolf von Harnack, *Porphyrius 'Gegen die Christen', 15 Bücher. Zeugnisse, Fragmente und Referate*, Abhandlungen der königlich preussischen Akademie der Wissenschaften, Jahrgang 1916, Philosophisch-historische Klasse 1 (Berlin: Verlag der Königl. Akademie der Wissenschaften, 1916), 93.

[107] Eusebius of Caesarea, *Hist. eccl.*, VIII,1,5: GCS Euseb. 9/2 [NF 6,2], 738.

[108] See Thümmel, 'Versammlungsraum, Kirche, Tempel', 492–493 and 499.

[109] The report from the *Acta Munati Felicis* is cited in the *Gesta apud Zenophilum*: CSEL 26,187.

[110] Jenn Cianca, *Sacred Ritual, Profane Space: The Roman House as Early Christian Meeting Place*, Studies in Christianity and Judaism 1 (Montreal; Kingston: McGill-Queen's University Press, 2018), 5.

highlighted ritual's active role in defining what is sacred; it does 'not simply react to the sacred as something already and for always fixed'.[111] While Cianca is aware of the largely hypothetical character of her argument, she establishes the conception of a ritually constructed sacrality, which 'allows for an organic, slower-moving development of early Christian sacred space, rather than reading a sea change into the building of the Lateran in Rome'.[112] In a similar way, Ann Marie Yasin concludes in her study of Christian social topography that,

regardless of their location or architectural form, as sites of ritual action, of community definition, and of prayer as a means of communicating with the divine, places in which Christians gathered to worship had been transformed into sacred spaces long before the development of the Constantinian world.[113]

While apologists of the second and third century reiterate that Christians have no temples, altars or images of deities, the same apologists employ cultic language for Christian worship. Just before 200, Minucius Felix speaks for the first time of Christian meeting places as 'sanctuaries' (*sacraria*).[114] The conflict between Christians and pagans also testifies to a fundamental antithesis in the conception of sacred space. The classical temple has an 'extroverted' character: its significant architectural and artistic elements, such as columns, friezes and sculptures, are placed on the outside of the building. This external magnificence and splendour were designed for worshippers who remained outside the inner sanctum. Christian sacred space, however, had an 'introverted' character since it needed above all a large room where the community could assemble under the leadership of the bishop (or, in his place, the presbyter). By virtue of their baptism, Christians considered themselves a priestly people who took a constitutive role in liturgical worship. Even in the monumental basilicas of the fourth century precious materials and decorative elements are above all found inside the building, which contrasts with the usually plain exterior.

---

[111] Catherine Bell, *Ritual: Perspectives and Dimensions* (New York: Oxford University Press, 1997), 37, with reference to Arnold van Gennep, *The Rites of Passage*, trans. Monika B. Vizedom and Gabrielle L. Caffee (Chicago: University of Chicago Press, 1960), 12.

[112] Cianca, *Sacred Ritual, Profane Space*, 167.

[113] Ann Marie Yasin, *Saints and Church Spaces in the Late Antique Mediterranean: Architecture, Cult, and Community*, Greek Culture in the Roman World (Cambridge: Cambridge University Press, 2009), 44. See also Heid, *Altar und Kirche*, 178–198.

[114] Minucius Felix, *Octavius*, 9,1: CSEL 2,12. See Heid, *Altar und Kirche*, 192–193.

The conception of a ritually constructed sacrality not only helps us to see elements of continuity in the creation of monumental church architecture in the fourth century but also illumines the disputed question of whether pre-Constantinian Christian references to 'altar' should be interpreted metaphorically or whether they designate material objects actually used in their worship. Stefan Heid argues that 'the table of the Lord' (1 Cor 10:21), which for Paul clearly has the function of an altar, was not identical with the (several) tables used for the regular meal of the community. Rather, a special table with the Eucharistic offerings of bread and wine was brought in at the end of the meal.[115] It is likely that such a ritualised and hence sacred table is meant by the 'altar' of Hebrews 13:10 and the letters of Ignatius of Antioch. Phenomenologically, the wooden tables for the early Christian Eucharist were very different from the stone altars associated with the slaughter of animals in pagan worship. However, as Heid shows, the sacrality of an altar did not depend on its form or material, but on its function. In classical antiquity, various objects could serve as an altar for offerings to the gods, including metal tripods, stone pillars, wooden tables and massive stone altars.[116] Moreover, the fact that an item was not fixed but mobile did not make it profane. The Israelites carried the table of the bread of the Presence and the altar of burnt offering through the desert (Ex 25:28; 27:7). In the Roman world, sacred objects were carried in procession, including the statues of gods. Against this background, a portable wooden table that was brought into a Christian meeting place for the Eucharist could nonetheless be considered an altar and be charged with sacredness.[117]

Scholarly critiques of the theory of 'house churches' and proposals for a sacred space constituted by ritual action raise doubts about the alleged domestic and familiar character of early Christian worship. Several recent contributions rather support the plausibility of a more sacred and hierarchical character of the Eucharist, even from its origins. In this chapter, I have made frequent use of the impressive and thoroughly researched study of Stefan Heid, *Altar und Kirche: Prinzipien christlicher Liturgie.*

---

[115] See Heid, *Altar und Kirche*, 31–32.   [116] See ibid., 54–67.

[117] See ibid., 149–157. The Christian prayer hall in Megiddo has a Greek mosaic inscription, 'The God-loving Akeptous has offered the table to God Jesus Christ as a memorial', which is placed next to stone foundations that would indicate a fixed altar. However, the dating of this inscription to the third century has been disputed. Compare Adams, *The Earliest Christian Meeting Places*, 96–99, with Heid, *Altar und Kirche*, 56, 179–181.

Where I do not agree with Heid is in his claim that, well into the fourth century, in any given town, even in cities as large as Rome and Alexandria, there was only one church building in the full sense of the word, where the Christians would gather around the bishop who was assisted by his presbyters and deacons in the celebration of the Eucharist. Heid offers an impressive array of second- and third-century sources that speak of one church and one altar, but the key problem of his argument is that he consistently interprets such texts as referring to material realities, when they could also express ecclesiological desiderata or pastoral ideals.[118] Archaeology cannot decide this question because, with very few exceptions, no unambiguous evidence of Christian sacred spaces has survived from the pre-Constantinian period. At the same time, while I think that Heid overstates his case, he shows that the widely held idea of an early diversity and subsequent centralisation of Christian communities and their worship is in need of revision.[119]

When we come to consider the day and time for the celebration of the Eucharist, the importance of the first day of the Jewish week is evident in early Christianity. This is the day of Christ's resurrection from the dead (Mk 16:2; Jn 20:1, 19), and it is observed in a special way by the community (1 Cor 16:2; Acts 20:7–12). The 'Lord's Day' (Rev 1:10) is most likely to be identified with the first day of the week, and on this day the Eucharist is held (*Didache* 14). While Robert Taft surmises that the Sunday celebration of the Eucharist may have started in the first half of the first century,[120] the earliest clear evidence for this practice stems from the second century. The *Epistle of Barnabas* has commonly been dated to 130–135, but in recent scholarship support has grown for an earlier date

---

[118] See Heid, *Altar und Kirche*, 69–160.

[119] See the contributions of Georg Schöllgen, 'Hausgemeinden, ΟΙΚΟΣ-Ekklesiologie und monarchischer Episkopat', in *Jahrbuch für Antike und Christentum* 31 (1988), 74–90; and 'Probleme der frühchristlichen Sozialgeschichte: Einwände gegen Peter Lampes "Buch Die stadtrömischen Christen in den ersten beiden Jahrhunderten"', in *Jahrbuch für Antike und Christentum* 32 (1989), 23–40, which is a critique of Peter Lampe, *Christians at Rome in the First Two Centuries: From Paul to Valentinus*, trans. Michael Steinhauser and ed. Marshall D. Johnson (London: Continuum, 2006).

[120] See Robert F. Taft, 'The Frequency of the Celebration of the Eucharist throughout History', in *Between Memory and Hope: Readings on the Liturgical Year*, ed. Maxwell E. Johnson (Collegeville: Liturgical Press, 2000), 77–96, at 77–78. For a more sceptical position and a good overview of different opinions, see Paul F. Bradshaw and Maxwell E. Johnson, *The Origins of Feasts, Fasts, and Seasons in Early Christianity* (Collegeville: Liturgical Press, 2011), 3–10.

around 96–98.[121] In this letter, which some churches accepted as part of the canonical Scriptures, Christians are instructed to celebrate not the Sabbath but the first day of the week, which is acclaimed as the 'eighth day, which is the beginning of another world'. This eighth day is marked by a new creation because it is the day of Jesus' resurrection.[122] In the middle of the second century, Justin Martyr also explains the special significance of 'the day of the sun' by reference to the beginning of God's creation and to Christ's resurrection.[123]

Given that the Jewish day is reckoned to begin with sunset, the weekly celebration of the Eucharist may initially have taken place on Sunday evening,[124] or on Saturday evening after the end of the Sabbath – as is increasingly argued by scholars.[125] An intriguing source is the letter sent by Pliny the Younger in his capacity as governor of the Roman province of Bithynia and Pontus to the Emperor Trajan in c. 112, with the request for instructions regarding how to deal with Christians. Pliny ascertained from them that they usually met 'on a fixed day' (*stato die*) before dawn to sing a hymn (*carmen*) to Christ as to a god and to commit themselves to moral conduct. After they departed, they would meet again (presumably on the same day) for a shared meal, but they ceased to do so after the governor banned such assemblies.[126] It would seem plausible that the morning service indicated here was held on Sunday.[127] Pliny's outside perspective does not allow for any conclusions about what kind of service was held. A morning celebration of the Eucharist would appear exceptional at the time but was more widely adopted once the Eucharist became

---

[121] See Stephen G. Wilson, *Related Strangers: Jews and Christians 70–170 CE* (Minneapolis: Fortress Press 1995), 231–232; and James Carleton Paget, *The Epistle of Barnabas: Outlook and Background* (Tübingen: Mohr, 1994), 9–30.

[122] *Epistle of Barnabas*, 15,8–9: ed. and trans. Holmes, 428 and 429.

[123] Justin Martyr, *First Apology*, 67,8: PTS 38,130.

[124] This was the widely received thesis of Willy Rordorf, *Der Sonntag: Geschichte des Ruhe- und Gottesdiensttages im ältesten Christentum*, Abhandlungen zur Theologie des Alten und Neuen Testaments 43 (Zurich: Zwingli Verlag, 1962); and *Sabbat und Sonntag in der Alten Kirche*, Traditio Christiana 2 (Zurich: Theologischer Verlag, 1972).

[125] See Gerard Rouwhorst, 'The Reception of the Jewish Sabbath in Early Christianity', in *Christian Feast and Festival: The Dynamics of Western Liturgy and Culture*, ed. Paul Post et al., Liturgia condenda 12 (Leuven: Peeters, 2001), 223–266; and Richard Bauckham, 'Sabbath and Sunday in the Post-Apostolic Church', in *From Sabbath to Lord's Day*, ed. Donald A. Carson (Grand Rapids: Zondervan, 1982), 251–298.

[126] Pliny the Younger, *Ep.* X,96: trans. Betty Radice, Loeb Classical Library 59 (Cambridge, MA: Harvard University Press, 1969), 284–291.

[127] For a different reading, see Klaus Thraede, 'Noch einmal: Plinius d.J. und die Christen', in *Zeitschrift für die Neutestamentliche Wissenschaft* 95 (2004), 102–128.

separated from the ordinary meal of the community. In early third-century North Africa, Tertullian records that the 'sacrament of the Eucharist' (*eucharistiae sacramentum*) or the 'sacrifice' (*sacrificium*) at the 'altar of God' (*ara Dei*) is celebrated in the morning.[128] Tertullian clearly distinguishes the Eucharist from the convivial 'supper of God' (*cena Dei*) or 'banquet of the Lord' (*convivium dominicum*) held in the evening.[129] Tertullian also testifies to the requirement to fast before receiving the Eucharist, as does the *Apostolic Tradition*, and this points to a morning celebration.[130] In the middle of the third century, Cyprian of Carthage confirms that the Eucharist, which he calls *dominicum* (literally, 'that which belongs to the Lord') is separate from the evening meal and is held in the morning in celebration of the Lord's resurrection.[131] In sum, while there was no uniformity regarding the day and time of the weekly Eucharist in the first two centuries, it was clearly was chosen for its sacred and symbolic meaning. Gradually, the celebration on a Sunday morning emerged as the common pattern throughout the Christian world.

In most religious traditions, the position taken in prayer and the layout of holy places is determined by a 'sacred direction'. For the history of religions, the term 'sacred direction' is more appropriate than 'orientation', since the latter implies a turning towards the geographical east. Orientation in prayer was a general custom among the various forms of sun-worship in the ancient world from the Mediterranean to India. The practice was common in Roman religion and became detached from the cult of the sun. The eastern sky was regarded as the home of the gods and thus as a symbol of fortune.[132] Jews stood out by praying towards Jerusalem or, more specifically, towards the presence of the transcendent God (*shekinah*) in the Holy of Holies of the Temple (e.g., Dan 6:10). Even after the destruction of the Temple, the custom of turning towards

---

[128] Tertullian, *De corona*, 3,3: CCL 2,1043, and *De oratione*, 19,1–3: CCL 1, 267–268.
[129] Tertullian, *Ad uxorem*, 2,8,8: CCL 1,388–389; *Apologeticum*, 39,16–17: CCL 1,152; *De spectaculis*, 13,4: CCL 1,239; see Heid, *Altar und Kirche*, 110–111; for different readings of Tertullian, see Andrew B. McGowan, 'Rethinking Agape and Eucharist in Early North African Christianity', in *Studia Liturgica* 34 (2004), 165–176; and J. Patout Burns Jr. and Robin M. Jensen, *Christianity in Roman Africa: The Development of Its Practices and Beliefs* (Grand Rapids: Eerdmans, 2014), 239–242.
[130] Tertullian, *Ad uxorem*, 2,5,3: CCL 1,389; *Apostolic Tradition*, 36: ed. Bradshaw, Johnson, Phillips, 180.
[131] Cyprian of Carthage, *Ep. 63*, 16: CSEL 3/2,714.
[132] See the seminal work of Franz Joseph Dölger, *Sol salutis: Gebet und Gesang im christlichen Altertum mit besonderer Rücksicht auf die Ostung in Gebet und Liturgie*, Liturgiegeschichtliche Forschungen, 4/5, 2nd ed. (Münster: Aschendorff, 1925), 38–60.

Jerusalem was kept in the liturgy of the synagogue. Thus, Jews have expressed their eschatological hope for the coming of the Messiah, the rebuilding of the Temple and the gathering of God's people from the Diaspora.

Facing Jerusalem in prayer was inseparably linked with the messianic hope of Israel.[133] For this reason, the sacred direction was part of the controversies that finally led to the separation of Christianity from Judaism. Christians no longer turned towards the earthly Jerusalem, but towards the new, heavenly Jerusalem. It was their firm belief that when the Lord comes again in glory to judge the world, he will gather his elect to make up this heavenly city. The rising sun was considered an appropriate expression of this eschatological hope. From very early on, it was a matter of course for Christians to pray facing east.[134]

In the New Testament, the special significance of the eastward direction for worship is not explicit. Even so, tradition has found many biblical references for this symbolism, for instance, the sun of righteousness (Mal 4:2), the day dawning from on high (Lk 1:78), the angel ascending from the rising of the sun with the seal of the living God (Rev 7:2), not to mention the Johannine light imagery. According to early Christian exegesis, the sign of the coming of the Son of Man with power and great glory, which appears as the lightning from the east and shines as far as the west, is the cross (Mt 24:27 and 30).

There is very strong evidence for eastward prayer from most parts of the Christian world from the second century onwards.[135] To give just a few examples, for Tertullian the practice was self-evident, both in liturgical and in private prayer, so that it did not need express justification.[136] In his treatise *On Prayer* (c. 231), Origen recurs to the symbolism of the Fourth Gospel, which presents Christ as the light of the world.[137] Elsewhere, Origen notes that the eastward position in prayer belongs to

---

[133] See Erik Peterson, *Frühkirche, Judentum und Gnosis: Studien und Untersuchungen* (Freiburg: Herder, 1959), 1–4; and Louis Bouyer, *Liturgy and Architecture* (Notre Dame: University of Notre Dame Press, 1967), 17–20.

[134] See Martin Wallraff, *Christus verus sol: Sonnenverehrung und Christentum in der Spätantike*, Jahrbuch für Antike und Christentum. Ergänzungsband 32 (Münster: Aschendorff, 2001), 60–88; Uwe Michael Lang, *Turning towards the Lord: Orientation in Liturgical Prayer*, 2nd ed. (San Francisco: Ignatius Press, 2009), 35–71; Stefan Heid, 'Gebetshaltung und Ostung in frühchristlicher Zeit', in *Rivista di Archeologia Cristiana* 82 (2006), 347–404.

[135] See the extensive documentation of Dölger, *Sol salutis*, 136–286.

[136] See Tertullian, *Ad nationes*, 1,13: CCL 1,32 and *Apologeticum* 16,9–11: CCL 1,116.

[137] Origen, *De oratione*, 32: GCS Orig. II,400.

that class of ecclesiastical customs that must be observed, even though their meaning is not familiar to everyone. He claims that, together with other rites, the turning to the east was 'handed on and entrusted to us by the high priest and his sons', that is, its origin goes back to Christ and his apostles.[138]

The *Didascalia apostolorum*, a fourth-century Syriac Church order based on a Greek original believed to date to the early third century, rules that the liturgical assembly, both clergy and laity, should stand and turn towards the east in prayer.[139] The Psalm verse adduced to authenticate this rule, 'Give glory to God, who rides upon the heaven of heavens toward the east' (Ps 67[68]:34), is understood as a prophecy of the Lord's ascension. Christ ascended towards the east, the place of Paradise (Gen 2:8), from where his second coming is expected.

A broad stream of liturgical sources from the fourth century onwards confirms the practice of facing east. In the liturgy of the eighth book of the late fourth-century *Apostolic Constitutions*, which is based on the text of the *Apostolic Tradition*, after the dismissals, the general prayer of the faithful and the kiss of peace, the deacon proclaims: 'Let us stand upright before the Lord with fear and trembling, to offer the oblation.'[140] It is likely that this would include turning towards the east. Other Greek, Coptic and Ethiopian liturgies have similar diaconal exhortations to stand upright and look towards the east at the beginning or during the anaphora.[141] In the early Church, the lifting up of heart that introduced the Eucharistic prayer (*Sursum corda – Habemus ad Dominum*) was accompanied by prayer gestures of the entire assembly: standing upright, raising one's arms, looking upwards and turning towards the east.[142]

CONCLUSION

While this chapter has covered a lot of ground, it is inevitable that the picture it offers of early Eucharistic liturgy remains fragmentary. As has been seen, the available sources raise more questions than they deliver

---

[138] Origen, *Hom. in Num.*, V,1: GCS Orig. VII,26–27.

[139] *Didascalia apostolorum*, 12: CSCO 407, 144.

[140] *Apostolic Constitutions*, VIII,12,2: SC 336, 176.

[141] See Dölger, *Sol salutis*, 327–330; also Michael J. Moreton, 'Εἰς ἀνατολὰς βλέψατε: Orientation as a Liturgical Principle', in *Studia Patristica* 18 (1982), 575–590.

[142] See Robert F. Taft, 'The Dialogue before the Anaphora in the Byzantine Eucharistic Liturgy. II: The *Sursum corda*', in *Orientalia Christiana Periodica* 54 (1988), 47–77, at 74–75.

answers. There is one leitmotif, however, that can be discerned in the first centuries of the Church, and it is the priestly and sacrificial understanding of the Eucharist, which was conceived as the 'pure offering' prophesied by Malachi. Rooted in the Last Supper and formed by 'Temple piety', the sacred meal that emerged as the heart of Christian worship came to be celebrated as a memorial in which the sacrifice of Christ became present and its saving effects were communicated to those who partook in it. Even in the modest material settings of the first two centuries, the sacred character of the Eucharist is evident in the place and time set apart for its celebration and in the personal conduct expected from those who shared in it. In the third century, which brought intellectual flourishing and organisational growth to the Church, the earliest texts of Eucharistic prayers emerge. Their common elements confirm the sacrificial and priestly understanding of the Eucharist. The evident changes the Constantinian settlement brought to the externals of Christian worship should not make us oblivious to the continuity in the understanding of the Eucharist and in its basic liturgical structure.

3

Development of Eucharistic Prayers in the Third and Fourth Century

At the heart of the liturgical celebration of the Eucharist stands the great prayer of thanksgiving, known in Eastern Christian traditions as anaphora (offering), in which the offerings of bread and wine are consecrated as the body and blood of Christ. Because of the oral character of early liturgical prayer, our knowledge of the formation of Eucharistic prayers in the first three centuries is very limited. This chapter will first examine several 'paleoanaphoras' that are generally held to have originated from the pre-Constantinian period, although questions of dating and possible earlier forms of these Eucharistic prayers continue to be debated in contemporary scholarship. The following section will briefly survey some of the 'classical' anaphoras of this period, which can be broadly divided into Antiochene and Alexandrian types. A consideration of scriptural readings and liturgical music will complete this chapter.

EARLY EUCHARISTIC PRAYERS: AN ATMOSPHERE OF 'CONTROLLED FREEDOM'

Historians of early Christianity generally agree that there was no fixed written form of liturgical prayer in the first three centuries and that room was given to improvisation. Nevertheless, this was conducted within a framework of stable elements and conventions that governed not only content but also structure and style, in a manner largely indebted to biblical language. Allan Bouley notes that such conventions 'are ascertainable in the second century and indicate that extempore prayer was not left merely to the whim of the minister. In the third century, and possibly even before, some anaphoral texts already existed in writing'.

Hence Bouley identifies an 'atmosphere of controlled freedom',[1] since concerns for orthodoxy limited the celebrant's liberty to vary the texts of the prayer. This need became particularly pressing during the doctrinal struggles of the fourth century, and from then onwards the texts of Eucharistic prayers, such as the Roman canon and the Anaphora of St John Chrysostom, were consolidated.

In a study on improvisation in liturgical prayer, Achim Budde analyses three oriental anaphoras used over a considerable geographical area: the Egyptian version of the Anaphora of St Basil, the West Syrian Anaphora of St James and the East Syrian Anaphora of Nestorius. Applying a comparative method, Budde identifies common patterns and stable elements of structure and rhetoric, which he argues go back to the pre-literary history of these Eucharistic prayers and may have been transmitted by memorisation.[2] Sigmund Mowinckel, known especially for his exegetical work on the Psalms, has observed that the rapid development of fixed forms of prayer corresponds to an essential religious need and constitutes a fundamental law of religion.[3] Budde's methodological approach is an important supplement and corrective to that of Bouley, who would appear to underestimate the significance of memorisation in an oral culture.[4] The formation of stable liturgical texts can thus be ascertained from early on as a strong force in the process of handing on the Christian faith.

Regarding the development of early Eucharistic prayers, Anthony Gelston identifies three categories of constitutive elements that were becoming fixed by the beginning of the third century, if not earlier. The first category consists of material from Holy Scripture, including the *Sanctus*, the institution narrative, and the congregational 'amen' at the conclusion of the Eucharistic prayer (see also 1 Cor 14:16). The second category involves the participation of the assembly (and overlaps

---

[1] Allan Bouley, *From Freedom to Formula: The Evolution of the Eucharistic Prayer from Oral Improvisation to Written Texts*, Studies in Christian Antiquity 21 (Washington, DC: The Catholic University of America Press, 1981), xv; see also Jürgen Hammerstaedt and Peri Terbuyken, 'Improvisation', in *Reallexikon für Antike und Christentum* 17 (1996), 1212–1284.

[2] Achim Budde, 'Improvisation im Eucharistiegebet: Zur Technik freien Betens in der Alten Kirche', in *Jahrbuch für Antike und Christentum* 44 (2001), 127–144, esp. 138; also *Die ägyptische Basilios-Anaphora: Text – Kommentar – Geschichte*, Jerusalemer theologisches Forum 7 (Münster: Aschendorff, 2004).

[3] Sigmund Mowinckel, *Religion und Kultus*, trans. Albrecht Schauer (Göttingen: Vandenhoeck & Ruprecht, 1953), 8, 14 and 53.

[4] See Budde, 'Improvisation im Eucharistiegebet', 137.

with the first and the third kind). It is a practical exigency that such elements should be stable and familiar to the participants. Examples are the opening dialogue and the concluding doxology of the Eucharistic prayer. The third category comprises stable elements of the Eucharistic prayer that were considered part of received tradition and tended towards a fixed form from early on. Such elements are found in Justin's themes of thanksgiving (see Chapter 2) and in Origen's testimony that the Eucharistic prayer is normally addressed to the Father through the Son.[5]

The largely oral practice of early liturgical prayer means that there are only a few written texts that may be dated to the pre-Nicene period. In the following section, I shall discuss the so-called *Apostolic Tradition*, the Anaphora of Addai and Mari and the Barcelona Anaphora in conjunction with the Strasbourg papyrus.[6] These important witnesses have received considerable scholarly scrutiny in the last few decades and questions as to their date and possible early form elude definitive answers. We do well to preface our enquiry with the warning of Kenneth Stevenson:

> Every liturgical expert on antiquity knows that Hippolytus might, conceivably, have been a sham Syrian archaizer, doing his own thing, out of favor with the Pope; Addai and Mari could have been mutilated beyond recognition at the time of Patriarch Iso'yahb's liturgical adjustments in the seventh century (which involved abbreviations) and the *Strasbourg* papyrus could be a fragment of an early anaphora that went on to include material now lost but quite different in style and content from the later (complete) Greek Mark. With compilers of liturgical texts, all things are possible.[7]

The Apostolic Tradition *Attributed to Hippolytus of Rome*

A text that played an important role in twentieth-century liturgical scholarship and reform is the Eucharistic prayer in the Church order known as *Apostolic Tradition*. When the document first attracted the attention of historians in the second half of the nineteenth century, it was called the 'Egyptian Church order'. Subsequently, the document was attributed to Hippolytus, a colourful figure in the Roman church who accused its

---

[5] See Anthony Gelston, *The Eucharistic Prayer of Addai and Mari* (Oxford: Clarendon Press, 1992), 20–21.

[6] See also the chapter on 'paleoanaphoras' in Bryan D. Spinks, *Do This in Remembrance of Me: The Eucharist from the Early Church to the Present Day*, SCM Studies in Worship and Liturgy (London: SCM Press, 2013), 52–67.

[7] Kenneth Stevenson, *Eucharist and Offering* (New York: Pueblo, 1986), 9.

Bishop Callistus (d. 222) of laxity in the reconciliation of sinners and set himself up as an 'anti-pope', but who was eventually reconciled and died a martyr in 235. The document in question, which bears no title or author, was identified with the work called 'Apostolic Tradition', which is included among a list of known writings by Hippolytus inscribed on the base of an ancient statue believed to represent the author (though this description has been disputed). This statue was discovered in 1551 and is now placed at the entrance of the Vatican Library. Hippolytus was believed to have been a conservative who compiled information about liturgical practice in Rome, which may already have been considered archaic in his time.

The theory of Hippolytan authorship has been radically challenged by more recent studies.[8] The document in question was written in Greek, but except for some fragments, it has come down to us in Coptic, Ethiopic and Arabic translations, as well as a partial Latin version in a manuscript dating from late fifth century (known as the Verona Palimpsest). As a Church order, it has no single author but consists of a compilation of liturgical texts that were in use and subject to frequent modifications. None of the extant translations preserves the whole text, which includes ordination rites for bishops, priests and deacons, regulations on various states of life in the Church, the rites of the catechumenate and of baptism and various prayers and blessings. The document influenced subsequent Church orders in the East, above all the eighth book of the *Apostolic Constitutions*, the *Canons of Hippolytus* and the *Testament of Our Lord Jesus Christ*. Its influence on the development of Western liturgy was

---

[8] See Bruno Steimer, *Vertex traditionis: Die Gattung der altchristlichen Kirchenordnungen*, Beihefte zur Zeitschrift für die neutestamentliche Wissenschaft 63 (Berlin; New York: de Gruyter, 1992); Marcel Metzger, 'À propos des règlements ecclésiastiques et de la prétendue *Tradition apostolique*', in *Revue des sciences religieuses* 66 (1992), 249–261; Christoph Markschies, 'Wer schrieb die sogenannte Traditio Apostolica? Neue Beobachtungen und Hypothesen zu einer kaum lösbaren Frage aus der altkirchlichen Literaturgeschichte', in *Tauffragen und Bekenntnis: Studien zur sogenannten 'Traditio Apostolica', zu den 'Interrogationes de fide' und zum 'Römischen Glaubensbekenntnis'*, ed. Wolfram Kinzig, Christoph Markschies and Markus Vinzent, Arbeiten zur Kirchengeschichte 74 (Berlin; New York: de Gruyter, 1999), 1–79; Paul F. Bradshaw, Maxwell E. Johnson and L. Edward Philips, *The Apostolic Tradition: A Commentary*, Hermeneia (Minneapolis: Fortress Press, 2002). These recent contributions confirm the insight of Louis Bouyer, *Eucharist: Theology and Spirituality of the Eucharistic Prayer*, trans. Charles Underhill Quinn (Notre Dame; London: University of Notre Dame Press, 1968), 188–191.

minimal until the twentieth-century liturgical reforms.[9] Hence, it is more likely that the ancient Church order stems from the Christian East, possibly Egypt or Syria.[10]

Because of the uncertainties about its date and place of origin, the Latin version of the *Apostolic Tradition* can hardly be taken as a source for Roman liturgy in the early third century. At the same time, there is no doubt that the document contains very ancient material. It is a typical example of 'living literature', which has been aptly described as 'an aggregation of material from different sources, quite possibly arising from different geographical regions and probably from different historical periods, from perhaps as early as the mid-second century to as late as the mid-fourth century'.[11] For the purpose of our study, the most interesting section of the ancient Church order is found in the ordination rite of a bishop, which includes the model of a Eucharistic prayer that features almost all of the essential elements of the classical anaphoras that are attested in the fourth century.

Enrico Mazza has argued that the Eucharistic prayer incorporates material from the literary genre of Easter homilies, such as that Melito of Sardis (d. 180) and Pseudo-Hippolytus (the author of *In Sanctum Pascha*). However, while parallels with these second-century texts are undeniable, they may be too generic to support a direct influence.[12]

[9] Believed to reflect liturgical practice in early third-century Rome, the *Apostolic Tradition* had significant impact on the liturgical reform after the Second Vatican Council. The Second Eucharistic Prayer in the renewed *Missale Romanum* of 1970 follows the 'Hippolytan' model. The reconstructed *Apostolic Tradition* was also a key source for the revised Rite of Ordination of a Bishop and for the Rite of Christian Initiation for Adults (RCIA).

[10] A West Syrian origin has been proposed by Matthieu Smyth, 'The Anaphora of the so-called "Apostolic Tradition" and the Roman Eucharistic Prayer', in *Issues in Eucharistic Praying in East and West: Essays in Liturgical and Theological Analysis*, ed. Maxwell E. Johnson (Collegeville: Liturgical Press, 2010), 71–97.

[11] Bradshaw, Johnson and Philips, *Apostolic Tradition*, 14. This English translation does not rely on a hypothetical earliest text but presents in parallel columns the four principal linguistic versions (Latin, Coptic, Arabic and Ethiopic), as well as the three important adaptations in *Apostolic Constitutions, Canons of Hippolytus*, and *Testamentum Domini*.

[12] See Enrico Mazza, *The Origins of the Eucharistic Prayer*, trans. Ronald E. Lane (Collegeville: Liturgical Press, 1995), 102–129; for a critique of this proposal, see Bradshaw, Johnson and Phillips, *Apostolic Tradition*, 44–45.

[1] When he has been made bishop, let all offer the mouth of peace (*os pacis*), greeting him because he has been made worthy.

[2] And let the deacons offer to him the oblations, and let him, laying [his] hands on it with all the presbytery, say, giving thanks:

[3] 'The Lord [be] with you.' (*Dominus vobiscum*) And let them all say: 'And with your spirit.' (*Et cum spiritu tuo*) 'Up [with your] hearts.' (*Sursum corda*) 'We have [them] to the Lord.' (*Habemus ad Dominum*) 'Let us give thanks to the Lord.' (*Gratias agamus Domino*) 'It is worthy and just.' (*Dignum et iustum est*) And so let him continue:

[4] 'We render thanks to you, God, through your beloved Child (*puerum*) Jesus Christ, whom in the last times you sent to us as Savior and Redeemer and angel of your will,

[5] who is your inseparable Word, through whom you made all things and it was well pleasing to you,

[6] you sent from heaven into the Virgin's womb, and who conceived in the womb was incarnate and manifested as your Son, born from the Holy Spirit and the Virgin;

[7] who fulfilling your will and gaining for you a holy people stretched out [his] hands when he was suffering, that he might release from suffering those who believed in you;

[8] who when he was being handed over to voluntary suffering, that he might destroy death and break the bonds of the devil, and tread down hell and illuminate the righteous, and fix a limit and manifest the resurrection,

[9] taking bread [and] giving thanks to you, he said: "Take, eat, this is my body that will be broken for you." (*Accipite, manducate, hoc est corpus meum quod pro vobis confringetur*) Likewise also the cup, saying: "This is my blood that is shed for you." (*Hic est sanguis meus, qui pro vobis effunditur*)

[10] When you do this, you do my remembrance.'

[11] Remembering therefore his death and resurrection, we offer (*offerimus*) to you the bread and cup, giving thanks to you because you have held us worthy to stand before and minister to you.

[12] And we ask that you would send your Holy Spirit in the oblation of [your] holy Church, [that] gathering (them) into one you will give to all who partake of the holy things [to partake] in the fullness of the Holy Spirit, for the strengthening of faith in truth,

[13] that we may praise and glorify you through your Child Jesus Christ, through whom [be] glory and honor to you, Father and Son with the Holy Spirit, in your holy church, both now and to the ages of ages. Amen.[13]

---

[13] *Apostolic Tradition*, 4: trans. Bradshaw, Johnson, Phillips, 38–40, slightly modified. The Latin text is available in Anton Hänggi – Irmgard Pahl, *Prex eucharistica. Volumen I: Textus e variis liturgiis antiquioribus selecti*, Spicilegium Friburgense 12, 3rd ed. (Freiburg; Schweiz: Universitätsverlag, 1998), 80–81.

The ordination of a bishop is followed by an exchange of the kiss of peace, which is described with the unique expression 'mouth of peace'. The subsequent presentation of bread and wine to the bishop by deacons is understood as an act of offering. The gesture of the bishop and presbyters laying hands on the offerings is not known from other early Christian sources. Bernard Botte has taken this as evidence for sacramental concelebration; however, it cannot be interpreted as a co-consecration as in contemporary Roman practice, since only the bishop says the Eucharistic prayer.[14]

The form of the introductory dialogue is very similar to that attested by Cyprian of Carthage in the mid-third century.[15] The bishop continues with an extended prayer of thanksgiving for the Incarnation, birth and Passion of Jesus Christ. The anaphora does not include the *Sanctus*, which would suggest the early fourth century as the latest possible date for the prayer. Two Christological elements are of particular note: first, the title 'child' or 'servant' (*puer*, παῖς), which is also used in the meal prayers of the *Didache* (see Chapter 2); second, the designation of Jesus as 'angel of your [i.e., the Father's] will', which is a variant on the 'angel of great counsel' from the Septuagint version of Isaiah 9:6. This vestige of what scholars have termed 'angel-Christology' is found in Justin and Irenaeus[16] and points to a pre-Constantinian origin of the prayer. The affirmation that it was among the intentions of Christ to 'fix a limit' when he underwent his voluntary suffering has received very divergent interpretations, from setting a limit to hell and separating the reigns of life and death to establishing a rule for the celebration of the Eucharist.[17] It might speak in favour of the latter reading that the peculiar phrase leads to the narrative of institution.

If this text from the *Apostolic Tradition* could be dated to the third century, it would be the earliest example of the words of institution

---

[14] Compare Bernard Botte, 'Note historique sur la concelebration dans l'Eglise ancienne', in *La Maison-Dieu* 35 (1953), 9–23, at 12, with Jean Michel Hanssens, 'La concelebrazione sacrificale della Messa', in *Divinitas* 2 (1958) 242–267, at 248–249.

[15] Cyprian of Carthage, *De dominica oratione*, 31: CSEL 3,289; *De lapsis*, 1: CSEL 3,237.

[16] Justin Martyr, *Dialogue with Trypho*, 76,3 and 126,1: PTS 47,201 and 288; also *First Apology*, 63,5: PTS 38,121; Irenaeus of Lyon, *Against Heresies*, III,16,3: SC 34,283 and *Demonstration of the Apostolic Preaching*, 55–56: SC 406,162.

[17] See Bradshaw, Johnson, Philips, *Apostolic Tradition*, 47–48.

forming part of the Eucharistic prayer. The actual wording does not simply follow any of the biblical accounts but shows clear signs of liturgical redaction. In the words over the bread, the addition 'that will be broken for you' creates a parallel with the words over the cup. The same addition, which is rare in early Christian sources, is found in the Eucharistic prayer cited by Ambrose of Milan in the late fourth century (see Chapter 4).[18] It is peculiar, however, that in the words of the cup the present rather than the future tense is used for the blood of Christ ('that is shed for you'; on the ambiguity of the Greek participle used in the New Testament accounts, see Chapter 1).[19] The dominical command is modified from the imperative to the indicative: 'When you do this, you do my remembrance. ' This has been considered a misunderstanding of the Greek verbal form, which is ambiguous (ποιεῖτε, Lk 22:19 and 1 Cor 11:24–25). On the other hand, Ambrose's Eucharistic prayer also presents the command as an indicative but in the future tense.[20]

The short anamnesis that recalls the death and resurrection of Christ is linked with the oblation (offering) of bread and wine. The following epiclesis invokes the Holy Spirit over the Church's oblation and prays that those who share in it may be gathered into one (in a manner reminiscent of the *Didache*) and be strengthened in faith. The Latin text is defective here and has prompted very different attempts at reconstruction that range from a fully developed epiclesis for the transformation of the Eucharistic offerings into the body and blood of Christ to a removal of any reference to the Holy Spirit. The Eucharistic prayer concludes with a Trinitarian doxology.

Elsewhere, the *Apostolic Tradition* makes clear that this anaphora is to be taken as a paradigm and the bishop does not need to say it exactly as it is written down; rather, he is to pray according to his ability, as long as the content is orthodox.[21] It should be noted that the document does not offer a complete liturgical description of the Eucharist. Chapter 4 begins

---

[18] Ambrose of Milan, *De sacramentis*, IV,5,21: CSEL 73,55.
[19] This might be a scribal error for the future tense *effundetur*, which has a correspondence in the Ethiopic version; see Bradshaw, Johnson and Philips, *Apostolic Tradition*, 40.
[20] Ambrose of Milan, *De sacramentis*, IV,6,26: CSEL 73,57.
[21] *Apostolic Tradition*, 9,3–5: ed. Bradshaw, Johnson and Phillips, 68.

with the kiss of peace and ends with the concluding 'Amen' of the Eucharistic prayer. The information given about the post-baptismal Eucharist in chapter 21 is sketchy and focuses on the breaking of the bread and the communion of the newly baptised, which is accompanied by the distribution of milk and honey.[22] There is no indication of a 'Liturgy of the Word', although the celebration most likely included some form of scriptural readings and preaching by the bishop.[23]

The Anaphora of Addai and Mari

The Anaphora of Addai and Mari, also known as the Anaphora of the Apostles, is the most ancient Eucharistic prayer of the East Syrian tradition and is still used today in the two branches of the Church of the East and, with some modifications, by the Chaldean Catholic and Syro-Malabar Churches. The earliest available manuscript dates from the tenth century and was discovered by William Macomber in the church of Mar Esh'aya in Mosul and published in 1966.[24] The Anaphora of Addai and Mari and the Anaphora of St Peter in the Maronite tradition, usually referred to by its opening word, *Sharar* ('Confirm' or 'Strengthen'), have the greater part of their text in common, suggesting that they derive from a single Eucharistic prayer that predates the separation of the churches after the Council of Ephesus in 431. This common anaphora may date from the late third century and would thus be the oldest anaphora in continuous liturgical use today. Liturgical scholars have observed that Syriac-speaking Christians in the Near East maintained Jewish customs in worship longer than Greek- and Latin-speaking churches. For this reason, it has been suggested that an early form of Addai and Mari can be reconstructed with the help of parallel material in the tripartite meal blessing (*birkat-ha-mazon*). The methodological difficulties of such comparisons have already been mentioned in the course of this study (see above on the *Didache*), and in fact the parallels found between Jewish sources and Addai and Mari remain generic.[25]

---

[22] Ibid., 21,25–40: ed. Bradshaw, Johnson, Phillips, 120–124.
[23] See Spinks, *Do This in Remembrance of Me*, 64–66.
[24] The text was discovered and edited by William F. Macomber, 'The Oldest Known Text of the Anaphora of the Apostles Addai and Mari', in *Orientalia Christiana Periodica* 37 (1966), 335–371.
[25] See Gelston, *The Eucharistic Prayer of Addai and Mari*, 8–11. The study of Sarhad Y. H. Jammo, 'The Anaphora of the Apostles Addai and Mari: A Study of Structure and

The Mar Esh'aya text begins with an introductory dialogue that culminates in the exhortation that praise and thanksgiving be offered to the name of the Triune God for his work of creation and redemption. Whether or not the *Sanctus* was part of the ancient form of the anaphora has been disputed. It would be the earliest witness to the inclusion of the *Sanctus* in the Eucharistic prayer.[26] The lengthy section that follows is addressed to God the Son (contrary to the principle stated by Origen) and has its own doxology. The prayer consists in thanksgiving for the Incarnation and for the graces and benefits that came from it.

The core of the anaphora has been the object of much discussion in liturgical scholarship because the Mar Esh'aya text lacks an institution narrative. The subsequent presentation of the text adopts the division into sections, which Gelston proposes in his edition of the Syriac text and English translation:

[E]
Do thou, O my Lord, in thy manifold and ineffable mercies
make a good and gracious remembrance
for all the upright and just fathers who were pleasing before thee,
in the commemoration of the body and blood of thy Christ,
which we offer to thee upon the pure and holy altar, as thou hast taught us,
and make with us thy tranquility and thy peace all the days of the age,
(Amen.)

[F]
that all the inhabitants of the world may know thee,
that thou alone art God the true Father,
and thou didst send our Lord Jesus Christ thy Son and thy Beloved,
and he, our Lord and God, taught us in his life-giving Gospel
all the purity and holiness of the prophets and apostles and martyrs and confessors,
and bishops and priests and deacons,
and of all the children of the holy catholic Church,
those who have been signed with the sign of holy Baptism.

[G]
And we also, O my Lord, thy unworthy, frail, and miserable servants, who are gathered and stand before thee,
and have received by tradition the example which is from thee,

---

Historical Background', in *Orientalia Christiana Periodica* 68 (2002), 5–35, leaves a far too confident impression of what can be achieved by this approach.

[26] See Spinks, *Do This in Remembrance of Me*, 55–57, and his earlier study, *The Sanctus in the Eucharistic Prayer* (Cambridge: Cambridge University Press, 1991).

rejoicing and glorifying and exalting and commemorating
and celebrating this great and awesome mystery
of the passion and death and resurrection of our Lord Jesus Christ.[27]

Above all, the rich Eucharistic theology of the text needs to be acknow-
ledged. Two essential elements of fully developed anaphoras are integrated into the intercessory structure of Addai and Mari: the memorial
of Christ's saving Passion, death and resurrection and the Church's
offering or oblation of the sacrifice of Christ's body and blood.[28]
A reference to the institution of the Eucharist at the Last Supper and the
Lord's command offer it in his memory seems implied in the phrases 'as
thou hast taught us' (Section E), even though the addressee is God the
Father. In the corresponding section of the *Sharar*, the prayer is addressed
to the Son and continues with a loose quotation of John 6:51. Then
follows the institution narrative, which is also addressed to Christ.[29]
According to Macomber, the *Sharar* would testify to the early common
form of the anaphora at this point.[30]

In Addai and Mari, a second implicit reference to the institution of the
Eucharist is found in Section G, after the depiction of the assembly as
being gathered and standing before God. This depiction recalls the liturgical worship of the people of Israel in Deuteronomy (Deut 10:8 and
elsewhere), which is also found in the Eucharistic prayer of the *Apostolic
Tradition* (see above, p. 83). The priest then continues the prayer: '[we
who] have received by tradition the example which is from thee'. Bryan
Spinks observes that the Syriac verb for 'receive' corresponds to the
technical rabbinic term for receiving tradition and that its Greek equivalent is used by Paul in his introduction to the institution narrative in
1 Corinthians 11:23.[31] By 'tradition' is meant precisely the oral
transmission to which the Eucharistic institution belongs and, according
to Gelston, the 'example' (corresponding to the Greek τύπος), which in
itself means a 'type' or 'likeness', in this context 'clearly implies that what

---

[27] Gelston, *The Eucharistic Prayer of Addai and Mari*, 50–55 (critical edition of the Syriac
text and English translation).
[28] See ibid., 108–109.
[29] See the Latin version of the *Sharar* available in Hänggi – Pahl, *Prex eucharistica*, I, 413.
[30] See William F. Macomber, 'The Ancient Form of the Anaphora of the Apostles', in *East
of Byzantium: Syria and Armenia in the Formative Period (Dumbarton Oaks
Symposium, 1980)*, ed. Nina G. Garsoïan, Thomas F. Mathews and Robert
W. Thomson (Washington, DC: Dumbarton Oaks, 1982), 73–88, at 79–80.
[31] See Bryan D. Spinks, *Addai and Mari – The Anaphora of the Apostles: A Text for
Students*, Grove Liturgical Study 24 (Bramcote: Grove Books, 1980), 28.

the Lord said and did at the Last Supper was a pattern that the Christian congregation is intended to follow'.[32]

Section G is difficult to interpret; above all, its series of participles appears to lack a main verb. Moreover, the connection with the rest of the anaphora is not clear, because the initial 'we also' can be understood either in continuity or in contrast with the groups of persons mentioned in Sections E and F. In a series of articles, Bernard Botte argued that this was the place where the early form of Addai and Mari had a narrative of institution, which was not written down in the later manuscript tradition. According to Botte, there is a hiatus between the first part of the anaphora, which consists of thanksgiving, and the second part, beginning 'And we also', which is anamnetical; the presence of an anamnesis would seem to require an institution narrative.[33] While in twentieth-century scholarship there was considerable support for the hypothesis that the early form of Addai and Mari contained the Eucharistic words of institution, today this is a marginal position. However, this shift depends to a large extent on a hermeneutic that presupposes a lack of normativity in early Christian history, which has come under critical scrutiny (see Chapter 2). Hence, I consider the case of Addai and Mari far from closed.[34]

Another open question regarding the anaphora is the presence of an epiclesis. The Mar Esh'aya text contains an invocation of the Holy Spirit on the Eucharistic offerings that they may be sanctified and bear spiritual fruits in those who share in them:

[H]
And let thy Holy Spirit come, O my Lord, and rest upon this offering of thy servants,
and bless and sanctify it that it may be to us, O my Lord, for the pardon of sins

---

[32] Gelston, *The Eucharistic Prayer of Addai and Mari*, 107.

[33] See Bernard Botte, 'L'Anaphore Chaldéenne des Apôtres', in *Orientalia Christiana Periodica* 15 (1949), 259–276; 'L'épiclèse dans les liturgies syriennes orientales', in *Sacris Erudiri* 6 (1954), 48–72; 'Problèmes de l'anamnèse', in *Journal of Ecclesiastical History* 5 (1954), 16–24; 'Problèmes de l'anaphore syrienne des Apôtres Addaï et Mari', in *L'Orient syrien* 10 (1965), 89–106.

[34] See my own contributions, 'Eucharist without Institution Narrative? The Anaphora of Addai and Mari Revisited', in *Die Anaphora von Addai und Mari. Studien zu Eucharistie und Einsetzungsbericht*, ed. Uwe Michael Lang (Bonn: nova & vetera, 2007), 31–65; and 'Zum Einsetzungsbericht bei ostsyrischen Liturgiekommentatoren', in *Oriens Christianus* 89 (2005), 63–76. The response by Nicholas V. Russo, 'The Validity of the Anaphora of *Addai and* Mari: Critique of the Critiques', in *Issues in Eucharistic Praying in East and West*, 21–62, is bracketed by infelicitous ecclesiastical polemics.

and for the forgiveness of shortcomings, and for the great hope of the resurrection
from the dead,
and for new life in the kingdom of heaven with all who have been pleasing before
thee.[35]

Recent scholarship has seen in the petition for the Holy Spirit to 'come',
following the primitive Christian invocation *maranatha* (see Chapter 2),
an early form of Eucharistic epiclesis. Later, with the full development of
Trinitarian theology in the fourth century, the epiclesis adopted the form
of petitioning the Father to send the Spirit. The jussive form of the
epiclesis in the Anaphora of Addai and Mari has a parallel in the early
third-century Syrian *Acts of Thomas*, which also contains petitions for the
pardon of sins and for eternal life.[36] There is, however, no scholarly
consensus whether the epiclesis in the Mar Esh'aya text already formed
part of the anaphora in the third-century.

A final word of caution: Any discussion of the Anaphora of Addai
Mari needs to be conscious of the far-ranging reform of the East Syrian
liturgy that was carried out in the seventh century by Catholicos-Patriarch
Isho'yabh III (c. 650–659). The eleventh-century author Ibn at-Tayyib
(d. 1043) records that in this process of revision the Anaphora of Addai
and Mari was abridged, presumably with the idea of making it the
principal Eucharistic prayer of the Church of the East.[37] Isho'yabh III
reduced the number of anaphoras in use, fixed liturgical ceremonies,
determined their theological interpretation and thus gave them a sacro-
sanct quality that would preclude any change. It would seem that the
impact of Isho'yabh's reform belongs to the phenomenon classified by
Anton Baumstark as a secondary movement of abbreviation in liturgical
development.[38] Baumstark even concludes: 'There is no liturgical domain
which has been more hermetically sealed than that of the Nestorian

---

[35] Gelston, *The Eucharistic Prayer of Addai and Mari*, 54–55.
[36] See Spinks, *Do This in Remembrance of Me*, 57–58.
[37] See William F. Macomber, 'The Maronite and Chaldean Versions of the Anaphora of the
Apostles', in *Orientalia Christiana Periodica* 39 (1971), 55–84, at 56 and 74. For further
literature on Isho'yabh III, see Anton Baumstark, *Geschichte der syrischen Literatur: Mit
Ausschluß der christlich-palästinensischen Texte* (Bonn: A. Marcus und E. Weber, 1922),
197–200; and Jean Maurice Fiey, 'Išo'yaw le Grand. Vie du catholicos nestorien Išo'yaw
III d'Adiabène (580–659)', *in Orientalia Christiana Periodica* 36 (1969) 305–333, and 36
(1970) 5–46.
[38] See Anton Baumstark, *Comparative Liturgy*, rev. Bernard Botte, trans. Frank Leslie Cross
(Westminster: The Newman Press, 1958), 21–23.

Church, whose Rite received such a personal turn from the revision to which it was subjected by the Catholicos Išoʻjahb.'[39]

The Barcelona Anaphora and the Strasbourg Papyrus

The Greek papyrus Strasbourg Gr. 254, which dates from the fourth to fifth century, contains prayers that have parallels in the Alexandrian Anaphora of St Mark and its Coptic counterpart, the Anaphora of St Cyril. The text consists of praise and thanksgiving for God's works of creation and redemption with a quotation of Malachi 1:11, of intercessory prayers and of a commemoration of the saints and of a doxology. When the text was published in 1928, its editors considered it as fragmentary, as is suggested by the actual state of the papyrus. Since then, however, similarities with Jewish meal prayers have led many scholars, including Enrico Mazza, to conclude that the Strasbourg papyrus comprises a complete Eucharistic prayer, even though it lacks not only an institution narrative but also the *Sanctus* and an epiclesis.[40] More recently, Bryan Spinks has noted that, just as the Anaphora of Addai and Mari is divided by a doxology, so the doxology at the end of the intercessions in the Strasbourg papyrus may suggest that we have only the first units of a longer anaphora.[41]

Of significant import is the research of Michael Zheltov on the anaphora of the papyrus P. Monts. Roca inv. 128–178, which is now held in the library of Montserrat abbey. This Greek text of Egyptian origin can be dated to the fourth century and hence precedes the Strasbourg papyrus as a physical witness and most likely in content (see Figure 3.1).[42] The Barcelona Anaphora (as it is known since its first publication by Ramón Roca-Puig in 1994) shows the fully developed Alexandrian pattern (see below): an opening dialogue, a prayer of praise and thanksgiving leading to the *Sanctus*, an oblation of the bread and the cup, a first epiclesis asking the Father to send the Holy Spirit on the bread and cup and so to make them the body and blood of Christ, an institution narrative followed by

---

[39] Ibid., 19. [40] See Spinks, *Do This in Remembrance of Me*, 59–61.
[41] Bryan D. Spinks, 'A Complete Anaphora? A Note on Strasbourg Gr. 254', in *Heythrop Journal* 35 (1984), 51–59.
[42] Michael Zheltov, 'The Anaphora and the Thanksgiving Prayer from the Barcelona Papyrus: An Underestimated Testimony to the Anaphoral History in the Fourth Century', in *Vigiliae Christianae* 62 (2008), 467–504.

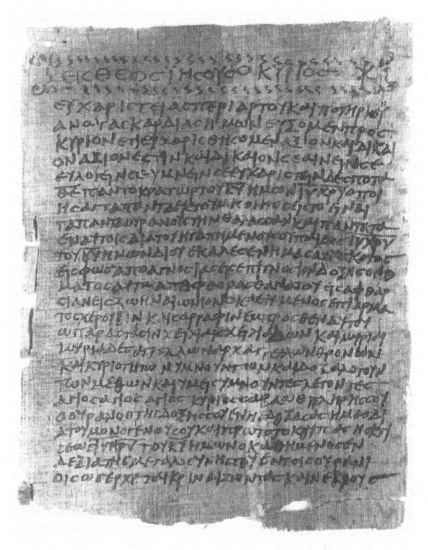

Figure 3.1 P. Monts. Roca inv. 154b, the first page of the Barcelona Anaphora / fourth century
(Abbadia de Montserrat, Biblioteca / Reprinted with kind permission)

an anamnesis, a second epiclesis asking for the spiritual fruits of communion and a concluding doxology:

One God.
Jesus the Lord.

'Thanksgiving for the bread and the cup.'

Up our hearts.
We have to the Lord.

Let us also give thanks.
Fitting and right.

It is fitting and right to praise you, to bless you, to hymn you, to give you thanks, o Master, God Pantocrator of our Lord Jesus Christ, who created all things from non-existence into being, all: heaven and the earth, the sea, and all that is in them, —through your beloved child Jesus Christ, our Lord, through whom you have called us from darkness into light, from ignorance to knowledge of the glory of his name, from decay of death into incorruption, into life eternal;

who sits on the chariot, Cherubim and Seraphim before it, who is attended by thousands of thousands and myriads of myriads of angels, archangels, thrones and dominions, hymning and glorifying, with whom we are also hymning, saying:

'Holy, Holy, Holy, Lord of Sabaoth! Heaven and earth are full of Your glory,'

in which you have glorified us through your Only-Begotten, the firstborn of every creature, Jesus Christ, our Lord, who sits on the right hand of your greatness in heaven, who is coming to judge the living and the dead, <the remembrance of whose death we do>.[43]

Through him we offer you these your creations, the bread and the cup: we ask and beseech you to send onto them your Holy and Comforter Spirit from heaven, to represent them materially and to make the bread the Body of Christ and the cup the Blood of Christ, of the New Covenant –

as he himself, when he was about to hand <himself>, having taken bread and given thanks, broke it and gave it to his disciples, saying:

'Take, eat, this is My body';

likewise after supper, having taken a cup and given thanks, he gave it to them, saying:

'Take, drink the blood, which is shed for many for remission of sins.'

And we also do the same in your remembrance, like those – whenever we meet together, we make the remembrance of you, of the holy mystery of our Teacher and King and Savior Jesus Christ.

---

[43] Angle brackets indicate insertions at places where the fragments Louvain Copt. 27 and P. Vindob. G 41043 agree together against the main papyrus.

Even so, we pray to you, Master, that in blessing you will bless and in sanctifying sanctify ... for all communicating from them for undivided faith, for communication of incorruption, for communion of the Holy Spirit, for perfection of belief and truth, for fulfillment of all your will,

so that in this and again we will glorify your all-revered and all-holy name, through your sanctified Child, our Lord Jesus Christ, through whom glory be to you, power unto the unblended ages of ages.

Amen.[44]

The evidence of the Barcelona Anaphora strongly supports the fragmentary character of the Strasbourg papyrus. At the same time, the anaphora lacks some elements of the fully developed Alexandrian tradition, such as the substantial intercessions. Zheltov also notes that the liturgical texts on the papyrus display archaic theological features (e.g., addressing Jesus as 'child' or 'servant' – παῖς – as in the *Didache* and the *Apostolic Tradition*), which might point to a third-century origin of the anaphora. The Barcelona Anaphora certainly calls for a revision of recent scholarship on the early development of Eucharistic prayers. At the very least, it questions the theory advanced, among others, by Paul Bradshaw that elements, such as the institution narrative and the epiclesis, should be considered a fourth-century interpolation. As Zheltov argues, 'these parts do not have an interpolated but an organic nature'.[45] If the Barcelona Anaphora can indeed be dated to the third century, it would increase the plausibility for a similar timeline for the Eucharistic prayer in the *Apostolic Tradition*.

AFTER CONSTANTINE: ANTIOCH AND ALEXANDRIA AS LITURGICAL CENTRES

The fourth and fifth centuries were a period of rapid and complex development of Christian doctrine and practice. In 313, the Emperor Constantine granted Christianity toleration and legal status. This act ended the last persecution of Christians in the Roman Empire, which had begun under Diocletian in 303, and it was hailed as the 'Peace of the Church'. Constantine also favoured the Christian faith and gave it substantial support, above all with the building and furnishing of churches throughout the Mediterranean world. In 380, the Emperor

---

[44] Ibid., 486–492. The layout of the text follows Zheltov, with some modifications.
[45] Ibid., 503. See also Spinks, *Do This in Remembrance of Me*, 99–102.

Theodosius made Catholic Christianity the official religion of the empire. These two dates mark important stages in – though by no means the conclusion of – a process of Christianisation in the Roman Empire. The period also witnessed bitter theological controversies over core Christian doctrines, the Trinity and Christology, which were addressed at the ecumenical councils of Nicaea (325), Constantinople (381), Ephesus (431) and Chalcedon (451). Beyond these disputes, the Constantinian settlement provided ideological and material conditions in which the religious practice of ordinary Christians could flourish and many new converts (though not all with pure motives) flocked into the newly built churches. The proliferation and elaboration of liturgical celebrations required a greater degree of regulation than before. From this period, therefore, the first written sources of liturgical texts emerge, and they usually carry the approbation of a bishop or a synod of bishops. It was widely considered necessary to formalise Christian worship in order to retain standards of doctrinal content and of prayer language.

With the Constantinian settlement, a process of liturgical standardisation began around the major urban centres of the Roman Empire (which would later be called 'patriarchates'): Rome, Alexandria, Antioch, Constantinople (dedicated as the new capital of the empire in 330) and – because of its special significance as the Holy City – Jerusalem. The socio-political importance of these cities and the high profile of their bishops enabled them to exert a great influence on the liturgical life of the local churches that surrounded them. Referring again to Robert Taft's linguistic simile (see Chapter 2), 'related but different liturgical "dialects" within a given zone of ecclesiastical politico-cultural influence gave way to the growing predominance of the "standard" language or rite – usually that of the metropolis'.[46] A 'rite' can be defined as a coherent body of liturgical forms and ordinances that are followed by local churches within a particular territory. It would be too early to speak of fully-fledged 'rites' in the fourth and fifth centuries; however, we can discern the development of liturgical families around the above-mentioned ecclesiastical centres.[47] The episcopal sees of Antioch and Alexandria are associated with the

[46] Robert F. Taft, *The Byzantine Rite: A Short History*, American Essays in Liturgy (Collegeville: Liturgical Press, 1992), 25.
[47] See the concise overview of early Christian liturgical families and rites by Hans-Jürgen Feulner, 'Liturgy', in *Dictionary of Early Christian Literature*, ed. Siegmar Döpp and Wilhelm Geerlings (New York: Herder and Herder, 2000), 384–388.

formation of the 'classical' anaphoras of the Eastern Christian traditions. These Eucharistic prayers were (and many of them still are) in liturgical use and have been modified, extended and occasionally shortened throughout the centuries. Hence, we can hardly determine when these anaphoras first appeared as written texts. Late fourth-century mystagogical preaching, for instance, by Cyril of Jerusalem (d. 386/387), Theodore of Mopsuestia (d. c. 428) and Ambrose of Milan (d. 397), contain allusions and citations that offer valuable information about the liturgical uses of their local churches. These catecheses and homilies are also important sources for Eucharistic theology and spirituality.[48]

Anaphoras of the Antiochene Type

Antioch in Syria (today in the southeastern corner of Turkey) was a major civil and ecclesiastical centre in late antiquity, with its sphere of influence extending to Syria, Palestine and Asia Minor. An early example of an Antiochene anaphora is found in the eighth book of the *Apostolic Constitutions*, a comprehensive Church order. Clement of Rome is listed as the purported editor of the document, but nineteenth-century research established that the *Apostolic Constitutions* were compiled in the region of Antioch between 375 and 400 and that they are based on early Church orders, such as the Syrian *Didascalia* and the *Apostolic Tradition*.[49] The eighth book contains a complete Eucharistic rite, which used to be known as the 'Clementine Liturgy'. This detailed account follows the pattern recorded by Justin in the mid-second century, but offers more detail, listing four Scripture readings (law, prophets, epistle, gospel), a sermon, litanies and prayers for the dismissal of catechumens, penitents and other groups, prayers of the faithful in the form of a litany, the exchange of peace, offertory, anaphora, communion rites, thanksgiving for communion and dismissal. The lengthy and carefully constructed Eucharistic prayer, which is based on the one in the *Apostolic Tradition*, shows parallels with other anaphoras that originated around Antioch, but it is not clear whether it has ever been in liturgical use and Allen Bouley calls it

---

[48] See Spinks, *Do This in Remembrance of Me*, 68–88; Hoping, *My Body Given for You*, 99–104 and 108–122.

[49] See Bruno Steimer, 'Apostolic Constitutions', in *Dictionary of Early Christian Literature*, 44.

an 'ideal text'.[50] The typical structure of the Antiochene anaphora can be summarised as follows:[51]

> Introductory dialogue with an initial Trinitarian greeting modelled on 2 Cor 13:13
>   ('The grace of . . .')
> Praise and thanksgiving ('It is truly right and just . . .')
> Introduction to the *Sanctus*
> *Sanctus*
> Post-*Sanctus*
> Institution Narrative
> Anamnesis
> Epiclesis
> Intercessions
> Doxology

The Byzantine Rite developed from the Antiochene liturgical family.[52] Within this tradition, the Eucharistic prayer with the greatest historical impact is the Anaphora of St John Chrysostom, which by the eleventh century had replaced the Byzantine version of the Anaphora of St Basil as the most frequently used in the Divine Liturgy (Eucharist). Robert Taft has made a compelling case that John Chrysostom, when he became bishop of Constantinople, introduced from his native Antioch an early form of the anaphora that bears his name, revising it for use in the capital.[53]

Another important influence on the Byzantine Rite was the liturgical practice of Jerusalem. The Anaphora of St James is ascribed to the 'Brother of the Lord' (Gal 1:19) and connected with the Holy City. The outline of the anaphora in the *Mystagogical Catecheses* attributed to

---

[50] Bouley, *From Freedom to Formula*, 231; see also Spinks, *Do This in Remembrance of Me*, 89–92.

[51] Anaphoras of the Antiochene type in the Greek original (where available) and in a Latin version are found in Hänggi – Pahl, *Prex eucharistica*, I, 204–373. For a selection of ancient anaphoras in English translation with useful introductions, see Ronald C. D. Jasper and Geoffrey J. Cuming, *Prayers of the Eucharist: Early and Reformed*, 3rd ed. (Collegeville: Liturgical Press, 1987).

[52] For a concise introduction with ample reference to further literature, see Taft, *The Byzantine Rite*; also Spinks, *Do This in Remembrance of Me*, 121–140.

[53] See Robert F. Taft, 'The Authenticity of the Chrysostom Anaphora Revisited: Determining the Authorship of Liturgical Texts by Computer', in *Orientalia Christiana Periodica* 56 (1990), 5–51.

Cyril of Jerusalem has points of contact with James.[54] After the Constantinian settlement, pilgrimages to the Holy Land increased rapidly and monumental churches were built on the sacred sites, especially the complex of buildings around the Holy Sepulchre. Stational liturgies were celebrated in the places connected with biblical events, especially the life of Christ, on particular days of the year. The 'travel diary' (*itinerarium*) of the fourth-century pilgrim known as Egeria is a fascinating source documenting this practice.[55] Stational liturgies proved to be very popular and imitated by pilgrims in their local churches, above all Constantinople and Rome.[56] The Jerusalem cycle of feasts had significant influence in both East and West. Moreover, the Divine Office of the Byzantine Rite bears the stamp of monasticism in the Holy Land.

The Syriac liturgical traditions belong to the Antiochene family but also show particular and complex developments.[57] Edessa in Mesopotamia became an important centre of Syriac language and culture, especially when the great light of Syriac Christianity, St Ephrem (d. 373), had to leave his native Nisibis, which fell to the Parthians in 363, and established himself at the school of Edessa. The Syriac tradition is usually divided into 'West Syrian' and 'East Syrian', which is not simply a geographical designation but also indicates different theological profiles

---

[54] Emmanuel J. Cutrone, 'Cyril's Mystagogical Catecheses and the Evolution of the Jerusalem Anaphora', in *Orientalia Christiana Periodica* 44 (1978), 52–64, has argued that the anaphora used in Jerusalem in the late fourth century did not contain an institution narrative, since it is not mentioned in Cyril's outline of the Eucharistic prayer in the fifth catechesis. This reading is unlikely, because the words of institution cited in the fourth catechesis do not follow any of the biblical accounts but appear to be taken from liturgical use. A strong case for the presence of an institution narrative in Cyril's Eucharistic Prayer has been made by Edward J. Yarnold, 'Anaphoras without Institution Narratives?', in *Studia Patristica* 30 (1997), 395–410; and Alexis Doval, *Cyril of Jerusalem, Mystagogue: The Authorship of the Mystagogic Catecheses*, Patristic Monograph Series 17 (Washington, DC: The Catholic University of America Press, 2001), 150–161. David S. Wallace-Hadrill, 'Eusebius and the Institution Narrative in the Eastern Liturgies', in *Journal of Theological Studies* N.S. 4 (1953), 41–42, sees evidence in Eusebius of Caesarea's *Demonstratio evangelica* that the anaphora used in Jerusalem had an institution narrative as early as the year 313.

[55] See *Egeria's Travels*, newly translated with supporting documents and notes by John Wilkinson, 3rd ed. (Warminster: Aris & Phillips, 1999).

[56] See John F. Baldovin, *The Urban Character of Christian Worship: The Origins, Development, and Meaning of Stational Liturgy*, Orientalia Christiana Analecta 228 (Rome: Pont. Institutum Studiorum Orientalium, 1987).

[57] See the overview of Spinks, *Do This in Memory of Me*, 141–170.

that resulted from the doctrinal controversies of the fifth century. These doctrinal differences also had an impact, albeit limited, on their liturgical rites.

The West Syrian tradition is more closely related to the liturgical customs of Antioch and Jerusalem. The large number of anaphoras (more than eighty have been identified and most of them are still unedited)[58] bespeaks the variety of this tradition, which is associated with the Middle Eastern churches that did not accept the Christological definition of the Council of Chalcedon in 451, because they regarded it as unfaithful to the teaching of the highly venerated St Cyril of Alexandria (d. 444).

The East Syrian tradition took a distinct path, which was to some extent owing to the fact that the Church of the East (in the Eastern part of Syria and Mesopotamia) became separate because it rejected the teaching of the Council of Ephesus in 431 as a betrayal of the Antiochene Christological school shaped by Theodore of Mopsuestia (d. c. 428) and Nestorius (d. c. 450). The most widely used Anaphora of Addai and Mari has early roots that go back to the third century, if not earlier. After the liturgical reforms of Catholicos-Patriarch Isho'yabh III, only two further anaphoras remained in use, those that bear the names of Theodore of Mopsuestia and Nestorius.[59]

Anaphoras of the Alexandrian Type

The anaphoral tradition of Alexandria, the centre of Christianity in Egypt, is well documented and may reach back to the third century (see above on the Barcelona Anaphora and the Strasbourg papyrus, pp. 91–94). Of particular interest is the euchologion (collection of prayers) attributed to Sarapion (d. after 360), which contains thirty texts, including an anaphora that integrates theological concepts and imagery from the Gospel of John. The prayers are likely to reflect the liturgical use of Thmuis in the Nile Delta, where Sarapion, a friend of Anthony and Athanasius, was bishop from c. 330 to his death.[60] The Eucharistic prayer in the euchologion shows typical

---

[58] See Hans-Jürgen Feulner, 'Zu den Editionen orientalischer Anaphoren', in *Crossroads of Cultures: Studies in Liturgy and Patristics in Honor of Gabriele Winkler*, ed. Hans-Jürgen Feulner, Elena Velkovska and Robert F. Taft (Rome: Pontificio Istituto Orientale, 2000), 251–282.

[59] Anaphoras of the East Syrian tradition in a Latin version are available in Hänggi – Pahl, *Prex eucharistica*, I, 374–420.

[60] See Spinks, *Do This in Remembrance of Me*, 94–99.

elements of the Alexandrian anaphoral tradition, which can be listed as follows:[61]

Introductory dialogue ('The Lord be with [you] all ...')
Praise and thanksgiving ('It is truly right and just ...')
Intercessions (including the deceased)
Introduction to the *Sanctus*
Sanctus
Epiclesis I
Institution Narrative
Anamnesis
Epiclesis II
Doxology

The two epicleses are a characteristic feature of the Alexandrian anaphora. Regarding the first epiclesis, there seem to be two strands of tradition. On the one hand, sources such as the Barcelona Anaphora and the fragmentary Deir Balyzeh papyrus from Upper Egypt (between sixth and eighth century) include a first epiclesis asking the Father to send the Holy Spirit upon the offerings of bread and wine and make them the body and blood of Christ. The second epiclesis, after the institution narrative, petitions for the spiritual fruits of sacramental communion. On the other hand, in the Eucharistic prayer of Sarapion, in the fully developed Greek Anaphora of St Mark and in its Coptic version, the Anaphora of St Cyril of Alexandria, the first epiclesis is less specific, asking for the blessing of the sacrifice through the coming of the Holy Spirit. Instead, the prayer for the consecration of the eucharistic offerings forms part of the second epiclesis. Perhaps this could be seen as an assimilation to the Antiochene pattern. The Egyptian version of the Anaphora of St Basil, which is related but distinct from the Byzantine Basil and can be classified as West Syrian in structure, might have been used in Egypt since the mid-fourth century (though the presumed connection with Basil of Caesarea visiting Egypt is tenuous). The anaphora is known in its original Greek as well as in Coptic dialects of Sahidic and Bohairic, and it became the standard anaphora of the Coptic Divine Liturgy.[62]

---

[61] Anaphoras of the Alexandrian type in the Greek original (where available) and in a Latin version are found in Hänggi – Pahl, *Prex eucharistica*, I, 101–203.

[62] On Egyptian anaphoras and the Coptic liturgy, see Spinks, *Do This in Remembrance of Me*, 94–120.

OTHER LITURGICAL DEVELOPMENTS

Scripture Readings

While there are no lectionary sources for the celebration of the Eucharist before the late fourth century, it is very likely that for major feasts and special seasons of the developing liturgical year the appropriate pericopes, that is, 'particular scriptural passages separated from their biblical context',[63] were used from very early on. The selection of particular biblical texts can be expected above all for the annual celebration of Easter and structured the pre-paschal period of preparation that was to become the forty days of Lent as well as the fifty days of the paschal season known since the late second century as Pentecost. The annual festivals of martyrs, such as Peter and Paul in Rome, Polycarp in Smyrna and Cyprian in Carthage, would also have been associated with particular readings. Fixed readings for liturgical feasts and seasons are indicated in sermons and writings of Ambrose of Milan and Augustine of Hippo.[64] A source of great importance is the fifth-century Armenian Lectionary, which is generally held to witness liturgical use in fourth-century Jerusalem and can be related to the preaching of Cyril of Jerusalem and the *Itinerarium Egeriae*.[65]

There is no evidence for the once popular theory that before the systematic organisation of pericopes in the fourth and fifth centuries, there was a continuous or consecutive reading (*lectio continua*) of Scripture at the Eucharist. When early Christian theologians comment on an entire biblical book in the form of consecutive homilies, such as Origen in the first half of the third century and John Chrysostom in the late fourth century, this did not happen in the context of the Eucharist – leaving aside the question of whether they delivered these homilies at all or whether they were literary products. At the celebration of the Eucharist, the presiding bishop would usually choose the readings and there is no suggestion that he was bound to a continuous reading of a biblical book.[66]

---

[63] Cyrille Vogel, *Medieval Liturgy: An Introduction to the Sources*, rev. and trans. William G. Storey and Niels Krogh Rasmussen (Washington, DC: The Pastoral Press, 1981), 300.

[64] For both Ambrose and Augustine, see the well-documented study of Geoffrey G. Willis, *St Augustine's Lectionary*, Alcuin Club Collections 44 (London: SPCK, 1962).

[65] *Le codex arménien Jérusalem 121*, ed. and trans. Athanase Renoux, 2 vol., Patrologia Orientalis 35.1, 36.2 (Turnhout: Brepols, 1969–1971).

[66] See Vogel, *Medieval Liturgy*, 300, with n. 38, where he refers to the work of Gerhard Kunze, *Die gottesdienstliche Schriftlesung*, Veröffentlichungen der evangelischen

Liturgy and Music

In Chapter 2, I argued that the sacrificial worship of the Jerusalem Temple offered concepts and images that formed the early Christian understanding of the Eucharist. At the same time, there was no continuity with the festive music of the Temple, which is described in various psalms.[67] Furthermore, early Christians were anxious to distance themselves from the musical practice of pagan rituals because of its association with idolatry and immorality. A consequence of this twofold demarcation is the exclusion of instruments, which is still maintained in Eastern Christian traditions and has been a strong current in the Latin West as well, leaving aside the special place of the organ, which it gradually acquired since the Carolingian period.[68]

There may have been interaction with synagogue practice – if indeed the prayer service of contemporary synagogues included music, which is a disputed point. It is often assumed that the chanting of psalms and the singing of hymns had a natural place in early Christian worship. However, Joseph Dyer cautions that '[p]salmody was not an essential component of the Mass from the beginning, and the *loci* appropriate for singing were only gradually occupied'.[69] In Greco-Roman culture, singing at evening banquets was common and Christians followed this custom, but this did not happen at celebrations of the Eucharist in the early morning.[70] Dyer also notes 'the possibly thin line that separated stylised

Gesellschaft für Liturgieforschung 1 (Göttingen: Vandenhoeck & Ruprecht, 1947); and 'Die Lesungen', in *Leiturgia* 2 (1955), 87–180.

[67] See James McKinnon, *Music in Early Christian Literature*, Cambridge Readings in the Literature of Music (Cambridge: Cambridge University Press, 1987, reprinted 1993), 1–11, with further bibliography; and *The Advent Project: The Later-Seventh-Century Creation of the Roman Mass Proper* (Berkeley; Los Angeles; London: University of California Press, 2000), 19–98.

[68] See Dietrich Schuberth, *Kaiserliche Liturgie: Die Einbeziehung von Musikinstrumenten, insbesondere der Orgel, in den frühmittelalterlichen Gottesdienst*, Veröffentlichungen der Evangelischen Gesellschaft für Liturgieforschung 17 (Göttingen: Vandenhoeck & Ruprecht, 1968); Ewald Jammers, *Musik in Byzanz, im päpstlichen Rom und im Frankenreich: Der Choral als Textaussprache*, Abhandlungen der Heidelberger Akademie der Wissenschaften, Philosophisch-historische Klasse, 1962/1 (Heidelberg: C. Winter, 1962); Egon Wellesz, *A History of Byzantine Music and Hymnography*, 2nd ed. revised and enlarged (Oxford: Clarendon Press, 1961).

[69] Joseph Dyer, Review of James McKinnon, *The Advent Project*, in *Early Music History* 20 (2001), 279–309, at 283.

[70] See Christopher Page, *The Christian West and Its Singers: The First Thousand Years* (New Haven; London: Yale University Press, 2010) 55–71 and his collection of sources at 72–83.

reading from simple song in the ancient world'.[71] Thus, the formal recitation of texts could have provided an opening for the introduction of chanting psalms. Communal psalmody is attested in the fourth century, and it seems to have originated not in the remote monastic communities of the desert but rather among urban ascetics who were associated with the city's cathedral or with a martyr's shrine. According to Dyer, the manner of singing psalms developed in such urban communities may have been similar to later Western psalm tones.[72] By the late fourth century, psalms were chanted in the Eucharistic liturgy between readings and during communion. The new practice seems to have been very popular, as is implied by the criticism of fourth-century Church fathers, including Athanasius, Basil of Caesarea, Jerome and Augustine, that singing in church should not be an occasion for aesthetic pleasure but should draw attention to the sacred words and draw the soul to love of God and to a virtuous life.[73]

CONCLUSION

This chapter has been dedicated to the formation of Eucharistic prayers, starting with those that are most likely to have pre-Nicene origins. The Constantinian settlement initiated a shift from an early oral practice within a framework of stable elements and conventions towards fixed written texts. From the fourth century onwards, sources for Eucharistic prayers flow abundantly, as has been shown in the concise survey of 'classical' anaphoras of the Greek- and Syriac-speaking East. While the fourth century re-shaped the celebration of the Eucharist – owing to the new public status of Christianity and the possibilities offered by monumental church architecture – the theological and spiritual contents of the 'classical' Eucharistic prayers build on the foundations that were laid in the previous centuries. The broader view of the first three chapters of this study has offered background and context for the more specific enquiry into the Latin liturgical tradition and the Roman Rite of Mass, on which my narrative will now focus.

---

[71] Dyer, Review, 284–285, with reference to Alfred Stuiber, 'Psalmenlesung oder Zwischengesang', in *Pietas: Festschrift für Bernhard Kötting*, ed. Ernst Dassmann and Karl Suso Frank, Jahrbuch für Antike und Christentum. Ergänzungsband 8 (Münster: Aschendorff, 1990), 393–398, at 393.

[72] See Joseph Dyer, 'The Desert, the City and Psalmody in the Late Fourth Century', in *Western Plainchant in the First Millennium: Studies in the Medieval Liturgy and Its Music*, ed. Sean Gallagher, James Haar, John Nádas and Timothy Striplin (Aldershot; Burlington: Ashgate, 2003), 11–43.

[73] See Uwe Michael Lang, 'Goodness of Forms: The Demand for the Artistic Quality of Music for the Liturgy', in *Antiphon* 23 (2019) 311–331, at 317–319.

4

The Formative Period of Latin Liturgy

This chapter will examine the process by which Latin came to be established as the liturgical language of the Western Church from the fourth century onwards. In this process, the elaboration of Christian revelation proved definitive in transforming a traditional style of prayer that was firmly embedded in the Roman world. Particular attention will be given to the development of the Roman Eucharistic prayer, the *Canon missae*. Characteristic features of the new liturgical idiom will be analysed with the help of selected examples, both from the canon and from the variable prayers of the Mass.

A CHRISTIAN LATIN CULTURE

Early Christian missions engaged primarily with *Kultursprachen*, that is, languages that carried a certain cultural and literary weight.[1] The wide diffusion of the Greek language facilitated the proclamation of the gospel in the Roman Empire, and Greek remained 'a fundamental "given" of eastern Christianity'.[2] The Greek spoken by the populace of Greece, Asia Minor, Syria, Palestine, Egypt and the Cyrenaica was not the classical

---

[1] See Peter Bruns, 'Kult(ur)- und Volkssprachen in der Alten Kirche', in *Forum Katholische Theologie* 29 (2012), 241–250, building on Karl Holl, 'Kultursprache und Volkssprache in der altchristlichen Mission', in *Kirchengeschichte als Missionsgeschichte: Band I. Die Alte Kirche*, ed. Heinzgünther Frohnes and Uwe W. Knorr (Munich: Kaiser, 1974), 389–396.

[2] Scott F. Johnson, 'The Social Presence of Greek in Eastern Christianity, 200–1200 CE', in *Languages and Cultures of Eastern Christianity: Greek*, ed. Scott F. Johnson, The Worlds of Eastern Christianity, 300–1500, vol. 6 (Farnham: Ashgate, 2015), 1–122, at 7.

idiom but the simplified Koine (derived from ἡ κοινὴ διάλεκτος, 'the common dialect'). Among the urban proletariat in the West, Koine Greek was spoken by uprooted people, prisoners of war, small merchants, sailors and other migrants from the Eastern territories. People who had left their home countries because of wars, or for social and economic reasons, flocked above all to the capital of the empire. Even if one takes into account satirical hyperbole, the poet Juvenal's caustic comment, 'I cannot, Romans, endure a Greek city',[3] suggests a strong presence of Hellenic speakers in Rome. Koine Greek was also current in the substantial Jewish diaspora and among the earliest Christians of the city, as the Apostle Paul's Letter to the Romans indicates.[4]

Greek was the language of the first known Christian literary works that originated in Rome, for instance, the *First Letter of Clement*, the *Shepherd of Hermas* and the writings of Justin Martyr. In the first two centuries, there were several popes with Greek names, and from this period Christian tomb inscriptions in Greek have come down to us.[5] It would be reasonable to assume that Greek had a considerable role in the worship of the first Christian communities in Rome. The decisive shift towards Latin seems to have begun in proconsular Africa, where the 'earliest known converts were Latin-speaking natives of the province rather than Greek-speaking immigrants'.[6] From the latter half of the second century, Latin translations of Greek works emerged in Rome, such

---

[3] 'Non possum ferre, Quirites, Graecam Vrbem'. Juvenal, *Satires*, 3,60–61: ed. Susanna Morton Braund, Loeb Classical Library 91 (Cambridge, MA; London: Harvard University Press, 1969), 170.

[4] See Gustave Bardy, *La question des langues dans l'Église ancienne*, Études de Théologie Historique (Paris: Beauchesne, 1948), 81–94; Wayne A. Meeks, *The First Urban Christians: The Social World of the Apostle Paul* (New Haven: Yale University Press, 1983), 37; also Peter Lampe, *Christians at Rome in the First Two Centuries: From Paul to Valentinus*, trans. Michael Steinhauser and ed. Marshall D. Johnson (London: Continuum, 2006).

[5] Maura K. Lafferty, 'Translating Faith from Greek to Latin: Romanitas and Christianitas in Late Fourth-Century Rome and Milan', in *Journal of Early Christian Studies* 11 (2003), 21–62, at 29, notes that epitaphs continued to be in Greek even for popes with Latin names, Urbanus, Pontianus, Fabianus and Lucius. The exception is Pope Cornelius (d. 253), whose epitaph is in Latin. On the presence of Greek-speaking Christians in Rome, see Carl Paul Caspari, *Ungedruckte, unbeachtete und wenig beachtete Quellen zur Geschichte des Taufsymbols und der Glaubensregel*, 3 vols. (Christiania: Malling, 1866–1875), vol. III, 303–466, esp. 456–457.

[6] Lafferty, *Translating Faith*, 29, n. 27, with reference to James B. Rives, *Religion and Authority in Roman Carthage from Augustus to Constantine* (Oxford: Clarendon Press, 1995), 223–226. See also Bardy, *La question des langues dans l'Église ancienne*, 57–63.

as the aforementioned *First Letter of Clement* and *Shepherd of Hermas*.[7] By the middle of the third century, this transition towards Latin was well advanced in the Roman church: some of its clergy corresponded in Latin with Cyprian of Carthage, and Novatian composed his *De trinitate* and other works in Latin, quoting from an already existing version of the Bible.[8] In addition, the stream of migrants from the East seems to have diminished in the second half of the third century. This demographic change meant that the life of the Roman church was increasingly dominated by native Latin speakers.

According to Optatus, bishop of Milevis in North Africa, writing between 364 and 367, there were 'forty and more churches (*basilicas*)' in Rome at the time when the Donatists set up their own bishop in the city, which happened not long after the origin of the schism in 312.[9] While the use of the term 'basilica' is anachronistic, the number of Christian communities is supported by the list of clergy in a letter of Pope Cornelius from the year 251.[10] Most of these pre-Constantinian congregations would certainly have been Latin-speaking in the third century, if not before. Latin would have been widely used for proclaiming the Sacred Scriptures. By the late fourth century, the Latin version of the psalms had acquired such an established status that Jerome only revised it with caution. Later he translated the Psalter from the Hebrew, as he said, not for liturgical purposes, but to provide a text for scholarship and controversy.[11] Around the same time, the Roman authors Marius

---

[7] Bardy, *La question des langues dans l'Église ancienne*, 106–107.

[8] The *Apostolic Tradition*, which used to be attributed to Hippolytus of Rome, remains an important early document (see Chapter 2), but it cannot be used as a source for Roman liturgy in the third century. Its influence on the subsequent development of Western liturgy was minimal until the Second Vatican Council.

[9] Optatus of Milevis, *Contra Parmenianum*, II,4: CSEL 26,39.

[10] The letter is transmitted in Eusebius, *Ecclesiastical History* VI,43,11: GCS 9/2 [NF 6/2],618: '[In Rome] there are 46 presbyters, 7 deacons, 7 sub-deacons, 42 acolytes, 52 exorcists, readers and door-keepers, and more than 1,500 widows and persons in distress, all of whom the grace and loving-kindness of the Lord nourishes.'

[11] See Jerome's two prefaces to the Psalter in *Biblia sacra iuxta Vulgatam versionem*, ed. Robert Weber et al., 4th ed. (Stuttgart: Deutsche Bibelgesellschaft, 1994), 767–769; see also Christine Mohrmann, 'The New Latin Psalter: Its Diction and Style', in *Études sur le latin des chrétiens*, 4 vols., Storia e letteratura 65, 87, 103, 143 (Rome: Edizioni di Storia e Letteratura, 1961–1977), vol. II, 109–131, at 110–111 (originally published in *The American Benedictine Review* 5 [1953], 7–33).

Victorinus and Ambrosiaster offer some evidence for a residual presence of Greek as a language of worship, especially in the Eucharistic prayer.[12]

Various answers have been given to the intriguing question as to why the transition from Greek to Latin in the liturgy did not keep pace with the changes in the social and cultural contexts of Roman Christianity. The German liturgical scholar Theodor Klauser attributed this phenomenon to the general conservatism of Romans and their tenacity in keeping religious traditions, which was shared by the Roman church.[13] According to the American Benedictine Allan Bouley, the need for a carefully formulated doctrinal language, especially during the Arian crisis of the fourth century, provided the leaven for creating an official Latin form of liturgical prayers.[14] Bouley's thesis, that it was the need for orthodox language that facilitated the development of Latin euchology (i.e., prayer texts), is certainly borne out by Ambrose's efforts to inculcate the Nicene faith in liturgical hymns to combat the presence of Arianism in Milan. Adding another dimension to the question, Christine Mohrmann argues that the formation of liturgical Latin became possible only after the Emperor Constantine gave peace and recognition to the Church, as there was no longer such a strong need for Christian communities to define themselves in opposition to the surrounding pagan culture. Their new secure status offered the local churches in the West greater freedom to draw, at least for purposes of style, if not for content, on the religious heritage of Rome for the development of their liturgies.[15]

From the perspective of sociolinguistics, Peter Burke observes that 'language is an active force in society, a means for individuals and groups to control others or resist such control, for changing society or for blocking change, for affirming or suppressing cultural identities'.[16] The formation of a Latin liturgical language can thus be understood as part of

---

[12] See my discussion in Uwe Michael Lang, *The Voice of the Church at Prayer: Reflections on Liturgy and Language* (San Francisco: Ignatius Press, 2012), 56–60.

[13] See Theodor Klauser, ‚Der Übergang der römischen Kirche von der griechischen zur lateinischen Liturgiesprache', in *Miscellanea Giovanni Mercati: 1. Bibbia, letteratura cristiana antica*, Studi e testi 121 (Vatican City: Biblioteca Apostolica Vaticana, 1946), 467–482.

[14] See Allan Bouley, *From Freedom to Formula: The Evolution of the Eucharistic Prayer from Oral Improvisation to Written Texts*, Studies in Christian Antiquity 21 (Washington, DC: The Catholic University of America Press, 1981), 202–207 and 212–213.

[15] See Christine Mohrmann, *Liturgical Latin: Its Origins and Character: Three Lectures* (London: Burns & Oates, 1959), 45–48.

[16] Peter Burke, *The Art of Conversation* (Ithaca: Cornell University Press, 1993), 26.

a wide-ranging effort by the leading bishops in Italy, above all Damasus in
Rome and Ambrose in Milan, to Christianise Roman culture. Pope
Damasus (r. 366–384) commissioned the renowned biblical scholar
Jerome to produce a revised translation of the Holy Scriptures, which
later came to be known as the *Vulgata* or 'Vulgate'. The extent of
Damasus' liturgical contribution is disputed by scholars: Klauser credits
him initiating efforts to establish Latin as the 'new' language of the
Roman liturgy, whereas Bernard Botte and Charles Pietri argue more
convincingly that Damasus' pontificate saw the conclusion of a development that had been underway for a considerable time.[17]

In the city of Rome, there remained a strong pagan presence, material
as well as intellectual, and the aristocracy in particular continued to
adhere to inherited customs, even if they had become nominal
Christians.[18] Rome was no longer the centre of political power, but its
culture maintained a grip on the thought-world of its elites; in fact, the
fourth century is now considered a period of literary renaissance, with a
renewed interest in the classics of Roman poetry and prose. There was
even a revival of Latin in the Eastern half of the empire.[19] With characteristic tenacity, Rome kept its ancient traditions.

The popes of the late fourth century and of the fifth century, beginning
with Damasus, made a conscious and comprehensive attempt to evangelise the symbols of Roman culture for the Christian faith. Part of this

[17] See Klauser, 'Der Übergang der römischen Kirche', followed by Massey H. Shepherd,
'The Liturgical Reform of Damasus I', in *Kyriakon: Festschrift Johannes Quasten*, ed.
Patrick Granfield and Josef A. Jungmann, 2 vols. (Münster: Aschendorff, 1970), vol. II,
847–863. For a different assessment of Damasus' role, see Bernard Botte and Christine
Mohrmann, *L'ordinaire de la messe: Texte critique, traduction et etudes*, Études
liturgique 2 (Paris; Louvain: Cerf; Abbaye du Mont César, 1953), 17; and Charles
Pietri, 'Damase évêque de Rome', in *Saecularia Damasiana: Atti del convegno
internazionale per il XVI centenario della morte di Papa Damaso I (11-12-384 – 10/
12-12-1984)*, Studi di antichità cristiana 39 (Vatican City: Pontificio Istituto di
Archeologia Cristiana, 1986), 29–58, at 50.
[18] On the difficulty of defining Christian identity in the late Roman Empire, see Robert
Marcus, *The End of Ancient Christianity* (Cambridge: Cambridge University Press,
1990), 19–83.
[19] See Lafferty, *Translating Faith from Greek to Latin*, 26–28, with references to Alan
Cameron, 'Latin Revival of the Fourth Century', in *Renaissances before the
Renaissance: Cultural Revivals of Late Antiquity and the Middle Ages*, ed. Warren
Treadgold (Stanford: Stanford University Press, 1984), 42–58; and Charles
W. Hedrick, *History and Silence: Purge and Rehabilitation of Memory in Late
Antiquity* (Austin: University of Texas Press, 2000). On the presence of the Latin
language in the Eastern half of the Roman Empire in the fourth century, see also Bardy,
La question des langues dans l'Église ancienne, 123–125 and 146–147.

project was the Christianisation of public space through extensive building projects. Once the Constantinian dynasty had taken the lead with the
monumental basilicas of the Lateran and St Peter's, as well as the cemetery basilicas outside the city walls, later emperors and popes continued
this building programme that was to transform Rome into a city dominated by churches. Perhaps the most prestigious project was the construction of a new basilica dedicated to St Paul on the Ostian Way, replacing
the small Constantinian edifice by a new church that would match the size
of St Peter's.[20] Another important part of this project was the
Christianisation of public time; a cycle of Christian feasts throughout
the year replaced pagan celebrations, as evident in the *depositio martyrum* of the Chronography of 354. This liturgical calendar, which can be
dated to the year 336, begins with the feast of the Nativity of Christ (25
December) and lists the celebrations of martyrs in Rome together with the
place in the city where they were commemorated.[21]

The formation of a Latin liturgical idiom was a major contribution to
this project of evangelising Roman culture and thus attracting the influential elites of the city and the empire to the Christian faith. It would not be
accurate to describe this process simply as the adoption of the vernacular
language in the liturgy, if 'vernacular' is taken to mean 'colloquial'. The
Latin of the canon, of the collects and prefaces of the Mass transcended
the conversational idiom of ordinary people. This highly stylised form of
speech, shaped to express complex theological ideas, would not have been
easy to follow by the average Roman Christian of late antiquity.[22]
Moreover, the adoption of *Latinitas* made the liturgy more accessible to
most people on the Italian peninsula but not to those in Western Europe
or in North Africa whose native language was Gothic, Celtic, Iberic
or Punic.

The Christian East was in a position to make use of several languages
that carried with themselves a certain cultural, social and political weight:

---

[20] See the beautifully illustrated volume by Hugo Brandenburg, *Ancient Churches of Rome
from the Fourth to the Seventh Century: The Dawn of Christian Architecture in the West*,
trans. Andreas Kropp, Bibliothèque de l'Antiquité Tardive 8 (Turnhout: Brepols, 2005).

[21] See Paul F. Bradshaw and Maxwell E. Johnson, *The Origins of Feasts, Fasts and Seasons
in Early Christianity* (Collegeville: Liturgical Press, 2011), 175.

[22] Mohrmann, *Liturgical Latin*, 53–54; see also Martin Klöckener, 'Zeitgemäßes Beten:
Meßorationen als Zeugnisse einer sich wandelnden Kultur und Spiritualität', in
*Bewahren und Erneuern: Studien zur Meßliturgie. Festschrift für Hans Bernhard Meyer
SJ zum 70. Geburtstag*, ed. Reinhard Meßner, Eduard Nagel und Rudolf Pacik,
Innsbrucker theologische Studien 42 (Innsbruck; Wien: Tyrolia, 1995), 114–142, at
126–127.

in addition to Greek, which retained a strong presence well into the fifth century, Syriac, Coptic Armenian, Georgian and Ethiopic began to be employed in the liturgy. In the Christian West, vernacular languages were not used in divine worship. The case of Roman North Africa is instructive: Augustine held Punic in esteem and made sure that the bishop chosen for a Punic-speaking region knew the language needed for his ministry.[23] However, there are no extant documents of a Punic liturgy, whether Catholic or Donatist. The religious prestige of the Roman church and its bishop helped Latin become the only liturgical language of the West. This would prove an important factor in furthering ecclesiastical, cultural and political unity. *Latinitas* became one of the defining characteristics of Western Europe.[24]

THE CANON OF THE MASS

The most important source for the early Roman Eucharistic prayer is Ambrose of Milan's series of catecheses for the newly baptised, dating from around 390, known under the title *De sacramentis*. This text is based on unrevised notes taken directly from Ambrose's preaching in Milan.[25] Unlike in *De mysteriis*, a series of homilies redacted for publication, Ambrose includes in the mystagogical instruction of *De sacramentis* extensive quotations from liturgical texts: the formula of renunciation, the formula of baptism – and substantial parts of the Eucharistic prayer. Elsewhere in *De sacramentis*, the bishop of Milan notes that he follows the 'pattern and form' of the Roman church in everything; this would

---

[23] Augustine *Ep.* 209,3: CSEL 57,348; see James N. Adams, *Bilingualism and the Latin Language* (Cambridge: Cambridge University Press, 2003), 238–240.

[24] As Christine Mohrmann notes, 'liturgical Latin was not brought to these people as an isolated linguistic phenomenon. At the same time, Latin was introduced as the language of higher civilisation, of the schools, and of ecclesiastical and governmental administration. Thus all through the Middle Ages, Latin as the language of the sacred liturgy was supported by Latin as the second language of the cultural élite'. Mohrmann, 'The Ever-Recurring Problem of Language in the Church', in *Études sur le latin des chrétiens*, vol. IV, 143–159, at 152 (originally published in *Theology of Renewal. Vol. II: Renewal of Religious Structures*, ed. Lawrence K. Shook [Montreal: Palm Publishers, 1968], 204–220).

[25] See Johannes Beumer, 'Die ältesten Zeugnisse für die römische Eucharistiefeier bei Ambrosius von Mailand', in *Zeitschrift für katholische Theologie* 95 (1973), 311–324; Josef Schmitz, *Gottesdienst im altchristlichen Mailand: Eine liturgiewissenschaftliche Untersuchung über Initiation und Meßfeier während des Jahres zur Zeit des Bischofs Ambrosius († 397)*, Theophaneia 25 (Köln: Hanstein, 1975); also Bouley, *From Freedom to Formula*, 200–215.

imply that the same Eucharistic prayer from which he quotes was also used in Rome.[26] The prayers included by Ambrose correspond to the core of the Gregorian *Canon missae*:[27] the first epicletic prayer[28] asking for the consecration of the Eucharistic offerings (*Quam oblationem*), the narrative of institution (*Qui pridie*), the anamnesis and act of offering (*Unde et memores*), the prayer for the acceptance of the sacrifice (*Supra quae*) and the second epicletic prayer for spiritual fruits of sacramental communion (*Supplices te rogamus*).

Since the first prayer cited by Ambrose begins with the words 'Fac nobis hanc oblationem ...', there must have been a preceding part to which the demonstrative 'this oblation' referred. Michael Moreton argues on the basis of Ambrose's own comments in *De sacramentis* that this section would have been very similar to the *Te igitur* of the later form of the canon,

in view of Ambrose's earlier statement *oratio petitur pro populo, pro regibus, pro caeteris*. This *oratio* for those who constitute the communion of the Church is coupled in *Te igitur* with the Church's *dona, munera, sancta sacrificia illibata*, to which Ambrose refers as the *sacramenta posita super altare*. Further, Ambrose's reference to the angels who watched the approach of the neophytes from the baptistery to the altar, *spectarunt angeli*, may conceivably contain an allusion to the pre-sanctus at the conclusion of the *laus*, to which he refers in the clause *laus deo defertur*.[29]

The table appended to this chapter (see Appendix) compares the evidence from Ambrose with the oldest available form of the Gregorian canon. Thus, the similarities and differences of the two sets of texts will be clearly visible. Moreover, the statements from *De sacramentis* indicated by

---

[26] Ambrose, *De sacramentis* III,1,5: CSEL 73,40: 'ecclesia Romana ... cuius typum in omnibus sequimur et formam .... In omnibus cupio sequi ecclesiam Romanam'. Explaining the baptismal ceremonies in Milan, Ambrose pays particular attention to the point where he differs from Roman usage, that is, in the washing of the feet of the candidates. The hypothesis of Klauser, 'Der Übergang der römischen Kirche', that the canon originated in Milan was refuted by Christine Mohrmann, '*Rationabilis* – λογικός', in *Études sur le latin des chrétiens*, vol. I, 179–187 (originally published in *Revue internationale des droits de l'antiquité* 5 [1950], 225–234).

[27] Ambrose, *De sacramentis* IV,5,21–22; 6,26–27: CSEL 73,55 and 57. The term 'canon' seems to have been used first in the sixth century; the oldest known reference to 'prex canonica' is Pope Vigilius, *Ep. ad Profuturum*, 5: PL 69,18; see Bouley, *From Freedom to Formula*, 208–209.

[28] This expression is used as distinct from the technical term 'epiclesis' for the explicit invocation of the Holy Spirit.

[29] Michael J. Moreton, 'Rethinking the Origin of the Roman Canon', in *Studia Patristica* 26 (1993), 63–66, at 65–66.

Moreton are paired with specific sections of the canon to which they might relate. The table will help to illustrate the discussion in the next section of this chapter.

From Praise to Petition

The Eucharistic prayer begins with the preface (*praefatio*). As a technical term that distinguishes the initial praise and thanksgiving from the canon properly speaking, *praefatio* appears in only about the seventh century. However, the word is already employed in a very similar way in the mid-third century by Cyprian of Carthage, who also cites the priest's exhortation 'Sursum corda' and the people's response 'Habemus ad Dominum'.[30] The model Eucharistic prayer of the so-called *Apostolica Tradition* (see Chapter 2) has a preface with an introductory dialogue that agrees with the typical Roman form, except for the addition 'Deo nostro' to the celebrant's last exhortation.[31] While this document can no longer be simply taken as a Roman source from the early third century, it is nonetheless an important witness to the classical structure and contents of the preface. The text shown in the table became known in the Roman tradition as the *Praefatio communis* for days when no proper preface was prescribed (on the characteristics of the preface as a variable prayer, see the section 'The Prefaces' below, pp. 138–143).

The *Sanctus–Benedictus* is not mentioned by Ambrose. The note in the *Liber pontificalis*, crediting Pope Xystus I (r. c. 117–127) with the introduction of the *Sanctus* in the Roman Mass, is of no historical value for the second century but rather reflects the established practice of the early sixth century, when the first edition of the work was compiled.[32] There is

---

[30] Cyprian of Carthage, *De dominica oratione*, 31: CSEL 3,289: 'Ideo et sacerdos ante orationem praefatione praemissa parat fratrum mentes dicendo: sursum corda, ut dum respondet plebs: Habemus ad Dominum, admoneatur nihil aliud se quam Dominum cogitare debet'; see also *De lapsis*, 1: CSEL 3,237.

[31] *Apostolic Tradition*, 4,3: ed. Paul F. Bradshaw, Maxwell E. Johnson and L. Edward Philips, *The Apostolic Tradition: A Commentary*, Hermeneia (Minneapolis: Fortress Press, 2002), 38.

[32] *Liber pontificalis*, VIII: ed. Louis Duchesne, *Le Liber pontificalis: Texte, introduction et commentaire*, Bibliothèque des Écoles françaises d'Athènes et de Rome, 2 vols. (Paris: E. Thorin, 1886, 1892), vol. I, 56. See also the edition by Theodor Mommsen, *Libri pontificalis pars prior*, in MGH Gestorum Pontificum Romanorum, vol. I, 11. The textual history of the *Liber pontificalis* is very complex. Duchesne and Mommsen offer different redactional hypotheses, but neither of them has considered all the available manuscripts. Duchesne's commentary is particularly useful, while Mommsen's edition is valuable for its critical apparatus. See Matthias Simperl, 'Eine Hinführung zum Umgang mit den

evidence for the liturgical use of the *Sanctus* (without any indication of the *Benedictus*) in two Latin writings from the beginning of the fifth century.[33] Bryan Spinks holds that the *Sanctus* was introduced into the Roman Eucharistic prayer at a date when the text of the canon was already established, at the end of the fourth or in the early fifth century – perhaps at first to be used only on specific occasions.[34]

The earliest evidence for an anaphoral *Benedictus* in the West comes from southern Gaul and is found in a sermon by Caesarius of Arles (c. 470–542).[35] Juliette Day argues that in the first half of the fifth century the Jerusalem Anaphora of St James provided the first known instance of combining the *Sanctus* with the *Benedictus* from Matthew 21:9, an acclamation from the Palm Sunday celebration in the Holy City. According to Day, Western churches most likely followed the example of the Jerusalem liturgy and soon afterwards integrated the *Benedictus* into the Eucharistic prayer.[36]

The section *Te igitur* ('To you, therefore, most merciful Father, we make humble prayer and petition through Jesus Christ, your Son, our Lord …') may originally have served to connect the petition to accept and bless the offerings (through Christ) with the preceding thanksgiving (through Christ).[37] It is often argued that with the introduction of the

Editionen des *Liber pontificalis'*, in *Das Buch der Päpste – Liber pontificalis: Ein Schlüsseldokument europäischer Geschichte*, Römische Quartalschrift. Supplementband 67 (Freiburg i. Br.: Herder, 2020), 458–481. Simperl suggests the use of both Duchesne's and Mommsen's edition, and for disputed passages he recommends a look at the manuscripts, many of which are accessible in digitised form (ibid., 479–481).

33 Ps.-Ambrose, *Libellus de Spiritu Sancto*, IV,2: ed. Lucien Chavoutier, 'Un Libellus Pseudo-Ambrosien sur le Saint-Esprit', in *Sacris Erudiri* 11 (1960), 136–192, at 149: 'Unde etiam tractum est per omnes fere orientale Ecclesias et nonnullas occidentales, voce populus utatur, id est: Sanctus, sanctus, sanctus Dominus Sabaoth. Plena est omnis terra maiestate eius'. Ps.-Athanasius, *Expositio fidei catholicae*, 63: CCL 9,145: 'perfectam trinitatem adorantes et magnificantes, sicut in mysteriis ore nostro dicimus, ita conscientia teneamus: Sanctus, sanctus, sanctus Dominus Deus omnipotens'.

34 See Bryan D. Spinks, *The Sanctus in the Eucharistic Prayer* (Cambridge: Cambridge University Press, 1991), 96. Robert F. Taft, 'The Interpolation of the Sanctus into the Anaphora: When and Where? A Review of the Dossier: Part I', in *Orientalia Christiana Periodica* 57 (1991), 281–308, at 306, suggests that the *Sanctus* was introduced into Western liturgies in the fourth century.

35 Caesarius of Arles, *Sermo* 73,2: CCL 103,307.

36 See Juliette Day, 'The Origins of the Anaphoral Benedictus', in *Journal of Theological Studies* NS 60 (2009), 193–211, at 210–211.

37 For a thorough discussion of this question, see Spinks, *The Sanctus in the Eucharistic Prayer*, 93–96.

Sanctus the flow of the Eucharistic prayer from praise to petition was interrupted; hence the meaning of *igitur* ('therefore') is no longer clear. On the other hand, Bernard Botte and Christine Mohrmann maintain that the postpositive conjunction *igitur* in fourth-century Latin has no greater force than the Greek particle δέ and they do not render it in their French translation of the *Te igitur*.[38] Be that as it may, with the addition of the *Benedictus*, the prayer of petition can be related to the Christological acclamation: 'Blessed is he who comes in the name of the Lord. Hosanna in the highest.' Bernard Capelle suggests that the reference to the commendation of the offerings by the priest in the Eucharistic prayer in Pope Innocent I's letter to Decentius, bishop of Gubbio, makes it likely that an early version of the *Te igitur* formed part of the canon before 416.[39]

Intercessions for the Living and the Dead

In the same passage from his letter to Decentius, Innocent I insists on observance of the Roman custom that the names of those making offerings be recited 'within the holy mysteries' and not before.[40] This would seem to confirm that the Roman Eucharistic prayer contained intercessions for the living by the early fifth century.[41] The second set of

---

[38] See Botte and Mohrmann, *L'ordinaire de la messe*, 75. In the *Hanc igitur*, however, they translate the conjunction as 'donc'; see ibid., 79.

[39] 'As to the recitation of the names before the priest says the canon (*precem sacerdos faciat*) and in his prayer commends the offerings of those whose names are recited (*eorum oblationes quorum nomina recitanda sunt sua oratione commendet*), it is useless – in your wisdom you can understand this – not to mention the names of the persons presenting the gifts till you offer the sacrifice to God'. Innocent I, *Ep. 25 (ad Decentium)*, 2: ed. Robert Cabié, *La lettre du pape Innocent I à Decentius de Gubbio (19 mars 416): Texte critique, traduction e commentaire*, Bibliothèque de la Revue d'histoire ecclésiastique 58 (Louvain: Publications Universitaires, 1973), 22. English translation: Lawrence J. Johnson, *Worship in the Early Church: An Anthology of Historical Sources*, 4 vols. (Collegeville: Liturgical Press, 2009), vol. III, 100 (no. 2785). See Bernard Capelle, 'Innocent Iᵉʳ e le canon de la messe', in*Travaux liturgiques de doctrine et d'histoire*, 3 vols. (Louvain: Centre Liturgique, 1955–1967), vol. II, 236–247, at 244–245 (originally published in *Recherches de théologie ancienne et médiévale* 19 [1952], 5–16).

[40] 'It is necessary first to commend the offerings (*oblationes*) and then to mention the names of those presenting them so that these persons be named within the holy mysteries (*inter sacra mysteria*) and not during what precedes them; by the mysteries themselves we open the way to the prayers that follow.' Innocent I, *Ep. 25 (ad Decentium)*, 2: ed. Cabié, 22; trans. Johnson, *Worship in the Early Church*, vol. III, 100 (no. 2785).

[41] See Josef A. Jungmann, *Missarum sollemnia: Eine genetische Erklärung der römischen Messe*, 2 vol., 5th ed. (Wien: Herder, 1962), vol. I, 70–71. For the difficulties of understanding the precise import of Innocent's letter, see the analysis of Richard Hugh

intercessions for the dead is considered a later insertion; it is absent from the canon in the earliest Gelasian and Gregorian sacramentaries but included in the largely Gallican Bobbio Missal (c. 700) as part of the 'daily Roman Mass' ('missa Romensis cottidiana'; see Figure 4.1). The use of the formula in Masses for deceased bishops in the *Hadrianum* would suggest that it had its original place in Masses for the dead. *Ordo Romanus* VII, a short rubrical directory for a Paduan-type sacramentary of Frankish origin, written sometime between the middle of the eighth and the late ninth century, notes that 'Memento . . . pacis' is prayed before and 'Ipsis . . . deprecamur' after reading out the names of the deceased from the diptychs (two plates linked with a hinge, which could be folded). This is to be done in daily Masses and only on appointed days, presumably excluding Sundays and feast days.[42] In the Carolingian reforms (see Chapter 6), the prayer became a fixed part of the canon.[43]

Intercessions for the living and the dead are part of the classical anaphoras emerging in the fourth century, and the names to be commemorated were recorded on diptychs. Anaphoras of the Antiochene type, such as that of St John Chrysostom, include intercessions after the epiclesis and before the doxology,[44] while anaphoras of the Alexandrian type, such as that of St Mark, place them between the initial thanksgiving (corresponding to the Roman preface), and the *Sanctus*.[45] The reading of the diptychs was an important expression of communion with other local churches, and the inclusion or exclusion of a name was the object of much controversy in the doctrinal struggles of the fifth and sixth centuries. In Greek, these intercessions are usually introduced with the formula μνήσθητι Κύριε, equivalent to the Latin 'Memento, Domine'. The Roman canon is unique in surrounding the core of the Eucharistic action with two distinct sets of intercessions, in the form of a literary diptych: the first for the living (*Memento, Domine*), including a special remembrance of the Church's hierarchy, and the second for the dead (*Memento etiam, Domine*).

Connolly, 'Pope Innocent I "De nominibus recitandis"', in *Journal of Theological Studies* 20 (1919), 215–226.

[42] *Ordo Romanus* VII,16: ed. Michael Andrieu, *Les Ordines Romani du haut moyen âge*, 5 vols., Spicilegium Sacrum Lovaniense 11, 23, 24, 28, 29 (Louvain: Peeters, 1931–1961), vol. II, 301: 'Hic orationes duae dicuntur una super dypticios, altera post lectionem nominum, et hoc cottidianis vel in agendis tantummodo diebus.'

[43] See Jungmann, *Missarum sollemnia*, vol. II, 295–298.

[44] See Anton Hänggi – Irmgard Pahl, *Prex eucharistica. Volumen I: Textus e variis liturgiis antiquioribus selecti*, Spicilegium Friburgense 12, 3rd ed. (Freiburg/Schweiz: Universitätsverlag, 1998), 228.

[45] See ibid., vol. I, 102.

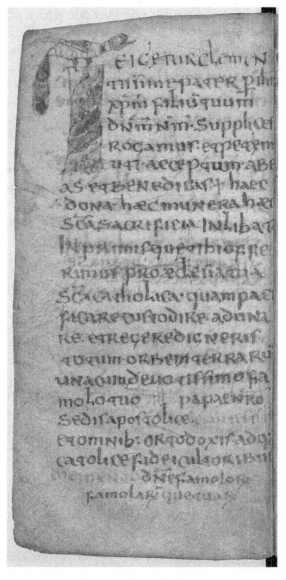

Figure 4.1 Bobbio Missal / c. 700 (Fol. 11v: Canon of the Mass [*Te igitur*] / Paris, Bibliothèque Nationale de France, MS lat. 13246 / Reprinted with kind permission)

The section following the first *Memento* raises the difficulty that the two initial participles stand on their own and do not form a grammatically complete sentence. Josef Andreas Jungmann offers a convincing reading of the *Communicantes*, when he proposes that the appeal to the saints resumes and strengthens the preceding petitions of the offerers.[46] The particular phrase 'communicantes et memoriam venerantes' ('In communion with those whose memory we venerate ...') may be indebted to an Old Latin variant of Romans 12:13: 'memoriis sanctorum communicantes', which has an equivalent in some Greek manuscripts,[47] is attested in the Vulgate tradition in place of the standard 'necessitatibus sanctorum communicantes' ('contributing to the needs of the saints'),[48] and is cited by fourth- and fifth-century Western authors.[49] For instance, Optatus of Milevis uses this Pauline verse in arguing against the Donatists who had established a community in Rome with a succession of their own bishops. Optatus accuses the Donatists of never approaching the memorial of the Apostle Peter, that is, his tomb in the Vatican Basilica built by Constantine. Thus, they violate the Apostle Paul's exhortation of 'communicating with the memorials of the saints (memoriis sanctorum communicantes)'.[50]

On major feasts of the liturgical year, a short embolism is added in the form 'Communicantes et diem [in the Easter Vigil: noctem] sacratissimum celebrantes ...'. The oldest Roman sacramentaries offer such a proper *Communicantes* for Christmas, Epiphany, Maundy Thursday, Easter, Ascension and Pentecost. These variations were given in the Mass formulary for the day after the proper preface under the heading 'infra actionem' ('within the action').[51] This heading was later included in the text of the canon and maintained in both manuscript and printed missals.

The *Hanc igitur*, which follows the *Communicantes*, renews the plea for the acceptance of the sacrifice of the clergy and of the whole family of God ('servitutis nostrae sed et cunctae familiae tuae') and it probably

---

[46] See Jungmann, *Missarum sollemnia*, vol. II, 213–225; for different readings, see Bernard Capelle, 'Problèmes du *Communicantes* de la Messe', in *Travaux liturgiques de doctrine et d'histoire*, vol. III, 269–275 (originally published in *Rivista liturgica* 40 [1953], 187–195); and Leo Eizenhöfer, '*Te igitur* und *Communicantes* im römischen Meßkanon', in *Sacris Erudiri* 8 (1956), 14–75.

[47] ταῖς μνείαις τῶν ἁγίων κοινωνοῦντες for the received ταῖς χρείαις τῶν ἁγίων κοινωνοῦντες. *The Greek New Testament*, ed. Barbara Aland et al., 4th rev. ed. (Stuttgart: Deutsche Bibelgesellschaft, 2013), ad loc.

[48] *Biblia sacra iuxta Vulgatam versionem*, ad loc.

[49] Passages from Hilary of Poitiers, Optatus of Milevis, Ambrosiaster, Rufinus, Gaudentius of Brescia, Pelagius, Augustine and Quodvultdeus are conveniently assembled by Eizenhöfer, '*Te igitur* und *Communicantes* im römischen Meßkanon', 65–68.

[50] Optatus of Milevis, *Contra Parmenianum*, II,4: CSEL 26,38.

[51] The Eucharistic prayer is called 'canon actionis' in the *Gelasianum Vetus* (Vat. Reg. Lat. 316): ed. Leo C. Mohlberg, *Liber Sacramentorum Romanae Aeclesiae Ordinis Anni Circuli*, Rerum Ecclesiasticarum Documenta. Series maior. Fontes IV, 3rd ed. (Rome: Herder, 1981), 183.

originated as a variable prayer inserted on important occasions in the liturgical year, not only for major feasts but also for the ordination of bishops, marriages and funerals.[52] The *Liber pontificalis* records that Pope Gregory the Great added the phrase 'diesque nostros in tua pace dispone atque ab aeterna damnatione nos eripi et in electorum tuorum iubeas grege numerari' ('order our days in your peace, and command that we be delivered from eternal damnation and counted among the flock of those you have chosen').[53] It is likely that with this addition the *Hanc igitur* became a permanent fixture in each Mass.

Institution Narrative and Consecration

The epicletic prayer *Quam oblationem* has an earlier parallel in Ambrose, who cites the petition that the oblation (of bread and wine) be made 'figura corporis et sanguinis Domini nostri Iesu Christi'. The formula 'figura/ὁμοίωμα /ἀντίτυπον of the body/blood of Christ' is found in both Western and Eastern sources as early as Tertullian and the *Apostolic Tradition*. Victor Saxer suggests this may have been part of a common core of early Christian Eucharistic prayers going back to the middle of the second century.[54] The use of *figura* should not be construed as denying the reality of Christ's Eucharistic presence. It is rather a key term of typological exegesis, which sees in the Old Testament anticipations or prefigurations of the New and in the New Testament itself prefigurations of eschatological realities.

Ambrose cites the formula as traditional but does not use it to explain the presence of Christ in the sacrament; instead, when he comments on the Eucharistic consecration, he insists that the elements of bread and wine have been changed (using verbs, such as *transfigurare*, *mutare*) into the Lord's Body and Blood.[55] Ambrose's theology appears to have had an impact on the revision of the Roman canon, which includes an implicit

---

[52] See Vincent L. Kennedy, 'The Pre-Gregorian Hanc Igitur', in *Ephemerides Liturgicae* 50 (1936) 349–358.

[53] *Liber pontificalis*, LXVI: ed. Duchesne, vol. I, 312; ed. Mommsen, 161; see also John the Deacon, *Vita Gregorii*, II.17: PL 75,94A; Bede the Venerable, *Hist. Eccl.* II.1: PL 95,80B.

[54] Victor Saxer, '"Figura Corporis et Sanguinis Domini": Une formule eucharistique des premiers siècles chez Tertullian, Hippolyte et Ambroise', in *Rivista di archeologia cristiana* 48 (1971), 65–89 (= *Pères saints et culte chrétien dans l'Eglise des premiers siècles*, Collected Studies Series 448 [Aldershot: Variorum, 1994], no. IV).

[55] This is shown, with many references from Ambrose, by Saxer, 'Figura Corporis', 79–84.

epiclesis asking that the offering 'may become for us the Body and Blood of your most beloved Son, our Lord Jesus Christ'.

Both in Ambrose's Eucharistic prayer and in the Gregorian canon, the institution narrative begins with the relative pronoun *qui* ('who', referring to Jesus Christ), which connects the whole section grammatically with the preceding prayer. In most historical anaphoras, the institution narrative rests on a liturgical tradition that is related to the Synoptic Gospels (Mt 26:26–28; Mk 14:22–24; Lk 22:19–21) but not wholly dependent upon them. In many Eastern Eucharistic prayers, the narrative is greatly embellished and rhetorically stylised, such as in the Anaphoras of St Mark, St Basil and especially St James. There are traits of such formalisation in the narrative of *De sacramentis*, where the introduction to the dominical words over the bread and over the chalice is constructed in parallel fashion ('pridie quam pateretur ... respexit ad caelum, ad te, sancte Pater omnipotens aeterne Deus ...'). By comparison with the oriental anaphoras, the narrative in Ambrose is more sober in character, but it nonetheless shows signs of a careful composition.

This is quite different in the Roman canon, which, as Edward Ratcliff notes, 'presents the Gospel tradition on a bolder relief than we have it in the oriental forms or in *De Sacramentis*'.[56] Ratcliff argues that the Roman narrative is not a combination of the narratives found in the Synoptics but follows in essence that of Matthew 26:26–28, though not in the familiar Vulgate version but in that of the Old Latin Gospels. Furthermore, the narrative is supplemented with distinctive elements of 1 Corinthians 11:23–26 in the words over the chalice and in the Lord's command to repeat these actions in memory of him. There are also a few additions to the biblical account, which serve to 'enhance the vividness of the Narrative, and to educe ... the full significance of the Institution'.[57] Most of them are, in fact, derived from Scripture, such as 'elevatis oculis in caelum' (Mt 14:19, Mk 7:34; Lk 9:16 – the miraculous feeding of the multitude); 'praeclarum (calicem)' (Ps 22[23]:5); 'mysterium fidei' (1 Tim 3:9).

Another indication of the biblical 'simplicity' of the narrative is the lack of rhythmic *clausulae*. This suggests that this part of the prayer did not undergo the same revision according to the rules of rhetoric as the

[56] Edward C. Ratcliff, 'The Institution Narrative of the Roman Canon Missae: Its Beginning and Early Background', in *Liturgical Studies*, ed. Arthur H. Couratin and David. H. Tripp (London: SPCK, 1976), 49–65, at 51 (originally published in *Studia Patristica* 2 [1957], 64–82).

[57] Ibid.

other parts of the canon. The only such reworking would seem to be the replacement of the paratactic 'respexit in caelum' in Ambrose's narrative to the ablative absolute 'elevatis oculis in caelum' ('with eyes raised to heaven').

The complex question of the Roman institution narrative's scriptural origins is advanced by Peter Burton's research on the Old Latin Gospels. Burton argues that 'the Matthaean Passion narrative contains various peculiarities of translation that may derive from a liturgical text incorporated within the common source'.[58] A significant case is the Latin rendering of the Greek ἐσθίειν (eat): in European witnesses of the *Vetus Latina*, the translation *manducare* is commonly found, while African witnesses use *manducare* and *edere* almost equally. It is remarkable that in the account of the Last Supper at Matthew 26:26, virtually all the manuscripts translate ἐσθίειν with the same verb: 'ipsis autem cenantibus' or 'cenantibus autem eis'. Most likely, *cenare* is intended to imply a special kind of 'eating', which justifies this unusual rendering.[59] Burton suggests, with some caution, that an earlier, separate liturgical version of the Last Supper account, or even of the whole Passion narrative, may have been incorporated into the Old Latin translation of Matthew's Gospel.

While Burton acknowledges that his theory is hard to verify, especially because of the variations among the manuscripts subsumed under the generic heading *Vetus Latina*, his argument would confirm the theological significance of the biblical institution narrative for the Roman liturgical tradition, which Ratcliff states succinctly:

> To such a liturgical tradition as this to which St. Cyprian is witness, an authentic scriptural, or rather Gospel, Institution Narrative is indispensable. For the function of the Narrative in the Canon is not merely to revive the memory of a significant historic event, or to provide a rationale for the celebration of the Eucharist, as the Greek Narratives do; its function is rather to make the significant historic event continuously present and operative. By means of the Narrative, therefore, the Church's *action* in the Eucharist is identified with, and becomes, the *action* of Christ in the Institution.[60]

The crucial testimony of Cyprian to which Ratcliffe refers is the bishop of Carthage's letter on the mixed chalice, which is addressed to Cecil, bishop of Biltha: 'As you well know, I have been admonished that the tradition of the Lord is to be followed when the chalice is offered, and that we are to

---

[58] Peter Burton, *The Old Latin Gospels: A Study of their Texts and Language* (Oxford: Oxford University Press, 2000), 34.
[59] See ibid., 36–44 and 92.   [60] Ratcliff, 'Institution Narrative', 62.

do nothing other than what the Lord was the first to do.'[61] At this point Cyprian invokes the 'tradition of the Lord (*dominica traditio*)', which he himself received. Later in the same letter, he formulates a sacramental principle based on divine institution:

If Jesus Christ, our Lord and God, is himself the high priest of God the Father, and was the first to offer himself as a sacrifice to the Father, and commanded that this be done in his own memory, certainly the office of Christ is carried out by the priest who imitates what Christ did and who in the Church offers a true and full sacrifice to God the Father when he offers it according to what he understands Christ to have offered.[62]

Both liturgical witness and patristic theology shaped what Geoffrey Willis calls 'the classical Roman pattern, which is a prayer containing two distinct offerings'. Willis describes the structure of the Roman Eucharistic prayer as follows:

It begins by offering to God the bread and wine and asking him that they may be made unto us the Body and Blood of Christ; it then consecrates the gifts by re-enacting the Lord's Supper; in virtue of the celebrant imitating the acts and words of Christ at the Supper and finally, after consecrating the gifts it offers them to the Father as the Body and Blood of Christ, and asks him to command the Son to carry this offering to the heavenly altar.[63]

Invocation of the Saints

The list of apostles and martyrs in the *Communicantes* is carefully constructed: after 'the glorious ever-Virgin Mary, Mother of our God and Lord, Jesus Christ'[64] are named twelve apostles, including Paul, and twelve male martyrs venerated in Rome in a descending hierarchy.[65]

---

[61] Cyprian, *Ep.* 63,2: CSEL 3/1,702; trans. Johnson, *Worship in the Early Church*, vol. I, 164–165 (no. 549), slightly modified.

[62] Cyprian, *Ep.* 63,14: CSEL 3/1,713; trans. Johnson, *Worship in the Early Church*, vol. I, 170 (no. 561).

[63] Willis, 'The New Eucharistic Prayers', 97.

[64] The name of 'blessed Joseph, her Spouse' was only added by Pope John XXII in 1962. Neil J. Roy, 'The Roman Canon: *Deësis* in Euchological Form', in *Benedict XVI and the Sacred Liturgy*, ed. Neil J. Roy and Janet E. Rutherford (Dublin: Four Courts Press, 2010), 181–199, at 190, speaks of 'an embolism of Marian devotion'.

[65] See Vincent L. Kennedy, *The Saints of the Canon of the Mass*, Studi di Antichità Cristiana 14, 2nd rev. ed. (Vatican City: Pontificio Istituto di Archeologia Cristiana, 1963); and the summary of Roy, 'The Roman Canon: *Deësis* in Euchological Form', 184–185: 'five popes or bishops of Rome, one bishop from abroad (Cyprian of Carthage, linked by bonds of friendship and correspondence with Cornelius); the Roman deacon Laurence who followed Pope Xystus II (d. 7 August 258) to martyrdom a few days later (10 August

The symbolic number of twenty-four is reminiscent of the elders surrounding the heavenly throne in the Book of Revelation (Rev 4:4,10 and elsewhere). A matching list of 'apostles and martyrs' comes after the *Memento* of the dead, in the prayer *Nobis quoque*: headed by John the Baptist, seven male martyrs, including the protomartyr Stephen and the apostle Matthias, again in a descending hierarchy, and seven female martyrs, who enjoyed a particular veneration in Rome.[66] The invocation of these and all the saints has a twofold dimension: not only does it express the bond and fellowship (*societas, consortium*) the liturgical assembly shares with those who worship God in the heavenly sanctuary, it is also a plea for God's forgiveness and protection through the intercession of those already perfected in glory.

In the sixth century, Rome witnessed an increasing devotion to early Christian martyrs, such as John and Paul, Cosmas and Damian, and hence Gregory the Great (r. 590–604) has been credited, with some plausibility, with the final redaction of both lists of saints.[67] Pope Gregory III (r. 731–741) stipulated that in the oratory dedicated to the relics of the saints, which he built in St Peter's Basilica, on feast days of saints the list of the *Communicantes* should be supplemented with a general commemoration.[68] Frankish sources added the names of saints of particular local veneration to the first, but not to the second Roman

---

258); the cleric and catechist Chrysogonus; finally four laymen, who actually constitute two sets of brothers: John and Paul associated if only by name with a *domus ecclesiae* on the Coelian Hill, and the eastern physicians Cosmas and Damian, under whose patronage a church in the Roman forum was dedicated in the sixth century'.

[66] The identity of Alexander is uncertain. Felicity is the Roman matron and mother of the seven brothers believed to have been martyred under Marcus Aurelius, not the North African companion of Perpetua. See Roy, 'The Roman Canon: *Deësis* in Euchological Form', 193–194, with reference to Kennedy, *The Saints of the Canon of the Mass*.

[67] See Jungmann, *Missarum sollemnia*, vol. II, 220 and 317–318. The Anglo-Saxon Aldhelm (c. 639–709) credits Gregory the Great with the addition of Agatha and Lucy: 'Mihi quoque operae pretium videtur, ut sanctae Agathae rumores castissimae virginis Luciae praeconia subsequantur, quas praeceptor et paedagogus noster Gregorius in canone cotidiano, quando missarum sollemnia celebrantur, pariter copulasse cognoscitur hoc modo in catalogo martyrum ponens: Felicitate, Anastasia, Agathe, Lucia.' *De virginitate* 42: MGH, Auctores Antiquissimi, Tomus XV, 293. The sequence of names in Aldhelm agrees with the one in the Bobbio Missal and Stowe Missal.

[68] 'Quorum sollemnitas hodie in conspectu tuae maiestatis celebratur, domine Deus noster, toto in orbe terrarum.' *Liber pontificalis*, XCII: ed. Duchesne, I, 417. For similar commemorations in later sources, see Jungmann, *Missarum sollemnia*, vol. II, 221–222.

list.[69] *Ordo Romanus* VII (see above, p. 115) notes that on a saint's feast day, this name be mentioned in the *Communicantes*.[70] The invocation of the saints, linked with the intercessions, also forms part of Eastern liturgies, and in the Antiochene tradition it typically begins with 'the God-bearer and ever-virgin Mary' and 'Saint John, the precursor and baptist'.[71] Again, the Roman canon stands out for framing the heart of the Eucharistic action with two distinct lists of saints in the *Communicantes* and *Nobis quoque* prayers. Neil J. Roy has made the felicitous proposal to see in this unique arrangement a '*Deësis* [literally: supplication] in euchological form':

> Just as in Christian iconography the *Deësis* presents the typical grouping of the Blessed Virgin Mary as Mother of God and St John the Baptist as Forerunner of the Lord, interceding on either side of Christ in majesty, so too the Roman Canon presents Mary and John the Baptist on either side of the Lord who became the central focus via the narrative of institution and consecration. The saints who follow Mary and those who follow John the Baptist express two elements or dimensions of the church: the hierarchic, and the charismatic.[72]

In Roy's reading, the *Nobis quoque* resumes the entreaty for the spiritual fruits of Holy Communion in the *Supplices*. Thus, the reference to 'us ... servants ... though sinners' is not understood to designate only the celebrant and his assisting clergy, as Jungmann argues,[73] but rather to the whole assembly – as would seem more likely. The earlier petition to

---

[69] The Old Gelasian Sacramentary (Vat. Reg. Lat. 316) adds the first martyrs of Paris, Bishop Denis with his companions Rusticus and Eleutherius; the bishops and confessors Hilary of Poitiers and Martin of Tours; the doctors Augustine of Hippo, Gregory the Great and Jerome; as well as the patriarch of Western monasticism, Benedict. Some of these names are erased but still legible in *Gelasianum Vetus*, no. 1246: ed. Mohlberg, 184.

[70] *Ordo Romanus* VII,8: ed. Andrieu, vol. II, 298: 'Si fuerit natale sanctorum hic dicat: *Sed et diem natalicii beati Illius celebrantes et omnium sanctorum*'.

[71] Θεωτόκου καὶ ἀειπαρθένου Μαρίας ... Τοῦ ἁγίου Ἰωάννου τοῦ προδρόμου καὶ βαπτίστοῦ; Anaphora of St John Chrysostom: Hänggi – Pahl, *Prex eucharistica*, vol. I, 228; Byzantine Anaphora of St Basil of Caesarea: ibid. 238; Anaphora of St James: ibid., 256.

[72] Roy, 'The Roman Canon: *Deësis* in Euchological form', 187. Roy refers to the description of a *deësis* in a passage by Sophronius of Jerusalem (634–639), which is often thought to be an interpolation by iconophiles in the eighth or ninth century. However, an image of a *deësis* in Santa Maria Antiqua in Rome has been dated to the seventh century. See Per Jonas Nordhagen, 'Constantinople on the Tiber: The Byzantines in Rome and the Iconography of their Images', in *Early Medieval Rome and the Christian West: Essays in Honour of Donald A. Bullough*, ed. Julia M. H. Smith, The Medieval Mediterranean 28 (Leiden; Boston: Brill, 2000), 113–134, at 116–118.

[73] See Jungmann, *Missarum sollemnia*, vol. II, 309–314.

'be filled with every grace and heavenly blessing' through sharing in the sacrament is given an ecclesiological dimension by the plea for sharing in the glorious fellowship of the saints.[74]

Christ the Mediator

In the definitive text of the Roman canon, from the earliest manuscript witnesses, the *Communicantes, Hanc igitur, Supplices te rogamus, Memento etiam* and *Nobis quoque* prayers conclude with the formula 'Per Christum Dominum nostrum'. This repeated conclusion makes clear that all prayer is offered through Christ the mediator between God and humanity (see 1 Tim 2:5). Jungmann considers this conclusion a secondary addition and relates it to the common form of the preface, in which thanksgiving is likewise made through the mediation of Christ ('gratias agere ... per Christum Dominum nostrum').[75] In the preface, the formula does not simply function as a conclusion but is expanded by a relative clause, and the same construction is used at the end of the *Nobis quoque*. At the other four places in the canon where the formula does conclude a prayer, post-Carolingian sources add 'Amen'.[76]

The Gregorian canon ends with two doxologies: the first, *Per quem*, takes the form of a relative clause governed by the conclusion to the *Nobis quoque* prayer, 'through Christ our Lord'. Jungmann recalls that the earliest sacramentaries insert the blessing of the sacred chrism on Maundy Thursday at this point in the Eucharistic prayer, as well as blessings of natural produce on specific occasions in the liturgical year.[77]

---

[74] Roy's interpretation is shared by Helmut Hoping, *My Body Given for You: History and Theology of the Eucharist*, trans. Michael J. Miller (San Francisco: Ignatius Press, 2019), 162, with reference to Josef Schmitz, 'Canon romanus', in *Prex eucharistica. Volumen III: Studia. Pars prima: Ecclesia antiqua et occidentalis*, ed. Albert Gerhards, Heinzgerd Brakmann and Martin Klöckener, Spicilegium Friburgense 42 (Fribourg: Academic Press, 2005), 281–310, at 308.

[75] See Jungmann, *Missarum sollemnia*, vol. II, 224–225.

[76] The earliest witness is the ninth-century *Sacramentary of St Thierry* (Rheims, Bibliothèque municipale, ms. 8). By the thirteenth century, the addition had become common.

[77] See Jungmann, *Missarum sollemnia*, vol. II, 323–328. The *Veronense* has a blessing of milk and honey in the baptismal Mass at Pentecost: *Sacramentarium Veronense (Cod. Bibl. Capit. Veron. LXXXV[80])*, ed. Leo C. Mohlberg, Rerum Ecclesiasticarum Documenta. Series Maior. Fontes I, 3rd ed. (Rome: Herder, 1978), 26 (no. 205). The *Hadrianum* contains a blessing of first grapes on the feast of Pope Xystus II on 6 August: *Le sacramentaire grégorien: Ses principales formes d'après les plus anciens manuscrits, Vol. I: Le sacramentaire, le supplément d'Aniane*, édition comparative Jean Deshusses, Spicilegium Friburgense 16, 3rd ed. (Fribourg Suisse: Édition Universitaires, 1992), 255

These prayers of blessing end with the invocation of Jesus Christ, which would find a natural conclusion in 'Through whom . . .'. Thus, 'all these good things' ('haec omnia . . . bona') may originally have indicated the natural gifts that had just been blessed, perhaps as an anti-Manichaean affirmation of the goodness of God's creation. When these blessings were no longer performed at this point in the canon, the prayer was understood to mean the consecrated offerings. Other scholars, however, including Jordi Pinell, argue that *Per quem* was a fixed part of the canon from an early stage and always referred to the Eucharist.[78]

The doxology *Per ipsum* completes the Roman canon with a Trinitarian act of praise: 'honour and glory' is offered to God the Father, to whom the whole Eucharistic prayer has been addressed, through the Son, the mediator and high priest, in the unity of the Holy Spirit. *Per ipsum* has a traditional ring to it, as it does not show traces of the Arian crisis of the fourth century, when the need to avoid any expression that might suggest a subordination of the Son and the Spirit to the Father led to a modification of orthodox doxologies to articulate the co-ordination of the three divine Persons.[79]

POSSIBLE ANTECEDENTS OF THE ROMAN EUCHARISTIC PRAYER

Parallels and resonances with the prayer language of the Roman canon have been identified in several fourth-century sources. Of particular note is again a passage from Optatus of Milevis, written in the 360s, where he accuses the Donatist schismatics of betraying the unity of the Church, while yet professing it in the offering of the Eucharistic sacrifice:

For who would doubt that you cannot pass over what is prescribed in the mystery of the sacraments (*illud legitimum in sacramentorum mysterio*) . . . . You say that you make an offering to God for the one Church, which is spread throughout the whole world (*offerre uos dicitis Deo pro una ecclesia, quae sit in toto terrarum orbe diffusa*).[80]

(no. 631). For the blessing of the sacred chrism in the *Hadrianum*, see ibid., 172–173 (no. 334).

[78] See Jordi Pinell, 'La grande conclusion du Canon romain', in *La Maison-Dieu* 88 (1966), 96–115.

[79] E.g., in the Anaphora of St John Chrysostom: Hänggi – Pahl, *Prex eucharistica*, vol. I, 228; see Jungmann, *Missarum sollemnia*, vol. II, 329.

[80] Optatus of Milevis, *Contra Parmenianum*, II,12: CSEL 26,47. The full passage reads: 'Iam et mendacium uestrum hoc loco iuste damnari potest, quo cotidie a uobis sacrificia condiuntur. Nam quis dubitet uos illud legitimum in sacramentorum mysterio praeterire

It would seem that Optatus is pointing here to the contents of the Eucharistic prayer that was used in North Africa – presumably by Catholic and Donatists alike. The reference to the offering made for the Church spread throughout the world has an obvious parallel in the section *Te igitur*.

Resonances with the Roman canon can also be found in the sermons of Zeno, bishop of Verona from 362 to 372: a description of Melchizedek as 'summus sacerdos' and of Abraham as 'patriarcha noster', as in the *Supra quae* prayer, and a reference to 'immaculata hostia'.[81] A geographical spread of the Roman Eucharistic prayer in northern Italy at this early stage in the history of Latin liturgy would be highly noteworthy.

In *Questions on the Old and the New Testaments*, a work attributed to Ambrosiaster, a Roman presbyter who wrote in the pontificate of Damasus (r. 366–384),[82] the author notes that in the Eucharistic prayer used in Rome, Melchizedek (whom he considers a manifestation of the Holy Spirit) is called 'summus sacerdos'.[83]

The period of formation of the Roman canon, between the important witness of Ambrose in the late fourth century and the Gregorian text from the late sixth century, cannot be traced for lack of sources, except for occasional modifications. The *Liber pontificalis* offers a snippet view, with the entry, generally considered reliable, that Pope Leo the Great (r. 440–461) added the phrase 'sanctum sacrificium, immaculatam hostiam' to the *Supra quae* prayer.[84] Louis Duchesne suggests that this acclamation of the bread and wine offered by Melchizedek (see Gen 14:18) as 'a holy sacrifice, a spotless victim' was directed against the Manichees, who had a horror of wine and would not use it for the Eucharist.[85]

---

non posse? Offerre uos Deo dicitis pro ecclesia, quae una est. Hoc ipsum mendacii pars est unam te uocare, de qua feceris duas; et offerre uos dicitis Deo pro una ecclesia, quae sit in toto terrarum orbe diffusa.' The initial phrase appears to imply a daily celebration of the Eucharist.

[81] See Gordon Jeanes, 'Early Latin Parallels to the Roman Canon? Possible References to a Eucharistic Prayer in Zeno of Verona', in *Journal of Theological Studies* N.S. 37 (1986), 427–431.

[82] Ambrosiaster was identified as the author of the *Quaestiones* by Alexander Souter, *A Study of Ambrosiaster*, Texts and Studies 7.4 (Cambridge: Cambridge University Press, 1905), whose arguments are now commonly accepted; see Sophie Lunn-Rockliffe, *Ambrosiaster's Political Theology*, Oxford Early Christian Studies (Oxford: Oxford University Press, 2007), 32.

[83] Ps.-Augustine [Ambrosiaster], *Quaestiones veteris ac novi testamenti*, 109,21: CSEL 50,268: 'sicut nostri in oblatione praesumunt'.

[84] *Liber Pontificalis*, XLVII: ed. Duchesne, I, 239.   [85] Ibid., 241, n. 12.

The earliest available physical witness to the canon, albeit in a somewhat garbled form, is the Bobbio Missal, an important source for the Gallican tradition dating from the turn of the eighth century (see Figure 4.1). The text that appears, with minor variations, in the eighth-century Old Gelasian Sacramentary, as well as in the slightly later Frankish Gelasian and the various Gregorian sacramentaries, reflects Roman liturgical practice of the mid-seventh century, if not earlier.[86] The differences between Ambrose's Eucharistic prayer and the Gregorian canon are far less remarkable than their similarities, given that the two centuries in between were a period of intense and dynamic liturgical development.

Despite the remarkable fact that a mature version of the Roman Eucharistic prayer emerges without apparent antecedents in the late fourth century, it is unlikely that it was composed from scratch.[87] Liturgical historians have tended to emphasise the disparate nature of the canon and have used the methods of higher criticism to explain the origin and development of its prayers. With a view to such hypothetical reconstructions (including his own), Anton Baumstark published a remarkable retraction, in which he proposes to consider the canon in its integrity[88] and explores its parallels in contents, structure and expression

---

[86] The skepticism of Yitzhak Hen regarding the early Roman Eucharistic prayer is overstated in his otherwise highly informative study, 'The Nature and Character of the Early Irish Liturgy', in *L'Irlanda e gli irlandesi nell'Alto Medioevo: Spoleto, 16–21 aprile 2009* (Spoleto: Centro italiano di studi sull'Alto Medioevo, 2010), 353–380, at 365–367.

[87] Moreton, 'Rethinking the Origin of the Roman Canon', 66, contends that 'the Latin canon in its earliest form, in Milan and therefore in Rome, was not a creation *de novo*, but was indebted to older anaphoral prayers, not only in the East, and perhaps especially in Egypt, but also in the Greek-speaking Church in the West'.

[88] See Anton Baumstark, 'Das "Problem" des römischen Messkanons, eine Retractatio auf geistesgeschichtlichem Hintergrund', in *Ephemerides Liturgicae* 53 (1939), 204–243. For earlier attempts at reconstructing the 'original' Roman canon, see the good overview of Adrian Fortescue, *The Mass: A Study of the Roman Liturgy*, 2nd ed. (London: Longmans, Green and Co, 1950), 138–171. On this subject, see also Geoffrey G. Willis, 'The Connection of the Prayers of the Roman Canon', in *Essays in Early Roman Liturgy*, Alcuin Club Collections 46 (London: SPCK, 1964), 121–133. Elsewhere, Willis cautions: 'The Roman Mass ought not to be treated as if it were the debased descendant of some Eastern rite. There is absolutely no warrant whatever for assuming that the ideal form of a liturgy is to be seen in any of the surviving Eastern rites.' Geoffrey G. Willis, 'The New Eucharistic Prayers: Some Comments', in *A Voice for All Time: Essays on the Liturgy of the Catholic Church since the Second Vatican Council*, ed. Christopher Francis and Martin Lynch (Bristol: Association for Latin Liturgy, 1994), 64–97, at 91–92 (originally published in *Heythrop Journal* 12 [1971], 5–28).

with the Alexandrian anaphora.[89] Baumstark even contended that the
Latin text of this Eucharistic prayer may have been introduced in Rome
not long after the pontificate of Cornelius (r. 251–253), the last pope
named among the martyrs in the *Communicantes* prayer and the first
pope whose epitaph was composed in Latin.[90]

While there is no evidence for a Latin Eucharistic prayer used in Rome
as early as the middle of the third century,[91] the canon contains material
that is at least as early.[92] The post-institution narrative prayers *Unde et
memores* and *Supra quae* include elements from a Judaeo-Christian background: in the *Unde et memores* it is above all the idea of a pure, holy and
perfect sacrifice ('hostiam puram, hostiam sanctam, hostiam
immaculatam'), which corresponds to ancient Jewish interpretations of
the sacrifice of Isaac, beginning with Philo of Alexandria.[93] In the *Supra
quae* there is the striking notion of the 'altar on high' (see Rev 8:3)[94] to
which the 'holy angel' – Christ himself, the 'angel of great counsel' (Is 9:6

[89] See Bouyer, *Eucharist*, 187–243, who undertakes a similar comparison and concludes
that 'the Roman canon appears ... as one of the most venerable witnesses of the oldest
tradition of the eucharistic prayer, at least contemporary in its totality with the most
archaic forms of the Alexandrian eucharist'; ibid., 243.

[90] See Baumstark, 'Das "Problem" des römischen Messkanons', 242–243; also 'Antik-
römischer Gebetsstil im Messkanon', in *Miscellanea Liturgica in honorem L. C.
Mohlberg*, Bibliotheca Ephemerides Liturgicae 22 (Rome: Ed. Liturgiche, 1948), vol. I,
301–331, at 301–305. Cornelius (d. 253) is placed after Xystus (d. 258) in the list of
popes, in order to link the latter with his correspondent and contemporary Cyprian of
Carthage (d. 258). See Roy, 'The Roman Canon: *Deësis* in Euchological form', 191.

[91] See Christine Mohrmann, 'Quelques observations sur l'évolution stylistique du Canon de
la Messe romain', in *Études sur le latin des chrétiens*, vol. III, 227–244, at 230–231
(originally published in *Vigiliae Christianae* 4 [1950], 1–19).

[92] There are passages in Tertullian that are reminiscent of the prayer language of the Roman
canon; these were identified by Eligius Dekkers, *Tertullianus en de geschiedenis der
liturgie*, Catholica 6,2 (Brussels; Amsterdam: De Kinkhoren; Desclée de Brouwer,
1947), 56–58. These passages may have been quotations from or allusions to
contemporary Eucharistic prayers, which were then (as prayer texts) incorporated into
the Roman canon. An alternative explanation would be that whoever composed the
canon deliberately took these phrases from Tertullian, without there being continuity
between earlier North African anaphoras and the later *Canon missae*. Martin Klöckener,
'Das eucharistische Hochgebet in der nordafrikanischen Liturgie der christlichen
Spätantike', in *Prex eucharistica*, vol. III, 43–128, at 53 (with n. 59), opts for the
second explanation.

[93] See Frédéric Manns, 'L'origine judéo-chrétienne de la prière "Unde et memores" du
Canon Romain', in *Ephemerides Liturgicae* 101 (1987), 60–68, esp. 64–67.

[94] Irenaeus of Lyon, *Against Heresies* IV,18,6: SC 100,614, writes: 'Est ergo altare in caelis,
illuc enim preces nostrae et oblationes diriguntur; et templum, quemadmodum Iohannes
in Apocalypsi ait.' This idea is already implicit in Clement of Rome, who calls Jesus Christ
'the high priest of our offerings'; *First Clement*, 36,1–2: SC 167,158.

LXX) according to primitive angel-Christology[95] – is asked to carry the Church's oblation. The references to Abel, Abraham and Melchizedek are deeply rooted in Jewish tradition, in particular Temple worship,[96] and the fact that these pre-Mosaic sacrifices are construed as types of the Eucharist would seem to indicate an apologetic context, such as that prevailing in the second century, when Christian authors insisted that the Levitical sacrifices were no longer acceptable to God and saw in the older sacrifices of Abel, Abraham and especially in the bread and wine offering of Melchizedek, fitting types of the Christian Eucharist.[97] This understanding is visually expressed in in the sanctuary of Sant'Apollinare in Classe in Ravenna, where a seventh-century mosaic showing the sacrifices of Abel, Abraham and Melchizedek is placed on the right-hand side of the sanctuary and thus relates to the altar where the Eucharistic sacrifice is offered (see Figure 4.2).

RHETORIC OF SALVATION

Liturgical prayer is a form of public speech, and hence in Christian antiquity, the threefold *officia* (duties or tasks) of classical rhetoric were applied to it as well: liturgical prayer is a means of teaching the faith (*docere*); the beauty of its language appeals to the worshippers' aesthetic sense (*delectare*) and its rhetorical force spurs the faithful on to right conduct (*movere*).[98] Hence, the euchological texts that have come down to us in the early medieval Roman sacramentaries were formed according

---

[95] Justin Martyr, *Dialogue with Trypho*, 76,3 and 126,1: PTS 47,201 and 288; also *First Apology*, 63,5: PTS 38,121; Irenaeus of Lyon, *Against Heresies*, III,16,3: SC 34,283; and *Demonstration of the Apostolic Preaching*, 55–56: SC 406,162. It is significant that this passage is modified in Ambrose's Eucharistic prayer to the plural 'per manus angelorum tuorum' (*De sacramentis*, IV,6,27: CSEL 73,57), presumably because by the late fourth century, angel-Christology had acquired an 'Arian' flavour.

[96] See Bellarmino Bagatti, 'L'origine gerosolimitana della preghiera Supra quae del Canone Romano', in *Bibbia e Oriente* 21 (1979), 101–108; and Frédéric Manns, 'Une prière judéo-chrétienne dans le Canon Romain', in *Antonianum* 54 (1979), 3–9.

[97] See Geoffrey G. Willis, *A History of Early Roman Liturgy to the Death of Pope Gregory the Great*, Henry Bradshaw Society, Subsidia 1 (London: Boydell Press, 1994), 30–31.

[98] See Mary Gonzaga Haessly, *Rhetoric in the Sunday Collects of the Roman Missal: With Introduction, Text, Commentary and Translation* (Cleveland: Ursuline College for Women, 1938), 5; also Peter Mack, 'Rhetoric and Liturgy', in *Language and the Worship of the Church*, ed. David Jasper and Ronald C. D. Jasper, Studies in Literature and Religion (Basingstoke: Macmillan: 1990), 82–109, at 86.

Figure 4.2 Mosaic panel / Sant'Apollinare in Classe, Ravenna / seventh century
(Sant'Apollinare in Classe, Ravenna / © José Luiz Bernardes Ribeiro / CC BY-SA 4.0)

to technical rules of composition.[99] The rhetorical character of these texts
is evident from the Eucharistic prayer cited by Ambrose. For instance, the
formula of petition 'et petimus et precamur'[100] ('we both ask and pray') is
an example of a doubling of the verb, which is typical of classical (pagan)
euchology, where formulae such as 'do dedicoque' ('I give and devote')
occur frequently.[101] This stylistic feature is also found in the *Te igitur*

---

[99] See Eduard Norden, *Die antike Kunstprosa vom VI. Jahrhundert v. Chr. bis in die Zeit
der Renaissance*, 2 vols., 2nd ed. (Leipzig: Teubner, 1909), vol. II, 457 ; and Christine
Mohrmann, 'Problèmes stylistiques dans la littérature latine chrétienne', in *Études sur le
latin des chrétiens*, vol. III, 147–170, at 147–148 (originally published in *Vigiliae
Christianae* 9 [1955], 222–246).

[100] Ambrose, *De sacramentis*, IV,6,27: CSEL 73,57.

[101] See Mohrmann, 'Quelques observations sur l'évolution stylistique du Canon de la Messe
romain', 239, with reference to Georg Appel, *De Romanorum Precationibus*,
Religionsgeschichtliche Versuche und Vorarbeiten VII.2 (Giessen: Töpelmann, 1909).

section of the Gregorian canon, though without the alliteration: 'supplices rogamus ac petimus' ('we make humble prayer and petition').[102] Such rhetorically dense expressions are also known from Greek Eucharistic prayers of the Alexandrian tradition: δεόμεθα καὶ παρακαλοῦμεν appears in the Strasbourg Papyrus and in the Anaphora of St Mark in the long intercessory part that leads to the *Sanctus*.[103]

Another example for effective rhetoric in liturgical prayer is the accumulation of near-synonyms. In the Ambrosian version of the Roman Eucharistic prayer, the petition to accept the oblation is intensified by three epithets: 'Make this offering for us approved, reasonable, acceptable (*scriptam, rationabilem, acceptabilem*)'.[104] In the prayer *Quam oblationem* of the Gregorian canon this sequence is increased to five epithets: 'Which oblation be pleased, O God, we pray, to make in all things blessed, approved, ratified, reasonable, and acceptable (benedictam, adscriptam, ratam, rationabilem, acceptabilemque)',[105] with the notable addition of the legal term 'ratus' ('ratified, valid').

These selected examples from the Eucharistic prayer may suffice to give a first impression of how this 'rhetoric of salvation' works to achieve its threefold end of teaching the faith, giving spiritual delight and persuading to a virtuous life.[106] The following sections of this chapter will extend this discussion to the variable prayers of the Roman Mass, especially the collects and prefaces.

The Collects

A full rhetorical analysis would also consider the relationship between author (or speaker) and audience, but the case of the liturgy raises a number of problems in this regard. In the first place, the authorship of liturgical prayers is usually not known. There is an interesting comment in Gregory the Great's letter to John, bishop of Syracuse, dating from October 598, in which the pope explains the reasons why in the Roman Mass he brought the Lord's Prayer forward from its previous position

---

[102] Hänggi – Pahl, *Prex eucharistica*, vol. I, 427.
[103] Ibid., vol. I, 116 and 102. For a discussion of rhetorical elements in Greek anaphoras, see Hieronymus Engberding, 'Die Kunstprosa des eucharistischen Hochgebetes der griechischen Gregoriusliturgie', in *Mullus: Festschrift Theodor Klauser*, Jahrbuch für Antike und Christentum. Ergänzungsband 1 (Münster: Aschendorff, 1964), 100–110.
[104] Ambrose, *De sacramentis*, IV,5,21: CSEL 73,55.
[105] Hänggi – Pahl, *Prex eucharistica*, vol. I, 433.
[106] For a more comprehensive analysis of rhetorical features in the Canon of the Mass, including prose rhythm, see Lang, *The Voice of the Church at Prayer*, 76–89.

immediately before the kiss of peace and Holy Communion, so that it would henceforth follow immediately after the canon, where it still is today. Gregory regarded it as very unfitting that the 'prex' that was composed by some 'scholasticus' should be said over the oblation, while the prayer composed by our Redeemer should not be said over his own Body and Blood.[107] The term *scholasticus* in late ancient Latin could indicate an advocate or, more generally, a scholar or learned man. In the context of Gregory's letter, it may well refer to an official of the papal chancery who was in charge of composing or revising liturgical prayers, or indeed putting together the Mass *libelli* that were the sources for the major sacramentaries. Such a *scholasticus* would also have recorded the prayers made by popes such as Leo, Gelasius and Gregory himself, but without noting the authors.

Secondly, the question of liturgical audience is a complex one; Mass prayers were originally composed for a specific assembly, in whose presence and name they were addressed to God. However, the use of these prayers soon transcended limits of space and time. In fact, the oldest euchological texts of the Roman Rite are of such a general nature that they could easily speak on behalf of diverse peoples in diverse situations and have done so ever since. These universal features of the Roman Mass, along with its 'simplicity' (in comparison with the more elaborate Eastern rites) made its wide diffusion possible. There are other elements, however, that show that the rite originated in the Roman church, such as the lists of saints in the Canon of the Mass or the collect for the feast of Saints Peter and Paul (29 June),[108] which express the local churches' communion with the Apostolic See.

The presidential prayers known as 'collects' (a term that is not of Roman but of Gallican derivation) are later in origin than the Eucharistic prayer and may go back to the first half of the fifth century.[109]

---

[107] Gregory the Great, *Ep.* IX, 26: MGH, Gregorii I Papae Registrum Epistolarum, vol. II, 59–60. See Geoffrey G. Willis, 'St Gregory the Great and the Lord's Prayer in the Roman Mass', in *Further Essays in Early Roman Liturgy*, Alcuin Club Collections 50 (London: SPCK, 1968), 175–188.

[108] This prayer, which is found in early Roman sacramentaries, contains the petition: 'da ecclesiae tuae eorum in omnibus sequi praeceptum, per quos religionis sumpsit exordium' ('grant that your Church may in all things follow the teaching of those through whom she received the beginning of religion'). *Corpus orationum*, ed. Eugène Moeller, Jean-Marie Clément and Bertrand Coppieters 't Wallant, CCL 160, 14 vols. (Turnhout: Brepols, 1992–2004), no. 1678.

[109] For a useful overview of recent research in this field, see James G. Leachman, 'History of Collect Studies', in *Appreciating the Collect: An Irenic Methodology*, ed. James

Their distinct style is well established already in the earliest examples that have come down to us in the Verona manuscript, which is from the first quarter of the seventh century, but contains material that has been dated from 400 to 560.[110] The Verona manuscript (also known incorrectly as 'Leonine Sacramentary') was probably not used in public worship in the actual form it has come down to us but was assembled as a private compilation of Roman formularies of different age and authority.

The typical style of early Roman collects is terse, well-balanced and economical in expression; each prayer consists generally of a single sentence, even if the syntax can at times be complex. In her study of the Sunday collects of the *Missale Romanum*, where the oldest euchological material of the Roman Rite is preserved, Mary Gonzaga Haessly distinguishes between a Protasis (Prelude), which is 'the basis or background for the Petition' and an Apodosis (Theme), which 'is, in general, the part of the Collect that expresses the purpose of the Prayer, or the goal toward which it gravitates'.[111] The Protasis usually in some way anticipates the Petition, which is in turn fulfilled in the Apodosis. Haessly also notes:

Besides the general division of the Collect into Protasis (Prelude) and Apodosis (Theme), every Collect has three parts: the Address, the Petition, the Conclusion. In the Address God is invoked under various titles, and frequently the invocation is accompanied by a relative clause, which I have called Statement of Fact. This clause refers to the feast of the day, or to an attribute of God .... The Petition, usually expressed by an imperative, is sometimes strengthened by the word 'quaesumus', which I have called the Formula of Petition.[112]

The collect, in its mature version, ends with the conclusion 'per Dominum nostrum Iesum Christum ...', which is at the same time a profession of faith and an act of praise in honour of the Triune God.

In its complete form, the collect has the following typical structure:

(1) an address to God, generally to the Father;
(2) a relative or participial clause referring to some attribute of God, or to one of his saving acts;
(3) the petition, either in the imperative or in the subjunctive;

G. Leachman and Daniel P. McCarthy, Liturgiam Aestimare: Appreciating the Liturgy 1 (Farnborough: St Michael's Abbey Press, 2008), 1–25. The history of the term *collecta* is traced by Patrick Regan, 'The Collect in Context', in ibid., 83–103.
[110] See Cyrille Vogel, *Medieval Liturgy: An Introduction to the Sources*, ed. and trans. William G. Storey and Niels Krogh Rasmussen (Washington, DC: The Pastoral Press, 1986), 38–45.
[111] Haessly, *Rhetoric in the Sunday Collects of the Roman Missal*, 13.   [112] Ibid., 14–15.

(4) the reason or desired result, for which the petition is made;
(5) the conclusion.[113]

This model can be illustrated with the example of a Sunday collect that is contained in the Old Gelasian Sacramentary and is used in the later Roman tradition for the Eleventh Sunday after Pentecost.[114] The prayer is remarkable for its literary beauty and theological richness:

(1) Omnipotens sempiterne Deus,
(2) qui abundantia pietatis tuae et merita supplicum excedis et vota,
(3) effunde super nos misericordiam tuam,
(4) ut dimittas quae consicentia metuit
(4) et adicias quod oratio non praesumit.
(5) Per Dominum ...

(1) Almighty, ever-living God,
(2) who in the abundance of your kindness surpass the merits and the desires of those who entreat you,
(3) pour out your mercy upon us:
(4) to pardon what conscience dreads
(4) and to give what prayer does not dare to ask.
(5) Through our Lord ....[115]

This typical structure need not always be rigidly followed; some elements may be rearranged, duplicated or omitted. For instance, in the following prayer, which is assigned in various ancient sacramentaries (and in the *Missale Romanum* of 1570) to the Third Sunday of Lent,[116] there is no relative or participial clause after the address to God, and the reason or desired result of the petition is omitted:

(1) Quaesumus, omnipotens Deus,
(3) vota humilium respice

---

[113] This structure is adapted from Willis, *A History of Early Roman Liturgy*, 63–64; a similar, more detailed methodology is presented by Renato De Zan, 'How to Interpret a Collect', in *Appreciating the Collect*, 57–82.

[114] *Gelasianum Vetus*, no. 1201: ed. Mohlberg, 179; see *Corpus orationum*, no. 3887.

[115] Translation from *Roman Missal: Renewed by Decree of the Most Holy Second Ecumenical Council of the Vatican, Promulgated by Authority of Pope Paul VI and Revised at the Direction of Pope John Paul II*, English translation according to the third typical edition (London: Catholic Truth Society, 2011).

[116] For instance, *Gellonense*, no. 389: ed. Antoine Dumas, *Liber Sacramentorum Gellonensis*, CCL 159A (Turnhout: Brepols, 1981), 48; *Gregorianum (Hadrianum)*, no. 229: ed. Deshusses, 147; *Paduanum*, no. 202: *Die älteste erreichbare Gestalt des Liber Sacramentorum anni circuli der römischen Kirche*, ed. Leo C. Mohlberg – Anton Baumstark, Liturgiegeschichtliche Quellen 11/12 (Münster: Aschendorff, 1927), 17; see *Corpus orationum*, no. 4915a.

(3) atque ad defensionem nostram dexteram tuae maiestatis extende.
(5) Per Dominum ...

(1) We beseech you, almighty God,
(3) look upon the prayers of the lowly;
(3) and for our defence stretch out the right hand of your majesty.
(5) Through our Lord ....[117]

This simpler and more direct form is less frequently used for the collect of the Mass but is found more often in the prayer over the offerings (secret) and the post-communion prayer.

The elements of the collects may also be inverted and rearranged, as in the following example, which is found with slight variation in a number of early sacramentaries.[118] The text appears in the *Missale Romanum* of 1570 as a Prayer over the People (*super populum*) for the Wednesday after the Fourth Sunday of Lent and as the collect for the Ninth Sunday after Pentecost:

(3) Pateant aures misericordiae tuae,
(1) Domine,
(3) precibus supplicantium,
(4) et ut desiderata consequantur,
(3) fac eos, quae tibi placita sunt, postulare.
(5) Per Dominum ...

(3) May the ears of your mercy be open,
(1) O Lord,
(3) to the prayers of those who call upon you;
(4) and that you may grant what they desire,
(3) have them ask what is pleasing to you.
(5) Through our Lord ....[119]

Mohrmann has noted parallels between the first and second element of the typical collect, that is, the address to God followed by a relative clause, and the pattern of pagan Roman prayers.[120] Mohrmann would

---

[117] The translation is from Lauren Pristas, 'The Post-Vatican II Revision of the Lenten Collects', in *Ever Directed Towards the Lord: The Love of God in the Liturgy of the Eucharist Past Present, and Hoped For*, ed. Uwe Michael Lang (London: T&T Clark [Continuum], 2007), 62–89, at 77, where she also offers a brief discussion of the prayer.

[118] It is used as a Sunday collect (e.g., *Gelasianum Vetus*, no. 1195) and as a collect or a *super populum* for weekdays in Lent (e.g., *Paduanum*, no. 245), see *Corpus orationum*, no. 4145.

[119] Translation from the *Roman Missal* 2011.

[120] Mohrmann, 'Quelques observations sur l'évolution stylistique du Canon de la Messe romain', 238, cites Scipio's prayer from Livy, *Ab urbe condita*, 29,27: 'Divi divaeque, qui maria terrasque colitis, vos precor quaesoque uti ...'.

seem correct in recognising in this structural parallel a general euchological form that is present in many religious traditions.[121] Anton
Baumstark already observed that in early Roman collects, the initial form
of praise is linked with a prayer of petition, according to the supreme
model of the Lord's Prayer: 'Our Father, who art in heaven ...'.[122] This
structure corresponds to the pattern of the Jewish *berakah*, where a
relative clause follows the invocation 'Blessed are you, Lord our
God ...'.[123]

Mohrmann describes the style of the collects as closer to the cultural
and literary traditions of classical Rome and their vocabulary as further
removed from Scripture than the canon and the prefaces.[124] While this
observation is generally correct, the biblical provenance of the collects'
vocabulary should not be overlooked; this is evident not so much from
direct quotations (although there are some) but from general resonances
and plays on scriptural words and concepts.[125] An example of this
pattern can be found in the initial petition of the above-mentioned collect
that the ears of God's mercy be open to the prayers of those who call upon
him. This striking anthropomorphism is typical of biblical expression; in
the Old Testament, God is attributed eyes (Am 9:3), ears (Deut 9:18),
hands (Is 5:25), feet (Gen 3:8), arms and so forth.

The variable prayers of the Mass originated in a given period and the
statements and petitions formulated in them often reflect a particular
moment in the history of the Roman church. As Willis notes:

[121] Thus Mohrmann, *Liturgical Latin*, 67–68. See the Egyptian prayer of a blind man and
the Babylonian prayer to Marduk in the collection *Cinq mille ans de prière: Textes
choisis et présentés par* Dom Pierre Miquel (Paris: Desclée de Brouwer, 1989), 29
and 36.

[122] See Anton Baumstark, *Liturgie comparée: Principes et méthodes pour l'étude historique
des liturgies chrétiennes*, Collection Irénikon, 3rd ed. (Chevetogne: Éditions de
Chevetogne, 1954), 73.

[123] See the collection of Jewish liturgical texts in Hänggi – Pahl, *Prex eucharistica*, vol. I,
5–57.

[124] See Botte and Mohrmann, *L'ordinaire de la messe*, 44–47.

[125] See Gerard Moore, 'The Vocabulary of the Collects: Retrieving a Biblical Heritage', in
Appreciating the Collect, 175–195; and Antoon A. R. Bastiaensen, 'Die Bibel in den
Gebetsformeln der lateinischen Kirche', in *The Impact of Scripture in Early Christianity*,
ed. Jan den Boeft and M. L. Van Poll-Van De Lisdonk, Supplements to Vigiliae
Christianae 44 (Leiden; Boston; Köln: Brill, 1999), 39–57. See also the two essential
reference works by Albert Blaise, *Le vocabulaire latin des principaux thèmes liturgiques*,
ouvrage revu par Antoine Dumas (Turnhout: Brepols, 1966); and Mary P. Ellebracht,
Remarks on the Vocabulary of the Ancient Orations in the Missale Romanum, Latinitas
Christianorum Primaeva 18, 2nd ed. (Nijmegen; Utrecht: Dekker & Van de Vegt, 1966).

In such cases the Pope, or somebody under his instructions, might compose the variable prayers and the preface of a mass, which would be used on the occasion for which it was designed, and then filed in the papal chancery for possible use on later occasions. Collections of such propers or masses began to be made, and these were called *libelli sacramentorum*.[126]

As these early liturgical texts show similarities in style and content to writings of some Church Fathers, scholars have attempted to infer their possible authors and to relate them to specific historical circumstances. To name a few examples: in his study of literary parallels between the Verona manuscript and the sermons of Leo the Great, Frank Leslie Cross argues that the pope actually cites phrases from texts already in liturgical use;[127] in a series of contributions, Arthur Paul Lang explores resonances between prayers from the Roman Rite and the preaching of Leo;[128] Antoine Chavasse identifies in the *Veronense* a number of Masses composed by Pope Gelasius (r. 492–496) and by Pope Vigilius (r. 537–555);[129] likewise Bernard Capelle sees in the *Veronense* some Masses by Gelasius and some retouches made by the same pope;[130]

---

[126] Geoffrey G. Willis, 'The Variable Prayers of the Roman Mass', in *Further Essays in Early Roman Liturgy*, 91–129, at 92.

[127] Frank Leslie Cross, 'Pre-Leonine Elements in the Proper of the Roman Mass', in *Journal of Theological Studies* 50 (1949), 191–197.

[128] Arthur P. Lang, *Leo der Grosse und die Texte des Altgelasianums mit Berücksichtigung des Sacramentarium Leonianum und des Sacramentarium Gregorianum* (Steyl: Steyler Verlagsbuchhandlung, 1957); 'Leo der Große und die Dreifaltigkeitspräfation', in *Sacris Erudiri* 9 (1957), 116–162; 'Anklänge an liturgische Texte in Epiphaniesermonen Leos des Grossen', in *Sacris Erudiri* 10 (1958), 43–126; 'Leo der Grosse und die liturgischen Texte des Oktavtages von Epiphanie', in *Sacris Erudiri* 11 (1960), 12–135; 'Anklänge an Orationen der Ostervigil in Sermonen Leos des Grossen', in *Sacris Erudiri* 13 (1962), 281–325; 'Leo der Grosse und die liturgischen Gebetstexte des Epiphaniefestes', in *Sacris Erudiri* 14 (1963), 3*–22*; 'Anklänge an Orationen der Ostervigil in Sermonen Leos des Grossen', in *Sacris Erudiri* 18 (1967–1968), 5–119; 'Anklänge an eine Heilig Geist Oration in einem Sermo Leos des Grossen auf die Fastenzeit', in *Sacris Erudiri* 23 (1978–1979), 143–170; 'Anklänge an Orationen der Ostervigil in Sermonen Leos des Grossen', in *Sacris Erudiri* 27 (1984), 129–149; 'Anklänge an Orationen der Ostervigil in Sermonen Leos des Grossen', in *Sacris Erudiri* 28 (1985), 155–381. See also Camille Callewaert, *S. Léon le Grand et les textes du Léonien*, Extrait de *Sacris Erudiri* I (Bruges; La Haye: Beyart; Nijhoff, 1948).

[129] Antoine Chavasse, 'Messes du pape Vigile dans le sacramentaire léonien', in *Ephemerides Liturgicae* 64 (1950), 161–213 and 66 (1952), 145–215.

[130] Bernard Capelle, 'Messes du pape s. Gélase dans le sacramentaire de Vérone'; 'Retouches gélasiennes dans le sacramentaire de Vérone' ; and 'L'œuvre liturgique de s. Gélase', in *Travaux liturgiques de doctrine et d'histoire*, vol. II, 79–105, 106–115 and 146–160 (originaly published in *Revue bénédictine* 56 [1945/1946], 12–41; *Revue bénédictine* 61 [1951], 3–14; *Journal of Theological Studies* NS 2 [1951], 129–144); see also Charles

Henry Ashworth holds that the Roman collects for Septuagesima, Sexagesima and Quinquagesima Sundays were written by Gregory the Great during the Lombard invasion at the beginning of his pontificate.[131]

While there are obvious parallels between Latin liturgical texts of late antiquity and the writings of Church Fathers of the same period, any effort to identify the author or redactor of a particular prayer will remain in the realm of probability. In the case of a well-known preacher, such as Leo the Great, it is difficult to determine whether he cites a prayer that is already in liturgical use, whether he is the author of the prayer or whether the prayer is formed later by putting together phrases and expressions from his preaching. Moreover, the precise historical origins of a prayer can hardly be determined, because ancient Roman collects are usually general in their content and would fit a variety of particular situations, especially in the turbulent period after the fall of the Western empire that was plagued by military crises and natural disasters.

The Prefaces

It is a characteristic of Western liturgies that the preface, originally considered the beginning of the Eucharistic prayer, varies according to the liturgical season or feast. Its general theme, which is praise and thanksgiving for the divine economy of salvation, leads into the heart of the Eucharistic sacrifice. The preface corresponds with the celebrant's call to the people 'Lift up your hearts (Sursum corda)' and shows a distinct lyrical tone. The great number of prefaces in ancient Roman sources suggests that improvisation and new composition prevailed here for a longer duration than for other parts of the Mass. The Verona manuscript has a proper preface for every formulary (267 altogether); the Old Gelasian limits the number of prefaces to 54, while the Frankish Gelasian sacramentaries of the eighth century feature some 200 of them. The exemplar of the Gregorian sacramentary, sent by Pope Hadrian I to Charlemagne in the late eighth century (the *Hadrianum*), has only 14 prefaces, and this pattern prevailed in the course of the Middle Ages, when the number of prefaces became strictly

Coebergh, 'S. Gélase Ier, auteur principal du soi-disant Sacramentaire léonien', in *Ephemerides Liturgicae* 65 (1951), 171–181.

[131] Henry Ashworth, 'The Influence of the Lombard Invasions on the Gregorian Sacramentary', in *Bulletin of the John Rylands Library, Manchester* 37 (1954), 305–327; also 'The Liturgical Prayers of St Gregory the Great', in *Traditio* 15 (1959), 107–161; and the earlier study by Bernard Capelle, 'La main de S. Grégorie dans le sacramentaire grégorien', in *Travaux liturgiques de doctrine et d'histoire*, vol. II, 161–175 (originally published in *Revue bénédictine* 49 [1937], 13–28).

limited. The *Missale Romanum* of 1570 has 11 prefaces, to which several were added in the twentieth century. The reform of the liturgy after the Second Vatican Council greatly expanded the corpus of prefaces to 81 in the *Missale Romanum* of 1970, to which more were added in the second and third typical editions.[132]

As Jungmann notes,[133] there were good reasons for the pruning of prefaces: many of the texts in the *Veronense* are exuberant in style and content, and they introduce idiosyncratic themes that can detract from the praise and thanksgiving to God, which marks the opening of the Eucharistic prayer. For instance, some of the prefaces in the Verona manuscript dwell excessively on the lives of martyrs and so become almost a panegyric for a Christian hero. The restriction that is evident from the Gregorian tradition was arguably too drastic but was needed to retain the distinctive prefatory character.

The introductory dialogue, which is common to most liturgical traditions in some form, reads, in the fully developed Roman model:

> Dominus vobiscum.
> Et cum spiritu tuo.
>
> Sursum corda.
> Habemus ad Dominum.
>
> Gratias agamus Domino Deo nostro.
> Dignum et iustum est.
>
> The Lord be with you.
> And with your spirit.
>
> Lift up your hearts.
> We lift them up to the Lord.
>
> Let us give thanks to the Lord our God.
> It is right and just.

---

[132] See *The Prefaces of the Roman Missal: A Source Compendium with Concordance and Indices*, ed. Anthony Ward and Cuthbert Johnson (Rome: C.L.V.–Edizioni liturgiche, 1989), esp. 10–12. The new prefaces are not simply retrieved from ancient sacramentaries but are either centonisations, with phrases from various liturgical sources being woven together, liturgical transpositions of biblical, patristic and Vatican II texts, or entirely new compositions. See Lauren Pristas, 'The Orations of the Vatican II Missals: Policies for Revision', in *Communio (US)* 30 (2003), 621–653, at 636–638.

[133] Jungmann, *Missarum sollemnia*, vol. II, 145–161.

This dialogue, which can be traced back to the third century, is thoroughly biblical and follows Jewish prayers of thanksgiving.[134] The people's final response 'Dignum et iustum' belongs to the kind of acclamations that were a common feature of popular assemblies in the ancient world. Such acclamations confirmed an important decision or election, including that of a Roman emperor.[135] They would later be used to approve the election of a bishop.[136]

The celebrant then takes up this response in the first part of the preface itself (also known by the technical term 'protocol'):

> Vere dignum et iustum est, aequum et salutare,
> nos tibi semper et ubique gratias agere:
> Domine, sancte Pater, omnipotens aeterne Deus:
> per Christum Dominum nostrum.

> It is truly right and just, our duty and our salvation,
> always and everywhere to give you thanks,
> Lord, holy Father, almighty and eternal God,
> through Christ our Lord.

The preface's rhetorical composition shows in the pleonastic emphasis on the fittingness of giving thanks and in the threefold address to God, where the shorter invocation precedes the longer and so a memorable climax is achieved: 'Lord, holy Father, almighty and eternal God'.[137] While there can be variations in the phrasing, the protocol always follows this pattern: the celebrant, in the name of the people present and indeed of the whole Church, proclaims that thanksgiving is due to God the Father through Jesus Christ.

The central part (or 'embolism') provides the motive for why the Church renders praise and thanks to God on this day and therefore varies according to the liturgical season or feast that is celebrated. As an example, I have chosen the Preface of the Nativity:

---

[134] See Ruth 2:4, Lk 1:24; 2 Tim 4:22 Col 3:1, Lam 3:41; 1 Thess 1:2. A full list of biblical references is compiled by Leo Eizenhöfer, *Canon Missae Romanae. Pars altera: Textus propinqui*, Rerum Ecclesiasticarum Documenta. Series minor. Subsidia studiorum 7 (Rome: Herder, 1966), 21–24.

[135] 'Aequm est, iustum est'; see the references in Eizenhöfer, *Canon Missae Romanae*, 25.

[136] Jungmann, *Missarum sollemnia*, vol. II, 139–140, also points to a similar response in Jewish morning prayer.

[137] In the *Missale Romanum* of 1570 and its subsequent editions, this was printed as 'Domine sancte, Pater omnipotens, aeterne Deus'. However, it has been shown that this punctuation is not correct, and so this has been changed in the *editio typica* of 1962; see Christine Mohrmann, 'Problèmes de ponctuation dans le préface', in Botte and Mohrmann, *L'ordinaire de la messe*, 105.

Quia per incarnati Verbi mysterium
nova mentis nostrae oculis lux tuae claritatis infulsit:
ut dum visibiliter Deum cognoscimus
per hunc in invisibilium amorem rapiamur.

For in the mystery of the Word made flesh
a new light of your glory has shone upon the eyes of our mind,
so that as we recognize in him God made visible,
we may be caught up through him in love of things invisible.[138]

This ancient Roman preface for Christmas[139] is a sublime expression of faith in the coming of the Son of God into this world, which is celebrated on one of the most festive days of the liturgical year. The text strongly draws on the Gospel of John, especially on its prologue (1:1–14) and more generally on the Johannine theology presenting Christ as the light of the world. There is also a clear echo of the angel's apparition to the shepherds, announcing the birth of the Saviour.[140] The themes of the preface resonate particularly in the writings of Gregory the Great.[141]

The word 'mysterium' has a wide-ranging meaning in liturgical texts and is found frequently in prayers for the celebration of the Nativity. When the first line of this passage evokes the 'mystery of the Incarnate Word', it employs the term for speaking of the divine revelation in Jesus Christ, much in the same way as St Paul uses μυστήριον (e.g., Rom 16:25). The reception of this revelation is indicated with the verb 'cognoscere' in the third line, which goes beyond intellectual knowledge and includes 'the idea of a real, effective experience of salvation'.[142] Moreover, the first and the third line are linked to each other by the same rhythmical ending (*cursus tardus*: 'Vérbi mystérium – Déum cognóscimus').[143]

---

[138] English translation from the *Roman Missal* 2011.

[139] *Gregorianum (Hadrianum)*, 38 and 51; *Paduanum*, 6; see *Corpus praefationum*, ed. Eugène Moeller, CCL 161, 4 vols. (Turnhout: Brepols, 1980–1981), no. 1322.

[140] The Vulgate version of Luke 2:9 reads: 'et claritas Dei circumfulsit illos' – 'and the glory of the Lord shone around them'.

[141] Gregory the Great, *In Ezech.* II, I, 15: SC 360,80: 'Redemptor itaque noster, pro nobis misericorditer incarnatus, ante humanos oculos quasi in porta stetit, quia et per humanitatem uisibilis apparuit, et sese inuisibilem in diuinitate seruauit.' See also *Moralia in Iob*, XVIII, LI, 83: CCL 143,946, and Fulgentius of Ruspe, *Ad Trasimundum*, 2, 6: PL 65,252B. For a full list of these biblical and patristic references, see Ward and Johnson, *The Prefaces of the Roman Missal*, 72–74.

[142] Ellebracht, *Remarks on the Vocabulary*, 70; see ibid., 67–71.

[143] The second line and fourth line have different rhythmical endings: 'claritátis infúlsit' (*cursus planus*) and 'amórem rapiámur' (*cursus trispondiacus*).

The theme of light, which suffuses the euchological texts for Christmas in the *Missale Romanum*, is greatly elaborated in the second line: the noun 'lux' is separated by its modifying adjective by three words. By means of this hyperbaton and of the prominent position of the adjective 'nova' at the beginning of the line, attention is drawn to the newness of Christian revelation in general and in particular of Christ's nativity, which renews the whole world and liberates it from sin.[144] The apposition 'tuae claritatis' can be construed as a genitive of identity or of inherence, as the two words have approximately the same meaning. In Latin Bible versions, 'claritas' is one of the possible translations for the Hebrew *kabod* and the Greek δόξα, which indicates the manifestation of God's glory, for example, in the sanctuary of the desert (Ex 40:33–35) and in the Temple of Jerusalem (1 Kgs 8:11). This glory now radiates from the new-born Christ child for those who look upon him with the eyes of faith.

The third line, with a subordinate clause in the indicative, explains the effect of the Incarnation, whereas the fourth line goes on to express the desired result with the subjunctive; in a very literal translation: 'so that we, while we know God visibly, may be caught up into love of things invisible'. The verb 'rapere', translating the Greek ἁρπάζειν, is adduced several times in the New Testament when a person is transported (in spirit or even physically) into the sphere of God. Thus, 'the Spirit of the Lord caught up' the deacon Philip, after he baptised the Ethiopian eunuch (Acts 8:39). The Apostle Paul speaks of being 'caught up to the third heaven' in his own description of his mystical experience (2 Cor 12:2,4).[145] Resonating with these scriptural passages, the embolism closes with a poetic invocation of enjoying eternal happiness, 'what no eye has seen … what God has prepared for those who love him' (1 Cor 2:9; see Is 64:4).

> Et ideo cum Angelis et Archangelis,
> cum Thronis et Dominationibus,
> cumque omni militia caelestis exercitus,
> hymnum gloriae tuae canimus, sine fine dicentes:

---

[144] This is another frequent theme in Christmas prayers; see Ellebracht, *Remarks on the Vocabulary*, 24–25; and Blaise, *Le vocabulaire latin*, 314 (§ 180). For instance, the striking phrase 'Unigeniti tui nova per carnem nativitas' appears in the collect for the *Missa in die* on Christmas Day (in *Missale Romanum* 1570).

[145] See also 1 Thess 4:17 and Rev 12:5.

> And so, with Angels and Archangels,
> with Thrones and Dominions,
> and with all the hosts and Powers of heaven,
> we sing the hymn of your glory
> as without end we acclaim:

The concluding part (or 'eschatocol') invokes the unending praise offered by the angels and saints to God in heaven, thus providing the transition to the *Sanctus*. A characteristic feature of many prefaces is the appeal to the choirs of angels, whose names are drawn from Scripture (e.g., Gen 3:24, Ez 28:14–16, Is 6:2–3, Eph 1:21 and Col 1:16).

This type of eschatocol makes the liturgical assembly join the angelic worship in a confident and quasi-natural manner. However, there is another type of eschatocol, for instance, in the *Praefatio communis*, in which such participation is not taken for granted; rather the Church on earth makes a humble plea that its voices may be admitted to the celestial song of praise:

> Cum quibus et nostras voces ut admitti iubeas deprecamur
> supplici confessione dicentes:

> May our voices, we pray, join with theirs
> in humble praise, as we acclaim:[146]

CONCLUSION

The fourth and fifth centuries were a crucial stage in the development of Latin liturgy and in the formation of the Roman Mass. An early version of the Eucharistic prayer, which became known as the *Canon missae*, is attested by Ambrose of Milan in the late fourth century. By the time of Pope Gregory the Great in the late sixth century, the canon reached its definitive form. This chapter has focussed on the liturgical texts of the emerging Roman Rite. The canon and the variable prayers of the Mass draw on the style of pagan prayer, but their vocabulary and content are distinctively Christian, indeed biblical. Their diction has Roman *gravitas*

---

[146] A similar plea is made in the introduction for the *Sanctus* of the Egyptian Anaphora of St Gregory of Nazianzus: ed. Hänggi – Pahl, *Prex Eucharistia I*, 360. See Albert Gerhards, 'Crossing Borders. The Kedusha and the Sanctus: A Case Study of the convergence of Jewish and Christian Liturgy', in *Jewish and Christian Liturgy and Worship: New Insights into its History and Interaction*, ed. Albert Gerhards and Clemens Leonhard, Jewish and Christian Perspectives Series 15 (Leiden: Brill, 2007), 27–40, at 35.

and eschews the exuberance of the Eastern Christian prayer style, which is also found in the Gallican tradition. Many of the early collects are considered literary masterpieces. Mohrmann rightly speaks of the fortuitous combination of a renewal of language, inspired by the newness of Christian revelation and a stylistic traditionalism that was deeply rooted in the Roman world. The formation of this liturgical idiom contributed significantly to the comprehensive effort of Church leaders in late antiquity to evangelise classical culture.

Appendix:

Ambrose's Eucharistic Prayer and the *Canon Missae*

Ambrose of Milan, *De sacramentis*[a]	*Canon missae*[b]
	Dominus vobiscum.
	Et cum spiritu tuo.
	Sursum corda.
	Habemus ad Dominum.
	Gratias agamus Domino Deo nostro.
	Dignum et iustum est.
laus deo defertur [IV,4,14]	Vere dignum et iustum est aequum et salutare nos tibi semper et ubique gratias agere, Domine, sancte Pater, omnipotens aeterne Deus, per Christum Dominum nostrum. Per quem maiestatem tuam laudant angeli, adorant dominationes, tremunt potestates, caeli caelorumque virtutes ac beata Seraphim socia exsultatione concelebrant. Cum quibus et nostras voces ut admitti iubeas deprecamur supplici confessione dicentes:
	Sanctus, sanctus, sanctus Dominus Deus Sabaoth. Pleni sunt caeli et terra gloria tua. Hosanna in excelsis. Benedictus qui venit in nomine Domino. Hosanna in excelsis.
sacramenta posita super altare [IV,3,8]	Te igitur, clementissime Pater, per Iesum Christum Filium tuum Dominum nostrum supplices rogamus et petimus, uti accepta habeas et benedicas haec dona, haec munera, haec sancta sacrificia illibata. In primis quae tibi offerimus pro Ecclesia tua sancta catholica, quam pacificare, custodire, adunare et regere digneris toto orbe terrarum, una cum famulo tuo papa nostro illo.[c]

(cont.)

Ambrose of Milan, *De sacramentis*	*Canon missae*
oratio petitur pro populo, pro regibus, pro ceteris [IV,1,4]	Memento, Domine, famulorum famularumque tuarum et omnium circum adstantium, quorum tibi fides cognita est et nota devotio. Qui tibi offerunt hoc sacrificium laudis: pro se suisque omnibus, pro redemptione animarum suarum, pro spe salutis et incolumitatis suae tibi reddunt vota sua aeterno Deo vivo et vero.
	Communicantes et memoriam venerantes in primis gloriosae semper virginis Mariae genetricis Dei et Domini nostri Iesu Christi, sed et beatorum apostolorum ac martyrum tuorum Petri, Pauli, Andreae, Iacobi, Ioannis, Thomae, Iacobi, Philippi, Bartholomaei, Matthaei, Simonis et Thaddaei, Lini, Cleti, Clementis, Xysti, Cornelii, Cypriani, Laurentii, Chrysogoni, Ioannis et Pauli, Cosmae et Damiani et omnium sanctorum tuorum, quorum meritis precibusque concedas, ut in omnibus protectionis tuae muniamur auxilio. Per Christum Dominum nostrum.[d]
	Hanc igitur oblationem servitutis nostrae sed et cunctae familiae tuae, quaesumus, Domine, ut placatus accipias diesque nostros in tua pace disponas atque ab aeterna damnatione nos eripi et in electorum tuorum iubeas grege numerari. Per Christum Dominum nostrum.
Fac nobis hanc oblationem scriptam, rationabilem, acceptabilem, quod est figura corporis et sanguinis Domini nostri Iesu Christi.	Quam oblationem tu, Deus, in omnibus, quaesumus, benedictam, adscriptam, ratam, rationabilem acceptabilemque facere digneris, ut nobis corpus et sanguis fiat dilectissimi Filii tui Domini Dei nostri Iesu Christi.
Qui pridie quam pateretur, in sanctis manibus suis accepit panem, respexit	Qui pridie quam pateretur accepit panem in sanctas ac venerabiles

(*cont.*)

Ambrose of Milan, *De sacramentis*	*Canon missae*
ad caelum, ad te, sancte Pater omnipotens aeterne Deus, gratias agens benedixit, fregit, fractumque apostolis et discipulis suis tradidit dicens: Accipite et edite ex hoc omnes; hoc est enim corpus meum, quod pro multis confringetur. Similiter etiam calicem, postquam cenatum est, pridie quam pateretur, accepit, respexit ad caelum, ad te, sancte Pater omnipotens aeterne Deus, gratias agens benedixit, apostolis et discipulis suis tradidit dicens: Accipite et bibite ex hoc omnes; hic est enim sanguis meus. quotienscumque hoc feceritis, totiens commemorationem mei facietis, donec iterum adveniam.	manus suas elevatis oculis in caelum ad te Deum Patrem suum omnipotentem tibi gratias agens benedixit, fregit, dedit discipulis suis dicens: Accipite et manducate ex hoc omnes. Hoc est enim corpus meum. Simili modo, posteaquam cenatum est, accipiens et hunc praeclarum calicem in sanctas ac venerabiles manus suas, item tibi gratias agens benedixit, dedit discipulis suis dicens: Accipite et bibite ex eo omnes. Hic est enim calix sanguinis mei, novi et aeterni testamenti, mysterium fidei, qui pro vobis et pro multis effundetur in remissionem peccatorum. Haec quotiescumque feceritis, in mei memoriam facietis.
Ergo memores gloriosissimae eius passionis et ab inferis resurrectionis et in caelum ascensionis offerimus tibi hanc inmaculatam hostiam, rationabilem hostiam, incruentam hostiam, hunc panem sanctum et calicem vitae aeternae.	Unde et memores sumus, Domine, nos tui servi sed et plebs tua sancta Christi Filii tui Domini Dei nostri tam beatae passionis nec non et ab inferis resurrectionis sed et in caelos gloriosae ascensionis offerimus praeclarae maiestati tuae de tuis donis ac datis hostiam puram, hostiam sanctam, hostiam immaculatam, panem sanctum vitae aeternae et calicem salutis perpetuae.
Et petimus et precamur, uti hanc oblationem suscipias in sublime altare tuum per manus angelorum tuorum, sicut suscipere dignatus es munera pueri tui iusti Abel et sacrificium patriarchae nostri Abrahae et quod tibi obtulit summus sacerdos Melchisedech.	Supra quae propitio ac sereno vultu respicere digneris et accepta habere, sicuti accepta habere dignatus es munera pueri tui iusti Abel et sacrificium patriarchae nostri Abrahae et quod tibi obtulit summus sacerdos tuus Melchisedech, sanctum sacrificium, immaculatam hostiam. Supplices te rogamus, omnipotens Deus, iube haec perferri per manus angeli tui in sublime altare tuum in conspectu divinae maiestatis tuae, ut quotquot ex hac altaris

(*cont.*)

Ambrose of Milan, *De sacramentis*	*Canon missae*
	participatione sacrosanctum Filii tui corpus et sanguinem sumpserimus, omni benedictione caelesti et gratia repleamur per Christum Dominum nostrum.
	Memento etiam, Domine, et eorum nomina qui nos praecesserunt cum signo fidei et dormiunt in somno pacis. Ipsis et omnibus in Christo quiescentibus locum refrigerii lucis et pacis ut indulgeas deprecamur. Per Christum Dominum nostrum.
	Nobis quoque peccatoribus famulis tuis de multitudine miserationum tuarum sperantibus partem aliquam et societatem donare digneris cum tuis sanctis apostolis et martyribus, cum Ioanne, Stephano, Matthia, Barnaba, Ignatio, Alexandro, Marcellino, Petro, Felicitate, Perpetua, Agatha, Lucia, Agnete, Caecilia, Anastasia et cum omnibus sanctis tuis, intra quorum nos consortium non aestimator meriti sed veniae, quaesumus, largitor admitte. Per Christum Dominum nostrum.
	Per quem haec omnia, Domine, semper bona creas, sanctificas, vivificas, benedicis et praestas nobis
	Per ipsum et cum ipso et in ipso est tibi Deo Patri omnipotenti in unitate Spiritus sancti omnis honor et gloria per omnia saecula saeculorum. Amen.
Ambrose of Milan, *On the Sacraments*[e]	*Canon of the Mass*[f] The Lord be with you. And with your spirit. Lift up your hearts. We lift them up to the Lord. Let us give thanks to the Lord our God. It is right and just.

(*cont.*)

Ambrose of Milan, *De sacramentis*	*Canon missae*
praise is offered to God [IV,4,14]	It is truly right and just, our duty and our salvation, always and everywhere to give you thanks, Lord, holy Father, almighty and eternal God, through Christ our Lord. Through him the Angels praise your majesty, Dominions adore and Powers tremble before you. Heaven and the Virtues of heaven and the blessed Seraphim worship together with exultation. May our voices, we pray, join with theirs in humble praise, as we acclaim: Holy, Holy, Holy Lord God of hosts. Heaven and earth are full of your glory. Hosanna in the highest. Blessed is he who comes in the name of the Lord. Hosanna in the highest.
sacraments placed on the altar [IV,3,8]	To you, therefore, most merciful Father, we make humble prayer and petition through Jesus Christ, your Son, our Lord: that you accept and bless these gifts, these offerings, these holy and unblemished sacrifices, which we offer you firstly for your holy catholic Church. Be pleased to grant her peace, to guard, unite and govern her throughout the whole world, together with your servant N. our Pope.
prayer is asked for the people, for kings and for others [IV,4,14]	Remember, Lord, your servants and all gathered here, whose faith and devotion are known to you. They offer you this sacrifice of praise for themselves and all who are dear to them: for the redemption of their souls, in hope of health and well-being, and paying their homage to you, the eternal God, living and true. In communion with those whose memory we venerate, especially the glorious ever-Virgin Mary, Mother

(*cont.*)

Ambrose of Milan, *De sacramentis*	*Canon missae*
	of our God and Lord, Jesus Christ, and your blessed Apostles and Martyrs, Peter and Paul, Andrew, James, John, Thomas, James, Philip, Bartholomew, Matthew, Simon and Jude; Linus, Cletus, Clement, Sixtus, Cornelius, Cyprian, Laurence, Chrysogonus, John and Paul, Cosmas and Damian and all your Saints; we ask that through their merits and prayers, in all things we may be defended by your protecting help. Through Christ our Lord. Amen.
	Therefore, Lord, we pray: graciously accept this oblation of our service, that of your whole family; order our days in your peace, and command that we be delivered from eternal damnation and counted among the flock of those you have chosen. Through Christ our Lord. Amen.
Make for us this offering approved, reasonable, acceptable, which is the figure of the body and blood of our Lord Jesus Christ.	Be pleased, O God, we pray, to bless, acknowledge, and approve this offering in every respect; make it spiritual and acceptable, so that it may become for us the Body and Blood of your most beloved Son, our Lord Jesus Christ.
Who on the day before he was to suffer, took bread in his holy hands, looked up to heaven, to you, holy Father, almighty, eternal God; giving thanks he blessed, broke, having broken delivered it to his apostles and disciples, saying: Take and eat of this, all of you; for this is my Body, which will be broken for many. In a similar way, when supper was ended, on the day before he was to suffer, he also took the chalice, looked up to heaven to you, holy	Who on the day before he was to suffer, took bread in his holy and venerable hands, and with eyes raised to heaven to you, O God, his almighty Father, giving you thanks, he said the blessing, broke the bread and gave it to his disciples, saying: Take this, all of you, and eat of it, for this is my Body. In a similar way, when supper was ended, he took this precious chalice in his holy and venerable hands, and once more giving you thanks, he said the

(cont.)

Ambrose of Milan, *De sacramentis*	*Canon missae*
Father, almighty, eternal God, giving thanks blessed it, delivered it to his apostles and disciples, saying: Take and drink of this, all of you; for this is my Blood. As often as you do this, so often will you make a memorial of me, until I come again.	blessing and gave the chalice to his disciples, saying: Take this, all of you, and drink from it, for this is the chalice of my Blood, of the new and eternal covenant, the mystery of faith, which will be poured out for you and for many for the forgiveness of sins. As often as you do these [actions], you will do them in memory of me.
Therefore, in memory of his most glorious Passion and Resurrection from the dead and Ascension into heaven, we offer to you this spotless victim, reasonable victim, unbloody victim, this holy bread and chalice of eternal life.	Therefore, O Lord, as we celebrate the memorial of the blessed Passion, the Resurrection from the dead, and the glorious Ascension into heaven of Christ, your Son, our Lord, we, your servants and your holy people, offer to your glorious majesty from the gifts that you have given us, this pure victim, this holy victim, this spotless victim, the holy Bread of eternal life and the Chalice of everlasting salvation.
We both ask and pray that you receive this offering on your altar on high by the hands of your angels, as you were pleased to receive the gifts of your servant Abel the just, and the sacrifice of our patriarch Abraham, and what the high priest Melchizedek offered to you.	Be pleased to look upon these offerings with a serene and kindly countenance, and to accept them, as once you were pleased to accept the gifts of your servant Abel the just, the sacrifice of Abraham, our father in faith, and the offering of your high priest Melchizedek, a holy sacrifice, a spotless victim.
	In humble prayer we ask you, almighty God: command that these gifts be borne by the hands of your holy Angel to your altar on high in the sight of your divine majesty, so that all of us, who through this participation at the altar receive the most holy Body and Blood of your Son, may be filled with every grace and heavenly blessing. Through Christ our Lord. Amen.

(*cont.*)

Ambrose of Milan, *De sacramentis*	Canon missae
	Remember also, Lord, the names of those who have gone before us with the sign of faith and rest in the sleep of peace. Grant them, O Lord, we pray, and all who sleep in Christ, a place of refreshment, light and peace. Through Christ our Lord. Amen.
	To us, also, your servants, who, though sinners, hope in your abundant mercies, graciously grant some share and fellowship with your holy Apostles and Martyrs: with John the Baptist, Stephen, Matthias, Barnabas, Ignatius, Alexander, Marcellinus, Peter, Felicity, Perpetua, Agatha, Lucy, Agnes, Cecilia, Anastasia and all your Saints; admit us, we beseech you, into their company, not weighing our merits, but granting us your pardon, through Christ our Lord.
	Through whom you continue to make all these good things, O Lord; you sanctify them, fill them with life, bless them, and bestow them upon us.
	Through him, and with him, and in him, O God, almighty Father, in the unity of the Holy Spirit, all glory and honour is yours, for ever and ever. Amen.

[a] Ambrose, *De sacramentis*, IV,5,21–22 and 6,26–27: CSEL 73,55 and 57, as found in Hänggi – Pahl, *Prex eucharistica*, vol. I, 421–422, supplemented with earlier references from Ambrose that may indicate parallels with the Gregorian canon.

[b] *Canon missae*, collated mainly from sacraments of the Gregorian type, as found in Hänggi – Pahl, *Prex Eucharistia I*, 426–438.

[c] Commemorating the pope alone reflects the original use of the canon in the city of Rome. Several early manuscripts add 'et antistite nostro illo' to commemorate the local bishop. The appended clause 'et omnibus orthodoxis atque catholicae et apostolicae fidei cultoribus' is found in a number of sources, and it may reflect ancient papal use.

^d The proper *Communicantes* and *Hanc igitur*, as well as the insertions in the *Quam oblationem* for the anniversary of an episcopal ordination and in the *Qui pridie* for Maundy Thursday are not listed here.

^e The translation is my own and attempts to follow Ambrose's Latin syntax as closely as possible.

^f The translation is taken from *Roman Missal* 2011, with some modifications where the early medieval text differs from the third typical edition of the post-Vatican II *Missale Romanum*.

5

Roman Stational Liturgy

This chapter will consider the ritual structure and elements of the Roman Mass in the crucial period of formation from the fifth to the early eighth century, which is especially associated with the decisive contributions of popes, such as Leo the Great (r. 440–461), Gelasius (r. 492–496) and Gregory the Great (r. 590–604). The reader will be introduced to the liturgical books that were compiled for the celebration of the Mass (sacramentaries, lectionaries, antiphoners, *ordines*). Particular attention will then be given to the papal stational liturgy as described in *Ordo Romanus I*, which was to have a fundamental impact on later development in the West. The chapter will include an extended discussion of the role of chant in the Mass, as well as sections on the renewed presence of Greek in the Roman liturgy and on the direction of liturgical prayer.

PONTIFICAL AND PRESBYTERAL CELEBRATIONS

In the late ancient and early medieval period, celebrations of the Roman Mass can be distinguished into two types: the first type is represented by the stational liturgy of the pope (or his delegate), which was held on Sundays and feast days during the liturgical year and especially during Lent. A particular church of the city (*statio*) was assigned for a given day, and the pope would move in solemn procession from his residence in the Lateran palace to the stational church to celebrate Mass. This type of stational or processional liturgy was first created in Jerusalem around the holy sites and later adopted in Constantinople, especially during the episcopate of John Chrysostom. The elaborate Roman stational liturgy evolved in the sixth and seventh century[1] and became such an integral part of the rite that the *statio* was recorded in the Mass formulary for specific days in the temporal cycle of the *Missale Romanum* until the post–Vatican II liturgical reform.

The second type of celebration, the simpler form of the rite, would have been observed in the twenty-five titular churches within the city walls, which can be compared to parish churches. We know very little about this presbyteral liturgy because the major sources from this time are mostly concerned with pontifical rites. What is known in historical scholarship as the Gelasian-type sacramentary for presbyteral use has been reconstructed by Antoine Chavasse from the so-called Old Gelasian Sacramentary from the middle of the eighth century.[2] This manuscript contains both presbyteral and pontifical rites,[3] and it is only later, in the Ottonian period (see Chapter 7), when liturgical books of a 'second generation' begin to appear (missal, pontifical, ritual, etc.), that we can identify a clearer differentiation between the two types of celebration. The Eucharist offered by a priest (*presbyter*) was understood as a reduced form of the bishop's liturgy. This idea was in continuity with the early Christian understanding that, theologically speaking, the bishop is the celebrant of each Eucharist in his diocese, even when he is not physically presiding over a particular assembly, as reflected in the practice of commemorating the bishop in the Eucharistic prayer and in the specifically Roman custom of the *fermentum*, the sending of a portion of the consecrated bread from the papal Mass to the presbyteral liturgies held in the titular churches of the city. While euchological texts for presbyteral celebrations have come down to us in the Gelasian-type sacramentaries, we know very little about their ritual shape, but it is likely that the Mass followed a simplified version of the pontifical ceremonial.[4] According to

[1] See John F. Baldovin, *The Urban Character of Christian Worship: The Origins, Development, and Meaning of Stational Liturgy*, Orientalia Cristiana Analecta 228 (Rome: Pont. Institutum Studiorum Orientalium, 1987).

[2] See Antoine Chavasse, *Le sacramentaire gélasien (Vaticanus Reginensis 316): Sacramentaire presbytéral en usage dans les titres romains au VIIe siècle*, Bibliothèque de théologie IV,1 (Tournai: Desclée, 1958).

[3] See Niels K. Rasmussen, 'Célébration épiscopale et célébration presbytérale: un essai de typologie', in *Segni e riti nella chiesa altomedievale occidentale, 11–17 aprile 1985*, Settimane di studio del Centro italiano di studi sull'alto medioevo 33 (Spoleto: Presso la Sede del Centro, 1987), vol. II, 581–607, at 584–585.

[4] Rasmussen comments: 'la plupart des textes nous montrent que la messe presbytérale ne peut être conçue que comme une messe épiscopale de forme réduite et non comme une eucharistie distincte de celle de l'évêque' (ibid., 602).

Hans-Joachim Schulz, a similar pattern of development can be identified in the celebration of the Eucharist according to the Byzantine Rite. Thus, the original function of the two processional entrances is still intelligible in the 'Hierarchical Divine Liturgy' but was obscured when the entrances were adapted to the reduced presbyteral form.[5] In its hierarchical (i.e., pontifical) form, the presiding bishop enters the sanctuary for the first time from his cathedra in the nave of the church at the Little Entrance. During the Great Entrance, the bishop remains in front of the altar to receive the offerings, which in the liturgy of the Great Church of Constantinople (Hagia Sophia) were prepared in a separate room, the skeuophylakion.

LITURGICAL BOOKS

The age of transition from late antiquity to the early Middle Ages saw a codification of liturgical books for the celebration of Mass and other sacramental rites. These books typically contained the texts needed for specific liturgical ministers, above all the sacramentary for the officiating bishop or priest, the lectionary (and its preceding forms) for deacon, subdeacon or lector and the gradual or Mass antiphoner for the singers.

Sacramentaries

The sacramentary can be described as the book containing the texts recited or chanted by the bishop or priest officiating at the celebration of Mass and other sacraments, as well as various consecrations and blessings. In the case of the Mass, formularies for particular occasions seem to have originated as small booklets (*libelli missarum*), which were collected and then organised into a book to be used throughout the liturgical year. Two types of Roman sacramentary have been identified, the Gelasian and the Gregorian. These differ from each other in significant ways but were both in use at the same time, in Rome and the Italian peninsula, as well as north of the Alps.[6]

---

[5] See Hans-Joachim Schulz, 'Liturgie, Tagzeiten und Kirchenjahr des byzantinischen Ritus', in *Handbuch der Ostkirchenkunde Bd. II*, ed. Wilhelm Nyssen, Hans-Joachim Schulz and Paul Wiertz (Düsseldorf: Patmos, 1989), 30–100, at 36–37. See also Alexander Schmemann, *Eucharist: Sacrament of the Kingdom*, trans. Paul Kachur (Crestwood: St Vladimir's Seminary Press, 1987), 15–16.

[6] This is a schematic and abbreviated presentation. For a more complete and detailed account see the indispensable work of Cyrille Vogel, *Medieval Liturgy: An Introduction to the Sources*, rev. and trans. William G. Storey and Niels Krogh Rasmussen

The Gelasian-type sacramentary[7] is believed to have been compiled originally for the use of priests in the city's titular churches. The earliest extant representative of this type is a Frankish manuscript, written in a nuns' scriptorium north-east of Paris (Chelles or possibly its mother house, Jouarre)[8] in the middle of the eighth century: Reg. lat. 316 from the Vatican Library, known as the Old Gelasian.[9] This sacramentary is essentially a Roman book, with additions of Gallican origin, for instance, consecration of virgins, dedication of churches and Masses of Advent. Moreover, the manuscript contains both presbyteral and episcopal rites, such as the consecration of bishops. Going beyond the heterogeneous composition of the manuscript, liturgical historians have considered the Old Gelasian a unique source for presbyteral use in Roman churches in the mid-seventh century. The archetype of this sacramentary is usually dated between 628 and 715, as can be inferred from the fact that the manuscript reflects the modifications made by Gregory the Great to the Canon of the Mass (above all, his addition to the prayer *Hanc igitur*) but does not yet feature the Masses for the Thursdays in Lent established by Gregory II (r. 715–731) or the *Agnus Dei* introduced by Sergius I (r. 687–701).

The Old Gelasian shows two major characteristics that are not found in Gregorian sacramentaries. First, the manuscript, which has the title 'Here begins the sacramentary of the Roman church ordered according to the yearly cycle (*Incipit liber sacramentorum romanae aecclesiae ordininis anni circuli*)', is organised in three distinct books and keeps the temporal and the sanctoral cycles separate. Secondly, Mass sets typically have two collects (*oratio*), a secret (*secreta*),[10] a proper preface (also called *contestatio* or *contestata*), a postcommunion (*post communionem*) and usually a

---

(Washington, DC: The Pastoral Press, 1981), 61–110. See also Éric Palazzo, *A History of Liturgical Books from the Beginning to the Thirteenth Century*, trans. Madeleine Beaumont (Collegeville: Liturgical Press, 1993).

[7] While there is no direct connection with Pope Gelasius, several scholars see his hand in some of the Mass formularies collected in the *Veronense* (see Chapter 4, p. 137).

[8] See Rosamond McKitterick, 'Nuns' Scriptoria in England and Francia in the Eighth Century', in *Francia* 19 (1992), 1–35.

[9] The last two quires, a supplement with a long exorcism, a penitential, and hagiographical notes on the apostles (*Breviarium apostolorum*), were separated from the original manuscript and are now kept in Paris, Bibliothèque Nationale, lat. 7193, fols. 41–56.

[10] The prayer more likely derives its name from the fact that it was said over the offerings that were 'set apart' for the Eucharistic consecration, rather than from its recitation at a low voice.

prayer of blessing (*ad populum*). It is not entirely clear why the Gelasian Mass sets, especially in the temporal cycle, include two prayers of a very similar kind before the secret (as do many formularies in the *Veronense*). Since these texts do not stem from stational liturgies, but from presbyteral use, the first prayer cannot be a stational collect. Antoine Chavasse has argued that the second collect originated as a conclusion to the intercessory prayers and corresponded to the *oratio super sindonem* (prayer over the veil covering the offerings) in the Ambrosian Rite of Milan.[11]

The Gregorian-type sacramentary emerged from the collection of Mass books for the use of the pope when he celebrated at the Lateran (his cathedral) and in the stational churches of the city. The sacramentary as such cannot be attributed to Gregory the Great, though it may contain material from his pontificate (see Chapter 4); it was redacted probably under Pope Honorius I (r. 625–638) and expanded in the course of the seventh and eighth centuries. In sacramentaries of the Gregorian type, the temporal and sanctoral cycles are not distinct, as in the Gelasian tradition; the *Hadrianum* and its followers combine the two cycles into one sequence of Sundays and feast days.[12] The Mass sets in the Gregorian tradition typically have three orations: a collect (*oratio*), a prayer over the offerings (*super oblata*) and a concluding prayer (*ad completa* or *ad complendum*); many formularies also include a prayer of blessing (*super populum*). The number of prefaces is much smaller than in the Gelasian sacramentaries: the *Hadrianum* only has fourteen, compared to fifty-four in the Old Gelasian.

Lectionaries

The lectionaries containing the texts of the scriptural readings (also called pericopes) for the Mass and the Divine Office developed, first, from marginal notes in biblical manuscripts designating the pericopes to be read and, secondly, from lists indicating the beginning (*incipit*) and the ending (*explicit*) of the readings for a particular liturgical celebration.

---

[11] See Antoine Chavasse, 'A Rome, au tournant du Ve siècle, additions et remaniements dans l'ordinaire de la messe', in *Ecclesia Orans* 5 (1988), 25–42, reprinted in *La liturgie de la ville de Rome du Ve au VIIIe siècle: Une liturgie conditionnée par l'organisation de la vie in urbe et extra muros*, Studia Anselmiana 112, Analecta Liturgica 18 (Rome: Centro Studi San Anselmo, 1993), 27–45, at 33–39.

[12] Benedict of Aniane's supplement (see Chapter 6) has the additional Mass formularies for the Sundays after Epiphany, Easter and Pentecost in appendices.

Such lists, to be used with a Bible manuscript, are known as *capitularia* and were compiled for the epistle readings (chosen from the New Testament letters, the Acts of the Apostles or the Old Testament) or for the gospel readings or for both sets of Mass readings. As a subsequent step, the full text of the scriptural readings was copied in a manuscript, either for the epistle (epistolary) or for the gospel (evangelary) or for all the readings in a single Mass lectionary (later to be included in a plenary missal together with the orations and the chants).[13]

While marginal notes seem to have been most widely used at an early stage, Cyrille Vogel cautions that

the various ways of indicating readings for the Eucharist coexisted for centuries, and we must not conceive of a rectilinear evolution from marginal notes through lists of readings to the complete Mass lectionary; actually, some of the full lectionaries are very old.[14]

In fact, the oldest known full lectionaries date from the sixth century[15] and hence are not far removed from the period when readings became fixed for the course of the liturgical year.

Non-Roman Western rites, such as the Gallican, Milanese or Visigothic, show considerable variety in the selection of biblical pericopes for the celebration of Mass; however, they have features in common that distinguish them from the Roman Rite, above all the use of three readings, the first from the Old Testament (usually a prophecy), the second from the New Testament and the third from the gospels. In the Easter season, the Acts of the Apostles and the Book of Revelation were read. On the feast day of a martyr, it was also customary to have a hagiographical reading in the celebration of the Eucharist.[16]

Anton Baumstark postulated that the arrangement of readings in the Eucharistic liturgy of the eighth book of the *Apostolic Constitutions* represented a primitive scheme that was later reduced in most liturgical traditions, except the East Syrian rite where it is still kept. Thus, to two readings from the Old Testament (law and prophets), adopted from the

---

[13] Manuscript sources for liturgical readings come under a variety of names; see Vogel, *Medieval Liturgy*, 314–355, based on the inventories of Theodor Klauser, *Das römische Capitulare Evangeliorum: Texte und Untersuchungen zu seiner ältesten Geschichte*, Liturgiegeschichtliche Quellen und Forschungen 28 (Münster: Aschendorff, 1935).

[14] Vogel, *Medieval Liturgy*, 344.

[15] For the Roman tradition, see the northern Italian fragment from the late sixth century: Munich, Bayerische Staatsbibliothek, Clm 29155.

[16] See Vogel, *Medieval Liturgy*, 303–304.

use of synagogue, were added two readings from the New Testament (epistle or Acts and gospel). In the Roman and Byzantine Rites, only two readings ordinarily remained, and in the Byzantine tradition the non-gospel reading was strictly limited to the New Testament.[17]

Taking issue with Baumstark's hypothesis of a single primitive scheme, Aimé-Georges Martimort argues that there are no unambiguous indications that the Roman Mass ever had a system of three readings.[18] When the *Liber pontificalis* records the liturgical changes introduced by Pope Celestine I (r. 422–433) (see the section on the introit below pp. 180–182), it affirms that the Mass only contained a Pauline epistle and a gospel reading.[19] While this may not be reliable information for the actual pontificate of Celestine, it would most likely reflect Roman practice in the early sixth century, when the book was compiled.[20] The fact that the *Comes*[21] of Würzburg, the oldest source for the Roman lectionary tradition, whose composition dates from as early as c. 600, lists an epistle and a prophecy (in this order) for important feast days of the year such as Christmas and Epiphany provides evidence for two parallel lists of pericopes. According to Antoine Chavasse, while one of these lists prevailed, the non-gospel reading from the other list may have been maintained because of local attachment to a particular tradition.[22] This interpretation would seem to be supported by the fact that the epistolary lists different readings from the same biblical books for a number of feasts, such as St John the Evangelist, St Silvester and Sts Agnes and Agatha.[23]

---

[17] See Anton Baumstark, *Comparative Liturgy*, rev. Bernard Botte, trans. Frank Leslie Cross (Westminster: The Newman Press, 1958), 44.

[18] See Aimé-Georges Martimort, 'À propos du nombre des lectures à la messe', in *Revue des Sciences Religieuses* 58 (1984), 42–51; and *Les lectures liturgiques et leurs livres*, Typologie des sources du Moyen Age occidental 64 (Turnhout: Brepols, 1992).

[19] See *Liber pontificalis*, XLV: ed. Louis Duchesne, *Le Liber pontificalis: Texte, introduction et commentaire*, Bibliothèque des Écoles françaises d'Athènes et de Rome, 2 vols. (Paris: E. Thorin, 1886, 1892), vol. I, 88–89 and 230; ed. Theodor Mommsen, *Libri pontificalis pars prior*, in MGH Gestorum Pontificum Romanorum, vol. I, 94.

[20] Following the hermeneutic principle Nicolas Huyghebaert applied to his study of the *Donation of Constantine*: 'si une légende n'offre que des fictions pour le temps dont elle parle, il lui arrive de révéler des choses intéressantes pour le temps où elle parle'. Nicolas Huyghebaert, 'Une legende de fondation: le *Constitutum Constantini*', in *Le Moyen Âge* 85 (1979), 177–209, at 194.

[21] The word *comes* literally means 'companion' and usually denotes a *capitulare* accompanying a Bible manuscript.

[22] See Antoine Chavasse, 'L'Epistolier romain du Codex de Wurtzbourg, son organisation', in *Revue Bénédictine* 91 (1981), 280–331, at 322.

[23] See German Morin, 'Le plus ancien *comes* ou lectionnaire de l'église romaine', in *Revue Bénédictine* 27 (1910), 41–74, at 46–49.

The preaching of Augustine is sometimes adduced as a source for the use of three Mass readings in North Africa.[24] There are a few instances in his vast corpus of preaching where he refers to three lessons. However, in sermons where Augustine mentions an Old Testament and a non-gospel New Testament reading, it is not clear whether he was preaching at the Eucharist or another liturgical celebration. The most common scheme that can be identified in Augustine's sermons for the Eucharist is apostle – psalm – gospel, with the psalm counted as one of the readings. Where he speaks of an OT lesson, it would seem to replace the apostle.[25]

The presence of both the gradual and alleluia in formularies of the Roman Mass *per annum* is often taken as a vestige of an earlier system of three readings, which would have been separated by the two chants. However, the alleluia is attested later than the hypothetical third reading, and it does not serve as an interlectionary chant in the same way as the gradual and tract.[26] William Mahrt suggests that the function of the alleluia would always have been 'the intensification of the effect of the gradual'.[27] To conclude this discussion, Roman lectionary sources, which begin to flow in c. 600, indicate only two readings for Mass: epistle (which can sometimes be from the Old Testament, from Acts or from Revelation) and gospel, except for special occasions in the liturgical year, such as Ember Saturdays.

The selection of biblical readings for these early sources does not follow a single and systematic pattern. The choice of scripture pericope was often related to the particular church in Rome where the stational

---

[24] See, for instance, Vogel, *Medieval Liturgy*, 304, with reference to Wunibald Roetzer, *Des heiligen Augustinus Schriften als liturgiegeschichtliche Quelle* (Munich: Hueber, 1930).

[25] For instance: 'Apostolum audivimus, psalmum audivimus, evangelium audivimus; consonant omnes divinae lectiones ut spem non in nobis, sed in Domino collocemus'; Augustine, *Sermo* 165,1: PL 38,902; also *Sermo* 176,1: PL 38,950. See Martimort, 'À propos du nombre des lectures à la messe', 45–47; and Gert Partoens, 'Prédication, orthodoxie et liturgie: Les sermons d'Augustine prononcés à Carthage en septembre-octobre 417', in *Prédication et liturgie au Moyen Âge*, ed. Nicole Bériou and Franco Morenzoni, Bibliothèque d'histoire culturelle du Moyen Âge 5 (Turnhout: Brepols, 2008), 23–51, at 27.

[26] See Aimé-Georges Martimort, 'Origine et signification de l'alleluia de la messe romaine', in *Kyriakon: Festschrift Johannes Quasten*, 2 vols. (Münster: Aschendorff, 1970), vol. II, 811–834; and Philippe Bernard, 'Les *Alleluia* mélismatiques dans le chant romain: Recherches sur la genèse de l'*alleluia* de la messe romaine', in *Rivista internazionale di musica sacra* 12 (1991), 286–362.

[27] William Mahrt, 'Gregorian Chant in the Season of Lent', in *Antiphon* 21 (2017), 93–114, at 95.

Mass was celebrated.[28] The surviving documents indicate a complex development that is connected with the progressive organisation of the liturgical year.[29] Cyrille Vogel notes that the strong liturgical seasons offer the earliest evidence for a stable arrangement of readings:

> (1) The period between Septuagesima and Easter, which had been organized before Gregory the Great, formed a fixed and autonomous liturgical unit throughout the Middle Ages ....
>
> (2) All Roman lectionaries agree on Easter Week, Pentecost Week and the intervening six Sundays. After Lent itself, this period contained the oldest section of lessons and remained stable for the future.
>
> (3) Lectionaries diverge for the period between Christmas and the last Sunday after Epiphany (= the Sunday before Septuagesima) and the period after Pentecost (= the Sunday after Pentecost to the last Sunday before Christmas), including Advent.

It is much easier to study the lessons of the *Sanctorale* than those of the *Temporale* since chronological data is far more exact for the former than the latter.[30]

Our understanding of the formative period of the Roman Mass lectionary in the seventh and early eighth century is greatly indebted to the seminal research of William Frere, Theodor Klauser and Antoine Chavasse.[31] These scholars established that epistle and gospel readings developed as two distinct cycles and were recorded in two kinds of liturgical books (according to the different forms mentioned above, ranging from marginal notes in biblical manuscripts to collections of the passages to be read), which remained independent during this period. There was certainly no systematic construction of the lectionary as happened in the liturgical reforms after the Second Vatican Council. At the same time, however, there was some correspondence

---

[28] See Baldovin, *The Urban Character of Christian Worship*, 153–158 and 240. Baldovin offers a few examples: 'The third Saturday of Lent has a station at Sta. Susanna. On this day the story of Susanna (Daniel 13:1–9, 15–17, 19–30, 33–62) is read. Sta. Anastasia is the station for the second Tuesday. This church faced two marked-places [*sic*] and the gold exchange; the gospel about Jesus driving the money-changers from the Temple is read' (ibid., 154).

[29] See the classic work of Thomas J. Talley, *The Origins of the Liturgical Year* (New York: Pueblo, 1986), and the excellent summary of Vogel, *Medieval Liturgy*, 304–314.

[30] Vogel, *Medieval Liturgy*, 349.

[31] See the concise account of Vogel, *Medieval Liturgy*, 349–355.

between the epistolary and the evangelary in the different stages of their development.[32]

The oldest extant lectionary source in which epistle and gospel readings are joined together for a complete cycle of Sundays and feast days is a document that was to assume a crucial role for the subsequent history of the Roman Mass: the late-eighth-century *Comes* of Murbach.[33] Originating from an abbey in Alsace that acquired considerable religious and political importance in the Carolingian age, the extant *capitulare* lists the initial and in many cases also the concluding words of the epistle and gospel readings and is meant to be used in conjunction with a book containing the full text. The temporal and sanctoral cycles are combined into one sequence, beginning with the Vigil of the Nativity of the Lord (24 December). Then follow lists of readings for the Common of Saints, for the ordinations of deacons, priests and bishops, for votive Masses and for Masses for the dead. The calendar of the *Comes* of Murbach is identical with that of the Frankish Gelasian sacramentary from the second half of the eighth century (see Chapter 6), which is based on both Gelasian and Gregorian models, with some Gallican additions. The arrangement of readings has been identified as a Frankish adaptation of earlier Roman epistolary and evangelary types. The fully developed cycle of Sundays and feast days in this 'essentially ... VIII-century Roman system'[34] was adopted in the missals according to the use of the Roman curia of the thirteenth century and is largely the same as in the *Missale Romanum* of 1570.

The *Comes* of Murbach also provides readings for Wednesdays (epistle and gospel) and Fridays (gospel only) in the liturgical year. Many diocesan missals of the later Middle Ages assign ferial pericopes for Wednesdays and Fridays unless the day has a proper Mass formulary. However, they were not included in the plenary missal of the Roman curia and hence are absent from the early printed editions of the *Missale Romanum*.

Chant Books

The earliest Western sources for chant texts in the Mass are of Gallican origin and are associated with scriptural readings. Gennadius notes that

---

[32] See Antoine Chavasse, *Les lectionnaires romains de la messe au VIIe et au VII^ee siècle: Sources et dérivés*, Spicilegii Friburgensis Subsidia 22, 2 vols. (Fribourg Suisse: Editions Universitaire, 1993).

[33] The text was edited by André Wilmart, 'Le Comes de Murbach', in *Revue Bénédictine* 30 (1913), 25–69. See also Vogel, *Medieval Liturgy*, 347 and 349–354.

[34] Vogel, *Medieval Liturgy*, 354.

the priest Musaeus of Marseilles (d. c. 460), at the behest of Bishop Venerius (d. 452), composed a lectionary that included psalm responsories ('responsoria psalmorum capitula'), but it is not clear whether this refers to the Mass or the Office.[35] More secure evidence is offered by the palimpsest Gallican lectionary from the late sixth century (Wolfenbüttel, Herzog-August-Bibliothek, Weissenburg 76), where incipits of chant texts are noted after some of the lessons.[36]

Roman chant books are mentioned in Anglo-Saxon sources from the mid-eighth century: Egbert (d. 766), who received diaconal ordination in Rome shortly before he was made bishop of York (c. 732), speaks of a 'liber antiphonarius' along with a sacramentary, both of which he believed to be works of Gregory the Great brought to England by Augustine of Canterbury a century before.[37] When the council of Clovesho in 747 insists on following the available written exemplars of the Roman church in liturgical celebrations, the 'manner of singing' is specifically included ('in modo cantilenae').[38] These testimonies may indicate that chant books for the celebration of the Eucharist developed, at least to some extent, in parallel with sacramentaries and lectionaries.[39]

However, the oldest available sources of chant texts for the Roman Mass only stem from the late eighth century and were written in northern Francia.[40] According to Joseph Dyer, these manuscripts, which do not contain musical notation, 'were copied in Francia from unnotated models brought from Rome by papal singers who taught the melodies that went with the texts. The originals have long since disappeared, perhaps taken back to Rome after they were copied'.[41] Chant notation is attested

---

[35] Gennadius, *De viris illustribus*, 80: PL 58,1103–1104; see James McKinnon, *Music in Early Christian Literature*, Cambridge Readings in the Literature of Music (Cambridge: Cambridge University Press, 1987, reprinted 1993), 170 (no. 398).

[36] Alban Dold edited the manuscript in 1936 and established correspondence of some of these incipits with the later gradual and offertory repertory; see David Hiley, *Western Plainchant: A Handbook* (Oxford: Clarendon Press, 1993), 296–297.

[37] Egbert of York, *Dialogus ecclesiasticae institutionis*: PL 89,440–442.

[38] Council of Clovesho (747), canon 13: *Councils and Ecclesiastical Documents Relating to Great Britain and Ireland*, ed. Arthur West Haddan and William Stubbs, vol. III (Oxford: Clarendon Press, 1871), 367.

[39] This is the view of Hiley, *Western Plainchant*, 293.

[40] The six oldest manuscripts were published by René-Jean Hesbert, *Antiphonale Missarum Sextuplex* (Paris; Brussels: Vromant, 1935; reprinted Rome: Herder, 1967).

[41] Joseph Dyer, 'Advent and the *Antiphonale Missarum*', in *Lingua mea calamus scribae: Mélanges offerts à madame Marie-Noel Colette par ses collègues, étudiants et amis*, ed. Daniel Saulnier, Katarina Livljanic and Christelle Cazaux-Kowalski, Études grégoriennes 36 (Solesmes: Éditions de Solesmes, 2009), 101–129, at 116.

sporadically in the ninth and fully developed in the tenth century; David Hiley remarks that these instances 'are the earliest musical notation of any kind in Western Europe'.[42] Hiley explains that chant melodies 'had previously been performed, learned, and transmitted without the aid of any written record (and thus they continued, to a considerable extent)'.[43]

The codification of chant melodies most likely resulted from the considerable expansion of their repertory in the Carolingian period (see Chapter 6). The increasing number of chants and the greater stylistic variety of liturgical music (including sequences, tropes and more settings of the ordinary) stretched the capacities for oral transmission and necessitated written aids for memorisation, at least for the purpose of rehearsal, if not performance.[44] Books with a complete cycle of notated chants emerge around the year 900, and the earliest examples are the manuscripts Chartres, Bibliothèque Municipale 47 (hailing from Brittany), Laon, Bibliothèque Municipale 239 and St Gall, Stiftsbibliothek 359.

Early medieval chant books come under different titles, and their actual contents vary significantly. The term *antiphonarius* (also spelled *antefonarius*) could indicate a book with chants for the Divine Office or for the Mass. In Roman use, the word *cantatorium* designates the book for the cantor, in particular the responsory and alleluia or tract.[45] The chant following the reading is known in some early sources as *responsum gradale*, and this name is possibly derived from the practice of the cantor ascending the steps (*gradus*) of the altar or of the ambo to sing.[46] In the early ninth century, Amalarius observes that the Romans use the term *cantatorium* for what the Franks call *gradale*.[47] In fact, manuscripts specifically compiled for the inter-lectionary chants are attested from the late ninth century, such as the above-mentioned St Gall, Stiftsbibliothek

---

[42] Hiley, *Western Plainchant*, 362. The oldest manuscripts with musical notation, in particular those of Chartres, St Gall and Laon, have been published in the series *Paléographie musicale* by the Benedictine monks of Solesmes.

[43] Ibid.   [44] See ibid., 520–521.

[45] See *Ordo Romanus* I, 57: ed. Michel Andrieu, *Les Ordines Romani du haut moyen âge*, 5 vols., Spicilegium Sacrum Lovaniense 11, 23, 24, 28, 29 (Louvain: Peeters, 1931–1961), vol. II, 86.

[46] Helmut Hucke, 'Graduale', in *Ephemerides Liturgicae* 69 (1955), 262–264, offers an alternative reading and argues that *gradalis* is used to distinguish the day offices from the night offices (*nocturnalis*). This use may be linked with the Vulgate title *canticum graduum* ('a song of ascents') for Psalms 119–133, which are assigned to the day hours of the Roman Office.

[47] Amalarius of Metz, *Prologus de ordine antiphonarii*, 17: ed. Jean Michel Hanssens, *Amalarii Episcopi Opera Liturgica Omnia*, Tomus I, Studi e testi 138 (Vatican City: Biblioteca Apostolica Vaticana, 1948), 363 (PL 105,1245).

359. In the same passage, Amalarius also notes that the Romans, unlike
the Franks, employ separate books for responsories (*responsoriale*) and
for antiphons (*antiphonarius*).[48] This information corresponds with Pope
Paul I writing to the Frankish King Pippin in 760 that the books he was
able to send him included an *antiphonale* and a *responsale*.[49] While the
precise import of Amalarius' comments is not wholly clear, he confirms
that in Rome chant books were organised according to distinct genres, for
use in both the Mass and Office. In Frankish practice, however, the chants
for the Mass were collected separately from those for the Office. The book
in which the Mass chants were gathered eventually came to be known as
the 'gradual' or 'Mass antiphoner'.[50]

Ordines

An invaluable source for our understanding of early medieval Western
liturgy is the collection known as *Ordines Romani*. The title is an early
modern coinage and has been widely employed since Jean Mabillon's
edition of fifteen *ordines* in his *Musaeum Italicum* of 1689. The term
ordo, which can be rendered as 'order' or 'arrangement' has a broad
range of meanings in the Middle Ages and can refer to a particular group
or class within society or to the clergy and its distinct ranks. The Latin
Vulgate uses the word for the proper ordering of worship or the correct
disposition of its ministers in the Old and New Testament.[51] The *Ordines
Romani* describe actual rites and serve as practical instructions for actors
in a variety of liturgical celebrations, including Mass, Divine Office,
baptism and other sacraments as well as sacramentals (to use the later,
scholastic distinction). According to the classification of Cyrille Vogel, an
ordo is a liturgical book in the proper sense, like a sacramentary or
lectionary, because it is written or compiled for use in divine worship.
Ordines articulate ritual prescriptions for carrying out a sacred action, as

[48] Ibid.
[49] Pope Paul I to Pippin: MGH, Epistolae Merowingici et Karolini aevi, Tomus III, VIII.
Codex Carolinus, no. 24, 529.
[50] See Hiley, *Western Plainchant*, 296–297 and 304. See also Michel Huglo, *Les livres de
chant liturgique* (Turnhout: Brepols, 1988).
[51] See, for instance, Ex 28:17; 28:20; 39:10; 39:13; 40:21; 40:23; Lev 17:15; Num 7:5; Deut
15:2; Ps 109:4; Lk 1:8; 1 Cor 14:40; 15:23; Col 2:5. For these references, I am indebted to
Joanne M. Pierce and John F. Romano, 'The *Ordo Missae* of the Roman Rite: Historical
Background', in *A Commentary on the Order of Mass of the Roman Missal*, ed. Edward
Foley et al. (Collegeville: Liturgical Press, 2011), 3–34, at 7.

proper to the time when a specific manuscript was produced and as long as it continued to be used as such. Recent research on early medieval pontifical manuscripts has questioned the clear-cut taxonomy of twentieth-century liturgical scholarship, and Helen Gittos rightly cautions: 'Given the oral nature of the transmission of liturgy in the Middle Ages it is even more important than ever to ask: Why were texts written down?'[52] The written record of a liturgical rite may have served didactic purposes, may have been instrumental in promoting reform or may have been intended to consolidate episcopal authority. Some scriptoria and scribes may even have had an antiquarian interest in collecting obsolete liturgical forms.[53] More commonly, however, *ordines* were written for pragmatic reasons and were copied, adapted and modified while being in liturgical use. For the history of the liturgy's actual performance (as well as its social and cultural impact) *ordines* are more informative than sacramentaries because they offer us ritual 'stage directions'.

The earliest manuscripts of the *Ordines Romani* from the Carolingian period do not originate from the city of Rome but were written in Frankish territory and document a process of reception and adaptation of the Roman liturgy.[54] *Ordo Romanus Primus* offers detailed instructions for the pope's solemn stational liturgy in Easter week and is in fact the oldest available description of the ritual shape of the Roman Mass. Michel Andrieu's critical edition from the mid-twentieth century documents the complex textual tradition of *Ordo Romanus I*. While the manuscript evidence, starting in the early ninth century, is Frankish, the document has been established as a record of the Roman church and its liturgy. Andrieu argues for a redaction of the document not long after the pontificate of Sergius I (r. 687–701) but before 750, when there is evidence for the use of *Ordo Romanus I* in Francia.[55] A *terminus post quem* can be established by the inclusion of the *Agnus Dei* to be sung during the fraction of the Eucharistic hosts, as introduced by Pope Sergius according

[52] Helen Gittos, 'Researching the History of Rites', in *Understanding Medieval Liturgy: Essays in Interpretation*, ed. Helen Gittos and Sarah Hamilton (London; New York: Routledge, 2018), 13–37, at 20.

[53] The discussion on the emergence of pontificals as distinct manuscripts from the late ninth century onwards is instructive in this regard. See Sarah Hamilton, 'Interpreting Diversity: Excommunication Rites in the Tenth and Eleventh Centuries', in *Understanding Medieval Liturgy*, 125–175, at 126–127.

[54] See the comprehensive survey of Vogel, *Medieval Liturgy*, 135–247.

[55] See Andrieu, vol. II, 38–51.

to his biography in the *Liber pontificalis*.[56] The codification of ritual for the papal stational liturgy would thus be contemporary with the systematic organisation of sacramentaries, lectionaries and chant books.

John F. Romano notes that the intention for recording such an elaborate ceremonial instruction is not entirely transparent, and he relates *Ordo Romanus I* not only to the liturgical developments but also to the political and social contexts of Sergius' pontificate.[57] The document displays two major concerns: 'first, to regulate the relationships of the ministers of the nascent papal court with one another and the people of Rome; and second, to keep track of and protect the precious liturgical furnishings employed in the liturgy'.[58] The first preoccupation with rank and precedence reflects the increasing social and political power of the papacy over the city in the late seventh century, when Rome still belonged to the Byzantine Empire.[59] The second preoccupation with the handling of valuable objects grants us insight into the material provisions for the papal liturgy at the time.

While Romano's broadening of perspective advances our understanding of this important document, there is little plausibility in his claim that 'it is misleading to assume that [*Ordo Romanus I*] was initially intended as a set of written instructions on how to execute a Mass', since '[t]here was no need to commit instructions to writing for the majority of medieval Masses'.[60] The papal Mass described in *Ordo Romanus I* is a rich and complex ritual for festive occasions in the liturgical year; it requires proficiency on the part of the liturgical actors and considerable logistical effort. Hence, it would seem plausible that a master of ceremonies compiled a written record and aide-mémoire that served to train the sacred ministers and to make the material preparations for the elaborate ceremonial. In fact, Romano also suggests that *Ordo Romanus I* was

---

[56] *Liber pontificalis*, LXXXVI: ed. Duchesne, vol. 1, 376; ed. Mommsen, 215.

[57] See John F. Romano, 'The Fates of Liturgies: Towards a History of the First Roman Ordo', in *Antiphon* 11 (2007), 43–77, at 46–50.

[58] Ibid., 49.

[59] See Paolo Delogu, 'The Papacy, Rome and the Wider World in the Seventh and Eighth Centuries', in *Early Medieval Rome and the Christian West: Essays in Honour of Donald A. Bullough*, ed. Julia M. H. Smith, The Medieval Mediterranean 28 (Leiden; Boston: Brill, 2000), 197–220; also Thomas F. X. Noble, *The Republic of St. Peter: The Birth of the Papal State, 680–825*, The Middle Ages Series (Philadelphia: University of Pennsylvania Press, 1984).

[60] Ibid., 49.

composed by the *ordinator* (literally, 'orderer'), an official at the papal court in charge of liturgical ceremonies.[61]

The ritual directions provided for the solemn stational liturgy are detailed but by no means comprehensive, and many questions that would interest us must be left unanswered. Nonetheless, *Ordo Romanus I* is a historical document of the greatest significance and, with hindsight, proved to be foundational for the further development of Western liturgy.

STATIONAL LITURGY ACCORDING TO *ORDO ROMANUS I*

Several manuscripts of the *ordo* give the title 'Here begins the order of ecclesiastical ministry of the Roman Church, or how Mass is celebrated'.[62] Accordingly, the document begins with an account of the seven ecclesiastical regions of the city of Rome and their officials. The fact that these officials have a particular ministry in the solemn Mass of the Roman pontiff gives this liturgical assembly an ecclesiological dimension: the stational liturgy can be understood as a representation of the Roman church, a hierarchical community led by the pope both as supreme pastor and civil administrator of the city.[63] The text goes on to outline the ritual functions exercised by the officials of each ecclesiastical region in the seven stational liturgies of the pope in Easter week, beginning with the Mass for Easter Sunday held in St Mary Major's (OR I, 5, 7 and 15–18).[64] This description does not just apply to the papal liturgy on this particular occasion or in this particular church, but sets a pattern for the cycle of stational Masses throughout the year.

---

[61] This office is mentioned only once in *Liber pontificalis*, XC: ed. Duchesne, 390; ed. Mommsen, 223: a certain Sergius held it under Pope Constantine (r. 708–715). Duchesne identifies the *ordinator* with a master of ceremonies (ibid., 394, n. 11).

[62] 'Incipit ordo ecclesiastici ministerii romanae ecclesiae vel qualiter missa caelebratur'; ed. Andrieu, vol. II, 67. English translation by John F. Romano, *Liturgy and Society in Early Medieval Rome*, Church, Faith and Culture in the Medieval West (Farnham: Ashgate, 2014), 229–248. An earlier translation, published before Andrieu's critical edition of the text, can be found in E. G. C. F. Atchley, *Ordo Romanus Primus* (London: Moring, 1905), 117–149.

[63] See Tommaso di Carpegna Falconieri, *Il clero di Roma nel medioevo: Istituzioni e politica cittadina (secoli VIII–XIII)* (Roma: Viella, 2002), 195–199 and 235–237; also Victor Saxer, 'L'utilisation de la liturgie dans l'espace urbain et suburbain: l'exemple de Rome', in *Actes du XIᵉ congrès international d'archéologie chrétienne (Lyon-Vienne-Grenoble-Genève et Aoste, 21–28 septembre 1986)*, Collection de l'École française de Rome 123 (Rome: École française de Rome, 1989), 917–1033.

[64] In the following, references to *Ordo Romanus I* are made as OR I in the body of the chapter, based on the critical text edited by Andrieu, vol. II, 67–108.

A Synopsis of the Papal Mass in the Early Eighth Century

At daybreak, the pope's entourage assembles at his residence in the Lateran palace, and from there the procession, with the pope at the end riding on horseback, advances to the stational church allocated for the celebration of Mass on the day.

On arrival at the stational church, the pope goes to the *secretarium*, the equivalent of the modern sacristy, where the preparations for Mass have been made. The pope is vested with the help of his assistants, lectors and cantors are assigned their ministries, the pope gives a sign for the singing of the introit with its psalm, the thurible is lit and incense is added. When these preliminaries are concluded, as soon as the choir (*schola cantorum*), placed in front of the altar on either side, starts to sing, the procession enters the nave of the church, with the pope being preceded by a subdeacon *sequens* (that is, designated to the assistance of the pope)[65] carrying the thurible (*thymiamaterium*) and seven acolytes with candles (*cereostata*), representing the seven ecclesiastical regions of the city. The attending bishops and priests have already taken their respective places in the *presbyterium*.

Having reached the steps leading up to the altar, the pope indicates to the head of the choir to finish the psalm with the doxology, then prays in silence until the repetition of the introit and ascends to the altar. The pope kisses the gospel book and the altar, and repairs to his seat in the centre of the apse. The choir sings the *Kyrie* and *Gloria* (which is intoned by the pope), the pope salutes the people for the first time ('Pax vobis' – 'Peace be with you') and prays the collect of the day.

The regional subdeacon ascends to the ambo to read the epistle, which is followed by the gradual response and the alleluia (or tract, according to the liturgical season). The deacon carries the gospel book in solemn procession with incense and candles to the ambo, where he proclaims the gospel, assisted by the subdeacon. No homily or creed is indicated.[66]

The pope's liturgical greeting and invitation to pray (which may have served at some point as an introduction to intercessions) is immediately followed by the preparing of the altar and the offertory. The pope receives

---

[65] The particular ministries of subdeacons in the papal Mass are discussed by Armando Cuva, 'Pagine di storia del ministero suddiaconale alla messa papale', in *Fons vivus – Miscellanea liturgica in memoria di don E.M. Vismara*, ed. Armando Cuva (Zurich: PaS, 1971), 287–314.

[66] On preaching at the papal stational Mass, see below. The creed only became part of the papal Mass in the year 1014 (see Chapter 7).

the offerings of bread and wine from notable laity (men and women separately) and from clergy, with the assistance of his liturgical ministers. This elaborately described ritual is accompanied by the singing of the offertory chant. No prayers over the offerings on the altar are mentioned in the manuscript tradition, with the exception of St Gall, Stiftsbibliothek, ms. 614 and ms. 140 (which is dependent on the former).[67] Both codices include the ecphonesis, 'Per omnia saecula [saeculorum]', which would indicate the use of the *oratio super oblata* from the Gregorian sacramentaries. The same two manuscripts also stand out for noting the preface dialogue.[68]

All the clergy bow for the singing of the *Sanctus*. Then the pope alone stands upright to pray the canon. He says the prayer with arms extended, but no further ritual gestures are indicated. During the doxology ('Per ipsum et cum ipso' – 'Through him and with him') the archdeacon comes up to the altar and elevates the chalice, while the pope touches its side with the Eucharistic bread.

The Lord's Prayer with the embolism follows. After the blessing 'Pax Domini sit semper vobiscum' ('May the peace of the Lord be with you always'), the pope takes a piece of the consecrated host from the previous Mass and immerses it in the chalice. He also breaks off some of the newly consecrated offerings for performing this particular rite at the next Mass.

Then, while the kiss of peace is exchanged, the pope begins with the fraction of the Eucharistic bread, which is continued by his assistants. During the lengthy rite of fraction, the *Agnus Dei* is sung. Meanwhile, the pope goes back to his seat and Holy Communion is brought to him there

---

[67] Michel Andrieu maintained that the collection St Gall, Stiftsbibliothek, ms. 614 contains an earlier, shorter redaction of *Ordo Romanus I*; see *Les Ordines Romani*, vol. II, 4–64. This theory has been widely accepted; see Vogel, *Medieval Liturgy*, 159–160. However, Romano, 'The Fates of Liturgies', 51–54, argues that 'there was no shorter redaction of OR I as Andrieu envisioned it: St Gall, Stiftsbibliothek, ms. 614 contains a copy of a mutilated manuscript, not a different Roman version of OR I. Its many divergences from the rest of the manuscript tradition are better explained as the interpolations of a Frankish scribe rather than evidence of a more pristine state of OR I'.

[68] See *Ordo Romanus I*, 87: ed. Andrieu, vol. II, 97. Josef Andreas Jungmann, Mario Righetti and Philippe Bernard have argued for the inclusion of the *oratio super oblata*, while Antoine Chavasse contends that it was not part of the papal stational liturgy. See Chavasse, 'A Rome, au tournant du Ve siècle, additions et remaniements dans l'ordinaire de la messe', in *La liturgie de la ville de Rome du Ve au VIIIe siècle*, 36–37, and Franck Quoëx, 'Ritual and Sacred Chant in the *Ordo Romanus* Primus (Seventh–Eighth Century)', in *Antiphon* 22 (2018), 199–219, at 211. This is a translation by Zachary Thomas of 'Ritualité et chant sacré dans l'*Ordo Romanus Primus* (VII–VIIIème siècle)', in *Aevum* 76 (2002), 253–265.

by deacons. The communion of the clergy and of the people follows, with the pope giving the host to a number of clergy and high-ranking laity; this is accompanied by the singing of the communion psalm.

When communion is finished, the pope goes to the altar for the concluding prayer. The deacon then dismisses the people with 'Ite, missa est' ('Go, this is the dismissal'). The word *missa*, which is related to *mittere* ('to send'), gave the Eucharist its name in the Roman tradition.[69] While its original meaning is dismissal, Klaus Gamber has argued that by the sixth century it was understood in the sense of sacrifice or offering, as the Eucharist was called in both East and West (*sacrificium*, προσφορά, *qurbana*).[70] After blessing the various orders of assisting clergy, the pope returns in solemn procession to the sacristy.

Imperial Ceremonial and Sacred Simplicity

Even though this schematic overview, focusing on the pope, barely renders justice to the intricacies of the elaborate ritual, we can discern two distinct cultural forces at work in the papal stational Mass: on the one hand, the ceremonial of the imperial court and administration and, on the other hand, the sacred (or hieratic) simplicity of the Roman Eucharist. Imperial ceremonial is evident especially in the procession of the pope on horseback with his court from the Lateran palace to the stational church and in the intricate entrance rite, wherein ecclesiastical officials carried before the pope a thurible and seven candles, which were signs of honour reserved to the emperor and senior magistrates. Some of this ceremonial is attached to the proclamation of the gospel: the evangelary is carried in solemn procession, with lights and incense, to the elevated ambo.

In an influential paper with the title 'The Genius of the Roman Rite', Edmund Bishop spoke of the 'simplicity' of the Roman Mass with specific reference to the early forms of the *Ordo Romanus*.[71] Such a

---

[69] See Franz Joseph Dölger, 'Zu den Zeremonien der Meßliturgie, III: *Ite missa est* in kultur- und sprachgeschichtlicher Bedeutung', in *Antike und Christentum* 6 (1940), 81–132; Christine Mohrmann, '*Missa*', in *Études sur le latin des chrétiens*, 4 vols., Storia e letteratura 65, 87, 103, 143 (Rome: Edizioni di Storia e Letteratura, 1961–1977), vol. III, 351–376 (originally published in *Vigiliae Christianae* 12 [1958], 67–92).

[70] See Klaus Gamber, *Missa Romensis: Beiträge zur frühen römischen Liturgie und zu den Anfängen des Missale Romanum*, Studia Patristica et Liturgica 3 (Regensburg: Pustet, 1970), 183–186.

[71] Edmund Bishop, 'The Genius of the Roman Rite', in *Liturgica Historica: Papers on the Liturgy and Religious Life of the Western Church* (Oxford: Clarendon Press, 1918), 1–19, at 8–12.

characterisation of the complex ceremonial displayed in the papal stational Mass may be surprising, even if one recalls that the comparison is not made with de-ritualised modern forms of worship but with the historical Byzantine and non-Roman Western rites. However, Bishop rightly notes that when we come to the core of the rite – the Eucharist – the atmosphere seems remarkably different: 'It may be said that with this [*sc.* the proclamation of the gospel] the ceremonial parts of the old Roman mass are over, just as the sacrifice is about to begin'.[72] In particular, the Eucharistic prayer is said by the pope at the altar, with few liturgical gestures: signs of the cross over the offerings are indicated in Gelasian and Gregorian sacramentaries, perhaps dating back to the middle of the seventh century (see Chapter 6); however, the elevation of the species and profound bows are added only later in the course of the Middle Ages. At the heart of the solemn papal liturgy, ritual simplicity prevails.

THE ROLE OF CHANT IN THE MASS

Ordo Romanus I brings into relief the fundamental role of chant in the celebration of Mass. Music does not simply serve as an ornament or embellishment but has a proper liturgical function. The choir (*schola cantorum*) fulfils a distinctive ministry in singing the ordinary chants (*Kyrie, Gloria, Sanctus-Benedictus* and *Agnus Dei*) on behalf of the worshipping assembly, and the proper chants that are generally drawn from Scripture (introit, gradual, alleluia or tract, offertory and communion), which, together with the prayers and readings, form an integral part of the Mass formulary.

The Chants of the Ordinary

While it is generally assumed that the ordinary of the Mass was originally sung by or at least involved the participation of the assembly, the earliest available sources that offer us a full picture of the ritual shape of the Roman Eucharist, in the form of the papal stational liturgy, assign these chants to a group of trained singers, known as the *schola cantorum*. The Western chant repertory contains a number of simple melodies for the ordinary chants that could well have been sung by the people. The evidence for such simpler chants appears later than for more sophisticated

[72] Ibid., 10.

pieces. This is not surprising, if one considers that most of the early extant chant manuscripts were composed for the use of the *schola cantorum* and for individual cantors. Chants to be sung by the assembly may have been transmitted in oral tradition, without the need for writing them down.

The origins of the *Kyrie eleison* ('Lord, have mercy') are not entirely clear. Building on observations by Edmund Bishop, Bernard Capelle saw in the *Kyrie* a remainder of the supplicatory litany known as *Deprecatio Gelasii*, named after Pope Gelasius. According to Capelle, Gelasius made this litany part of the entrance rites of the Mass. Gregory the Great later reduced the litany to the acclamation 'Kyrie eleison' and added 'Christe eleison'.[73] Antoine Chavasse refined this thesis by arguing that the *Deprecatio Gelasii* originally served as a substitute for the general intercessions (*orationes sollemnes*) that preceded the preparation of the altar at the offertory. It was only later, perhaps in the pontificate of Gregory the Great, that this litany was moved to the beginning of the Mass. According to Chavasse, the second collect that is attested in the Old Gelasian Sacramentary originally served as the concluding prayer of the litany and was kept even when the litany itself was discarded.[74]

More recently, Paul de Clerck and John F. Baldovin have argued that the *Kyrie* derived from the rogational litanies that formed part of the procession towards the stational church of the day. This type of litanic prayer, modelled on the *ektene* from Constantinopolitan stational practice, ended in a threefold 'Kyrie eleison'. Moreover, in Roman stational processions, antiphonal psalmody preceded the litany. When from the end of the sixth century the litany fell out of use on ordinary days, only the introit and the *Kyrie* remained after the pattern of the earlier stational practice.[75]

The earliest tangible information about the *Kyrie* in the Roman Mass actually stems from southern Gaul.[76] The council of Vaison in 529, under the presidency of Caesarius of Arles (d. 542), decreed its introduction into the Mass and the Office, following the example of Rome, Italy and the East. Only the Greek invocation 'Qurieleison' [*sic*] is mentioned and no

---

[73] See Bernard Capelle, 'Le Kyrie de la messe et le pape Gélase', in *Travaux liturgiques de doctrine et d'histoire*, 3 vols. (Louvain: Centre Liturgique, 1955–1967), vol. II, 116–134 (originally published in *Révue bénédictine* 46 [1934], 126–144).

[74] See Chavasse, 'A Rome, au tournant du Ve siècle, additions et remaniements dans l'ordinaire de la messe', in *La liturgie de la ville de Rome du Ve au VIIIe siècle*, 33–39.

[75] See Paul de Clerck, *La prière universelle dans le liturgies latines anciennes: temoignages patristiques et textes liturgiques*, Liturgiewissenschaftliche Quellen und Forschungen 63 (Münster: Aschendorff, 1977), 282–295. De Clerck's argument is further advanced by Baldovin, *The Urban Character of Christian Worship*, 243–247.

[76] See Chavasse, 'A Rome, au tournant du Ve siècle, additions et remaniements dans l'ordinaire de la messe', 27–28; and Hiley, *Western Plainchant*, 151–152.

indication is given of the form in which it is sung.[77] In 598, however, Pope Gregory the Great notes in a letter to John, bishop of Syracuse, that in Rome the *Kyrie* is not sung after the Greek manner, that is, by the whole congregation, but in alternation between clerics (presumably the *schola cantorum*) and people. Moreover, the Roman practice is to sing 'Christe eleison' as often as 'Kyrie eleison', while the Greeks do not have the invocation to Christ. Gregory also remarks that in daily Masses other verses, which he implies are sung at special occasions, are omitted.[78]

In *Ordo Romanus I*, the *Kyrie* (no invocation to Christ mentioned) is reserved to the schola, and its chanting is repeated until the pope gives the sign to conclude (OR I, 52). *Ordo Romanus IV*, a Frankish adaptation of *Ordo Romanus I* dating from the late eighth century, testifies to the ninefold structure of the *Kyrie* that would later become canonical:[79]

Kyrie eleison	Lord, have mercy
Kyrie eleison	Lord, have mercy
Kyrie eleison	Lord, have mercy
Christe eleison	Christ, have mercy
Christe eleison	Christ, have mercy
Christe eleison	Christ, have mercy
Kyrie eleison	Lord, have mercy
Kyrie eleison	Lord, have mercy
Kyrie eleison	Lord, have mercy

The opening lines of the *Gloria in excelsis* repeat the hymn of praise of the angels who announced the birth of Christ to the shepherds in Bethlehem (Lk 2:14). The *Gloria* originated in Greek as an example of a

---

[77] Council of Vaison (529), can. 3: CCL 148A,79. Baldovin, *The Urban Character of Christian Worship*, 246, argues that the council of Vaison had the stational practice of Constantinople in mind and introduced a Western form of the litany known as *synapte*. The 'Sanctus' mentioned in can. 3 would thus would not be the 'Holy, Holy, Holy . . .' of the Eucharistic prayer, but the Greek *Trisagion* ('Holy God, Holy Strong, Holy Immortal, have mercy on us').

[78] Gregory the Great, *Ep.* IX, 26: MGH, Gregorii I Papae Registrum Epistolarum, vol. II, 59.

[79] *Ordo Romanus IV*, 20: ed. Andrieu, vol. II, 159. The invocations are sung in alternation by the *schola* and the *regionarii* (originally the clerics from the ecclesiastical region of Rome that offered liturgical service on a particular day). Another Frankish recension of *Ordo Romanus I* from around the same time, *Ordo Romanus XV*, 16: ed. Andrieu, vol. III, 98, confirms the ninefold structure of the *Kyrie* but without mentioning 'Christe eleison'.

'private psalm' that follows the model of the biblical psalm – a genre that was popular in the early Christian centuries.[80] The hymn is widely attested as part of morning prayer in the cathedral office of the Greek-speaking East by the late fourth century.[81] According to the *Liber pontificalis*, Pope Symmachus (r. 498–514) decreed that the *Gloria* was to be sung in Masses on Sundays and the feast days of martyrs.[82] The entry about Pope Telesphorus (r. c. 126–c. 137) introducing the *Gloria* into the Midnight Mass at Christmas is anachronistic for the second century but might help to shed light on sixth-century practice. The long version of the *Liber pontificalis* (P), which is attested in most manuscripts, does not have the restriction that under Telesphorus the *Gloria* was sung 'tantum noctu natale Domini' ('only in the night of the birth of the Lord'). Louis Duchesne sees here the work of the second redaction of the *Liber pontificalis*, which breaks off in the middle of the brief pontificate of Pope Silverius (r. 536–537) and would have been compiled not long after that date. By the 540s at the latest, the *Gloria* would have been in wider use and for this reason the redactor dropped the qualifying note of the earlier version.[83]

The earliest available Latin version of the *Gloria* is found in the late-seventh-century Irish collection of texts for the Divine Office, known as the Antiphonary of Bangor. The wording of the hymn shows some differences from the version used in the Roman Mass, and there are still textual variants in some of the earliest notated manuscripts from the tenth century onwards.[84] The *Gloria*'s structure is Trinitarian: its first stanza is addressed to God the Father, its second stanza to God the Son and the Holy Spirit is included in the final doxology:

[80] Bernard Capelle, 'Le texte du "Gloria in excelsis"', in *Travaux liturgiques de doctrine et d'histoire*, vol. II, 176–191 (originally published in *Revue d'histoire ecclesiastique* 44 [1949], 439–457), argues that the Δόξα ἐν ὑψίστοις Θεῷ found in the fifth-century *Codex Alexandrinus* preserves the authentic text (which is very close to the received Latin version) and that the text of *Apostolic Constitutions* VII,47 is the result of Arianising interpolations.

[81] See Robert F. Taft, *The Liturgy of the Hours in East and West: The Origins of the Divine Office and Its Meaning for Today*, 2nd rev. ed. (Collegeville: Liturgical Press, 1993), 45, 55 and *passim*. The hymn is still used in *Orthros* (Matins) of the Byzantine Rite.

[82] *Liber pontificalis*, LIII: ed. Duchesne, vol. I, 263; ed. Mommsen, 125.

[83] *Liber pontificalis*, IX: ed. Duchesne, vol. I, 129; ed. Mommsen, 12. See Duchesne's observations, ibid., 130, n. 5. Note, however, that Duchesne's redactional hypothesis is not generally accepted and that recent scholarly contributions offer different models for the textual history of the *Liber pontificalis*; see Matthias Simperl, 'Beobachtungen und Überlegungen zur frühen Redaktionsgeschichte des Liber pontificalis', in *Das Buch der Päpste – Liber pontificalis: Ein Schlüsseldokument europäischer Geschichte*, Römische Quartalschrift. Supplementband 67 (Freiburg i. Br.: Herder, 2020), 52–77.

[84] See the synoptic table in Frederick B. Warren, *The Antiphonary of Bangor: An Early Irish Manuscript in the Ambrosian Library at Milan*, Henry Bradshaw Society 10, 2 vols. (London: Harrison and Sons, 1893–1895), vol. II, 76–77.

Gloria in excelsis Deo.
Et in terra pax hominibus bonae voluntatis.
Laudamus te.
Benedicimus te.
Adoramus te.
Glorificamus te.
Gratias agimus tibi propter magnam gloriam tuam.
Domine Deus, Rex caelestis,
Deus Pater omnipotens.

Domine Fili unigenite, Iesu Christe.
Domine Deus, Agnus Dei, Filius Patris.
Qui tollis peccata mundi, miserere nobis.
Qui tollis peccata mundi, suscipe deprecationem nostram.
Qui sedes ad dexteram Patris, miserere nobis.

Quoniam tu solus Sanctus,
Tu solus Dominus,
Tu solus Altissimus, Iesu Christe.
Cum Sancto Spiritu,
in gloria Dei Patris.
Amen.

Glory to God in the highest,
and on earth peace to people of good will.
We praise you,
we bless you,
we adore you,
we glorify you,
we give you thanks for your great glory,
Lord God, heavenly King,
O God almighty Father.

Lord Jesus Christ, Only Begotten Son,
Lord God, Lamb of God, Son of the Father,
who take away the sins of the world, have mercy on us;
who take away the sins of the world, receive our prayer;
who are seated at the right hand of the Father, have mercy on us.

For you alone are the Holy One,
you alone are the Lord,
you alone are the Most High, Jesus Christ,
with the Holy Spirit,
in the glory of God the Father.
Amen.

Ordo Romanus I and the documents dependent on it indicate that the *Gloria* was intoned by the pope and continued by the choir (OR I, 53). However, some of the early musical settings of the *Gloria* are quite plain and could at some point have been sung by the congregation.[85]

The origins of the *Sanctus-Benedictus* and its insertion into the Roman Eucharistic prayer have been discussed in the previous chapters. In the Roman Mass, the *Sanctus* appears as an acclamation in which the people joined in, and this use still echoed in Charlemagne's *Admonitio generalis* (see Chapter 6). The chant numbered as XVIII in the early-twentieth-century Vatican editions, which simply continues one of the preface tones, could have been sung by a regular congregation without difficulties.[86] Against this background, the indication in OR I, 87 that the regional subdeacons sing the *Sanctus* may be specific to the solemn papal Mass and possibly involve a more elaborate musical setting.

> Sanctus, Sanctus, Sanctus Dominus Deus Sabaoth.
> Pleni sunt cæli et terra gloria tua.
> Hosanna in excelsis.
> Benedictus, qui venit in nomine Domini.
> Hosanna in excelsis.
>
> Holy, Holy, Holy Lord God of hosts.
> Heaven and earth are full of your glory.
> Hosanna in the highest.
> Blessed is he who comes in the name of the Lord.
> Hosanna in the highest.

The *Agnus Dei* is addressed to Christ and takes up John the Baptist's exclamation, 'Behold, the Lamb of God, who takes away the sin of the world' (Jn 1:29). As has already been mentioned, Pope Sergius I is recorded to have introduced the chant to be sung during the Eucharistic fraction 'by the clergy and the people', perhaps with the clergy invoking 'Agnus Dei, qui tollis peccata mundi' and the people responding 'miserere nobis'.[87] While OR I, 99 and 105 only mention clergy singing the chant, the existence of settings such as Vatican XVIII, which is a straightforward musical continuation of the dialogue 'Pax Domini sit semper vobiscum' – 'Et cum spiritu tuo', may imply popular participation. While the earliest material witnesses for this *Agnus Dei* setting date from the twelfth

---

[85] See Hiley, *Western Plainchant*, 156–157.   [86] See ibid., 161–165.
[87] *Liber pontificalis*, LXXXVI: ed. Duchesne, vol. I, 376; ed. Mommsen, 215.

century, it is likely to be much older.[88] *Ordo Romanus III*, a Romano-Frankish supplement to *Ordo Romanus I* from the late eighth century, specifies that the schola will sing the *Agnus Dei* until the actual fraction is completed.[89] Thus, the original purpose of the chant is to accompany a particular liturgical action, in a manner similar to the introit or communion. Several Frankish sources from the ninth/tenth century show the *Agnus Dei* being sung at the *pax* or during communion. This shift coincides with the introduction of small, unleavened hosts that made the rite of fraction superfluous. While previously the *Agnus Dei* was repeated as often as needed to accompany this rite, the invocations were limited to the symbolic number three, and around the turn of the millennium we find the first instances of the final petition being changed to 'dona nobis pacem', no doubt because the chant was now associated with the kiss of peace.[90]

> Agnus Dei, qui tollis peccata mundi: miserere nobis.
> Agnus Dei, qui tollis peccata mundi: miserere nobis.
> Agnus Dei, qui tollis peccata mundi: dona nobis pacem.
>
> Lamb of God, you take away the sins of the world: have mercy on us.
> Lamb of God, you take away the sins of the world: have mercy on us.
> Lamb of God, you take away the sins of the world: grant us peace.

The Proper Chants

As has been discussed above, the proper chants of the Roman Mass came to be collected in the book known as the gradual or (Mass) antiphoner. While we have a partial understanding of how the variety of sacramentaries and lectionaries developed, the gradual presents us with the problem that its first specimens appear almost fully developed. Joseph Dyer

---

[88] See Hiley, *Western Plainchant*, 149, pointing to Peter Wagner, *Einführung in die gregorianischen Melodien: Ein Handbuch der Choralwissenschaft. Dritter Teil: Gregorianische Formenlehre: Eine choralische Stilkunde* (Leipzig: Breitkopf & Härtel, 1925), 448–449.

[89] *Ordo Romanus III*, 2: ed. Andrieu, vol. II, 131–132.

[90] See Josef A. Jungmann, *Missarum sollemnia: Eine genetische Erklärung der römischen Messe*, 2 vol., 5th ed. (Wien: Herder, 1962), vol. II, 419–421; and Hiley, *Western Plainchant*, 165–168.

observes that the earliest available Frankish sources from the late eighth
century offer a largely complete repertory of proper chants for the
temporal and the sanctoral cycles of the liturgical year. No previous forms
of noting chant, such as marginal notes or lists as in the case of the Mass
readings, have come down to us in the Roman tradition. Even so, some
kind of written record was needed, as can be inferred from the frequent
variations on the biblical text in the proper chants: words are added,
grammatical constructions are modified or different phrases are combined
into a cento.[91] As for the choice of chant texts, Dyer notes:

> Apart from a few notable examples of coordination like the Advent-Christmas
> block of Propers, the chants of the Mass seem to have been organised 'vertically'
> by genre in smaller or larger groups covering specific portions of the liturgical year
> rather than 'horizontally' as groups of diverse chants for a specific liturgical
> celebration.[92]

Such a grouping of chants by genre for particular seasons might suggest
the existence of smaller booklets that were at some stage combined into a
book for the entire liturgical year.

As already noted in my discussion of the *Kyrie*, the introit is believed to
have developed from the practice of antiphonal psalmody preceding the
litany in stational processions. According to the *Liber pontificalis*, Pope
Celestine I decreed that psalms should be sung 'before the sacrifice (*ante
sacrificium*)', which had not been done before, and the second edition of
the *Liber pontificalis* adds here that the psalms should be sung alternately
by all.[93] This note has commonly been interpreted as a reference to the
introit chant as early as Amalarius and Hrabanus Maurus in the ninth
century. Peter Jeffery challenged this reading and argued that *sacrificium*
refers to the Eucharistic liturgy in the strict sense, beginning with the
offertory. Hence, the passage in question might instead refer to the

---

[91] See Joseph Dyer, Review of James McKinnon, *The Advent Project*, in *Early Music
History* 20 (2001), 279–309, at 280–282.

[92] Ibid., 281–282.

[93] 'Hic multa constituta fecit et constituit ut psalmi David CL ante sacrificium psalli
antefanatim ex omnibus, quod ante non fiebat, nisi tantum epistula beati Pauli apostoli
recitabatur et sanctum euangelium, et sic missas fiebant.' *Liber pontificalis*, XLV: ed.
Duchesne, vol. I, 88–89 and 230; ed. Mommsen, 94. The text shows considerable
variants in the manuscript tradition, but these do not impact the point under discussion
here. See Joseph Dyer, '*Psalmi ante sacrificium* and the Origin of the Introit', in *Plainsong
and Medieval Music* 20 (2011), 91–121, at 92.

responsorial psalm between the epistle and the gospel, which would later be changed to the gradual responsory.[94] In his answer to Jeffery, Dyer has shown that in late ancient sources *sacrificium* commonly indicates the Mass as a whole and he made a compelling case that the passage most likely refers to the introit, which would have been sung by the time the *Liber pontificalis* was redacted in the early sixth century.[95] In the absence of other sources, however, it remains uncertain whether the introit was introduced in the first half of the fifth century.

What is intriguing in the text from the *Liber pontificalis* is the implication that before the intervention of Celestine, the Mass seems to have begun with the scriptural readings. This would correspond to the opening of the Good Friday afternoon liturgy according to the directory from the first half of the eighth century known as the *Ordo of Einsiedeln*: after the pope has entered the basilica of the Holy Cross in Jerusalem, has prostrated himself in prayer before the altar and has exchanged the kiss of peace with the clergy and the people, the liturgical action commences straightaway with readings interspersed by chants.[96] It has been argued that the Good Friday liturgy preserves a primitive pattern of the Roman Eucharist, following one of the 'laws of liturgical evolution' formulated by Anton Baumstark, that 'primitive conditions are maintained with greater tenacity in the more sacred seasons of the Liturgical Year'.[97] However, there is no evidence that this particular ritual, which was reserved to one of the most special days of the whole year when no Mass is offered, would have been an early paradigm for the regular celebration of the Eucharist. The section from the *Liber pontificalis* would be consistent with the practice of stational liturgy in the early sixth century (if not earlier), which opened with a procession from the pope's residence to the church where Mass was to be celebrated. This procession included psalms and litanies, and the first liturgical action to take place after the pope and his assistants entered the stational church and reached their designated places in the area around the altar may well have been the reading from the epistle.

---

[94] See Peter Jeffery, 'The Introduction of Psalmody into the Roman Mass by Pope Celestine I (422–432)', in *Archiv für Liturgiewissenschaft* 26 (1984), 147–165.

[95] See Dyer, '*Psalmi ante sacrificium* and the Origin of the Introit', 98–103.

[96] *Ordo Romanus* XXIII,17: ed. Andrieu, vol. III, 271; for a description of the manuscript, see ibid., 265–266.

[97] Baumstark, *Comparative Liturgy*, 27.

Dyer connects the introduction of the introit, both the chant and
the ritual, to the installation of a long, narrow passageway (*solea*) in the
central nave of Roman basilicas. This enclosed corridor served for
the processions of the clergy, while leaving the rest of the nave free for
the faithful. Several Roman churches, including the Lateran basilica,[98]
show traces of a *solea* from the sixth or possibly fifth century (the precise
dating of the archaeological remains is beset with difficulties).[99] In the
development of the entrance rites, there may well have been a mutual
influence between music, ceremonial and architecture, as Dyer concludes:
'The Roman *soleae* were thus visual analogues to the *psalmi* sung by the
schola cantorum as the pope and his clergy approached the altar to
celebrate the *sacrificium*.'[100]

In *Ordo Romanus I*, the introit appears as an antiphon ('antiphona ad
introitum') with several psalm verses as needed to accompany the pope's
procession to the altar. The antiphon is repeated after each verse and
probably after each part of the final doxology (*Gloria Patri* and *Sicut
erat*),[101] which is followed by extra psalm verses (*versus ad repetendum*),
as needed, and the final repetition of the antiphon (OR I, 44, 50–51). The
oldest available chant texts mostly indicate only one psalm verse and, in
some cases, an added *versus ad repetendum*. The vast majority of introits
are drawn from biblical texts, and about two-thirds of them are taken
from the psalms, especially those belonging to the oldest strata of the
repertory. Thus, the note in the *Liber pontificalis* about psalm-singing at
the beginning of the Mass gains credence for the early sixth century, if not
before.[102]

The inter-lectionary chants underwent considerable development in the
formative period of the Roman Rite. Since the late fourth century, it seems
to have been common practice in Rome and elsewhere (such as in
Augustine's North Africa) that a young lector (often an adolescent boy)

---

[98] For the Lateran basilica, see Sible de Blaauw, *Cultus et decor: Liturgia e architettura
nella Roma tardoantica e medievale. Basilica Salvatoris, Sanctae Mariae, Sancti Petri*,
Studi e testi 355–356, 2 vols. (Vatican City: Biblioteca Apostolica Vaticana, 1994), vol.
I, 127–129 and 159–160.

[99] See Dyer, '*Psalmi ante sacrificium* and the Origin of the Introit', 109–114.

[100] Ibid., 120.

[101] This seems to be implied in *Ordo Romanus I*, 50–51: ed. Andrieu, vol. II, 83, and it is
clearly specified in *Ordo Romanus XV*, 121–122: ed. Andrieu, vol. III, 120.

[102] See Hiley, *Western Plainchant*, 109; and Dyer, '*Psalmi ante sacrificium* and the Origin of
the Introit', 120.

sang a psalm (*psalmus responsorius*) in a simple tone after the epistle and before the gospel, with the people responding with an acclamation between verses. As already discussed in Chapter 3, there may not have been a significant musical difference between the stylised recitation of the reading and simple chanting.[103] Possibly in the early or mid-seventh century, the psalm was remade into the gradual, a highly melismatic responsorial chant consisting of only two psalm verses, that is, a respond and a solo verse. The respond would have been repeated after the solo verse (unlike in today's chant practice).[104] Unlike the introit, the gradual does not accompany a liturgical action with a variable number of psalm verses but offers a more contemplative reflection on the word of God. Other liturgical traditions also developed ornate inter-lectionary chants, such as the Ambrosian *psalmellus*, the Mozarabic *psalmo* and the Byzantine *prokeimenon*.[105] The short note in *Ordo Romanus I* offers very little information about the performance of the gradual: 'a cantor ascends [*sc.* presumably the ambo mentioned just before] and says (*dicit*) the response (*responsum*)' (OR I, 57).

The alleluia as a distinct chant consisting of the choral respond 'alleluia' with a melismatic *jubilus* on the final syllable '-ia', a verse and a repetition of the respond appears relatively late (OR I, 57). The assignment of a particular alleluia to a Mass formulary remains fluid for longer than is the case with the other propers, and chant historians have noted that in early medieval sources the musical repertory is limited to a number of core melodies.[106] If the Greek church historian Sozomenos, writing in Constantinople before 450, offers reliable information in his comparison of customs in different local churches, then in Rome the alleluia was sung only once a year, on Easter Sunday.[107] Perhaps this refers to the solemn

---

[103] See Dyer, Review McKinnon, 284–285;and Alfred Stuiber, 'Psalmenlesung oder Zwischengesang', in *Pietas: Festschrift für Bernhard Kötting*, ed. Ernst Dassmann and Karl Suso Frank, Jahrbuch für Antike und Christentum. Ergänzungsband 8 (Münster: Aschendorff, 1990), 393–398, at 397.

[104] See Dyer, Review McKinnon, 297.

[105] See Hiley, *Western Plainchant*, 495 and 500–501. The *prokeimenon*, however, precedes the epistle reading in the Divine Liturgy.

[106] See ibid., 130–131. Hiley also notes that the Antiphoner of Mont-Blandin, one of the oldest available graduals from around 800, for the Easter Octave, the Sundays after Easter, the Pentecost Octave and the Sundays after Pentecost 'simply gives the rubric "alleluia quale volueris", meaning that the singer must at this point dip into a pool of suitable alleluias gathered elsewhere (in this case at the end of the manuscript)' (ibid., 298).

[107] Sozomenus, *Ecclesiastical History*, VII,19: PG 67,1476B. He adds that it was customary among Romans to swear an oath on having heard or sung the alleluia.

chanting of the alleluia at the Easter Vigil. By the year 500, John the
Deacon states that in Rome the alleluia was sung only during the seven
weeks between Easter and Pentecost, whereas in other churches it was
sung throughout the whole liturgical year.[108] At the end of the sixth
century, John, bishop of Syracuse, asks in a letter to Pope Gregory the
Great whether it was his decision to extend the singing of the alleluia
beyond the Paschal season. The precise meaning of Gregory's response,
that 'in this matter we have somewhat limited (*amputavimus*) a former
tradition, one handed down to us from the Greeks',[109] is not clear. David
Hiley plausibly argues that the pope may have cut back an even more
extended use of the alleluia, which had spread to Rome from the East in
the course of the sixth century. It is doubtful that his intervention concerned the musical structure and form of the alleluia as known to us from
the later repertory.[110] The alleluia mentioned by Gregory may well have
been the refrain or end-phrase of the responsorial psalm. Such a reading
would support the theory of James McKinnon that the alleluia goes back
to the earlier practice of singing one of the psalms that begin with the
acclamation 'alleluia' as the responsorial psalm for Eastertide.[111] At a
second stage, the alleluia as an additional chant following the gradual was
created. McKinnon sees here the influence of the Byzantine alleluia, which
took its inspiration from the distinct alleluia-psalm that was sung after the
responsorial psalm and before the gospel in the Jerusalem liturgy of the
early fifth century. The difficulty with this genealogy, Dyer notes, is that
Byzantine musical influence in Rome is scarce and seems to be limited to
the five alleluias in Greek transliteration in the solemn Vespers at the
Lateran basilica in Easter week.[112] Moreover, the Byzantine *alleluiaria*
are rather short and not as melismatic as their Roman counterparts.

[108] John the Deacon, *Letter to Senarius*, XIII: *Analecta Reginensia: Extraits des manuscrits latins de la reine Christine conservés au Vatican*, ed. André Wilmart, Studi e testi 59 (Vatican City: Biblioteca Apostolica Vaticana, 1933), 178. English translation: Lawrence J. Johnson, *Worship in the Early Church: An Anthology of Historical Sources*, 4 vol. (Collegeville: Liturgical Press, 2009), vol. IV, 43–44 (no. 4171).

[109] Gregory the Great, *Ep.* IX, 26: MGH, Gregorii I Papae Registrum Epistolarum, vol. II, 59; trans. Johnson, *Worship in the Early Church*, vol. IV, 68 (no. 4248).

[110] See Hiley, *Western Plainchant*, 502.

[111] See James McKinnon, *The Advent Project: The Later Seventh-Century Creation of the Roman Mass Proper* (Berkeley; Los Angeles; London: University of California Press, 2000), 249–252.

[112] See Dyer, Review McKinnon, 298.

While the origin of the distinct alleluia chant in the Roman Mass remains unclear, William Mahrt rightly describes its liturgical function as 'the intensification of the effect of the gradual ... for the purpose of recollection and meditation' on the epistle reading. The jubilant melismatic character of the fully developed alleluia 'creates a sense of expectation, which places the gospel as its object and as the peak of the whole Liturgy of the Word'.[113]

The tract, in the words of Dyer, 'remains the most puzzling of the Mass chants, both with respect to its form and its exclusive liturgical assignment to penitential occasions, the Paschal vigil excepted'.[114] Most of the relatively few tracts in the chant repertory are appointed to the penitential season from Septuagesima until Holy Week. Mahrt describes the tract as 'meditation chant, with its own style of melismatic expression, but without the *jubilus* of the alleluia'.[115] The tract is first documented in *Ordo Romanus I* (OR I, 57), and it may have originated as a late addition to the Mass Propers to replace the alleluia after the gradual. On the other hand, the typical structure of the tract, which consists in a succession of psalm verses, sung without a refrain, might indicate that the tract derived from the psalm sung by a soloist without congregational responses (*in directum*) between epistle and gospel – a theory already proposed by Peter Wagner and tentatively supported by McKinnon.[116]

Ordo Romanus I does not give any intimations about the form of the offertory but states pithily that the *schola cantorum* should stop singing when the altar is fully prepared (OR I, 85), without any indication of when to start. The origin of the offertory chant has often been seen in a psalm with an antiphon accompanying a liturgical action in the same way as introit and communion. The schola would have sung as many psalm verses as needed to cover the offertory procession. A serious difficulty with this theory lies in the fact that the earliest available offertory chants do not have the form of an antiphon but rather that of a long, melismatic

---

[113] William Mahrt, 'Gregorian Chant in the Season of Lent', in *Antiphon* 21 (2017), 93–114, at 95. Regarding the musical performance of the alleluia and possible differences between early medieval and today's practice, see Hiley, *Western Plainchant*, 130.
[114] Dyer, Review McKinnon, 301.
[115] Mahrt, 'Gregorian Chant in the Season of Lent', 96.
[116] See the discussion of McKinnon, *The Advent Project*, 280–283.

responsory. Some of them only have responds, while others have up to four verses, with a complete or partial repetition of the respond after each verse. The texts of the earliest extant offertory chants are often not taken directly from a scriptural passage; rather, phrases are neatly combined to create what has been termed a 'libretto' for a particular musical setting.[117] This structure and melismatic character of the Roman offertory, which is removed from antiphonal psalmody, is paralleled in the Old Spanish *sacrificium* and the Milanese *offerenda*.[118]

Philippe Bernard surmises that the oldest Roman offertories may not have had a processional character at all (like the introit) but were short chants to mark the (rather straightforward) preparation of the altar. Bernard argues that the offertory procession, which is particularly protracted in the civic ceremonial of *Ordo Romanus I*, was added to the Roman Mass at some point in the development of the stational liturgy (see my discussion below, pp. 192–194).[119]

Sources from the late fourth century indicate that during the distribution of communion, Psalm 33 was sung by a cantor – an obvious choice because of the verse: 'Taste and see that the Lord is good.'[120] This practice is attested around 380 in the *Mystagogical Catecheses* of Cyril of Jerusalem and in the eighth book of the *Apostolic Constitutions*.[121] There is no contemporary evidence for the Roman practice. *Ordo Romanus I* leaves precise instruction for the communion chant: the 'antiphona ad communionem' is to start as soon as the pope administers the sacrament to the notable laymen in the area of the church called *senatorium*. The singing of psalm verses lasts as long as the distribution of communion; once this is completed, the chant concludes with the *Gloria*, *Sicut erat* and the 'versus', which I take to indicate the extra *versus ad repetendum*, as in the introit (OR I, 117, 122). The structure of the chant for distributing communion thus resembles the chant for the

---

[117] McKinnon, *Advent Project*, 305; see Kenneth Levy, 'Toledo, Rome, and the Legacy of Gaul', in *Early Music History* 4 (1984), 49–99.

[118] See Hiley, *Western Plainchant*, 121 and 499–500.

[119] See Philippe Bernard, *Du chant romain au chant grégorien (IVᵉ–XIIIᵉ siècle)*, Collection Patrimoines – Christianisme (Paris: Cerf, 1996), 437–438.

[120] Ps 33:8 in the Greek Septuagint, Ps 33:9 in the Latin Vulgate, and Ps 34:8 in the Hebrew numbering used in most modern translations.

[121] Cyril of Jerusalem, *Mystagogical Catecheses*, V,20; *Apostolic Constitutions*, VIII, 13,16; for the texts, see McKinnon, *Music in Early Christian Literature*, 76–77 (no. 158) and 109 (no. 235).

entrance procession.[122] Despite this similar structure and function, the oldest extant communion chants show a diversity in musical form that sets them apart from the introit. The earliest communions vary considerably both in length and in complexity. David Hiley speaks of a 'fragmented repertory' with many layers of material, which raises difficult questions for chant historians.[123]

The Schola Cantorum

The ordinary and proper chants of the Mass have been discussed at some length because the ritual description of *Ordo Romanus I* shows them as integral elements of the rite. The singers of the *schola cantorum* have a twofold liturgical ministry in the hierarchically ordered assembly: firstly, in the proper chants they proclaim texts that are (with some exceptions) drawn from the Sacred Scriptures. According to Franck Quoëx, this musical proclamation serves to accompany and elucidate the meaning of a specific ritual (introit, offertory, communion), and it offers a meditation on the word of God (gradual, alleluia or tract). Secondly, in the ordinary chants, the *schola* sings on behalf of the entire congregation and thus forms a link between the pontiff with his assistants in the sanctuary and the faithful in the body of the church.[124] The liturgical ministry of the *schola* is accentuated by the participation of its officials in the rite, for instance, the *archiparafonista* offering water at the offertory (OR I, 80).

Historians have proposed different theories about the origins of the *schola cantorum*, which in *Ordo Romanus I* appears as a formally structured association of trained singers in clerical orders.[125] The earliest indisputable information about the existence of the *schola* stems from the pontificate of Adeodatus II (r. 672–676), when the future Pope Sergius I, who had arrived in Rome from Sicily, became a cleric and since he proved to be a talented singer, was entrusted to the *prior cantorum* for

---

[122] As is the case with the introit, *Ordo Romanus XV*, 151: ed. Andrieu, vol. III, 124, details the performance of the communion chant.

[123] Hiley, *Western Plainchant*, 120; see ibid., 116–120 and 498–499.

[124] See Quoëx, 'Ritual and Sacred Chant', 218–219.

[125] See McKinnon, *The Advent Project*, 84–89; Rebecca Maloy, *Inside the Offertory: Aspects of Chronology and Transmission* (Oxford: Oxford University Press, 2010), 22–23.

instruction.[126] This office can safely be identified with the *prior scholae* mentioned in *Ordo Romanus I*. Hence the *schola cantorum* must have been established as a recognisable body by c. 675.

At the Roman synod held under Gregory the Great in July 595, it was decreed that deacons were no longer to act as cantors at Mass. Apparently, the custom had arisen that cantors would be ordained to the diaconate because of their good voices. As James McKinnon rightly notes, deacons had an important role in the Roman church and it was Gregory's view that they should above all be dedicated to the liturgical and charitable ministry proper to their order; the proclamation of the gospel remained their prerogative, while 'psalms and other readings' belonged to the subdeacons or, if necessary, those in minor orders.[127] This passage does not yet imply the existence of the *schola cantorum* as an organised school of clerics dedicated to singing. The strong presence of monks at Rome's major basilicas makes it likely that they had a dominant role in liturgical chant. McKinnon concludes from the available evidence that the Roman *schola cantorum* as a professional body was founded in the second third of the seventh century.[128] Philip Bernard proposes to see the origins of the *schola* in an association of the cantors of the Roman titular churches that gradually became a stable institution providing musically talented boys with an education in the liberal arts. The *schola cantorum* in the form of a well-organised choir school, as it is presented in *Ordo Romanus I*, may not be older than the late seventh or early eighth century.[129]

Old Roman Chant

So far, my overview of chant in the solemn papal liturgy has largely focused on texts and I have only touched upon questions of musical form. The repertory of liturgical chant sung in Rome (and the surrounding territories in central Italy) in the early medieval period is known as Old Roman chant.[130] The codification of this plainchant 'dialect' occurred considerably later than that of the Gregorian repertory, and the five complete manuscripts with musical notation that have come down to us

---

[126] See *Liber pontificalis*, LXXXVI: ed. Duchesne, vol. I, 371; ed. Mommsen, 210.
[127] Gregory the Great, *Ep.* V, 57a: MGH, Gregorii I Papae Registrum Epistolarum, vol. I, 363; see McKinnon, *The Advent Project*, 85.
[128] See McKinnon, *The Advent Project*, 89.
[129] See Bernard, *Du chant romain au chant grégorien*, 412.
[130] See Hiley, *Western Plainchant*, 530–540.

date from the eleventh to the thirteenth century, beginning with the gradual copied at Santa Maria in Trastevere in 1071. These manuscripts were created in a period when Gregorian chant was gaining ground in the city of Rome and eventually replaced the Old Roman tradition in the pontificate of Innocent III (r. 1198–1216).

Most of the chants of the Old Roman repertory have the same text as the Gregorian repertory. The two musical idioms are clearly related but also show significant differences, as David Hiley illustrates with the example of communion chants:

> The two settings agree on where phrases begin and end, and the settings of those phrases usually have the same shape and tonal character. One finds the same structural elements in both types of chant: intonation figures, recitation passages, cadence figures. The main difference between the Gregorian and Old Roman chant concerns surface detail. Old Roman Chant is more ornate.[131]

Old Roman chant shares stylistic features with Milanese and Beneventan chant. As Rebecca Maloy notes, these three 'Italian dialects . . . are unified by a tendency toward stepwise motion and ornateness'.[132] Their melodies proceed on a limited range of scale, avoiding larger intervals, but tend to be ornate and melismatic, with more individual notes. Byzantine influence on the Old Roman repertory can be detected only in particular instances, and similarities between Greek and Latin chant might indicate common roots of liturgical music rather than a direct influence of the former on the latter. Independent developments in East and West are to be expected, because 'chant is bound to a text and often shapes itself according to the needs of text declamation. Differences of language have far-reaching musical consequences', as Hiley observes.[133]

Since the earliest notated books for Old Roman chant only date from the eleventh century, we have to assume that oral transmission played a key role in the handing-on of the repertory prior to this. With a gap of almost four centuries, it is doubtful that the extant manuscripts record in every aspect the liturgical chant of the papal Mass as Frankish cantors experienced it in the Carolingian period. McKinnon has even argued that the Gregorian repertory may be 'closer to the Roman original than the

[131] Hiley, *Western Plainchant*, 532.
[132] Maloy, *Inside the Offertory*, 147; see Hiley, *Western Plainchant*, 540–552.
[133] Hiley, *Western Plainchant*, 526, with reference to Ewald Jammers, *Musik in Byzanz, im päpstlichen Rom und im Frankenreich: Der Choral als Textaussprache*, Abhandlungen der Heidelberger Akademie der Wissenschaften, Philosophisch-historische Klasse, 1962/ 1 (Heidelberg: C. Winter, 1962).

extant version'[134] and that 'the general stylistic homogeneity of the extant Roman melodies might reflect a blurring of distinctions from melody to melody in the course of centuries of oral transmission'.[135] However, the stylistic parallels of the (codified) Old Roman with the Milanese and Beneventan dialects does not sustain such a hypothesis. The similarities with Beneventan chant are particularly instructive since it went into decline after the eighth century and conserved its earlier form.[136]

The Old Roman repertory has been described as 'formulaic' in the tonal characteristics of its melodies, especially its graduals and tracts, and to a lesser extent in the offertories.[137] As Emma Hornby has shown for Old Roman tracts in the eighth mode, the formulaicism of their melodies, with particular words associated with particular musical phrases, had a mnemonic function and enabled a remarkably stable oral transmission and performance.[138] In fact, as William T. Flynn argues with reference to the work of Anna Maria Busse Berger, 'words alone are a powerful form of musical notation, and perhaps the most common form, even after more specialized notations were invented and transmitted by cantors and clerics'.[139] In the light of these considerations, it is thus most likely that 'Old Roman chant preserves the spirit, if not always the letter, of the eighth-century state'.[140]

Ordo Romanus XIX, a Frankish customary for meals in monastic communities, contains a list of popes who organised and developed a repertory of chant for the liturgical year (*annalis cantus*), beginning with its institution by Leo the Great.[141] While the contribution of popes as early as the fifth and sixth century to this project is not certain, the creation and organisation of this repertory was a remarkable musical

---

[134] McKinnon, *the Advent Project*, 377.   [135] Ibid., 379.

[136] See Thomas Forrest Kelly, *The Beneventan Chant* (Cambridge: Cambridge University Press, 1989), 25–40.

[137] See Maloy, *Inside the Offertory*, 88–146; and Joseph Dyer, '*Tropis semper variantibus*: Compositional Strategies in the Offertories of the Old Roman Chant', in *Early Music History* 17 (1998), 1–59.

[138] See William T. Flynn, 'Approaches to Early Medieval Music and Rites', in *Understanding Medieval Liturgy*, 57–71, at 66–67; and Emma Hornby, *Gregorian and Old Roman Eighth-Mode Tracts: A Case Study in the Transmission of Western Chant* (Aldershot: Ashgate, 2002; reissued London; New York: Routledge, 2009).

[139] Flynn, 'Approaches to Early Medieval Music and Rites', 65; see Anna Maria Busse Berger, *Medieval Music and the Art of Memory* (Berkeley: University of California Press, 2005).

[140] Hiley, *Western Plainchant*, 562; see also the discussion of Dyer, Review McKinnon, 305–307.

[141] *Ordo Romanus XIX*, 36: ed. Andrieu, vol. III, 223–224.

achievement. Even when we take into consideration the formulaic character of Old Roman melodies and the use of the same pieces for various
celebrations, their mastery required expertise and training. The *schola
cantorum* provided liturgical singing for the papal stational liturgies, but
we cannot assume that the many titular churches of the city were able to
offer similarly high musical standards. At the beginning of this chapter,
I noted that the presbyteral liturgies of these titular churches remain
largely obscure to us. Dyer notes that these smaller churches may have
had few singers (perhaps only one), who would 'possess only a basic,
passepartout repertory, suitable for ordinary occasions of the Temporale
and small repertory for whatever saints' feasts were celebrated'.[142] The
momentous work of the Roman *schola cantorum* would have had a direct
impact on the Lateran (the pope's cathedral), St Peter's, St Mary Major's
and other large churches, but the musical conditions in the *tituli* would
have changed at a much slower pace.

PARTICULAR QUESTIONS RELATING TO THE PAPAL STATIONAL LITURGY

Preaching at Mass

Notably, *Ordo Romanus I* does not include a provision for a sermon, but
can this be taken to mean that preaching at Mass was not known in Rome
at the time?[143] It is striking that, in comparison with bishops of other
important sees both in the Greek East and in the Latin West, relatively few
homilies of popes have come down to us from late antiquity. The two
outstanding examples are Leo the Great and Gregory the Great. Leo's
almost one hundred sermons are fine examples of liturgical preaching, but
they were delivered only on particular feast days (including Christmas,
Epiphany, Easter, Ascension, Pentecost, Saints Peter and Paul), penitential
days (especially Lent and Ember Days) and on special occasions (such as
the anniversary of his episcopal ordination or the commemoration of
Alaric's invasion of Rome in 410). Gregory has left us a cycle of forty
homilies on the gospels preached in the course of the liturgical year, which
can be dated between 590 and 592. These homilies were either delivered

---

[142] Dyer, Review McKinnon, 308.
[143] The tantalizing information offered by Sozomenus that in Rome 'neither the bishop nor
anyone else teaches (διδάσκει) in churches' (*Ecclesiastical History*, VII,19: PG 67,1476B)
is hard to gauge.

by the pontiff himself or read by a notary because of his ill health and weak voice. There are several sixth- and seventh-century sources, including Gregory's *Regula pastoralis*, that insist on the bishop's duty of preaching.[144] John Romano observes that the instructions of *Ordo Romanus I* 'concern ceremonial duties that were ambiguous as to who performed them. In the case of the sermon, however, there would have been no ambiguity as to who was to preach: the pope would have preached a sermon without any assistance'.[145] On the other hand, the silence of the document may reflect the recognition that the liturgical setting of the papal stational Mass in a large Roman basilica was not conducive to preaching. The pope speaking from his cathedra in the centre of the apse could have been heard easily by the clergy surrounding him but only with difficulty by the people who stood at a considerable distance in the naves. Martin Morard tentatively suggests that the night vigil in preparation for a major feast day could have provided the moment for preaching rather than the stational Mass in the morning, at least as long as vigils were widely attended by clergy and people.[146] The actual practice of preaching at papal liturgies may have varied according to different occasions and in different pontificates.[147]

Offertory Rite and Procession

Antoine Chavasse saw the Eucharistic liturgy of *Ordo Romanus I* characterised by two complementary processional movements that involve the whole assembly and are accompanied by the chanting of psalmody: offertory and communion.[148] It is often assumed that the offertory

---

[144] See Romano, *Liturgy and Society in Early Medieval Rome*, 50.   [145] Ibid.

[146] See Martin Morard, 'Quand liturgie épousa predication: Note sur la place de la prédication dans la liturgie romaine au Moyen Âge (VIIIᵉ–XIVᵉ siècle)', in *Prédication et liturgie au Moyen Âge*, ed. Nicole Bériou and Franco Morenzoni, Bibliothèque d'histoire culturelle du Moyen Âge 5 (Turnhout: Brepols 2008), 79–126, at 117–118.

[147] A similar suggestion is offered by Geoffrey G. Willis, *A History of Early Roman Liturgy to the Death of Pope Gregory the Great*, Henry Bradshaw Society. Subsidia 1 (London: Boydell Press, 1994), 6.

[148] Chavasse, 'A Rome, au tournant du Ve siècle, additions et remaniements dans l'ordinaire de la messe', in *La liturgie de la ville de Rome du Vᵉ au VIIIᵉ siècle*, 37: 'L'offertorium se réalise en deux mouvements coordonnés et complémentaires: APPORT (*offerre*, une fois; *oblationes*, 3 fois; *oblatas*, 5 fois) et RECEPTION (*susceptio*, n. 77; *suscipere*, 7 fois). Chaque mouvement est effectué par l'Assemblée comme telle, selon la structure de base: les Apportants, nommés au moment où ils interviennent (hommes et femmes, Pontife, évêques, prêtres, diacres, etc.); les Recevants, les ministres qui réceptionnent les oblats

procession by the laity is a custom reaching back to the early Christian centuries.[149] More recent scholarship, however, has built on the observation by scholars, such as Edward Yarnold, that there is no unequivocal fourth- or fifth-century evidence in the Latin West, with the possible exception of Augustine in North Africa, 'whether or not there was a formal offertory procession, or at what point in the Eucharist (or before it) this offering took place'.[150] There is no indication of it in any sources of the papal liturgy before *Ordo Romanus I*, including the passages where Gregory the Great comments on liturgical questions. This silence corresponds to the complete lack of evidence for an early 'processional' form of the offertory chant in analogy to introit and communion. The musical form of the early offertories for the Roman Mass is responsorial, not antiphonal.

In his studies of the musical and liturgical history of the offertory, Joseph Dyer draws attention to the fact that the offertory procession in *Ordo Romanus I* does in fact not involve all the laity but only the nobility.[151] Involving the leading men and women of the city in the elaborate liturgical offering, Dyer argues, was a symbolic gesture to exhort them to assist the Roman church with the task of providing grain for the city's populace – a task that had become more urgent in the turbulent seventh century marked by the constant threat of Lombard invasions and by tensions with the Byzantine Empire. The offertory procession as a symbolic gesture of social involvement may have been instituted in the mid-seventh century.[152]

(du Pontife aux acolytes). Ces deux groupes, coacteurs, gardent chacun sa propre structure. D'un côté: Hommes et Femmes, avec leurs hiérarchies ... de l'autre: les ministres, coopérant selon leur position ....'

[149] See, for instance, Theodor Klauser, *A Short History of the Western Liturgy: An Account and Some Reflections*, trans. John Halliburton, 2nd ed. (Oxford: Oxford University Press, 1979), 109.

[150] Edward J. Yarnold, 'The Liturgy of the Faithful in the Fourth and Early Fifth Centuries', in *The Study of Liturgy*, ed. Cheslyn Jones et al., rev. ed. (London: SPCK, 1992), 230–244, at 231; see also Alan Clark, 'The Function of the Offertory Rite in the Mass', in *Ephemerides Liturgicae* 64 (1950), 309–344. J. Patout Burns Jr. and Robin M. Jensen, *Christianity in Roman Africa: The Development of Its Practices and Beliefs* (Grand Rapids: Eerdmans, 2014), 266, n. 252, argue that even in Augustine there is no clear evidence for an offertory procession after the intercessions.

[151] See Joseph Dyer, 'The Offertory Chant of the Roman Liturgy and Its Musical Form', in *Studi Musicali* 11 (1982), 3–30; also Maloy, *Inside the Offertory*, 15–26.

[152] The Old Gelasian Sacramentary, which is dated between 628 and 715, contains a rubric in the Mass for the reconciliation of penitents on Maundy Thursday, 'Post haec offert plebs, et confitiuntur sacramenta', which is followed by the *secreta*. This offering of the people may be connected to the particular occasion; *Gelasianum Vetus* (Vat. Reg.

In the adaptation of the papal stational Mass north of the Alps a
'popular' offertory procession was introduced. While the particulars of
the ceremony may vary, several Frankish *ordines* as well as testimonies by
bishops, such as Haito of Basel and Theodulf of Orleans, confirm that
ordinary laypeople presented their offerings to the bishop or priest for the
Eucharistic sacrifice. It would be misleading simply to see Gallican influence here, because in the dramatic offertory procession of the Gallican
Mass, which compares with the 'Great Entrance' of the Byzantine liturgy,
deacons carried the offerings to be consecrated from a separate *sacrarium*
to the altar in tower-shaped vessels (*turres*), without lay participation.[153]
The lay offering of bread and wine seem to have taken place before the
Mass. By comparison, the offertory procession of the Frankish-Roman
ordines unfolds on a simpler scale and, as Rebecca Maloy suggests, 'is
probably best seen as an adaptation of the principles of *Ordo I* to the
specific needs of northern congregations'.[154]

Fermentum, *Communion and Pax*

A notable feature of the solemn papal Mass consists in the two rites of
commingling of the Eucharistic species. The first commingling happens at
the altar after the *Pater noster* and its embolism. The pope says 'Pax
Domini sit semper vobiscum' ('The peace of the Lord be always with you')
and drops a fragment of the *sancta* into the chalice (OR I, 95). *Sancta* is
the name given to the consecrated bread from the previous papal Mass,
which is shown to the pope during the entrance procession and venerated
by him (OR I, 48). Adding the *sancta* to the newly consecrated chalice
was a symbol of unity and continuity between the offering of one Mass
and the next. After this first commingling, the archdeacon passes the kiss

Lat. 316): ed. Leo C. Mohlberg, *Liber Sacramentorum Romanae Aeclesiae Ordinis Anni Circuli*, Rerum Ecclesiasticarum Documenta. Series maior. Fontes IV, 3rd ed. (Rome: Herder, 1981), no. 368.
[153] See Matthieu Smyth, *La liturgie oubliée: La prière eucharistique en Gaule antique et dans l'Occident non romain*, Patrimoines – Christianisme (Paris: Cerf, 2003), 197–203. The procession was accompanied by the singing of the *sonus* concluding with a threefold alleluia known as *laudes*. The Byzantine *Cherubikon*, the troparion sung at the Great Entrance, likewise concludes with a triple alleluia; see Hiley, *Western Plainchant*, 500.
[154] Maloy, *Inside the Offertory*, 21. The second description of Mass in the Frankish *Capitulare ecclesiastici ordinis* (*Ordo Romanus XV*) from the late eighth century, which Michel Andrieu considered a sort of compromise between the Roman and the Gallican tradition, testifies to an extensive offertory procession. *Ordo Romanus XV*, 133–144: ed. Andrieu, vol. III, 122–123; see ibid., 74–79.

of peace to the clergy in hierarchical order and to the people. Meanwhile, the pope initiates the fraction of the Eucharistic bread and returns to his seat. When the exchange of peace is completed, the assisting clergy resume the rite of fraction to prepare for communion, while the *schola cantorum* is singing the *Agnus Dei*.

The second commingling takes place at the pontiff's seat. A deacon brings the consecrated host to the pope, who saves a fraction of it before he communicates and then drops it into the chalice, held by the archdeacon, with the words, 'Fiat commixtio et consecratio corporis et sanguinis domini nostri Iesu Christi accipientibus nobis in vitam aeternam. Amen' ('May the mingling and consecration of the body and blood of our Lord Jesus Christ bring eternal life to us who receive it. Amen'; OR I, 107). After offering the salutation 'Pax tecum' ('Peace be with you') to the archdeacon, who replies 'Amen', the pope drinks from the chalice.

This second commingling has been traced back to the *fermentum* (lit. 'leaven'). Our understanding of this Roman practice hinges on the following passage from Innocent I's letter to Decentius, bishop of Gubbio, dating from 416:

As to the *fermentum* which we send on Sunday to the various titular churches, there is no reason for you to consult us on this matter. Here, in fact, all the churches are located within the city. Because of the people entrusted to their care the presbyters of these churches cannot celebrate with us, and so by means of the acolytes they receive the *fermentum* prepared by us so that on Sunday they do not feel separated from communion with us. But this should not, I believe, be done in rural areas of the diocese because the sacraments are not to be carried great distances. We ourselves do not send the *fermentum* to presbyters located in the various cemetery churches since these can rightfully and lawfully consecrate it themselves.[155]

The *fermentum* is thus a portion of the consecrated bread from the papal Mass, which was sent to the titular churches within the walls of the city. The *Liber pontificalis* attributes the institution of this practice to Pope Miltiades (r. 310/311–314).[156] Innocent's letter was generally taken to imply that the presbyters received the *fermentum* during the celebration of Mass in their titular churches. Adding the consecrated bread from the

---

[155] Innocent I, *Ep. 25 (ad Decentium)*, 5: ed. Cabié, 26–28; trans. Johnson, *Worship in the Early Church*, vol. III, 101–102 (no. 2788).

[156] *Liber pontificalis*, XXXIII: ed. Duchesne, vol. I, 168; ed. Mommsen, 46; trans. Johnson, *Worship in the Early Church*, vol. IV, 56 (no. 4214).

papal Mass to the chalice was a visible symbol of the unity of the Eucharist offered in different churches of the city.

Recent scholarship, however, has questioned this consensus, and John Baldovin succinctly presents the different readings now offered:

(1) There was only one eucharistic celebration within the city walls of Rome in the early fourth century. The presbyters alone were given communion in the *tituli*. They received under both kinds by placing the *fermentum* into a chalice of unconsecrated wine . . ..

(2) The bishop (or his representative) alone celebrated on Sundays but communion was sent to the *tituli* so that all might receive. The fragments *(fermentum)* were placed in the chalice of unconsecrated wine by the presbyters. Thereby they were consecrated by contact and distributed to the people in the manner that Eastern Christians still distribute communion today, i.e. in spoons . . ..

(3) The major celebration of the eucharist took place at the stational church and was presided over by the bishop or his representative. The eucharistic celebrations in the *tituli* must have begun somewhat later in the morning so that the acolytes could bring the *fermentum* to those churches and all could recognize by this very tangible sign that there was in principle only one eucharistic celebration on a given Sunday . . ..[157]

The first hypothesis was proposed by Pierre Nautin, who argued that only one Sunday Mass was offered in Rome, following the ancient principle (articulated above all by Ignatius of Antioch in the early second century)[158] that in a local Christian community, there should be only one altar and one Eucharist, at which the bishop presides. Presbyters in titular churches conducted aliturgical, that is, non-eucharistic synaxes (similar to today's 'celebration of the word') for catechumens and penitents who were not admitted to Holy Communion anyway. The presbyter would drop the *fermentum* into a chalice of wine, which would be consecrated by contact (*consecratio per contactum*), and only he would communicate as a visible sign of his *communio* with the pope.[159]

---

[157] John F. Baldovin, 'The Fermentum at Rome in the Fifth Century: A Reconsideration', in *Worship* 79 (2005), 38–53, at 50.

[158] Ignatius of Antioch, *Philadelphians*, 4: *The Apostolic Fathers: Greek Texts and English Translations*, ed. and trans. Michael W. Holmes after the earlier work of J. B. Lightfoot and J. R. Harmer, 3rd ed. (Grand Rapids: Baker Academic, 2007), 238 and 239; see also *Smyrneans*, 8,1: ibid., 254 and 255.

[159] See Pierre Nautin, 'Le Rite du "Fermentum" dans les Eglises Urbaines de Rome', in *Ephemerides Liturgicae* 96 (1982), 510–522; likewise Robert F. Taft, *A History of the*

The second hypothesis was advanced by Victor Saxer, who agrees with Nautin that the *fermentum* effected a consecration by contact, a practice that was known in Rome and is echoed in the words accompanying the second commingling of OR I, 107 ('Fiat commixtio et consecratio . . .').[160] Only one Mass was offered within the city walls on any given day (by the pope or a representative) and from it the *fermentum* was sent to the non-eucharistic assemblies in the titular churches to consecrate a chalice of wine. Departing from Nautin, however, Saxer argues that the contents of this chalice was then distributed into other chalices of wine for an extended consecration by contact, so as to provide communion for the people.[161]

Baldovin surmises that '[t]here may have been no need to celebrate the eucharist in very many locations within the city since the practice of receiving communion had declined so drastically by the end of the fourth century'.[162] Leading bishops at the time, such as John Chrysostom, deplored that among the masses who joined the Church in the post-Constantinian period, many showed a lack of commitment to the moral demands of their new faith and this led them to abstain from communion even at the Sunday Eucharist. What effect would this development have had on regular worship in late fourth-century Rome? Estimating the total urban population of Rome depends on variables that are hard to determine with certainty, but it is likely that the city, despite urban decline, still had several hundred thousand inhabitants at the time.[163] On the basis of Pope Cornelius' letter to Fabian, bishop of Antioch, which lists 46 priests, the number of Christians in Rome in the mid-third century has been estimated to be about 30,000.[164] This number must have risen in the relatively calm decades before the Diocletianic persecution and especially

Liturgy of St John Chrysostom, Vol. V: The Precommunion Rites, Orientalia Christiana Analecta 261 (Rome: Pontifical Oriental Institute 2000), 412–421.

[160] See the study of Michel Andrieu, *Immixtio et consecratio: La consécration par contact dans les documents liturgiques du moyen âge* (Paris: A. Picard, 1924).

[161] Victor Saxer, 'L'utilisation de la liturgie dans l'espace urbain et suburbain: l'exemple de Rome', in *Actes du XIᵉ congrès international d'archéologie chrétienne (Lyon-Vienne-Grenoble-Genève et Aoste, 21–28 septembre 1986)*, Collection de l'École française de Rome 123 (Rome: École française de Rome, 1989), 917–1033. See Baldovin, 'The Fermentum at Rome in the Fifth Century', 48–49.

[162] Baldovin, 'The Fermentum at Rome in the Fifth Century', 52.

[163] See Neville Morley, 'Population Size and Social Structure', in *The Cambridge Companion to Ancient Rome*, ed. Paul Erdkamp (Cambridge: Cambridge University Press, 2013), 29–44, at 31–35.

[164] Eusebius, *Ecclesiastical History* VI.43.11: GCS 9/2 [NF 6/2],618; see Adolf von Harnack, *The Mission and Expansion of Christianity in the First Three Centuries*,

since the Constantinian settlement, even though by the late fourth century Christians may not yet have formed a majority in the city. The Lateran basilica, dedicated in 324, served as the seat of the pope as the bishop of Rome and may have held a few thousand worshippers, but even with a marked drop in the number of communicants, making the sacrament available only in a single church within the city walls, as Nautin postulates, is a very unlikely scenario.

With more plausibility, Saxer maintains that the *fermentum* served precisely to provide communion for the people assembled in the titular churches by means of a protracted consecration by contact. While Baldovin offers guarded support for Saxer's hypothesis,[165] he recognises the arguments that speak in favour of the 'common opinion' that the titular churches had full Eucharistic celebrations on Sundays. The crux lies in interpreting the above-mentioned passage from Pope Innocent – whose tantalisingly terse prose tells us much less than we would like to know about worship in early fifth-century Rome.[166] The letter offers two reasons why *fermentum* was not sent to the cemetery basilicas outside the city walls: first, because of the distance and, second, because the priests in charge of these churches had 'the right and the freedom to confect [the sacraments] (*eorum conficiendorum ius habeant atque licentiam*)'. It could be inferred from this statement that the priests in the titular churches were not permitted to celebrate the Eucharist independently, or it could mean that for their legitimate celebration of the sacrament, it was necessary for them to receive the *fermentum* from the Mass offered by the pope (or his representative). This second reading would agree with the record of the *Liber pontificalis* that Pope Siricius (r. 384–399) decreed 'that no presbyter should celebrate Mass (*missas celebraret*) every week unless he receives the *fermentum*, namely, the indicated consecrated [portion] from the designated bishop of the place'.[167]

How likely is it that by the time of Innocent, the priests in charge of the titular churches within the city would not have the right to offer Mass

trans. and ed. James Moffatt, 2 vols., 2nd ed. (London; New York: Williams and Norgate, 1908), vol. II, 247–248.

[165] Baldovin, 'The Fermentum at Rome in the Fifth Century', 51–52; Romano, *Liturgy and Society in Early Medieval Rome*, 114–115, also follows Saxer; however, he does so without presenting the different positions on the question.

[166] See the careful analysis of Richard Hugh Connolly, 'Pope Innocent I "De nominibus recitandis"', in *Journal of Theological Studies* 20 (1919), 215–226.

[167] *Liber pontificalis*, XL: ed. Duchesne, 216; ed. Mommsen, 85; trans. Johnson, *Worship in the Early Church*, vol. IV, 57 (no. 4216).

themselves? From the fourth century onwards, there is growing evidence for the frequent, even daily celebration of the Eucharist in the Latin West. While the Roman church was relatively slow to institute daily Masses, the custom is clearly attested in Ambrose's Milan and Augustine's North Africa.[168] Daniel Callam has shown that at the time the link between the continence required from clerics in major orders and the frequency of the Eucharist is not as straightforward as is sometimes claimed. At the same time, however, the impact of the monastic movement on the clergy, which is exemplified in the monk-bishop, led to a diffusion of an ascetical piety that included the frequent offering of Mass.[169]

Moreover, historical scholarship has emphasised the ethnic and linguistic diversity of the Christian communities in Rome in the first two centuries.[170] In the fourth century, the pre-Constantinian buildings where such congregations gathered were transformed into titular churches.[171] In a city as large as Rome, assembling the whole Christian people around the bishop for a single Eucharistic celebration may have been an ecclesiological ideal rather than a pastoral-liturgical reality. As the church was growing in the post-Constantinian period, the *fermentum* may have been instituted as a tangible sign of unity between the pope and his presbyterate in offering the Eucharist. As for the significance of the formula *Fiat commixtio et consecratio*, Josef Andreas Jungmann suggests that 'consecratio' should not be understood in the narrow sense of 'consecration' but rather as a form of 'hallowing' that effects a union of the two sacramental species, which symbolises the risen Christ.[172]

The decreasing number of communicants in the course of the fourth century may have led to one of the distinguishing features of the Roman Mass: the place assigned to the kiss of peace. In all other historical rites,

---

[168] Daniel Callam presents a range of sources that speak against daily Mass in Rome in the late fourth century; see 'The Frequency of Mass in the Latin Church ca. 400', in *Theological Studies* 45 (1984), 613–650, at 648–650.

[169] See Callam, 'The Frequency of Mass in the Latin Church ca. 400'; and 'Clerical Continence in the Fourth Century: Three Papal Decretals', in *Theological Studies* 41 (1980), 3–50.

[170] See esp. Peter Lampe, *Christians at Rome in the First Two Centuries: From Paul to Valentinus*, trans. Michael Steinhauser and ed. Marshall D. Johnson (London: Continuum, 2006).

[171] Optatus of Milevis, writing between 364 and 367, says there were more than forty churches in Rome, when the Donatists set up their own bishop in the city not long after 312; *Contra Parmenianum*, II,4: CSEL 26,39.

[172] See Jungmann, *Missarum sollemnia*, vol. II, 391–394, where he points to parallels in the Greek Anaphora of St James and in the Visigothic liturgy.

both East and West, the peace is exchanged before the offertory; in the Roman Rite, however, it is exchanged right before Holy Communion. In his description of the post-baptismal Eucharist at Rome from the middle of the second century, Justin Martyr places the kiss of peace after the intercessory prayers and before the preparing of the offerings.[173] Dominic Serra sees the change in the location of the peace in relation to the declining number of communicants. As many faithful did not receive the sacrament by the end of the fourth century, a rite of dismissal was instituted for them and they would leave the church before communion. In fact, Robert Taft argues that the 'inclination prayer' of the Byzantine Rite had just this function when it was introduced at the time of John Chrysostom.[174] Serra interprets this dismissal in terms of Aidan Kavanagh's idea of the '*missa* structure' of certain rites, that is, the 'sending' into another stage of the liturgical celebration.[175] In this particular instance, those who did not receive communion were 'sent' to leave the liturgical assembly. The peace had been associated with the offering of the Eucharistic sacrifice, based on the exhortation from the Sermon on the Mount to be reconciled to one's brother before offering one's gift at the altar (Mt 5:23–24), and participation in this sacrifice is completed in its reception. With the new phenomenon of many non-communicants, the reason for moving the peace right before communion may have been that it was to be given only to those who would receive the sacrament.[176] Early medieval sources beginning with Gregory the Great in the late sixth century specifically associate the kiss of peace with the reception of communion.[177] The earliest witness for the new location of the *pax* in Rome (which is attested around the same time in North Africa)[178] is

---

[173] Justin Martyr, *First Apology*, 65,2: PTS 38,125. This is the first post-biblical source that mentions the kiss of peace; see Michael P. Foley, 'The Whence and Whither of the Kiss of Peace in the Roman Rite', in *The Fullness of Divine Worship: The Sacred Liturgy and Its Renewal*, ed. Uwe Michael Lang (Washington, DC: The Catholic University of America Press, 2018), 81–142, at 87 (originally published in *Antiphon* 14 [2010], 45–94).

[174] Robert F. Taft, 'The Inclination Prayer Before Communion in the Byzantine Liturgy of St John Chrysostom: A Study in Comparative Liturgy', in *Ecclesia Orans* 3 (1986), 29–60.

[175] See Aidan Kavanagh, *Confirmation: Origins and Reform* (New York: Pueblo 1988), 3–38.

[176] See Dominic E. Serra, 'The Kiss of Peace: A Suggestion from Ritual Structure', in *Ecclesia Orans* 14 (1997), 79–94, at 91–92.

[177] See Jungmann, *Missarum sollemnia*, vol. II, 401–404.

[178] See Augustine, *Sermo* 227: PL 38,1101; for more references, see Roetzer, *Des heiligen Augustinus Schriften als liturgiegeschichtliche Quelle*, 130–131. Hence the *fermentum* alone, which was not known in North Africa, is not sufficient to account for this particular difference, as suggested by Paul Bradshaw, 'The Genius of the Roman Rite

Innocent I, who states that it must be given after the Eucharistic prayer. His interpretation of the ritual gesture, that as a concluding sign or seal (*signaculum*) by which 'the people consent to all that has taken place in the mysteries and to what is celebrated in the Church', might confirm the theory that at this time only the communicants, who were fully committed to the Christian life, received the peace.[179]

The two rites of commingling were copied in the Frankish recensions of *Ordo Romanus I*, but their origin and meaning were not understood outside Rome. After some hesitation, the place of the first commingling was chosen. The commingling of the Eucharistic species is preceded by the much-reduced rite of fraction, and it is accompanied by the formula *Fiat commixtio et consecratio* (or a variation of it). The salutation *Pax Domini sit semper vobiscum* and the kiss of peace follow. As Jungmann suggests, the burgeoning of allegorical liturgical commentary may have consolidated this new arrangement. The commingling of the Eucharistic species now represents the resurrection of Christ: the uniting of his body and blood that were separated when he died on the cross signify his rising again to life.[180] In the light of this reading, the *pax* acquires a distinctively paschal meaning: it evokes the peace Christ offers to his disciples when he appears to them after his resurrection (Jn 20:21–22; also Lk 24:35–36).[181] As Michael P. Foley rightly notes: 'It is this paschal model that proved to be the decisive hermeneutic for the liturgical kiss in the Roman Rite and for its further development.'[182]

Revisited', in *Ever Directed Towards the Lord: The Love of God in the Liturgy of the Eucharist Past, Present, and Hoped For*, ed. Uwe Michael Lang (London: T&T Clark, 2007), 49–61, at 60–61.

[179] 'Pacem igitur asseris ante confecta mysteria quosdam populis imperare, vel sibi inter sacerdotes traddre, cum post omnia quae aperire non, debeo pax sit necessaria indicenda per quam constet populum ad omnia quae in mysteriis aguntur atque in ecclesia celebrantur praebuisse consensum ac finita esse pacis concludentis signaculo demonstrentur.' Innocent I, *Ep. 25* (*ad Decentium*), 1: ed. Cabié, 20–22; trans. Johnson, *Worship in the Early Church*, vol. III, 100 (no. 2784).

[180] Amalarius of Metz, *Liber officialis* III,31,1–3 and 35,2: ed. Jean Michel Hanssens, *Amalarii Episcopi Opera Liturgica Omnia*, Tomus II, Studi e testi 139 (Vatican City: Biblioteca Apostolica Vaticana, 1948), 361–362 and 367–368 (PL 105,1151–1152 and 1154); see Jungmann, *Missarum sollemnia*, vol. II, 395–396.

[181] See Foley, 'The Whence and Whither of the Kiss of Peace in the Roman Rite', 105–108; also Dominic E. Serra's 'The Greeting of Peace in the Revised Sacramentary: A New Pastoral Option', in *Liturgy for the New Millennium: A Commentary on the Revised Sacramentary*, ed. Mark R. Francis and Keith F. Pecklers (Collegeville: Liturgical Press, 2000), 97–110, at 110.

[182] Foley, 'The Whence and Whither of the Kiss of Peace in the Roman Rite', 105.

The Renewed Presence of Greek in the Roman Liturgy

There is no evidence for a continued use of Greek in the Roman liturgy after the late fourth century (see Chapter 4). In the seventh century, however, the rapid Islamic expansion in the Eastern Mediterranean led to an influx of Greek-speaking Christian refugees in Rome,[183] and Greek elements were again introduced into the Roman liturgy. The best-known examples are adoption of the *Trisagion* ('Holy God, Holy Strong, Holy Immortal, have mercy on us') in the *Improperia* (Reproaches) of the Good Friday liturgy and the doubling of the scriptural readings in Latin and Greek on solemn celebrations in the liturgical year, such as Christmas and Easter (Sunday and Monday), the Vigils of Easter and Pentecost, the four Ember Saturdays and the Mass for the ordination of a pope.[184] The twofold proclamation certainly helped the Greek-speaking residents of the city to follow the biblical text,[185] but it also served the purpose to affirm the universal claims of the papacy over the Church in both West and East.

In the course of the Middle Ages, Hebrew, Greek and Latin came to be known as the 'three sacred languages (*tres linguae sacrae*)' of Christianity. Church Fathers, such as Hilary of Poitiers and Augustine of Hippo, already honoured the three languages that were used on the title of the cross according to John 19:20, because they had a special significance in the history of salvation and the preaching of the Gospel. Thus, Hilary attributed particular merit to Hebrew, Greek and Latin, not because of some inherent quality, but because in these languages 'is preached above all the mystery of the will of God and the expectation of the coming Kingdom of God'.[186] Likewise, Augustine commented on the title of the cross: 'These three languages were prominent there before all others:

---

[183] See Hans-Georg Beck, 'Die frühbyzantinische Kirche', in *Handbuch der Kirchengeschichte, Bd. II/2: Die Reichskirche nach Konstantin dem Großen – Die Kirche in Ost und West von Chalkedon bis zum Frühmittelalter 451–700*, ed. Hubert Jedin et al. (Freiburg im Breisgau: Herder, 1975), 3–92, at 87–92.

[184] See Radek Tichý, *Proclamation de l'Évangile dans la messe en occident: Ritualité, histoire, comparaison, théologie*, Studia Anselmiana 168 (Rome: Pontificio Ateneo S. Anselmo, 2016), 243–248; also Vogel, *Medieval Liturgy*, 296–297.

[185] The baptismal liturgy of *Ordo Romanus XI*, 62–66: ed. Andrieu, vol. II, 434–435, from the second half of the seventh century, includes the chanting of the creed in either Greek (as the first option) or Latin. Moreover, the choice of the Niceno-Constantinopolitan Creed may also have been an accommodation to Greek speakers, since it was more widely used in the East than in Rome, where the Apostles' Creed predominated. See John F. Romano, 'Baptizing the Romans', in *Acta ad archaeologiam et artium historiam pertinentia* 31 (2019), 43–62, at 44–45.

[186] Hilary of Poitiers, *Tractatus super psalmos*, prol. 15: CSEL 22, 13.

Hebrew on behalf of the Jews who boasted in the law of God; Greek on behalf of the wise men among the pagans; Latin on behalf of the Romans who at that time were dominating many and almost all peoples.'[187] This patristic reading entered medieval exegesis, and Augustine's commentary in particular was regularly quoted by later theologians.

It would appear that no author actually called these three languages 'sacred' before Isidore of Seville (c. 560–636).[188] He considered Hebrew, Greek and Latin sacred because they were the languages of Sacred Scripture and insisted that familiarity with them was necessary for correct exegesis. There is no reference, however, whether explicit or implicit, to the Church's liturgy in Isidore.

The oldest reflection on the use of the three languages in the liturgy is found in the collection of letters known as *Expositio antiquae liturgiae gallicanae*, which used to be attributed to Germanus of Paris (c. 496–576), but which is now dated to the seventh or early eighth century. In the brief account of the Gallican Mass, it is noted that the *Trisagion*, which precedes the Canticle of Zechariah (*Benedictus*) and the scriptural readings, is sung first in Greek, then in Latin and finishes with the Hebrew 'amen', thus symbolising the 'trinitas linguarum' of the title of the cross.[189] No normative conclusions are drawn from this factual description. Likewise, when later Western authors, for instance, Thomas Aquinas in his *Scriptum* on the Sentences of Peter Lombard, comment on the use of the three sacred languages of Scripture in divine worship, this is simply meant to be an elucidation of liturgical practice in the Latin Church.[190]

This idea of *tres linguae sacrae*, which was widely received in the Middle Ages, is manifestly different from the ideological position that has been denounced as 'trilinguism', according to which the liturgy could be celebrated only in Hebrew, Greek and Latin (and not be translated into

---

[187] Augustine of Hippo, *In Iohannis evangelium tractatus*, 117,4: CCL 36,653.

[188] Isidore of Seville, *Etymologiae*, IX, 1, 3–4: PL 82,326: 'Tres autem sunt linguae sacrae ....'

[189] The text of Martène's *editio princeps* in PL 72 is not reliable; see now the critical edition by Philippe Bernard, *Epistulae de ordine sacrae oblationis et de diversis charismatibus ecclesiae Germano Parisiensi episcopo adscriptae: Epistola I, 3*: CCM 187, 339.

[190] 'Sciendum autem, quod in officio Missae, ubi passio repraesentatur, quaedam continentur verba Graeca, sicut, *kyrie eleison*, idest domine miserere: quaedam Hebraica, sicut *alleluja*, idest laudate Deum; *Sabaoth*, idest exercituum; *hosanna*, salva obsecro; *amen*, idest vere, vel fiat: quaedam Latina, quae patent: quia his tribus linguis scriptus est titulus crucis Christi, *Joan. 19*.' Thomas Aquinas, *Super Sent.*, lib. 4, d. 8, q. 2, a. 4, qc. 3 expos.

any other language). While it is often claimed that this was a widely held view among the Franks who opposed the missionary work of Cyril and Methodius,[191] Francis Thomson has shown that 'trilinguism' was rather a generic piece of Byzantine polemics against the Latin West. As he concludes from his comprehensive study of the available material, 'the notion that the Western Church ever propagated trilinguism in the Cyrillo-Methodian sense belongs to the realm of myth, not history'.[192]

THE DIRECTION OF LITURGICAL PRAYER IN ROMAN BASILICAS

Even before the Peace of the Church, Christian communities in the city of Rome had their own buildings, which also served for liturgical celebrations; as for the shape, furnishings and use of these pre-Constantinian edifices, we are very much in the dark.[193] The oldest surviving monuments are the basilicas built under Constantine, but the interior of these buildings has changed considerably over the centuries. Arguably, the Constantinian plan can be discerned most clearly from the Lateran basilica. Here, the bishop's *cathedra* was placed at the end of the apse, which corresponded to the seat of honour occupied by the magistrate in secular basilicas, which were used as court or market halls, and to the emperor's seat in the senate. In Christian basilicas, the altar usually stood at the entrance to the apse, its sacred character being marked by its exalted position, by the steps leading up to it, and sometimes by a ciborium, a superstructure that was particularly apt to emphasise the altar's importance.

---

[191] See, for instance, Keith Pecklers, *Dynamic Equivalence: The Living Language of Christian Worship*, (Collegeville: Liturgical Press, 2003), 4–7.

[192] Francis J. Thomson, 'SS. Cyril and Methodius and a Mythical Western Heresy: Trilinguism. A Contribution to the Study of Patristic and Mediaeval Theories of Sacred Languages', in *Analecta Bollandiana* 110 (1992), 67–122, at 96. Thomson argues that 'Western opposition to Cyril and Methodius' innovations was not so much directed against the use of Slavonic as against the invention of an entirely new alphabet' (ibid., 75); see also Tia M. Kolbaba, *The Byzantine Lists: Errors of the Latins*, Illinois Medieval Studies (Chicago: University of Illinois Press, 2000), 66–67.

[193] See Charles Pietri, *Roma christiana: Recherches sur l'Eglise de Rome, son organisation, sa politique, son idéologie de Miltiade à Sixte III (311–440)*, Bibliothèque des écoles françaises d'Athènes et de Rome 224, 2 vols. (Rome: École française de Rome, 1976), vol. I, 3–4 ; and Federico Guidobaldi, 'L'inserimento delle chiese titolari di Roma nel tessuto urbano preesistente: osservazioni ed implicazioni', in *Quaeritur inventus colitur: Miscellanea in onore di Padre Umberto Maria Fasola*, ed. Philippe Pergola, 2 vols., Studi di antichità cristiana 40 (Vatican City: Pontificio Istituto di Archeologia Cristiana, 1989), vol. I, 382–396.

There is no clear evidence for the original position of the main altar in the Constantinian building of St Peter's. The Vatican basilica was a *martyrium*, distinguished by the tomb of the apostle, and its design was governed primarily not by the needs of a liturgical assembly but by the peculiar site of the *memoria*. John Ward Perkins has argued that there would hardly have been room for an altar within the precinct of the tomb, let alone within the shrine itself.[194] Hence it is quite possible that the (portable) main altar of the church was originally placed in the body of the nave and was not connected with the tomb, which would have been freely accessible to the faithful. Achim Arbeiter has observed that the basilica was partitioned into two main areas: the nave, which served for the celebration of the Eucharist, and the transept with the shrine of the apostle, which formed the sacred area for pilgrims. The position of the altar may have been under the triumphal arch or in the nave but not under the crossing.[195] On the other hand, Sible de Blaauw has made a case for the main altar's position in the area of the tomb.[196] Werner Jacobsen has argued that the altar stood near the tomb and that it could be approached only from the side of the nave, because its rear side was blocked by the second-century martyr memorial (*tropaion*) that was incorporated into the basilica to indicate the burial place of St Peter.[197] Most recently, Stefan Heid suggests that the fourth-century shrine enclosing the *tropaion* had a niche that could be accessed and used as an altar. Heid argues that it was the prerogative of the pope to offer Mass above the venerated tomb.[198]

At any rate, there is no doubt that the arrangement at the apostle's tomb was changed significantly during the pontificate of Gregory the Great in the late sixth century. The floor of the apse was raised by almost

---

[194] See John B. Ward Perkins, 'The Shrine of St. Peter and Its Twelve Spiral Columns', in *Studies in Roman and Early Christian Architecture* (London: Pindar Press, 1994), 469–488, at 470; also Pietri, *Roma christiana*, vol. I, 69.

[195] See Achim Arbeiter, *Alt-St. Peter in Geschichte und Wissenschaft: Abfolge der Bauten, Rekonstruktion, Architekturprogramm* (Berlin: Mann, 1988), 204–206; also 181–184.

[196] See de Blaauw, *Cultus et decor*, vol. II, 481–482.

[197] See Werner Jacobsen, 'Organisationsformen des Sanktuariums im spätantiken und mittelalterlichen Kirchenbau: Wechselwirkungen von Altarraum und Liturgie aus kunsthistorischer Perspektive', in *Kölnische Liturgie und ihre Geschichte: Studien zur interdisziplinären Erforschung des Gottesdienstes im Erzbistum Köln*, ed. Albert Gerhards and Andreas Odenthal, Liturgiewissenschaftliche Quellen und Forschungen 87 (Münster: Aschendorff, 2000), 67–97, at 70–71.

[198] See Stefan Heid, *Altar und Kirche: Prinzipien christlicher Liturgie* (Regensburg: Schnell & Steiner, 2019), 285–310.

one and a half metres and the elevated platform was extended nearly six metres into the body of the church. The altar with canopy was erected directly over the tomb; and on its western end, a semi-circular crypt was added, which gave the faithful easy access to the highly venerated shrine. The raised apse with the bishop's seat and the bench for the clergy was separated from the body of the church by a screen of columns. Gregory's primary motive for visibly uniting the altar with the *memoria* can be seen in the desire to respond to the strongly felt association between the celebration of the Eucharist and the cult of the martyrs.[199] It might also have been the pope's intention to assimilate the plan of St Peter's to that of the Lateran basilica.[200]

In general, the eastward direction of prayer determined the position of the priest at the altar during the Eucharistic liturgy.[201] In a church with an oriented apse, the celebrant would usually stand in front of the altar, facing east just as the people did. Several Roman basilicas are not aligned along the east-west axis for various reasons: churches rested on ancient foundations or secular buildings were turned to Christian use; in the majority of cases, the variation from the east-west axis was owing to the constraints of the location, for the entrance to the church usually lay on the street side, as in the case of the church of St Clement, where the doors open to the south-east.[202]

Churches with the entrance in the east and the apse in the west, such as the Vatican basilica, are found mainly in Rome and North Africa. Regarding the direction of liturgical prayer in these churches, different hypotheses have been proposed. According to Louis Bouyer, the whole assembly, both the celebrant who stood behind the altar and the people in

---

[199] 'Hic fecit ut super corpus beati Petri missae celebrarentur'; *Liber pontificalis*, LXVI: ed. Duchesne, vol. I, 312; ed. Mommsen, 162. See Hugo Brandenburg, 'Altar und Grab: Zu einem Problem des Märtyrerkultes im 4. und 5. Jh.', in *Martyrium in Multidisciplinary Perspective: Memorial Louis Reekmans*, ed. Mathijs Lamberigts and Peter van Deun, Bibliotheca Ephemeridum Theologicarum Lovaniensium 117 (Leuven: Peeters, 1995), 71–98.

[200] See de Blaauw, *Cultus et decor*, vol. I, 117–127; and Jacobsen, 'Organisationsformen des Sanktuariums im spätantiken und mittelalterlichen Kirchenbau', 71–72.

[201] See Uwe Michael Lang, *Turning towards the Lord: Orientation in Liturgical Prayer*, 2nd ed. (San Francisco: Ignatius Press, 2009), 35–93; also Cyrille Vogel, 'L'orientation vers l'Est du célébrant et des fidèles pendant la célébration eucharistique', in *L'Orient syrien* 9 (1964), 3–37; and Marcel Metzger, 'La place des liturges à l'autel', in *Revue des sciences religieuses* 45 (1971), 113–145.

[202] See Sible de Blaauw, *Met het oog op het licht: Een vergeten principe in de oriëntatie van het vroegchristelijk kerkgebouw*, Nijmeegse Kunsthistorische Cahiers 2 (Nijmegen: Nijmegen University Press, 2000), 17–23.

the nave, turned towards the east for the Eucharistic prayer.[203] This suggestion has met severe criticism on the grounds that it would have been unthinkable for the people to turn their back on the altar, since from early on the altar was considered a holy object, indeed a symbol of Christ.[204] Klaus Gamber holds that the congregation, separated by male and female, mainly occupied the lateral naves, of which St Peter's and the Lateran had four and some churches even six. The central nave would have been left free for liturgical actions, such as the entrance procession, the reception of the offerings and the distribution of communion.[205] An analogy for this particular arrangement can be seen in the use of the Christian East, where the faithful stand somewhat removed from central space under the dome, which is left free for liturgical ceremonies.[206]

Consequently, in basilicas with an eastward entrance, the faithful did not face the altar directly, but did not turn their back on it either. To do this would indeed have been inconceivable on account of the sacred character of the altar and of the sacrifice offered on it. The people in the side naves needed only to change their position slightly in order to face east; the altar would have been more or less on their right or their left. During the Eucharistic liturgy, the congregation would face the same direction as the celebrant, looking towards the eastern entrance where windows may have allowed the light of the rising sun, the symbol of the risen Christ and his second coming in glory, to flood into the nave. The practice of priest and people facing each other arose when the profound symbolism of liturgical orientation was no longer understood and the faithful no longer turned eastward for the Eucharistic prayer. This happened especially in those churches where the altar was moved from the middle of the nave to the apse.

There are two serious objections to the hypothesis offered by Bouyer and developed by Gamber. First, while the central nave was used for liturgical rites, it is questionable that during the Eucharistic prayer the

---

[203] See Louis Bouyer, *Liturgy and Architecture* (Notre Dame: University of Notre Dame Press, 1967), 55–56.

[204] See, for instance, Vogel, 'L'orientation vers l'Est', 26–29.

[205] See Klaus Gamber, *Liturgie und Kirchenbau: Studien zur Geschichte der Meßfeier und des Gotteshauses in der Frühzeit*, Studia Patristica et Liturgica 6 (Regensburg: Pustet, 1976), 23–25 and 131–136; also Thomas F. Mathews, 'An Early Roman Chancel Arrangement', in *Rivista di Archeologia Cristiana* 38 (1962), 73–96, at 83.

[206] See Robert F. Taft, 'Some Notes on the Bema in the East and West Syrian Traditions', in *Orientalia Christiana Periodica* 34 (1968), 326–359, at 327; see also Richard Krautheimer, with Slobodan Ćurčić, *Early Christian and Byzantine Architecture*, 4th ed. (New Haven; London: Yale University Press, 1986), 101–102 and 217–218.

people stood mainly in the side naves, which were also used for extra-liturgical purposes. In his reconstruction of the early Lateran basilica, de Blaauw identified a long narrow corridor (*solea*) in the nave that served the clergy for ceremonial functions, thus leaving the rest of the spacious nave free for the faithful.[207] Secondly, the idea that in basilicas with an eastern entrance the whole assembly should have turned towards the doors appears very implausible. However, our judgement in this question should not be governed by modern sensibilities. In the context of religious practice in the ancient world, this gesture would not appear as extraordinary as it may do today. A common custom in antiquity was to lift one's eyes and hands in prayer upwards, towards the sky, which meant that in a closed room, one would turn to a window or an open door. This is well attested in Jewish and early Christian sources, for example, Daniel 6:10, Tobit 3:11 and Acts 10:9. The Babylonian Talmud transmits a ruling of Rabbi Hiyya bar Abba to the effect that one must not pray in a room without windows.[208] In his treatise *On Prayer*, Origen discusses the problem that arises if a house has no doors or windows facing east. He argues that one should turn towards the east, because this is a basic principle of Christian prayer, whereas turning towards the open sky is just a convention.[209] Against this background, it would not appear impossible that in a church with a westward apse, the people, along with the priest, turned towards the entrance in the east for the Eucharistic prayer.[210]

Another line of argument can be developed from the observation that facing east was accompanied by looking upwards, namely towards the sky, which was considered the place of paradise and the scene of Christ's

---

[207] See de Blaauw, *Cultus et decor*, vol. I, 127–129 and 159–160.

[208] Babylonian Talmud, *Berakhot* 5,1 (31a); 5,5 (34b).

[209] Origen, *De oratione* 32: GCS Orig. II, 400–401.

[210] The church of Tyre from the early fourth century and the Constantinian *martyrion* at the Holy Sepulchre in Jerusalem are among the few churches in the Levant that have an eastward entrance. John Wilkinson, 'Orientation, Jewish and Christian', in *Palestine Exploration Quarterly* 116 (1984), 16–30, at 26–29, thinks that even there the liturgical assembly prayed towards the east, that is, in the direction of the entrance. For a description of these two buildings, see Eusebius, *Hist. eccl.* X, 4, 37–46: GCS Euseb. 9/2 [NF 6,2], 873–876; and *Vita Constantini* III, 36–39: GCS Euseb. I, 100. Alternatively, de Blaauw, *Met het oog op het licht*, 36, proposes that this type of church was meant to imitate the layout of the Jerusalem Temple, which had its entrance in the east. Following Ezekiel 8:16–18, it would have been inconceivable for the congregation to turn away from the altar.

second coming.[211] The lifting up of hearts for the canon or anaphora, in response to the admonition *Sursum corda*, included the bodily gestures of standing upright, raising one's arms and looking heavenward. It is not mere accident that the apse and triumphal arch of many basilicas were decorated with magnificent mosaics; their iconographic programmes often show close relationships with the Eucharist that is celebrated underneath.[212] The bishop or priest at the altar prayed with outstretched, raised arms (like the female figure known from the Roman catacombs as *orans*) and ritual gestures, such as signs of the cross, were added only gradually. Where the altar was placed at the entrance of the apse or in the central nave, such as in St Peter's before Gregory the Great, the celebrant standing in front of it could easily have looked towards the apse. With splendid mosaics representing the celestial world, the apse may have indicated the 'liturgical east' and hence the focus of prayer for the whole assembly. This theory is rather conjectural and requires much closer scrutiny. However, it has the definite advantage that it accounts better for the correlation between worship, art and architecture than the ideas of Bouyer and Gamber, which need to accommodate a discrepancy between the liturgical rite and the space created for it.[213]

At some point – and in St Peter's this may have been after the Gregorian fusion of altar with the apostle's tomb – celebrant and people were certainly facing one another in a basilica with an eastward entrance. The difference in liturgical directionality is evident from two versions of *Ordo Romanus I*. After the entrance procession, the pontiff kisses the gospel book and the altar, goes to his seat and stands facing east ('stat versus orientem'; OR I, 51). Most manuscripts give no further indications of direction. However, the collection St Gall, Stiftsbibliothek, ms. 614, which is often – though not universally – held to contain an earlier,

---

[211] See Mario Righetti, *Manuale di storia liturgica. Volume 1: Introduzione generale*, 3rd ed. (Milan: Editrice Ancora, 1964), 377–379.

[212] See Ursula Nilgen, 'Die Bilder über dem Altar: Triumph- und Apsisbogenprogramme in Rom und Mittelitalien und ihr Bezug zur Liturgie', in *Kunst und Liturgie im Mittelalter: Akten des internationalen Kongresses der Bibliotheca Hertziana und des Nederlands Instituut te Rome. Rom, 28.–30. September 1997*, ed. Nicolas Bock, Sible de Blaauw, Christoph L. Frommel and Herbert Kessler, Römisches Jahrbuch der Bibliotheca Hertziana. Beiheft zu Band 33 (1999/2000) (Munich: Hirmer, 2000), 75–89; and Christa Belting-Ihm, *Die Programme der christlichen Apsismalerei vom 4. Jahrhundert bis zur Mitte des 8. Jahrhunderts*, Forschungen zur Kunstgeschichte und christlichen Archäologie 4, 2nd ed. (Stuttgart: Steiner, 1992).

[213] On liturgical orientation and church architecture in Rome, see now Heid, *Altar und Kirche*, 279–349.

shorter redaction, notes that, after the *Kyrie*, the pontiff turns towards the people ('se dirigens contra populum'), intones the *Gloria in excelsis Deo* and immediately turns east again ('statim regerat se ad orientem') until the chant is completed. Then he turns again towards the people ('ad populum') for the liturgical salutation *Pax vobis*, and turns to the east ('ad orientem') for the *Oremus* and the collect (OR I, 53). This version of *Ordo Romanus I* presupposes a church with an oriented apse, with the seat of the pontiff facing west. The more widely attested version was evidently composed for a Roman basilica with the entrance at the east end. In this case, when the pontiff stood at his seat, he was already facing east and at the same time facing the people; hence there was no need for an instruction to turn around. Even with this arrangement, there were structures that impaired visual contact with the altar (and, to a greater degree, with bishop's seat in the apse), such as the relatively high screens (*cancelli*) that enclosed the *presbyterium*, a ciborium above the altar that was supported by columns, or the *fastigium* of the Lateran basilica, a monumental colonnade with silver statues.[214] At any rate, Christians in the late ancient and early medieval periods would not have associated liturgical participation with looking at the celebrant and his sparse ritual actions.

The Carolingian programme to renew the Roman imperial heritage in a Christian key (see Chapter 6) led to the adoption of particular features of Roman church architecture. The addition of a second apse to the west, for instance, in Cologne cathedral and the abbey church at Fulda (to house the body of Boniface), was inspired by the Gregorian plan of St Peter's. The ideal monastic plan of St Gall shows a church with two apses: the one to the east is dedicated to St Paul and the one in the west is dedicated to St Peter.[215] Such arrangements, however, were episodic, and the eastward direction of the apse with the main altar remained the norm in the Western Middle Ages.

The well-known ivory panel produced in Lorraine c. 875 and exhibited in the Liebieghaus, Frankfurt (see Figure 5.1) shows a solemn pontifical Mass. The scene can be read as an illustration of *Ordo Romanus I*. The celebrant is the pope or a metropolitan archbishop (as implied by the

---

[214] See Allan Doig, *Liturgy and Architecture from the Early Church to the Middle Ages* (Aldershot: Ashgate, 2008), 26–27.

[215] See ibid., 143–146; also Richard Krautheimer, 'The Carolingian Revival of Early Christian Architecture', in *The Art Bulletin* 24 (1942), 1–38; and Charles B. McClendon, *The Imperial Abbey of Farfa: Architectural Currents of the Early Middle Ages* (New Haven; London: Yale University Press, 1987), 69–71.

Figure 5.1 Depiction of a solemn pontifical Mass at the *Sanctus* / Ivory, Lorraine /
c. 875
(Liebighaus Skulpturensammlung, on permanent loan from Universitätsbibliothek Frankfurt
am Main / © Liebieghaus Skulpturensammlung, Frankfurt am Main / Reprinted with kind
permission)

pallium he is wearing) and he stands with his arms raised in prayer at the altar, which is prepared with chalice, paten and liturgical books. He is surrounded by assisting clergy as indicated after the conclusion of the offertory: in the background five deacons vested in dalmatic (OR I, 86); in the foreground five subdeacons of the *schola cantorum* vested in the *planeta* and facing the pontiff to make the liturgical responses (OR I, 87) . The subdeacons are depicted as singing – possibly the *Sanctus*. The artistic composition of the relief places the ciborium supported by four columns and crowned by angels behind the altar, but it should be imagined as covering it. This is a representation of the sanctuary, not of the nave of the church. Thus, the frontal depiction of the pontiff need not be understood as a celebration 'facing the people'. More likely, he is facing east towards the apse at a free-standing altar surrounded by his clergy (the *circumstantes* mentioned in the Canon of the Mass).[216]

CONCLUSION

In this chapter, I have traced the emergence of the ritual form and structure of the Roman Mass in the papal stational liturgy of the late ancient and early medieval periods. The codification of liturgical books in this period has left us a body of prayers, scriptural readings and chants, which are arranged according to the still developing liturgical year. This organisation of liturgical texts is by no means uniform, and two distinct traditions can be identified for the sacramentary: the Gelasian type for the use of priests in the city's titular churches and the Gregorian type for the papal stational liturgies. Different forms of indicating the Mass readings are known from this period (marginal notes, *capitularia*, epistolary, evangelary, full lectionary), and the cycles of epistle and gospel are arranged separately though they are not completely unrelated. Of particular importance is *Ordo Romanus I*, a detailed description of the pope's stational liturgy in Easter week and the oldest available description of the ritual shape of the Roman Mass. My discussion of this foundational document has had a particular focus on the role of chant (and of the *schola cantorum* that executes it), which is conceived as an integral element of the liturgy and thus helps us to understand the actual celebration of the Mass.

---

[216] See the comments of Heid, *Altar und Kirche*, 461–462.

Interpreting the extant sources of the papal stational liturgy present us with a fundamental problem, since they are prescriptive texts that communicate how the rite *should* be enacted. As historical scholarship has made us increasingly aware, however, we cannot simply assume that such prescriptions are identical with the way in which the liturgy was in fact carried out.[217] *Ordo Romanus I* was originally designed for the solemn papal Mass on Easter Sunday, Monday and Tuesday; as a template for other occasions, it was likely to be adapted to the spatial arrangements, local resources and (quite possibly) particular observances of the stational church chosen for the day. Moreover, it is a script for liturgical actors who were, for the most part, clerics (the papal court included also lay officials). As such, *Ordo Romanus I* can easily give the impression of a 'clericalised' liturgy, but such a view would be misleading since it abstracts from the genre and purpose of the document. Liturgical books in the strict sense are not concerned with how people in general participated in the rite, let alone how they experienced it. The difficulties of understanding the *fermentum* in relation to the reception of Holy Communion illustrate how limited our knowledge of popular liturgical practice actually is. Homiletic and hagiographical literature may give us glimpses into how liturgical celebrations were perceived, but such texts are scarce for the period studied in this chapter. While the significance of *Ordo Romanus I* for the history of Western liturgy cannot be disputed, the document leaves us with many open questions.

---

[217] This is a theme running through the contributions of the important volume *Understanding Medieval Liturgy*; see also Paul F. Bradshaw, *The Search for the Origins of Christian Worship: Sources and Methods for the Study of Early Liturgy*, 2nd ed. (Oxford: Oxford University Press, 2002), 1–20.

6

The Expansion and Adaptation of the Roman Liturgy in the Carolingian Age

The Carolingian age – which, for the purposes of this chapter, can be dated from 751, when Pippin the Short became King of the Franks, to 888, when the empire shaped by Charlemagne was divided after the overthrow and death of Charles the Fat – was pivotal for the development of Western liturgy. In the Frankish realm, the encounter and transformation of Roman and Franco-German traditions gave the Mass a ritual structure and shape that would essentially be retained for over a millennium. Recent contributions from a variety of historical disciplines offer a better understanding of this multifaceted development. Gallican patrimony was not simply replaced but to some degree integrated into the Roman Rite. The chapter will discuss key elements of liturgical reform in the Carolingian age and show their slow pace and gradual implementation, their dependence on local initiative and their focus on education, first of the clergy and, through them, of the whole people.

EXPANSION OF ROMAN LITURGICAL PRACTICE

By the early eighth century, the Roman Rite had been established as a recognisable body of liturgical forms and ordinances that was codified in liturgical books (see Chapter 5). These books were not composed originally with the intention of being copied and adopted beyond the city and its environs. In fact, they contain much material that has local Roman ambience. Rome was by no means the only centre of the Western liturgy in late antiquity. There were distinctive local and regional traditions on the Italian peninsula, such as those in Milan, Ravenna and Benevento, as well as in North Africa, Spain and Gaul. Popes saw liturgical unification as beneficial for tightening the bonds of local churches to the papacy. Innocent I (r. 402–417) was notable in this regard, stating in his letter to Bishop Decentius of Gubbio in 416 that, because the Roman church is the see of Peter, all churches in the Latin West should follow not only its doctrine but also its worship.[1] Innocent's letters were known in Gaul through collections of canon law. However, demands for Romanisation remained generic, and until the middle of the eighth century, we know only of a handful of concrete instructions on liturgical matters sent by popes to bishops north of the Alps.[2] Certain Roman practices were introduced in Merovingian Gaul through conciliar legislation; for instance, at the council of Vaison in 529 the incorporation of the *Kyrie* and the *Sanctus* into every celebration of Mass was decreed.[3] However, there was no concerted effort to Romanise the Gallican liturgical tradition, and popes did not exercise jurisdiction in liturgical matters beyond the local churches of *Italia suburbicaria*, which included central and southern Italy, as well as Sicily, Sardinia and Corsica.[4]

---

[1] 'Who does not know or fails to notice what has been transmitted to the Roman church by Peter, the first of the apostles, and has been maintained up to the present? This is what all of us are to follow so that nothing is added or introduced that lacks this authority or pretends to have received its model elsewhere. It is clear that in all Italy, Gaul, Spain, Africa, Sicily and the islands scattered among these countries no one has established a church except those to whom the venerable apostle Peter or his successors made priests (*sacerdotes*).' Innocent I, *Ep. 25 (ad Decentium)*: ed. Robert Cabié, *La lettre du pape Innocent I à Decentius de Gubbio (19 mars 416): Texte critique, traduction e commentaire*, Bibliothèque de la Revue d'histoire ecclésiastique 58 (Louvain: Publications Universitaires, 1973), 18–20. English translation: Lawrence J. Johnson, *Worship in the Early Church: An Anthology of Historical Sources*, 4 vols. (Collegeville: Liturgical Press, 2009), vol. III, 100 (no. 2783). See also Innocent's letter to Victricius of Rouen (416): PL 56, 519–527.

[2] These are listed by Cyrille Vogel, *Medieval Liturgy: An Introduction to the Sources*, ed. and trans. William G. Storey and Niels Krogh Rasmussen (Washington, DC: The Pastoral Press, 1986), 148.

[3] Council of Vaison (529), can. 3: CCL 148A,79. However, John F. Baldovin, *The Urban Character of Christian Worship: The Origins, Development, and Meaning of Stational Liturgy*, Orientalia Cristiana Analecta 228 (Rome: Pont. Institutum Studiorum Orientalium, 1987), 246, argues that 'Sanctus' here refers to the Greek *Trisagion*.

[4] See Vogel, *Medieval Liturgy*, 147–148 and 297–298; as well as Yitzhak Hen, *The Royal Patronage of Liturgy in Frankish Gaul: To the Death of Charles the Bald (877)*, Henry Bradshaw Society. Subsidia 3 (London: Boydell Press, 2001), 54–55.

Notwithstanding such a lack of official reach, the extension of Roman liturgical practice beyond the Alps was already underway under Merovingian rule, and this for a variety of religious, cultural and political reasons:

Firstly, Rome, as the hallowed place of the martyrdom of the Apostles Peter and Paul and the episcopal see of the successor of Peter, attracted many pilgrims – clerics, religious and laypeople – who were deeply impressed by the liturgical celebrations they witnessed and were keen to see some of their elements introduced back in their homelands.

Secondly, although Rome had been in political, social and economic decline owing to the sweeping transformations of the migration period, which culminated in the fall of the Western Empire in 476, the cultural and artistic prestige of the city was still considerable and was enhanced by the spiritual authority of the papacy.

Thirdly, Germanic rulers, above all the Franks, decided to promote the use of the Roman liturgy in their territories, because they considered it an expedient for political unification and social cohesion, although we need to be careful not to reduce such efforts to the criteria of modern sociology. The desire to unite a people in the true worship of God was seen as a sacred duty of rulers; this is especially clear in the case of Charlemagne, as we shall see.

An important landmark for the papacy was Gregory the Great's sending of Augustine and his monastic companions to England in the late sixth century. The highly successful evangelisation of the Anglo-Saxons and its wider cultural impact were specifically linked with Roman observances and customs,[5] strengthened the position of the popes and laid the ground for the work of English missionaries to the continent in the following century, especially the re-organisation of the Frankish church by Boniface (originally called Wynfreth, d. 754). Boniface insisted on the Roman practice of an episcopal imposition of hands and a second post-baptismal anointing and hence established the sacrament of confirmation as a

---

[5] See canon 13 of the council of Clovesho in 747: 'Ut uno eodemque modo Dominicae dispensationis in carne sacrosanctae festivitates, in omnibus ad eas rite competentibus rebus, id est, in Baptismi officio, in Missarum celebratione, in cantilenae modo celebrantur, juxta exemplar videlicet quod scriptum de Romana habemus Ecclesia.' *Councils and Ecclesiastical Documents Relating to Great Britain and Ireland*, ed. Arthur West Haddan and William Stubbs, vol. III (Oxford: Clarendon Press, 1871), 367.

separate stage in the process of Christian initiation. However, there is no evidence that Boniface's reform efforts had any particular impact upon the liturgy of the Mass beyond generic calls to follow Roman practice.[6]

THE MASS IN MEROVINGIAN GAUL

Clovis (c. 466–511), who united the Frankish tribes under his own kingship, converted to Catholic Christianity in 496 and made the Merovingian dynasty into leading patrons of the Church in Western Europe. Historiography has generally seen in this period the decline and decay of sophisticated Gallo-Roman civilisation, as evident in a reversion to oral tradition in proceedings of court, culture and religion.[7] On the other hand, recent scholarship draws attention to the vitality of literary production in both civil and ecclesiastical life under Merovingian rule. Yitzhak Hen argues that the role of formal correspondence and legal documentation was just as important then as was it was at the time of the Roman Empire.[8] Extant manuscripts testify to the productivity and creativity of Frankish liturgical scriptoria in adverse social and economic conditions. For our purpose, it is significant to note that among Merovingian liturgical sources, none of which is earlier than the seventh century, there are only a few that bear little or no trace of Romanisation, among them the collection of seven Masses published by Franz Mone (also known as Reichenau Fragments) and the Lectionary of Luxeuil. Most liturgical documents that are classified as Gallican already contain some Roman material, such as the *Missale Gothicum*, the Bobbio Missal, the *Missale Francorum* and the *Missale Gallicanum vetus*.

---

[6] Compare Arnold Angenendt, 'Keine Romanisierung der Liturgie unter Karl dem Großen? Einspruch gegen Martin Morards '*Sacramentarium immixtum*' *et uniformisation romaine*', in *Archiv für Liturgiewissenschaft* 51 (2009), 96–108, at 97–103, with the different assessment of Yitzhak Hen, *Culture and Religion in Merovingian Gaul: A.D. 481–751*, Cultures, Beliefs and Traditions 1 (New York: Brill, 1995), 44–46.

[7] See Matthew Innes, 'Memory, Orality and Literacy in an Early Medieval Society', in *Past & Present*, no. 158 (1998), 3–36, at 4–8.

[8] See Hen, *Culture and Religion in Merovingian Gaul*, 40–41 and 43–44.

The Order of Mass in the Gallican Rite according to the so-called *Exposition of the Gallican Liturgy* (seventh or early eighth century),[9] and the Masses of Mone:[10]

Salutations
Trisagion[11] and *Kyrie eleison*
Prophetia (Canticle of Zechariah: *Benedictus*)
Collect *post Prophetiam*
Prophetia (Old Testament reading)
Apostolus (Epistle reading)
Hymnus (Canticle of the Three Young Men: *Benedicite*)
De Aius ante Evangelium (*Trisagion*)
Evangelium (Gospel)
Sanctus post Evangelium
Sermon
Preces (litany) with Collect
Dismissal of catechumens and penitents
Offertory[12] with *Sonus* (chant) and *Laudes* (alleluias)
Praefatio (admonition to earnest prayer) and *Collectio* (prayer for acceptance of prayers)
Recital of names of the deceased and Collect *post nomina*
Collect *ad pacem* and Kiss of peace
Eucharistic Prayer
    Sursum corda
    Contestatio or *Immolatio* (Preface)
    Sanctus
    Post-*Sanctus*
    Secreta (Words of Institution)
    Post-*Secreta* or Post-*Mysterium*
    Doxology

[9] Although the description of the Mass already contains Roman elements, it is an important witness to Gallican tradition; see the critical edition by Philippe Bernard, *Epistulae de ordine sacrae oblationis et de diversis charismatibus ecclesiae Germano Parisiensi episcopo adscriptae* CCM 187 (Turnhout: Brepols, 2007).

[10] The schema is adapted from Ronald C. D. Jasper and Geoffrey J. Cuming, *Prayers of the Eucharist: Early and Reformed*, 3rd ed., revised and enlarged (New York: Pueblo, 1987), 148–150; and Bryan D. Spinks, *Do This in Remembrance of Me: The Eucharist from the Early Church to the Present Day* (SCM Studies in Worship and Liturgy (London: SCM Press, 2013), 197. See also Matthieu Smyth, '*Ante Altaria*': *Les rites antiques de la messe dominicale en Gaule, en Espagne et en Italie du Nord* (Paris: Cerf, 2007).

[11] 'Holy God, Holy Strong, Holy Immortal, have mercy on us.' It could be chanted in Latin and Greek.

[12] Bread and wine, which have been prepared beforehand, are brought to the altar by a deacon in a formal procession.

Fraction with chant
Lord's Prayer
Blessing by the bishop
Communion
Post Eucharistiam (thanksgiving) and Collect
Dismissal

The differences in character between Roman and other Western liturgical traditions have been highlighted in a seminal essay by Edmund Bishop. While one need not follow the value judgement that is implied in Bishop's pitting the linear and austere simplicity of the Roman Rite against the florid and repetitive style of the Gallican and Visigoth Rites, much of his analysis is still valid.[13] The Gallican tradition displays liturgical themes that are spiritually and culturally distinct from the Roman tradition. Some of these elements will be explored in the course of this chapter: an emotive, interior focus on the celebrant's role at Mass, a tendency to verbal embellishment, a preference for the allegorical interpretation of the liturgy and a fusion of liturgical prayer and ritual gesture.

THE RISE OF THE CAROLINGIAN DYNASTY AND LITURGICAL PATRONAGE

The eighth century saw the rise to the Frankish throne of the Carolingian family, whose members had successively occupied the key office of 'mayors of the palace', with increasing control over the executive power in civil affairs.[14] As Merovingian authority was waning, Charles Martel and his sons Carloman and Pippin III (also known as Pippin the Short), while still holding on to their ministerial title, began to consider themselves kings in all but name. After Carloman withdrew to the monastic life, the way was open to Pippin to become the first Carolingian King of the Franks, with the approval of Pope Zacharias, in 751.[15] Pope Stephen

---

[13] See Edmund Bishop, 'The Genius of the Roman Rite', in *Liturgica Historica* (Oxford: Clarendon Press, 1918), 1–19, esp. 4–5, where he compares and contrasts the Roman and Mozarabic prefaces for Pentecost. See also Paul Bradshaw, 'The Genius of the Roman Rite Revisited', in *Ever Directed Towards the Lord: The Love of God in the Liturgy Past, Present, and Hoped For*, ed. Uwe Michael Lang (London: T&T Clark, 2007), 49–61.

[14] A good overview of the period is offered by Joseph H. Lynch and Phillip C. Adamo, *The Medieval Church: A Brief History*, 2nd ed. (London; New York: Routledge, 2014), 72–84.

[15] See Chris Wickham, *The Inheritance of Rome: A History of Europe from 400 to 1000* (London: Penguin Books, 2010), 376–377.

II, who succeeded Zacharias in 752, travelled to Francia to anoint Pippin king in the abbey church of St Denis near Paris in 754, thus investing his kingship with a sacred character. Stephen also started the practice of addressing the King of the Franks as 'Patrician of the Romans'. While the precise import of this title is not clear, it certainly symbolised the political and religious alliance between the Carolingian dynasty and the papacy, which was to shape the history of Europe. In his own realm, Pippin continued the exercise of royal patronage over the church as in Merovingian times and took an interest in ecclesiastical affairs, including clerical and sacramental discipline.[16] He has often been credited with authoritative attempts to unify and standardise divine worship in his kingdom through the adoption of Roman liturgical books. It is only in retrospect that we hear of Pippin's efforts to replace Gallican chant with Roman chant. In a much-discussed chapter from his *Admonitio generalis* of 789, his son and successor Charlemagne stipulates that the clergy

are to learn Roman chant (*cantum Romanum*) thoroughly and that it is to be employed throughout the office, night and day, in the correct form, in conformity with what our father of blessed memory, King Pippin, strove to bring to pass when he abolished Gallican chant (*quando Gallicanum tulit*) for the sake of unanimity with the apostolic see and the peaceful concord of God's holy church.[17]

Two further sources, the *Libri Carolini* of c. 790 and Walafrid Strabo in the early 840s,[18] associate this particular reform with Pope Stephen's visit

---

[16] The council of Soisson in 744 confirmed for Neustria (the north-western territory of the realm) the decrees passed for Austrasia (the north-eastern territory) by the *Concilium Germanicum*, held in an unknown location in 742 under the leadership of Carloman and Boniface. See, e.g., *Concilium Suessonense* (744), can. 4: 'And each priest, who is in a parish [*parrochia*], should be obedient and subject to the bishop, and always on Maundy Thursday [*in caena Domini*] he should give an account of his ministry to the bishop, and should request chrism and oil, and whenever the bishop according to canon law visits the parish to confirm the people, bishops, abbots and priests should be ready to assist the bishop in his needs': MGH, Legum Sectio III, Concilia, Tomus II, Concilia Aevi Karolini, Pars I, 35.

[17] *Admonitio generalis*, c. 80: MGH, Legum Sectio II, Capitularia Regum Francorum, Tomus I, 61. See also Charlemagne's *Epistola generalis*: ibid., 80. The 2012 MGH edition by Hubert Mordek, Klaus Zechiel-Eckes and Michael Glatthaar lists this paragraph as c. 78, without significant variations in the text; see Daniel J. DiCenso, 'Revisiting the *Admonitio Generalis*', in *Chant, Liturgy, and the Inheritance of Rome: Essays in Honour of Joseph Dyer*, ed. Daniel J. DiCenso and Rebecca Maloy, Henry Bradshaw Society. Subsidia 8 (London: Boydell Press, 2017), 315–367, at 334–335.

[18] See *Opus Caroli Regis contra Synodum (Libri Carolini)*, c. I.6: MGH, Concilia, Tomus II, Supplementum I, 135–136; and Walafrid Strabo, *Libellus de exordiis et incrementis quarundam in observationibus ecclesiasticis rerum*, c. 26; ed. and trans. Alice L. Harting-Correa, Mittellateinische Studien und Texte 19 (Leiden: Brill, 1995), 168–169.

to the Frankish court residing in the *villa* of Ponthion (Champagne) in January 754. According to Christopher Page, the pope would most likely have travelled with some members of his *schola cantorum*, and this is in fact confirmed by Walafrid:

In fact, the more perfect knowledge of plain-chant (*cantilenae ... perfectiorem scientiam*), which almost all Francia now loves, brought Pope Stephen, when he came into Francia to Pippin, Emperor Charles the Great's father, to seek justice for St Peter against the Lombards, through his clerics (*per suos clericos*) at the request of the same Pippin, and from that time onward its use prevailed far and wide.[19]

There can be little doubt, therefore, of a concerted effort not just to complement but to transform the Gallican musical tradition with the introduction of Roman chant, and that this effort was supported by leading bishops in Pippin's reign, above all Chrodegang of Metz (d. 766), a close advisor to the king, and Remedius of Rouen (d. 771), Pippin's half-brother. Both bishops founded schools of liturgical chant according to the Roman model, and Metz became a centre of Carolingian liturgical renewal.[20] Thanks to the 'Frankish absorption and transformation of the Roman chant', the repertory we know as 'Gregorian' was created (see the section on Gregorian chant below, pp. 232–234).[21]

My discussion of *Ordo Romanus I* in Chapter 5 has shown the ordinary and proper chants of the Mass as integral elements of the rite. Thus, the introduction of Roman chant books into Francia was not just a matter of musical style and technique but also had implications for the selection of texts to be sung, and hence for the structure and content of the entire liturgical year. As Donald Bullough notes:

Ordo psallendi, like *cantilena*, in the usage of the day embraces words as well as music, structure as well as content (much like our 'a good paper'). The most influential and effective instruments of even an incomplete Romanisation were, on the one hand, those who had received a musical education in a Roman *schola* and, on the other, *ordines* rather than sacramentaries.[22]

---

[19] Walafrid Strabo, *Libellus de exordiis et incrementis*, c. 26: ed. Harting-Correa, 168–169; trans. Donald A. Bullough, *Carolingian Renewal: Sources and Heritage* (Manchester: Manchester University Press, 1991), 7–8. Christopher Page, *The Christian West and Its Singers: The First Thousand Years* (New Haven; London: Yale University Press, 2010), 281–328 (two chapters on 'Pippin and his Singers').

[20] See Page, *The Christian West and Its Singers*, 302, 305–306 (on Remedius) and 339–353 (on Metz).

[21] James McKinnon, *The Advent Project: The Later Seventh-Century Creation of the Roman Mass Proper* (Berkeley; Los Angeles; London: University of California Press, 2000), 3.

[22] Bullough, *Carolingian Renewal*, 8. See also Jesse D. Billett, 'The Liturgy of the "Roman" Office in England from the Conversion to the Conquest', in *Rome across Time and Space: Cultural Transmission and the Exchange of Ideas c. 500–1400*, ed. Claudia Bolgia,

Around 760, Pope Paul I sent Pippin an *antiphonale* and a *responsale*, the two separate books used in Rome for antiphons and for responsories (see Chapter 5).[23] The reception of these Roman chant books would imply an adoption of the fully formed Mass Proper. While there is no need to accept in its entirety James McKinnon's ground-breaking though disputed thesis that the cycle of chants had been created in the preceding century at the initiative of the Roman *schola cantorum*, it may have been the key element (rather than prayers and readings) that structured the liturgical year in the seasons between Epiphany and (Pre)Lent, and between Pentecost and Advent.[24]

In sum, the adoption of Roman chant books and the formation of singers in the practice of the Roman *schola cantorum* during the reign of Pippin was a significant step towards the Romanisation of the liturgy as a whole. What remains controverted among scholars is the king's personal interest and involvement in liturgical reform. Cyrille Vogel follows Anton Baumstark in arguing for a broadly conceived intention of standardising divine worship in the Kingdom of the Franks according to Roman models already under Pippin. The chief motives were to 'foster unity within the kingdom and [to] help consolidate the alliance between the Holy See and the Frankish monarchy, the protector of the *iustitia sancti Petri*'.[25]

On the other hand, Yitzhak Hen notes that there is scant evidence for crediting Pippin with such a sweeping initiative and contends that royal patronage of the liturgy continued in a more haphazard way, just as in the

---

Rosamond McKitterick and John Osborne (Cambridge: Cambridge University Press, 2011), 84–110, at 85: 'In the Middle Ages the term *cantus* could embrace not just musical melody but the whole of the liturgy, and when Bede and other Anglo-Saxon authors speak of Roman music they imply the adoption of a whole liturgical system of texts, ceremonies, feasts, and seasons.'

[23] Pope Paul I to Pippin: MGH, Epistolae Merowingici et Karolini aevi, Tomus III, VIII. Codex Carolinus, no. 24, 529.

[24] For critical yet sympathetic discussions of the late James McKinnon's thesis, see the extended reviews by Joseph Dyer, in *Early Music History* 20 (2001), 279–309; and by Peter Jeffery, in *Journal of the American Musicological Society* 56 (2003), 167–179.

[25] Vogel, *Medieval Liturgy*, 150; see also by the same author: 'Les échanges liturgiques entre Rome et les pays francs jusqu'à l'époque de Charlemagne', in *Le chiese nei regni dell'Europa occidentale e i loro rapporti con Roma sino all'800: 7–13 aprile 1959*, Settimane di studio del centro italiano di studi sull'alto Medioevo 7, 2 vols. (Spoleto: Presso la sede del Centro, 1960), 185–295; 'La réforme cultuelle sous Pépin le Bref et sous Charlemagne', in Erna Patzelt and Cyrille Vogel, *Die karolingische Renaissance: Beiträge zur Geschichte der Kultur des frühen Mittelalters*, 2nd ed. (Graz: Akademische Druck-u. Verlagsanstalt, 1965), 172–242; and 'Les motifs de la romanisation du culte sous Pépin le Bref (751–768) et Charlemagne (774–814)', in *Culto cristiano, politica imperiale carolingia: 9–12 ottobre 1977*, Convegni del Centro di studi sulla spiritualità medievale 18 (Todi: Accademia tudertina, 1979), 13–41.

Merovingian period. Liturgical books were compiled with Roman and Gallican material juxtaposed, above all in the mixed type of sacramentary known as the Frankish Gelasian or eighth-century Gelasian (*Gelasianum saeculi octavi*).[26] We have about a dozen examples of this sacramentary, which are presumed to derive from a lost archetype dating from the middle of the eighth century. Vogel sees in this archetype the work of a Frankish cleric close to Pippin, who composed, possibly in the monastery of Flavigny in Burgundy and even at the suggestion of the king, a sacramentary based on Roman models both Gelasian and Gregorian (which had been in circulation in Francia for some time), with generous additions of Gallican material. The general structure follows the Gregorian type, while the Mass formularies follow the Gelasian arrangement (two *orationes, secreta, contestatio, post communionem* and *super populum*) and have more Gelasian than Gregorian texts. In addition, Hen points to Frankish particularities, such as 'rogation days, consecration of churches and more significantly, the Frankish episcopal blessings which were despised and harshly condemned by Pope Zacharias in a letter to Boniface'.[27] The Frankish Gelasian enjoyed a wide circulation, which may indicate that it was promoted with Pippin's own authority. However, in the absence of any documentary evidence for such an official character, Bernard Moreton suggests that the sacramentary was disseminated because it was 'a manifestly convenient collection of the tradition',[28] which naturally included Gallican elements.

To conclude this section, the most far-reaching reform measure under Pippin was the decision, supported by leading bishops, to introduce Roman chant, which was not just a matter of musical preference but had profound implications for the liturgical texts. However, such initiatives were of their very nature local and dependent on resources that could be mustered only in ecclesiastical centres, such as Metz. While there were efforts to update liturgical books, they would not seem to amount to a general policy to unify divine worship in the Frankish kingdom.

CHURCH REFORM IN THE AGE OF CHARLEMAGNE

Pippin's son and successor Charles, known as 'the Great' or Charlemagne (born c. 742, king 768, crowned emperor 800, d. 814), resumed the work

---

[26] See Hen, *Royal Patronage*, 57–61, with further literature.

[27] Hen, *Royal Patronage*, 60. See the reply of Pope Zacharias to Boniface, *Ep. 87*: MGH, Epistulae Selectae, I, 198.

[28] Bernard Moreton, *The Eighth-Century Gelasian Sacramentary: A Study in Tradition*, Oxford Theological Monographs (Oxford: Oxford University Press, 1976), 173–174.

of his father with energy and dedication. Charlemagne understood himself as a Christian Caesar who would renew the Roman Empire in union with the papacy. According to his friend and biographer Einhard, no objective was closer to his heart than 'to restore to the city of Rome her ancient authority' through his own labours.[29]

Charlemagne not only enlarged the Frankish empire until it extended from central Italy to the North Sea and from the Spanish March to the Elbe river but also promoted a programme of reform aiming at 'the Christianization of society through education'.[30] Susan Keefe emphasises that this reform 'was primarily concerned with the Christianization of *every individual*, and not with political unity'.[31] Charlemagne is infamous for the forced baptism of the Saxons, which was linked with an act of feudal submission to himself (a decision that provoked a protest from Alcuin). However, this decision formed part of a particular military campaign and was not typical of his overall effort gradually to shape a new mindset by means of education, which would range from the elite of scholars he assembled at his court to the local pastors instructing their people in the essentials of Christian faith and living. In his *Admonitio generalis* (789), Charlemagne called for church reform and in the *Epistola de litteris colendis* (c. 794–797), a letter to Abbot Baugulf of Fulda, he outlined his plan for cultural reform, which included a revival not only of Latin but also of Greek antiquity in a Christian key, also known in modern scholarship as the 'Carolingian Renaissance'; both ends were to be achieved in the first place by the foundation of schools attached to cathedrals and monasteries. For the production of books, the Carolingian minuscule was developed, a clear and elegant script based on Roman letters. Charlemagne reclaimed the observance of canon law, for which purpose he obtained in 774 from Pope Hadrian the collection known as *Dionysio-Hadriana*, based on the compilation by Dionysius Exiguus in the early sixth century. Ecclesiastical reform also included efforts to establish an amended, authoritative version of the Latin Bible, the compilation of a model homiliary for the clergy by the Lombard Paul the Deacon and the general introduction of the Rule of St Benedict for monastic communities, based on what was considered an autograph version from Monte Cassino.[32] Charlemagne took a

---

[29] Einhard, *Vita Karoli Magni*, c. 27: MGH, Scriptores Rerum Germanicarum, Tomus XXV, 32.

[30] Susan Keefe, *Water and the Word: Baptism and the Education of the Clergy in the Carolingian Empire*, Publications in Medieval Studies, 2 vols. (Notre Dame: University of Notre Dame Press, 2002), vol. I, 2.

[31] Ibid., vol. I, 5.   [32] See Hen, *Royal Patronage*, 73–74, with further literature.

personal interest in the efforts of the churchmen and scholars he surrounded himself with, such as the Anglo-Saxon Alcuin of York (d. 804) and the Visigoth Theodulf of Orleans (d. 820), to standardise liturgical books.

The principles of Charlemagne's church reform have been identified as *correctio, unanimitas* and *secundum Romanum usum.*[33] While the benefits of such a programme for the social and political cohesion of his realm lay at hand, it also needs to be understood as religiously motivated. The king and (from 800) emperor saw it as his sacred duty to unite his people in the right worship of the one true God and so lead them to salvation. The idea of the Franks as the 'New Israel' had some currency' and among the scholars at his court, Charlemagne was 'David' and his son Louis as 'Solomon'. Charlemagne himself chose another Old Testament model in the prologue to his *Admonitio generalis*, namely Josiah, the King of Judah in the seventh century BC who purified the worship of the Israelites from pagan elements and centralised it at the Temple of Jerusalem, which he restored (see 2 Kgs 22–23 and 2 Chr 34–35).[34]

The Hadrianum *and Its Supplement*

A key moment in Charlemagne's grand project was his request to Pope Hadrian, made in the early 780s through Paul the Deacon, to provide him with the authentic sacramentary of the Roman church, which was presumed to come from Gregory the Great. It may have been on his visits to Rome in 774 and 781 that Charlemagne realised that the type of sacramentary circulated during the reign of his father Pippin, the Frankish Gelasian, was in fact not used for papal liturgies. Pope Hadrian responded with some delay between 784 and 791, and he sent Charlemagne the sacramentary known as the *Hadrianum*, most likely redacted under Pope Honorius I (d. 638) and subsequently revised and enlarged. The motives and circumstances of this donation remain disputed. Hen surmises that in Rome a real effort was made to produce the oldest available exemplar of the Gregorian-type sacramentary. Vogel, by contrast, suggests that the pope and his advisors misunderstood the

---

[33] See Rosamond McKitterick, *Charlemagne: The Formation of a European Identity* (Cambridge: Cambridge University Press, 2008), 306–320.

[34] *Admonitio generalis*, prologue: MGH, Legum Sectio II, Capitularia Regum Francorum, Tomus I, 53–54. Josiah is singled out for praise by Theodulf of Orleans, *Carmen* 28 (*Contra Iudices*), ll. 77–82: MGH, Poetae Latini Aevi Karolini, Tomus I, 495. See also Hen, *Royal Patronage*, 81–84.

nature of Charlemagne's request and sent him a venerable manuscript as a personal gift.[35] Hadrian's letter that accompanied the manuscript, with its irregular Latin, continues to raise difficulties of interpretation. Martin Morard makes a strong philological case that the attribute 'immixtum' Hadrian uses to describe the sacramentary should not be understood as an 'unmixed', as often assumed, but should rather be translated as 'intermingled'. Hence the phrase would not indicate a 'purely' Gregorian sacramentary but rather a compilation from different sources, in use for papal celebrations in Rome.[36]

The manuscript had indeed been compiled for the Roman stational Masses and hence did not include a complete cycle of Masses for the liturgical year. It lacked more than half of the Sunday formularies, including those after the Epiphany, after Easter and after Pentecost. There were no Masses for the deceased, no texts for the reconciliation of penitents and no votive Masses. As it stood, the *Hadrianum* was not fit for liturgical use in the Frankish realm. Nonetheless, the manuscript from Rome was given a place of honour in the palace library at Aachen to serve as an 'authentic' sacramentary, from which reproductions were to be made. It is not surprising that the diffusion of what is called *Hadrianum ex authentico* was very slow, and only a few copies of it have come down to us. The only complete and uncorrected copy that has survived is the sacramentary commissioned by Bishop Hildoard of Cambrai, which is dated to c. 811–812 (Figure 6.1). An influential figure like Alcuin did not see the need for a new sacramentary and continued with his own adaptations of pre-Hadrianic Gregorian as well as Gelasian material.[37]

The limits of the *Hadrianum* were clearly seen, and it was either Charlemagne himself or his successor Louis the Pius who took the initiative to supplement the sacramentary. The work of restructuring, amending and augmenting the *Hadrianum* used to be attributed to Alcuin, but since the ground-breaking work of Jean Deshusses on the Gregorian sacramentaries, it is now almost unanimously ascribed to Benedict of Aniane (d. 821) and dated between 810 and 815. The supplement known by the incipit of its prologue as *Hucusque* includes above all Sunday Masses but also many votive Masses and a range of occasional services, such as weddings and funerals, as well as texts and rites for

---

[35] Compare Vogel, *Medieval Liturgy*, 85 with Hen, *Royal Patronage*, 75.

[36] Martin Morard, '"Sacramentarium immixtum" et uniformisation romaine: de l'*Hadrianum* au *Supplément* d'Aniane', in *Archiv für Liturgiewissenschaft* 46 (2004), 1–30, at 5–7.

[37] See Hen, *Royal Patronage*, 79–80, with further literature.

Figure 6.1 Sacramentary of Hildoard of Cambrai / Northern France / 811–812
(Cambrai, Bibliothèque Municipale, 164 [olim 159]), fols. 35v–36r / © 2013 Institut de
recherche et d'histoire des textes / CC BY-NC 3.0)

monastic communities and prayers for the kings of the Franks. A separate appendix features 221 Gelasian prefaces, 51 Gallican episcopal blessings given before the distribution of Holy Communion, as well as texts and rubrics for the conferral of the minor orders. Morard argues that most of the supplemented material is taken from eight-century Gelasian sources, which had already taken root in Frankish use. Far from being an 'unmixed' Roman sacramentary, the result of Benedict's reworking can justly be described as a 'hybrid' (Vogel) or 'amalgam' (Hen) of Roman-Gregorian, Roman-Gelasian and Gallican traditions.

Romanisation and Liturgical Diversity

Notwithstanding the forceful Carolingian rhetoric of unanimity and Romanisation, there remained in fact a plurality of liturgical books – and hence liturgical uses – under Charlemagne and his successor Louis the Pious: along with the circulation of the supplemented *Hadrianum*, the Old Gelasian, Frankish Gelasian, type-II Gregorian sacramentaries,[38] as well as those of the still vital Gallican patrimony co-existed well into the ninth century. Amalarius, after visiting Rome in 831, commented on the differences between Roman and Frankish liturgy.[39] In the 840s, Walafrid Strabo noted the lack of uniformity in liturgical practice within the Frankish Kingdom.[40]

   In recognition of this diversity, scholars have reconsidered the scope and reach of liturgical reform in the age of Charlemagne. Mention has already been made of the work of Yitzhak Hen, who emphasises the limited extent of Charlemagne's actions and sees in them a continuation of Merovingian and earlier Carolingian royal patronage.[41] Martin Morard has challenged long-held convictions of a consistent programme of Romanisation (let alone 'Gregorianisation') of the liturgy in the Frankish Kingdom, especially regarding the role of Charlemagne and

---

[38] As exemplified in the Sacramentary of Padua: 'It is referred to as a Gregorian sacramentary, type II, because it is now considered to be an adaptation of the Lateran sacramentary (= type I) of the mid-VII century for presbyteral use at the Vatican.' Vogel, *Medieval Liturgy*, 94.

[39] Amalarius, *Liber officialis*, Praefatio altera: ed. Jean Michel Hanssens, *Amalarii Episcopi Opera Liturgica Omnia*, Tomus II, Studi e testi 139 (Vatican City: Biblioteca Apostolica Vaticana, 1948), 13–19.

[40] Walafrid Strabo, *Libellus de exordiis et incrementis*, c. 26 : ed. Harting-Correa, 162–165.

[41] For a concise presentation of his thesis, see Yitzhak Hen, 'The Romanization of the Frankish Liturgy: Ideal, Reality and the Rhetoric of Reform', in *Rome Across Time and Space: Cultural Transmission and the Exchange of Ideas c. 500–1400*, ed. Claudia Bolgia, Rosamond McKitterick and John Osborne (Cambridge: Cambridge University Press, 2011), 111–123.

his court.[42] The lack of positive evidence that the use of the 'authentic' *Hadrianum* was actually imposed by royal authority[43] may reflect awareness on the part of Charlemagne and his trusted advisors that no programme of reform could be simply legislated and enforced, given the very limited structures of communication and administration in early medieval society. As Vogel observes: 'Liturgical unification depended entirely upon a few famous scriptoria and their patrons and was never accomplished in a uniform manner ... there was no religious authority capable, or even desirous, of imposing uniformity.'[44] Extant liturgical manuscripts continued to be used, partly for economic reasons, as book production was very costly and partly because of their venerable prestige. For instance, the important abbey of St Riquier in 831 records in its sacristy the following books for the ministry of the altar: three Gelasian Mass books, nineteen Gregorian ones and one 'missalis Gregorianus et Gelasianus modernis temporis ab Albino ordinatus', referring to one of Alcuin's abovementioned editions.[45]

The morally charged rhetoric of Charlemagne's ecclesiastical capitularies goes beyond positive legislation.[46] These documents are shot through with admonitions and appeals for a reform that is meant to promote 'unanimity with the Apostolic See and the peaceful harmony of

[42] The argument of Morard, '"Sacramentarium immixtum" et uniformisation romaine' has provoked a fervent objection from Angenendt, 'Keine Romanisierung der Liturgie unter Karl dem Großen?'

[43] See Morard, '"Sacramentarium immixtum" et uniformisation romaine', 9, in response to the entirely hypothetical suggestion of Jean Deshusses, 'The Sacramentaries: A Progress Report', in *Liturgy* 18 (1984), 13–60, at 48: 'Though we have no extant copies of any royal edicts imposing the use of the Roman sacramentary in the Carolingian kingdom, one feels that such decrees must have existed'.

[44] Vogel, *Medieval Liturgy*, 92.

[45] Hariulf of Oldenburg, *Chronicon Centulense*, III,3: PL 174,1261; see Bullough, *Carolingian Renewal*, 163.

[46] See Angenendt, ,Keine Romanisierung der Liturgie unter Karl dem Großen?', 104, with reference to Thomas Martin Buck, *Admonitio und Praedicatio: Zur religiös-pastoralen Dimension von Kapitularien und kapitulariennahen Texten (507–814)*, Freiburger Beiträge zur mittelalterlichen Geschichte 9 (Frankfurt am Main: Peter Lang, 1997), 13. Rosamond McKitterick, *The Frankish Church and the Carolingian Reforms, 789–895* (London: Royal Historical Society, 1977), 25, argues that a capitulary was first issued as an act of legislation, but 'eventually intended to serve a didactic purpose ... and to supply a source of regulative and admonitory canons for reference and guidance, rather than have the force of statutory law'. Morard, '"Sacramentarium immixtum" et uniformisation romaine', 10, observes: 'Dans l'empire carolingien, d'ailleurs, celui qui n'avait pas entendu la loi n'était pas tenu d'obéir, ce qui relativise considérablement la portée réelle des capitulaires.'

God's holy Church'.[47] Hen's reading would seem too narrow when he argues that Charlemagne was intent only on 'doctrinal conformity with Rome'.[48] The idea of *unanimitas apostolicae sedis* cannot be dissociated from unity in divine worship, and Arnold Angenendt rightly points to a plethora of contemporary ecclesiastical sources that demand conformity with the liturgical use or custom (*consuetudo*) of the Roman church.[49] Decisive impulses came from episcopal and monastic centres, such as Metz, Laon, Lorsch, St Gall and naturally from Charlemagne's palatine chapel in Aachen. According to Morard, the story of the *Hadrianum* and its supplement shows that the lasting success of a Roman liturgical book beyond the confines of the city was owing to its inherent qualities that met the cultural, spiritual and missionary needs of local churches at the time.[50]

So far, this discussion has largely focused on the history of sacramentaries, which assemble the prayer texts used in the Church's public worship, but offer us little, if any, information about its ritual performance. These euchological resources on their own were not sufficient to convey the rites and ceremonies of the Roman Mass. A fuller picture emerges only when we consider the Frankish adaptation of the *Ordines Romani* (see Chapter 5), which Bullough justly acclaims as the 'most influential and effective instruments of even an incomplete Romanisation'.[51] It is of singular significance for the further development of Western liturgy that, as part of the Carolingian reforms, the elaborate rite of the papal stational Mass, as documented in *Ordo Romanus I*, became the model for

---

[47] *Admonitio generalis*, c. 80: MGH, Legum Sectio II, Capitularia Regum Francorum, Tomus I, 61.

[48] Hen, *Royal Patronage*, 86.

[49] The synod of Riesbach (Bavaria) in 798, held under Archbishop Arno of Salzburg decreed: 'missas secundum consuetudinem caelebrare, sicut Romana traditio nobis tradidit'. *Concilium Rispacense* (798), can. 2: MGH, Legum Sectio III, Concilia, Tomus II, Concilia Aevi Karolini, Pars I, 198. See also the examination of priests dating from 803, in *Additamenta ad Pippini et Karoli M. Capitularia*, no. 116: 'Missam vestram secundum ordinem Romanam quomodo nostis vel intellegistis.' MGH, Legum Sectio II, Capitularia Regum Francorum, Tomus I, 234. *Ordo Romanus XV*, a Frankish directory for the liturgical year from the late eighth century, stipulates: '155. Hoc iterum aque iterum super omnia admonemus, ut om[nis] sacerdos q[ui] desiderat racionabiliter sacrificum Deo offerre, ut et conplaciat, secundum sanctae institutionis ortodoxorum patrum, beati atque gloriosa sedis sancti Petri apostoli, isto more, cum omni devotione retinire atque celebrare stodit ... 156. Qui enim isto modo non offert, postquam cognoverit, non recto ordine offert se barbarico et suo arbitrio sequitur ...'; ed. Michel Andrieu, *Les Ordines Romani du haut moyen âge*, 5 vol., Spicilegium Sacrum Lovaniense 11, 23, 24, 28, 29 (Louvain: Peeters, 1931–1961), vol. III, 125.

[50] Morard, '"Sacramentarium immixtum" et uniformisation romaine', 24.

[51] Bullough, *Carolingian Renewal*, 8.

liturgical celebrations north of the Alps. The process of reception and adaptation of *Ordo I* resulted in a variety of *ordines*, some of them maintaining their Roman character, others showing different grades of Gallican influence. As is the case with the sacramentaries, the extant manuscripts of the *ordines* are all of Frankish or Germanic production.[52]

Ordo Romanus II, a supplement to *Ordo I*, is concerned with the celebration of a stational Mass by a bishop or priest in the absence of the pope. While the document clearly reflects the liturgical settings of the city of Rome, its final instruction would point to a Frankish context: 'The bishops who preside over cities must perform in the same way as the Supreme Pontiff.'[53] Theodor Klauser suggests with some plausibility that this phrase may have been added 'by an editor commissioned by the Frankish court or by a Synod'.[54]

In their efforts to adopt the Roman Mass, Frankish clerics and monks were not looking at its simpler, presbyteral form, which they could have observed in the titular churches of the papal city but rather at its solemn pontifical form. As has been discussed in Chapter 5, the oldest available Roman sources, both sacramentaries and *ordines*, are chiefly concerned with the liturgical celebrations of a bishop. The Eucharist celebrated by a priest was understood as a simpler form of the episcopal liturgy, with reduced ceremonial.[55] The Carolingian liturgists adapted *Ordo Romanus I* as the standard and measure of the celebration of Mass, to the local conditions and customs of cathedrals and churches of the Frankish realm. In doing so, they ensured that the solemn pontifical liturgy remained the normative exemplar, in which all other celebrations of Mass participated to a greater or lesser degree. Sven Conrad summarises the observations of scholars, such as Joaquim Nabuco and Josef Andreas Jungmann, when he notes: 'Through many steps of liturgical reduction, we arrive from there [*Ordo Romanus I*] to the simple *Missa lecta* or to what is known as the Private Mass. The principles are given from the top and in their

---

[52] Vogel, *Medieval Liturgy*, 135–247, offers an excellent overview of the *Ordines Romani*.

[53] 'Episcopi, qui civitatibus praesedent, ut summus pontifex ita omnia agant.' *Ordo Romanus II*, 10: ed. Andrieu, vol. II, 116.

[54] Theodor Klauser, *A Short History of the Western Liturgy: An Account and Some Reflections*, trans. John Halliburton, 2nd ed. (Oxford: Oxford University Press, 1979), 71.

[55] See Niels K. Rasmussen, 'Célébration épiscopale et célébration presbytérale: un essai de typologie', in *Segni e riti nella chiesa altomedievale occidentale: 11–17 aprile 1985*, Settimane di studio del Centro italiano di studi sull'alto medioevo 33 2 vol. (Spoleto: Presso la Sede del Centro, 1987), 581–607.

implementation are simply reduced.'[56] In a similar way, the Divine Liturgy of the Byzantine Rite is intelligible only from its hierarchical (i.e., pontifical) form.[57]

Susan Keefe has confirmed the local character and gradual pace of liturgical reform in the Carolingian age in her study of baptismal instructions, which were composed as tools for the formation of the pastoral clergy to enable them to educate the people in the Christian faith.[58] Across the Carolingian territories and even in the late ninth century, there remained a range of observances 'from Amiens, where some form of [*Ordo Romanus*] XI was observed ... to southern France, where the Old Gallican *pedilavium* persisted'.[59] Religious practice was indeed meant to be 'corrected', and this implied a standardisation according to the Roman pattern in a generic sense, but significant variations remained and non-Romans observances continued.[60]

Gregorian Chant

The repertory that was created by the Frankish adoption and adaptation of Roman chant was invested with the authority of Pope Gregory the Great (r. 509–604) and is still known as 'Gregorian chant'. One of the oldest extant Roman graduals and a source for Hesbert's edition of the

---

[56] Sven Conrad, 'Renewal of the Liturgy in the Spirit of Tradition: Perspectives with a View Towards the Liturgical Development of the West', in *Antiphon* 14 (2010), 95–136, at 119; see also Joaquim Nabuco, 'La liturgie papale et les origines du cérémonial des évêques', in *Miscellanea liturgica in honorem L. Cuniberti Mohlberg*, 2 vols., Bibliotheca Ephemerides Liturgicae 22–23 (Rome: Edizioni Liturgiche, 1948–1949), vol. I, 283–300; Josef Andreas Jungmann, *Missarum sollemnia: Eine genetische Erklärung der römischen Messe*, 2 vols., 5th ed. (Wien: Herder, 1962), vol. I, 263–265; and Franck Quoëx, 'Ritualité et chant sacré dans l'*Ordo Romanus Primus* (VII–VIIIème siècle)', in *Aevum* 76 (2002), 253–265.

[57] See Hans-Joachim Schulz, 'Liturgie, Tagzeiten und Kirchenjahr des byzantinischen Ritus', in *Handbuch der Ostkirchenkunde Bd. II*, ed. Wilhelm Nyssen, Hans-Joachim Schulz and Paul Wiertz (Düsseldorf: Patmos, 1989), 30–100, at 36–37; also Alexander Schmemann, *Eucharist: Sacrament of the Kingdom*, trans. Paul Kachur (Crestwood: St Vladimir's Seminary Press, 1987), 15–16.

[58] The lasting impact of these baptismal instructions is evident from the fact they continued to be copied until the twelfth century; see Keefe, *Water and the Word*, vol. I, 154–155.

[59] See Keefe, *Water and the Word*, vol. I, 114.

[60] Surveying the extant baptism instructions from the Carolingian period, Keefe, *Water and the Word*, vol. I, 150, notes: 'These Texts show that the Roman *ordo* of baptism was not a single text, such as *OR XI* or the Reginensis, which had acquired some sort of official recognition. The "Roman *ordo* of baptism" meant a type of rite, of which there could be numerous legitimate variations.'

Antiphonale Missarum Sextuplex, the Antiphoner of Mont-Blandin (Brussels, Bibliothèque Royale 10127–10144), dating from around 800, bears the name of Saint Gregory.[61] The manuscript Lucca, Biblioteca Capitolare 490 of the *Liber pontificalis* includes a poem beginning with the words 'Gregorius praesul', which celebrates the pope for instituting the *schola cantorum* and for composing 'this book', which indicates that the text served as the introduction to a chant volume.[62] Two further sources for the *Antiphonale Missarum Sextuplex*, Monza, Basilica S. Giovanni CIX and Paris, Bibliothèque Nationale, lat. 17436, both written in north-east France in the second half of the ninth century, have a shorter version of 'Gregorius praesul', which identifies the pope as the author of the 'hunc libellum musicae artis scholae cantorum'.[63] How are we to interpret this attribution, which is found in unnotated chant books? David Hiley argues that there is some continuity of texts between Gregory's lifetime and the earliest available books with musical notation, but the intervening space of almost three centuries makes it highly unlikely that these books contain the melodies sung in the late sixth century:

No doubt many of the same texts were sung with the same liturgical assignment in Gregory's time as later, but we must reckon with both more subtle and more radical changes in singing practice in the interim . . . . In this context, the very idea of a 'composer' of chant is anachronistic.[64]

The legendary ascription to Gregory the Great ignores the fact that the musical form of Roman liturgical chant was changed when it was established in Francia in the eighth century. This process of transformation is hard to grasp, and Hiley even calls it 'a hazardous undertaking',[65] since the training of Frankish singers in the substantial Roman repertory relied largely on oral transmission and memorisation. In his *vita* of Gregory the Great, the Roman deacon John Hymonides, writing between 873 and

---

[61] See *Antiphonale Missarum Sextuplex*, ed. René-Jean Hesbert (Rome: Herder, 1935), xv–xviii.

[62] The text of the poem is found in *Paléographie musicale: Les principaux manuscrits de chant grégorien, ambrosien, mozarabe, gallican, publiés en fac-similés phototypiques, par les Bénédictins de Solesmes*, vol. II (Solesmes: Imprimerie Saint-Pierre, 1891), 21; see plate 3 for a reproduction of the manuscript page.

[63] See David Hiley, *Western Plainchant: A Handbook* (Oxford: Clarendon Press, 1993), 510–511; also 297–298.

[64] Ibid., 513; see the careful survey of sources that ascribe the creation of chant to Gregory, ibid., 503–513.

[65] Ibid., 517.

875, claims that the constitution of the northern singers was too coarse to master the ornate modulations of Roman chant.[66] The abilities of Frankish cantors may have varied, but the evident chauvinism of this assertion obscures the fact that their aesthetic criteria were in many ways different from those of their Roman teachers. Thus, Hiley observes,

it seems conceivable that the Franks sang the Roman chants in a more straightforward idiom than the Romans themselves, something perhaps more akin to that of their native traditions. That is a matter of surface detail. As regards learning the standard formulas, type-melodies and the methods of using them, the Frankish singers were evidently very successful.[67]

Despite their royal commission to learn Roman melodies thoroughly and employ them in the liturgy, the Frankish cantors actually transformed them and so created a new chant dialect. The presumed authority of Gregory the Great, who in contemporary manuscript illustrations is often depicted as writing (or dictating) under the inspiration of the Holy Spirit in the form of a dove, no doubt helped to establish what musicologists recognise as the remarkable diffusion and stability of this new repertory. William T. Flynn, who questions this consensus and argues against the assumption underlying the 'Gregorian semiology' of the Solesmes monk Eugène Cardine (1905–1988) that 'dissimilar notational signs' carry 'the same melodic meaning when occurring in similar musical contexts', nonetheless acknowledges that '[l]ater notated transmission show at most a correspondence of about 80–90 per cent of melodic content' – which is still a very high percentage.[68] The performance of Gregorian chant certainly differed from region to region and even from place to place in aspects, such as sound, tempo and dynamics, but the repertory is remarkably consistent.[69]

PERSONAL AND EMOTIVE LITURGICAL EXPRESSION

We are now in a better position to appreciate the Romanisation of the liturgy in the Frankish Kingdom as a long process, which had begun in Merovingian times and was accelerated under the Carolingian dynasty.

---

[66] See John the Deacon, *Vita Gregorii*, II,7: PL 75,90D–91A.
[67] Hiley, *Western Plainchant*, 562.
[68] William T. Flynn, "Approaches to Early Medieval Music and Rites", in *Understanding Medieval Liturgy: Essays in Interpretation*, ed. Helen Gittos and Sarah Hamilton (London and New York: Routledge, 2018), 57–71, at 60.
[69] See Hiley, *Western Plainchant*, 563–564.

It would not be adequate to think of this process as a one-way street, because with the reception of Roman liturgical books, Gallican elements were maintained and inserted into them. In a study on the Divine Office in early medieval England, Jesse Billett proposes that any enquiry into the transmission and transformation of Roman liturgy needs to distinguish between elements that are 'structural' and 'incidental' (or, in Aristotelian-Thomistic terms, 'substantial' and 'accidental').[70] Billett explains:

> By 'structural' non-Roman elements is meant things that alter or add to the structure of the liturgy itself. By 'incidental' non-Roman elements is meant things not themselves of Roman origin, but that perform the same liturgical function as if they were Roman.[71]

For instance, codex Vat. Reg. Lat. 316 (the 'Old Gelasian') has non-Roman elements, some of which are structural, such as the addition of blessings of the people before communion, some of which are incidental, such as the use of Gallican euchological texts in the place of Roman ones. However, these elements are not significant enough to change the Roman character of the sacramentary. On the other hand, Gallican liturgical sources, such as the Bobbio Missal, include Roman elements both structural (the *Canon missae*) and incidental (proper orations), but preserve a particular ritual pattern and form that is distinctively non-Roman. In the light of this discussion, I intend to illustrate with select examples that the Frankish adoption of the Roman Mass introduced both structural and incidental elements from the Gallican tradition, without breaking the continuity of a rite that remained substantially 'Roman'.

The Frankish adaptation of the Roman Rite has been described as a shift towards a more personal, emotive understanding of and approach to the liturgy.[72] The Gallican tradition shows a strong sense of spiritual introspection and of personal involvement in ministering at the altar. Such tendency can be identified in the incorporation of specific prayers of a distinct style or register into the already existing structure of the Roman Mass. Prayers composed in the first person (singular or plural) make the bishop or priest celebrant enter into a personal dialogue with

[70] See Billett, 'The Liturgy of the "Roman" Office in England from the Conversion to the Conquest', at 92–94.

[71] Ibid., 93.

[72] See, for instance, Herman Wegman, *Christian Worship in East and West: A Study Guide to Liturgical History*, trans. Gordon W. Lathrop (New York: Pueblo, 1985), 190–191.

God, in which he acknowledges his sinfulness and expresses his fervent hope of receiving divine mercy in the form of a worthily offered Mass.

Such 'apologies' are also known in the Byzantine tradition and the oldest known example from the Divine Liturgy is the prayer 'No one is worthy' (Οὐδεὶς ἄξιος), which is said by the priest in a low voice during the singing of the *Cherubikon* at the Great Entrance. This text is attested in the Liturgy of St Basil of the eighth-century Euchologion Barberini Gr. 336 and was later adopted in the Liturgy of St John Chrysostom. The parallels between the prayer and the disciplinary canons of the Council in Trullo of 692 suggests that it may have been composed shortly afterwards.[73]

A good example of this priestly liturgical spirituality in the Western tradition is found in the Sacramentary of Echternach, compiled at the end of the ninth century from both Gregorian and Gelasian sources. The sacramentary features a short order of Mass, which extends from the preface dialogue to the *Agnus Dei*. This is preceded by a collection of personal prayers to be said by the priest (and in one case by the deacons) before, during and after the celebration of Mass. The prayer 'Quando sacerdos ad immolandum accedit ante altare' exemplifies the dynamic of fear and trust, sorrow and joy that characterises this form of clerical introspection. The priest presents himself before God both as a sinner and, by virtue of his ministry, as a mediator of salvation:

Deus qui te praecipis a peccatoribus exorare, tibique contriti cordis sacrificium offerri, hoc sacrificium quod ego indignus de tua misericordia confisus tuae pietati offerre praesumo acceptare dignare, et ut ipse tibi et sacerdos et ara et templum et sacrificum esse merear propitius concede, quo per huius ministerii exhibitionem, peccatorum meorum adipisci merear remissionem, mihique et his pro quibus offertur tuam miserissimam proptiationem.

O God, who command that you be entreated by sinners and that the sacrifice of a contrite heart be offered to you, deign to accept this sacrifice, which I, unworthy and confident in your mercy, presume to offer to your kindness, and graciously grant that I myself may be to you both priest and altar and temple and sacrifice, so that, through the exercise of this ministry, I may obtain the remission of my sins, and, both for me and for those for whom [this sacrifice] is offered, your most merciful pardon.[74]

---

[73] See Alain-Pierre Yao, *Les 'apologies' de l'Ordo Missae de la Liturgie Romaine: Sources – Histoire – Théologie*, Ecclesia orans. Studi e ricerche 3 (Naples: Editrice Domenicana Italiana, 2019), 37–42.

[74] *The Sacramentary of Echternach: (Paris Bibliothèque Nationale, MS. Lat. 9433)*, ed. Yitzhak Hen, Henry Bradshaw Society 110 (London: Boydell Press, 1997), 86–87.

Such prayers known as apologies (*apologiae*) are to be said privately by the celebrant at different moments of the Mass. They display an emphasis on personal sin as well as trust in God's mercy and election, which is expressed in dramatically ascending language and verbal repetition.

Devotions of this kind were also included in the prayer books for the personal use of the Carolingian elites. The small but splendid volume produced between 846 and 869 for Charles the Bald (King of West Francia 843, emperor 875, d. 877) by his court school[75] contains variations of prayers that became part of the *Ordo Missae* (see Chapter 7): a prayer to the Holy Trinity for the acceptance of the sacrifice offered through the hands of the priest with a plea for particular intentions (*Suscipe sancta Trinitas*), a confession of sins (*Confiteor*), a response to the priest's petition for prayer (*Orate, fratres*), as well as a prayer before and after communion.[76]

The incorporation of these prayers into the Roman Mass highlights the evolving understanding of the priest's distinct liturgical role in relation to God and to the lay congregation. Bonifaas Luykx has classified the 'Apology type' as the first of three major stages in the development of the *Ordo Missae* (for an extended discussion, see Chapter 7). There are three moments in particular when the priest offers these apology prayers: at the beginning of Mass, at the offertory and in preparation for taking communion.[77] In the case of the introductory rites, it can be argued that the addition of personal prayers verbalise a non-verbal liturgical element that is already present in the earlier Roman tradition. The papal Mass as

---

[75] See Robert Deshman, 'The Exalted Servant: The Ruler Theology of the Prayerbook of Charles the Bald', in *Viator* 11 (1980), 385–417; Rosamond McKitterick, 'Charles the Bald (823–877) and his Library: The Patronage of Learning', in *The English Historical Review* 95 (1980), 28–47; and the overview of Pierre Salmon, 'Libelli Precum du VIIIᵉ au XIIᵉ siècle', in *Analecta liturgica: Extraits des manuscrits liturgiques de la Bibliothèque vaticane. Contribution à l'histoire de la prière chrétienne*, Studi e testi 273 (Vatican City: Biblioteca Apostolica Vaticana, 1974), 121–194.

[76] The only printed edition is still *Liber precationum, quas Carolus Calvus imperator Hludovici Pij Caesaris filius et Caroli Magni nepos sibi adolescenti pro quotidiano usu ante annos viginti quinque septingentos in unum colligi et literis scribi aureis mandavit*, ed. Feliciano Ninguarda (Ingolstadt: Sartorius, 1583), 112–116.

[77] Bonifaas Luykx, 'Der Ursprung der gleichbleibenden Teile der heiligen Messe (Ordinarium Missae)', in *Liturgie und Mönchtum* 29 (1961), 72–119. See now the overview of Joanne M. Pierce and John F. Romano, 'The *Ordo Missae* of the Roman Rite: Historical Background', in *A Commentary on the Order of Mass of the Roman Missal*, ed. Edward Foley et al. (Collegeville: Liturgical Press, 2011), 3–34, at 16–23, with a review of more recent scholarship refining Luykx's typology.

described in *Ordo Romanus I* contains a moment of prayer and recollection of the pontiff and his assistants in front of the altar, and it is in these
moments that the Frankish apologies are inserted.[78] These prayers tend in
a more penitential direction, which corresponds with the increasing focus
on the priest as acting in the person of Christ in the re-presentation of the
sacrifice of the cross. Although Gallican clerical prayers introduce a
personal and emotive register of liturgical prayer, which is distinct from
the objective and hieratic character of the Roman Mass as inherited from
late antiquity, these texts can be read as an articulation of the celebrant's
interior preparation to offer the acceptable sacrifice in the sight of God for
the salvation of souls.

Silence and Liturgical Prayer

A development parallel, and at first glance contradictory, to the Frankish
spirituality of verbalisation, is the extension of silence during liturgical
prayer. The earliest clear evidence for a partial recitation of the
Eucharistic prayer in a low voice is found in the East Syrian tradition,
in Narsai's *Homily on the Mysteries* from the late fifth or early sixth
century. The inaudible recitation of large parts of the anaphora by the
celebrant spread to Greek-speaking churches by the middle of the sixth
century.[79] Gallican and Mozarabic liturgies also witness to the practice of
saying prayers quietly, while the cantors would sing.

Ordo Romanus I, which describes the papal Mass in Rome in the first
half of the eighth century, notes that after the singing of the *Sanctus*
'surgit pontifex solus et intrat in canonem'.[80] This passage has sometimes
been read as an indication that the canon was prayed in a low voice, but
this is not entirely clear. It is merely said that the pope alone, having
bowed with his assistants during the *Sanctus*, stands upright and 'enters

---

[78] *Ordo Romanus I*, 50: ed. Andrieu, vol. II, 83. For this moment of prayer, an 'oratorium'
was placed before the altar. This was not a kneeler or faldstool, as often assumed, but a
rug or mat; see John F. Romano, *Liturgy and Society in Early Medieval Rome*, Church,
Faith and Culture in the Medieval West (Farnham: Ashgate, 2014), 257. According the
Frankish recension of *Ordo Romanus I* in the late-eighth-century *Capitulare ecclesiastici
ordinis*, the pope prostrates himself in prayer: *Ordo Romanus XV*, 15: ed. Andrieu, vol.
III, 98.

[79] See the section on 'Speech and Silence' in Uwe Michael Lang, *The Voice of the Church at
Prayer: Reflections on Liturgy and Language* (San Francisco: Ignatius Press, 2012),
122–135.

[80] *Ordo Romanus I*, 88: ed. Andrieu, vol. II, 95–96.

into the canon', that is, he alone continues with the prayer *Te igitur*,[81] while the clergy assisting him remain bowing. The passage does not specify whether or not the pontiff prays in an audible voice, as was the earlier Roman tradition. However, a clear distinction is introduced between the preface, which is chanted and culminates in the *Sanctus* sung by the schola, and the canon, now defined as beginning with the words *Te igitur*.[82] This distinction is then reflected in liturgical manuscripts from the ninth century onwards, where the title 'Canon missae' or 'Canon actionis' is often inserted before *Te igitur*.

Ordo Romanus III, an addition to the first *Ordo Romanus* dating from the late eighth century, specifies the concelebration of cardinal priests with the pope on the four most solemn occasions of the liturgical year: Easter, Pentecost, St Peter (and St Paul) and Christmas. The cardinal priests standing close to the altar are to say the canon with the pope, though in a lower voice: 'ut vox pontificis valentius audiatur'.[83] This would obviously imply that the pope prays the canon in a voice audible to the concelebrants so that they can join in the prayer.

The early Frankish recension of the *Ordo Romanus I* from the late eighth century contained in *Ordo Romanus XV* (also known under its title *Capitulare ecclesiastici ordinis*) distinguishes between various ways of reciting the different parts of the Eucharistic prayer. The preface is sung in an elevated voice so that it may be heard by all;[84] after the singing of the *Sanctus*, the pontiff begins to recite the canon in a different voice so that it may be heard only by those standing around the altar.[85] He only

---

[81] Jungmann, *Missarum sollemnia*, vol. II, 130, n. 15, observes that the verb 'intrare' is used precisely in this sense in the *Gelasianum Vetus* (Vat. Reg. Lat. 316): ed. Leo C. Mohlberg, *Liber Sacramentorum Romanae Aeclesiae Ordinis Anni Circuli*, Rerum Ecclesiasticarum Documenta. Series maior. Fontes IV, 3rd ed. (Rome: Herder, 1981), nos. 195, 319 and 381.

[82] However, the same *Ordo Romanus I* still reflects the older understanding of the canon beginning with the preface, when it indicates: 'Nam quod intermisimus de patena, quando inchoat canonem, venit acolytes sub humero habens sindonem in collo ligatam, tenens patenam ante pectus suum in parte dextera usque medium canonem'; *Odo Romanus I*, 91: ed. Andrieu, vol. II, 96–97.

[83] *Ordo Romanus III*, 1: ed. Andrieu, vol. II, 131.

[84] *Ordo Romanus XV*,37: ed. Andrieu, vol. III, 103: 'Inde vero pontifex, elevans vocem et dicit ipsa prefationem, ita ut ab omnibus audiatur.'

[85] *Ordo Romanus XV*,39: ed. Andrieu, vol. III, 103: 'Et incipit canire [varia lectio: pontifex canone] dissimili voce <et melodia>, ut a circumstantibus altare tantum audiatur.' The variant readings at this point need not concern us. Whether or not the canon was chanted in a reciting tone, it would still be audible only to by-standers.

raises his voice again at the end, for the ecphonesis, 'Per omnia saecula saeculorum'.[86]

The Romano-Germanic *Ordo Romanus V*, dating from the later ninth century, notes that after the singing of the *Sanctus*: 'surgit solus pontifex et tacito intrat in canonem',[87] adding the specification 'tacito' or 'silently' to the original rubric. This would not necessarily mean that the canon was said completely inaudibly; but at any rate, only those who were close to the altar would be able to hear it.

This brief review of selected documents indicates a development from the understanding of the Canon of the Mass as a 'holy of holies', into which only the pontiff could enter, towards its recitation *submissa voce*. It is conceivable that this practice was introduced in Rome by the popes of Greek and Syrian origin, who were elected to the see of Peter in the second half of the seventh century and the first half of the eighth century. We also need to keep in mind that, before the age of electrical amplification, when the pope celebrated Mass in one of the larger Roman basilicas, such as the Lateran, or St Peter's in the Vatican, it would have been impossible in most parts of the church to follow the prayers he recited or chanted at the altar. Even in a smaller church (such as St Sabina on the Aventine), the audibility of the liturgical prayers would be limited. Just as there were *visible* barriers, such as the relatively high *cancelli* separating various precincts of the church's interior,[88] and a *ciborium* over the main altar, sometimes decorated with curtains, likewise the physical dimensions of the church interior created an *acoustic* separation between the pope and his assistants at the altar and the faithful in the naves.[89]

The Frankish adaptation of the Roman liturgy goes beyond pragmatic considerations and draws attention to the nature of the Eucharistic sacrifice. The sacred silence of the canon dramatically highlights the heart and centre of the liturgy, when the celebrant, acting in the person of Christ the eternal high priest, enters into the holy of holies and makes present Christ's own Body and Blood under the appearance of bread and wine as the sacrifice of our redemption. Such dramatic emphasis is elaborated

---

[86] *Ordo Romanus XV*,43: ed. Andrieu, vol. III, 104: 'usquedum dixerit pontifex alta voce: Per omnia saecula saeculorum'.

[87] *Ordo Romanus V*,58: ed. Andrieu vol. II, 221.

[88] The Roman basilica of St Clement contains such *cancelli*, which date from late antiquity and were re-used in the medieval church.

[89] See Geoffrey G. Willis, 'The Variable Prayers of the Roman Mass', in *Further Essays in Early Roman Liturgy*, Alcuin Club Collections 50 (London: S.P.C.K., 1968), 91–129, at 128–129.

in the allegorical reading of Amalarius and it is visually expressed in the ivory plaques of the back plate for the mid-ninth century sacramentary produced for Bishop Drogo of Metz, a son of Charlemagne (see Figure 6.2). The individual plaques (which are out of sequence) show distinct moments in the pontifical celebration of Mass.[90]

Allegorical Reading of the Liturgy

Allegory can be defined as a literary or rhetorical device to convey a meaning that transcends the plain sense of language. A classic example for biblical allegory is given by the Apostle Paul in his Letter to the Galatians, where he reads the figures of Hagar and Sarah from the Book of Genesis as an allegory of the two covenants (Gal 4:21–31). With the momentous contribution of Origen (c. 185–254), allegorical reading became dominant in early Christian exegesis of Scripture: the spiritual meaning is considered latent in the literal meaning.[91] The method was also adopted in expositions on the liturgy, beginning with patristic authors in the fourth century, such as Cyril of Jerusalem, Ambrose of Milan, Theodore of Mopsuestia and leading in the sixth century to Ps.-Dionysius the Areopagite, who would later have a strong impact on the Latin West.

The Frankish spirituality and aesthetic of the Mass described in the previous section resonated particularly with allegorical liturgical commentary, which was advanced by Amalarius in his *Liber officialis* (or *De ecclesiasticis officiis*), written around 823 and later revised.[92] In this commentary on the liturgy, Amalarius privileges the spiritual over the literal meaning, according to the threefold distinction familiar from scriptural exegesis: the allegorical sense, by which the Old Testament

---

[90] See Robert G. Calkins, 'Liturgical Sequence and Decorative Crescendo in the Drogo Sacramentary', in *Gesta* 25 (1986), 17–23, and Allan Doig, *Liturgy and Architecture from the Early Church to the Middle Ages* (Aldershot: Ashgate, 2008), 120–123.

[91] For a brief, magisterial introduction to the topic, see Robert Louis Wilken, 'Interpreting Job Allegorically: The Moralia of Gregory the Great', in *Pro Ecclesia* 10 (2001), 213–230.

[92] In 813/814, Amalarius served as Frankish envoy to the Byzantine court, and he might have become familiar with allegorical liturgical commentary during his stay in Constantinople; see Wolfgang Steck, *Der Liturgiker Amalarius: Eine quellenkritische Untersuchung zu Leben und Werk eines Theologen der Karolingerzeit*, Münchener theologische Studien. Historische Abteilung 35 (St Ottilien: EOS-Verlag, 2000).

Figure 6.2 Drogo Sacramentary / Metz / c. 850
(Metal back plate with ivory plaques showing various moments in the celebration of a pontifical Mass / Paris, Bibliothèque Nationale de France, MS lat. 9428/ Reprinted with kind permission)

announces and foreshadows the New; the tropological or moral sense; and the anagogical sense, relating to the 'things that are above' (Col 3:2).

Amalarius has a strong preference for reading the liturgy in a 'reme-morative' manner: in particular, he consistently interprets the rites and ceremonies of the Mass as re-enacting the saving acts of Christ.[93] Every word and gesture of the priest and his assistants is charged with symbolic meaning, because it manifests the presence of Christ and his work of redemption in the solemn worship of the Church. Although Amalarius' rememorative-allegorical interpretation provoked considerable opposition in his own time, as exemplified by the deacon Florus of Lyon in his *Opusculum de actione missarum* (between 835 and 838), this method was widely received and became dominant among medieval liturgical commentators. The Dominican theologian Albert the Great (d. 1280) was somewhat critical of it and his disciple Thomas Aquinas (d. 1274) attempted a balance between a literal and an allegorical reading of the prayers and rites of the Mass.[94] Still, the most widely read liturgical commentators of the age of the cathedrals were disciples of Amalarius, among them John Beleth (d. 1182) in his *Summa de ecclesiasticis officiis*; Prevostinus of Cremona (d. 1210) in his *Summa de officiis*; Lothar of Segni (later Pope Innocent III, d. 1216) in his *De sacro altaris mysterio*; Sicard of Cremona (d. c. 1215) in his voluminous *Mitralis de officiis* and, above all, William Durandus (d. 1296) in his *Rationale divinorum officiorum*, the most complete and most widely read liturgical *Summa* of the Middle Ages, which is still extant in about 200 codices and in many early printed edition (from as early as 1459).

The allegorical reading of the Mass would also seem to account for a particular development that has raised considerable difficulties of interpretation: the multiple signs of the cross the priest makes over the offerings during the Eucharistic prayer.[95] The earliest available source supports a Roman origin of this practice: the Old Gelasian Sacramentary (compiled between 628 and 715) stipulates that the priest should make five signs of the cross in the *Te igitur* section of the canon,

---

[93] The method of rememorative allegory has been severely criticised by twentieth-century liturgists; more recently, however, it has been viewed more favourably: see Franck Quoëx, 'Thomas d'Aquin, mystagogue: l'*Expositio Missae* de la *Somme de théologie* (IIIa, q. 83, a. 4–5)', in *Revue Thomiste* 105 (2005), 179–225 and 435–472; Michael P. Foley, 'The Mystic Meaning of the *Missale Romanum*', in *Antiphon* 13 (2009), 103–125; and Claude Barthe, 'The "Mystical" Meaning of the Ceremonies of the Mass: Liturgical Exegesis in the Middle Ages', in *The Genius of the Roman Liturgy: Historical Diversity and Spiritual Reach: Proceedings of the 2006 Oxford CIEL Colloquium*, ed. Uwe Michael Lang (Chicago: Hillenbrand Books, 2010), 179–197.

[94] See Foley, 'The Mystic Meaning of the *Missale Romanum*', 109–110 and 120.

[95] See Daniel Cardó, *The Presence of the Cross and the Eucharist: A Theological and Liturgical Investigation* (Cambridge: Cambridge University Press, 2019), 118–121.

while he is saying 'that you accept and bless + these gifts +, these offerings +, these holy + and unblemished sacrifices +'.[96]

Later witnesses to this practice date from the Carolingian period: firstly, in 751 Pope Zacharias wrote in a letter to Boniface, in response to a query concerning the signs of the cross to be made during the canon:

> You ask us, most holy brother, to inform Your Holiness where the sign of the Cross should be made during the recitation of the holy canon. In compliance with your request we have marked in the roll we have given to your monastic priest Lullus the places where the sign of the Cross is to be made.[97]

This letter suggests that by the middle of the eighth century the signing of the Eucharistic offerings during the canon already had some currency, while there was no uniform observance. In particular, it would not seem to have been standard practice to indicate the signs of the cross at the appropriate place in the text of the canon.

Secondly, *Ordo Romanus VII*, a short rubrical directory, which in most manuscripts has the title 'Qualiter quaedam orationes et cruces in *Te igitur* agendae sunt', specifically indicates where signs of the cross are to be made.[98] This directory has been identified as an extract from a Paduan-type sacramentary, that is, the adaptation of the Lateran pontifical sacramentary for presbyteral use at the Vatican, which was produced in one of the ecclesiastical centres of the Frankish realm, with reference to *Ordo Romanus I*, between the second half of the eighth and the late ninth century.[99] The longer and more primitive version from Carolingian times offers the entire text of the *Canon missae* with its rubrics, while the shorter version, which is associated with the tenth-century pontifical, only provides the rubrical instructions along with the incipit and explicit of the distinct prayers of the canon. While there is some ambiguity in these instructions and the manuscript tradition is not unanimous, Johannes Nebel identifies twenty-four signs of the cross in the canon – a number charged with biblical symbolism, for instance, the twenty-four divisions of priests and Levites (1 Chr 24) and the twenty-four elders of the

---

[96] *Gelasianum Vetus*, no. 1244.

[97] Boniface, *Ep. 7*: MGH, Epistulae Selectae I, 200; English translation: *The Letters of Saint Boniface*, trans. Ephraim Emerton, with a new introduction and bibliography by Thomas F. X. Noble (New York: Columbia University Press, 2000), 142, slightly modified.

[98] *Ordo Romanus VII*: ed. Andrieu, vol. II, 295–305.

[99] Vogel, *Medieval Liturgy*, 162, describes the author as 'a Frankish scribe favourable to the Romanization of the liturgy'.

Apocalypse (Rev 4:4).[100] Most importantly and unlike the Old Gelasian, *Ordo Romanus VII* stipulates that multiple signs of the cross be made over the *oblata* not only during the prayers *Te igitur* and the *Quam oblationem*, but also during the *Unde et memores*, and before the doxology, that is, after the words of institution and the consecration of the Eucharistic offerings. Finally, this practice is confirmed in the *Hadrianum*: while the signs of the cross there add to a total number of sixteen, some of them are to be made over the already consecrated elements.[101]

Since Christian antiquity, the cruciform signing of a person or an object had been understood as a gesture of blessing and consecration. For this reason, the extension of the signs of the cross to the consecrated elements raised a theological problem that is addressed by Thomas Aquinas in his exposition of the rite of Mass in the *Summa Theologiae*. Aquinas' liturgical commentary is firmly rooted in his theological synthesis and, more specifically, in his understanding of the Eucharist as a visible, albeit figurative representation of the redemptive Passion of Jesus Christ.[102] He argues that the priest makes multiple signs of the cross 'to express the Passion of Christ, which came to an end on the cross' and then proceeds to explain these signs with recourse to the method of rememorative allegory: the different sets of crosses to be made correspond to the stages of Christ's Passion. Aquinas concludes that

the consecration of this sacrament, and the acceptance of the sacrifice, and its fruits, proceed from the virtue of the cross of Christ. And therefore, wherever mention is made of these, the priest makes use of the sign of the cross.[103]

---

[100] Johannes Nebel, *Die Entwicklung des römischen Meßritus im ersten Jahrtausend anhand der Ordines Romani: Eine synoptische Darstellung*, Pontificium Athenaeum S. Anselmi de Urbe, Pontificium Institutum Liturgicum, Thesis ad Lauream 264 (Rome, 2000), 418–419.

[101] *Gregorianum (Hadrianum)*, nos. 5–15: ed. Jean Deshusses, *Le sacramentaire grégorien: Ses principales formes d'après les plus anciens manuscrits*, vol. 1, Spicilegium Friburgense 16, 3rd ed. (Fribourg: Éditions Universitaires, 1992), 87–91.

[102] Notably, the Eucharist is also a representation of Christ's resurrection; see *Summa theologiae*, III, q. 83, a. 5, ad 6 and ad 8. Hence, Aquinas' idea of sacramental representation, whilst being focussed on the cross encompasses the whole of the Paschal Mystery. Accordingly, he prefaces his brief exposition of the rite of Mass by emphasising that 'the whole mystery of our salvation is comprised in this sacrament'; III, q. 83, a. 4, resp. See Bruce D. Marshall, 'The Whole Mystery of our Salvation: Saint Thomas Aquinas on the Eucharist as Sacrifice', in *Rediscovering Aquinas and the Sacraments: Studies in Sacramental Theology*, ed. Matthew Levering and Michael Dauphinais (Chicago: Hillenbrand, 2009), 39–64.

[103] Thomas Aquinas, *Summa Theologiae*, III, q. 83, a. 5, ad 3.

Regarding the historical origins of the practice, Jungmann suggested the use of gestures in Roman rhetoric. Pointing to people or objects that were relevant to the argument was a common device for visually reinforcing the words of the speaker.[104] Most (though not all) signs of the cross in the *Canon missae* are associated with the offerings placed on the altar, and hence the physical gesture serves to highlight the verbal reference.[105]

More recently, Daniel Cardó has made a strong case that the original meaning of the signs of the cross during the canon was in fact benedictory, as evidenced in the Old Gelasian. At the same time, the cross appears 'as an indication of the relation of the Eucharistic offering with the sacrifice of the Cross'.[106] This relation was dramatically highlighted by the Carolingian additions, which corresponded to the Frankish preference for personal and emotive liturgical expression. As a consequence, the signs of the cross in their entirety could no longer be understood as benedictory and were allegorically re-interpreted as commemorating the Passion of Christ.

RAISING THE LEVEL OF LATINITY

A particular aspect of the Carolingian *renovatio* was the revision of liturgical texts according to standards of classical Latinity. This effort is to be understood as a corrective to the extensive vulgarisation of Latin, that is, the introduction of non-classical forms of orthography, grammar and syntax in the Merovingian period. The narrative of a Latin liturgical culture in decline has been questioned by Els Rose in her substantial work on the language of the *Missale Gothicum*, which accompanies her magisterial critical edition of this late seventh-century witness to the Gallican tradition.[107] At the same time, Rose provides examples of how the Bobbio Missal radically shortens prayers of the *Missale Gothicum* to the point

---

[104] See Timothy McNiven, 'Rhetorical Gesture and Response in Ancient Rome', in *Semiotica* 139 (2002), 327–330.

[105] See Jungmann, *Missarum sollemnia*, vol. II, 179–184; likewise Nebel, *Die Entwicklung des römischen Meßritus im ersten Jahrtausend*, 419.

[106] Cardó, *The Presence of the Cross and the Eucharist*, 99; see also 121. Cardó supports the interpretation of Ernest Beresford-Cooke, *The Sign of the Cross in the Western Liturgies* (London: Longmans, Green and Co., 1907), 13.

[107] H. G. E. Rose, ed., *Missale gothicum e codice Vaticano Reginensi latino 317 editum* (CCL 159D), Turnhout: Brepols, 2005; see also 'Liturgical Latin in the Missale Gothicum (Vat. Reg. Lat. 317). A reconsideration of Christine Mohrmann's approach', in *Sacris Erudiri* 42 (2003), 97–121.

that their grammar becomes confused and their contents can be understood only with difficulties.[108] Rose observes that, in some cases, 'the
scissor and paste work of the compiler of the Bobbio Missal has led to
grammatically incorrect and incomprehensible texts'.[109] Robert Coleman
likewise notes the 'garbled form' of the Roman Canon of the Mass in the
Bobbio Missal.[110] Some of the variations could be interpreted as ortho-
graphic peculiarities that would be typical of a period of transition from
Latin to the Romance vernaculars. However, as Coleman observes, 'in a
religion where departures from the prescribed form of words could raise
doubts about the validity of the rites enacted by them, the motivation to
restore was strong'.[111]

Churchmen and scholars under Charlemagne were not only concerned
with classical standards of morphology and syntax in written Latin. The
philologist Roger Wright maintains that the most significant change of the
Carolingian age was the adoption of a standard spoken form of Latin, still
employed today, which is based 'on the phonographic assumption, that
every written letter of the standard spelling should be given a regular
sound'.[112] This manner of pronunciation was already in use among
Anglo-Saxon and Germanic scholars, such as Alcuin and Hrabanus
Maurus, who were not native speakers. However, it was foreign to those
who spoke Latin as their first language in those parts of Europe where
Romance languages would subsequently develop. This area was still a

---

[108] See Els Rose, 'Liturgical Latin in the Bobbio Missal', in *The Bobbio Missal: Liturgy and Religious Culture in Merovingian Gaul*, ed. Yitzhak Hen and Rob Meens, Cambridge Studies in Palaeography and Codicology (Cambridge: Cambridge University Press, 2004), 67–78, at 71–76.

[109] Ibid., 72.

[110] For instance, the phrase 'intra quorum nos consortium non aestimator meriti sed ueniae, quaesumus, largitor admitte' ('admit us, we beseech you, into their company, not weighing our merits, but granting us your pardon') becomes 'intra quorum nos consorcio non stimator meritis sed ueniam quesomus largitur admitte'. Robert Coleman, 'Vulgar Latin and the Diversity of Christian Latin', in *Actes du Ier Colloque international sur le latin vulgaire et tardif (Pécs, 2–5 septembre 1985)*, ed. József Herman (Tübingen: Niemeyer, 1987), 37–52, at 47.

[111] Ibid.

[112] Roger Wright, *A Sociophilological Study of Late Latin*, Utrecht Studies in Medieval Literacy 10 (Turnhout: Brepols, 2002), 347. This volume contains papers published in various places, some of them revised; see also his *Late Latin and Early Romance in Spain and Carolingian France*, ARCA: Classical and medieval texts, papers, and monograph 8 (Liverpool: Francis Cairns, 1982). Wright makes frequent reference to Michel Banniard, *Viva voce: communication écrite et communication orale du IVe au IXe siècle en occident latin*, Collection des études augustiniennes. Série Moyen-âge et temps modernes 25 (Paris: Institut des études augustiniennes, 1992).

'monolingual speech community' in the early-eighth century, despite local and sociolinguistic variations within the one language.[113] The standard pronunciation of Latin that was promoted effectively by the Carolingian scholars would have sounded artificial to native speakers, who in different regions assigned different sounds to the same written letter of a word. The new system eventually led to the 'conceptual separation of Latin from Romance' and made Latin a foreign language, although this process was not completed until the Renaissance of the twelfth century or even, in a sense, of the sixteenth century.[114]

As a consequence of the Carolingian efforts to restore the grammatical standards of the Latin language and to use a normative pronunciation the gap widened between the language of the liturgy and the developing vernacular of the people, even in countries where this vernacular derived from Latin.[115]

It would seem that Wright's theory can also shed light on an exchange of letters between Boniface and Pope Zacharias in 746: the missionary found in Bavaria that children had been baptised 'in nomine patria et filia et spiritus sancti' and considered it necessary to re-administer the sacrament. This decision, however, met with the disapproval of the pope, who did not see this necessity.[116] Zacharias came from a Greek family in Calabria, then belonging to the Byzantine Empire, but had spent many years in Rome, where he was a deacon before his election to the see of Peter in 741 and can thus be considered as belonging to the monolingual

---

[113] Wright, *Sociophilological Study of Late Latin*, 99.

[114] Ibid., 34; see also 14–15. One need not agree with Wright's damning judgement of the Carolingian reform of education and his apparent aversion towards establishing standards of grammar and orthography. Likewise, his claim that the pre-Carolingian monolingualism could have continued for centuries without developing into the various Romance languages, in a similar way as English is spoken in the world today, would appear highly speculative. A very different evaluation is given by Francis J. Thomson, 'SS. Cyril and Methodius and a Mythical Western Heresy: Trilinguism. A Contribution to the Study of Patristic and Mediaeval Theories of Sacred Languages', in *Analecta Bollandiana* 110 (1992), 67–122, at 93: 'Merovingian Latin had … degenerated into a confused system in which solecism and incongruity were commonplace and it had become necessary to restore correct norms for use throughout the Empire and to instruct the nobility's children in these norms. It is surely no exaggeration to state that the restoration of the *norma rectitudinis* ensured the maintenance of Latin as the language of west European culture until the Renaissance.'

[115] See Lang, *The Voice of the Church at Prayer*, 119–122; also the pertinent observations of Ernst Auerbach, *Literatursprache und Publikum in der lateinischen Spätantike und im Mittelalter* (Bern: Francke, 1958), 88 and 197.

[116] See the reply of Pope Zacharias to Boniface, *Ep. 68*: MGH, Epistulae Selectae I, 141 (dated 1 July 746).

Romance area. As a quasi-native Latin speaker, he was obviously not preoccupied by the grammatically incorrect endings of the sacramental formula and did not see any reason to suspect a deviation from the profession of faith in the Blessed Trinity. For the Anglo-Saxon Boniface, on the other hand, the departure from standard grammar and pronunciation was so serious that it raised doubts about the validity of the sacrament.

LOCAL REFORM AND PRACTICAL REACH

As we have seen, a major concern of Carolingian liturgical reform was the emendation and correction of liturgical books, and there is considerable evidence that such measures were followed on a regional and local level. The widely diffused capitulary of Bishop Haito of Basel, dating from before 813, features a list of books that were deemed necessary for priests in their ministry, and the list included a sacramentary, a lectionary, an antiphoner and a homiliary for the Sundays and feast-days of the year. The capitulary warns that without these books, a man would hardly deserve to be called a priest, and the Gospel saying would apply to him: 'If a blind man leads a blind man, both will fall into a pit' (Mt 15:14; Lk 6:39).[117]

According to Donald Bullough, by the middle of the ninth century, 'prescription was partly matched by practice in widely scattered Frankish rural churches – ones that had evidently benefited from generous donors, lay and ecclesiastical, and presumably from actively interventionist bishops'.[118] This state of affairs is corroborated for the areas of modern France, Germany and northern Italy by charters and other texts that list the possessions of churches. These lists are not as clear as we would wish regarding the precise nature and contents of liturgical books. The revised sacramentaries, whether Gelasian or Gregorian, emerged from scriptoria attached to cathedrals and major monasteries, where they would have been first adopted for liturgical use.[119] Rural and minor urban churches may well have continued for some time with the older books, perhaps

---

[117] Haito of Basel, *Capitula*, VI: MGH, Capitula Episcoporum, Pars I, 211.

[118] Donald A. Bullough, 'The Carolingian Liturgical Experience', in *Continuity and Change in Christian Worship: Papers Read at the 1997 Summer Meeting and the 1998 Winter Meeting of the Ecclesiastical History Society*, ed. Robert N. Swanson, Studies in Church History 35 (Woodbridge: Boydell Press, 1999), 29–64, at 44.

[119] See ibid., 47, and McKitterick, *The Frankish Church*, 127.

with the occasional insertion of new material. It is quite possible that priests in rural settlements used a more limited range of texts for the Mass and the Divine Office. While Bullough cautions not to overstate the standardising effect of the Carolingian liturgical reform, his survey of the extant evidence leads him to the affirm that the 'picture of the first Carolingian century as one in which many more books, in a generally improved Latinity, were copied and circulated, and even reached segments of society that had previously been book-less, is not to be questioned".[120] The contributions of Carine van Rhijn on handbooks for the pastoral care of local priests show that the ideals of the Carolingian reforms had a remarkably broad reach. These unassuming manuscripts covered many aspects of the priest's daily ministry and usually include explanations of the Mass and of baptism, commentaries on the creed and the Lord's Prayer, sample homilies, collections of canons and other material.[121]

Most of the written sources that have come down to us from the period are prescriptive; that is, they decree a particular liturgical practice in wording that is meant to convey authority, either ecclesiastical or civil, or both. Is it possible to say anything about how these reform measures were received in local communities and affected the ordinary faithful? This important though demanding question has found an exemplary treatment in Bullough, who begins his enquiry by surveying the physical settings of liturgical worship in central and western Europe, which were for the most part very simple. There was a considerable gap between the cathedrals of episcopal towns and the humble churches associated with rural settlements (to describe these as parish churches would carry

---

[120] Bullough, 'The Carolingian Liturgical Experience', 49–50.
[121] See Carine van Rhijn, 'Carolingian Rural Priests as Local (Religious) Experts', in *Gott handhaben: Religiöses Wissen im Konflikt um Mythisierung und Rationalisierung*, ed. Steffen Patzold and Florian Bock (Berlin: Walter de Gruyter, 2016), 131–146; '"Et hoc considerat episcopus, ut ipsi presbyteri non sint idiothae": Carolingian Local *Correctio* and an Unknown Priests' Exam from the Early Ninth Century', in *Religious Franks: Religion and Power in the Frankish Kingdoms. Studies in Honour of Mayke de Jong*, ed. Rob Meens et al. (Manchester: Manchester University Press, 2016), 162–180; 'Manuscripts for Local Priests and the Carolingian Reforms', in *Men in the Middle: Local Priests in Early Medieval Europe*, ed. Carine van Rhijn and Steffen Patzold, Ergänzungsbände zum Reallexikon der Germanischen Altertumskunde 93 (Berlin: Walter de Gruyter, 2016), 177–198; 'The Local Church, Priests' Handbooks and Pastoral Care in the Carolingian Period', in *Chiese locali e chiese regionali nell'alto medioevo: Spoleto, 4–9 aprile 2013*, Settimane di studio del Centro italiano di studi sull'alto medioevo 61, 2 vols. (Spoleto: Centro Italiano di studi sull'alto medioevo, 2014), 689–710.

associations that are quite anachronistic for the early medieval period), with the churches of religious communities somewhere in between. Bullough observes:

We are bound to assume that the majority of western Europe's Christian laity would in this period normally have worshipped, if anywhere, in rural churches, whether these were located in a 'central place' and served probably by a small group of clergy who were also responsible for subordinate *oratoria*, or one of those oratories or chapels, typically on a private estate ('seignorial lands'), with a single priest who may only have been an occasional visitor.[122]

It is extremely difficult to estimate the density of these places of worship in a society that was predominantly rural. However, the numbers that have come down from some dioceses, such as Lucca, Trier or Paris, suggest an existing network of churches with parochial rights along with subordinate chapels to serve the pastoral needs of the people.[123] Many, if not most of these rural churches would have been simple wooden constructions, with or without stone footings, such as the 'basilica lignea modica' near Michelstadt, which Einhard found on the estate he secured from Louis the Pious in 815, and which he rebuilt as a large and impressive edifice of red sandstone, modelled on Roman basilicas and still standing today. Bullough notes that even in rural northern and central Italy the first extant masonry constructions that used to be considered Carolingian now tend to be dated to later periods, up to the eleventh century. At the same time, even plain buildings could have a relatively ornate interior, especially around the altar. Churches in economically prosperous areas were certainly provided with liturgical objects made of precious materials.[124]

Synodal decrees and ecclesiastical capitularies from the early Middle Ages insist that priests should know and understand the texts they recite, celebrate the Divine Office diligently, care for their churches, look after relics, make sure bells are rung to call the faithful to prayer and so on. Likewise, synods and individual bishops exhort the faithful not to talk idly when they are in church but to be attentive and prayerful during

---

[122] Ibid., 31.

[123] See ibid., where Bullough refers to the works of Luigi Nanni, *La parrochia studiata nei documenti lucchesi dei secoli VIII–XIII*, Analecta Gregoriana 47 (Rome: Apud aedes Universitatis Gregorianae, 1948), esp. 66–75; Eugen Ewig, *Trier im Merowingerreich: Civitas, Stadt, Bistum* (Trier: Paulinus-Verlag, 1954), 149–165 and 182–282; Michel Roblin, *Le terroir de Paris aux époques gallo-romaine et franque: Peuplement et défrichement dans la Civitas des Parisii (Seine, Seine-et-Oise)*, 2nd ed. (Paris: A. et J. Picard, 1971), esp. 151–154.

[124] See Bullough, 'The Carolingian Liturgical Experience', 39–40.

liturgical services – and not leave before the Mass has ended.[125] However, before the twentieth century, prescriptive documents of the Roman Rite provide hardly any indication of just *how* the laity are meant to participate in the sacred liturgy.[126] Elevated Latinity and its normative pronunciation further raised obstacles for the comprehension of liturgical prayers even among Romance-speakers. Lay literacy was very limited in the early Middle Ages, and collections of devotional prayers (*preces privatae*) were the privilege of a small elite. When it came to musical resources, there must have been a considerable gap between episcopal and monastic centres, and the rural churches that served the majority of the people. Complex chant melodies required trained singers and only simple responses and refrains would allow for popular involvement.[127] Still, Charlemagne's *Admonitio generalis* assumes that the people join in the acclamations at Mass and explicitly includes the *Sanctus*.[128] At any rate, it would be anachronistic to evaluate liturgical life in the Carolingian period by modern criteria of active participation, which are largely based on speaking roles. The efforts to raise the dignity and splendour of divine worship, along with the emphasis on a broad education in the essentials of the Christian faith, no doubt increased the lay faithful's ability to enter into the celebration of the sacred mysteries.[129]

EAST AND WEST

The Carolingian period is usually seen as a significant step in the process of alienation between Eastern and Western Christianity. The papacy severed its political ties with the Byzantine Empire and turned westward through its alliance with the Frankish kings, which culminated in the

---

[125] See the references in Andreas Amiet, 'Die liturgische Gesetzgebung der deutschen Reichskirche in der Zeit der sächsischen Kaiser 922–1023', in *Zeitschrift für schweizerische Kirchengeschichte* 70 (1976), 1–106 and 209–307, at 103 and 269.

[126] Bullough, 'The Carolingian Liturgical Experience', 32, observes: 'If ... we ask what went on in those churches, for the greater part of this period we are faced with an almost total silence: a collection of contemporary texts descriptive of ordinary *fideles*, observant Christians joining in worship in their local church or oratory, would be at most a very slim volume, perhaps not even a short periodical article.'

[127] See ibid., 51–55.

[128] *Admonitio generalis*, c. 70: MGH, Legum Sectio II, Capitularia Regum Francorum, Tomus I, 59.

[129] Philippe Bernard, *Du chant romain au chant grégorien (IVe–XIIIe siècle)*, Collection Patrimoine – Christianisme (Paris: Cerf, 1996), 413, dismisses the idea of the 'passivity' of the faithful as an anachronistic cliché ('un poncif anachronique').

creation of a Western Empire in 800. The iconoclast controversy in Byzantium (726–780 and 815–843) contributed to further estrangement. However, John Osborne has recently argued that the bonds between Rome and Constantinople were strengthened again after the defeat of iconoclasm in the East, known as the 'Triumph of Orthodoxy', in 843. The issues surrounding the Photian schism were finally resolved at the council of 879–880:[130]

In sum, the revival of regular contacts between emperor, pope, and patriarch following the 'Triumph of Orthodoxy' in 843 created a climate in which political and cultural exchange could once again flourish. With one foot planted firmly in each world, the city of Rome remained at the centre of developments in both Greek and Latin Christianity, functioning as the most important point of contact for the transmission of cultural ideas between Western Europe and Byzantium.[131]

Frankish esteem for Greek as a liturgical language is especially evident from the set of chants known as *Missa graeca*. Manuscripts from the ninth to the eleventh century contain chants of the Roman Mass ordinary written in Greek, but in Latin characters, and they are sometimes provided with musical notation: *Doxa en ipsisis Theo* (*Gloria*), *Pisteuo eis hena Theon* (*Credo*),[132] *Agios, agios, agios* (*Sanctus*) and *O amnos tu theu* (*Agnus Dei*). Charles Atkinson has argued for the abbey of Saint-Denis near Paris as the origin of the *Missa graeca* and has suggested that it may have been composed between 827 and 835, when the Byzantine Emperor Michael II sent a copy of the works of Ps.-Dionysius the Areopagite to the Frankish Emperor Louis the Pious. A few years later, the *Corpus Areopagiticum* was translated into Latin under the guidance of Abbot Hilduin (a cousin of Louis the Pious).[133] Walter Berschin has

---

[130] John Osborne, 'Rome and Constantinople in the Ninth Century', in *Rome Across Time and Space: Cultural Transmission and the Exchange of Ideas c. 500–1400*, ed. Claudia Bolgia, Rosamond McKitterick and John Osborne (Cambridge: Cambridge University Press, 2011), 222–236.

[131] Ibid., 236. Tia M. Kolbaba, 'Latin and Greek Christians', in *The Cambridge History of Christianity. Vol. 3: Early Medieval Christianities, c. 600–c. 1100*, ed. Thomas F. X. Noble, Julia M. H. Smith (Cambridge: Cambridge University Press, 2008), 213–229, at 229, notes: 'Sources that report friendly interaction between Latin and Greeks in the early Middle Ages are as numerous as sources that report conflict.'

[132] At the time, the creed was part of the Mass ordinary in Carolingian Francia, but not in Rome (see Chapter 7).

[133] See Charles M. Atkinson, 'Zur Entstehung und Überlieferung der "Missa graeca"', in *Archiv für Musikwissenschaft* 29 (1982), 113–145; and '*Doxa in ipsistis Theo*: Its Textual and Melodic Tradition in the "Missa graeca"', in *Chant, Liturgy, and the Inheritance of Rome*, 3–32.

highlighted the fact that the phenomenon of the *Missa graeca* spread throughout Europe even to places where Greek culture was quite remote. Hence this phenomenon illustrates the cultural and religious prestige of Greek in Western Christendom.[134]

A particular case of Western impact on the Byzantine liturgy might be the introduction of verbal concelebration (in the sense of co-consecration) in a rubric that is attested in the Latin version of the Liturgy of St John Chrysostom by Leo Tuscan (1173/74). On the basis of comparative liturgical criteria, it has been established that this *diataxis* (comparable to the Western *ordo*) reflects the use of the Great Church of Constantinople, Hagia Sophia, in the tenth century.[135] The text is also the first witness (in East or West) for a sacramental concelebration among priests without the presidency of a bishop. Referring to growing alienation and ritual disagreements between the Byzantine and Latin churches, Robert Taft considers it unlikely that the rubric for concelebration is owing to Western influence.[136] However, it seems remarkable that this Byzantine source dates from a time when sacramental concelebration was known in the solemn papal Mass. The Ottonian period (see Chapter 7) is characterised by lively, albeit tense, relations between the papacy and the Byzantine Empire.[137] Against this background, the question of possible Latin influence cannot be categorically ruled out and would merit further investigation.

CONCLUSION

In this chapter, I have discussed key aspects of the Carolingian liturgical reform. Recent studies from a variety of historical disciplines offer a more

[134] See Walter Berschin, *Griechisch-lateinisches Mittelalter: Von Hieronymus zu Nikolaus von Kues* (Bern; Munich: Francke, 1980), 31–38.
[135] See André Jacob, 'La concélébration de l'anaphore à Byzance d'après le témoignage de Léon Toscan', in *Orientalia Christiana Periodica* 35 (1969), 249–256. See also Robert F. Taft, 'Eucharistic Concelebration Revisited: Problems of History, Practice, and Theology in East and West', in *Orientalia Christiana Periodica* 76 (2010), 277–313 and 77 (2011), 25–80, at 42–46.
[136] See Robert F. Taft, 'Ex Oriente Lux? Some Reflections on Eucharistic Concelebration', in *Beyond East & West: Problems in Liturgical Understanding*, 2nd revised and enlarged edition (Rome: Edizioni Orientalia Christiana, 2001), 111–132, at 116 (revised version of an article originally published in *Worship* 54 [1980] 308–324).
[137] Jonathan Shepard, 'Western Approaches (900–1025)', in *The Cambridge History of the Byzantine Empire c. 500–1492*, ed. Jonathan Shepard (Cambridge: Cambridge University Press, 2008), 537–559, at 540, speaks of 'the intensity of imperial relations with Rome' in the first half of the tenth century.

nuanced understanding of this complex process of exchange and trans-formation of Roman and Franco-Germanic traditions. These scholarly contributions impress upon us the need to leave behind anachronistic ideas about a sweeping unification of liturgical practice effected by royal and ecclesiastical legislation. The main vehicles of Romanisation were the *Ordines Romani* in their Frankish adaptation. Moreover, the long-term impact of the *Hadrianum*, with its Carolingian supplement, was consider-able, as it formed the prototype of would later become the *Missale Romanum*. The success of the Roman-Gregorian liturgy throughout Western Europe was not simply a result of its imposition by authority, but owing to its religious and cultural appeal, as well as its ability to integrate Gallican elements.[138] As we shall see in Chapter 7, at the beginning of the second millennium this process came full circle: the mixed Roman-Frankish rite was established in the papal city itself and became the foundation for further liturgical development in the Latin Church. It was not rare in liturgical scholarship of the mid-twentieth century to present this synthesis in disparaging terms and to call for a return to pure and pristine Roman tradition (a principle that was imple-mented in the reforms after Vatican II only in parts). We are now in a better position to appreciate the enrichment that the Carolingian reforms brought to the Roman Rite, and I would suggest that, because of its (necessarily) slow and gradual pace, its dependence on local initiative and its focus on education (first of the clergy and, through them, of the whole people), it is a reform that merits the disputed epithet 'organic'.

---

[138] I follow here the assessment of Morard, '"Sacramentarium immixtum" et uniformisation romaine', 22: 'Il convient cependant de souligner que c'est en vertu de ses qualités propres qu'il rencontra le succès que l'on sait, lent, progressif, non exclusif, mais aussi massif. Si uniformisation il y eut, elle s'opéra par le biais des réseaux monastiques, de manière pragmatique, non absolue, conforme sans doute aux ambitions des souverains carolingiens, encouragée par l'Eglise romaine, favorisée par l'esprit de saine liberté prôné par *Hucusque*, mis non imposée d'une façon qua seule l'invention de l'imprimerie e le plein épanouissement de la suprématie romaine rendra possible a partir du XVIe siècle.'

7

From the Ottonian Revival to the High Middle Ages

The period from the tenth to the twelfth centuries has often been over-shadowed by the momentous liturgical developments that both preceded and followed it, but recent scholarship has highlighted its distinct contributions to the complex history I endeavour to trace in this book. This chapter will examine the genesis of the *Ordo Missae* as a distinctive set of prayers and rubrics for the priest, which would come to exert significant impact upon the ritual shape of the Roman Mass, especially with the spread of what is known as 'private Mass'. From a broader perspective, due consideration will be given to the emerging tradition of the Romano-Germanic Pontifical and to the claims of the papal reform movement regarding the prevalence of the Roman liturgy in the Western Church. The thirteenth century proved pivotal in several ways, above all when a major step towards liturgical standardisation was taken by the decision of the rapidly expanding Franciscan Order to adopt the liturgical use of the Roman curia. Moreover, the profound veneration of the Eucharist at the time brought new elements to the rite of the Mass, such as the elevation of the consecrated species, and led to the institution of the feast of Corpus Christi. This chapter will conclude with a discussion of preaching at Mass in the central and later Middle Ages.

FROM THE CAROLINGIAN TO THE OTTONIAN AGE

The empire created by Charlemagne was divided into three parts after the death of Louis the Pious in 840: West Francia (roughly modern France), East Francia (roughly modern Germany), and the intermediate territory running from the North Sea to Italy, named Lotharingia after Lothair I (d. 855) who inherited it along with the imperial title. Despite the political instability, the Carolingian reform efforts continued and actually gained new momentum under Charles the Bald (d. 877). The city of Rome, however, entered into a veritable period of crisis, which has with some justification been called a 'dark age' (*saeculum obscurum*) of the papacy, lasting well into the eleventh century. Spiritual and cultural leadership was found north of the Alps, and this held for the liturgy too, which flourished in episcopal cities and Benedictine monasteries on both sides of the Rhine, such as Mainz, Tours, Corbie, Lorsch, Metz, Fulda, Reichenau and St Gall. New impulses came with the monastic reform that originated from Cluny in Burgundy and reached into Italy, including Rome, and with the German emperors of the Ottonian dynasty.

The Ottonians originated as a ducal family from Saxony and rose to royal power in Germany. In 936, Otto I, known as Otto the Great, was crowned king at Aachen; in 962, the pope invested him with the imperial title, which he held until his death in 973. Under his leadership, and that of his son and grandson who succeeded him, Otto II (r. 973–983) and Otto III (r. 983–1002), the 'Holy Roman Empire' took shape. This empire included the lands that now make up Germany, Switzerland, northern and central Italy, but not the area of modern France. Nonetheless, the Ottonian rulers renewed the Roman and imperial aspirations of Charlemagne. They maintained a palace in Rome and spent long periods there near the pope, both seeking his religious authority to support their own claims and exercising control over him. Pursuing ties with Byzantium, which was still a major power and a culture of greater sophistication, they sealed a strategic alliance when Otto II married the Byzantine princess Theophano in 972. Like their Carolingian predecessors, the Ottonians took a direct and vivid interest in ecclesiastical matters and showed themselves patrons of the liturgy in their realm, which also led to a flourishing of sacred architecture and art.

THE *ORDO MISSAE*

For the purposes of our enquiry, the most momentuous step in early medieval liturgical development is the collection of the recurring parts of the Eucharistic celebration into what is known to this day as the *Ordo Missae* (Order of Mass). Andrew Hughes offers a useful definition of its fully developed form:

Presenting the common texts and, by means of rubrics, referring to the proper items and generally giving many directions for performance, the Ordo transmits this information mostly in the order in which it is required in the service. Designed for the celebrant, the Ordo gives texts, music, and instructions where it is necessary that he should speak, sing, or act.[1]

The earliest vestiges of an Order of Mass are already found in many Gregorian-type sacramentaries, which begin with a separate section 'How the Roman Mass is to be celebrated (*Qualiter missa romana caelebratur*)'. This instruction corresponds with the description of the papal stational liturgy in *Ordo Romanus I* and may go back to the late seventh century.[2] Its most important textual sources are the Sacramentary of Hildoard of Cambrai (c. 811–812), a copy of the *Hadrianum ex authentico* (see Figure 6.1),[3] and the Sacramentary of Trent (first third of the ninth century), which is based on a pre-Hadrianic source.[4] The first part of section *Qualiter missa romana caelebratur* lays out the structure of the Mass:

- Introit
- *Kyrie*
- *Gloria* (when ordained)[5]
- Collect *(oratio)*
- Epistle (*apostolus*)
- Gradual and alleluia
- Gospel
- Offertory
- Prayer over the offerings (*super oblata*)

After this brief summary, the wording of the recurring liturgical texts (with responses) are provided:

---

[1] Andrew Hughes, *Medieval Manuscripts for Mass and Office: A Guide to Their Organization and Terminology* (Toronto; Buffalo: University of Toronto Press, 1982), 148.

[2] See Joanne M. Pierce and John F. Romano, 'The *Ordo Missae* of the Roman Rite: Historical Background', in *A Commentary on the Order of Mass of the Roman Missal*, ed. Edward Foley et al. (Collegeville: Liturgical Press, 2011), 3–34, at 17.

[3] *Hadrianum ex authentico*, nos. 1–20: ed. Jean Deshusses, *Le sacramentaire grégorien: Ses principales formes d'après les plus anciens manuscrits*, vol. 1, Spicilegium Friburgense 16, 3rd ed. (Fribourg: Éditions Universitaires, 1992), 85–92; see Cyrille Vogel, *Medieval Liturgy: An Introduction to the Sources*, ed. and trans. William G. Storey and Niels Krogh Rasmussen (Washington, DC: The Pastoral Press, 1986), 82–83.

[4] See Vogel, *Medieval Liturgy*, 97–98. This manuscript includes a selection of Mass orations.

[5] The *Gloria* was reserved to bishops, to be used on Sundays and feast days; priests could only say it at Easter.

- *Per omnia saecula saeculorum*
- Preface dialogue
- Common preface
- Canon of the Mass
- Lord's Prayer with embolism
- *Pax Domini*
- *Agnus Dei*

This embryonic Order of Mass simply organises the structure and content that is known to us from other liturgical books of Roman descent. A subsequent step is taken with the collections of private prayers to be said by the celebrant at different moments of the rite. The earliest known example of such a collection is attested in the Sacramentary of Amiens (Paris, Bibliothèque Nationale, lat. 9432), dating from the second half of the ninth century.[6] In this sacramentary, a series of prayers for the priest is arranged in two parts, before and after the section 'How the Roman Mass is to be celebrated' (fols. 12v–16r). The first part (fols. 10r–12r) begins with prayers for the preparation for Mass, including the penitential Psalm 50, for the washing of hands and for putting on each of the liturgical vestments. In procession to the altar, the priest reflects on his unworthiness, confesses his sins and asks for the grace of justification. Prayers are indicated for the blessing of incense and for the incensation itself, and brief verses of praise are prescribed before and after the gospel. The placing of the gifts of bread and wine on the altar is accompanied by a plea of acceptance. A different hand, dated by Victor Leroquais to the tenth century, then adds three mementos that are to be inserted into the canon: for the priest himself, for the living and for the deceased. The second part of these prayers, in the original hand (fols. 16r–17v), follows after the *Agnus Dei* but begins with the placing of the offerings on the altar and lists five texts with the incipit *Suscipe, sancta Trinitas* ('Receive, O holy Trinity'), which implore the acceptance of this offering and intercede for various intentions. The invitation to the people *Orate, fratres* ('Pray, brethren . . .') elicits a plea that the Lord accept the sacrifice from the mouth and the hands of the priest for the salvation of all. During

---

[6] See Victor Leroquais, 'L'ordo missae du sacramentaire d'Amiens, B.N. lat. 9432', in *Ephemerides Liturgicae* 41 (1927), 435–445, at 439–444. However, Leroquais presents the text in a way that obscures the fact that the prayers are arranged in two distinct groups. The digitised manuscript is accessible at https://gallica.bnf.fr/ark:/12148/btv1b9065879n. See also Victor Leroquais, *Les sacramentaries et les missels manuscrits des bibliothèques publiques de France*, 4 vols. (Paris: s.n., 1924), vol. I, 39–41.

the *Sanctus*, which the priest is meant to recite 'speedily (*cursim*)', he adds a lengthy apology that expresses his sense of unworthiness and reliance on divine mercy. Another petition for absolution from sins precedes the *Te igitur*. Then follow prayers for the commingling of the body and blood of Christ, before and after taking communion, including *Domine Iesu Christe, Fili Dei vivi* ('Lord Jesus Christ, Son of the living God ...').[7] The kissing of the altar at the end of Mass is attended by the prayer *Placeat tibi, sancta Trinitas* ('May it please you, O holy Trinity ...'), and the removal of liturgical vestments by a short commendation to God's protection.

Most of these prayer texts, some of which consist of a single psalm verse, accompany and elucidate the spiritual meaning of particular ritual actions for the celebrant priest. They thus serve to sustain his personal piety and help the devout offering of the sacrifice of the Mass. How are these prayers meant to be used? Several of these texts follow after the heading 'alia' or 'item alia', which suggests that the priest is not required to recite the whole series of them but can select one or another.[8]

It is a distinctive feature of this developing *Ordo Missae* that it contains prayers addressed to the Holy Trinity, especially at the offertory. In the Roman Rite, liturgical prayer is generally addressed to God the Father through the Son in the Holy Spirit. In response to Arian influences on Germanic tribes, including the Goths, the Lombards and the Burgundians, the Gallican tradition emphasised the full divinity of Christ by addressing liturgical prayer to him as God and by directly invoking the Trinity.[9] Both forms of prayer entered the Roman Mass when it was received and adapted north of the Alps.

The *Ordo Missae* as a distinct liturgical genre flourished between the ninth and eleventh centuries. Contents and form varied considerably: for prayers, the opening word or phrase or the complete text is given; more or

---

[7] A version of this prayer is recorded by Alcuin in the early ninth century; see Gerald Ellard, 'The Odyssey of a Familiar Prayer', in *Theological Studies* 2 (1941), 221–241.

[8] As observed by Joanne M. Pierce, 'Early Medieval Prayers Addressed to the Trinity in the *Ordo Missae* of Sigebert of Minden', in *Traditio* 51 (1996), 179–200, at 183.

[9] See ibid., 182–198. See also Helmut Hoping, 'Liturgy and the Triune God: Rethinking Trinitarian Theology', in *Authentic Liturgical Renewal in Contemporary Perspective: Proceedings of the Sacra Liturgia Conference held in London, 5th – 8th July 2016*, ed. Uwe Michael Lang (London: Bloomsbury T&T Clark, 2017), 21–30, at 24–26, for a critical appreciation of the influential work on this question by Josef A. Jungmann, *Die Stellung Christi im liturgischen Gebet*, Liturgiewissenschaftliche Quellen und Forschungen 19–20, 2nd ed. (Münster: Aschendorff, 1962), originally published in 1925.

less detailed ritual instructions are sometimes provided[10] and occasionally musical notation is added. Moreover, *ordines* can be found not only in sacramentaries or missals but also in handbooks for priests or collections of prayers (*libelli precum*).[11] According to the widely received classification of Bonifaas Luykx, *ordines* developed in distinct stages and the extant specimen can be classified in three types:[12]

(1) The 'Apology type' is characterised by groups of personal prayers (possibly of Gallican inspiration) that are simply inserted into the rite: (a) apology prayers at the beginning of Mass (*ante altare*), in which the priest expresses his own sinfulness and commends himself to God's mercy; (b) offertory prayers (*ad munus offerendum*), often in the form *Suscipe, sancta Trinitas*, with various intentions; (c) prayers to prepare for communion.

(2) The 'Frankish type' signals an advancement on the Apology type in that it integrates personal prayers into the rite of Mass by means of rubrical headings and instructions. Thus, specific ritual actions are linked with prayers, psalmody and versicles, beginning with the spiritual preparation in the sacristy (including washing of hands and vesting) and concluding with the un-vesting of the priest after Mass. While some of these texts can be classified as apologies, many of them offer the celebrant a spiritual reading of each ritual action. The *ordo* of Amiens, which has been discussed above, is considered the earliest and best representative of this type, which spread especially in West Francia.

---

[10] Because of the red ink commonly used for such instructions, they have become known as 'rubrics' (from 'ruber', the Latin word for red).

[11] For partial lists of *ordines* that are available in the (outdated) eighteenth-century collection of Edmond Martène or in a recent critical edition, see Joanne M. Pierce, 'The Evolution of the *Ordo Missae* in the Early Middle Ages', in *Medieval Liturgy: A Book of Essays*, ed. Lizette Larson-Miller, Garland Medieval Casebooks 18 (New York: Garland, 1997), 3–24, at 6–8. See also Pierre Salmon, 'L'*Ordo missae* dans dix manuscrits du Xe au XVe siècle', in *Analecta liturgica: Extraits des manuscrits liturgiques de la Bibliothèque vaticane. Contribution à l'histoire de la prière chrétienne*, Studi e testi 273 (Vatican City: Biblioteca Apostolica Vaticana, 1974), 195–221; Alain-Pierre Yao, *Les 'apologies' de l'Ordo Missae de la Liturgie Romaine: Sources – Histoire – Théologie*, Ecclesia orans. Studi e ricerche 3 (Naples: Editrice Domenicana Italiana, 2019), 355–358.

[12] See Bonifaas Luyxk, 'Der Ursprung der gleichbleibenden Teile der heiligen Messe (Ordinarium Missae)', in *Liturgie und Mönchtum* 29 (1961), 72–119, which is the translation by Johannes Madey of *De oorsprong van het gewone der Mis*, De Eredienst der kerk 3 (Utrecht; Antwerp: Spectrum, 1955).

(3) The development of the *Ordo Missae* culminated in the 'Rhenish type', which retains the structure of the Frankish type but increases the number of prayers, adds the recitation of entire psalms and connects these elements by rubrics. This *ordo* was composed for the solemn celebration of a bishop and also includes private prayers for his assistants. Building on its Frankish predecessor, exemplars of the Rhenish *Ordo Missae* may include the following elements:[13]

- Washing of hands with a prayer (*Largire sensibus nostris* or *Largire clementissime Pater*);
- Psalmody during the preparation in the sacristy (Psalms 83, 84, 85) with versicles and prayers;
- During the entrance procession Psalm 42 (*Iudica me*), with the antiphon *Introibo ad altare Dei*, confession of sins (*Confiteor*) and the prayer *Aufer a nobis*;
- Apology prayers during the *Gloria*;
- Prayer for the incensation of the gospel;
- Offertory prayers and dialogue *Orate, fratres*;
- Psalmody recited by deacon and subdeacons during the canon (Psalms 19, 24, 50, 89, 90), followed by prayers;
- Prayers for the commingling of body and blood;
- Prayers for the kiss of peace (such as *Habete vinculum caritatis, Pax Christi et ecclesiae*);
- Prayers for communion (such as *Panem caelestem accipiam, Quid retribuam*);
- Prayer at the conclusion of Mass (*Placeat tibi, sancta Trinitas* or *Meritis et intercessionibus*);
- Rite of thanksgiving in the sacristy, including Psalm 150 and Daniel 3:57–88 from the Canticle of the Three Young Men, with prayers.

---

[13] This typical scheme is based on Luyxk, 'Der Ursprung der gleichbleibenden Teile', 91–93; see also Joseph Lemarié, 'A propos de l'Ordo Missae du Pontifical d'Hugues de Salins (Montpellier, Bibl. Fac. de Médecine 303)', in *Didaskalia* 9 (1979), 3–9; and Andreas Odenthal, '"Ante conspectum diuinae maiestatis tuae reus assisto": Liturgie- und frömmigkeitsgeschichtliche Untersuchungen zum "Rheinischen Messordo und dessen Beziehungen zur Fuldaer Sakramentartradition', in *Liturgie vom frühen Mittelalter zum Zeitalter der Konfessionalisierung: Studien zur Geschichte des Gottesdienstes*, Spätmittelalter, Humanismus, Reformation 61 (Tübingen: Mohr Siebeck, 2011), 16–49, at 21–25 (originally published in *Archiv für Liturgiewissenschaft* 49 [2007] 1–35).

Luykx named this type of the *Ordo Missae* 'Rhenish' because he saw it radiate from the leading monasteries and episcopal sees along the river Rhine in the tenth century, especially St Gall, but also Reichenau and Mainz. Stephen van Dijk and Joan Hazelden Walker prefer to speak of the 'Lotharingian type' but likewise highlighted the active role of the abbey of St Gall, 'a centre of embellishment and dramatization of public worship: tropes, sequences, proses, offertory verses, *jubili*, liturgical drama, etc.'[14] Luykx's typology has been a remarkable success despite its preliminary character – he never published the extended study of the manuscript tradition, which he announced in his original contribution of 1955.[15] In the meantime, the study of *ordines* has been given a broader footing and scholars have expanded and refined Luykx's taxonomy. Still more work remains to be done: many sources that are now available in a critical edition raise questions about the geographical diffusion of *ordines*. Andreas Odenthal has pointed to the importance of ecclesiastical centres beyond the Rhine, above all the abbey of Fulda in central Germany.[16] The prayers of the *Ordo Missae* are not always organised in a distinct section but may be dispersed throughout a sacramentary; hence, more *ordines* are likely to be discovered and published. Moreover, the development of the *Ordo Missae* needs to be understood as more fluid than the three discrete types suggest. For instance, vesting prayers, which Luykx identifies as an innovation of the Frankish type over the Apology type, may have been used by priests before they were codified in a written *ordo*.

This consideration leads us again to the question of how these collections of the priest's (or bishop's) personal prayers were meant to be used. As has been noted in the discussion of the Amiens *ordo*, many prayers are introduced by the heading 'alia', which suggests that the celebrant could choose one or another. This characteristic corresponds to the first of two forms of the Rhenish *Ordo Missae* identified by Luykx, which consists in a repertory of alternative texts.[17] The best-known example of such a repertory is the *ordo* that is contained in a prayer book produced

---

[14] Stephen J. P. van Dijk, O.F.M. and Joan Hazelden Walker, *The Origins of the Modern Roman Liturgy: The Liturgy of the Papal Court and the Franciscan Order in the Thirteenth Century* (Westminster; London: The Newman Press; Darton, Longman & Todd, 1960), 50; see ibid., 49–51.

[15] See Luyxk, 'Der Ursprung der gleichbleibenden Teile', 96.

[16] See Odenthal, 'Ante conspectum diuinae maiestatis tuae reus assisto', 38–45.

[17] See Luykx, 'Der Ursprung der gleichbleibenden Teile', 95.

probably in St Gall for Sigebert, bishop of Minden from 1022–1036.[18] The text has achieved some notoriety since it was published in 1557 by the Lutheran theologian and historian Matthias Flacius Illyricus (1520–1575). In the Reformation controversies, Flacius Illyricus wanted to demonstrate the historical diversity of the Catholic liturgy and in particular to construct a narrative of decline and decay from the purity of Christian origins. For this purpose, he published several documents, including the Minden *ordo*, which he dated around the year 700. Thus the text became known as *Missa Illyrica*.[19] Its character as a repertory of private prayers is particularly clear, for example, in the part between the epistle and gospel readings, where sixteen prayers (some of them are quite lengthy) are indicated during the chanting of the gradual, alleluia and sequence.[20] For the offertory, fourteen (albeit short) prayers beginning with *Suscipe sancta Trinitas* are listed; most of them are dedicated to particular intentions (including the celebrant himself, his congregation and benefactors, the king and the Christian people, the Church, the sick and the deceased).[21]

The second form of the Rhenish *Ordo Missae* according to Luykx is 'sober, perfectly balanced [and] strictly follows the course of the Mass'.[22] There are three outstanding examples of this form in the monastic library of St Gall: Cod. Sang. 339 (c. 980–1000), Cod. Sang. 338 (1050–1060), and Cod. Sang. 340 (c. 1050–1075).[23] The *ordines* in these manuscripts have clearly grown over time: prayers were added by different hands at various stages, presumably while the books were in liturgical use.

---

[18] See Joanne M. Pierce, 'New Research Directions in Medieval Liturgy: The Liturgical Books of Sigebert of Minden (1022–1036)', in *Fountain of Life*, ed. Gerard Austin (Collegeville: Liturgical Press, 1986), 51–67, which reports the summary conclusions of her *Sacerdotal Spirituality at Mass: Text and Study of the Prayerbook of Sigebert of Minden (1022–1036)* (PhD dissertation, University of Notre Dame, 1988). Martène's edition is available in PL 138:1301–1336.

[19] See Oliver K. Olson, 'Flacius Illyricus als Liturgiker', in *Jahrbuch für Liturgik und Hymnologie* 12 (1967), 45–69; also 'Matthias Flacius Illyricus, 1520–1575', in *Shapers of Religious Traditions in Germany, Switzerland, and Poland, 1560–1600*, ed. Jill Raitt (New Haven: Yale University Press, 1981), 1–17.

[20] PL 138:1315B-1321A. See Pierce, 'Early Medieval Prayers', 182–184.

[21] PL 138:1325A-1327D. See Pierce, 'Early Medieval Prayers', 187–196.

[22] Luykx, 'Der Ursprung der gleichbleibenden Teile', 95; my translation.

[23] See ibid., 96–97. The texts have been edited by Michael G. Witczak, 'St. Gall Mass Orders (I): MS. Sangallensis 338: Searching for the Origins of the "Rheinish Mass Order"', in *Ecclesia Orans* 16 (1999), 393–410; 'St. Gall Mass Orders (II): MS. Sangallensis 339', in *Ecclesia Orans* 22 (2005), 47–62; and 'St. Gall Mass Orders (III): MS. Sangallensis 340', in *Ecclesia Orans* 24 (2007), 243–261. The digitised manuscripts are available on www.e-codices.unifr.ch/en.

However, the main body of prayers, meeting Luyxk's description, progresses in a linear fashion and is integrated into the structure of the Mass. While this form of the Rhenish *ordo* shares the penitential emphasis of the genre, its overall tone is more measured and less likely to overlay the traditional sequence of the rite of Mass. It may be asked whether, in liturgical history, undue weight has been given to Sigebert of Minden's *ordo* because of the role that Flacius Illyricus' 1557 edition secured for it in post-Reformation controversies. The prominent place this *ordo* obtains in Josef Andreas Jungmann's magisterial work *Missarum sollemnia*[24] may have created a lop-sided narrative. The aforementioned St Gall *ordines* testify to a pruning and aligning of personal prayers, and this effort resonates with views of the chronicler and Gregorian reformer Bernold of Constance (c. 1050–1100), who objects to the length and the private character of such prayers.[25] The substantial differences that can be observed between these individual *ordines* raises the question whether it is appropriate to subsume them under the same Rhenish category.[26]

The creation of the *Ordo Missae* epitomised the Frankish tendency to verbalise non-verbal liturgical actions (see Chapter 6). This verbalisation introduced a personal and emotive register that was different from the 'official' register of liturgical prayer as codified in the sacramentaries. Modern liturgical scholarship has tended to interpret this process as a departure from the 'classical form' of the Roman Rite that was determined by the cultural needs of the Franco-Germanic people. Joanne Pierce and John F. Romano offer a balanced version of this critique:

The Roman Mass before this point was known for its soberness, simplicity, and straightforwardness. These OMs filled out the framework of the Roman Rite with new prayers, psalms, and gestures, elaborating the 'soft spots' of the liturgy that had not previously received full elaboration, especially actions that occur without

---

[24] See the entry 'Missa Illyrica' in the index of Josef A. Jungmann, *Missarum sollemnia: Eine genetische Erklärung der römischen Messe*, 2 vol., 5th ed. (Wien: Herder, 1962), vol. II, 590. Pierce, 'The Evolution of the *Ordo Missae*', 12, also notes that 'Jungmann singles out the Minden OM for special attention'.

[25] Bernold of Constance, *Micrologus de ecclesiasticis observationibus*, 18: PL 151,989BC; see Odenthal, 'Ante conspectum diuinae maiestatis tuae reus assisto', 46–47.

[26] Given our better (though far from complete) knowledge of the manuscript tradition, Luykx's typology of the *Ordo Missae* may well be one of the 'traditional landmarks in liturgical history' that are rife for critical revision, as argued by Helen Gittos and Sarah Hamilton, 'Introduction', in *Understanding Medieval Liturgy: Essays in Interpretation*, ed. Helen Gittos and Sarah Hamilton (London; New York: Routledge, 2018), 1–10, at 8.

words. They imbued the Roman Eucharistic liturgy with new embellishment, drama, and allegorical symbolism.[27]

This assessment is not without problems; first of all, the characterisation of the Roman Mass as sober, simple and straightforward. The ritual shape of the Mass, for which *Ordo Romanus I* is our key witness, certainly featured lavish and dramatic elements, especially in its processional parts, which were indebted to imperial ceremonial (see Chapter 5). Secondly, the elaboration of the 'soft spots' can be understood as offering genuine development and even enrichment. For instance, the pontiff's moment of silent prayer before he approached the altar[28] occasioned the recitation of Psalm 42[43], with the evocative antiphon 'Introibo ad altare Dei ...' ('I will go to the altar of God ...'; Ps 42[43]:4).[29]

Thirdly, and perhaps most importantly, when we enquire into the effect the inclusion of the priest's private prayers had on the ritual shape of the Mass, we find that, rather than offering drama and embellishment, it paved the way for the wide diffusion of the 'private Mass' (a term fraught with difficulties that will be discussed below), with its much-reduced ceremonial. As Stephen van Dijk and Joan Hazelden Walker note, the prayers of the Rhenish *Ordo Missae* could be used in the solemn Mass and in the low Mass but with a fundamentally different effect on the rite. In the solemn Mass, the celebrant's personal prayers 'remained accidental' and did not impinge upon its structure and form, which were shaped by the ordinary and proper chants.[30] In the low Mass, however, the Rhenish order 'became both a guide to the ritual and its framework', into which 'were fitted the variable and invariable texts of the Mass'.[31] The *Ordo Missae* thus created a coherent (and memorable) scheme that facilitated the success of the private Mass. The Frankish adaptation of the Roman Rite certainly added dramatic elements that accommodated more tangible forms of piety, especially in the principal celebrations of the liturgical year, such as Holy Week and Easter, and it encouraged the composition of tropes, sequences and proses that gave particular feasts

---

[27] Pierce and Romano, 'The *Ordo Missae* of the Roman Rite', 21.

[28] *Ordo Romanus I*, 50: 7: ed. Michel Andrieu, *Les Ordines Romani du haut moyen âge*, 5 vols., Spicilegium Sacrum Lovaniense 11, 23, 24, 28, 29 (Louvain: Peeters, 1931–1961), vol. II, 83.

[29] This psalm verse was already employed by Ambrose of Milan in his mystagogical catecheses for the newly baptised to evoke the approach to the altar of the Eucharist: *De sacramentis* IV,2,7: SC 25bis,104–105, and *De mysteriis* 8,43: SC 25bis,178–179.

[30] Van Dijk and Hazelden Walker, *The Origins of the Modern Roman Liturgy*, 50.

[31] Ibid.

a more exuberant character. However, it would seem that the contribution of the *Ordo Missae* was at the same time more fundamental and less visible, since it shifted the rite towards an interiorisation of liturgical action and a focus on the personal devotion of the offering priest, with a particular stress on his personal sinfulness and need for divine mercy. While this aspect of priestly spirituality is no doubt important (the recent clerical abuse scandals illustrate very painfully the consequence of priests becoming oblivious to the ascetical dimension of their ministry), there is some foundation for the oft-repeated charge that the early medieval period saw a 'clericalisation' of the Mass and a detachment of the laity from its liturgical enactment. I shall take up this question again below in my more extended discussion of the private Mass.

In a seminal contribution, Paul Tirot has drawn attention to another type of *Ordo Missae* that originated from the Benedictine abbey of Cluny, which was founded in 910 and became a centre of monastic and ecclesiastical reform. The Cluniac *Ordo Missae*, which was probably established by the middle of the eleventh century,[32] stands out for its very sparing use of apology prayers. The introductory rites include a moment of silent prayer before the altar and a short *Confiteor*, but not Psalm 42 (*Iudica me*) or the prayer *Aufer a nobis*. At the offertory, no private prayers are indicated for the placing of the offerings on the altar, for the incensation or for the washing of hands, except for *In spiritu humilitatis* (which incorporates Daniel 3:39–40 from the Latin Vulgate), a humble and contrite plea that the sacrifice offered by the priest may be pleasing in God's sight. The invitation to prayer is recorded in the form *Orate pro me peccatore*, but no response follows; rather, it leads directly to the *secreta* that concludes the offertory. There is no private prayer to prepare for communion or to accompany the elaborate purification of the sacred vessels. The priest concludes the Mass by saying *Placeat tibi, sancta Trinitas* and kissing the altar, without a blessing.

Tirot argues that this monastic *Ordo Missae* intended to reproduce *Ordo Romanus I* as closely as possible. Thus, it can be understood as a liturgical expression of the particular character of Cluny's foundation: by invoking the protection of the Apostles Peter and Paul, the monastery placed itself under the direct authority of the pope, not the local bishop.

---

[32] See Paul Tirot, 'Un "Ordo Missae" monastique: Cluny, Cîteaux, La Charteuse', in *Ephemerides Liturgicae* 95 (1981), 44–120 and 220–251, at 234–235. The study was also published separately in the series Biblioteca Ephemerides Liturgiae. Subsidia 21 (Rome: C.L.V. – Edizioni Liturgiche, 1981).

While it is conceivable that monastic customaries do not include all the liturgical formulas that were in actual use, for instance, for the blessing of incense and for the incensation of the offerings,[33] the Cluniac *ordo* is distinguished from other *ordines*, both diocesan and monastic, by its sobriety and restraint. These qualities recommended this *ordo* to the Cistercians and Carthusians who adopted it in their own monastic uses (with modifications reflecting the austere spirit of the newly founded orders). Tirot draws attention to the fact that, contrary to what is often assumed, the Cluniac, Cistercian and Carthusian liturgical uses do not depend on the particular customs and observances of the dioceses where these orders were founded. In the case of the Cluniac *ordo*, which stands at the origin of this development, there seems to be a conscious effort to imitate ancient Roman liturgical sources.[34] As Tirot documents, late medieval and early modern liturgical books in all three traditions depart from this original simplicity and gradually supply the *Ordo Missae* with private prayers of different origins.

THE ROMANO-GERMANIC PONTIFICAL AND THE OTTONIAN CHURCH

The compilation of the Romano-Germanic Pontifical (*Pontificale Romano-Germanicum* = PRG) has been considered a milestone of liturgical development in the Ottonian age. The critical edition of Cyrille Vogel and Reinhard Elze, which built on the ground-breaking but unfinished work of Michel Andrieu,[35] has established a generally accepted history: between 950 and 963, in the monastery of St Alban's in Mainz a new kind of liturgical book was compiled, with the authority of Archbishop William (r. 954–968), a natural son of Emperor Otto I. The volume assembled a variety of *ordines*, comprising both prayer texts and rubrical instructions, which were proper to a bishop (or his delegate) and which had formerly been found in different books. These included rites for the ordination of clerics, for the consecration of virgins, for the dedication of churches and altars, for coronations, for a range of blessings, for the reconciliation of penitents, Mass ceremonials (*Ordo Romanus V* and *X*), as well as liturgical and canonical treatises. These

---

[33] See ibid., 89.   [34] See ibid., 246–249.
[35] *Le Pontifical romano-germanique du dixième siècle*, ed. Cyrille Vogel and Reinhard Elze, 3 vols., Studi e testi 226, 227, 269 (Vatican City: Biblioteca Apostolica Vaticana, 1963–1972). See also the overview of Vogel, *Medieval Liturgy*, 230–239.

texts are both of Roman and of German origin; hence the name given to the pontifical. After its rapid dissemination north of the Alps, it was thanks to the Ottonian presence in Rome that the book was introduced in the city and helped to establish there the mixed form of the Roman Rite that had gone through a process of adaptation and enrichment in the Frankish-Germanic realms. The PRG became the foundational document for the subsequent development of liturgical books for episcopal celebrations.

Henry Parkes' study of the manuscript tradition has revealed the conjectural character of this account. His thorough codicological investigation shows that there is no original source for the text edited by Vogel and Elze, which is better described as 'a hypothetical corpus of tenth-century material formed by surgically combining representatives of Andrieu's two principal manuscript groups'.[36] Postulating a single origin of this remarkable compendium of liturgical texts, which survives in some forty variations, has no basis in the evidence. What we can credibly affirm is that

a very significant textual tradition rose to prominence in late tenth- or early eleventh-century Germany, that its eclectic contents were broadly liturgical in scope, and that it metamorphosed wildly in its remarkable transmission across Europe in a manner which is not yet understood.[37]

With this important caveat in mind, the edition by Vogel and Elze can still be used, but note should be taken of the sources and dates of its component texts.[38]

In a recent contribution, Parkes connects the creation of the PRG with the last Ottonian ruler, the devout Henry II (king 1002, emperor 1014, d. 1024), who took great interest in ecclesiastical matters, even to the point of being acclaimed in his time as *coepiscopus,* and was canonised a saint in 1146. Henry II is known to liturgical historians above all for his

---

[36] Henry Parkes, 'Questioning the Authority of Vogel and Elze's *Pontifical romano-germanique*', in *Understanding Medieval Liturgy*, 75–101, at 85. See also *The Making of Liturgy in the Ottonian Church: Books, Music and Ritual in Mainz, 950–1050*, Cambridge Studies in Medieval Life and Thought. Fourth Series 100 (Cambridge: Cambridge University Press, 2015).

[37] Parkes, 'Questioning the Authority of Vogel and Elze's *Pontifical romano-germanique*', 100.

[38] Parkes has also created a website that shows how the standard edition makes use of a selection of known manuscripts, with links to digitised sources of the PRG tradition: 'PRG Database: A tool for navigating *Le Pontifical Romano-Germanique*, ed. Cyrille Vogel & Reinhard Elze', at http://database.prg.mus.cam.ac.uk.

initiative to insert the creed into the Roman Mass. Bern, abbot of Reichenau (d. 1048) reports that Henry, staying in the city of Rome in 1014 for his coronation as emperor, was surprised to find that, unlike in Germany, the creed did not form part of the rite of Mass and inquired about the reasons for this absence. He received the response that the Roman church had always stood firm in the Catholic faith according to the teaching of St Peter. Hence, it was not necessary to have the creed sung at Mass in Rome, unlike in those local churches that were at some point tainted by heresy. However, the newly crowned emperor persuaded Pope Benedict VIII (r. 1012–1024) to add the creed to the main celebration of Mass ('ad publicam missam').[39] The creed in question was that of the first two ecumenical councils of Nicaea (325) and Constantinople (381), which had been used as a baptismal profession of faith in the Christian East since the fourth century. Peter the Fuller, anti-Chalcedonian patriarch of Antioch (r. 471–488), is credited with the introduction of the creed into the Eucharistic liturgy, to be recited after the kiss of peace. In the Latin West, the creed became part of the Mass first in Visigothic Spain, after the conversion of King Reccared and his nobles to Catholic Christianity. At the third synod of Toledo in 589, it was decreed that the Niceno-Constantinopolitan Creed should be said with the *filioque* clause, affirming the procession of the Holy Spirit from the Father and the Son, at every Mass, in preparation for Holy Communion, preceding the Lord's Prayer.[40] The Stowe Missal (c. 792–803), an important source for Irish liturgical use, places the creed after the gospel. Towards the end of the eighth century, Charlemagne had the singing of the creed (including the *filioque*) inserted after the gospel at the celebration of Mass in his Palatine chapel at Aachen. This decision was part of the Carolingian struggle against Adoptionist Christology in Spain. Pope Leo III (r. 795–816) approved of the use of the creed at Mass, though without the *filioque*, and he did not adopt the practice in Rome itself. The new custom spread slowly throughout the Carolingian realms

---

[39] See Bern of Reichenau, *Libellus de quibusdam rebus ad missae officium pertinentibus*, 2: PL 142, 1060D–1061A. See now also the critical edition of Henry Parkes published as CCM 297.

[40] The Latin translation of the creed used in Mozarabic sources is different from the version later introduced in the Roman Rite. Interestingly, the loanword 'homusion' is used, where the Roman version translates 'consubstantialis'; see Marius Férotin, *Le Liber Mozarabicus Sacramentorum et les manuscrits mozarabes*, Monumenta Ecclesiae Liturgica 6 (Paris: Firmin-Didot, 1912), 773.

and was commonly accepted in Franco-German churches by the tenth century.[41]

The episode recorded by Bern of Reichenau most likely happened at the Roman synod of 1014, which was held on the occasion of Henry's imperial coronation. It is interesting to note that the emperor is presented as petitioning the insertion of the creed into the Roman Mass and the pope as making the decision.[42] The confident abbot of Reichenau, a champion of the Ottonian imperial church, records with satisfaction that Franco-German use prevailed over the claim of the Roman church, not least since the matter of the creed forms part of his lengthy discussion on the differences regarding the use of the *Gloria in excelsis* (see below, pp. 274–275). At the same time, Bern remains sceptical whether the Romans abided by the decision made at the synod of 1014. In fact, the creed was adopted in Rome only on Sundays and major feasts in the liturgical year – and not at every *missa publica* – as is confirmed towards the end of the eleventh century by Bernold of Constance.

> Credo in unum Deum,
> Patrem omnipotentem,
> factorem caeli et terrae,
> visibilium omnium et invisibilium.
> Et in unum Dominum, Iesum Christum,
> Filium Dei unigenitum.
> Et ex Patre natum ante omnia saecula.
> Deum de Deo, lumen de lumine, Deum verum de Deo vero.
> Genitum, non factum, consubstantialem Patri:
> per quem omnia facta sunt.

---

[41] See the excellent documentation of Andreas Amiet, 'Die liturgische Gesetzgebung der deutschen Reichskirche in der Zeit der sächsischen Kaiser 922–1023', in *Zeitschrift für schweizerische Kirchengeschichte* 70 (1976), 1–106 and 209–307, at 222–228; also Bernard Capelle, 'L'introduction du symbole à la messe', in *Travaux liturgiques de doctrine et d'histoire*, 3 vols. (Louvain: Centre Liturgique, 1955–1967), vol. III, 60–81 (originally published in *Mélanges Joseph de Ghellinck, S.J.*, Museum Lessianum. Section historique 13–14, 2 vols. [Gembloux: Duculot, 1951], vol. II, 1003–1028). For the Carolingian background, see Thomas F. X. Noble, 'Kings, Clergy and Dogma: The Settlement of Doctrinal Disputes in the Carolingian World', in *Early Medieval Studies in Memory of Patrick Wormald*, ed. Stephen Baxter et al., Studies in Early Medieval Britain (Farnham: Ashgate, 2009), 237–252.

[42] This is also the gist of the tantalisingly generic comment in the *Vita* of Meinwerk, bishop of Paderborn, ch. 26: MGH Scriptores Rerum Germanicarum in Usum Scholarum LIX, 31.

Qui propter nos homines et propter nostram salutem
descendit de caelis.
Et incarnatus est de Spiritu Sancto
ex Maria Virgine: et homo factus est.
Crucifixus etiam pro nobis:
sub Pontio Pilato passus, et sepultus est.
Et resurrexit tertia die, secundum Scripturas.
Et ascendit in cælum: sedet ad dexteram Patris.
Et iterum venturus est cum gloria
iudicare vivos et mortuos:
cuius regni non erit finis.
Et in Spiritum Sanctum, Dominum et vivificantem:
qui ex Patre Filioque procedit.
Qui cum Patre et Filio simul adoratur et conglorificatur:
qui locutus est per prophetas.
Et unam, sanctam, catholicam et apostolicam Ecclesiam.
Confiteor unum baptisma in remissionem peccatorum.
Et exspecto resurrectionem mortuorum.
Et vitam venturi saeculi.
Amen.

I believe in one God,
the Father almighty,
maker of heaven and earth,
of all things visible and invisible.
And in one Lord Jesus Christ,
the Only Begotten Son of God,
born of the Father before all ages.
God from God, Light from Light,
true God from true God,
begotten, not made, consubstantial with the Father;
through him all things were made.
For us men and for our salvation
he came down from heaven,
and by the Holy Spirit was incarnate of the Virgin Mary,
and became man.
For our sake he was also crucified;
under Pontius Pilate he suffered death and was buried,
and rose again on the third day
in accordance with the Scriptures.
He ascended into heaven
and is seated at the right hand of the Father.
He will come again in glory
to judge the living and the dead
and his kingdom will have no end.
And in the Holy Spirit, the Lord, the giver of life,

who proceeds from the Father and the Son,
who with the Father and the Son is adored and glorified,
who has spoken through the prophets.
And in one, holy, catholic and apostolic Church.
I confess one Baptism for the forgiveness of sins
and I look forward to the resurrection of the dead
and the life of the world to come.
Amen.

The ecclesiastical interests of Henry II form the background to Parkes' argument that the monarch initiated the PRG tradition as a new kind of liturgical compilation not for practical use but as a scholarly resource for the newly founded episcopal see of Bamberg in the early eleventh century.[43] It will be seen whether this new hypothesis of the PRG's origin, which is presented with impressive documentation, holds up to scrutiny. What Parkes' revisionist approach shows convincingly is that the often uneven and inconsistent PRG tradition can no longer be understood as a decisive turning point or paradigm shift in the history of the Western liturgy.[44] As we have seen in the case of the Carolingian reforms, processes of liturgical change are more fluid and drawn-out than the tendency of modern scholarship to identify discrete stages allows for.

By dating the PRG tradition in the eleventh and twelfth century (rather than the period between 950 and 1050, as is still widely held), Parkes associates it with the papal reform movement, which also afforded bishops a heightened sense of their sacred authority.[45] In the liturgy, the impetus for reform translated into a renewed emphasis on order and harmony by means of the prescriptive force of the written text. However, books compiled for the episcopal liturgy were not simply practical tools but also functioned as 'sites of institutional memory'.[46] Parkes brings into relief the agency of scribes in producing liturgical manuscripts and notes that almost all PRG sources 'display evidence of

---

[43] Henry Parkes, 'Henry II, Liturgical Patronage and the Birth of the "Romano-German Pontifical"', in *Early Medieval Europe* 28 (2020), 104–141.

[44] See Parkes, 'Questioning the Authority', 86; and 'Henry II', 140.

[45] See Parkes, *The Making of Liturgy*, 222–223.   [46] Ibid., 179.

local scribal initiative or intervention'.[47] The intention to fix in writing what used to be unwritten codifies existing ritual practice, but this determination does not necessarily lead to uniformity. Paradoxically, as Parkes observes, '[t]he more that writing intervenes in the running of the liturgy, the more a scribe has to commit to performance decisions in advance, hence the greater the potential for these books to differ among themselves'.[48] We will encounter a similar phenomenon with early printed liturgical books in the late fifteenth and early sixteenth century.

Present-day historians are inclined to highlight elements of diversity and innovation, and historians of the liturgy make no exception to this trend. However, it needs to be recognised that there are significant differences in the evolution of liturgical forms and genres; for instance, Christopher Jones notes that pontificals 'tend to be much less conservative than sacramentaries'.[49] Helen Gittos strikes a similar chord when she recalls a 'widely accepted'[50] insight of Mary C. Mansfield:

> Undoubtedly some rites hardly altered over many centuries. The canon of the mass, to take the most obvious example, remained stable because of its central importance from ancient times. Generally, as one moved outward from the canon first to the rest of the liturgy of the mass, then to the daily office, and finally to occasional rites like penance, one finds at each step more tolerance for alteration.[51]

The core of the Eucharistic liturgy, inherited from its formative period between the fifth and the seventh century, showed remarkable continuity throughout the Middle Ages. Local variations concerned more peripheral aspects of the celebration of Mass. Nonetheless, the importance of ritual in medieval society ensured that such disparities could provoke tension and even conflict. A telling illustration is Bern of Reichenau's lengthy discussion on the use of the *Gloria in excelsis* at Mass: Roman custom

---

[47] Ibid., 188. Parkes does not appear to address sufficiently the question on whose authority these scribes may act. Would they follow the instructions of their bishop, or of a cleric acting as master of ceremonies, or do they intervene at their own initiative?

[48] Ibid., 10.

[49] Christopher A. Jones, 'The Chrism Mass in Later Anglo-Saxon England', in *The Liturgy of the Late Anglo-Saxon Church*, ed. Helen Gittos and M. Bradford Bedingfield, Henry Bradshaw Society. Subsidia 5 (London: Boydell Press, 2005), 105–142, at 128.

[50] Helen Gittos, 'Researching the History of Rites', in *Understanding Medieval Liturgy*, 13–37, at 33.

[51] Mary C. Mansfield, *The Humiliation of Sinners: Public Penance in Thirteenth-century France* (Ithaca; London: Cornell University Press, 1995), 160.

reserved its use to bishops (except at Easter), while in Germany any priest could intone it on the appropriate days. Bern defends the practice of the imperial church with reference to Gregory the Great's instruction to Augustine of Canterbury, encouraging him in his mission to accept sound practice where he finds it, since the unity of faith does not require the imitation of every Roman custom.[52] Another instance of such differences and their potential for controversy is reported from the celebration of St Stephen's Day on 26 December 1052 at Worms, in which Pope Leo IX (r. 1049–1053) and Henry III (king 1028, emperor 1046, d. 1056) participated. At the solemn Mass celebrated by Archbishop Liutpold of Mainz (r. 1051–1059), a deacon chanted the epistle, which in Roman use would pertain to the ministry of a subdeacon. Stirred by his curial advisors, Leo IX intervened against this practice, but the archbishop and his deacon stood their ground, and in order to avoid scandal, the pope did not insist on the matter.[53] This episode is indicative both of the increasing confidence that the papal reform movement (of which Leo IX is considered a 'moderate' exponent) gave to the pope and his curia in liturgical affairs, and of the persistence of local customs.

THE REFORM PAPACY AND THE ROMAN LITURGY

As the papal reform movement gained momentum in the course of the eleventh century, the papacy moved to take charge of the development of the Roman Rite again. The role of Gregory VII (r. 1073–1085) is crucial in this process – not, however, because of a consistent liturgical agenda (which he did not have), but rather because of his claims to papal leadership that set the tone for things to come. A good source for Gregory's liturgical ideas is Bernold of Constance, who stayed in Rome from 1079 to 1084 and between 1086 and 1090 and wrote a commentary on the Mass known as *Micrologus de ecclesiasticis observationibus*, a work that enjoyed considerable circulation and influence in the Middle Ages.[54] Bernold reports the pope's interest in studying apostolic traditions

---

[52] Bern of Reichenau, *Libellus de quibusdam rebus ad missae officium pertinentibus*, 2: PL 142, 1060D–1061A; see the discussion by Amiet, 'Die liturgische Gesetzgebung der deutschen Reichskirche', 222–223.

[53] The incident is reported by Frutolf of Michelsberg, *Chronica*, A.D. 1053: MGH Scriptores VI, 196–197; see Amiet, 'Die liturgische Gesetzgebung der deutschen Reichskirche', 279.

[54] Forty-six manuscripts of the work have come down to us; see Vincent L. Kennedy, 'For a New Edition of the Micrologus of Bernold of Constance', in *Mélanges en l'honneur de*

and his aim of restoring what was held to be Roman use in the age of Gregory the Great.[55]

Against this backdrop, it may appear ironic that the Mass 'iuxtam Romanam consuetudinem',[56] which Bernold expounds in the first of the three distinct treatises that make up the *Micrologus*, shows that the Rhenish *Ordo Missae* tradition had become an integral part of the rite followed by the pope and his curia. However, despite his repeated insistence on Roman custom (*consuetudo*), manner (*mos*), authority (*auctoritas*) and order (*ordo*), Bernold was not a naïve observer, and he was aware that not all of the prayers used at Mass were of Roman origin. In particular, he mentions the Gallican provenience of the *Veni sanctificator* at the offertory,[57] and he concedes that the *Suscipe sancta Trinitas* is derived 'from ecclesiastical custom' but is not found in the Roman *ordines*, which foresee no prayer after the presentation of bread and wine except the *secreta*.[58] Likewise, the prayer *Domine Iesu Christe qui ex voluntate Patris* in preparation for communion is based only on the tradition of 'religious men',[59] and it has already been noted above that Bernold is critical of an excessive use of long private prayers.

The *Micrologus* reports with disapproval that during the canon some priests interpolate prayers in the commemoration of the living (*Memento, Domine*) and of the dead (*Memento etiam, Domine*). Priests who insert the Incarnation into the anamnetic section of *Unde et memores* and extend the lists of the saints are likewise censured.[60] Bernold thus witnesses to the increasing insistence on the written ritual, as well as to priests being inclined to add to the received text. The importance of fidelity to the written text is also stressed in the Rule of St Augustine, which categorically instructs in its short chapter on prayer: 'Do not sing except what you read is to be sung; but what is not written that it should

---

[55] See Bernold of Constance, *Micrologus de ecclesiasticis observationibus*, 5, 14, 17, 43 and 56: PL 151,980CD, 986B, 988B, 1010AB and 1018BC. See Reinhard Elze, 'Gregor VII. und die römische Liturgie', in *La Riforma Gregoriana e l'Europa: Congresso internazionale, Salerno, 20–25 maggio 1985*, ed. Alfons M. Stickler et al., Studi Gregoriani 13–14, 2 vols. (Rome: LAS, 1989–1991), vol. I, 179–188, esp. 180.
[56] Ibid., 1: PL 151,979A; see also the brief description of a priest's Mass, ibid., 23: PL 151,992B–995C.
[57] Ibid., 11: PL 151,984A.   [58] Ibid., 11: PL 151,984B.
[59] Ibid., 18: PL 151, 989B: 'ex religiosorum traditione habemus'.
[60] Ibid., 13: PL 151,985B–986A.

be sung, should not be sung.'[61] After its influence had been eclipsed by the
Rule of St Benedict in the early medieval period, the Rule of St Augustine
was widely adopted in the eleventh century by canons regular, that is,
clerics living in community. Subsequently, it was embraced by a number
of new religious orders, including the Premonstratensians (Norbertines) in
1120, the Trinitarians in 1198 and the Dominicans in 1216.

A committed advocate for the Gregorian reform, Bernold does not
seem to be overly concerned with establishing the 'purely' Roman tradition but rather with following the liturgical order of the contemporary
papacy. Thus, the *Micrologus* may echo the policy of Pope Gregory VII,
who demanded that the Roman tradition, purged of recently introduced
German customs, should be the norm for the whole Latin Church but
only enacted very minor liturgical changes to implement this demand.
Most of Gregory's reforms were decreed at two Roman synods in Lent
and in November 1078, which determined the date of the Ember days in
Lent and after Pentecost Sunday (against the different German legislation
of the synod of Seligenstadt in 1023) and added feasts of holy popes to the
universal calendar.[62] Gregory VII also insisted that at solemn occasions
every Christian should contribute to the offering at solemn Mass. He
refers to the biblical injunction given through Moses for the feast of
unleavened bread, 'You shall not appear in my sight empty-handed' (Ex
23:15) and 'the custom of the holy fathers', which presumably reflects the
Roman nobility's offering of bread and wine recorded in the *Ordines
Romani* for papal Masses.[63] This practice seems to have fallen into disuse
as monetary offerings became more customary, and it is telling that
Bernold makes no mention of it being observed or of Gregory's attempt
at restoring it.[64]

---

[61] *Praeceptum* II,4: ed. Luc Verheijen, *La règle de Saint Augustin*, 2 vols. (Paris: Études
Augustiniennes, 1967), vol. I, 420–421. The passage is taken literally from Augustine, *Ep.*
211,7.

[62] Moreover, in the Divine Office Gregory VII made marginal changes in the chants for
Matins of Sexagesima Sunday and modified the psalms and lessons in the night office
throughout the year; see H. E. J. Cowdrey, *Pope Gregory VII, 1073–1085* (Oxford:
Clarendon Press, 1998), 319–320; and esp. H. E. J. Cowdrey, 'Pope Gregory VII
(1073–85) and the Liturgy', in *Journal of Theological Studies* NS 55 (2004), 55–83.
See also Uta-Renate Blumenthal and Detlev Jasper, '"Licet nova consuetudo" – Gregor
VII. und die Liturgie', in *Bishops, Texts and the Use of Canon Law Around 1100: Studies
in Honour of Martin Brett*, ed. Bruce C. Brasington and Kathleen G. Cushing, Church,
Faith and Culture in the Medieval West (Aldershot: Ashgate, 2008), 45–68.

[63] See *Ordo Romanus I*, 69–75 and *IV*, 38–45: ed. Andrieu, vol. II, 91–92 and 161–162.

[64] See Cowdrey, 'Pope Gregory VII (1073–85) and the Liturgy', 73–74; also Jungmann,
Missarum sollemnia, vol. II, 28–29.

Of wider impact were the calls for local churches, such as those of Denmark and Scotland,[65] to follow Roman customs and observances, in order to guarantee doctrinal purity and ecclesiastical unity. Reform popes before Gregory VII had already made such demands in Italy with regard to the Ambrosian tradition in the north and the Beneventan tradition in the south. While Gregory refused to concede the use of the Slavonic language in territories he claimed for the Latin Church (Croatia and Bohemia), he did not insist on liturgical conformity in relation to the Greek and Armenian churches. Regarding Eastern Christianity, his main concern was a recognition of the primacy of the papacy.[66]

In continuity with his immediate predecessors, Gregory VII was persistent in his efforts to have the Hispanic (Mozarabic) Rite replaced by the Roman Rite throughout the Iberian Peninsula, with the intention of binding the re-conquered Christian territories to the see of Rome and forging the unity of Latin Christendom. This momentous change had been initiated in the Kingdom of Aragón in the pontificate of Alexander II (r. 1061–1073) through the activities of his legate Cardinal Hugo Candidus, and it was facilitated by Cluniac influence on monasteries in northern Spain. Gregory's campaign was crowned with success when at the council of Burgos in May 1080, King Alfonso VI of León and Castile decided to adopt the Roman Rite in his realm.[67] Rose Walker concludes from her comparative study of Mozarabic and Roman liturgical manuscripts that were produced in northern Spain in the late eleventh or early twelfth century that the Roman Mass was introduced swiftly and radically, while some elements of transition can be identified in the case of the Divine Office. The rupture is also visible in a shift from a 'Mozarabic' to a 'Romanesque' style of illumination and decoration in liturgical manuscripts.[68]However, the substitution was not complete, and the Mozarabic liturgy continued to be celebrated in some places, especially in Toledo, its traditional centre, which was captured from the Muslims in 1085.[69]

---

[65] See van Dijk and Hazelden Walker, *The Origins of the Modern Roman Liturgy*, 71–74; and Elze, 'Gregor VII. und die römische Liturgie', 185.

[66] See Cowdrey, 'Pope Gregory VII (1073–85) and the Liturgy', 79–81.

[67] See ibid., 78–79.

[68] See Rose Walker, *Views of Transition: Liturgy and Illumination in Medieval Spain*, The British Library Studies in Medieval Culture (London; Toronto: The British Library and University of Toronto Press, 1998), 208–224.

[69] See Ludwig Vones, 'The Substitution of the Hispanic Liturgy by the Roman Rite in the Kingdoms of the Iberian Peninsula', in *Hispania Vetus: Musical-Liturgical Manuscripts:*

In his decree *In die resurrectionis* about the psalms and lessons at the night office, Gregory VII stated that he had investigated 'the Roman order and the ancient custom of our church (*ordinem Romanum ... et antiquum morem nostrae ecclesiae*)' and intended to restore the older usage, which had been changed under German influence.[70] Notwithstanding this strong claim, liturgical sources of the Gregorian period show the continued impact of the Romano-Germanic tradition, especially in the reception of the Rhenish *Ordo Missae* and the pontifical compilations.[71] Interestingly, the oldest extant books of Old Roman chant with musical notation, beginning with the gradual of Santa Maria in Trastevere of 1071, hail from a period when this repertory may have been threatened. The lack of evidence does not permit us to reconstruct this process, but it would seem likely that the Ottonian presence in Rome and the election of German popes in the late tenth and the eleventh century led to the introduction of the significantly different Gregorian chant that was in use north of the Alps. At this point, a particular need may have been perceived to codify the Old Roman melodies.[72]

H. E. J. Cowdrey has described Gregory's policy regarding the city of Rome as 'quieta non movere',[73] and in the context of his whole pontificate, his liturgical interventions appear very restrained. Within the framework established by the rite of Mass, there was no strict uniformity in particular ceremonies and observances even within the city of Rome. The Lateran basilica, the cathedral of the pope as bishop of Rome, which claimed the title 'mother and head of all the churches in the city and the world (*omnium urbis et orbis ecclesiarum mater et caput*)', had no claim to impose its use on the many churches and monasteries of the city, and certainly not on St Peter's in the Vatican, its rival for honour and prestige. At the time, the cycle of papal stational Masses was still a living reality, and proper customs (as well as local prerogatives) were maintained with tenacity.[74] It would seem that, like Bernold, the champion of his cause in the empire, Gregory VII was above all intent that obedience should be shown to the Roman church by following the pattern of papal liturgy,

From Visigothic Origins to the Franco-Roman Transition, 9th–12th Centuries, ed. Susana Zapke (Bilbao: Fundación BBVA, 2007), 43–59.

[70] See Cowdrey, 'Pope Gregory VII (1073–85) and the Liturgy', 60.

[71] See Vogel, *Medieval Liturgy*, 249–251.

[72] See David Hiley, *Western Plainchant: A Handbook* (Oxford: Clarendon Press, 1993), 594.

[73] See Cowdrey, *Pope Gregory VII (1073–85)*, 314–329.

[74] See Cowdrey, 'Pope Gregory VII (1073–85) and the Liturgy', 57–58.

without insisting on uniformity in every detail. The demand to 'purify' the
Roman liturgy of Germanic accretions did not translate into a practical
programme but remained an ideological gesture towards the emperor.
The scope of Gregory VII's liturgical legislation is so limited that it hardly
qualifies as significant in the history of the Roman Rite.[75] However, his
strong statement for papal authority, epitomised in the *Dictatus papae*,
was of long-term consequences for the Western Church in general and for
the ordering of its divine worship in particular. Moreover, the (then
largely rhetorical) emphasis on investigating apostolic traditions and
restoring the purity of ancient Roman observance helped create a mentality that was to have a lasting effect on conceptions of liturgical renewal.

For some time, however, diversity of observances in worship remained,
as is attested in a letter of Peter Abelard to Bernard of Clairvaux, written
probably in 1131 and certainly before 1135. Abelard defends himself
against criticism of liturgical innovations he introduced at the community
of the Paraclete with a counterattack on innovations in the Cistercian
liturgy. In a more conciliatory tone, he observes that there is a legitimate
variety of liturgical practice in the Latin Church, even within the city of
Rome:

For who does not know that, in divine offices, there are diverse and innumerable
customs of the Church, even amongst the clergy themselves? Assuredly, not even
the very City holds to the ancient custom of the Roman see, but only the Lateran
church, which is the mother of all, holds to the ancient office; none of its daughters
follows it in this respect – not even the very basilica of the Roman palace.[76]

In a recent study dedicated to the Roman liturgy in the pontificate of
Innocent II (r. 1130–1143), during which Abelard wrote this letter, John
F. Romano has refuted the claim of earlier scholars, such as Anton
L. Mayer, that the nascent Gothic spirit effected a fundamental shift in
attitudes towards the liturgy, with a new emphasis in 'subjectivity, indi-
vidualism, and Christ-centered piety'.[77] The spiritual and intellectual

[75] This is implied in the *Breviarium Romanum* of 1568, where Gregory VII is mentioned as
the restorer of the Divine Office, and it is reflected in the periodisation of modern
liturgical scholarship. See Elze, 'Gregor VII. und die Liturgie', 179 and 185–187.
[76] Peter Abelard, *Ep. 10*: ed. Edmé Reno Smits, *Peter Abelard: Letters IX–XIV. An Edition
with Introduction* (Doctoral thesis, Rijksuniversiteit te Groningen, 1981), 246–247 (PL
178, 340BC); for the dating of the letter, see ibid., 135–136. The translation is taken from
Cowdrey, 'Pope Gregory VII (1073–85) and the Liturgy', 57.
[77] John F. Romano, 'Innocent II and the Liturgy', in *Pope Innocent II (1130–43): The
World vs the City*, ed. John Doran and Damian J. Smith, Church, Faith and Culture in the
Medieval West (Abingdon; New York: Routledge, 2016), 326–351, at 335, with

dynamic of the Gothic period certainly had an impact on the Church's forms of worship, for example, in the compilation of offices for new saints and in the composition of various types of chant (e.g., sequences, tropes, processional hymns). Specific changes were made to the Paschal Triduum, stational churches were re-assigned and the papal ceremonial acquired imperial elements, such as the cone-shaped Phrygian mitre ringed with a crown and the imperial *laudes* (acclamations of praise) addressed to the pope – means by which Innocent II intended to bolster the legitimacy of his pontificate, which was challenged by the antipope Anacletus II (1130–1138).[78] The Roman Rite developed, but 'in reality changes came in small steps and did not necessarily accompany large-scale historical movements'.[79] Romano relates an episode that shows how even minor liturgical modifications could be met with resistance: Nicola Magnacozza (Latinised: Maniacutius), a deacon at the urban church of St Laurence in Damaso who later became a Cistercian monk at the abbey of Tre Fontane, strongly objected to the altering of the readings at some of the stational Masses in Lent and on the feast of the Apostles Peter and Paul (29 June). For Magnacozza, the Roman liturgy had been composed with the guidance of the Holy Spirit and hence it should be left unchanged.[80] Evidently, not everyone in Rome shared such an uncompromisingly conservative attitude, but an embattled pope like Innocent II realised that '[b]eing able to carry out time-honoured liturgical forms … enforced his authority and legitimacy in Rome'.[81] The continuing momentum of the reform papacy in the twelfth century led to the diffusion of Roman liturgical books in places that had their own particular traditions, including the venerable Benevento. Innocent II put his seal on this shift by personally celebrating the Roman Mass in the city's cathedral. However, the Roman Rite was not adopted wholesale, and local features were integrated into it.[82]

THE PAPAL CHAPEL AND THE FRANCISCAN LITURGY
IN THE THIRTEENTH CENTURY

The twelfth and thirteenth centuries (there is no agreement about the precise boundaries) are widely acclaimed as the highpoint of the

---

reference to Anton L. Mayer, 'Die Liturgie und der Geist der Gotik', in *Jahrbuch für Liturgiewissenschaft* 6 (1926), 68–97.

[78] See ibid., 338–341.   [79] Ibid., 335.

[80] See ibid.; also Vittorio Peri, '"Nichil in ecclesia sine causa": Note di vita liturgica romana nel XII secolo', in *Rivista di archeologia cristiana* 50 (1974), 249–273.

[81] Ibid., 345.   [82] See ibid., 344.

millennial period that Renaissance Humanists unfavourably termed 'Middle Ages' (*media aetas*). Many European countries enjoyed considerable growth in population, economic prosperity, technological advances and wider access to education. The cultural achievements of this epoch include the founding of the universities, the development of scholastic philosophy and theology, the systematic ordering of canon law, Gothic art and architecture and polyphonic music. The Gregorian reform movement provided the ferment for a religious renewal with the papacy at its head. The Fourth Lateran Council in November 1215, effectively organised by Pope Innocent III, combined concerns for doctrinal orthodoxy with particular attention to Catholic practice. Raising the standards of the clergy provided inspiration and leadership for the lay faithful; vice versa, a better education of the laity in the faith and a deeper spiritual (especially sacramental) life made greater demands on the formation and life of the clergy.[83] For our topic, it is beneficial that the increasing level of literacy in society brought a flourishing of historical, pastoral and devotional literature, not only for the clergy but also for the educated laity, which offer us glimpses of ordinary Catholics at worship beyond the prescriptive liturgical sources.[84]

In the city of Rome, the aforementioned letter of Abelard is indicative of a specific development that was to have a decisive impact on liturgical development, as H. E. J. Cowdrey neatly summarises:

> The separation of the papal household and the Lateran basilica gave rise to a gathering duality of observance which, in the thirteenth century, under Franciscan influence, led to the liturgy of the papal court's becoming the general standard for the Western Church.[85]

The Gregorian reform strengthened the power and prestige of the papal curia (often rendered 'household' or 'court'), and gradually the papal chapel, rather than the Lateran basilica, became the model for

---

[83] See Brenda Bolton, *The Medieval Reformation*, Foundations of Medieval History (London: Edward Arnold, 1983); Robert N. Swanson, *Religion and Devotion in Europe, c. 1215–c. 1515*, Cambridge Medieval Textbooks (Cambridge: Cambridge University Press, 1995), 10–41; James Watt, 'The Papacy', in *The New Cambridge Medieval History: Volume 5, c.1198–c.1300*, ed. David Abulafia (Cambridge: Cambridge University Press, 1999), 107–163, esp. 119–126.

[84] See the exemplary study of Augustine Thompson, *Cities of God: The Religion of the Italian Communes 1125–1325* (University Park: The Pennsylvania State University Press, 2005), 245–271 and 343–349.

[85] Cowdrey, 'Pope Gregory VII (1073–85) and the Liturgy', 57.

liturgical observance in Rome and beyond.[86] The curial liturgy was conducted with solemnity, especially in the splendid thirteenth-century setting of the chapel of St Laurence in the Palace, known as the *Sancta Sanctorum* for its outstanding collection of relics. Beginning with the pontificate of Innocent III (r. 1198–1216), popes increasingly used the Vatican palace as a residence and its 'great chapel' (*capella magna*) for liturgical celebrations. However, these ceremonial spaces were relatively small and did not allow for the processional elements that characterised stational liturgies in the churches of the city. Moreover, the papal court often travelled in this period, and, for reasons of expediency, its liturgical use was given a standard form that could also be transferred to places with fewer resources, such as Anagni or Orvieto.

Still, the impact of the papal chapel remained geographically limited, and general conformity with Roman liturgical practice began to be observed throughout the Latin Church only with the rapid expansion of the new Franciscan Order in the thirteenth century. The mendicant orders constituted a new type of religious life that did not observe a vow of stability. Instead, friars would periodically move from house to house. With Latin as the common language of the Church, of higher education and culture, the friars enjoyed high mobility throughout Europe. It proved onerous for them to adapt to local liturgical variations and so the desire arose for a unified practice within the orders. After an initial period of diversity, the Dominicans adopted a proper use of the Roman Rite that was established in 1256 by the Master of the Order, Humbert de Romans.[87]

The Franciscans accepted the liturgical books of the Roman Rite in the form used by the papal curia. The detailed reconstruction of this history in the seminal work of Stephen van Dijk (and Joan Hazelden Walker) has come under criticism in recent scholarship.[88] The greatest difficulty lies in van Dijk's hypothesis of unified liturgical prototypes, the so-called Regula missal and breviary, for which there is no manuscript evidence. Hence, to more recent scholarship, early Franciscan liturgical life, both in the Mass and the Divine Office, appears more varied and less organised than van

---

[86] See van Dijk and Hazelden Walker, *The Origins of the Modern Roman Liturgy*, 80–87.
[87] See the still valid work of William R. Bonniwell, *A History of the Dominican Liturgy 1215–1945*, 2nd ed. revised and enlarged (New York: Joseph F. Wagner, 1945).
[88] See Anna Welch, *Liturgy, Books and Franciscan Identity in Medieval Umbria*, Medieval Franciscans 12 (Leiden: Brill, 2015).

Dijk's narrative suggests.[89] However, the liturgical books the early friars adopted generally followed the pattern of the Roman curia. The diocese of Assisi under Bishop Guido II (d. 1228), who had a close relationship with Francis and his early disciples, used the liturgical books of the papal curia, and the priests among the friars would most likely have done the same, in accordance with the instructions of the holy founder.[90] The *Regula bullata* of 1223 determined that clerics should 'perform the Divine Office according to the *ordo* of the holy Roman church except for the psalter'.[91] The *ordo* refers to the liturgical use of the papal curia, which was consolidated under Innocent III and gradually extended to other churches in the city. The thirteenth century also offers the first indisputable corroboration that Gregorian chant was used in the liturgy of the papal chapel (even though it may already have been introduced earlier).[92]

A momentous step in the history of early Franciscan liturgy is the work of Haymo of Faversham, who served as minister general from 1240 until his death in 1244, after the turbulent second tenure of Elias of Cortona (1232–1239). At the order's chapter in Bologna in 1243, Haymo presented the ordinal known by its opening words *Indutus planeta* ('Wearing the chasuble . . .'), which describes itself as an 'ordo agendorum et dicendorum', that is, an order regulating the ceremonies to be carried out and the texts to be recited, in the private Mass of a priest or the simple conventual Mass on a ferial day.[93] *Indutus planeta* was based on the liturgical use of the papal curia; it was adopted by the Friars Minor and helped to create a unified liturgy of the Mass in the mendicant

---

[89] This is one of the main correctives brought to van Dijk's work by Welch, *Liturgy, Books and Franciscan Identity*, 51–81.

[90] See ibid., 66.

[91] *Regula bullata*, ch. 3; see Richard W. Pfaff, *The Liturgy in Medieval England: A History* (Cambridge: Cambridge University Press, 2009), 320.

[92] See Hiley, *Western Plainchant*, 594–595.

[93] A critical edition of *Indutus planeta* is included in *Sources of the Modern Roman Liturgy: The Ordinals by Haymo of Faversham and Related Documents, 1243–1307*, ed. Stephen J. P. van Dijk, 2 vols., Studia et documenta franciscana 1–2 (Leiden: Brill, 1963) vol. II, 1–14. The text was also edited by Vincent L. Kennedy, 'The Franciscan *Ordo Missae* in the Thirteenth Century', in *Medieval Studies* 2 (1940), 204–222, at 217–222. See van Dijk and Hazelden Walker, *The Origins of the Modern Roman Liturgy*, 292–301. Welch, *Liturgy, Books and Franciscan Identity*, 77–78, notes that Haymo's authorship of *Indutus planeta* is not beyond doubt; however, his decisive reform of the Franciscan order, including its liturgical practice, is certain.

order.[94] A detailed rubrical analysis would go beyond the scope of this book; hence, in the following section, I shall limit myself to the features of *Indutus planeta* that are most relevant to the further development of the 'soft spots' in the Mass of the Roman Rite.

The description of the Mass begins with the prayers at the foot of the altar and end with the final blessing. Hence, the prayers of preparation and of thanksgiving, which feature prominently in the Rhenish *Ordo Missae*, are not included. The introductory rites set the pattern that was to remain stable in the Roman Rite until the reforms of the 1960s: Psalm 42 (*Iudica me*) with the antiphon *Introibo ad altare Dei*; the priest's confession of sins and the ministers' prayer for forgiveness (no confession of the ministers is indicated); a series of versicles leading to the oration *Aufer a nobis*, which is said while the priest ascends the altar steps; the prayer *Oramus te Domine* (with a reference to relics, if they are present on the altar) and the kissing of the altar. Then follow several sections on ceremonial actions (joining of hands, bowing, kissing the altar, the manner of kissing,[95] raising and extending of hands) before the description of the Mass continues.

The offertory is presented in the form that would later become normative for the Roman Rite, except for a few ceremonial details. The paten with the host is offered with the prayer *Suscipe sancte Pater*. In the conventual Mass, the subdeacon will have prepared the altar with the host and the chalice, the latter filled with wine only, after the reading of the epistle; in the private Mass, the priest does this either before the Mass or after the gospel, whatever appears opportune to him. The priest blesses water and pours some of it into the chalice with the prayer *Deus qui humanae substantiae*. He then offers the chalice with the prayer *Offerimus tibi Domine*. The host is placed on the left and the chalice on the right (while in the Tridentine rubrics the host is placed in front of the chalice). Liturgical commentators since Amalarius associated this particular custom with the allegorical reading of the altar as the cross of Christ:

---

[94] This unification of the ritual structure of the Mass did of course not exclude local variations, especially in the sanctoral calendar, as Welch argues in *Liturgy, Books and Franciscan Identity*, 87–91.

[95] Under the heading 'De modo osculandi', *Indutus planeta* stipulates that the liturgical book is never to be kissed, except after the reading of the gospel (ed. van Dijk, 6). Thus, it proscribed the widely known liturgical custom of the celebrant kissing the image of Christ before beginning the prayer *Te igitur* of the canon, which fell out of use in the standardised form of the Roman Mass. See Uwe Michael Lang, 'Kissing the Image of Christ in the Medieval Mass', in *Antiphon* 22 (2018), 262–272.

the bread represents his crucified body and, on its right, the chalice with wine and water points to his pierced side, from which blood and water flowed as a mystical sign of the sacraments.[96] The chalice is then covered with a 'simple folded corporal' (what would later become the pall), while the prayer *In spiritu humilitatis* is said. This is followed by the invocation *Veni sanctificator*, which is accompanied by the sign of the cross over host and chalice together. The blessing of incense and the incensation is not explained, but reference is made to the Franciscan *Ordinationes divini officii*, which cover the solemn conventual Mass. After the incensation, the priest returns to the middle of the altar where he says the prayer, *Suscipe sancta Trinitas*, kisses the altar and turns around to the people with the invitation *Orate fratres*. Those in proximity ('circumstantes') respond *Suscipiat Dominus*, and the praying of the *secreta* concludes the offertory.

Notably, the section on the offertory regulates the celebrant's actions in a precise and comprehensive way, and the same holds for the subsequent sections from the canon until communion. These instructions are much more extended than the rubrics found in the concise *Ordo Missae* of contemporary Franciscan missals, known from its incipit as 'Paratus sacerdos' ('The priest being ready . . .'). Some missals of the late thirteenth and early fourteenth century insert *Indutus planeta* before the *Ordo Missae* or incorporate it into the latter.[97] The priest's physical postures and gestures are described with attention to detail, for instance, the manner of making the signs of the cross during the canon. It is interesting to note that no imposition of hands over the offerings at the prayer *Hanc igitur* is indicated; this gesture is attested only in the fourteenth century. Unlike in the modern reading, it was not interpreted as epicletic, but rather 'as a way of calling attention (pointing – *hanc*) to the oblation being offered at that moment'.[98] After pronouncing the words 'Hoc est enim corpus meum' and bowing in adoration, the priest elevates the consecrated host reverently so that those present can see it. This gesture was an innovation inspired by increased devotion to the sacrament of the

[96] See Amalarius, *Liber officialis*, l. IV, c. 47: ed. Jean Michel Hanssens, *Amalarii Episcopi Opera Liturgica Omnia*, Tomus II, Studi e testi 139 (Vatican City: Biblioteca Apostolica Vaticana, 1948), 542–543. William Durandus notes that this custom was observed in Rome, in *Rationale divinorum officiorum*, IV, 30, 22: CCM 140,388.
[97] See Kennedy, 'The Franciscan *Ordo Missae* in the Thirteenth Century', 210–217.
[98] Daniel Cardó, *The Presence of the Cross and the Eucharist: A Theological and Liturgical Investigation* (Cambridge: Cambridge University Press, 2019), 145; see Jungmann, *Missarum sollemnia*, vol. II, 233–234.

altar. There is no elevation of the consecrated chalice at this point, presumably because the precious blood it contained could not actually be seen; the second elevation would be added at a later stage (see the section below on the veneration and reservation of the Eucharist). *Indutus planeta* specifically notes that from the consecration of the host until the purification of hands, the priest keeps his thumb and index finger, which touched the body of the Lord, closed, except for signs of the cross and when he touches the sacred host – a practice first attested in reformed Benedictine monasticism of the tenth century (Cluny, Hirsau).[99]

The presentation of the concluding rites is remarkably terse, especially in comparison to the preceding sections. The postcommunion prayer, the dismissal *Ite missa est* (or *Benedicamus Domino*) and the prayer *Placeat sancta Trinitas* are not mentioned,[100] perhaps because they did not require a specific regulation. Only the priest's bowing and kissing of the altar are treated in their respective separate sections. The Mass finishes with the blessing 'In unitate Sancti Spiritus benedicat nos Pater et Filius. Amen'.

The extensive instructions of *Indutus planeta*, regarding both the prayers to be said and the ritual postures and gestures of the celebrant, were integrated into the liturgical practice of the Roman curia. Moreover, as Radulphus de Rivo (d. 1403) reported with disapproval, Pope Nicholas III (r. 1277–1280) imposed the 'new' liturgical books of the Franciscans, including the missal, on the churches of the city of Rome,[101] which would otherwise have maintained their proper customs and observances. Subsequently, the 'Ordo missalis secundum consuetudinem Romane curie' was gradually incorporated into missals of local dioceses and religious orders throughout Europe. Thus, through the agency of the Franciscans, a unification of the ritual structure and shape of the Mass was achieved in the Latin Church to a degree that previous popes may have demanded but were never able to implement effectively. Needless to

[99] See Jungmann, *Missarum sollemnia*, vol. II, 100 and 255–256. Kennedy, 'The Franciscan *Ordo Missae* in the Thirteenth Century', 217, observes that 'the elevation of the host ... does not appear in the Franciscan *Ordo missae*' and adds in n. 75 that '*Indutus planeta* is the earliest liturgical document of Roman origin to mention it.'

[100] See, however, the Franciscan *Ordo Missae* in Kennedy, 'The Franciscan *Ordo Missae* in the Thirteenth Century', 215.

[101] Radulphus de Rivo, *Liber de canonum observantia*, Propositio XXII: ed. Cunibert Mohlberg, *Radulph de Rivo: Der letzte Vertreter der altrömischen Liturgie*, 2 vols., Recueil de travaux publiés par les membres des conférences d'histoire et de philologie 29 and 42 (Louvain: Bureaux du recueil, 1911–1915), vol. II, 128. See Kennedy, 'The Franciscan *Ordo Missae* in the Thirteenth Century', 204 and 206.

say, such standardisation of the missal (and the breviary), for which the Franciscans acted as a catalyst, did not happen overnight but through a long and complex process of manuscript transmission. Variations in the missals of dioceses and religious orders remained, and even where the Order of Mass followed essentially the Roman use, differences in the texts and ceremonies of the liturgical 'soft spots' – the introductory rites, the offertory and the concluding rites – still remained. Rubrical instructions originated from private annotations as a practical help for priests in the celebration of Mass; they were a far cry from the consistency and detail of *Indutus planeta*.

THE PLENARY MISSAL AND THE EXPANSION OF PRIVATE MASSES

Between the ninth and the thirteenth century, manuscripts compiled and arranged for distinct liturgical actors (sacramentary, lectionary, antiphoner) were gradually supplanted by manuscripts containing the complete texts of a particular ritual celebration (pontifical, missal, breviary). In his study of pontificals, Niels Krogh Rasmussen has spoken of a transition from liturgical books of a 'first generation' to those of a 'second generation'.[102] This process of transition, however, was anything but uniform and needs to be considered separately for each genre of liturgical book. In his study of the Romano-Germanic Pontifical tradition, Henry Parkes has argued that beyond their practical purpose, these codices of a new kind that assembled the rites proper to a bishop also served as 'sites of institutional memory' that communicated a theology of the episcopacy.[103]

The evolution of liturgical manuscripts for the Mass and the Divine Office happened in parallel and produced a similar type of book: the missal and the breviary, which contained all the texts needed for enactment of the rite. Hence, it is often assumed that the origins and motives underlying this parallel development are the same, namely 'private celebration and private recitation'.[104] On the other hand, Stephen van Dijk

---

[102] See Niels K. Rasmussen, 'Célébration épiscopale et célébration presbytérale: un essai de typologie', in *Segni e riti nella chiesa altomedievale occidentale, 11–17 aprile 1985*, Settimane di studio del Centro italiano di studi sull'alto medioevo 33 (Spoleto: Presso la Sede del Centro, 1987), vol. II, 581–607, at 584–585.

[103] See Parkes, *The Making of Liturgy*, 166–179.

[104] Van Dijk and Hazelden Walker, *The Origins of the Modern Roman Liturgy*, 61.

and Joan Hazelden Walker contend that the missal and breviary, while apparently developing in parallel, are products of very different rationales. The indistinct title *breviarium*, deriving from *brevis* ('short', 'brief') and implying an abridgment, could, in general refer to a smaller-format volume in which texts from different choir books were assembled. Increasing literacy in monastic communities led to a heightened desire for participation in the Divine Office by means of the written text. In the twelfth century, a *breviarium* of this kind was still a choir book and not intended for private recitation. Religious and clerics in higher orders, who were bound to the Divine Office, normally sang it in a monastic or secular community, or in parishes. There is scattered manuscript evidence for private (and possibly lay) recitation in the Carolingian and the Ottonian period,[105] but there was no sense that this could be a substitute for chanting the office in choir. If a monk or cleric was impeded from participating in choir, he was expected to make up for it in some form, but he was not obliged to say the canonical hours privately. With the arrival of the friars, the breviary developed into a portable volume with all the texts needed for saying the Divine Office outside choir, for instance, when travelling, and subsequently this practice began to be imposed as a canonical obligation for clerics.[106]

While the genesis of the breviary is associated with increased literacy and an emphasis on the written text in liturgical participation, the plenary missal (*liber missalis*, *missale*) came into being for entirely different reasons, which are to some extent practical. Cathedrals, monasteries and collegiate churches could easily muster the human and material resources for the solemn celebration of the liturgy, including the set of books for distinct clerical functions. But as the network of parish churches and chapels of ease was growing even in remote areas of northern and western Europe, Mass was frequently celebrated in modest circumstances that would only permit a simpler form of the rite. A single manuscript that contains all the texts of the Mass, which is first attested in the ninth

---

[105] See Susan Rankin, 'Carolingian Liturgical Books: Problems of Categorization', in *Gazette du livre medieval* 62 (2016), 21–33, at 21–24.
[106] See Van Dijk and Hazelden Walker, *The Origins of the Modern Roman Liturgy*, 26–44. Thompson, *Cities of God*, 243, relates an episode from the *Annales Foroiuliensis* (MGH Scriptores XIX, 209), which illustrates – with disapproval – changing attitudes to the Divine Office. On the feast of St John, the Baptist (24 June) in 1299, lightning damaged the cathedral of Cividale dei Friuli and killed several people, as the canons were singing Matins in choir. They remained unharmed, but several canons who had anticipated Matins the evening before and were not in choir (and presumably in bed) were killed.

century, proved to be eminently useful and it 'grew in popularity among the clergy along with the development of pastoral care'.[107] The popularity of the plenary missal was also facilitated by the growing practice of private Masses, which led to the concentration of liturgical roles in the person of the offering priest. However, van Dijk and Hazelden Walker rightly caution that the relationship between the two phenomena is not as close or straightforward as is often assumed.[108] There is considerable variety in Mass books between the ninth and the twelfth century: some sacramentaries are supplied with marginal notes to indicate the incipits of chants (presumably sung from memory); some manuscripts represent a full sacramentary-gradual, and in some cases a lectionary is added so that all the Mass texts are contained in one book, though in separate sections.[109] The daily offering of private Masses with a votive formulary did not require a plenary missal for the full cycle of the liturgical year; a modest fascicle (*libellus missarum*) with the specific texts would be sufficient.

The very expression 'private Mass' can easily be misleading and needs clarification.[110] Small gatherings for the Eucharist are attested in the first three centuries, when Christian communities found themselves in a vulnerable position and subject to occasional persecutions. Such circumstances demanded a simplicity of external ritual, which continued in places where congregations were small and resources were limited. However, despite the objection of van Dijk and Hazelden Walker, Jungmann still appears correct in asserting that the private Mass of the early medieval period is not simply defined by its simplicity of ritual. The novelty consisted in the celebration of Mass by a priest with only one or two assistants; unlike in conventual or parochial Masses, the participation of the lay faithful would be merely accidental.[111] As discussed in

---

[107] Van Dijk and Hazelden Walker, *The Origins of the Modern Roman Liturgy*, 65; also Rankin, 'Carolingian Liturgical Books: Problems of Categorization'.

[108] See Van Dijk and Hazelden Walker, *The Origins of the Modern Roman Liturgy*, 57–66.

[109] See Éric Palazzo, *A History of Liturgical Books from the Beginning to the Thirteenth Century*, trans. Madeleine Beaumont (Collegeville: Liturgical Press, 1993), 107–110.

[110] From the perspective of liturgical theology, Helmut Hoping, *My Body Given for You: History and Theology of the Eucharist*, trans. Michael J. Milller (San Francisco, Ignatius Press, 2019), 171, notes: 'Since every celebration of the Mass ... with or without the participation of the faithful, has an ecclesial character, the expression "private Mass" is not entirely appropriate. Today we speak about *missa sine populo* [Mass without the people].'

[111] See Jungmann, *Missarum sollemnia*, vol. I, 279–283; van Dijk and Hazelden Walker, *The Origins of the Modern Roman Liturgy*, 45–48.

Chapter 5, from the fourth century onwards, there is growing evidence for the frequent, even daily offering of the Eucharist in the Latin West, which is associated with the ascetical movement. However, the process by which the private celebration of Mass spread first in monasteries raises questions that require some elucidation. Monasticism started as a lay movement in late antiquity, and monastic communities may or may not have had members who were in priestly orders. The Rule of St Benedict prescribed caution regarding the admittance of priests into the monastery and insisted on the priority of monastic observance.[112] The abbot may elect a monk who has suitably proved himself for ordination to the priesthood, but again obedience to the Rule was emphasised.[113] Originally, the Eucharist did not have a particular place in the daily life of the monks, which was shaped above all by the Divine Office, and if there was a communal celebration, it may have been held only on Sundays and feast days.[114] Nonetheless, the conventual Mass soon became a staple of daily monastic life, and by the ninth century, it was widespread to have a Mass in the early morning (*missa matutinalis*) in addition to the main Mass of the day (*missa maior*).[115] When monks began to undertake missionary work (as in the case of Augustine of Canterbury and his companions), the number of priest-monks increased continuously, since their work required the administration of the sacraments. The devout ideal of each priest celebrating Mass daily for the spiritual benefit of the living and the dead became prevalent, and it was probably the general rule in monasteries by the eighth century. For this purpose, monastic churches were supplied with separate oratories or with side altars (of which the model plan of St Gall numbers seventeen).[116]

Taking issue with this narrative, Angelus Häussling has argued that the great increase of altars and Masses within monastic communities does not derive from the personal devotion of priest-monks but is connected with a new liturgical vision of the Benedictine abbey in the early medieval period.

---

[112] *Regula Sancti Benedicti*, c. LX: SC 182,634–636.
[113] Ibid., c. LXII: SC 182,640–642.
[114] See Adalbert de Vogüé, 'Problems of the Monastic Conventual Mass', in *Downside Review* 87 (1969), 327–338; and 'Eucharist and Monastic Life', in *Worship* 59 (1985), 498–510.
[115] See Angelus A. Häussling, *Mönchskonvent und Eucharistiefeier: Eine Studie über die Messe in der abendländischen Klosterliturgie des frühen Mittelalters und zur Geschichte der Messhäufigkeit*, Liturgiewissenschaftliche Quellen und Forschungen 58 (Münster: Aschendorff, 1973), 324–327.
[116] See Otto Nußbaum, *Kloster, Priestermönch und Privatmesse: Ihr Verhältnis im Westen von den Anfängen bis zum hohen Mittelalter*, Theophaneia 145 (Bonn: Hanstein, 1961).

In analogy to the episcopal town, with its churches and shrines, above all the city of Rome, the abbey was considered a family of churches (*Kirchenfamilie*), which consisted of the churches on its territory (a large abbey could have several) and of the side altars in the main abbey church. In imitation of the Roman stational liturgy, these many altars, which were dedicated to different saints and contained their relics, served as 'stational' shrines that were honoured by a cycle of Masses that were celebrated in addition to the daily conventual Masses. For some time, the ancient principle was maintained that only one Eucharist per day should be offered on a particular altar. According to Häussling, this conception of the abbey as a liturgical organism required a greater number of priests in the community.[117]

While Häussling's thesis sheds light on the 'clericalisation' of monasticism and on the architectural layout of monastic churches in the early medieval period, as exemplified in the plan of St Gall, it does not account for the individual monk-priest's incentive to offer Mass daily (or even more frequently). Personal devotion surely had a part in this development, and another important factor needs to be considered, namely, the laity's growing desire to have Masses offered for specific intentions (*vota*). This practice of votive Masses (known as *missa specialis, peculiaris* or *familiaris*)[118] had its roots in late antiquity: for instance, the *Veronense* has several sets of Mass prayers in times of drought ('De siccitate temporis'),[119] as well as a formulary against the enemies of the Catholic faith ('Contra inimicos catholicae professionis').[120] The third book of the Old Gelasian Sacramentary mainly consists of votive Masses for a variety of personal and public intentions, such as for travel, illness, preventing the death of livestock, petitioning rain, rulers, times of war and Masses for the dead.[121] The *Hucusque* supplement to the Gregorian *Hadrianum* contains an extended section with prayers for

---

[117] See Häussling, *Mönchskonvent und Eucharistiefeier*, 298–347.

[118] See Arnold Angenendt, ‚Missa specialis: Zugleich ein Beitrag zur Entstehung der Privatmesse', in *Frühmittelalterliche Studien* 17 (1983), 153–221.

[119] *Sacramentarium Veronense (Cod. Bibl. Capit. Veron. LXXXV[80])*, XXXII, 1111–1137: ed. Leo C. Mohlberg, Rerum Ecclesiasticarum Documenta. Series Maior. Fontes I, 3rd ed. (Rome: Herder, 1978), 141–143. This discussion follows Jungmann, *Missarum sollemnia*, vol. I, 285–292.

[120] Ibid. XII, 218–221: ed. Mohlberg, 28.

[121] See the various sets of prayers in *Gelasianum Vetus* (Vat. Reg. Lat. 316), Book III, XXIIII–CVII: ed. Leo C. Mohlberg, *Liber Sacramentorum Romanae Aeclesiae Ordinis Anni Circuli*, Rerum Ecclesiasticarum Documenta. Series maior. Fontes IV, 3rd ed. (Rome: Herder, 1981), 191–248.

votive Masses, which are likely drawn from eighth-century Frankish Gelasian sources.[122] Of particular significance was the increasing demand for Masses for the dead, especially on fixed days for memorials. The founding of prayer fraternities to offer suffrages for the deceased also added to the increase in private Masses. Another contributing factor was connected with the tariff penance, which had been introduced in continental Europe by Celtic and Anglo-Saxon monks. In the Carolingian period, it became possible to commute an imposed penance into a specific number of 'penitential' Masses to be offered.[123]

Secular priests followed the monastic example and began to offer Mass more often, sometimes even several times a day, to fulfil particular Mass intentions (for which it was customary to offer a stipend). This practice was repeatedly censured in ecclesiastical legislation, until Innocent III in 1206 definitely limited the number of Masses a priest could offer to one a day, except on Christmas Day (where the Roman tradition lists three papal Masses in different stational churches) and in case of necessity.[124] In the ninth and tenth centuries, bishops and synods also repeatedly proscribed the *missa solitaria*, that is, the priest's offering of Mass with no attendants at all. Even a private Mass should be celebrated with the assistance of one or two clerics in minor orders (in accordance with the plural form of the liturgical salutation 'Dominus vobiscum').[125]

In the private celebration of Mass, the parts assigned in its solemn form to distinct liturgical ministries were recited by the priest himself, and they were increasingly spoken rather than chanted. As the space on side altars was smaller, the ceremonial was reduced and eventually the lessons were read by the priest at the altar. The ascendancy of private Masses seems gradually to have given rise to the custom that in the solemn Mass the celebrant would recite in a low voice the ordinary and proper chants that were sung by the schola, as well as the readings proclaimed by the subdeacon and deacon. The first known indication of this new practice

---

[122] *Supplementum Anianense (Hucusque)*, nos. LXIII–XCVI: ed. Deshusses, 424–451.

[123] See Philippe Rouillard, *Histoire de la penitence: Des origines à nos jours* (Paris: Cerf, 1996), 47–48; also Cyrille Vogel, 'La vie quotidienne du moine en occident à l'époque de la floraison des messe privées', in *Liturgie, spiritualité, cultures: Conférences Saint-Serge, XXIXe semaine d'études liturgiques. Paris, 29 juin–2 juillet 1982*, ed. Achille M. Triacca et al., Bibliotheca Ephemerides Liturgicae: Subsidia 29 (Rome: C.L.V. – Edizioni Liturgiche, 1983), 341–360.

[124] See Amiet, 'Die liturgische Gesetzgebung der deutschen Reichskirche', 263–267; also Adolph Franz, *Die Messe im deutschen Mittelalter: Beiträge zur Geschichte der Liturgie und des religiösen Volkslebens* (Freiburg im Breisgau: Herder, 1902), 74–77.

[125] See Amiet, 'Die liturgische Gesetzgebung der deutschen Reichskirche', 21–24.

comes from the description of the pontifical Mass on Easter Sunday in the
ordo of the Lateran basilica, composed by its prior Bernard in the mid-
twelfth century. Here the bishop says with his assistants the introit and
the *Kyrie* at his seat with his assistants, while the cantors are singing.[126]
After intoning the *Gloria*, the bishop continues reciting the text with the
deacon, subdeacon and assisting priest, while the singing of the hymn
continues.[127] The bishop is also meant to read the epistle after it has been
proclaimed – but no such indication is given for the gospel.[128] The *Credo*
is intoned and recited in the same manner as the *Gloria*.[129] The *Sanctus* is
recited by the bishop with the deacon and subdeacon, while it is sung by
the choir; when it has been said, the bishop starts praying the canon.[130]
Similarly, the bishop recites the *Agnus Dei* privately with the deacon right
before exchanging the kiss of peace.[131]

The Dominican *ordinarium* of 1256 takes a step further by prescribing
that at the (solemn) conventual Mass the priest celebrant and his liturgical
assistants recite all the ordinary and proper chants, while they are being sung
in choir. However, the priest does not double the epistle and gospel readings.[132] While deploring this development, which separates the priest from
the *schola cantorum* and facilitates the secularisation of church music, Josef
Andreas Jungmann caustically remarks that there is some progress in the fact
that the priest, instead of filling every available moment with lengthy *apologiae*, actually recites the biblical texts of the Mass propers.[133] In fact, the
new practice might have been motivated by the desire to curb the priest's
private prayers and to align them with the official liturgical texts.

Notwithstanding the strong impact of the private Mass, the solemn
Mass (*missa solemnis*) with the assistance of deacon and subdeacon
remained the normative form of the rite.[134] Notably, Francis of Assisi in a

---

[126] *Bernhardi cardinalis et Lateranensis ecclesiae prioris, Ordo officiorum ecclesiae
Lateranensis*, ed. Ludwig Fischer, Historische Forschungen und Quellen 2–3 (Munich;
Freising: Datterer & Cie. 1916), 80 (l. 32–34). It is not entirely clear what 'officium
legendo' refers to, but I take it to mean the previously mentioned introit *and* the *Kyrie*,
not just the introit, as suggested by Jungmann, *Missarum sollemnia*, 140.

[127] Ibid., 80 (l. 34–36).   [128] Ibid., 81 (l. 11–13).   [129] Ibid., 81 (l. 15–17).

[130] Ibid., 83 (l. 38)–84 (l. 1).   [131] Ibid., 85 (l 15–16).

[132] *Ordinarium juxta ritum Sacri Ordinis Fratrum Praedicatorum*, ed. Francesco
M. Guerrini (Rome: Collegium Angelicum, 1921), 235–244 (nos. 47–100).

[133] See Jungmann, *Missarum sollemnia*, vol. I, 140–141.

[134] Jungmann notes that the first unambiguous reference to the *missa sollemnis* with one
deacon and one subdeacon (as opposed to an unspecified number of each) is found in the
De officiis ecclesiasticis by John of Avranches, written in the 1060s, and that it was
customary at the conventual Mass in Cluny around the same time; see ibid., vol. I,
265–266.

letter addressed to all Friars Minor in the autumn of 1224, after his retreat on Mount La Verna, commanded that in the houses of his order only one Mass a day should be celebrated. If there was more than one priest in a house, he should assist at the conventual Mass and not celebrate individually. Augustine Thompson comments on this instruction:

> Most likely, with the growing number of clerics and the facilitation of the daily Masses by the privilege of portable altars, Franciscan celebration of the liturgy was becoming routine and sloppy, the very sin that Francis had so abominated in the clergy . . .. Rather than waiting in line to rush through their own private Mass in assembly-line fashion, or even to mumble Mass at a side altar while the other brothers are chanting the Office (a not-uncommon solution to the multiplying of Masses), friar priests were to take turns celebrating the solemn sung community liturgy with deacon, subdeacon, and all the proper ministers and rites.[135]

Francis' concern is thus consistent with the great care he showed for the dignity and decorum of the liturgy; it is also indicative of a certain reaction to the detrimental effects of the enormous proliferation of private Masses.[136]

Thirteenth-century theological treatises on the liturgy naturally comment on the solemn Mass. In his widely copied *De mysterio missae*, the Dominican master Albert the Great takes the liturgical roles of deacon and subdeacon for granted.[137] The same can be said of Thomas Aquinas, when he discusses the rite of Mass in both his commentary on the *Sentences* and in the *Summa*.[138]

VENERATION AND RESERVATION OF THE EUCHARIST

The two great Eucharistic controversies of the Middle Ages had a lasting impact not only on Catholic doctrine but also on liturgy and

---

[135] Augustine Thompson, *Francis of Assisi: A New Biography* (Ithaca: Cornell University Press, 2012), 120–121.

[136] A slightly earlier example for such a reaction would be the statutes Alberto di Morra (the future Pope Gregory VIII) composed in 1186 for a congregation of Augustinian canons in Benevento; see Paul Kehr, 'Papst Gregor VIII. als Ordensgründer', in *Miscellanea Francesco Ehrle. Vol. II: Per la storia di Roma e dei papi*, Studi e testi 38 (Rome: Biblioteca Apostolica Vaticana, 1924), 248–276, at 272 (no. 29). Except for the hebdomadary (who is appointed for one week to sing the chapter Mass), each priest of the community is to celebrate Mass only once a week and, with due preparation, may on other days receive Holy Communion.

[137] For instance, Albert the Great, *De mysterio missae*, tr. II, c. 3, c. 4, c. 7, tr. III, c. 23: *Opera Omnia*, vol. 38, ed. Auguste Borgnet (Paris: Vivès, 1899), 45, 46–47, 52–57, 162–165.

[138] Thomas Aquinas, *Super Sent.*, lib. 4, d. 8, q. 2, a. 4, qc. 3 expos.; *Summa Theologiae*, III, q. 83, a. 4 co.

devotion.[139] The first controversy in the late Carolingian period involved two monks of the abbey of Corbie in Picardy, Paschasius Radbertus (d. c. 859) and Ratramnus (d. c. 870). The second controversy in the age of papal reform was prompted by the teachings of Berengar of Tours (d. 1088), whose main opponent was Lanfranc of Bec (d. 1089). From this time onwards, popular piety was incited by an increasing number of Eucharistic miracles, such as bleeding hosts, which purported to offer proof to the senses of the real presence of Christ in the consecrated species of bread and wine.[140] In the middle of the twelfth century, the term 'transsubstantiatio' was invented to account for the effect of the Eucharistic consecration of bread and wine. Under the leadership of Pope Innocent III, the author of an influential treatise on the Mass (*De sacro altaris mysterio*), the Fourth Lateran Council in 1215 taught the doctrine of transubstantiation in its profession of faith:

There is indeed one universal Church of the faithful . . . in which the priest himself, Jesus Christ, is also the sacrifice. His Body and Blood are truly contained in the sacrament of the altar under the appearances of bread and wine, the bread being transubstantiated (*transsubstantiatis*) into the body by the divine power and the wine into the blood, to the effect that we receive from what is his what he has received from what is ours in order that the mystery of unity may be accomplished.[141]

The doctrine of transubstantiation received an extended treatment in St Thomas Aquinas' treatise on the Eucharist in the *Summa theologiae* and was restated by the Second Council of Lyon in 1274.[142]

---

[139] See the excellent treatment of both controversies by Hoping, *My Body Given for You*, 175–198.

[140] See Peter Browe, 'Die eucharistischen Verwandlungswunder des Mittelalters', in *Die Eucharistie im Mittelalter: Liturgiehistorische Forschungen in kulturwissenschaftlicher Absicht*, ed. Hubertus Lutterbach and Thomas Flammer, Vergessene Theologen 1, 7th ed. (Münster: Lit Verlag, 2019), 265–289 (originally published in *Römische Quartalsschrift* 37 [1929], 137–169). The variety of scholastic explanations of these miracles are documented by Peter Browe, 'Die scholastische Theorie der eucharistischen Verwandlungswunder', in ibid., 251–263 (originally published in *Theologische Quartalsschrift* 110 [1929], 305–332).

[141] Fourth Lateran Council, *Constitutiones, 1. De fide catholica* (30 November 1215): trans. *Enchiridion symbolorum definitionum et declarationum de rebus fidei et morum*, ed. Heinrich Denzinger and Peter Hünermann, 43rd ed. (San Francisco: Ignatius Press, 2012) [henceforth cited as DH], no. 802.

[142] Thomas Aquinas, *Summa theologiae*, III, q. 75, a. 2–8; Second Council of Lyon, Session 4, *Letter of Emperor Michael to Pope Gregory* (6 July 1274): DH 860. See the discussion of Hoping, *My Body Given for You*, 198–207.

The interplay of doctrinal clarification and popular devotion led to a heightened sense of the real presence of Christ in the liturgy of the Mass.[143] Kneeling during the Eucharistic prayer had become increasingly common among the laity since the ninth century as the adequate posture of worshipping Christ made present in the sacrament. Starting from France, possibly as a reaction to the Albigensian denial of incarnational and sacramental reality,[144] priests would elevate the consecrated host for the adoration of the faithful, after pronouncing the words of Christ over it. The practice was confirmed by the bishop of Paris, Odo of Sully (d. 1208), and in the course of the thirteenth century, the elevation of the consecrated chalice was likewise introduced. Both elevations could be accompanied by an elevation candle (see Figure 7.1), by the ringing of a handbell or even by the tolling of the church bells.[145] Francis of Assisi promoted these new forms of Eucharistic devotion enthusiastically and strongly encouraged the lay faithful to kneel at the elevation of the consecrated species at Mass and when the Blessed Sacrament is carried in procession.[146]

Fourth- and fifth-century sources indicate that, by that period, the reception of communion by the laity had already become less frequent than in former times (see Chapter 5). Some Carolingian bishops encouraged the faithful to receive the sacrament more often, but these efforts had little apparent success, and ecclesiastical legislation largely followed the pattern set by the council of Agde in the south of France, held under Caesarius of Arles in 506, which obliged general communion three times a year, at Christmas, Easter and Pentecost.[147] The people's vivid faith in Christ's presence in the Eucharistic species and the sense of their own sinfulness made the reception of communion a rare occasion. The Fourth Lateran Council even saw the need to legislate that the faithful had to receive the sacrament at least once a year in the Easter season ('in pascha').[148] By that time, the chalice was no longer given to the laity in

---

[143] See the overview of Hoping, *My Body Given for You*, 208–210.

[144] See Gerard G. Grant, 'The Elevation of the Host: A Reaction to Twelfth-Century Heresy', in *Theological Studies* 1 (1940), 228–250.

[145] See Peter Browe, 'Die Elevation in der Messe', in *Die Eucharistie im Mittelalter*, 475–508 (originally published in *Bonner Zeitschrift für Theologie und Seelsorge* 8 [1931], 20–66).

[146] See Thompson, *Francis of Assisi*, 62, and 83–86.

[147] Council of Agde (506), can. 18: CCL 148,202. See Amiet, 'Die liturgische Gesetzgebung der deutschen Reichskirche', 82–84.

[148] Fourth Lateran Council, *Constitutiones*, 21. *De confessione facienda et non revelanda a sacerdote et saltem in pascha communicandos* (30 November 1215): DH 812.

Figure 7.1 Simone Martini / The Miraculous Mass of St Martin / c. 1325
(Lower Basilica of St Francis, Assisi / © Archivio fotografico del Sacro Convento di
S. Francesco in Assisi / Reprinted with kind permission)

most churches, and since the eighth or ninth century a thin wafer of
unleavened bread, made of water and wheat, had become the norm.[149]
From the eleventh century, the use of hosts that were consecrated in

---

[149] There is some evidence for the use of unleavened bread in the Eucharist from the
Christian East in the late sixth century. This has been the practice of the Armenian
church practice since at least the synod of Dvin in 719 and may go back to the seventh
century. See Jean Michel Hanssens, *Institutiones liturgicae de ritibus orientalibus,*

another Mass began to spread. Until then, this practice was limited to the 'Mass of the Presanctified' (*missa de praesanctificatis*) on Good Friday, when the sacrament that had been confected on Maundy Thursday was distributed (since the seventh or eighth century in the form of bread alone, presumably for practical reasons).[150] If at a Mass consecrated hosts were left over, they were ordinarily consumed by the priest.[151] The administration of Holy Communion outside Mass is first attested in the twelfth century. Until the sixteenth century, this seemed to happen only at Easter and other major feasts when there were many communicants, and the sacrament was distributed right after Mass so as to maintain a connection with the offering of the sacrifice.[152]

The reservation of the Eucharist to make it available to the sick and the dying has its roots in Christian antiquity. In the early medieval period, it was established to keep the consecrated hosts in churches, to protect them from profanation and to prevent superstitious practices, and various places and forms of reservation are attested. The *conditorium* mentioned in *Ordo Romanus I*[153] probably means a cupboard or chest kept in the sacristy (a custom maintained in northern Italy, including Milan, until the sixteenth century). When the sacrament was reserved in the church itself, it could be placed on the altar in a casket made of precious metal. In England and France, it was common to suspend a pyx (a round receptacle, sometimes resembling a tower) or a dove-shaped vessel (*columba* or *peristerium*) with the sacrament before the high altar. The recessed cabinet in the side wall of the sanctuary, known as ambry or aumbry, was rarely used for Eucharistic reservation. In late medieval Germany, the consecrated hosts were often kept in a monumental and ornate 'sacrament house' (*Sakramentshaus*) on the gospel side of the chancel.[154]

Tomus II: De missa rituum orientalium, Pars prima (Rome: Apud Aedes Pont. Universitatis Gregorianae, 1930), 133–141.

[150] See Peter Browe, 'Die Kommunion an den drei letzten Kartagen', in *Die Eucharistie im Mittelalter*, 309–324 (originally published in *Jahrbuch für Liturgiewissenschaft* 10 [1930], 56–76).

[151] See Peter Browe, 'Wann fing man an, die in einer Messe konsekrierten Hostien in einer anderen Messe auszuteilen?', in *Die Eucharistie im Mittelalter*, 383–393 (originally published in *Theologie und Glaube* 30 [1938], 388–404).

[152] See Peter Browe, 'Wann fing man an, die Kommunion außerhalb der Messe auszuteilen?', in *Die Eucharistie im Mittelalter*, 303–308 (originally published in *Theologie und Glaube* 23 [1931], 755–762).

[153] *Ordo Romanus I*, 48: ed. Andrieu, vol. II, 83.

[154] See Otto Nußbaum, *Die Aufbewahrung der Eucharistie*, Theophaneia 29 (Bonn: Hanstein, 1979); still valuable is William H. Freestone, *The Sacrament Reserved: A Survey of the Practice of Reserving the Eucharist, with Special Reference to the*

The Fourth Lateran Council decreed that the Eucharist should be kept in a safe place and locked but did not specify a particular location.[155] The ordinal of the Dominican missal of 1256[156] and the ceremonial *ordinationes* of the Augustinian friars of 1290 stipulate that the sacrament is to be reserved on the high altar (*altare maius*).[157] Van Dijk and Hazelden Walker argue that the common source for the practice of these orders (there is apparently no similarly precise indication in contemporary Franciscan documents) is the papal curia, where the sacrament was customarily (though with exceptions) kept at the high altar.[158]

From the late thirteenth century, the word *tabernaculum* ('tent') was employed to indicate the receptacle for the sacrament of the altar. The widely read liturgical commentator William Durandus notes that, in imitation of the Ark of the Covenant and of the Tent of Meeting (e.g., Ex 25–26, 33:7–11), 'in some churches an ark or tabernacle (*archa seu tabernaculum*) is placed, in which the body of the Lord and relics are kept'.[159] The biblical association is significant, since the Tent of Meeting was God's presence among the people of Israel in the desert. The prologue of St John's Gospel states that the divine Word 'was made flesh and dwelt (ἐσκήνωσεν, literally: pitched his tent) among us' (Jn 1:14). In the Apocalypse, the heavenly Jerusalem is evoked with the words: 'Behold the dwelling of God is with men', which reads in the Vulgate: 'Ecce tabernaculum Dei cum hominibus' (Rev 21:3).

Medieval veneration of the Eucharist reached its climax with the introduction of the feast of Corpus Christi and the forms of popular devotion associated with it: procession, exposition and benediction of the Blessed Sacrament. The proximate origins of Corpus Christi are

---

Communion of the Sick, During the First Twelve Centuries, Alcuin Club Collections 21 (London: Mowbray, 1917).

[155] Fourth Lateran Council, *Constitutiones*, 20: *De chrismate et eucharistia sub sera conservanda* (30 November 1215): *Conciliorum Oecumenicorum Decreta*, ed. Giuseppe Alberigo et al., 3rd ed. (Bologna: Istituto per le Scienze Religiose, 1973), 244.

[156] *Ordinarium juxta ritum Sacri Ordinis Fratrum Praedicatorum*, ed. Guerrini, 246 (no. 107).

[157] *Ordinationes Ordinis Eremitarum Sancti Augustini*, c. 37: Biblioteca Apostolica Vaticana, Codex Reg. lat. 1806 (13th–14th c.), fol. 24r (accessible at https://digi.vatlib .it/view/MSS_Reg.lat.1806). The manuscript transcription by Pancratius C. Langeveld, *Ordinationes et ordinarium cum notis OESA* (Nijmegen, 1960) has not been available to me.

[158] See van Dijk and Hazelden Walker, *the Origins of the Modern Roman Liturgy*, 369–370.

[159] William Durandus, *Rationale divinorum officiorum*, I, 2, 4: CCM 140,30.

connected with the visions of Juliana of Cornillon (d. 1258), a lay sister serving in a *leprosarium* (leper house) connected with the Premonstratensian house of Mont-Cornillon near Liège.[160] The idea of a new liturgical feast dedicated to the Eucharist resonated widely, was promoted especially by the Dominicans and its observance spread through the Low Countries and Germany. Jacques Pantaleon, archdeacon of Campines in the diocese of Liège and a great supporter of Juliana, became pope as Urban IV (r. 1261–1264), and in his bull *Transiturus* of 1264 decreed the celebration of Corpus Christi for the whole Church on the Thursday after Trinity Sunday. The date was chosen to connect the new feast with Maundy Thursday, when the institution of the Eucharist is commemorated, and it was in fact the first available Thursday after the conclusion of the Easter season. The institution of the new liturgical feast is often connected with the Eucharistic miracle of Bolsena (1263), when a priest from Bohemia, who had asked for a sign to dispel his doubts about the presence of Christ in the sacrament, during the celebration of Mass saw the consecrated host turn in to flesh and several drops of blood sprinkling on the corporal. The blood-stained corporal is still venerated in the cathedral of Orvieto. However, the earliest sources for the miracle of Bolsena date from 1337, and there is no reference to it in any of Urban's writings.[161]

Urban IV died shortly after *Transiturus* and his immediate successors seemed to have little interest in the new feast; nonetheless, its celebration spread throughout the Western Church thanks to the initiatives of local bishops and religious orders, and in northern Europe it was particularly associated with processions of the Blessed Sacrament. The first Corpus Christi procession is attested in Cologne between 1265 and 1277.[162]

---

[160] See *The Life of Juliana of Cornillon*, trans. Barbara Newman, in *Living Saints of the Thirteenth Century: The Lives of Yvette, Anchoress of Huy; Juliana of Cornillon, Author of the Corpus Christi Feast; and Margaret the Lame, Anchoress of Magdeburg*, ed. Anneke B. Mulder-Bakker (Turnhout: Brepols, 2012), 177–302. On the institution of the feast, see Miri Rubin, *Corpus Christi: The Eucharist in Late Medieval Culture* (Cambridge: Cambridge University Press, 1991), 164–199.

[161] See Browe, 'Die eucharistischen Verwandlungswunder des Mittelalters', 286–287. See also Kristen van Ausdall, 'Art and Eucharist in the Late Middle Ages', in *A Companion to the Eucharist in the Middle Ages*, ed. Ian C. Levy, Gary Macy and Kristen van Ausdall, Brill's Companions to the Christian Tradition 26 (Leiden: Brill, 2012), 541–617, at 582–587.

[162] A date between 1275 and 1277 is most likely, given the violent conflict between the city of Cologne and its archbishop, which prompted a papal interdict between 1268 and 1275. See Theodor Schnitzler, 'Die erste Fronleichnamsprozession: Datum und Charakter', in *Münchener Theologische Zeitschrift* 24 (1973), 352–362.

At this early stage, the consecrated host was carried in a closed pyxis, but soon a monstrance or ostensory (from the Latin *monstrare* or *ostendere*, which both mean 'to show') with a glass frame was used that exposed the sacrament for the adoration of the people. The universal observance of the feast was renewed by the Avignon Pope John XXII (r. 1316–1334) in 1317, when he promulgated the collection of canon law authorised by his predecessor Clement V (r. 1305–1314) and known as the *Clementine Constitutions* (*Constitutiones clementinae*), which included the bull *Transiturus*.

Recent research by Ronald Zawilla and Pierre-Marie Gy has confirmed the traditional ascription of the Mass and Office for Corpus Christi to Thomas Aquinas.[163] It is most likely that the Dominican theologian compiled and composed the liturgical texts during his stay at the papal court in Orvieto between 1261 and 1265, including the sequence *Lauda Sion*, and the hymns *Pange lingua* (for Vespers), *Sacris solemniis* (for Matins) and *Verbum supernum* (for Lauds), as well as *Adoro te devote*.[164]

PREACHING AT MASS

There is scarce evidence from the post-Carolingian period for preaching in a liturgical context. This does not mean that there was no proclamation of the Gospel and transmission of the faith; however, Christian teaching was embedded in a culture that was largely oral, and it was not considered an integral part of the Church's public worship, which relied on a written text.[165] In *Ordo Romanus X*, which forms part of the Romano-Germanic Pontifical tradition, the bishop's 'sermon to the people' after the gospel appears as optional.[166] From the twelfth century, however,

---

[163] See Ronald Zawilla, *The Biblical Sources of the Historiae Corporis Christi Attributed to Thomas Aquinas: A Theological Study to Determine Their Authenticity* (PhD dissertation, University of Toronto, 1985); Pierre-Marie Gy, 'L'office du Corpus Christi et s. Thomas d'Aquin: État d'une recherche', in *Revue des sciences philosophiques et théologiques* 64 (1980), 491–507; also Jean-Pierre Torrell, *Saint Thomas Aquinas, Vol. I: The Person and His Work*, trans. Robert Royal (Washington, DC: The Catholic University of America Press, 1996), 129–136.

[164] See the discussion of Aquinas as 'Poet of the Eucharist' by Paul Murray, *Aquinas at Prayer: The Bible, Mysticism and Poetry* (London: Bloomsbury, 2013), 155–259.

[165] See R. Emmet McLaughlin, 'The Word Eclipsed? Preaching in the Early Middle Ages', in *Traditio* 46 (1991), 77–122.

[166] *Ordo Romanus X*, 32: ed. Andrieu, vol. II, 346; see Martin Morard, 'Quand liturgie épousa predication: Note sur la place de la prédication dans la liturgie romaine au moyen âge (VIIIᵉ-XIVᵉ siècle)', in *Prédication et liturgie au Moyen Âge*, ed. Nicole Bériou and Franco Morenzoni, Bibliothèque d'histoire culturelle du Moyen Âge 5 (Turnhout: Brepols, 2008), 79–126, at 89–90.

'preaching' (*praedicare, praedicatio*) is given increasing importance in both liturgical and canonical sources. While sermons could be given on various occasions, some of them extra-liturgical, they acquire a stable place in pontifical celebrations. In the mid-twelfth-century *ordo* of the Lateran basilica by prior Bernard, the description of the pontifical Mass includes a sermon after the gospel.[167] A sermon by the pope is specifically recorded on Maundy Thursday,[168] and on Easter Sunday a priest instructs the faithful about receiving communion worthily after they made their Mass offering.[169] The contemporary *ordo* by Benedict, a canon and cantor of St Peter's, notes papal preaching – usually after the proclamation of the gospel – at several stational Masses, including the third Mass of Christmas Day, Septuagesima Sunday, Laetare Sunday, Maundy Thursday and the Sunday after the Ascension.[170]

The pastoral turn of the thirteenth century, as exemplified by the Fourth Lateran Council, also brought a new focus on liturgical preaching. The *ordo* of the papal Mass established by Gregory X (r. 1271–1276) includes a sermon by the pope after the gospel, partly in Latin and partly in the vernacular, which is followed by a general confession, (non-sacramental) absolution and a blessing.[171] In the pontifical of William Durandus, written between 1292 and 1295, the bishop's preaching is particularly associated with such a penitential rite, to which indulgences are attached.[172] Martin Morard suggests that the repetition of the *Confiteor* after the sermon can be explained by a greater desire of the lay faithful for sacramental participation. Since they were not able to follow the alternating confession of sins by the celebrant and his assistants at the foot of the altar, which was said in a low voice while the introit was sung, it was replicated for the congregation after the sermon.

---

[167] *Ordo officiorum ecclesiae Lateranensis*, ed. Fischer, 82 (l. 8–9).   [168] Ibid., 50 (l. 32).
[169] Ibid., 78 (l. 21–30).
[170] Benedict, *Liber politicus*, 20, 30, 35, 40, 61: *Le Liber censuum de l'Église romaine*, ed. Paul Fabre and Louis Duchesne, 3 vols., Bibliothèque des Écoles Françaises d'Athènes et de Rome 6 (Paris: Fontemoing, 1910–1952) vol. II, 146a, 149a, 150a, 151a, 157a. John F. Romano, 'The Ceremonies of the Roman Pontiff: Rereading Benedict's Twelfth-Century Liturgical Script', in *Viator* 41 (2010), 133–150, shows that the *ordo* is a reliable source for the mid-twelfth century, rather than a compilation of liturgical sources that were obsolete by this time.
[171] *Ordinal of Gregory X (c. 1274)*, in *The Ordinal of the Papal Court from Innocent III to Boniface VIII and Related Documents*, ed. Stephen J. P. van Dijk and Joan Hazelden Walker, Spicilegium Friburgense 22 (Fribourg Switzerland: University Press, 1975), 586.
[172] William Durandus, *Pontificale*, III,18,34: ed. Michel Andrieu, *Le pontifical romain au moyen-âge*, vol. 3, Studi e testi 88 (Vatican City: Biblioteca Apostolica Vaticana, 1940), 639; see Morard, 'Quand liturgie épousa predication', 95–97.

The reconciliation effected by the penitential rite thus expresses what contemporary scholastic theology called the *res tantum* or fruit of the Eucharist, that is, the unity of the Church as the mystical Body of Christ.[173] The practice of a sermon, combined with a penitential rite and the proclamation of indulgences was soon adopted in the Mass celebrated by a priest. While other liturgical commentators already discuss the bishop's 'sermon to the people',[174] Durandus is the first who dedicates a chapter to preaching in general, which follows the one on the creed. He begins by stating that preaching takes place after the gospel and the profession of faith, because it is 'as it were an exposition of the words of the gospel and of the creed, or of the New and the Old Testament'.[175] At the end of the same section, however, Durandus adds that the creed is sung after the sermon, because it is the Church's profession of the faith that has just been preached; in the second redaction of the work, he qualifies this statement as 'nonetheless commonly observed (*communiter tamen*)'.[176] The lack of clarity in Durandus' comments may reflect different practices. Morard raises the question of whether preaching after the creed, which is also known from northern Italy,[177] is a distinctly presbyteral use, since pontifical sources habitually place the sermon within Mass after the gospel.[178] Other moments in the liturgy could be chosen as well: for instance, at high Mass in early-thirteenth century Siena, it was customary to preach after the gospel only at Easter and on major feast days, while on other days during the year a 'sermo ad populum' was given after the *Sanctus* or, in some churches, after receiving the offering of the faithful.[179]

In the later Middle Ages, parish priests throughout Europe were expected to preach on Sundays and major feast days.[180] Not all of them

---

[173] See Morard, 'Quand liturgie épousa predication', 112–113; also Gilles Emery, 'The Ecclesial Fruit of the Eucharist in St. Thomas Aquinas', in *Nova et Vetera* (English Edition) 2 (2004), 43–60, at 47–51.

[174] See, for instance, Honorius Augustodunensis, *Gemma animae* I, 25: PL 172,352CD (after the gospel); Sicard of Cremona, *Mitralis de officiis* III,4: CCM 228,163 (before or after the gospel).

[175] William Durandus, *Rationale divinorum officiorum*, IV, 26, 1: CCM 140,372.

[176] Ibid.   [177] See Thompson, *Cities of God*, 251.

[178] See Morard, 'Quand liturgie épousa predication', 110–111.

[179] This particular practice is noted with disapproval in the *Ordo officiorum* composed by the Sienese canon Odericus. See Jean-Baptiste Molin, 'Le prières du prône en Italie', in *Ephemerides Liturgicae* 76 (1962), 39–42, at 39.

[180] For further references, see Thompson, *Cities of God*, 251 and 335–337, for northern Italy; McLaughlin, 'The Word Eclipsed?', 77, for Germany; Eamon Duffy, *The Stripping*

may have been sufficiently trained to do so and not all of them may have fulfilled their duty conscientiously, but in general preaching was popular among the ordinary faithful.[181] As Thompson suggests, denunciations that Italian laypeople were notorious for evading sermons may have been a cliché of reformers and moralists, rather than an accurate reflection of pastoral reality. Hagiographical literature, on the other hand, is full of examples of 'avid sermon-goers', even if it is rather the non-liturgical 'solemn sermons', preached by religious, especially of the mendicant orders, that made the deepest impression.[182] North of the Alps, benefices were founded for secular priests to exercise the office of preacher (*Prädikatur*) from the late fourteenth century and especially in the second half of the fifteenth century. In some places, altar benefices were even converted into preaching benefices. The canonist Francesco Zabarella (1360–1417) was not the only voice that equated the spiritual benefit of preaching the word of God with the sacramental reception of the Body of Christ.[183] The importance of regular sermons was widely recognised and was promoted by the conciliarist reform movement.

CONCLUSION

Perhaps the most significant development of the Mass in the post-Carolingian period is the creation of the *Ordo Missae* as a coherent body of prayers and rubrics for the celebrant (including, in some cases, his

---

of the Altars: Traditional Religion in England 1400–1570, 2nd ed. (New Haven: Yale University Press, 2005), 57–58, for England.

[181] Martin Luther's formidable opponent Johann Eck (1486–1543) was exemplary in discharging his preaching duties as a parish priest in Ingolstadt; see Marco Benini, 'Johannes Eck als achtsamer Liturgie: Sein Ingolstädter Pfarrbuch als liturgiehistorische Quelle unter besonderer Berücksichtigung der szenischen Liturgie des Osterfestkreises', in *Archiv für Liturgiewissenschaft* 57 (2015), 72–95, esp. 77.

[182] Thompson, *Cities of God*, 336.

[183] See Gabriela Signori, *Räume, Gesten, Andachtsformen: Geschlecht, Konflikt und religiöse Kultur im europäischen Mittelalter* (Ostfildern: Jan Thorbecke Verlag, 2005), 22–25; and 'Einheit in der Vielfalt? Annäherungen an den "vorreformatorischen" Kirchenraum', in *Konfessionen im Kirchenraum: Dimensionen des Sakralraums in der frühen Neuzeit*, ed. Susanne Wegmann and Gabriele Wimböck, Studien zur Kunstgeschichte des Mittelalters und der frühen Neuzeit 3 (Korb: Didymos-Verlag, 2007), 215–234, at 221–223, with reference to Bernhard Neidiger, 'Wortgottesdienst vor der Reformation: Die Stiftung eigener Predigtpfründen für Weltkleriker im späten Mittelalter', in *Rheinische Vierteljahrsblätter* 66 (2002), 142–189; and Paul Ourliac, 'L'institution paroissiale dans le droit canonique du XVe siècle', in *Revue de droit canonique* 25 (1975), 93–112, at 96.

assistants). Personal priestly prayers known as *apologiae* were added, at
first with varying success, to the traditional structure of Mass that was
inherited from the formative period of the Roman Rite. These prayers
could be excessive in their length and in their penitential emphasis, as
exemplified in the *Missa Illyrica* and criticised by Bernold of Constance in
the eleventh century, but a process of pruning resulted in their integration
into the rite. The shift from an oral to a written culture in the high
medieval period gave the codified liturgical text a renewed importance,
and the *Ordo Missae*, with its increasingly sophisticated rubrication,
became normative for the celebration of the Eucharist. In the thirteenth
century, the rapidly growing Franciscan Order decided to follow the
liturgical use of the papal curia, and their ordinal *Indutus planeta* was
gradually adopted in missals of local dioceses and religious orders. The
papal reform movement had provided the ferment for this momentous
step of standardising the ritual shape of the Mass after the Roman model.
At the same time, the extension of private Masses had a lasting effect on
the form of celebration. While the solemn, sung form remained the
liturgical norm in parishes and religious houses, an increasing number
of Masses was offered without a regular congregation and with a much-
reduced ceremonial. Elements of the private Mass were introduced into
the solemn Mass, such as the doubling of the sung texts by the celebrant.
Finally, ever-greater devotion to the Eucharist culminated in the introduction of the feast of Corpus Christi, whose impact on later medieval society
can hardly be overestimated. Miri Rubins' acclaimed study offers a lively
account of how Corpus Christi 'became the central symbol of a culture'
that was universally shared in Western Christendom until c. 1500.[184]

---

[184] Rubin, *Corpus Christi*, 347.

8

Decline and Vitality in the Later Middle Ages

Standard liturgical textbooks have generally tended to give the later medieval period (from about 1200 onwards) short shrift: the early Christian Eucharist, which originated as a spirit-filled expression of communal worship, is said to have become an almost exclusively clerical exercise of a hypertrophied ritual system. The formation of national languages and cultures meant that Latin as the language of the liturgy became even more removed from the language of the people. Consequently, it is argued, lay participation largely disappeared, including the reception of Holy Communion. The faithful would rather occupy themselves with private, largely visual devotions while the priest as the ritual professional offered Mass at some distance, in a language they could not comprehend.[1] This reading fitted into a general narrative of a Church in crisis that almost inevitably led to the Protestant Reformation of the sixteenth century. In recent decades, however, historians have offered new perspectives on Christianity in the later Middle Ages and have highlighted that elements of decline and vitality existed side by side. In liturgical scholarship, the traditional focus on texts has been widened in favour of multidisciplinary studies of late medieval worship from musical, artistic, literary, social and, more generally, religious perspectives. In this chapter, I will, after a general historical introduction, pursue

---

[1] See, for example, the devastating assessments of Theodor Klauser, *A Short History of the Western Liturgy: An Account and Some Reflections*, trans. John Halliburton, 2nd ed. (Oxford: Oxford University Press, 1979), 97; and Anscar J. Chupungco, 'History of the Roman Liturgy until the Fifteenth Century', in *Handbook for Liturgical Studies, Vol. I: Introduction to the Liturgy*, ed. Anscar J. Chupungco (Collegeville: Liturgical Press, 1997), 131–152, at 150.

several themes, which in the end will join to offer us a more complete picture of this rich and complex period, namely: religion as a system of symbols, popular participation, unity and diversity in the development of the missal, codification of ritual, the Mass and sacred polyphony and transformations in church architecture.

THE AUTUMN OF THE MIDDLE AGES?

Modern historiography has habitually depicted the later Middle Ages as an age marked by social decline and cultural exhaustion, as reflected in Johan Huizinga's classic work, *The Autumn of the Middle Ages* (*Herfstij der Middeleeuwen*), first published in 1919.[2] Accordingly, medieval religious culture was believed to display a state of accelerating decay and disintegration, which led inexorably to the Protestant Reformation of the sixteenth century. However, a strong revisionist trend in historical scholarship in the last few decades has questioned long-held positions about the alleged decadence of the late medieval Church and has successfully exposed and challenged teleological narratives that were oriented towards the Reformation.[3] Huizinga's thesis has some factual basis, insofar as the late medieval world did suffer a general sense of crisis that threatened its cohesion; yet this was for a variety of reasons, only some of which were religious. The end of the Medieval Warm Period in the early fourteenth century had a detrimental effect on agriculture and caused a series of famines. The Black Death, a plague epidemic that raged from 1346 to 1353, wiped out about a third of Europe's population. The long, enervating conflict of the Hundred Years' War between England and France from 1337 to 1453 brought a further decline in population and prosperity for both countries. In 1453, Constantinople was conquered by the Ottoman Turks and the Byzantine Empire ceased to exist.

The move of the papal court to Avignon (1309–1377) was a turning point in the history of the papacy and had serious consequences for the Roman liturgy, as will be seen below. The papal schism that followed

---

[2] See now the translation of the second Dutch edition of 1921: Johan Huizinga, *The Autumn of the Middle Ages*, trans. Rodney J. Payton and Ulrich Mammitzsch (Chicago: University of Chicago Press, 1996).

[3] See, for instance, Robert N. Swanson, *Religion and Devotion in Europe, c. 1215–c. 1515*, Cambridge Medieval Textbooks (Cambridge: Cambridge University Press, 1995), 342: 'Does that mean that "the Reformation" was unforeseeable in 1515? Probably. Does it mean that pre-Reformation religion was in fact vital and progressing (whatever progress is) rather than decadent and ready to fall? Almost certainly.'

(1378–1417) deeply affected the Church and generated the conciliarist movement to resolve this acute crisis. Conciliarism favoured a more corporate form of ecclesiastical government and placed limits on the pope's exercise of power, thus attempting to check the claims of the Gregorian reform.[4] The later Middle Ages also brought the growth of the state, which can be understood as the consolidation and centralisation of political authority over a particular geographical area – also described in terms of 'sovereignty'. As the sense of belonging to a united Christendom, headed by the pope, declined among European elites in favour of identification with their own nation, civil rulers began to take greater control over the church in their territories.

This was not a 'Golden Age' of Christianity, as nineteenth-century Romantics may have imagined, but it is also mistaken to regard late medieval Europe as 'almost a mission country', as historians such as Jacques Le Goff and Jean Delumeau have proposed.[5] While a belief in magic persisted and certain folk practices could easily be classified as superstitious, there was a thoroughly Christian religious culture that permeated and shaped people's lives from birth to burial. The Church was remarkably successful in its 'primary' pastoral role, which is the care of souls (*cura animarum*). The failings of priests and religious were depicted in contemporary literature even to the point of caricature (see Giovanni Boccaccio's *Decameron*, Geoffrey Chaucer's *Canterbury Tales* or William Langland's *Piers Plowman*). However, denunciations of abuses were usually linked with calls for reform; in general, the sacramental system and the ordained priesthood as such were not contested, except by the most radical dissidents in the Lollard and Hussite movements. What made the Church vulnerable was its 'secondary' role that resulted from the seemingly inseparable entanglement of spiritual and

---

[4] See Norman Tanner, *The Church in the Later Middle Ages* (London; New York: I. B. Tauris, 2008), 1–32; Francis Oakley, 'Conciliarism', in *The Oxford Encyclopedia of the Reformation*, ed. Hans J. Hillerbrand, 3 vols. (New York: Oxford University Press, 1996), vol. I, 394–397; Bruce Gordon, 'Conciliarism in Late Mediaeval Europe', in *The Reformation World*, ed. Andrew Pettegree (London; New York: Routledge, 2000), 31–50.

[5] Jacques Le Goff, 'Le christianisme médiévale en occident du concile de Nicée (325) à la Réforme (début du XVIᵉ siècle)', in *Histoire des religions, tome II*, ed. Henri-Charles Pueh, Encyclopédie de la Pléiade (Paris: Gallimard, 1972), 749–868, at 856; see Jean Delumeau, *Catholicism between Luther and Voltaire: A New View of the Counter-Reformation*, trans. Jeremy Moiser (London: Burns & Oates, 1977); and the overview of John Van Engen, 'The Christian Middle Ages as an Historiographical Problem', in *The American Historical Review* 91 (1986), 519–552.

temporal spheres. Questions of jurisdiction, taxation and land ownership brought conflicts with local communities as well as the emerging nation states. The papacy in particular, ruling over a territory in central Italy, was involved in the politics and warfare between Europe's leading powers.[6]

Renaissance Humanism opened up new intellectual and spiritual horizons. While the artist and art historian Giorgio Vasari spoke of a 'rebirth' (*rinascita*) in his *Lives of the Most Excellent Painters, Sculptors, and Architects* (first edition 1550, second edition 1568), nineteenth-century historians extended the use of the term, now in its French form 'Renaissance', to designate a historical epoch that witnessed a new flowering of European civilisation.[7] While elements of continuity with the medieval world should not be overlooked,[8] the Renaissance introduced a new understanding of man and of the world that saw as its point of reference the legacy of Greek and Roman antiquity. But Humanism also aspired to a revival of Christian antiquity, as shown by a renewed interest in the early Church Fathers, especially the Greek. Christian Humanists, above all Erasmus, offered a trenchant critique of contemporary scholastic theology and advocated a return to a 'simpler' theology founded on the Bible (read in its original languages) and the patristic tradition. Humanism was by no means the only current in a varied intellectual landscape: at the same university (for instance, Tübingen in southern Germany), the *via moderna* of William of Ockham (d. 1349), which was associated with philosophical nominalism, was taught side-by-side with the *via antiqua*, which was associated with philosophical realism; among the theological schools, Thomism as well as Augustinianism experienced a revival. Many of the different currents, however, joined in the conciliarist call for a reform of the Church 'in head and members'.

Religious practice in the later Middle Ages is characterised by diverse, if not contrary tendencies. On the one hand, historians have been

---

[6] See Euan Cameron, *The European Reformation*, 2nd ed. (Oxford: Oxford University Press, 2012), 1–98; and Robert Bireley, *The Refashioning of Catholicism 1450–1700: A Reassessment of the Counter Reformation* (Washington, DC: The Catholic University of America Press, 1999), 1–24.

[7] See especially Jacob Burckhardt's *The Civilization of the Renaissance in Italy* (*Die Cultur der Renaissance in Italien*) of 1860.

[8] The art historian Erwin Panofsky argues that 'the Renaissance was connected with the Middle Ages by a thousand ties' and that 'the heritage of classical Antiquity had never been lost beyond recuperation'. Erwin Panofsky, 'Renaissance and Renascences', in *The Kenyon Review* 6 (1944), 201–236, at 202.

accustomed to claim for this period an internalisation of man's relationship to God to such an extent that private forms of devotion came to be regarded as more important than public acts of worship. This tendency developed fully in early modernity, through both Protestant and Catholic reform movements. Christopher Dawson has singled out the flowering of mysticism in Spain and Italy, and the ascetic spirituality as represented in the Ignatian *Spiritual Exercises*, with their roots in the personalism of the *devotio moderna*.[9] On the other hand, more recent scholarship, such as the work of Caroline Walker Bynum, has emphasised the sheer materiality of religious devotion, with its focus on miraculous phenomena, relics and pilgrimages.[10] It would not seem adequate to separate these divergent experiences into the categories of elite and popular piety. Rather, they are found across the social spectrum, as shown, for instance, in the tangible devotion to the holy face of Christ, which was shared equally among the illiterate populace, well-educated nuns and the powerful Duke of Burgundy.[11]

RELIGION AS A SYSTEM OF SYMBOLS

Ritual is about symbolic performance and communication. It generally consists of prescribed actions that are carried out in a deliberate and stylised manner; its use of language is highly formalised. The best definition of ritual I have found is that of Stanley J. Tambiah:

Ritual is a culturally constructed system of symbolic communication. It is constituted of patterned and ordered sequences of words and acts, often expressed in multiple media, whose content and arrangement are characterised in varying degree by formality (conventionality), stereotypy (rigidity), condensation (fusion), and redundancy (repetition).[12]

---

[9] See Christopher Dawson, *The Dividing of Christendom* (San Francisco: Ignatius Press, 2009; originally published in 1965), 33.

[10] See Caroline Walker Bynum, *Christian Materiality: An Essay on Religion in Late Medieval Europe* (New York: Zone Books, 2011).

[11] See the papers from a conference held at Magdalene College, Cambridge in April 2016, which explore medieval devotion to the holy face from a variety of disciplines, including history of art and literature: *The European Fortune of the Roman Veronica in the Middle Ages*, ed. Amanda Murphy, Herbert L. Kessler, Marco Petoletti, Eamon Duffy and Guido Milanese, Convivium Supplementum 2 (Turnhout: Brepols, 2017).

[12] Stanley J. Tambiah, 'A Performative Approach to Ritual', in *Proceedings of the British Academy* 65 (1979), 113–169, at 119.

As a highly structured and ordered system of communication, ritual is often compared with play. However, Tambiah insists that there is an important difference between them: games 'appear to have a disjunctive effect: they end in the establishment of a difference between the individual players or teams where originally there was no indication of inequality'. Ritual, by contrast, has the effect of establishing or confirming solidarity or communion between separate groups.[13]

What both ritual and play have in common is the fact that their end or purpose lies in itself: thereby, they effect a change or transformation in those who participate in them. As such, ritual is efficacious and acts by means of symbols.[14] In a Christian context, the sacraments would be obvious examples of actions and words effecting a state that would not be present otherwise, for instance, in the symbolic act of pouring water three times over a person's head with the formula 'I baptise you in the name of the Father and of the Son and of the Holy Spirit'.

While ritual behaviour is part of our daily lives and is not limited to religion, it is in the religious sphere where it is most widely perceived and practised. In his seminal work on the interpretation of cultures, Clifford Geertz describes religion as a

(1) system of symbols which acts to (2) establish powerful, pervasive, and long-lasting moods and motivations in men by (3) formulating conceptions of a general order of existence and (4) clothing these conceptions which such an aura of factuality that (5) the moods and motivations seem uniquely realistic.[15]

This dense description hinges on Geertz's understanding of 'symbol' by which he means 'any object, act, event, quality or relation which serves as a vehicle for a conception'. The conception is the symbol's 'meaning': thus the cross, when spoken about, represented visually or formed as a physical gesture, is a symbol. Geertz further describes symbols as 'tangible formulations of notions, abstractions from experience fixed in perceptible forms, concrete embodiments of ideas, attitudes, judgments, longings, or beliefs'.[16] Through such symbols, religion shapes and directs the dispositions, attitudes, ideas and incentives of its adherents. As a system of symbols, religion articulates and communicates conceptions about the

---

[13] Ibid., 118.
[14] See David Torevell, *Losing the Sacred: Ritual, Modernity and Liturgical Reform* (Edinburgh: T&T Clark, 2000), 36, with reference to the work of Richard Schechner.
[15] Clifford Geertz, 'Religion as a Cultural System', in *The Interpretation of Cultures: Selected Essays* (New York: Basic Books, 1973), 87–125, at 90.
[16] Ibid., 91.

whole cosmos. In doing so, it offers a model *of* reality as well as a model *for* reality, that is, it claims to represent things as they are and to show how they should be. In other words, religion provides a worldview and creates an ethos.

For Geertz, religion as a system of symbols does not simply reflect social structure (as Émile Durkheim proposed); however, it is not totally independent of it either. The symbolism relates to such human experiences as ignorance, pain and injustice and gives them meaning by integrating them into a cosmic order. In ritual, this general order of existence (the world as it is) and the ethos (the world as it should be and what we should do about it) meet. The complex of symbols imbues 'the metaphysic they formulate and the style of life they recommend' with 'persuasive authority'. In fact, Geertz even speaks of a fusion of the two in ritual: 'the world as lived and the world as imagined, fused under the agency of a single set of symbolic forms, turn out to be the same world'. Religious convictions emerge from such 'concrete acts of religious observance'.[17] Here Geertz appears to reformulate the Christian principle *lex orandi, lex credendi*: the liturgy is an expression of and witness to belief.[18] Geertz's description of religion as a system of symbols is particularly relevant for the European Middle Ages, when divine worship was an 'important indicator of cultural creativity and social development'[19] in societies that identified themselves as a Christian commonwealth.

POPULAR PARTICIPATION

The prevailing use of Latin as a sacred language certainly removed the liturgy from the vast majority of the lay faithful, but it did not raise an impenetrable barrier to popular participation, as is often assumed. In

---

[17] Ibid., 112.

[18] The principle 'ut legem credendi lex statuat supplicandi' was first formulated in the fifth century by Prosper of Aquitaine, *Indiculus de gratia Dei* (*Capitula Caelestini*), 8: PL 51,209. See also *Enchiridion symbolorum definitionum et declarationum de rebus fidei et morum*, ed. Heinrich Denzinger and Peter Hünermann, 43rd ed. (San Francisco: Ignatius Press, 2012), no. 246. There is, however, a significant difference here that Geertz does not account for. In the Christian understanding, rite 'forms and constitutes but does not "produce" the *lex credendi*, as noted by Aidan Kavanagh, *On Liturgical Theology: The Hale Memorial Lectures of Seabury-Western Theological Seminary, 1981* (Collegeville: Liturgical Press, 1984), 100.

[19] Yitzhak Hen, 'Key Themes in the Study of Medieval Liturgy', in *T&T Clark Companion to Liturgy*, ed. Alcuin Reid (London: Bloomsbury T&T Clark, 2016), 73–92, at 73.

Romance-speaking countries, where the vernacular language developed from Latin, there was a basic understanding at least of the meaning conveyed in liturgical texts. Contrary to claims advanced by dissident groups, such as the Waldensians, the gist of the Mass was accessible even to the lesser educated, at least if they chose to follow attentively, as Augustine Thompson shows in his study of ordinary religious practice in the Italian cities of the high Middle Ages.[20] A telling example is offered in the decree of the synod of Grado in 1296 that deacons were not to use melismatic tones in their chanting of the gospel, because 'these impeded the understanding of the hearers and so the devotion in the minds of the faithful is reduced' – note the concern for the comprehension of the sacred text among the laity. Elaborate tones were permitted only for the proclamation of the genealogies of Christ on Christmas and Epiphany and for 'the first Gospel chanted by a newly ordained deacon'.[21]

Claire Taylor Jones argues that historians have underestimated the grasp of Latin among women religious in the later medieval period. She exemplifies that with Dominican nuns a certain degree of Latin comprehension was expected (though not an active command of the language, as in the case of the friars). Choir nuns had (or at least were meant to have) a working understanding of the Latin Office, which comprised a much wider range of texts than the Mass, including biblical, patristic, homiletic and hagiographical literature. Hence, Taylor Jones speaks of 'liturgical literacy', especially among the Dominican nuns of the Observant reform movement in fifteenth-century Germany.[22]

Writing about early modern Europe, Peter Burke records that an increasing part of the laity was studying Latin, including a small but growing group of learned women.[23] The cultural impact of the sacred language in everyday speech is also evident from the resonances of

[20] See Augustine Thompson, *Cities of God: The Religion of the Italian Communes 1125–1325* (University Park: The Pennsylvania State University Press, 2005), 239–241.
[21] As quoted in ibid., 240.
[22] Claire Taylor Jones, *Ruling the Spirit: Women, Liturgy, and Dominican Reform in Late Medieval Germany*, The Middle Ages Series (Philadelphia: University of Pennsylvania Press, 2018), 5–9, 20–26, 73–85 and 92–96.
[23] See Peter Burke, *Languages and Communities in Early Modern Europe: The 2002 Wiles Lectures given at Queen's University, Belfast* (Cambridge: Cambridge University Press, 2004), 49, where he names 'Isotta Nogarola and Laura Cereta in Italy, Caritas Pirckheimer in Germany, Beatriz Galindo, nicknamed "La Latina", in Spain, and Mildred Cooke'.

liturgical Latin in vernacular expressions of Romance-speaking countries.[24] The use of Latin in the later medieval and early modern period provided an example of 'diglossia', which means that 'it was considered appropriate to use that language in some situations and domains'.[25] It was the language of the cultural elites and served to bind together international communities of ideas, above all the Church and the Republic of Letters. Objections to the use of Latin not only in the liturgy but also in other aspects of the Church's life were advanced by heterodox movements and became dominant in the Protestant Reformation. On the other hand, the Humanists' call for a return to the purity of Ciceronian Latinity aggravated this situation, because it meant that a 'living second language' was discarded in favour of reviving a language that had been truly 'dead'.[26]

The vernacular prayer of the faithful at the main Sunday Mass in the parish church offered a form of popular participation that corresponded to the needs of the community. The oldest known example of such vernacular prayer from England precedes the Norman Conquest and has been dated to the early eleventh century.[27] Further examples survive from twelfth-century Germany, thirteenth-century Italy and France and fifteenth-century Poland and Spain. Notably, the prayer of the faithful

---

[24] Burke, *Languages and Communities*, 50–51, provides a few delightful examples: 'In the Venetian of Chioggia, for instance, an authoritarian person is nicknamed *potente de sede*, and someone full of himself *un egosum*, derived respectively from the Magnificat, *Deposuit potentes de sede*, and from St John's Gospel 11.25, *Ego sum resurrectio et vita*. Some of the Italian examples are simple borrowings, like *introibo* for "preamble" or *confiteor* for "apology" .... Yet other examples express playfulness, irony and mockery, including the mockery of liturgical Latin itself .... A woman regarded as too pious, for instance, was known in the sixteenth century as *una magnificatte*, while shouting was described as "singing Vespers", *cantare il vespro*'. See also Remo Bracchi, 'Il latino liturgico sulla bocca del popolo', in *Il latino e i cristiani: Un bilancio all'inizio del terzo millennio*, ed. Enrico dal Covolo and Manlio Sodi, Monumenta Studia Instrumenta Liturgica 17 (Vatican City: Libreria Editrice Vaticana, 2002), 489–507.

[25] Burke, *Languages and Communities*, 43.

[26] See ibid., 144–145; and Christine Mohrmann, 'The Ever-Recurring Problem of Language in the Church', in *Études sur le latin des chrétiens*, 4 vols., Storia e letteratura, 65, 87, 103, 143 (Roma: Edizioni di Storia e Letteratura, 1961–1977), vol. IV, 143–159, at 152 (originally published in *Theology of Renewal. Vol. II: Renewal of Religious Structures*, ed. Lawrence K. Shook [Montreal: Palm Publishers, 1968], 204–220).

[27] See *The Lay Folks Mass Book or the Manner of Hearing Mass: With Rubrics and Devotions for the People in Four Texts, and Offices in English According to the Use of York from Manuscripts of the Xth to the XVth century*, ed. Thomas Frederick Simmons, Early English Text Society 71 (London: Trübner, 1879), 61–80 ('Bidding Prayers according to the Use of York') and 315–346 (notes and commentary).

employs local languages, such as Castilian, Catalan, Basque and Breton, as well as Occitan and German dialects.[28] This vernacular rite was inserted at some point during the offertory (after the initial *Oremus* and before the *secreta*) and most commonly after the incensation of the gifts and the altar and before the priest's washing of hands (*lavabo*). Italian sources stand out for placing the prayer of the faithful after the *Sanctus* (and sometimes after the *Agnus Dei*).[29] The priest left the altar and went to the door of the chancel screen or mounted the pulpit.[30] As the English name 'bidding of the bedes' indicates, the rite consisted in the priest's call to prayer for particular intentions, which would typically include: peace; the welfare of the Church, especially the pope, the hierarchy and all in the service of God; the government of the realm, especially the king or prince; the Holy Land; the bounty of the harvest; merchants and labourers; pregnant women; the sick; pilgrims; perseverance in grace; conversion of sinners and the faithful departed, especially those related to the local community and those buried in the church's cemetery. The actual prayer could take different forms and usually entailed saying the Our Father (and the Hail Mary) once or several times. The commemoration of the dead was more formalised: a recitation of Psalm 129 (*De profundis*) was followed by a series of short petitions and a concluding collect. Either before or after the prayer, the priest announced the liturgical feasts of the coming week. In French sources from the fifteenth century onwards, the vernacular rite known as *prône* included not only the prayer of the faithful but also the publication of indulgences, banns of marriage and excommunications, and in the early modern period became an important place of catechesis.[31]

---

[28] See Jean-Baptiste Molin, 'L'*Oratio fidelium*: Ses survivances', in *Ephemerides Liturgicae* 73 (1959), 310–317. Molin has published collections of medieval formularies in various European languages in 'L'*oratio communis fidelium* au Moyen Âge en Occident du Xe au XVe siècle', in *Miscellanea liturgica in onore di Sua Eminenza il Cardinale Giacomo Lercaro*, 2 vols. (Rome: Desclée, 1966–1967), vol. II, 315–468; see also 'Quelques textes médiévaux de la prière universelle', in *Traditio et Progressio: Studi liturgici in onore del Prof. Adrien Nocent, OSB*, ed., Giustino Farnedi, Studia Anselmiana 95, Analecta liturgica 12 (Rome: Pontificio Ateneo S. Anselmo, 1988), 338–358.

[29] See Jean-Baptiste Molin, 'Le prières du prône en Italie', in *Ephemerides Liturgicae* 76 (1962), 39–42; also Thompson, *Cities of God*, 252.

[30] The French name 'prières du prône' may be derived from *prothyra*, which could indicate the grill separating the chancel from the nave or the ambo in front of that grill.

[31] See Katharine J. Lualdi, 'Change and Continuity in the Liturgy of the Prône from the Fifteenth to the Seventeenth Century', in *Prédication et liturgie au Moyen Âge*, ed. Nicole Bériou and Franco Morenzoni, Bibliothèque d'histoire culturelle du Moyen Âge 5 (Turnhout: Brepols, 2008), 373–389.

So far this discussion of popular participation in the late medieval Mass has been concerned with language comprehension. This initial focus is legitimate, insofar as the Church's public worship is ordered by official texts; at the same time, however, we need to beware of a narrowing tendency in twentieth-century liturgical scholarship and renewal that 'sees liturgy only as text and limits participation to speaking roles'.[32] Thus, the Lutheran liturgist Frank Senn has proposed a broader conception of liturgical participation:

The laity have always found ways to participate in the liturgy, whether it was in their language or not, and they have always derived meaning from the liturgy, whether it was the intended meaning or not. Furthermore, the laity in worship were surrounded by other 'vernaculars' than language, not least of which were the church buildings themselves and the liturgical art that decorated them.[33]

Senn's 'vernaculars' are echoed in the work of Éric Palazzo, who has explored the sensory dimensions of the liturgy: the stimulation of seeing, hearing, smelling, touching and tasting made participation in the Mass a synesthetic experience.[34] The research project *Experience of Worship in Late Medieval Cathedral and Parish Church*, initiated by Bangor University (2009–2013), has aimed at recreating such a synesthetic

---

[32] Frank C. Senn, *The People's Work: A Social History of the Liturgy* (Minneapolis: Fortress Press, 2006), 145.

[33] Ibid. Kavanagh, *On Liturgical Theology*, 103–107, traces the reduction of liturgy to *text* to the Renaissance and Reformation periods, and connects it with the invention of printing. 'A Presence which had formerly been experienced by most as a kind of enfolding embrace had now modulated into an abecedarian printout to which only the skill of literacy could give complete access .... The truth lies now exclusively in the text; no longer on the wall, or in the windows, or in the liturgical activity of those who occupy the churches' (ibid., 104). On the detrimental effect of printing on ritual, see also John Bossy, *Christianity in the West, 1400–1700* (Oxford: Oxford University Press, 1985), 103.

[34] Among Éric Palazzo's numerous publications, see the English account of his work, 'Art, Liturgy and the Five Senses in the Early Middle Ages', in *Viator* 41 (2010), 25–56; and the recent monograph, *L'invention chrétienne des cinq sens dans la liturgie et l'art au Moyen Âge* (Paris: Cerf, 2014). Palazzo retraces the appeal to the sensory dimensions of the liturgy and their ritual 'activation' to the splendid book illuminations of the Carolingian period. However, John H. Arnold, 'Belief and the Senses for the Medieval Laity', in *Les cinq sens au Moyen Âge*, ed. Éric Palazzo (Paris: Cerf, 2016), 623–647, notes that such liturgical manuscripts were accessible only to a small clerical elite and had no popular reach. Thus, Arnold cautions that for understanding how the medieval laity may have encountered the sacred by means of sensory stimuli, the wider context of these elements needs to be considered. For instance, it needs to be asked who was able to see imagery in churches and how the knowledge acquired through preaching and catechesis (or the lack of it) impacted their perception of the iconography.

experience through liturgical enactment. For this purpose, the material conditions for the celebration of Mass in late medieval English settings (including buildings, objects and texts) were carefully reconstructed. The subsequent analysis and interpretation of the participants' engagement with the ritual offers a lively complement to the new perspectives offered by historical study.[35]

It remains true that the laity's participation in the Mass was at a remove from the action of the officiating priest. Even where lay devotion was literate, as was increasingly the case in the later medieval period, especially with the invention of printing, there was a clear separation between the clergy and the faithful. Primers and other devotional books did not contain translations of the Latin liturgical texts but rather offered spiritual and moral commentary on the Mass.[36] Lay participation was by its very nature 'untexted' and 'unscripted': it was not regulated by the official liturgical books that gave detailed instructions to the clergy regarding what to say and how to perform the sacred rites. Thus, the faithful were able to engage with the Mass in a variety of ways that are not easy for us to grasp precisely because they were not scripted. Paul Barnwell speaks of 'the meditative and affective nature of much lay devotion in the period'.[37] The sensory dimensions of the late medieval liturgy offered important stimuli for such meditation: the images on the rood screen and on the walls of the church visualised the communion of the saints, while funeral monuments were a reminder of purgatory and the need to pray for the dead. The faithful who attended Mass weekly (and many of them daily) would be familiar with the stable chants of the ordinary. Barnwell contends that 'key words and phrases would easily be recognised: their significance would be apprehended even if they were not understood in the way necessary to translate them'.[38] It is worth noting

---

[35] Key contributions to this research project are published in *Late Medieval Liturgies Enacted: The Experience of Worship in Cathedral and Parish Church*, ed. Sally Harper, Paul S. Barnwell and Magnus Williamson (London; New York: Routledge, 2016). For further documentation, see www.experienceofworship.org.uk/.

[36] See Paul S. Barnwell, 'The Nature of Late Medieval Worship: The Mass', in *Late Medieval Liturgies Enacted*, 207–218, at 211–213; and Katherine Zieman, *Singing the New Song: Literacy and Liturgy in Late Medieval England* (Philadelphia: University of Pennsylvania Press, 2008), 80–92. On female literacy and devotion, see Gabriela Signori, *Räume, Gesten, Andachtsformen: Geschlecht, Konflikt und religiöse Kultur im europäischen Mittelalter* (Ostfildern: Jan Thorbecke Verlag, 2005), 147–169.

[37] Paul S. Barnwell, 'How to Do Without Rubrics: Experiments in Reconstructing Medieval Lay Experience', in *Late Medieval Liturgies Enacted*, 235–254, at 238.

[38] Barnwell, 'The Nature of Late Medieval Worship', 214.

here that the laity would have found the parish Mass celebrated at the high altar less approachable, since they were at considerable physical distance from the priest and their view was restricted not only by the rood screen but also by servers and singers in the chancel. 'Private' Masses at a side altar or in a chantry chapel offered a more direct way for the faithful to engage with the liturgical action both visually and aurally, and this contributed to their popularity.[39] Woodcut representations of the Mass in moral and devotional literature from the late fifteenth and early sixteenth century show lay men and women in close proximity to the priest at a side altar of a church; for instance, Hans Baldung Grien's illustration of the Third Commandment for the 1516 print of the widely read explanation of the Decalogue by the Franciscan Marquard of Lindau (Figure 8.1).[40]

An important element that distinguished the laity's participation in the Mass in the period under discussion was the scarcity of fixed seating. For most of the Middle Ages, people usually stood or knelt in the nave, with men and women separated and aligned according to social rank. Hence, there was an albeit restricted freedom to move within the church building. Seating was provided for elderly and infirm members of the congregation in the form of ledges at the walls of the nave or portable stools. It is commonly held that fixed benches began to appear in northern and western Europe in the thirteenth century and became more widespread from the late fourteenth century onwards. Retracing the history of church benches is beset with intractable difficulties for lack of material evidence. Early examples of wooden benches or pews are likely to have been replaced either because they were worn out or because more elaborate ones were produced.[41] Late medieval benches have survived above all in English parish churches, while examples from continental Europe are rare. The reasons for this discrepancy are not clear; however, written sources confirm that fixed seating in churches spread in the territory of the Holy Roman Empire from the fourteenth century as well.[42]

[39] See Barnwell, 'How to Do Without Rubrics', 245.
[40] See Signori, *Räume, Gesten, Andachtsformen*, 43 and 70.
[41] See Paul S. Barnwell, 'Seating in the Nave of the Pre-Reformation Parish Church', in *Pews, Benches and Chairs: Church Seating in English Parish Churches from the Fourteenth Century to the Present*, ed. Trevor Cooper and Sarah Brown (London: Ecclesiological Society, 2011), 69–86.
[42] See Signori, *Räume, Gesten, Andachtsformen*, 87–88.

Figure 8.1 Hans Baldung Grien / The Third Commandment / 1516
(Woodcut in Marquard of Lindau, *Frag und Antwurt der zehen gebott wie man die halte sol*
(Straßburg: Grüninger, 1516), XIIIv / Bayerische Staatsbibliothek München,
Rar. 2312#Beibd.1, urn:nbn:de:bvb:12-bsb00014698-6 / CC BY-NC-SA 4.0)

A permanent seat could be purchased; this became an expression of
social status (and, occasionally, social conflict).[43] The development of
fixed benches in churches is usually associated with an increased frequency of preaching in the later medieval period. Barnwell argues that
this was only one factor among others and points to the flourishing of
meditative piety in the period, which focused on the crucified Christ
visible on the monumental rood screen, a focus sharpened by the installation of permanent seating.[44] Sitting was associated with the contemplative life, and this is illustrated from contemporary iconography of the

---

[43] See Barnwell, 'Seating in the Nave of the Pre-Reformation Parish Church', 78–82; also
Gabriela Signori, 'Umstrittene Stühle: Spätmittelalterliches Kirchengestühl als soziales,
politisches und religiöses Kommunikationsmedium', in *Zeitschrift für Historische
Forschung* 29 (2002), 189–213.
[44] See Barnwell, 'Seating in the Nave of the Pre-Reformation Parish Church', 83.

Annunciation, which often shows Mary seated in prayerful reading.[45] At any rate, the increasing presence of benches and pews changed the dynamic of the congregation, at least in the part of the nave closest to the chancel.

The 'vernaculars' other than language of the late medieval Mass, evoked by Senn, spoke eloquently to worshippers both as private individuals and – in a juxtaposition typical of the religious practice of the age – as a body. The social anthropologist Mary Douglas has spoken of 'non-verbal symbols', which 'are capable of creating a structure of meanings in which individuals can relate to one another and realize their own ultimate purposes'.[46] To quote an influential essay by the historian John Bossy, the Mass was a 'social institution'[47] and created a bond that was not only expressed verbally through praying for one another (see above on the bidding of the bedes) but became tangible in two particular rites: the pax and blessed bread.[48] The kiss of peace was exchanged by means of the pax (also known as pax-brede or *pacificale*), a tablet made of glass, wood or metal and often adorned with an image, such as the crucifixion or the Lamb of God. The pax was passed from the clergy to the laity and was kissed in turn. A particular custom on Sundays and feast days was the blessing of bread that had been prepared and offered by the women of a household in the village or a neighbourhood in the city (organised by rota). After the Mass, the priest blessed the bread and it was distributed to the congregation. Some of the blessed bread ('holy loaf' in English sources) was taken to the sick and the elderly and people kept it because they believed in its protective powers.[49] Both the pax and the blessed

[45] See Signori, *Räume, Gesten, Andachtsformen*, 86–87 and 158–161.
[46] Mary Douglas, *Natural Symbols: Explorations in Cosmology*, 2nd ed. (London; New York: Routledge, 1996), 53. While describing this system of symbols as a language with grammatical rules and a specific vocabulary, it is not necessary to commit oneself to a structuralist model. On the usefulness and limits of 'linguistic' approaches to the liturgy, see Victor Turner, 'Ritual, Tribal and Catholic', in *Worship* 50 (1976), 504–526, at 510.
[47] John Bossy, 'The Mass as a Social Institution, 1200–1700', in *Past & Present*, no. 100 (August 1983), 29–61; see also Thompson, *Cities of God*, 235–271 ('The City Worships'); and Eamon Duffy, *The Stripping of the Altars: Traditional Religion in England 1400–1570*, 2nd ed. (New Haven; London: Yale University Press, 2005), 91–130 ('The Mass').
[48] For England, see Duffy, *The Stripping of the Altars*, 125; for northern Italy, see Thompson, *Cities of God*, 253–255.
[49] On the customs surrounding *panis benedictus* in medieval and early modern Europe, see Peter Browe, 'Der Kommunionersatz im Mittelalter', in *Die Eucharistie im Mittelalter: Liturgiehistorische Forschungen in kulturwissenschaftlicher Absicht*, ed. Hubertus Lutterbach and Thomas Flammer, Vergessene Theologen 1, 7th ed. (Münster: Lit

bread were obvious substitutes for the sacramental communion, which had become rare in parish life; and for most laypeople, it did not extend beyond the annual reception at Easter as prescribed by Lateran IV. However, these particular rites contributed significantly to the community-building power of the Mass, which Augustine Thompson describes with a view of the medieval city-state (*commune*) of northern Italy: 'Celebration of Mass, especially Sunday Mass, sealed the unity of a community or neighbourhood . . .. This ritual created and vivified the community. The Mass was its very life, as the midday meal was the life of the family'.[50]

UNITY AND DIVERSITY IN THE DEVELOPMENT OF THE MISSAL

As discussed in Chapter 7, the ideological foundation for the unification of the liturgy emerged from the papal reform movement of the eleventh century, especially the pontificate of Pope Gregory VII (r. 1073–1085). However, general conformity with Roman liturgical practice began to be achieved only with the rapid expansion of the new Franciscan Order in the thirteenth century. The Friars Minor settled on the missal and breviary of the Roman Rite in the form used by the papal curia. These books were simplified by comparison with the fuller ceremonial observed in the major churches of Rome, especially the Lateran basilica. Thus, the later Middle Ages witnessed a standardisation of the Latin liturgy according to the model of the Roman curia, which increasingly shaped local diocesan uses.

While episcopal and monastic centres throughout Europe shaped and retained their particular liturgical customs within the Roman tradition, a movement towards unifying the rite of Mass can also be observed on a regional level, as in the case of the Sarum use. The liturgical use associated with the post-Norman Conquest see of Old Sarum, which was transferred to the new location of Salisbury in 1220, was followed, with local adaptations, in most of the fourteen dioceses of the ecclesiastical province of Canterbury by the later medieval period. By comparison, the use of York was limited to a much smaller province of three dioceses and the use

Verlag, 2019), 415–424 (originally published in *Ephemerides Liturgicae* 8 [1934], 534–548).
50 Thompson, *Cities of God*, 246.

of Hereford was observed only in the diocese itself.[51] Several reasons may have facilitated the prevalence of the Sarum use: Firstly, Canterbury Cathedral was a monastic foundation dating from the mission of Augustine, and its use could not simply be imitated by secular (i.e., non-monastic) cathedrals. Secondly, by the fifteenth century the Chapel Royal had adopted the Sarum use and gave it normative force, exercising an influence analogous to that of the papal chapel on the Roman Mass.[52] Thirdly, the material conditions of book production and trade favoured the Sarum use, as David Hiley notes:

> from the thirteenth century onward, professional workshops in Oxford, London, and later Cambridge appear to have been able to supply books of Salisbury use 'on demand', so to speak, making it easy for churches to acquire books of this type rather than those of their diocesan cathedral.[53]

With the invention of printing, a comprehensive set of liturgical books for the Sarum use was available in the early sixteenth century.[54]

Despite such tendencies towards standardisation, variations in the missals of dioceses and religious orders remained and were noteworthy in certain respects: in the formal presentation of liturgical formularies (such as the headings of the Mass propers); in the prayers, readings and chants assigned to particular feasts; in the sanctoral cycle of the calendar and in the structure and sequence of sections within the missal. Even where the Order of Mass essentially followed the use of the Roman curia ('Ordo missalis secundum consuetudinem Romane curie'), there were differences in the texts and rubrics of the introductory and the concluding rites. Likewise, the ritual shape and the prayers of the offertory were by no means uniform.[55] Liturgical diversification increased with the addition of new saints' feasts, the proliferation of prefaces, tropes

---

[51] See Richard W. Pfaff, *The Liturgy in Medieval England: A History* (Cambridge: Cambridge University Press, 2009), 350–387 and 412–480.

[52] See Christopher Hohler, 'Reflections on Some Manuscripts Containing 13th-Century Polyphony', in *Journal of the Plainsong & Mediaeval Music Society* 1 (1978), 2–38, at 37, n. 28.

[53] David Hiley, *Western Plainchant: A Handbook* (Oxford: Clarendon Press, 1993), 584, with reference to Diane Lynne Droste, *The Musical Notation and Transmission of the Music of the Sarum Use, 1225–1500* (PhD dissertation, University of Toronto, 1983).

[54] See John Harper, 'Enacting Late Medieval Worship: Locations, Processes and Outcomes', in *Late Medieval Liturgies Enacted*, 31–45, at 32.

[55] See the thoroughly documented study of Paul Tirot, 'Histoire des prières d'offertoire du VIIᵉ au XVIᵉ siècle', in *Ephemerides Liturgicae* 98 (1984), 148–197 and 323–391; also published separately in the series Biblioteca Ephemerides Liturgiae. Subsidia 34 (Rome: C.L.V. – Edizioni Liturgiche, 1985).

and sequences (of uneven quality) and the multiplication of votive Masses, some of which were attached to questionable practices, such as the use of a symbolic number of candles for specific Masses: seven for the Mass of St Sophia along with seven orations, twelve for the apostles and twenty-four for the elders of the Apocalypse.[56]

In general, diocesan bishops did not have effective control over the making of liturgical books in their territories. Before the invention of printing, manuscripts for liturgical use were usually copied at the initiative of local churches and their clergy, who would engage scribes for this particular purpose.[57] Local nobility or other patrons would often donate missals and be involved in their production. Episcopal leadership was mostly reactive and its limits are illustrated by the largely unsuccessful efforts of Nicholas of Cusa, who as bishop of Brixen tried to enforce the correction of missals in use according to approved normative manuscripts at two diocesan synods in 1453 and 1455.[58] The new, fast-growing and largely unregulated printing industry dramatically simplified the production of liturgical books and gave printers an important role in this process. Leaving aside the stable parts, above all in the Order of Mass and the temporal cycle of the liturgical year, the actual composition of a diocesan missal seems to have been, to a considerable extent, in the hands of the printers themselves, as the eminent historian of the Catholic Reform and Counter-Reformation Hubert Jedin noted.[59] Rather than leading towards uniformity, the possibility of printing missals introduced an even greater diversity. Amato Pietro Frutaz has drawn attention to the categorical differences in the sanctoral calendars of early printed editions of the *Missale Romanum* from the last quarter of the fifteenth century, most of them coming from Italy. The *editio princeps*, printed by Antonio Zarotto in Milan in 1474, simply lists a saint or a group of saints for each day of the year, in the manner of the martyrology. Other early printed

---

[56] See the still valuable work of Adolph Franz, *Die Messe im deutschen Mittelalter: Beiträge zur Geschichte der Liturgie und des religiösen Volkslebens* (Freiburg im Breisgau: Herder, 1902), esp. 268–291.

[57] Natalia Nowakowska, 'From Strassburg to Trent: Bishops, Printing and Liturgical Reform in the Fifteenth Century', in *Past & Present*, no. 213 (November 2011), 3–39, at 24, points to the evidence provided by contracts from fifteenth-century Poland and England.

[58] See Hubert Jedin, 'Das Konzil von Trient und die Reform des Römischen Meßbuches', in *Liturgisches Leben* 6 (1939), 30–66, at 40–41.

[59] 'Die gedruckten Missalien waren allzuhäufig Privatunternehmungen tüchtiger Drucker'; ibid., 41.

missals use a version of the Franciscan calendar, with a motley addition of saints.[60]

Some bishops denounced this rank growth, as well as the errors introduced by careless printers. A particular problem concerned rubrics, which did not have official character and varied both in quality and in usefulness.[61] However, only a few bishops across Europe, mostly in the Holy Roman Empire, took the initiative to create officially approved printed editions for liturgical use. Based on international incunabula catalogues that document European printing until the year 1500, Natalia Nowakowska has compiled a list of diocesan liturgical books that were produced with episcopal commission by leading master printers, such as Erhard Ratdolt in Augsburg and Venice, Georg Stuchs in Nuremberg, Georg Reyser in Wurzburg and Michael Wenssler in Basel. With the caution that our knowledge of early printed books is far from complete and any quantitative survey must remain provisional, she concludes that these '107 episcopally commissioned editions ... in fact formed only a small part of the wider market in printed liturgical books in the fifteenth century; they existed alongside a separate genre, the uncommissioned or unofficial diocesan printed liturgy'.[62] Most of these books are in fact breviaries and hence primarily for the use of clergy; only 28 of the 107 incunabula listed are missals.

Nowakowska also observes that episcopal commissions of liturgical books reached their height in the last decade of the fifteenth century and then fell sharply in most dioceses. The reasons for this fluctuation are complex, and they probably include a saturation of the market as a result of the success of the earlier initiatives. Liturgical books, once acquired, continued to be used as long as they remained in adequate condition. Going beyond such pragmatic motives, however, disagreements between reformers who inclined towards corrected editions of the current liturgical books and Humanists who argued for a further-ranging reform returning

[60] *Missale Romanum Mediolani, 1474*, ed. Robert Lippe, 2 vols., Henry Bradshaw Society 17 and 33 (London: Harrison and Sons, 1899 and 1907), vol. I, xiii–xxiv. See Amato Pietro Frutaz, 'Contributo alla storia della riforma del Messale promulgato da san Pio V nel 1570', in *Problemi di vita religiosa in Italia nel Cinquecento: Atti del Convegno di storia della Chiesa in Italia (Bologna, 2–6 sett. 1958)*, Italia Sacra 2 (Padua: Editrice Antenore, 1960), 187–214, at 201–203.

[61] See Nowakowska, 'From Strassburg to Trent', 19–20.

[62] Ibid., 19; see 32–39 for the list detailing date of printing, diocese, commissioning bishop, printer, place of printing and ISTC (= Incunabula Short Title Catalogue) reference.

to ideals of Christian antiquity may have stifled the bishops' efforts in overseeing the publication of liturgical books.[63]

The digitised collection of early printed missals from the Diocese of Passau in the Bavarian State Library (Bayerische Staatsbibliothek) in Munich allows us to illustrate this convoluted history with the example of the votive Mass of the Holy Face of Christ.[64] Two editions of the *Missale Patauiense* (after 1491 and 1494, reprinted 1498), published with the mandate of Christoph von Schachner, bishop of Passau from 1490 to 1500, do not have such a votive formulary;[65] neither does the exquisitely illuminated missal printed by Johann Winterburger in Vienna in 1503, apparently without episcopal commission.[66] The first of two copies of the *Liber missalis secundum chorum Patauiensem*,[67] printed in Augsburg by Erhard Ratdolt in 1503, with the mandate of Wiguleus Fröschl von Marzoll, bishop of Passau from 1500 to 1517, does not include the votive Mass.[68] In the second copy of the same edition, however, Erhard Ratdolt added an appendix with votive Masses, which he introduced with the rubric: 'The printer added the following special Masses to incite a greater

---

[63] See Nowakowska, 'From Strassburg to Trent', 25–26 and 31, with reference to Hubert Jedin, 'Das Konzil von Trient und die Reform der liturgischen Bücher', in *Ephemerides Liturgicae* 59 (1945), 5–38. Jedin mentions the provincial synod of Bourges in 1528, under the presidency of Archbishop (later Cardinal) François de Tournon, which stipulated that henceforth breviaries, missals and rituals could be printed only with the prior approbation of the competent bishops. This would imply that such had not been done before. The synod also recalled that a reduction of feast days was the remit of ordinaries (see ibid., 12).

[64] See Uwe Michael Lang, 'Votive Masses of the Holy Face of Christ in Early Printed Diocesan Missals', in *Mediaeval Studies* 79 (2017), 165–203.

[65] *Missale Patauiense* (Passau: Johann Petri, after 1491), Bayerische Staatsbibliothek (= BSB), 2 Inc.c.a. 2590; *Missale Patauiense* (Augsburg: Erhard Ratdolt, 1494), BSB, Rar. 331; reprinted with a renewed episcopal mandate: *Missale Patauiense* (Augsburg: Erhard Ratdolt, 1498), BSB, 2 Inc.c.a. 3666. These pre-1501 editions are not listed by Nowakowska, 'From Strassburg to Trent'.

[66] *Missale Patauiense* (Vienna: Johann Winterburger, 1503), BSB, Rar. 2149.

[67] This and similar titles do not indicate that the use of the missal was limited to the choir area (also spelled 'quire') of the cathedral, which was reserved to the clergy. Rather, the cathedral liturgy is meant to be the normative for the whole diocese, with the intention to unify the celebration of Mass. See Dominik Daschner, *Die gedruckten Meßbücher Süddeutschlands bis zur Übernahme des Missale Romanum Pius V. (1570)*, Regensburger Studien zur Theologie 47 (Frankfurt am Main: Peter Lang, 1995), 21–22 and 25–29.

[68] *Liber missalis secundum chorum Patauiensem* (Augsburg: Erhard Ratdolt, 1503), BSB, Rar. 1739.

love of God, and for the glory of his work.'[69] In this section, we find the
votive Mass of the Holy Face, entitled 'Officium sancte Veronice: hoc est
de facie Iesu Christi'.[70] A subsequent edition of the *Missale Patauiense* also
printed in Augsburg by Erhard Ratdolt in 1505, and commissioned by Bishop
Wiguleus Fröschl, does not include these additional votive Masses.[71] This
evidence would seem to suggest that Ratdolt's initiative did not meet with the
approval of the diocesan bishop, at least not immediately. Subsequent editions of the *Missale Patauiense* – printed by Johann Winterburger in Vienna
(1507, 1509, 1512), by Jobst Gutknecht, with Jakob Heller and Heinrich
Hermann von Wimpffen, in Nuremberg (1514), and by Lucas Alantsee, for
Peter Liechtenstein, in Vienna (1522) – have the appendix with 'Missae
speciales' that includes the formulary of the Holy Face.[72]

In conclusion, printers of diocesan missals would confidently supply
their editions with Mass formularies that corresponded to devotions
popular at the time, perhaps with the collaboration and the advice of
local clergy. This phenomenon accounts for the haphazard inclusion of
the votive Mass of the Holy Face in diocesan missals from the late
fifteenth and early sixteenth century, some of them printed for use in the
same diocese in the space of a few years. In certain respects, the new
possibility of printing missals initially generated greater diversity, rather
than leading towards uniformity.

CODIFICATION OF RITUAL

The urban stational liturgy, which had in many ways shaped the development of the Roman Mass (see Chapter 5), fell into decline in the twelfth
and thirteenth centuries, when popes began to turn away from the city,

---

[69] *Liber missalis secundum chorum Patauiensem* (Augsburg: Erhard Ratdolt, 1503), BSB, 4
Liturg. 400, fol. 305r: 'Subsequentes missas speciales per maiori diuini amoris incentiuo
et operis decore subiunxit impressor.' A similar rubric introducing a section with votive
Masses is found in *Missale Saltzeburgense* (Vienna: Johann Winterburger, 1510),
fol. 234v; and in the *Missale secundum chorum alme ecclesie Strigoniensis* (Venice:
Petrus Liechtenstein, 1512), fol. 284v.

[70] Ibid., fols. 306v–308r.

[71] *Missale Patauiense* (Augsburg: Erhard Ratdolt, 1505), BSB, Rar. 2139.

[72] *Missale Patauiense* (Vienna: Johann Winterburger, 1507), BSB, ESlg/2 Liturg. 227, fols.
284v–285r; *Missale Patauiense* (Vienna: Johann Winterburger, 1509), BSB, Res/4
Liturg. 402, fols. 255v–256v; *Missale Patauiense* (Vienna: Johann Winterburger, 1512),
BSB, Rar. 2150, fols. 299v–300r; *Missale Patauiense* (Nuremberg: Jobst Gutknecht, with
Jakob Heller and Heinrich Hermann von Wimpffen, 1514), BSB, Rar. 2150, fols. 331r–
332e. *Missale Patauiense* (Vienna: Lucas Alantsee, for Peter Liechtenstein, 1522),
Regensburg, Staatliche Bibliothek, 999/4Liturg.96, fols. 338r–339r.

and the papal curia frequently moved between central Italian towns, such as Orvieto, Viterbo and Anagni. The preferred place for papal celebrations was no longer the city with its basilicas and titular churches – and processional spaces between them – but the chapel of the palace. The simplified ritual observed in the court setting became the model for the Roman liturgical books promoted in the thirteenth century by the rapidly expanding Franciscan Order (see Chapter 7). The transfer of the papacy to Avignon in 1309 brought the cycle of stational liturgies in Rome to a definite halt. In Avignon, papal liturgical celebrations were also held in the setting of the palace. Even after the return of the pope to Rome in 1378 and the end of the Western schism in 1417, the intimate link of the papal liturgy with the urban churches was never resumed.[73] The Vatican palace became the pope's preferred residence, and major liturgical celebrations were held in its 'great chapel' (*capella magna*), known as the Sistine Chapel since its rebuilding under Pope Sixtus IV (r. 1471–1484).

As the conciliarist movement diminished because of its failure to deliver its stated programme of renewing the Church 'in head and members', the papacy regained momentum, and its liturgical celebrations once again began to be imitated by bishops throughout the Latin Church. In the late fifteenth and early sixteenth century, the papal masters of ceremonies Agostino Patrizi Piccolomini (d. 1495), Johann Burchard (d. 1506) and Paride Grassi, also referred to by his Latinised name Paris de Grassis (d. 1528), were responsible for organising and recording both liturgy and court ceremonial. They left us three categories of written works: prescriptive ceremonial books, descriptive diaries and treatises. These sources offer us not only detailed accounts of papal and curial liturgies but also insight into life at the papal court in the Renaissance period. For musicologists, the close relationship between music and ritual in the Sistine Chapel is of particular interest. The *Caeremoniale Romanum* composed in 1488 for the papal curia by Patrizi with the assistance of Burchard offered a model that was increasingly adopted by cardinals who served as diocesan bishops outside Rome for their own celebrations.[74]

[73] See John F. Romano, 'Innocent II and the Liturgy', in *Pope Innocent II (1130–43): The World vs the City*, ed. John Doran and Damian J. Smith, Church, Faith and Culture in the Medieval West (Abingdon; New York: Routledge, 2016), 326–351, at 344–345.

[74] See Jörg Bölling, 'Zur Erneuerung der Liturgie in Kurie und Kirche durch das Konzil von Trient (1545–1563). Konzeption – Diskussion – Realisation', in *Papsttum und Kirchenmusik vom Mittelalter bis zu Benedikt XVI: Positionen – Entwicklungen – Kontexte*, ed. Klaus Pietschmann, Analecta musicologica 47 (Kassel: Bärenreiter, 2012),

The papal masters of ceremonies of the Renaissance period were working in a tradition that can be traced back to the *Ordines Romani* of the early medieval period. From the late thirteenth century onwards, these ceremonial instructions became more systematic and specific, and they had considerable impact beyond their immediate purpose throughout the Latin Church.[75] A text of considerable influence was the ceremonial for the Mass of a cardinal-bishop from the hand of the Dominican Cardinal Latino Malabranca Orsini (d. 1294),[76] which was extensively used by William Durandus (d. 1296) in the ritual instructions he compiled for the celebration of Mass in his diocese of Mende, France.[77] As James Monti observes, the 'medieval codification of liturgical rites also served to guarantee the validity and authenticity of the sacramental celebrations'.[78] The concern for sacramental validity, especially of the Eucharist, goes back at least to the early medieval period, as is attested in Irish sources, including the treatise on the Mass in the Stowe Missal (c. 800), where the dominical words of consecration are called a 'dangerous prayer' (*periculosa oratio*).[79] Irish penitentials prescribe set penances for priests who make mistakes in pronouncing them. At least since the thirteenth century, the idea that the celebration of Mass is *periculosa* was included in the rite of ordination to the priesthood.[80] Scholastic medieval theologians and

124–145; and *Das Papstzeremoniell der Renaissance: Texte – Musik - Performanz, Tradition – Reform – Innovation* 12 (Frankfurt am Main: Peter Lang, 2006).

[75] The papal ceremonials have been edited by Marc Dykmans, S.J., *Le cérémonial papal de la fin du Moyen-Âge à la Renaissance*, 4 vols., Bibliothèque de l'Institut Historique Belge de Rome 24–27 (Brussels; Rome: Institut Historique Belge de Rome, 1977–1985).

[76] The text is part of Mabillon's *Ordo Romanus XIV* (PL 78:1165). See now the critical edition by Dykmans, *Le cérémonial papal de la fin du Moyen-Âge à la Renaissance*, vol. I, 220–263.

[77] Joseph Berthelé and Marcellin Valmary, ed., 'Les instructions et constitutions de Guillaume Durand le Spéculateur, publiées d'après le manuscrit de Cessenon', *Académie des Sciences et Lettres de Montpellier: Mémoires de la Section des Lettres*, 2ᵉ Série, Tome III, 1905, 1–148, at 54–77 ('De officio misse'); see James Monti, *A Sense of the Sacred: Roman Catholic Worship in the Middle Ages* (San Francisco: Ignatius Press, 2012), 27–28.

[78] Monti, *A Sense of the Sacred*, 13.

[79] *The Stowe Missal: Ms. D. II. 3 in the Library of the Royal Irish Academy, Dublin*, ed. George F. Warner, 2 vols., Henry Bradshaw Society 32 (London: Harrison and Sons, 1915), vol. II, 37 (text) and 40 (translation). In the Gaelic original, the expression appears in Latin.

[80] See Balthasar Fischer, '"Oratio periculosa": Eine altirische Bezeichnung für die Einsetzungsworte in der Messe', in *Prex eucharistica, Volumen III: Studia, Pars prima: Ecclesia antiqua et occidentalis*, ed. Albert Gerhards, Heinzgerhard Brakmann and Martin Klöckener, Spicilegium Friburgense 42 (Fribourg: Academic Press, 2005), 237–241.

canonists usually include in their treatment of the Eucharist a discussion of liturgical requirements that are necessary for a valid confection of the sacrament. From the late fifteenth century, printed missals often contained a section entitled *Cautelae missae* ('Cautions for the Mass'), dealing with 'defects' that could compromise the integrity of the sacramental celebration and how to remedy them.[81]

Care for precise ceremonial instruction found a visual expression in a series of diagrams inserted into processional from the late fourteenth or early fifteenth century, which represents an adaptation of the Sarum use for the diocese of Norwich. The manuscript was in all likelihood produced for the community of chaplains at the Hospital of St Giles (also known as the Great Hospital) in the city. Nine diagrams in this book indicate the choreography of important processions, most of which were unique in the liturgical year and hence required special preparation, especially those in Holy Week and on Easter Day. The liturgical ministers are identified by signs that indicate their role, such as a thurible, processional cross or a pair of candlesticks. A tonsured head (a small white circle surrounded by a thick circle of hair) marks the priest, the deacon and the subdeacon, and the celebrant is usually shown by a stylised cope (see Figure 8.2). For particular ceremonies, material objects are on display, such as the paschal candle, the baptismal font or vessels for the holy oils.[82] These illustrations are the earliest of their kind and do not seem to have been imitated until the sixteenth century, when similar diagrams appear in printed Sarum processionals (in the form of woodcuts).[83] Francis Wormald, who owned the manuscript and first drew attention to the diagrams, notes their unique character in comparison with the figurative depictions of ceremonies found in deluxe pontificals and coronation books: 'These are idealized representations and are quite distinct from the more utilitarian diagrams of our manuscript, which record the exact positions of those in the procession at certain specified points in the

---

[81] See Monti, *A Sense of the Sacred*, 13–14.

[82] See Francis Wormald, 'A Medieval Processional and Its Diagrams', in *Kunsthistorische Forschungen: Otto Pächt zu seinem 70. Geburtstag*, ed. Artur Rosenauer and Gerold Weber (Salzburg: Residenz Verlag, 1972), 129–134, at 131; also Aden Kumler, '*Imitatio Rerum*: Sacred Objects in the St. Giles's Hospital Processional', in *Journal of Medieval and Early Modern Studies* 44 (2014), 469–502.

[83] See Karl Drew Hartzell, 'Diagrams for Liturgical Ceremonies: Late 14th Century', in *Local Maps and Plans from Medieval England*, ed. Raleigh A. Skelton and Paul D. A. Harvey (Oxford: Clarendon Press, 1986), 339–341.

Figure 8.2 Processional of Sarum Use, adapted for the Diocese of Norwich / The blessing of holy water on Sunday / Late fourteenth or early fifteenth century (© The British Library Board, Add. MS 57534, fol. 3v / Reprinted with kind permission)

ceremony'.[84] Wormald suggests that 'the diagrams grew out of the roster or tabula on which were set out day by day the various [liturgical] duties' of the clerical community.[85]

Against the backdrop of increasing concern for precise performance of liturgical ceremonial emerged the work that was to become decisive for the further development of the ritual shape of the Roman Mass, the *Ordo Missae* of Johann Burchard. The first edition of 1496 is presented as an 'Order to be observed by a priest in the celebration of Mass without chant and without ministers according to the rite of the holy Roman church', which is compiled for the purpose of 'the instruction of newly ordained priests'.[86] The 1498 reprint, which is largely identical with its predecessor except for a few minor additions, notes at this point that the *ordo* is written not with rhetorical flourish but in plain and accessible language.[87] The second edition of 1502 retains the initial description but omits the phrase about the educational scope of the work. However, in his dedication letter to Cardinal Bernardino López de Carvajal, then Cardinal-Priest of Santa Croce in Gerusalemme, Burchard explains the reasons for compiling and publishing this *Ordo Missae*:

Engaged from my youth in the sacred ceremonies ... when I saw that not a few priests in the celebration of Mass frequently imitated many abuses, and diverse rites and unsuitable gestures, I thought it unworthy that there is no definite norm transmitted to the priests by the holy Roman Church, Mother and Teacher of all the churches, to be universally observed in the celebration of Mass. Therefore, I have gathered these ceremonies together and published them; they are taken from the various decrees of the holy fathers, which the Supreme Pontiffs have instituted for the above-mentioned celebration. And when I recently reviewed the collection of the same, I discovered that more ceremonies had been omitted than handed on. I added, therefore, what was necessary, and as much as I was able, completed the work.[88]

---

[84] Wormald, 'A Medieval Processional and Its Diagrams', 132.   [85] Ibid.

[86] Johann Burchard, *Ordo missae secundum consuetudinem Romanae ecclesiae* (Rome: Andreas Fritag and Johann Besicken, 1496) (ISTC ib01284400). There are no page numbers in the copy of the Niedersächsische Staats- und Universitätsbibliothek Göttingen, which was made available to me through the good offices of Professor Jörg Bölling.

[87] See Johann Burchard, *Ordo missae secundum consuetudinem Romanae ecclesiae* (Rome: Stephan Plannck, 1498) (ISTC ib01284500), 2r. The book has been digitised by the Biblioteca Apostolica Vaticana and is accessible at https://digi.vatlib.it/view/Inc.IV.528.

[88] Johann Burchard, *Ordo missae* (Rome: Johannes Besicken, 1502); cited after *Tracts on the Mass*, ed. John Wickham Legg, Henry Bradshaw Society 27 (London: Harrison, 1904), 121–174, at 121–122. The English translation is taken, with minor modifications, from Cassian Folsom, 'Gestures Accompanying the Words of

Complaints about a lack of uniformity and abuses in the liturgy, owing to the poor formation of priests and the lack of reliable books, are somewhat commonplace in this period. There can be no doubt that such problems existed, but we can hardly gauge how widespread they were. Any reformer (and Burchard urges the rhetoric of 'reformare' in the letter to his patron) tends to paint the present situation in dark colours so as to motivate his own agenda. The scope of the 1502 *ordo*, which was printed with a letter of approval from Pope Alexander VI, is much broader than its predecessor: Burchard insists that its ceremonial instructions also apply to cardinals and prelates, including the Supreme Pontiff, when they celebrate Mass not pontifically but in private ('non ... pontificaliter sed in priuato').[89] The *Ordo Missae* of 1502 was widely received, was published in an Italian translation in 1534 and was inserted into some printed editions of the *Missale Romanum* from 1541.[90]

Burchard thoroughly reworked his earlier *ordo* for the new edition, which offers much more detailed and comprehensive rubrical instructions. Now the ritual performance of gestures and movements is precisely regulated and meticulously explained. By contrast, the *Ordinarium Missae* (named after its incipit 'Paratus sacerdos'), which was integrated into the Roman Missal and contained the recurring parts of the rite, was largely limited to prayer texts and only had room for very few rubrics.[91] Thus, Burchard's *ordo* can be best understood in continuity with the ordinal *Indutus planeta* (see Chapter 7).

The *Ordo Missae* edited by Burchard follows the use of the Roman curia, which had been established in the thirteenth century, with important specifications at three stages of the rite: Firstly, in the introductory rites, Psalm 42 (*Iudica me*) is recited at the foot of the altar (which was Roman practice at least since *Indutus planeta*), rather than in the sacristy or in procession to the sanctuary, as was common in diocesan uses.[92]

Consecration in the History of the *Ordo Missae*', in *The Veneration and Administration of the Eucharist: The Proceedings of the Second International Colloquium on the Roman Catholic Liturgy Organised by the Centre International d'Etudes Liturgiques* (Southampton: Saint Austin Press, 1997), 75–94, at 78–79.

[89] Burchard, *Ordo missae* 1502; ed. Wickham Legg, *Tracts on the Mass*, 126.

[90] See Pierre Jounel, *Les rites de la Messe: Ritus servandus in celebratione Missae* (Tournai: Desclée, 1963), 10.

[91] See the *Ordinarium Missae* in the *editio princeps* of 1474 and subsequent editions, in *Missale Romanum Mediolani, 1474*, ed. Lippe, vol. I, 198–211 and vol. II, 98–117.

[92] Burchard, *Ordo missae* 1502, ed. Wickham Legg, *Tracts on the Mass*, 133–135; see Josef A. Jungmann, *Missarum sollemnia: Eine genetische Erklärung der römischen Messe*, 2 vols., 5th ed. (Wien: Herder, 1962), vol. I, 381–382.

Secondly, while the offertory rite is fixed in its curial form, the 1502 *ordo* (but not the earlier edition) includes an offertory procession, which still had some currency at the time.[93] After reading the offertory verse, the celebrant goes to the epistle side of the altar, removes his maniple and accepts the (undetermined) gifts from the faithful who each kiss his hand. The celebrant responds by saying either 'May your sacrifice be acceptable to almighty God' or 'May you receive a hundredfold, and possess eternal life' (see Mt 19:29). Having received the offering, the celebrant takes the maniple again, goes to the middle of the altar and continues with the offertory rite. Thirdly, in the concluding rites the final blessing follows after the prayer *Placeat tibi sancta Trinitas*, not vice versa, as in some diocesan uses and in early printed Roman Missals.[94] The 'Last Gospel' (Jn 1:1–14), which was not yet in general use and is not included in early printed Roman Missals, is to be read at the altar rather than said in a low voice from memory as the celebrant returns to the sacristy (as was the practice in the Roman pontifical high Mass and in some diocesan uses).[95] The rationale for this particular change may have been to focus on the sacred texts and their authentic meaning and to avoid a perfunctory recitation.

The most significant innovation in Burchard's *ordo* concerns the reverential gesture for the consecrated Eucharist: when the celebrant has pronounced the dominical words over the bread, he is instructed to genuflect as a sign of adoration ('genuflexus eam adorat'). Then he elevates the host and after having placed it on the corporal again he genuflects a second time. In the same manner, the consecration of the chalice is followed by a genuflection before and after the elevation.[96] The genuflection replaces the 'medium bow' that is indicated in *Indutus planeta* for the adoration of the body of the Lord.[97] Until the later Middle Ages, bowing towards the consecrated species remained the priest's liturgical gesture of adoration, while kneeling in the presence of

[93] Burchard, *Ordo missae* 1502, ed. Wickham Legg, *Tracts on the Mass*, 149; see Jungmann, *Missarum sollemnia*, vol. II, 23–25.

[94] Burchard, *Ordo missae* 1502, ed. Wickham Legg, *Tracts on the Mass*, 166–167; see Jungmann, *Missarum sollemnia*, vol. II, 552–553.

[95] Burchard, *Ordo missae* 1502, ed. Wickham Legg, *Tracts on the Mass*, 167–168; see Jungmann, *Missarum sollemnia*, vol. II, 556–557.

[96] Burchard, *Ordo missae* 1502, ed. Wickham Legg, *Tracts on the Mass*, 156–157.

[97] 'Adorato corpore Domini cum mediocri inclinatione …'; *Indutus planeta*, in *Sources of the Modern Roman Liturgy: The Ordinals by Haymo of Faversham and Related Documents, 1243–1307*, ed. Stephen J. P. van Dijk, 2 vols., Studia et documenta franciscana 1–2 (Leiden: Brill, 1963) vol. II, 11.

the sacrament was a characteristic expression of lay piety. Some priests in Germany introduced a genuflection on both knees after the words of consecration, but this appeared impractical in the ritual setting of the Mass. Peter Browe surmises that there was reticence to adopt the short genuflection on one knee only, either because it could be interpreted as a lack of reverence or because it was used in court ceremonial.[98] Nonetheless, the new practice was gaining currency in the late fifteenth and early sixteenth century.[99] The Roman pontifical of 1485 (*Pontificalis liber*), edited by Patrizi with the collaboration of Burchard, appears to be the first liturgical book prescribing a genuflection instead of a bow for the adoration of the consecrated host.[100] Burchard's *ordo* of 1502 systematically stipulates genuflections, not only for the double consecration of bread and wine but also in subsequent moments of the rite when a sign of reverence to the body and blood of Christ is called for (when the priest uncovers or covers the chalice with the pall, and when he takes the consecrated host).

Burchard's innovation met with the sharp disapproval of his successor, Paride Grassi, who tried to strip the papal ceremonial of a number of elements that had been adopted in the later medieval period. In particular, Grassi accuses Burchard of failing to cite an authority or precedent for his new practice, since bowing was the traditional liturgical sign of reverence for the body and blood of Christ.[101] However, Grassi's critique remained a passing episode, as Burchard's rubrics were gaining currency and were adopted in the post-Tridentine *Missale Romanum* of 1570 (see Chapter 9).

THE MASS AND SACRED POLYPHONY

In the Western tradition, the relationship between liturgy and music had been settled for centuries by the creation of Gregorian chant (see Chapter 6), which achieved a remarkable harmony between theological demands on sacred music and the natural desire for artistic expression. As the musicologist William Mahrt notes, the musical form created by

---

[98] See Peter Browe, 'Die Elevation in der Messe', in *Die Eucharistie im Mittelalter*, 475–508 (originally published in *Bonner Zeitschrift für Theologie und Seelsorge* 8 [1931], 20–66), at 493.

[99] See ibid., 495–496.

[100] *Il 'Pontificalis liber' di Agostino Patrizi Piccolomini e Giovanni Burcardo (1485)*, Edizione anastatica, ed. Manlio Sodi, Monumenta Studia Instrumenta Liturgica 43 (Vatican City: Libreria Editrice Vaticana, 2006), 567 (no. 1909).

[101] See Bölling, *Das Papstzeremoniell der Renaissance*, 97–99.

different genres of chant for the liturgical text is integrated into the structure and movement of the ritual action.[102]

However, the question was bound to come up again with the expansion of sacred polyphony, which had its roots in the early medieval period and flourished especially in twelfth- and thirteenth-century Paris. The move of the papacy to Avignon in 1309 brought into contact the traditional Roman practice of plainchant and the French and Burgundian polyphonic *ars nova*, which was introduced to the papal court. In 1324/25, the Avignon Pope John XXII (r. 1316–1334) issued the decree *Docta Sanctorum Patrum*, which is the first known papal document dealing directly with sacred music.[103] The decree is a remarkable combination of canonical norms, technical observations and comments on the moral effects of music. The pope invokes the authority of the 'holy fathers' and follows Thomas Aquinas in stating that the purpose of singing in the liturgy is to kindle the devotion of the faithful.[104] The decree goes on to censure the rhythmic complexities of the *ars nova*, but it does not attempt to ban polyphonic singing altogether, as the Dominican Order did at its Chapter General in Bologna in 1242.[105] John XXII states that he does not intend

to forbid the occasional use – principally on solemn feasts at Mass and in the Divine Office – of certain consonant intervals superposed upon the simple ecclesiastical chant, provided these harmonies are in the spirit and character of the melodies themselves, as, for instance, the consonance of the octave, the fifth, the fourth, and others of this nature: but always on condition that the melodies themselves remain intact in the pure integrity of their form and that no innovation take place against true musical discipline, for such consonances are pleasing to the ear and arouse devotion, and they prevent torpor among those who sing in honour of God.[106]

Going into considerable musical detail, the decree approves the use – on festive occasions – of organum, which is based on plainchant and belongs

---

[102] See William Mahrt, 'Toward a Revision of *Music in Catholic Worship*', in *Sacred Music* 134 (2007), 54–60, esp. 56.

[103] See Robert F. Hayburn, *Papal Legislation on Sacred Music: 95 A.D. to 1977 A.D.* (Collegeville: Liturgical Press, 1979, reprinted Harrison: Roman Catholic Books, 2006), 17–23. For a critical analysis of the decree, see Helmut Hucke, 'Das Dekret "Docta Sanctorum Patrum" Papst Johannes' XXII.', in *Musica Disciplina* 38 (1984), 119–131.

[104] 'Dulcis quippe omnino sonus in ore psallentium resonat, quum Deum corde suscipiunt, dum loquuntur verbis, in ipsum quoque cantibus devotionem accendunt'; cited in Hucke, 'Das Dekret', 121.

[105] 'Cantus debet fieri ... sollemnius in diebus festivis, semper vero sine discantu et organo'; cited in Hucke, 'Das Dekret', 123.

[106] Translation Hayburn, *Papal Legislation on Sacred Music*, 21, slightly modified.

to the practice of *ars antiqua*. John XXII stipulates that in sacred music the formal structure of chant be preserved both in its tonality (modes) and in its particular rhythmic movement. What makes plainchant eminently suitable to the liturgy can be understood in comparison with the more elaborate forms of polyphony that do not meet with approval in the papal document.[107] Although this is not made explicit in *Docta Sanctorum Patrum*, it would seem right to conclude, as Joseph Ratzinger does, that a primary concern is the music's relation to the text – and, we may add, to the rite; on both counts, plainchant is considered exemplary. For this reason, the decree makes 'reference to the formal structures of the chant as the point of departure for ecclesiastical polyphony'.[108]

The papal intervention had only limited success in steering the development of sacred music. The burgeoning of polyphony in the late medieval and early modern periods led to Mass settings that were conceived as autonomous works of art and tended to overlay the liturgical rite. As Josef Andreas Jungmann has argued, the practice emerging in the twelfth and thirteenth centuries that the celebrant would recite the ordinary and proper chants separately in the sung Mass detached the choir from its original liturgical role and gave it a more secular character.[109] Against this backdrop, it is noteworthy that a string of conciliar and episcopal legislation from the fifteenth century onwards condemns the abbreviation or even omission of parts of the rite for the sake of musical compositions. The problem was considered serious enough that it was included in the condemnation of liturgical abuses at the seventeenth general council of the Roman Catholic Church, which was convoked in Basel in 1431, moved to Ferrara and then to Florence, where it was concluded in 1449. In 1435, the Council of Basel denounced the malpractice 'of some churches' where the creed is not sung in its entirety, or where the preface or the Lord's Prayer is omitted.[110] Sources from the middle of the

---

[107] See Karl Gustav Fellerer, 'Die Constitutio Docta SS. Patrum Johannes XXII.', in *Geschichte der katholischen Kirchenmusik. Bd. 1: Von den Anfängen bis zum Tridentinum*, ed. Karl Gustav Fellerer (Kassel: Bärenreiter, 1972), 379–380.

[108] See Joseph Ratzinger, 'The Artistic Transposition of the Faith: Theological Problems of Church Music', in *Theology of the Liturgy: The Sacramental Foundation of Christian Existence*, ed. Michael J. Miller, trans. John Saward, et al., Joseph Ratzinger Collected Works 11 (San Francisco: Ignatius Press, 2014), 480–493 (originally published in 1978), at 492.

[109] See Jungmann, *Missarum sollemnia*, vol. I, 141.

[110] Council of Basel, 21st Session (9 June 1435), in *Conciliorum Oecumenicorum Decreta*, ed. Giuseppe Alberigo et al., 3rd ed (Bologna: Istituto per le Scienze Religiose, 1973), 491.

sixteenth century add the epistle to the parts of the Mass that are trun-
cated or left out.[111] Wolfgang Fuhrmann associates such phenomena with
the emergence of the cyclic Mass composition, in which the disparate
movements of the ordinary are unified by sharing a musical theme (*cantus
firmus*). The idea of omitting certain parts of the Mass would seem
motivated by the desire to experience the unity of the musical composition.[112] Evidently, such issues could arise only in places where the
material resources were available to employ a considerable number of
professional singers, including cathedrals, collegiate churches, major religious houses and court chapels. Salisbury Cathedral offers an interesting
example of changing attitudes: between about 1450 and 1549 (when the
first edition of the *Book of Common Prayer* was published) its choir was
transformed from a large group of up to fifty-two vicars choral and
fourteen boy choristers whose main duty consisted in liturgical plainchant to a compact and highly skilled ensemble of some twenty men
(some of them professional lay musicians) and fourteen boys who were
mainly occupied with the new polyphonic repertory.[113] Such a shift did
not automatically lead to an emphasis on aesthetic performance at the
expense of the integrity of the rite. However, the gap between liturgy
and music certainly widened in the period of transition to
early modernity.

TRANSFORMATIONS IN CHURCH ARCHITECTURE

The typical interior of a late medieval church was not conceived as a
unified space but was structured by a complex system of limits and
barriers. While the Western Church never went as far as the Byzantine
tradition, which introduced an iconostasis that separates the sanctuary
completely from the nave, screens served to emphasise the sacredness of

---

[111] See the documentation by Wolfgang Fuhrmann, '"Semper reformanda": Motiv- und
Argumentationstraditionen der liturgisch-musikalischen Reform', in *Papsttum und
Kirchenmusik vom Mittelalter bis zu Benedikt XVI*, 28–56, at 52–56.
[112] See ibid., 48. For an introduction to the cyclic Mass, see Richard Taruskin, *Music from
the Earliest Notations to the Sixteenth Century*, The Oxford History of Western Music 1
(Oxford: Oxford University Press, 2006), 459–460; and, for a revisionist account,
Andrew Kirkman, 'The Invention of the Cyclic Mass', in *Journal of the American
Musicological Society* 54 (2001), 1–47.
[113] See Roger Bowers, 'The Reform of the Choir of Salisbury Cathedral, *c.*1450–1549', in
Late Medieval Liturgies Enacted, 157–176.

the high altar. While such structures impeded the view of the laity, they also engaged their devotion by appealing to a mystical reality. From the late twelfth century, a rood screen (*jubé* in French and *Lettner* in German) was installed in larger churches to divide the chancel with the high altar from the nave. Cathedral, collegiate and monastic churches generally had an altar in front of the rood screen where Masses were offered for the laity (see Figure 8.3). Hence this altar was known in Germany as 'altar of the laity' (*Laienaltar*) or 'altar of the cross' (*Kreuzaltar*). Side altars and enclosed chapels added to the 'liminal zones' within the edifice, and the crossing of such a threshold (*limen*) was associated with a particular ritual, for instance, entrance to the body of the church by the sacrament of baptism and access to the altar by the sacrament of holy orders.[114] The late medieval winged altarpiece, which could be opened and closed, as well as veiled with lateral curtains or with a Lenten cloth, highlighted the altar as the liminal sphere par excellence that creates a passage between heaven and earth by means of the Eucharistic sacrifice. Textile furnishings had no liturgical function in Western tradition but were employed to conceal and reveal distinct sacred spaces within the church building. Moreover, decorated curtains had their own iconography and so offered forms of visual participation to the faithful. In the fourteenth and fifteenth centuries, two particular focal points were added in churches north of the Alps: a monumental 'sacrament house' (*Sakramentshaus*) in the chancel for the reservation of the Eucharist and an elevated and often ornate pulpit, made of wood or stone, in the nave (usually on the gospel side), in keeping with the late medieval emphasis on preaching.[115]

Around the same time and starting in Italy, new architectural ideas were to have significant consequences for the performance and

---

[114] See the various contributions in *The Notion of Liminality and the Medieval Sacred Space*, ed. Klára Doležalová and Ivan Foletti, Convivium Supplementum 3 (Turnhout: Brepols, 2020). The work of social anthropologists, such as Arnold van Gennep and Victor Turner, has brought into relief the concept of liminality – a state 'betwixt and between' that can be fruitfully applied to liturgy as a spatial, temporal, and ritual category.

[115] See Gabriela Signori, 'Einheit in der Vielfalt? Annäherungen an den "vorreformatorischen" Kirchenraum', in *Konfessionen im Kirchenraum: Dimensionen des Sakralraums in der frühen Neuzeit*, ed. Susanne Wegmann and Gabriele Wimböck, Studien zur Kunstgeschichte des Mittelalters und der frühen Neuzeit 3 (Korb: Didymos-Verlag, 2007), 215–234, at 219–226; and *Räume, Gesten, Andachtsformen*, 24–35.

Figure 8.3 Rogier van der Weyden / Seven Sacraments Altarpiece / c. 1445–1450
(In the background of the central panel a priest offers Mass at the altar in front of the chancel
screen. In the chancel behind the screen, a solemn Mass is celebrated and a deacon is depicted
singing the gospel at an eagle lectern. The left panel of the triptych shows another Mass at a
side altar with a small congregation. / Antwerp, Royal Museum of Fine Arts / Wikipedia
Commons, Public Domain)

experience of the sacred liturgy. Renaissance architecture transformed the typical church interior by creating a unified space. There
was an unobstructed view of the main sanctuary from the nave, with
its focal point on the high altar and, increasingly, on the reserved

Eucharist.[116] The introduction of a fixed tabernacle on the high altar is usually associated with the liturgical reforms that were implemented after the Council of Trent. However, this practice was already promoted by reforming bishops before Trent and can be traced back to fifteenth-century Tuscany. High-altar tabernacles were introduced in several churches of this Italian region, including the cathedrals of Volterra (1471) and Prato (1487); perhaps the best-known example is the splendid bronze tabernacle made between 1467 and 1472 by Vecchietta for the high altar of the church of the Santa Maria della Scala hospital in Siena, which was transferred to the city's cathedral in 1506, where it replaced Duccio's *Maestà*.[117]

The unified church interior gave the liturgical rites in the sanctuary greater visibility and so enhanced their potential for engaging the congregation. At the same time, the pastoral functions of the nave as the place of preaching and of sacramental confession were brought into greater relief. Such transformations would come to full fruition in the post-Tridentine reform.

CONCLUSION

The approaches to the liturgy of the Mass in the later Middles Ages that I have pursued in this chapter do not yield a homogeneous picture. The period is marked by complex and diverse phenomena. A personal and reflective faith as epitomised in the *devotio moderna* movement existed alongside a buoyant religious practice centred on the tangible and material. The *Ordo Missae* after the model of the Roman curia was widely adopted throughout the Western Church, while increasingly detailed rubrication supported a standardised form of celebrating Mass. At the same time, a variety of diocesan and religious uses persisted and liturgical texts were composed locally, especially for votive Masses that arose from particular devotions, such as the holy face of Christ. The laity's experience of the liturgy was clearly separate from that of the officiating clergy, not least because of the use of Latin as a sacred language. Nonetheless, forms

---

[116] See Jörg Stabenow, 'Introduzione', in *Lo spazio e il culto: Relazioni tra edificio ecclesiale e uso liturgico dal XV al XVI secolo*, ed. Jörg Stabenow (Venice: Marsilio, 2006), 9–23, at 11–13.

[117] See Hans Caspary, *Das Sakramentstabernakel in Italien bis zum Konzil von Trient: Gestalt, Ikonographie und Symbolik, kultische Funktion*, 3rd ed. (Munich: Uni-Druck, 1969), 52–67.

of popular participation were offered not only by verbal elements, such as the prayer of the faithful, but also by non-verbal symbols, such as the pax, that spoke powerfully to the people and made the Mass a social institution that was deeply rooted in their cycle of life. There were aspects of the Church's role in society that made it vulnerable and called for reform, but the sacramental system and its liturgical expression proved to be remarkably resilient.

9

The Tridentine Reform

The final chapter of this book will examine the liturgical reform that was initiated by the Council of Trent (1545–1563), with particular focus on the 1570 edition of the *Missale Romanum*, which was promulgated in its aftermath. After a consideration of the state of the Roman Mass on the eve of the council, I will survey the conciliar deliberations and decrees concerning the liturgy. Against the background of early modern developments, I will the discuss the significance of the post-Tridentine missal, giving special attention to the ritual shape of the Mass.

LITURGICAL LIFE ON THE EVE OF TRENT

As discussed in Chapter 8, the liturgical practice of the late medieval Western Church was not in a general state of decay and decadence, but there were certainly aspects in need of correction. Early modern reformers observed that priests exhibited signs of greed, a lack of preparation, carelessness in liturgical functions or disregard for rubrics. Such grievances can be seen as part of the general critique of the state of the clergy and the appeals for renewal, which were concerns widely shared at the time. A good example for the changing mentality is the *missa sicca* ('dry Mass'), which consisted of a complete Mass formulary, except the offertory, the canon and communion. This form of devotion was used for funerals or marriages held in the afternoon when (because of strict fasting rules) no Mass could be celebrated, at sea when there would be a danger of spilling the chalice, or when visiting the sick and the dying. The dry Mass was considered acceptable in the later Middle Ages, and

Johannes Burchard's *Ordo Missae* provides instructions for it.[1] By the time of the Council of Trent, however, it was denounced as a liturgical abuse.

As shown in Chapter 8, along with the standardisation effected by the adoption of the *Ordo Missae* according to the custom of the Roman curia, the variety of liturgical uses for dioceses and religious orders continued in the later medieval period. The invention of printing added to this diversity, since missals and other liturgical books were often produced at the initiative of master printers and without episcopal control. Calls for greater liturgical unification made themselves heard long before Trent. In the early period of the Council of Constance (1414–1418) the anonymous author of a treatise calling for a reform of the church lamented the 'discordia et discordancia magna' of different liturgical uses and called for a conformity to the practice of the Roman church.[2] About a century later, in 1513, the *Libellus* addressed to Pope Leo X by two hermits of Camaldoli, Paolo Giustiniani and Pietro Quirini, included among its considerations for church reform an appeal for a unified celebration of Mass and other ceremonies.[3]

The profound rupture of the Protestant Reformation had a momentous impact on liturgical life. Martin Luther (1483–1546) offered a radical critique of the sacrificial character of the Mass and condemned the Roman canon. However, he changed the ritual structure of the Mass only gradually and in many Lutheran church orders some elements that had a popular appeal were retained, including Eucharistic vestments and the

---

[1] Johann Burchard, *Ordo missae* (Rome: Johannes Besicken, 1502), cited after *Tracts on the Mass*, ed. John Wickham Legg, Henry Bradshaw Society 27 (London: Harrison, 1904), 173–174. See Adolph Franz, *Die Messe im deutschen Mittelalter: Beiträge zur Geschichte der Liturgie und des religiösen Volkslebens* (Freiburg im Breisgau: Herder, 1902), 73–86. The *missa bifaciata* or *trifaciata*, in which the priest would say the parts of the Mass from the introit to the preface two or three times, and then continue with the canon, with the idea of fulfilling several Mass intentions, was already condemned in the high Middle Ages. This practice is not mentioned in synodal legislation after the early fourteenth century and seems to have died out by the early modern period.

[2] *Acta Concilii Constantiensis*, ed. Heinrich Finke, 4 vols. (Münster: Regensbergsche Buchhandlung, 1896–1928), vol. II, 591.

[3] Stephen M. Beall has published a revised version of the text from *Annales Camaldulenses Ordinis Sancti Benedicti*, ed. Giovanni B. Mittarelli and Anselmo Costadoni, vol. IX (Venice: Monasterium Sancti Michaelis De Muriano, 1773), 612–719, as well as an English translation, available at https://marquette.academia.edu/StephenBeall. See Jedin, 'Das Konzil von Trient und die Reform der liturgischen Bücher', 8–9.

elevation of the consecrated species.[4] In central and northern Europe, an ever-greater liturgical divergence ensued, which, contrary to the well-known adage *lex orandi lex credendi*, would not always reflect doctrinal differences. Other Reformers, such as Huldrych Zwingli (1484–1531) in Zurich, as well as the compilers of the English *Book of Common Prayer* (especially in its second edition of 1552), went much further in their rejection of the medieval liturgical tradition. The varied history of Reformed and Anglican worship is beyond the scope of this book.[5]

THE COUNCIL OF TRENT

The rivalry between the Kingdom of France and the House of Habsburg, which ruled Spain and held the throne of the Holy Roman Empire, delayed the convocation of a general council to address the acute crisis of the Catholic Church for several years. When the council finally assembled in the city of Trent, which was part of the empire but on Italian soil, its twofold agenda was shaped by the doctrinal challenges of the Protestant Reformers and the need for reform of the Church's discipline. This included a reaffirmation of Catholic doctrine on the sacraments and the Mass, as well as the demand to address liturgical abuses. The compromise that had been reached between pope and emperor meant that matters of doctrine and of church reform were treated in parallel. Hence, calls for renewed liturgical discipline were heard already during the council's first period from December 1545 to March 1547. However, the question was resumed in earnest only in its last period, from January 1562 to December 1563, alongside the deliberations about the decree on the sacrifice of the Mass.

As Hubert Jedin has observed, the nations represented at the council expressed a strong desire for a unified missal.[6] The request was included

---

[4] See Bryan D. Spinks, *Do This in Remembrance of Me: The Eucharist from the Early Church to the Present Day* (London: SCM Press, 2013), 246–271; and Helmut Hoping, *My Body Given for You: History and Theology of the Eucharist*, trans. Michael J. Milller (San Francisco: Ignatius Press, 2019), 223–235.

[5] See Spinks, *Do This in Remembrance of Me*, 272–312 ('The Reformed Tradition: From Ulrich Zwingli to Eugène Bersier') and 313–346 ('The Anglican Tradition: From Thomas Cranmer to Tractarian Disputes').

[6] The following discussion is largely based on Hubert Jedin, 'Das Konzil von Trient und die Reform des Römischen Meßbuches', in *Liturgisches Leben* 6 (1939), 30–66, at 37–45; and 'Das Konzil von Trient und die Reform der liturgischen Bücher', in *Ephemerides Liturgicae* 59 (1945), 5–38, at 28–30.

in the substantial list of petitions submitted in 1561 by Bartolomeu dos
Mártires (1514–1590), archbishop of Braga in Portugal.[7] In early March
1562, a memorandum from a group of Italian prelates close to the
Augustinian Cardinal Girolamo Seripando (1493–1563) recommended
the reform and standardisation of liturgical books.[8] A clear statement
came from the Spanish bishops in early April 1562. In a memorandum
presented to the legates of the council, they suggested a unified breviary
and missal 'used in all churches' with a separate proper of saints for each
diocese.[9] Emperor Ferdinand I (1503–1564) had a *libellus reformationis*
sent to the assembly, in which he petitioned the revision of liturgical
books and the removal of apocryphal elements, as well as the permission
to sing psalms and hymns in German.[10] The emperor's intervention is
significant in that it signals the failure of attempts to reform the liturgy on
a local and regional level, by means of provincial councils and imperial
diets. The matter was handed over to the initiative of the general council.
A contrasting voice came from France: in January 1563, the French
representatives at Trent presented their own *libellus reformationis* with
a list of liturgical reform measures, which included the demand for more
extensive use of the vernacular in the Mass and in the administration of
the sacraments but said nothing about a reform of missal or breviary.[11]
The French bishops wanted to keep the oversight over liturgical books for
themselves rather than relinquish it to the council or to the pope.

The conciliar debates on the doctrine of the sacrifice of the Mass were
accompanied by a discussion of concrete steps towards liturgical reform.
At a general congregation of the council on 20 July 1562, a commission
was instituted to study this question. On 8 August 1562, this commission

---

[7] *Petitiones, quas Venerabilis servus Dei Bartholomaeus a Martyribus in concilio facere intendebat*, in *Concilium Tridentinum: Diariorum, Actorum, Epistularum, Tractatuum Nova Collectio*, ed. Societas Goerresiana (Freiburg: Herder, 1901–), vol. XIII/1, 544: 'Sacerdotes celebrent iuxta missale Romanum, nihil addentes vel minuentes, et quae alta voce et intelligibili et quae secrete dicenda sunt, [ita] dicant.'

[8] *Quae potissimum restituenda et emendanda videntur*, in ibid., 610: 'Tam breviaria quam missalia reformanda essent et a multis ineptiis purganda.'

[9] *Reformatio ab Hispanis concepta Tridenti sub Pio IV*, in ibid., 627: 'Videatur, an expediret unum breviarium et unum missale fieri, quod ad omnes ecclesias deserviret, exceptis sanctis cuiusque dioceseos, de quibus in brevi libello posset notari varietas.'

[10] *Petitiones a S. Caes. M.tis consiliariis et aliis a S. M. deputatis exhibitae, ut earum a s. synodo Tridentina aliqua habeatur ratio et consideratio*, in ibid., 671.

[11] See Jedin, 'Das Konzil von Trient und die Reform des Römischen Meßbuches', 39–40; and 'Das Konzil von Trient und die Reform der liturgischen Bücher', 29–30.

produced a dossier on liturgical issues,[12] the contents of which can be divided into three broad categories:

Firstly, there were observations of a doctrinal character. For instance, the question was raised whether it was correct to refer to the unconsecrated elements of bread and wine as *immaculata hostia* ('spotless victim') and *calix salutaris* ('chalice of salvation') in the offertory prayers. Likewise, the legitimacy of making the sign of the cross over the consecrated species after the words of institution in the Canon of the Mass was proposed for discussion.

Secondly, there were comments that reflected the new historical consciousness of Renaissance Humanists, who promoted a return *ad fontes*, that is, to the (biblical and patristic) sources of the Catholic tradition. The concrete proposals for reform include the purging from liturgical texts of apocryphal material that was clearly not historical, and of texts that were considered superstitious, especially in votive Masses. These concerns reflect the aspiration to give priority to the traditional order of the Roman liturgy over forms of private devotion and personal piety. The ideal of the *norma patrum* ('norm of the fathers') would later be enshrined in the bull promulgating the *Missale Romanum* of 1570.

Thirdly, there were indications of liturgical malpractice on the part of the clergy, which had been denounced by reformers both Protestant and Catholic. These included the neglect of sacred vessels, ignorance of or disregard for rubrics on the part of priests and dubious practices, such as the *missa sicca*. There can be no doubt that such abuses really happened, but it is hard to say how pervasive they really were. Any reformer is inclined to make the picture of the present situation as bleak as possible. Rhetorical emphasis, if not exaggeration, is often used as a tool to advance one's own reforming agenda.

In late August 1562, the dossier on liturgical abuses was condensed to a compendium, which retained the demand for a unified missal and stated the need for standardised rubrics very clearly; it also claimed the project of reforming the missal for the agenda of the council itself, so that the local ordinaries would then have a secure foundation for their own particular reform measures.[13] However, this shorter text did not make

---

[12] Council of Trent, Session XXII, *Abusus, qui circa venerandum missae sacrificium evenire solent, partim a patribus deputatis animadversi, partim ex multorum praelatorum dictis et scriptis excerpti* (8 August 1562), in *Concilium Tridentinum*, vol. VIII, 916–921.

[13] Council of Trent, Session XXII, *Compendium abusuum circa sacrificium missae* (c. 25 August 1562), in ibid., 921–924.

it to the council floor, as there was a concern that focusing on specific aspects of the problem would provoke objections from some council fathers, delay the current session or even threaten its successful conclusion. There was a strong desire for the widest possible consensus and hence the *Doctrine and canons on the sacrifice of the Mass* was followed by a brief *Decree concerning the things to be observed, and to be avoided, in the celebration of Mass* of 17 September 1562. The decree warns priests against avarice, idolatry, irreverence and superstition in matters of divine worship, addresses liturgical abuses in a generic sense and instructs local ordinaries to exercise oversight and to correct errors, but does not mention an actual revision of liturgical books.[14]

A new impetus for reform was given, when after the death of the Cardinal legates Ercole Gonzaga and Girolamo Seripando in March 1563, Cardinals Giovanni Morone (1509–1580) and Bernardo Navagero (1507–1565) were appointed in their stead. The discussion on liturgical books continued over the summer, and in October 1563, Charles de Guise, Cardinal of Lorraine (1524–1574), on a visit to Rome, arranged for the sending of a manuscript of the Gregorian sacramentary tradition from the Vatican Library to Trent. The Cardinal of Lorraine was not an official legate at the council but was treated as such by Morone, in order to ensure his support for Morone's energetic reform programme. The arrival of the manuscript on 25 October 1563 was a tangible symbol of the desire to prune and revise the existing missal in light of the ancient Roman tradition.[15] It is, however, extremely difficult to trace the progress of the conciliar deliberations at this point because of a lack of sources. The bishop of Salamanca, Pedro González de Mendoza (c. 1518–1574), notes in his council diary that in the general congregation of 26–27 October 1563 deputies were appointed to produce a reformed missal and breviary, but this is not noted in the official acts. Jedin suggests that no special commission (*deputatio*) was instituted but that the task of revising the liturgical books was entrusted to already existing commissions, either the one working on the index, or, more likely, the one working on the catechism. These commissions did not

<hr>

[14] Council of Trent, Session XXII, *Decretum de observandis et evitandis in celebratione missarum* (17 September 1562), in ibid., 962–963.
[15] See Amato Pietro Frutaz, 'Contributo alla storia della riforma del Messale promulgato da san Pio V nel 1570', in *Problemi di vita religiosa in Italia nel Cinquecento: Atti del Convegno di storia della Chiesa in Italia (Bologna, 2–6 sett. 1958)*, Italia Sacra 2 (Padova; Editrice Antenore, 1960), 187–214, at 188–189.

leave any minutes; at least there is no record in the acts of the council.[16] In his diary, González de Mendoza also expressed his apprehension that the work on the missal and the breviary could not be completed at the council, because it had been left so late. In fact, it seems to have been the prevailing view among the council fathers that they were not in a position to undertake the revision of liturgical books themselves.

The council was concluded prematurely on 4 December 1563, because of alarming news about the ill health of Pope Pius IV. In the final session, it was decided that several reform measures, which the council was not able to complete, should be left to the pope, among them the reform of the breviary and of the missal. The discussions among the council fathers served to establish two fundamental principles for this work: in the first place, the council fathers supported a unification of the Order of Mass and its rubrics; any celebration of Mass was meant to conform to this general standard. Secondly, there was a broad consensus that the Roman Rite should be pruned of more recent accretions, especially those containing apocryphal material, those reflecting private devotions and those judged to be superstitious.

THE *MISSALE ROMANUM* OF 1570

Soon after the council, Pope Pius IV set up commissions for the revision of liturgical books. Since the need for a reform of the breviary was considered more pressing, this task was given priority. However, work on the missal was probably undertaken in parallel, since the revised *Missale Romanum* of 1570 appeared only one and a half years after the revised *Breviarium Romanum* of 1568, a relatively short interval given the complexity of curial proceedings and the limited capacities for printing in large quantities. Once again, we face the difficulty that we do not have official records of this ongoing labour but are dependent on occasional information, found especially in personal correspondence. We have hardly any sources on the working principles and methods of the commission entrusted with the missal. Amato Pietro Frutaz discovered a *Missale secundum morem Sancte Romane Ecclesie*, printed by Giovanni Battista di Sessa in Venice in 1497, containing many annotations and corrections from the hand of Cardinal Guglielmo Sirleto (1514–1585), a

---

[16] See Jedin, 'Das Konzil von Trient und die Reform der liturgischen Bücher', 35–37; also Frutaz, 'Contributo alla storia della riforma del Messale', 188–192.

key collaborator in the post-Tridentine revision of the Vulgate text, the composition of the catechism and the reform of liturgical books. Sirleto's notes are found mainly in the calendar section, where he deleted many feasts of saints, and in the Mass Propers, where he made various changes. There are only few suggestions for modifications in the Order of Mass. The annotations show a work in progress, and by no means all of Sirleto's proposals were accepted in the 1570 edition of the *Missale Romanum*.[17]

Frutaz also discovered two relevant hand-written documents in the Vatican Library: the first is an Italian memorandum of a few pages signed by Leonardo Marini, archbishop of Lanciano, with the title *Information for the correction of the missal*.[18] This document can be dated some time before 13 October 1568, when Marini's successor, Ettore Piscicelli, was appointed to the see of Lanciano. The author's first objective is the harmonisation of the missal with the breviary, especially regarding the calendar and the biblical readings (there had been discrepancies in this regard in the existing liturgical books). The second document is an anonymous list of twelve questions in Latin, presumably emerging from the reform commission.[19] There is scope for further research here, since the longer memorandum would suggest that a study of the reform of the breviary, for which more sources are available, could shed light on the reform of the missal. Within the limits of this chapter, I shall concentrate on a comparison between the post-Tridentine missal and its predecessors.

Pope Pius V's bull of promulgation *Quo primum* of 14 July 1570 states that the missal has been restored 'to the original norm and rite of the holy fathers (*ad pristinam ... sanctorum patrum normam ac ritum*)'.[20] This statement reflects the Renaissance Humanist ideas that animated some of the proposals for reform at the council. However, caution is needed in interpreting the declared return to the fathers. Above all, we need to be aware that limiting the title '(Church) father' to normative theologians in the early centuries of Christianity is a late modern conception. The Benedictine scholar Jean Mabillon (1632–1707) still considered Bernard of Clairvaux, who died in 1153, as the last of the fathers. Even in the mid-nineteenth century, one of the great editorial projects of Jacques-Paul Migne (1800–1875), the *Patrologia Latina*, concluded with the works

---

[17] Sirleto's annotations are presented by Frutaz, 'Contributo alla storia della riforma del Messale', 197–208.

[18] Ibid., 210–213.   [19] Ibid., 213–214.

[20] *Missale Romanum: Editio Princeps (1570)*, Edizione anastatica, ed. Manlio Sodi and Achille Maria Triacca, Monumenta Liturgica Concilii Tridentini 2, 2nd ed. (Vatican City: Libreria Editrice Vaticana, 2012).

of Pope Innocent III, who died in 1216.[21] It is thus consonant with the early modern understanding of *norma patrum* that the Tridentine reform in essence follows the mixed Franco-Roman order that had been established in the city of Rome since the pontificate of Gregory VII (1073–1085) and had since then been adopted in most of the Western Church.

The process of publication of the actual missal of Pius V is somewhat obscure to us.[22] Three early printings from 1570 are known: two folio editions produced by the heirs of Bartolomeo Faletti, Giovanni Varisco and associates in Rome and in Venice, and a smaller quarto edition produced by the same printers in Rome. These three editions show the signs of hasty work: they have variants between them and contain a considerable number of errors, which were corrected in subsequent printings of 1571. From then onwards, the production of the missal was taken on by the leading printers of Europe, including Christophe Plantin in Antwerp. This peculiar episode appears to confirm the important and sometimes questionable role enterprising printers had in the making of liturgical books in the early modern period (see also Chapter 8). Despite such vicissitudes, the Roman printing of 1570 is generally considered the *editio princeps* of the Tridentine missal (see Figure 9.1).

The Order of Mass

The 'Ordinary of Mass' (*Ordinarium Missae*) in the *Missale Romanum* of 1570 (for the Latin text and an English translation, see the Appendix to this chapter) follows the use of the Roman curia and Burchard's *Ordo Missae* in its second edition of 1502 (see Chapter 8). Burchard's rubrical instructions are the main source for the *Ritus servandus in celebratione*

---

[21] See Hubertus R. Drobner, *Lehrbuch der Patrologie* (Freiburg i. Br: Herder, 1994), 3. On the question of *norma patrum* see also Stefan Heid, 'Tisch oder Altar? Hypothesen der Wissenschaft mit weitreichenden Folgen', in *Operation am lebenden Objekt: Roms Liturgiereformen von Trient bis zum Vaticanum II*, ed. Stefan Heid (Berlin: be.bra wissenschaft, 2014), 351–374, at 352–353 and 372–374.

[22] See the seminal studies by Louis Duval-Arnould, 'Notes sur l'édition princeps du Missel Tridentin', in *Memoriam Sanctorum Venerantes: Miscellanea in onore di Monsignor Victor Saxer*, Studi di antichità cristiana 48 (Vatican City: Pontificio Istituto di Archeologia Cristiana, 1992), 269–284; and 'Nouvelles recherches sur les premières impressions du "Missel tridentin" (1570–1571)', in *De l'histoire de la Brie à l'histoire des réformes: Mélanges offerts au chanoine Michel Veissière*, ed. Michèle Bardon et al. (Paris: Fédération des Sociétés historiques et archéologiques de Paris et de l'Ile de France, 1993), 121–137.

Figure 9.1 *Missale Romanum* / 1570
(Quarto edition, Rome: Heirs of Bartolomeo Faletti, Giovanni Varisco and associates, 1570,
fol. 149v–150r: Canon of the Mass [*Te igitur*] / Bischöfliche Zentralbibliothek Regensburg,
ILR 541-1570 / Reprinted with kind permission)

Missae ('Rite to be observed in the celebration of Mass') that is placed at
the beginning of the missal. The rubrics for the introductory rites specify
that Psalm 42 (*Iudica me*) is said at the foot of the altar. In liturgical
books from the later Middle Ages, we find a wide use of tropes, that is,
texts (in both poetry and prose) added to embellish or augment chant
from the Order or from the Proper of the Mass. The missal of 1570 explicitly proscribes the troping of the introit, the *Kyrie* and the *Gloria*. The
offertory follows the use of the Roman curia as codified by Burchard.
However, the offertory procession that is still included in Burchard's *ordo*
of 1502, is not retained. Anthony Chadwick suggests that this was
'probably for fear of pecuniary abuses on the part of the clergy'.[23] The
elevation of the consecrated species is preceded and followed by a
genuflection of the celebrant. As stipulated by Burchard, the final blessing
is given after the prayer *Placeat tibi sancta Trinitas*, not before, as in

---

[23] Anthony Chadwick, 'The Roman Missal of the Council of Trent', in *T&T Clark
Companion to Liturgy*, ed. Alcuin Reid (London: Bloomsbury T&T Clark, 2016),
107–131, at 115.

earlier printed editions of the Roman Missal. The Last Gospel is read in a low voice at the altar.

Calendar and Mass Propers

Considerable work was done on the liturgical calendar.[24] The very full sanctoral cycle of the pre-Tridentine books was substantially reduced, with the aim of bringing the temporal cycle to the fore again. The Roman calendar of 1568 and 1570 has 157 ferial days, not counting the octaves of feasts (which were simplified). Especially in the months of March and April, many entries of saints were removed to keep Lenten ferias as free as possible. The 'norm of the fathers' is shown in a preference for the early Christian saints, especially martyrs. From later periods mainly popes, doctors of the church, and founders of religious orders are included.[25]

There were no alterations in the structure of the temporal cycle of the liturgical year, which had been established since the early Middle Ages, and few modifications were made in its prayers, chants and readings. The most substantial change was the purging of the poetic sequences to be sung before the gospel, except those for Easter, Pentecost and Corpus Christi (as well as the Requiem Mass).

The Common of Saints was laid out more systematically, with complete Mass formularies. The number of votive Masses was reduced; their use was strictly regulated and restricted to weekday ferias.

The pruning of the sanctoral cycle and the restoration of ferial days meant that ordinarily on weekdays the Mass formulary of the preceding Sunday would be used, including its scriptural readings. The memorandum of Leonardo Marini reports a proposal to select three passages each from the Letters of St Paul and from the Gospels, which are not contained in other Mass formularies, to be used every week on ferial days, in order

---

[24] See ibid., 116–117 for a concise overview.

[25] Scholars disagree about the archetype chosen for the revision of the calendar. Theodor Klauser argued that the idea was to restore the calendar of the *ordo* of the Lateran basilica, composed by its prior Bernard in the mid-twelfth century (see Chapter 7), that is, the calendar used in the cathedral church of Rome around the time of the Gregorian reform, with the addition of more recently canonised saints. By contrast, Frutaz argues, on the basis of Sirleto's annotations, that the direct model for the work of the commission was rather the Franciscan calendar of the thirteenth century, which in turn is based on the Lateran *ordo* from the mid-twelfth century. See Frutaz, 'Contributo alla storia della riforma del Messale', 203–205.

to avoid repeating the Sunday readings.[26] Many diocesan missals in the later Middle Ages contained specific readings for Wednesdays and Fridays during the liturgical year, unless the day had a proper Mass formulary. These ferial pericopes stem from the early Roman-Frankish lectionary tradition, which was consolidated in the Carolingian period (see Chapter 5). They were not included in the plenary missal of the Roman curia and hence in the early printed editions of the *Missale Romanum*. Marini may have been aware of the ferial readings in existing diocesan missals, but he offers a wider selection of scriptural passages. The intention clearly is to present the treasury of Holy Scripture more fully in the course of the liturgical year. However, this proposal was not heeded in the 1570 edition, which rather followed the tradition of the pre-Tridentine curial missals.

THE SHAPE OF THE 'TRIDENTINE MASS'

The *Missale Romanum* of Pius V thus stands in continuity with the plenary missals of the Roman Rite in the form used by the papal curia, which go back to the thirteenth century. This continuity extends even further to the time of the Gregorian reform in the eleventh century and, in the essential structure and contents of the rite, to the papal stational Mass of *Ordo Romanus I*. Perhaps the most significant novelty concerns the form of celebration or the 'shape' of the Tridentine Mass. As has been discussed in Chapter 7, in the course of the Middle Ages the phenomenon of 'private Masses' spread widely and brought with it a simplification of ritual and a concentration of liturgical roles in the person of the priest. At the same time, the solemn or high Mass (*Missa solemnis*), with the assistance of deacon and subdeacon and the participation of cantors, remained the normative liturgical form.

The *Ordinarium Missae* of 1570 still contains some rubrical instructions for the solemn Mass and musical notation for the parts of the rite that are to be sung, including the intonations of *Gloria* and *Credo*, the prefaces, the Lord's Prayer and the dismissal. However, the comprehensive and detailed *Ritus servandus* in the opening section of the missal seems to give priority to the low Mass (*Missa lecta*),[27] which was said (rather than sung) by a priest with the assistance of one or more servers.

---

[26] See Frutaz, 'Contributo alla storia della riforma del Messale', 211–212.

[27] The term literally means 'read Mass' – compare the German phrase 'Messe lesen'.

The indications for the solemn Mass appear as additions to an underlying shape and structure, which is that of the low Mass. Hence, it can be argued that the *Ritus servandus* ratifies the shift, which began with the Franciscan ordinal *Indutus planeta* (see Chapter 7), towards an understanding that the ritual forms of the Mass were, as Chadwick has aptly put it, 'based on low Mass rather than low Mass being a reduction of the normative pontifical Mass, from which the solemn form with deacon and subdeacon is also a reduction'.[28] There were practical reasons in favour of the low Mass: above all, it was better suited to the demands of pastoral care, especially in the countryside, since it could be celebrated in places that lacked the human resources needed for the solemn liturgy. Furthermore, the simpler form of the Mass proved to be extremely useful in the worldwide missionary expansion of the Catholic Church in the early modern period. The sung liturgy was still cultivated, especially on important occasions of the Church's year[29] and the post-Tridentine period brought a flourishing of sacred music. At the same time, the conceptual shift that can be observed in the 1570 missal reversed a liturgical principle that the solemn pontifical liturgy is the normative exemplar, in which all other celebrations of Mass participate to a greater or lesser degree. This principle had shaped the development of the Roman Mass since the late ancient and early medieval periods.

The increasing prevalence of the simplified, spoken ritual meant that the sensory dimensions of the liturgy and hence the stimuli for the meditative and affective participation of the laity were curtailed. The structure of the solemn Mass is not a linear sequence but rather a complex fabric of different ritual actions that are performed simultaneously. Paul Barnwell applies to this fabric the musical concept of 'polytextuality'[30] and argues that it offered the laity various ways of engaging with it, unlike the said Mass, which shifts emphasis to the spoken word, a movement that was supported by Renaissance Humanist culture. At the same time,

---

[28] Chadwick, 'The Roman Missal of the Council of Trent', 108–109.

[29] This is shown by reports about Jesuit missionaries making every effort to sing the Office of *Tenebrae* (in polyphonic settings) even as they were sailing to their overseas destinations. Once they had established themselves in their African or South Asian missions, they introduced the celebration of *Tenebrae* there. See Robert L. Kendrick, *Singing Jeremiah: Music and Meaning in Holy Week* (Bloomington: Indiana University Press, 2014), 9–12.

[30] Paul S. Barnwell, 'The Nature of Late Medieval Worship: The Mass', in *Late Medieval Liturgies Enacted: The Experience of Worship in Cathedral and Parish Church*, ed. Sally Harper, Paul S. Barnwell and Magnus Williamson (London; New York: Routledge, 2016), 207–218, at 216–218.

the question of liturgical language came to the fore in the sixteenth century, when the Protestant Reformers, in continuity with dissident movements of the later Middle Ages, such as that of the Hussites, attacked the use of Latin in the liturgy. There was a theological rationale at the root of this critique: The Protestants' idea of divine worship being essentially a proclamation of the Word of God made them conclude that using a language that was not intelligible to the assembly was contrary to the Gospel. Martin Luther was happy to allow for some Latin, insofar as it was understood by the people, and this custom was followed for some time in Lutheran communities. John Calvin (1509–1564), on the other hand, categorically rejected the use of Latin in worship.[31]

At the Council of Trent, the question of liturgical language was debated with remarkable depth, and the arguments produced by the Protestant Reformers were seriously considered.[32] The *Decree on the sacrifice of the Mass* of the council's twenty-second session in 1562, resulting from this discussion, contains a carefully worded doctrinal exposition on the subject, stating that it 'did not seem expedient (*expedire visum est)*' to the Fathers that the Holy Mass should be celebrated in the vernacular 'throughout (*passim)*'.[33] However, they recognised the value of the texts of the liturgy for the instruction of the faithful in a language that was intelligible to them. Therefore, pastors and those entrusted with the care of souls should preach frequently about what is read at Mass, especially on Sundays and feast days. Moreover, canon nine of the same *Decree on the sacrifice of the Mass* declares anathema anyone who says that the Mass 'must be celebrated only in the vernacular language (*lingua tantum vulgari missam celebrari debere)*'; again, the subtle wording of this conciliar text is to be noted.[34] As a result of the shift from ritual complexity towards the spoken word and the retention of almost exclusive use of Latin, the gap widened in the post-Tridentine period between the 'official' liturgy that was performed by the priest at the altar and the devotional exercises the laity used to follow it.

One form of popular participation in the Mass that had spread in the later medieval period was vernacular singing, especially the German *Ruf*

---

[31] See Herman A. P. Schmidt, *Liturgie et langue vulgaire : Le problème de la langue liturgique chez les premiers Réformateurs et au Concile de Trente*, Analecta Gregoriana 53 (Rome: Apud Aedes Unversitatis Gregorianae, 1950), 23–79.

[32] See ibid., 81–198.

[33] Council of Trent, Session XXII, *Doctrina et canones de sanctissimae Missae sacrificio* (17 September 1562), cap 8: *Concilium Tridentinum*, vol. VIII, 961.

[34] Ibid., can. 9: 962.

(acclamation) and *Leise* (refrain). The *Leise* (the word is supposedly derived from *Kyrie eleison*) had its origins in brief responses to Latin chants, especially the sequences for major feasts. For instance, as early as the mid-twelfth century, the Easter sequence *Victimae paschali laudes* could be interpolated by the congregation with the stanza *Christ ist erstanden* ('Christ is risen'). In the mid-thirteenth century, the Pentecost sequence *Veni Sancte Spiritus* was joined with the stanza *Nun bitten wir den heiligen Geist* ('Now we implore the Holy Spirit'). Vernacular singing was also introduced at the end of the sermon or the end of the Mass. This tradition served as the basis for the flourishing of Lutheran hymnody.[35]

RESERVATION OF THE EUCHARIST AND CHURCH ARCHITECTURE

The Council of Trent did not give specific directives on church architecture and furnishing. However, by affirming the Catholic doctrine of the Eucharist, the conciliar decrees gave clear theological indications that were to shape the building of new churches and the restructuring of already existing ones. The canons of the *Decree on the Eucharist*, dating from the council's thirteenth session on 11 October 1551, confidently asserted the Catholic position in the face of Protestant criticism, especially that of Martin Luther who argued that Christ was present in the sacrament of the Eucharist only during the actual liturgical celebration, when it would be received in faith by the communicants. Trent restated the teaching of the Fourth Lateran Council of 1215 about the real and abiding presence of Christ under the form of bread and wine after their consecration by the priest and the need for an appropriate and secure reservation of the consecrated hosts after Mass, which were also used for bringing Holy Communion to the sick.[36] Canon seven speaks in apparently general terms about the reservation of the Holy Eucharist 'in sacrario'. In medieval use, *sacrarium* could indicate any place for Eucharistic reservation, including the sacristy. However, in the

---

[35] See Volker Mertens, 'Leisen und Rufe', in *Die Musik in Geschichte und Gegenwart*, 2nd ed., *Sachteil*, vol. 5 (Kassel: Bärenreiter, 1996),1075–1078.

[36] Council of Trent, Session XIII, *Decretum de sanctissimo Eucharistiae sacramento* (11 October 1551), cap. 5–6 and can. 6–7: *Concilium Tridentinum*, vol. VII, 202 and 203–204. Fourth Lateran Council, *Constitutiones*, 20. *De chrismate et eucharistia sub sera conservanda* (30 November 1215): *Conciliorum Oecumenicorum Decreta*, ed. Giuseppe Alberigo et al., 3rd ed. (Bologna: Istituto per le Scienze Religiose, 1973), 244.

Tridentine context, it would be safe to assume that many council fathers would have understood *sacrarium* to mean the tabernacle at the high altar.[37]

This arrangement had already gained some currency in fifteenth-century Italy (see Chapter 8) and was vigorously promoted by Gian Matteo Giberti (1495–1543), bishop of Verona from 1524 until his death. Giberti's *Constitutiones*, which were issued in 1542 with the approval of Pope Paul III, aimed at a reform of ecclesiastical life in his diocese and in many ways anticipated post-Tridentine developments.[38] Reserving the sacrament on the high altar in the centre of the church, where it would be exposed for the veneration of both clergy and laity, formed an important part of Giberti's pastoral programme. The tabernacle was intended to be the heart of the church, both in a spatial and in a spiritual sense. Giberti applied this new arrangement to his own cathedral in Verona and prescribed it for every parish church of his diocese.[39] During the reign of Mary Tudor in England (1516–1558), the Legatine Synod, convoked by Cardinal Reginald Pole (1500–1558) and held between November 1555 and February 1556, decreed that the Eucharist was to be reserved at the high altar, and this was implemented by installing tabernacles in several English cathedrals.[40] Without ever being strictly prescribed in the Roman liturgical books,

[37] On the difficulty of interpreting *sacrarium*, see Susanne Mayer-Himmelheber, *Bischöfliche Kunstpolitik nach dem Tridentinum: Der Secunda-Roma-Anspruch Carlo Borromeos und die mailändischen Verordnungen zu Bau und Ausstattung von Kirchen* (Munich: Tuduv, 1984), 113 and 318–319. Hans Caspary, *Das Sakramentstabernakel in Italien bis zum Konzil von Trient: Gestalt, Ikonographie und Symbolik, kultische Funktion*, 3rd ed. (Munich: Uni-Druck, 1969), 9 and 124, n. 20, notes that a contract made for the collegiate church at Empoli in Tuscany in 1484 states: 'tabernacul[um] sive sacrari[um] ... poniturum super altare'.

[38] See Christoph Jobst, 'Liturgia e culto dell'Eucaristia nel programma spaziale della chiesa: I tabernacoli eucaristici e la trasformazione dei presbiteri negli scritti ecclesiastici dell'epoca introno al Concilio di Trento', in *Lo spazio e il culto: Relazioni tra edificio ecclesiale e uso liturgico dal XV al XVI secolo*, ed. Jörg Stabenow (Venice: Marsilio, 2006), 91–126, at 92–93: also Enrico Cattaneo, 'Influenze veronesi nella legislazione di san Carlo Borromeo', in *Problemi di vita religiosa in Italia nel Cinquecento: Atti del convegno di storia della Chiesa in Italia (Bologna, 2–6 sett. 1985)*, Italia sacra 2 (Padua: Editrice Antenore, 1960), 122–166.

[39] On Giberti, see also the collected papers in *Atti del Convegno di Studi Gian Matteo Giberti (1495–1543)*, ed. Marco Agostini and Giovanna Baldissin Molli (Cittadella: Biblos, 2012).

[40] See Eamon Duffy, *Fires of Faith: Catholic England under Mary Tudor* (New Haven and London: Yale University Press, 2009), 192–193.

the high-altar tabernacle was gradually adopted throughout post-Tridentine Catholicism.

Carlo Borromeo (1538–1584) has often been held up as a model reforming bishop, who implemented the Tridentine decrees in the Archdiocese of Milan with exemplary diligence and dedication. The diocesan and provincial synods Borromeo held for the reform of his vast diocese also dealt with matters of church building and maintenance, and the relevant norms were published by a group of authors under Borromeo's supervision in 1577 as *Instructiones fabricae et supellectilis ecclesiasticae*.[41] The treatise was widely distributed among clergy, architects and builders in the diocese, and a system of visitations and inspections was instituted to make sure that its norms were implemented. The impact of the *Instructiones* was not limited to Milan but extended throughout Europe and the Americas.

In his letter introducing the treatise, Borromeo affirms that church architecture needs to be 'in agreement with the thinking of the Fathers', as demanded by the Tridentine liturgical reform.[42] Borromeo shows familiarity with *Rationale divinorum officiorum* by William Durandus, the most influential liturgical commentator of the later Middle Ages. However, the *Instructiones* do not follow Durandus' highly symbolic reading of churches and their ornamentation. There is a practical side to Borromeo's guidelines, which serve the end of creating and maintaining a building fit for the worship of God and for the sanctification of God's people.

The sections that directly affect the celebration of Mass concern the layout and furnishing of the main sanctuary (*cappella major*). It is to be oriented, with the main altar facing east, and where this is impossible, it can be directed towards another cardinal point (except north), preferably towards the west, as in some Roman basilicas. The floor of the main sanctuary should be elevated by at least three steps above the floor level of the rest of the church.[43] The chapter on the high altar lays down that the

---

[41] Carlo Borromeo, *Instructionum Fabricae et Supellectilis Ecclesiaticae Libri II*, ed. Stefano Della Torre, Monumenta Studia Instrumenta 18 (Vatican City: Libreria Editrice Vaticana, 2000). See Matthew E. Gallegos, 'Charles Borromeo and Catholic Tradition Regarding the Design of Catholic Churches', in *Sacred Architecture* 9 (2004), 14–19.

[42] The translation of Borromeo's letter is taken from Evelyn C. Voelker, *Charles Borromeo's Instructiones Fabricae et Supellectilis Ecclesiasticae, 1577: A Translation with Commentary and Analysis* (PhD dissertation, Syracuse University 1977), 22 and 23.

[43] Borromeo, *Instructiones*, lib. I, c. X: *De cappella majori*. At the fourth provincial council Borromeo convened in Milan in 1576, it was decreed: 'Let him [bishop] see to it that in

arrangement in the main sanctuary must be spacious enough for solemn Mass with priest, deacon, subdeacon and assistants.[44] The Eucharistic tabernacle should be solidly made and firmly installed on the high altar of the church.[45] The archbishop of Milan set the example by transferring the reserved sacrament in his own cathedral from the sacristy to the high altar. Borromeo also dedicates a chapter to ambo and pulpit. Evoking the example of ancient Roman basilicas, he stipulates that the ambo should be preferably constructed of marble or stone (though brick is permissible) and decorated with sculptures. There can be two ambones, one for the gospel and one for the epistle reading, as seen in the two elaborate pulpits he commissioned for the *duomo* of Milan; they were completed under his younger cousin and successor Federico Borromeo (1564–1631) in 1602. If there is one ambo only, it should be placed on the gospel side, with different levels for the proclamation of the gospel and the epistle. Parish churches should have a pulpit in place of the ambo, for the proclamation of the gospel and for preaching. Both ambo and pulpit should be located in the body of the church, in a prominent position so that the preacher or the reader can be seen and heard by all. At the same time, they must not be too far from the high altar, in keeping with the plan of the church, as this will be more convenient for the priest who is to preach at solemn Mass.[46]

According to the *Instructiones*, every part of the church building is ordered towards the celebration of the liturgy as that is its principal purpose and end. This does not mean that every detail is regulated. In many places, Borromeo shows practical sense and refers to the skill and expertise of architects. The norms of 1577 are not tied to any specific style of art and architecture[47] but found their immediate expression in the Mannerist style of the day. A model implementation can be seen in the Milanese church of San Fedele (dedicated to St Fidelis of Como), which Borromeo commissioned from the architect Pellegrino Tibaldi in 1569 for

---

every respect it [church] be built in such a manner that it not depart from ancient custom and approved tradition, that the priest celebrating Mass at the main altar may face east.' Translation from Voelker, *Charles Borromeo's* Instructiones, 64.

[44] Ibid., lib. I, c. XI: *De altari majori*.

[45] Ibid., lib., I, c. XIII: *De tabernaculo sanctissimae Eucharistiae*.

[46] Ibid., lib. I, c. XXII: *De ambonibus et suggestu*.

[47] Compare the critical comment of Anthony Blunt, *Artistic Theory in Italy, 1450–1600* (Oxford: Oxford University Press, 1962), 129: "In every case ecclesiastical reasons predominate, and purely artistic considerations are only allowed in questions which are ecclesiastically indifferent."

Figure 9.2 San Fedele, Milan / Commissioned in 1569
(© Luca Casonato / Reprinted with kind permission)

the Society of Jesus and consecrated in 1579 (see Figure 9.2).[48] Borromeo also employed Tibaldi in the remodelling of Milan cathedral.

By means of his highly influential *Instructiones* and the building activity in his diocese, Borromeo made significant contributions towards the conception of liturgical space as 'sacred theatre' (*teatro sacro*), which came to full fruition in the Baroque period. Designing the church as a *teatro* implies a unified space that offers a clear view of the sanctuary with a focus on the high altar and the tabernacle. The ideas of 'stage' and 'audience' have negative connotations when applied to the liturgy, because they suggest a separation of the clerical actors from the lay spectators. Such criticism was already voiced in the sixteenth century. However, the theatrical analogy was aiming above all at the visibility of the liturgical action, which was meant to facilitate the participation of the faithful. Jörg Stabenow also notes the great attention given to the layout and artistic decoration of the space for the laity. Particular features were the monumental pulpit and

[48] The choir and the dome were built in the first half of the seventeenth century but largely followed Tibaldi's plan. The altar ciborium was added only in 1835, modelled on Tibaldi's design for the *duomo*. See Richard Haslam, 'Pellegrino Tibaldi and the Design of S. Fedele, Milan', in *Arte Lombarda* 42/43 (1975), 124–153.

several confessionals, which highlighted the importance of preaching and Christian living (which was exemplified in biblical and hagiographical imagery). The installation of organs and choir offered opportunities for dramatic musical expression. Thus, Stabenow even speaks of a new appreciation for the laity in post-Tridentine church architecture.[49]

SACRED MUSIC

The question of defining criteria for sacred music, which arose with the development of polyphony in the later Middle Ages, presented itself more acutely with the flourishing of Renaissance culture, and it was discussed at the Council of Trent, although not before its final period between 1559 and 1563. Two main issues that had occupied local synods and individual bishops even before Trent emerged in the council's deliberations: first, the integrity and intelligibility of the text set to music (which was also a general concern of musical humanists in the sixteenth century) and, secondly, the use of music of secular origin in divine worship.[50]

In the twenty-second session of the council in 1562, a committee drafted a series of canons on liturgical abuses, one of which included directives on sacred music:

Everything should indeed be regulated so that the Masses, whether they be celebrated with the plain voice or in song, with everything clearly and quickly executed, may reach the ears of the hearers and quietly penetrate their hearts. In those Masses where measured music and organ are customary, nothing profane should be intermingled, but only hymns and divine praises .... But the entire manner of singing in musical modes should be calculated, not to afford vain delight to the ear, but so that the words may be comprehensible to all; and thus

---

[49] See Jörg Stabenow, 'Auf dem Weg zum "theatrum sacrum": Bedeutungen der theatralen Analogie im Kirchenraum der Gegenreformation in Italien', in *Konfessionen im Kirchenraum: Dimensionen des Sakralraums in der frühen Neuzeit*, ed. Susanne Wegmann and Gabriele Wimböck, Studien zur Kunstgeschichte des Mittelalters und der frühen Neuzeit 3 (Korb: Didymos-Verlag, 2007), 115–136; also Ralf van Bühren, 'Kirchenbau in Renaissance und Barock: Liturgiereformen und ihre Folgen für Raumordnung, liturgische Disposition und Bildausstattung nach dem Trienter Konzil', in *Operation am lebenden Objekt: Roms Liturgiereformen von Trient bis zum Vaticanum II*, ed. Stefan Heid (Berlin: be.bra wissenschaft, 2014), 93–119.

[50] See the study of Craig A. Monson, 'The Council of Trent Revisited', in *Journal of the American Musicological Society* 55 (2002), 1–37 (reprinted in *Music and the Renaissance: Renaissance, Reformation and Counter-Reformation*, ed. Philippe Vendrix [London; New York: Routledge, 2017], 487–524). For a translation of essential sources, Robert F. Hayburn, *Papal Legislation on Sacred Music: 95 A.D. to 1977 A.D.* (Collegeville: Liturgical Press, 1979, reprinted Harrison: Roman Catholic Books, 2006), 25–31.

may the hearts of the listeners be caught up into the desire for celestial harmonies and contemplation of the joys of the blessed.[51]

However, this text was not included in the final *Decree concerning the things to be observed, and to be avoided, in the celebration of Mass*, which contains only this very short paragraph on the matter:

Let them keep away from the churches compositions in which there is an intermingling of the lascivious or impure, whether by instrument or voice.[52]

Thus, only an admonition to maintain a distinction between sacred and secular music entered the council's decree but not the central argument of the original draft on the intelligibility of the text sung at Mass, with its theological emphasis on the priority of the word.

The question of sacred music was taken up again in the council's twenty-fourth session in 1563, when an attempt was made to ban polyphony from the sacred liturgy, as some prelates had already tried to do previously, including Cardinal legate Giovanni Morone during his first stint as bishop of Modena from 1529 to 1550.[53] Among those who strongly opposed such a proposal were Cardinal Otto Truchseß von Waldburg (1514–1573), bishop of Augsburg,[54] and even the Emperor Ferdinand I, who was alerted to the debate at the council and intervened with a letter in August 1563.[55] Historical scholarship has refuted the story that polyphony was saved when Pope Marcellus II, who reigned for less than a month in 1555, heard the *Missa Papae Marcelli* by Giovanni Pierluigi da Palestrina (c. 1525–1594), because the composer had no influence on the debates about musical reform at Trent.[56] As for

---

[51] Council of Trent, Session XXII, *Canones de abusibus circa celebrantes vel audientes missam, propositi examinandi* (10 September 1562), can. 8: *Concilium Tridentinum*, vol. VIII, 927; trans. Monson, 'The Council of Trent Revisited', 9. This draft canon is sometimes mistaken for an official conciliar decree, even in standard works of musicology, as noted by Monson, ibid., 11–12.

[52] Council of Trent, Session XXII, *Decretum de observandis et evitandis in celebratione missarum* (17 September 1562): *Concilium Tridentinum*, vol. VIII, 963; trans. Monson, 'The Council of Trent Revisited', 11.

[53] See Monson, 'The Council of Trent Revisited', 13–14.

[54] See Christian T. Leitmeir, 'Catholic Music in the Diocese of Augsburg c. 1600: A Reconstructed Tricinium Anthology and its Confessional Implications', in *Early Music History* 21 (2002), 117–173, at 121–122.

[55] See Monson, 'The Council of Trent Revisited', 13–14.

[56] The composer who can claim to have had some bearing on Trent's deliberations was the Franco-Flemish Jacobus de Kerle, whose *Preces speciales*, a set of polyphonic devotional responsories, were sung several times a week at prayer services during the last sessions of the council. The musical setting was commissioned by Cardinal Truchseß von Waldburg.

the *Missa Papae Marcelli*, it is more probable to see in it Palestrina's creative response to the council's reforming idea on sacred music.[57] In the end, the only pronouncement on the matter was included in the *Decree on reform*, which delegates decisions on the Divine Office, including 'the proper manner of singing or playing therein' to provincial synods. In the interim period before such synods are held, the local bishop, with the help of at least two canons, may provide as seems expedient.[58]

The debate flared up once again in the twenty-fifth session, when the practice of music in female religious houses was discussed and an attempt was made to exclude polyphony from convents altogether. However, there was opposition to this move, and in the end, it was agreed that decisions on music should be made by the competent religious superiors.[59]

In sum, the Council of Trent said as little as possible on sacred music, but its discussion of it gave a strong impulse to local synods and bishops who implemented the council's programme for the reform of ecclesiastical life and discipline. In the years after Trent, concerns for the intelligibility of the text and for an exclusion of secular music from the liturgy were perceived as being in conformity with the council ('secundum formam concilii'). Practical solutions differed considerably from one place to the other, and this is reflected in the rich variety of polyphonic music at the time.[60]

CONCLUSION

The Council of Trent's decision to leave the reform of the missal and breviary in the hands of the pope (and thus also his curia) inaugurated a period of unprecedented standardisation of the Latin liturgical tradition. Pius V published the *Breviarium Romanum* in 1568 and the *Missale Romanum* in 1570. In 1588, Sixtus V created the Sacred Congregation

See Patrick Bergin Jr., '*Preces Speciales*: Prototype of Tridentine Musical Reform', in *The Ohio State Online Musical Journal* 2 (2009), at www.osomjournal.org/issues/2/bergin .html?, with ample bibliography. The idea of Palestrina as the 'saviour' of sacred polyphony seems to have been presented first by the Sienese composer and music theorist Agostino Agazzari in 1607 and was then often repeated.

[57] This was suggested by Karl Gustav Fellerer and Moses Hadas, 'Church Music and the Council of Trent', in *The Musical Quarterly* 39 (1953), 576–594.

[58] Council of Trent, Session XXIV, *Decretum de reformatione* (11 November 1563), c. 12: *Concilium Tridentinum*, vol. IX, 983–984.

[59] See Monson, 'The Council of Trent Revisited', 19–22.

[60] See Monson, 'The Council of Trent Revisited', 24; also Lewis H. Lockwood, 'Vincenzo Ruffo and Musical Reform after the Council of Trent', in *The Musical Quarterly* 43 (1957), 342–371.

of Rites, which was to give authentic answers to questions arising from the new liturgical books and ensure the observance of liturgical norms. For pontifical celebrations, Clement VIII promulgated the *Pontificale Romanum* in 1596 and the *Caeremoniale Episcoporum* in 1600. In 1614, Paul V issued the *Rituale Romanum* for all those sacraments and sacramentals not reserved to bishops.[61] The medium of printing – now closely supervised by ecclesiastical authority – meant that uniform liturgical books could much more easily be produced and distributed throughout the Catholic Church. Thus, the sixteenth century marks a decisive moment in the long shift from oral to written culture, with profound consequences for the celebration of the liturgy.

The changes and developments that subsequent popes introduced to the missal were minor and did not alter the basic structure and shape of Mass. Thus, the period between 1570 and the mid-twentieth century was marked by a stable ritual that came to be known as the 'Tridentine Mass'. It is important to recall that the *Missale Romanum* of Pius V was not compulsory for dioceses or religious orders that could legitimately claim a particular liturgical tradition older than 200 years. However, the desire to strengthen the visible unity and cohesion of the Church, which had already been felt at Trent, led to the adoption of the Roman books even where an older tradition existed, with some notable exceptions that included the Ambrosian Rite in Milan, the Mozarabic Rite in Toledo and the particular uses of the Carmelite and Dominican Orders. This liturgical unification was not forced by the papacy but was widely thought to be an appropriate step taken for the good of the Catholic Church at the time. The English polymath Adrian Fortescue (1878–1923), who had misgivings about this course of events, observed that 'the Protestant revolt of the sixteenth century had its natural result in increased centralisation among those who remained faithful'.[62] At the same time, the prevalence of a prescriptive liturgical book does not produce simple uniformity in the ways in which the liturgy is enacted, let alone experienced. Each celebration of the Mass is conditioned by its

---

[61] The *Rituale Romanum* was never imposed as such, like the other liturgical books of the post-Tridentine reform, but was rather intended as a model to be adapted in local rituals. See Neil J. Roy, 'The Development of the Roman Ritual: A Prehistory and History of the *Rituale Romanum*', in *Antiphon* 15 (2011), 4–26.

[62] Adrian Fortescue, *The Early Papacy to the Synod of Chalcedon in 451*, 4th ed. by Alcuin Reid (San Francisco: Ignatius Press, 2008), 36.

particular setting and circumstances. In an increasingly global church, the Tridentine reforms were applied in varying degrees and with different speeds. Local customs and traditions not only persisted but also gained new vigour where dedicated pastors implemented the council's decrees effectively.[63]

[63] See Simon Ditchfield, *Liturgy, Sanctity and History in Tridentine Italy: Pietro Maria Campi and the Preservation of the Particular*, Cambridge Studies in Italian History and Culture (Cambridge: Cambridge University Press, 1995); and 'Giving Tridentine Worship Back Its History', in *Continuity and Change in Christian Worship*, ed. Robert N. Swanson, Studies in Church History 35 (Woodbridge: Boydell Press, 1999), 199–226. Ditchfield's work concentrates on the breviary and the cult of the saints but is also relevant to the history of the Mass.

Appendix

The *Ordinarium Missae* of the 1570 *Missale Romanum*

The Latin text is taken from the folio edition that was produced in Rome by the heirs of Bartolomeo Faletti, Giovanni Varisco and associates.[64] In the transcription, I generally follow the particular spelling, capitalisation and punctuation of the printed text. Abbreviations are written out. Rubrical instructions, printed in red ink, are shown in italics. For the translation, I have made use of the Latin-English missal published in the United States in 1966 and the *Roman Missal* of 2011.[65]

Ordinarium Missę	The Ordinary of the Mass
Sacerdos cum ingreditur ad altare signans se signo crucis clara voce dicit.	*When the priest proceeds towards the altar, signing himself with the sign of the cross he says in a clear voice:*
In nomine patris, et filij, et spiritus sancti. Amen.	In the name of the Father, and of the Son, and of the Holy Spirit. Amen.
Deinde iunctis manibus ante pectus dicit.	*Then, with his hands joined before his breast, he says:*

---

[64] *Missale Romanum: Editio Princeps (1570)*, 233–292 (in the original pagination) and 293–352 (in the pagination of the anastatic reprint edited by Sodi and Triacca).

[65] *English-Latin Roman Missal for the United States of America: Containing the Mass Text from the Roman Missal and the Prayers of the Celebrant together with the Ordinary of the Mass from the English-Latin Sacramentary*, English translations approved by the National Conference of Bishops of the United States of America and confirmed by the Apostolic See (New York: Benziger Brothers, 1966); and *Roman Missal: Renewed by Decree of the Most Holy Second Ecumenical Council of the Vatican, Promulgated by Authority of Pope Paul VI and Revised at the Direction of Pope John Paul II*, English translation according to the third typical edition (London: Catholic Truth Society, 2011).

(cont.)

Ordinarium Missę	The Ordinary of the Mass
V. Introibo ad altare dei.	V. I will go to to the altar of God.
R. Ad deum qui lętificat iuuentutem meam.	R. To God who gives joy to my youth.
Postea alternatim cum ministris dicit sequentem Psalmum.	*Afterwards, alternating with the ministers, he says the following psalm:*
Iudica me deus, et discerne causam meam de gente non sancta: ab homine iniquo et doloso erue me.	Judge me, O God, and distinguish my cause from the nation that is not holy: deliver me from the unjust and deceitful man.
Quia tu es deus fortitudo mea, quare me repulisti, et quare tristis incedo dum affligit me inimicus?	For you are God, my strength; why have you cast me off, and why do I go sorrowful while the enemy afflicts me?
Emitte lucem tuam, et veritatem tuam: ipsa me deduxerunt et adduxerunt in montem sanctum tuum, et in tabernacula tua.	Send forth your light and your truth; they have conducted me, and brought me to your holy hill, and to your tabernacles.
Et introibo ad altare dei, ad deum qui lętificat iuuentutem meam.	And I will go in to the altar of God, to God who gives joy to my youth.
Confitebor tibi in cithara deus deus meus: quare tristis es anima mea, et quare conturbas me?	I will give praise upon the harp to you, O God my God; why are you sad, O my soul, and why do you disquiet me?
Spera in deo, quoniam adhuc confitebor illi, salutare vultus mei et deus meus.	Hope in God, for I will still give praise to him, the salvation of my countenance, and my God.
Gloria patri et filio et spiritui sancto. Sicut erat in principio, et nunc et semper, et in secula seculorum. Amen.	Glory be to the Father, and to the Son, and to the Holy Spirit. As it was in the beginning, is now, and ever shall be, world without end. Amen.
In missis mortuorum omittitur pręfatus Psalmus, et post In nomine patris, statim dicitur vt sequitur.	*In Masses for the dead, the preceding psalm is omitted, and after, In the name of the Father, it is immediately said as follows:*
V. Introibo ad altare dei.	V. I will go to the altar of God.
R. Ad deum qui lętificat iuuentutem meam.	R. To God who gives joy to my youth.
Signat se dicens.	*Signing himself, he says.*
V. Adiutorium nostrum in nomine domini.	V. Our help is in the Name of the Lord.
R. Qui fecit cęlum et terram.	R. Who made heaven and earth.

(*cont.*)

Ordinarium Missę	The Ordinary of the Mass
Deinde iunctis manibus inclinatus facit confessionem. Confiteor deo omnipotenti, beatę Marię semper virgini, beato Michaeli archangelo, beato Ioanni Baptistę, sanctis apostolis Petro et Paulo, omnibus sanctis, et vobis, fratres: quia peccaui nimis cogitatione, verbo et opere, *percutit sibi pectus dicens* mea culpa, mea culpa, mea maxima culpa. Ideo precor beatam Mariam semper virginem, beatum Michaelem archangelum, beatum Ioannem Baptistam, sanctos apostolos Petrum et Paulum, omnes sanctos, et vos, fratres, orare pro me ad dominum deum nostrum.	*Then, with his hands joined and bowing, he makes the confession:* I confess to almighty God, to blessed Mary ever Virgin, to blessed Michael the Archangel, to blessed John the Baptist, to the holy apostles Peter and Paul, to all the Saints, and to you, brethren, that I have greatly sinned in thought, word, and deed, *he strikes his breast three times, saying*, through my fault, through my fault, through my most grievous fault. Therefore I beseech blessed Mary ever Virgin, blessed Michael the Archangel, blessed John the Baptist, the holy apostles Peter and Paul, all the saints, and you, brethren, to pray for me to the Lord our God.
Ministri respondent. Misereatur tui omnipotens deus, et dimissis omnibus peccatis tuis, perducat te ad vitam ęternam. *Sacerdos dicit.* Amen.	*The ministers respond:* May almighty God have mercy on you, forgive all your sins, and bring you to everlasting life. *The priest says:* Amen.
Deinde ministri repetunt Confessionem: et vbi a sacerdote dicebatur Vobis fratres *et* Vos, fratres, *a ministris dicitur* Tibi pater, *et* Te pater.	*Then the ministers repeat the Confession, and where it was said by the priest* to you, brethren, *and* you, brethren, *by the ministers it is said* to you, father, *and* you, father.
Postea sacerdos iunctis manibus facit absolutionem, dicens. Misereatur vestri omnipotens deus, et dimissis omnibus peccatis vestris, perducat vos ad vitam ęternam. *R.* Amen.	*Afterwards the priest, with his hands joined, gives absolution, saying:* May almighty God have mercy on you, forgive all your sins, and bring you to everlasting life. *R.* Amen.
Signat se signo crucis dicens.	*He signs himself with the sign of the cross, saying:*
Indulgentiam, absolutionem, et remissionem omnium peccatorum nostrorum, tribuat nobis omnipotens et misericors dominus. *R.* Amen.	May the almighty and merciful Lord grant us pardon, absolution, and remission of all our sins. *R.* Amen.

(*cont.*)

Ordinarium Missę	The Ordinary of the Mass

Inclinatus prosequitur.
V. Deus tu conuersus viuificabis nos.
 	
R. Et plebs tua lętabitur in te.
V. Ostende nobis domine
    misericordiam tuam.
R. Et salutare tuum da nobis.
V. Domine exaudi orationem meam.
R. Et clamor meus ad te veniat.
V. Dominus vobiscum.
R. Et cum spiritu tuo.
	Bowing, he proceeds:
	V. O God, you will turn to us and give
	    us life.
	R. And your people will rejoice in you.
	V. Show us, Lord, your mercy.
	
	R. And grant us your salvation.
	V. Lord, hear my prayer.
	R. And let my cry come to you.
	V. The Lord be with you.
	R. And with your spirit.

Ascendens ad altare dicit.
Oremus.
Aufer a nobis, quęsumus domine,
    cunctas iniquitates nostras, vt ad
    sancta sanctorum puris mereamur
    mentibus introire. Per Christum
    dominum nostrum. Amen.
	Ascending to the altar, he says:
	Let us pray.
	Take away from us, Lord, we pray, all
	    our sins, that we may enter into the
	    Holy of Holies with pure minds.
	    Through Christ our Lord. Amen.

Manibus iunctis super altare, inclinatus
    dicit.
Oramus te domine per merita
    sanctorum tuorum, *osculatur altare*
    dicens quorum reliquię hic sunt, et
    omnium sanctorum: vt indulgere
    digneris omnia peccata mea. Amen.
	Bowing with his hands joined over the
	    altar, he says:
	We ask you, Lord, by the merits of
	    your saints, *he kisses the altar,*
	    saying, whose relics are here, and of
	    all the saints, that you may pardon
	    all my sins. Amen.

Deinde diaconus recepto thuribulo a
    celebrante, incenset illum tantum.
    Postea signans se signo crucis, incipit
    Introitum, *quo finito, iunctis*
    manibus alternatim cum ministris
    dicit.
	Then the deacon, having received the
	    thurible from the celebrant, incenses
	    him alone. Afterwards [the
	    celebrant] signs himself with the sign
	    of the cross, begins the Introit, *and*
	    when finished, with his hands joined,
	    he says alternating with the
	    ministers:

Kyrie eleison. Kyrie eleison. Kyrie
    eleison. Christe eleison. Christe
    eleison. Christe eleison. Kyrie
    eleison. Kyrie eleison. Kyrie eleison.
	Lord, have mercy. Lord, have mercy.
	    Lord, have mercy. Christ, have
	    mercy. Christ, have mercy. Christ,
	    have mercy. Lord, have mercy. Lord,
	    have mercy. Lord, have mercy.

Postea ad medium altaris extendens et
    iungens manus, caputque
	Afterwards at the middle of the altar,
	    with his hands extended and joined,

(*cont.*)

Ordinarium Missę	The Ordinary of the Mass
aliquantulum inclinans, dicit si dicendum est. Gloria in excelsis deo: *et prosequitur iunctis manibus: cum dicit.* Adoramus te, *et* Iesu Christe *et* Suscipe deprecationem, *inclinat caput: et in fine dicens* Cum sancto spiritu, *signat se.*	*and bowing his head somewhat, he says, if it is to be said,* Glory to God in the highest, *and he proceeds with his hands joined. When he says* we adore you, *and* Jesus Christ *and* receive our prayer, *he bows his head. And at the end, when saying* with the Holy Spirit, *he signs himself.*
[*Then follow musical intonations for* Gloria in excelsis deo.]	
Gloria in excelsis deo. Et in terra pax hominibus bonę voluntatis. Laudamus te. Benedicimus te. Adoramus te. Glorificamus te. Gratias agimus tibi propter magnam gloriam tuam. Domine deus, rex cęlestis, deus pater omnipotens. Domine fili vnigenite Iesu Christe. Domine deus, agnus dei, filius patris. Qui tollis peccata mundi, miserere nobis. Qui tollis peccata mundi, suscipe deprecationem nostram. Qui sedes ad dexteram patris, miserere nobis. Quoniam tu solus sanctus. Tu solus dominus. Tu solus altissimus, Iesu Christe. Cum sancto spiritu in gloria dei patris. Amen.	Glory to God in the highest, and on earth peace to people of good will. We praise you, we bless you, we adore you, we glorify you, we give you thanks for your great glory, Lord God, heavenly King, O God almighty Father. Lord Jesus Christ, Only Begotten Son, Lord God, Lamb of God, Son of the Father, who take away the sins of the world, have mercy on us; who take away the sins of the world, receive our prayer; who are seated at the right hand of the Father, have mercy on us. For you alone are the Holy One, you alone are the Lord, you alone are the Most High, Jesus Christ, with the Holy Spirit, in the glory of God the Father. Amen.
Sic dicitur Gloria in excelsis, *etiam in missis beatę Marię.*	*Thus* Glory in the highest *is said, also in the Masses of blessed Mary.*
Deinde osculatur altare in medio, et versus ad populum dicit: V. Dominus vobiscum. R. Et cum spiritu tuo.	*Then he kisses the altar in the middle and turning towards the people, he says:* V. The Lord be with you. R. And with your spirit.
Postea dicit Oremus. *Deinde* Orationes, *vnam aut plures: Sequitur* Epistola Graduale, Alleluia *vel* Tractus, Sequentia, *vt tempus postulat.*	*Afterwards he says* Let us pray. *Then* the Collects, *one or several. There follows* the Epistle, Gradual, Alleluia or Tract, Sequence, *as the time demands.*

(*cont.*)

Ordinarium Missę	The Ordinary of the Mass
His finitis si est missa sollemnis diaconus deponit librum euangeliorum super altare, et benedicto incenso vt supra, genuflexus manibus iunctis ante medium altaris dicit:	*When this is completed, if it is a solemn Mass, the deacon places the Book of Gospels on the altar, and when the incense is blessed, as above, [the deacon] kneeling and with his hands joined, says before the middle of the altar:*
Munda cor meum ac labia mea omnipotens deus, qui labia Isaię prophetę calculo mundasti ignito: ita me tua grata miseratione dignare mundare, vt sanctum euangelium tuum digne valeam nunciare. Per Christum dominum nostrum. Amen.	Cleanse my heart and my lips, almighty God, who cleansed the lips of the Prophet Isaiah with a burning coal. In your gracious mercy be pleased so to purify me that I may worthily proclaim your holy Gospel. Through Christ our Lord. Amen.
Deinde accipit librum, et rursus genuflectus petit benedictionem a sacerdote dicens: Iube, domne benedicere. *Sacerdos respondet.* Dominus sit in corde tuo et in labijs tuis: vt digne et competenter annuncies euangelium suum: in nomine patris et filij ✠ et spiritus sancti.	*Then he accepts the book and again kneeling he asks for a blessing from the priest, saying:* Lord, grant your blessing. *The priest responds:* The Lord be in your heart and on your lips, that you may worthily and fittingly proclaim his holy Gospel, in the name of the Father, and of the Son, ✠ and of the Holy Spirit. Amen.
Deinde accepta benedictione osculatur manum sacerdotis: et cum alijs ministris incenso et luminaribus accedens ad locum euangelij, stans iunctis manibus dicit.	*Then having received the blessing he kisses the hand of the priest and with the other ministers for the incense and the lights he goes to the place of the gospel; standing with his hands joined, he says:*
V. Dominus vobiscum.	V. The Lord be with you.
R. Et cum spiritu tuo.	R. And with your spirit.
Pronuncians Sequentia sancti euangelij secundum N.ᵃ *pollice dextrę manus, signat librum euangelij, deinde frontem, labia, et pectus: et dum ministri respondent,* Gloria tibi domine, *incensat ter librum, postea dicit euangelium iunctis manibus.*	*Proclaiming* The continuation of the Holy Gospel according to N., *he signs with the thumb of his right hand the Book of Gospels, then his forehead, lips and breast, while the ministers respond,* Glory to you, Lord. *He incenses the book three times and afterwards reads the Gospel with his hands joined.*
Quo finito subdiaconus defert librum sacerdoti, qui osculatur euangelium,	*When he has finished, the subdeacon brings the book to the priest, who*

(*cont.*)

Ordinarium Missę	The Ordinary of the Mass
dicens, Per euangelica dicta deleantur nostra delicta: *deinde a diacono sacerdos incensatur.*	*kisses the Gospel, saying:* Through the words of the Gospel may our sins be wiped away. *Then the priest is incensed by the deacon.*
Si vero sacerdos sine diacono et subdiacono celebrat, delato libro ad aliud cornu altaris, stans ad medium altaris iunctis manibus et aliquantulum inclinatus, dicit Munda cor meum, *et* Iube domne benedicere, *vt supra, et* Dominus sit in corde meo et in labijs meis, vt digne et competenter annunciem euangelium suum.	*If, however, the priest celebrates without deacon and subdeacon, when the book has been brought to the other corner of the altar, he stands in the middle of the altar with his hands joined, bowing somewhat, and says* Cleanse my heart *and* Lord, grant your blessing, *as above, and* The Lord be in my heart and on my lips, that I may worthily and fittingly proclaim his holy Gospel.
Deinde ad librum conuersus iunctis manibus dicit. V. Dominus vobiscum. R. Et cum spiritu tuo: *et pronuncians* Initium *siue* sequentia sancti euangelij etc.[b] *signat se, et legit euangelium, vt dictum est. Quo finito, respondent ministri.* Laus tibi Christe: *et sacerdos osculatur euangelium, vt supra.*	*Then turning towards the book, with his hands joined, he says:* V. The Lord be with you. R. And with your spirit. *And proclaiming* The beginning *or* The continuation of the Holy Gospel *etc., he signs himself and reads the Gospel, as said above. When he has finished, the ministers respond,* Glory to you, Lord, *and the priest kisses the Gospel, as above.*
In missis defunctorum dicitur Munda cor meum: *sed non petitur benedictio, non deferuntur luminaria, nec osculatur liber.*	*In Masses for the dead,* Cleanse my heart *is said, but no blessing is requested, no lights are carried, and the book is not kissed.*
Deinde ad medium altaris extendens et iungens manus, dicit si dicendum est: Credo in vnum deum: *et prosequitur iunctis mani- bus. Quando autem ventum est ad illud,* Et incarnatus est, *genuflectit usque dum dicitur,* Crucifixus etiam pro nobis. *In fine ad* Et vitam venturi, *signat se signo crucis.*	*Then in the middle of the altar, extending and joining his hands, he says, if it is to be said:* I believe in one God, *and he proceeds with his hands joined. But when he has come to,* And was incarnate, *he genuflects until it is said,* He was also crucified for us. At the end, at *And the life of [the world] to come,* he signs himself with the sign of the cross.

(cont.)

Ordinarium Missę	The Ordinary of the Mass

[*Then follows a musical intonation for* Credo in vnum deum.]

Credo in vnum deum. Patrem omnipotentem, factorem cęli et terrę, visibilium omnium et inuisibilium. Et in vnum dominum Iesum Christum, filium dei vnigenitum. Et ex patre natum, ante omnia secula. Deum de deo, lumen de lumine, deum verum de deo vero. Genitum, non factum, consubstantialem patri: per quem omnia facta sunt. Qui propter nos homines, et propter nostram salutem descendit de cęlis. Et incarnatus est de spiritu sancto ex Maria virgine: *et homo factus est.* Crucifixus etiam pro nobis: sub Pontio Pilato passus et sepultus est. Et resurrexit tertia die, secundum scripturas: Et ascendit in cęlum: sedet ad dexteram patris. Et iterum venturus est cum gloria iudicare viuos et mortuos: cuius regni non erit finis. Et in spiritum sanctum dominum et viuificantem: qui ex patre filioque procedit. Qui cum patre, et filio simul adoratur et conglorificatur: qui locutus est per prophetas. Et vnam sanctam catholicam et apostolicam ecclesiam. Confiteor vnum baptisma in remissionem peccatorum. Et exspecto resurrectionem mortuorum. Et vitam venturi sęculi. Amen.

I believe in one God, the Father almighty, maker of heaven and earth, of all things visible and invisible. And in one Lord Jesus Christ, the Only Begotten Son of God, born of the Father before all ages. God from God, Light from Light, true God from true God, begotten, not made, consubstantial with the Father; through him all things were made. For us men and for our salvation he came down from heaven, and by the Holy Spirit was incarnate of the Virgin Mary, *and became man.* For our sake he was also crucified; under Pontius Pilate he suffered death and was buried, and rose again on the third day in accordance with the Scriptures. He ascended into heaven and is seated at the right hand of the Father. He will come again in glory to judge the living and the dead and his kingdom will have no end. And in the Holy Spirit, the Lord, the giver of life, who proceeds from the Father and the Son, who with the Father and the Son is adored and glorified, who has spoken through the prophets. And in one, holy, catholic and apostolic Church. I confess one Baptism for the forgiveness of sins and I look forward to the resurrection of the dead and the life of the world to come. Amen.

Deinde osculatur altare, et versus ad populum dicit:
V. Dominus vobiscum.
R. Et cum spiritu tuo.
Postea dicit Oremus *et Offertorium.*

The he kisses the altar, and turning to the people he says:
V. The Lord be with you.
R. And with your spirit.
Then he says Let us pray *and the* Offertory.

(*cont.*)

Ordinarium Missę	The Ordinary of the Mass
Quo dicto, si est missa sollemnis, diaconus, porrigit patenam celebranti: si priuata, sacerdos ipse accipit patenam cum hostia, quam offerens dicit.	*When he has said this, if it is a solemn Mass, the deacon hands the paten to the celebrant; if it is a private [Mass], the priest himself takes the paten with the host and offering it he says:*

Suscipe, sancte pater, omnipotens ęterne deus, hanc immaculatam hostiam: quam ego indignus famulus tuus offero tibi deo meo viuo et vero, pro innumerabilibus peccatis et offensionibus et negligentijs meis, et pro omnibus circumstantibus, sed et pro omnibus fidelibus Christianis viuis atque defunctis: vt mihi, et illis proficiat ad salutem in vitam ęternam. Amen.

Receive, holy Father, almighty and eternal God, this spotless host, which I, your unworthy servant, offer to you, my living and true God, for my innumerable sins, offenses, and negligences, and on behalf of all here present but also for all the Christian faithful, living and dead, that it may profit me and them for salvation to life everlasting. Amen.

Deinde reposita hostia super corporale, ministrat diaconus vinum, subdiaconus vero aquam in calice: vel si priuata est missa, vtrumque infundit sacerdos, et aquam miscendam in calice benedicit dicens.

Then, having put the host back on the corporal, the deacon supplies the wine and the subdeacon the water in the chalice. Or, if it is a private Mass, the priest pours both and he blesses the water that is mixed in the chalice, saying:

Deus, qui humanę substantię dignitatem mirabiliter condidisti, et mirabilius reformasti: da nobis per huius aquę et vini mysterium, eius diuinitatis esse consortes, qui humanitatis nostrę fieri dignatus est particeps, Iesus Christus filius tuus dominus noster. Qui tecum viuit et regnat, in vnitate spiritus sancti deus: per omnia secula seculorum. Amen.

O God, who wonderfully created the dignity of human nature and still more wonderfully restored it, grant that through the mystery of this water and wine we may be partakers in the divinity of him, who deigned to share in our humanity, Jesus Christ, your Son, our Lord. Who lives and reigns with you in the unity of the Holy Spirit, God, for ever and ever. Amen.

In missis pro defunctis dicitur prędicta oratio: sed aqua non benedicitur.

In Masses for the dead the preceding prayer is said, but the water is not blessed.

Accipiens calicem, offert dicens.

He takes the chalice and offers it, saying:

Offerimus tibi domine calicem salutaris, tuam deprecantes

We offer you, Lord, the chalice of salvation, begging your mercy that it

(cont.)

Ordinarium Missę	The Ordinary of the Mass
clementiam: vt in conspectu diuinę maiestatis tuę, pro nostra et totius mundi salute, cum odore suauitatis ascendat. Amen.	may arise in the sight of your divine majesty for our salvation and for that of the whole world, with the odour of sweetness. Amen.
Deinde posito calice super corporale, et palla cooperto, iunctis manibus aliquantulum inclinatus dicit.	*Then having placed the chalice on the corporal and having covered it with the palla, with his hands joined and bowing somewhat, he says:*
In spiritu humilitatis, et in animo contrito suscipiamur a te domine: et sic fiat sacrificium nostrum in conspectu tuo hodie, vt placeat tibi domine deus.	With humble spirit and contrite heart may we be accepted by you, O Lord, and may our sacrifice in your sight this day be pleasing to you, Lord God.
Erectus expandit manus, easque in altum porrectas iungens eleuatis ad cęlum oculis, et statim demissis dicit.	*Standing erect, he stretches out his hands and holding them high he joins them, and elevating his eyes and immediately lowering them, he says:*
Veni sanctificator, omnipotens ęterne deus: *benedicit oblata prosequendo:* et bene✠dic hoc sacrificium, tuo sancto nomini pręparatum.	Come, O Sanctifier, almighty and eternal God, *he blesses the offerings as follows,* and bless ✠ this sacrifice prepared for your holy name.
Postea, si sollemniter celebrat, benedicit incensum, dicens.	*Then, if he celebrates in a solemn way, he blesses the incense, saying:*
Per intercessionem beati Michaelis archangeli stantis a dextris altaris incensi, et omnium electorum suorum, incensum istud dignetur dominus bene✠dicere, et in odorem suauitatis accipere. Per Christum dominum nostrum. Amen.	Through the intercession of blessed Michael the Archangel, standing at the right hand of the altar of incense, and of all his elect, may the Lord bless ✠ this incense and receive it in the odour of sweetness. Through Christ our Lord. Amen.
Et accepto thuribulo a diacono, incensat oblata, dicens.	*And having taken the thurible from the deacon, the incenses the offerings, saying:*
Incensum istud a te benedictum, ascendat ad te domine: et descendat super nos misericordia tua.	May this incense blessed by you arise before you, O Lord, and may your mercy descend upon us.
Deinde incensat altare, dicens.	*Then he incenses the altar, saying:*
Dirigatur domine oratio mea sicut incensum in conspectu tuo: eleuatio manuum mearum sacrificium	Let my prayer, O Lord, be directed as incense in your sight, the lifting up of my hands as an evening sacrifice. Set

(cont.)

Ordinarium Missę	The Ordinary of the Mass
vespertinum. Pone domine custodiam ori meo, et ostium circumstantię labijs meis: vt non declinet cor meum in verba malitię ad excusandas excusationes in peccatis.	a watch, O Lord, before my mouth, and a door round about my lips, that my heart may not incline to evil words, to make excuses in sins.
Dum reddit thuribulum diacono dicit.	*When he gives the thurible to the deacon, he says:*
Accendat in nobis dominus ignem sui amoris, et flammam ęterne charitatis. Amen.	May the Lord enkindle in us the fire of his love, and the flame of everlasting charity. Amen.
Postea incensatur sacerdos a diacono, deinde alij per ordinem.	*Afterwards the priest is incensed by the deacon, then the others according to rank.*
Interim sacerdos lauat manus, dicens.	*In the meantime the priest washes his hands, saying:*
Lauabo inter innocentes manus meas: et circumdabo altare tuum domine. Ut audiam vocem laudis: et enarrem vniuersa mirabilia tua. Domine dilexi decorem domus tuę, et locum habitationis glorię tuę. Ne perdas cum impijs animam meam: et cum viris sanguinum vitam meam. In quorum manibus iniquitates sunt: dextera eorum repleta est muneribus. Ego autem in innocentia mea ingressus sum: redime me, et miserere mei. Pes meus stetit in directo: in ecclesijs benedicam te domine. Gloria patri et filio et spiritui sancto. Sicut erat in principio, et nunc et semper: et in sęcula sęculorum. Amen.	I will wash my hands among the innocent and will go around your altar, O Lord, that I may hear the voice of your praise and tell of all your wondrous works. O Lord, I have loved, the beauty of your house and the place where your glory dwells. Take not away my souls with the wicked, nor my life with men of blood. On their hands are crimes, and their right hands are full of gifts. But as for me, I have walked in my innocence; redeem me, and have mercy on me. My foot has stood in the direct way: in the assemblies I will bless you, O Lord. Glory be to the Father, and to the Son, and to the Holy Spirit. As it was in the beginning, is now, and ever shall be, world without end. Amen.
In missis pro defunctis omittitur pars pręcedentis psalmi.	*In Masses for the dead, part of the preceding psalm is omitted.*
Deinde ad medium altaris, et aliquantulum inclinatus iunctis manibus, dicit.	*Then, in the middle of the altar and bowing somewhat, with his hands joined, he says:*

(*cont.*)

Ordinarium Missę	The Ordinary of the Mass
Suscipe, sancta Trinitas, hanc oblationem, quam tibi offerimus ob memoriam passionis, resurrectionis, ascensionis Iesu Christi domini nostri: et in honore beatę Marię semper virginis, et beati Ioannis Baptistę, et sanctorum apostolorum Petri et Pauli, et istorum, et omnium sanctorum: vt illis proficiat ad honorem, nobis autem ad salutem: et illi pro nobis intercedere dignentur in cęlis, quorum memoriam agimus in terris. Per Christum dominum nostrum. Amen.	Receive, Most Holy Trinity, this offering which we make to you in remembrance of the Passion, Resurrection, and Ascension of Jesus Christ, our Lord, and in honour of blessed Mary ever Virgin, blessed John the Baptist, the holy apostles Peter and Paul, and of these, and of all the saints: that it may avail to their honour and to our salvation; and may they deign to intercede for us in heaven whose memory we keep on earth. Through Christ our Lord. Amen.
Postea osculatur altare, et versus populum dicit.	*Afterwards he kisses the altar and turning to the people, he says:*
Orate fratres: vt meum ac vestrum sacrificium, acceptabile fiat apud deum patrem omnipotentem.	Prayer, brethren, that my sacrifice and yours may be acceptable to God the almighty Father almighty.
Circumstantes respondent: alioquin ipsemet sacerdos.	*Those present respond; otherwise the priest himself:*
Suscipiat dominus sacrificium de manibus tuis *vel* meis, ad laudem et gloriam nominis sui: ad vtilitatem quoque nostram, totiusque ecclesię suę sanctę. Amen.	May the Lord receive the sacrifice from your *or* my hands, for the praise and glory of his name, for our good and that of all his holy Church.
Deinde manibus extensis absolute subiungit orationes secretas. Quibus dictis, cum peruentum fuerit ad conclusionem clara voce dicit. Per omnia sęcula sęculorum, *cum Pręfatione, vt in sequentibus.*	*Then, with his hands extended, he straightaway adds the secret prayers. Having said them, when he has reached the conclusion, he says in a clear voice,* for ever and ever, *with the Preface, as in the following.*
Pręfatio incipitur ambabus manibus positis hinc et inde super altare: quas aliquantulum eleuat, cum dicit: Sursum corda. *Iungit manus et caput inclinat, cum dicit* Gratias agamus domino deo nostro. *Deinde disiungit manus, et disiunctas tenet vsque ad finem Pręfationis, et iterum iungit cum dicit* Sanctus etc.	*The Preface is commenced with both hands placed on the altar on either side. He raises them somewhat, when he says:* Lift up your hearts. *He joins his hands and bows his head, when he says:* Let us give thanks to the Lord our God. *Then he extends his hands and keeps them extended until the end of the Preface, and he joins them again when he says* Holy etc.

(*cont.*)

Ordinarium Missę	The Ordinary of the Mass
[*Then follow the Prefaces with musical notation in the festive and the ferial tone, as well as proper* Communicantes *and* Hanc igitur. *Here I include only the text of the Common Preface, which is used on days to which no proper preface is assigned.*]	
Per omnia secula seculorum.	For ever and ever.
R. Amen.	R. Amen.
V. Dominus vobiscum.	V. The Lord be with you.
R. Et cum spiritu tuo.	R. And with your spirit.
V. Sursum corda.	V. Lift up your hearts.
R. Habemus ad dominum.	R. We lift them up to the Lord.
V. Gratias agamus domino deo nostro.	V. Let us give thanks to the Lord our God.
R. Dignum et iustum est.	R. It is right and just.
Prefatio.	*Preface*
Vere dignum et iustum est, ęquum et salutare, nos tibi semper et ubique gratias agere, domine sancte, pater omnipotens, ęterne deus, per Christum Dominum nostrum. Per quem maiestatem tuam laudant angeli, adorant dominationes, tremunt potestates. Cęli cęlorumque virtutes, ac beata Seraphin, socia exultatione concelebrant. Cum quibus et nostras voces, vt admitti iubeas deprecamur, supplici confessione dicentes.	It is truly right and just, our duty and our salvation, always and everywhere to give you thanks, holy Lord, almighty Father, eternal God, through Christ our Lord. Through him the Angels praise your majesty, Dominions adore and Powers tremble before you. Heaven and the Virtues of heaven and the blessed Seraphim worship together with exultation. May our voices, we pray, join with theirs in humble praise, as we acclaim:
Sanctus, Sanctus, Sanctus dominus deus sabbaoth. Pleni sunt cęli et terra gloria tua. Osanna in excelsis. Benedictus qui venit in nomine domini. Osanna in excelsis.	Holy, Holy, Holy Lord God of hosts. Heaven and earth are full of your glory. Hosanna in the highest. Blessed is he who comes in the name of the Lord. Hosanna in the highest.
[*Then follow musical intonations for the* Gloria, *for the dismissal, for the introduction to prayer on penitential days, and for the invitation to the* Oratio super populum.]	

(*cont.*)

Ordinarium Missę	The Ordinary of the Mass
Sacerdos extendens et iungens manus, eleuans ad cęlum oculos et statim demittens, inclinatus ante altare dicit.	*The priest extends and joins his hands, raises his eyes to heaven and immediately lowers them; bowing before the altar, he says:*

Te igitur clementissime Pater, per Iesum Christum filium tuum dominum nostrum, supplices rogamus, ac petimus, *Osculatur altare*, uti accepta habeas, et benedicas, *Ter signet super oblata*, hęc ✠ dona, hęc ✠ munera, hęc ✠ sancta sacrificia illibata. *Extensis manibus prosequitur.* In primis quę tibi offerimus pro Ecclesia tua sancta catholica: quam pacificare, custodire, adunare et regere digneris toto orbe terrarum: vna cum famulo tuo papa nostro *N.* et antistite nostro *N.* et omnibus orthodoxis, atque catholicę et apostolicę fidei cultoribus.

To you, therefore, most merciful Father, we make humble prayer and petition through Jesus Christ, your Son, our Lord, *he kisses the altar*: that you accept and bless, *he signs the offerings three times*, these ✠ gifts, these ✠ offerings, these ✠ holy and unblemished sacrifices. *With his hands extended, he proceeds.* Which we offer you firstly for your holy catholic Church: be pleased to grant her peace, to guard, unite and govern her throughout the whole world, together with your servant *N.* our Pope and *N.* our Bishop, and all and all the true believers and professors of the Catholic and apostolic faith.

Commemoratio pro viuis
Memento domine famulorum famularumque tuarum *N. Iungit manus, orat aliquantulum pro quibus orare intendit: et extensis manibus prosequitur.* Et omnium circumstantium, quorum tibi fides cognita est et nota deuotio, pro quibus tibi offerimus: vel qui tibi offerunt hoc sacrificium laudis, pro se, suisque omnibus: pro redemptione animarum suarum, pro spe salutis et incolumitatis suę tibi reddunt vota sua ęterno deo viuo et vero.

Commemoration of the living
Remember, Lord, your servants *N. He joins his hands, prays for a short while for those he intends to pray for, and with his hands extended he proceeds.* And all gathered here, whose faith and devotion are known to you. For them, we offer you this sacrifice of praise, and they offer it for themselves and all who are dear to them: for the redemption of their souls, in hope of health and well-being, and paying their homage to you, the eternal God, living and true.

Infra actionem.
Communicantes, et memoriam venerantes: in primis gloriosę semper virginis Marię genetricis dei et domini nostri Iesu Christi. Sed et beatorum apostolorum, ac martyrum tuorum: Petri et Pauli, Andreę, Iacobi, Ioannis, Thomę,

Within the action
In communion with those whose memory we venerate, especially the glorious ever Virgin Mary, Mother of our God and Lord, Jesus Christ, and your blessed Apostles and Martyrs, Peter and Paul, Andrew, James, John, Thomas, James, Philip,

(*cont.*)

Ordinarium Missę	*The Ordinary of the Mass*
Iacobi, Philippi, Bartholomęi, Matthęi, Simonis et Thaddęi: Lini, Cleti, Clementis, Xisti, Cornelij, Cypriani, Laurentij, Chrysogoni, Ioannis et Pauli, Cosmę et Damiani. Et omnium sanctorum tuorum: quorum meritis precibusque concedas, vt in omnibus protectionis tuę muniamur auxilio. *Iungit manus.* Per eundem Christum dominum nostrum.	Bartholomew, Matthew, Simon and Jude; Linus, Cletus, Clement, Sixtus, Cornelius, Cyprian, Laurence, Chrysogonus, John and Paul, Cosmas and Damian and all your saints; we ask that through their merits and prayers, in all things we may be defended by your protecting help. *He joins his hands.* Through the same Christ our Lord. Amen.
Tenens manus extensas super oblata dicit. Hanc igitur oblationem seruitutis nostrę, sed et cunctę familię tuę, quęsumus domine, vt placatus accipias: diesque nostros in tua pace disponas, atque ab ęterna damnatione nos eripi, et in electorum tuorum iubeas grege numerari. *Iungit manus.* Per Christum dominum nostrum.	*Holding his hands extended over the offerings, he says:* Therefore, Lord, we pray: graciously accept this oblation of our service, that of your whole family; order our days in your peace, and command that we be delivered from eternal damnation and counted among the flock of those you have chosen. *He joins his hands.* Through Christ our Lord. Amen.
Quam oblationem tu deus in omnibus, quęsumus: *signat ter super oblata* bene✠dictam, ascri✠ptam, ra✠tam, rationabilem, acceptabilemque facere digneris: *signat semel super hostiam: et semel super calicem:* vt nobis cor✠pus, et san✠guis fiat dilectissimi filii tui domini nostri Iesu Christi.	Be pleased, O God, we pray, *he signs the offerings three times,* to ✠ bless, ✠ acknowledge, and ✠ approve this offering in every respect; make it spiritual and acceptable, *he signs the host once and the chalice once* so that it may become for us the ✠ Body and ✠ Blood of your most beloved Son, our Lord Jesus Christ.
Qui pridie, quam pateretur: *accipit hostiam:* accepit panem in sanctas ac venerabiles manus suas: *eleuat oculos ad celum:* Et eleuatis oculis in cęlum ad te deum patrem suum omnipotentem: tibi gratias agens: *signat super hostiam,* bene✠dixit, fregit, deditque discipulis suis dicens. Accipite et manducate ex hoc omnes. *Tenens ambabus manibus hostiam, profert verba consecrationis distincte, secrete, et attente.*	Who on the day before he was to suffer, *he takes the host,* took bread in his holy and venerable hands, *he raises his eyes to heaven,* and with eyes raised to heaven to you, O God, his almighty Father, giving you thanks, *he signs the host,* he said the ✠ blessing, broke the bread and gave it to his disciples, saying: Take this, all of you, and eat of it. *Holding the host in both hands he pronounces the words of consecration distinctly, in a low voice and attentively.*

(cont.)

Ordinarium Missę	The Ordinary of the Mass
Hoc est enim corpus meum.	For this is my Body.
Prolatis verbis consecrationis, statim hostiam consecratam genuflexus adorat: surgit, ostendit populo: reponit super corporale, iterum adorat: et non disiungit pollices et indices, nisi quando hostia tractanda est, vsque ad ablutionem digitorum. Tunc detecto calice dicit.	*After pronouncing the words of consecration, he immediately adores the host kneeling; he rises and shows it to the people. Having put it back on the corporal, he adores it again, and he does not disjoin his forefingers and thumbs, except when he is to take the host, until after the washing of his fingers. Then, uncovering the chalice, he says:*
Simili modo, postquam cenatum est: *ambabus manibus accipit calicem:* accipiens et hunc pręclarum calicem in sanctas ac venerabiles manus suas: item tibi gratias agens, *sinistra tenens calicem, dextra signat super eum,* bene✠dixit, deditque discipulis suis, dicens: Accipite et bibite ex eo omnes. *Profert verba consecrationis super calicem tenens illum parum eleuatum.*	In a similar way, when supper was ended: *he takes the chalice with both hands,* he took this precious chalice in his holy and venerable hands, and once more giving you thanks, *he takes the chalice in his left hand, and with his right he signs it,* he said the ✠ blessing and gave the chalice to his disciples, saying: Take this, all of you, and drink from it. *He pronounces the words of consecration over the chalice, holding it a little raised.*
Hic est enim calix sanguinis mei: noui et ęterni testamenti: mysterium fidei: qui pro vobis et pro multis effundetur in remissionem peccatorum.	For this is the chalice of my Blood, of the new and eternal covenant, the mystery of faith, which will be poured out for you and for many for the forgiveness of sins.
Prolatis verbis consecrationis deponit calicem super corporale, et genuflexus adorat: surgit et ostendit populo: dicens. Haec quotiescumque feceritis, in mei memoriam facietis. *Deponit, cooperit, et iterum adorat. Deinde disiunctis manibus dicit.*	*After pronouncing the words of consecration, he sets down the chalice on the corporal and kneeling he adores it; he rises and shows it to the people, saying:* As often as you do these [actions], you will do them in memory of me. *He sets down [the chalice], covers it and adores it again. Then, with his hands extended, he says:*
Unde et memores domine nos serui tui, sed et plebs tua sancta eiusdem Christi filii tui domini nostri, tam beatę passionis, nec non et ab inferis Resurrectionis, sed et in cęlos gloriosę Ascensionis, offerimus	Therefore, O Lord, as we celebrate the memorial of the blessed Passion, the Resurrection from the dead, and the glorious Ascension into heaven of Christ, your Son, our Lord, we, your servants and your holy people, offer to

(*cont.*)

Ordinarium Missę	The Ordinary of the Mass
pręclarę maiestati tuę, de tuis donis ac datis, *signat ter super hostiam et calicem simul,* hostiam ✠ puram: hostiam ✠ sanctam: hostiam ✠ immaculatam, *signat semel super hostiam, et semel super calicem,* panem ✠ sanctum vitę ęternę et calicem salutis perpetuę. *Extensis manibus prosequitur.*	your glorious majesty from the gifts that you have given us, *he signs the host and the chalice together three times,* this pure ✠ victim, this holy ✠ victim, this spotless ✠victim, *he signs the host once and the chalice once,* the holy Bread of ✠ eternal life and the Chalice of ✠ everlasting salvation. *He proceeds with his hands extended.*
Supra quę propitio ac sereno vultu respicere digneris: et accepta habere, sicuti accepta habere dignatus es munera pueri tui iusti Abel, et sacrificium patriarchę nostri Abrahę: et quod tibi obtulit summus sacerdos tuus Melchisedec, sanctum sacrificium, immaculatam hostiam.	Be pleased to look upon these offerings with a serene and kindly countenance, and to accept them, as once you were pleased to accept the gifts of your servant Abel the just, the sacrifice of Abraham, our father in faith, and the offering of your high priest Melchizedek, a holy sacrifice, a spotless victim.
Profunde inclinatus iunctis manibus dicit. Supplices te rogamus omnipotens deus: iube hęc perferri per manus sancti Angeli tui in sublime altare tuum in conspectu diuinę maiestatis tuę. Ut quotquot, *osculatur altare,* ex hac altaris participatione, sacrosanctum filii tui, *signat semel super hostiam, et semel super calicem,* cor✠pus et san✠guinem sumpserimus, omni benedictione cęlesti et gratia repleamur. Per eundem Christum dominum nostrum. Amen.	*Bowing profoundly and with his hands joined, he says:* In humble prayer we ask you, almighty God: command that these gifts be borne by the hands of your holy Angel to your altar on high in the sight of your divine majesty, so that all of us, *he kisses the altar,* who through this participation at the altar receive, *he signs the host once and the chalice once* the most holy ✠ Body and ✠ Blood of your Son, may be filled with every grace and heavenly blessing. Through the same Christ our Lord. Amen.
Commemoratio pro defunctis. Memento etiam domine famulorum famularumque tuarum: qui nos pręcesserunt cum signo fidei et dormiunt in somno pacis. *N. Iungit manus, orat aliquantulum pro his defunctis pro quibus orare intendit: et extensis manibus prosequitur.* Ipsis domine, et omnibus in Christo quiescentibus, locum refrigerij, lucis,	*Commemoration of the dead* Remember also, Lord, your servants who have gone before us with the sign of faith and rest in the sleep of peace. *N. He joins his hands, prays for a short while for the dead for whom he intends to pray and with his hands extended, he proceeds.* Grant them, O Lord, we pray, and all who sleep in Christ, a place of

(cont.)

Ordinarium Missę	The Ordinary of the Mass
et pacis, vt indulgeas deprecamur. Per eundem Christum dominum nostrum. Amen.	refreshment, light and peace. Through the same Christ our Lord. Amen.

Percutit pectus elata parum voce dicens.

Nobis quoque peccatoribus famulis tuis, de multitudine miserationum tuarum sperantibus, partem aliquam et societatem donare digneris, cum tuis sanctis apostolis et martyribus: cum Ioanne, Stephano, Mathia, Barnaba, Ignatio, Alexandro, Marcellino, Petro, Felicitate, Perpetua, Agatha, Lucia, Agnete, Cecilia, Anastasia: et omnibus sanctis tuis. Intra quorum nos consortium, non ęstimator meriti, sed venię, quęsumus, largitor admitte. Per Christum Dominum nostrum.

Striking his breast he says in a slightly raised voice:

To us, also, your servants, who, though sinners, hope in your abundant mercies, graciously grant some share and fellowship with your holy Apostles and Martyrs: with John the Baptist, Stephen, Matthias, Barnabas, Ignatius, Alexander, Marcellinus, Peter, Felicity, Perpetua, Agatha, Lucy, Agnes, Cecilia, Anastasia and all your Saints; admit us, we beseech you, into their company, not weighing our merits, but granting us your pardon, through Christ our Lord.

Per quem hęc omnia domine semper bona creas: *signat ter super hostiam et calicem simul dicens.* San✠ctificas, viui✠ficas: bene✠dicis et pręstas nobis, *discooperit calicem, genuflectit, accipit sacramentum dextera, tenens sinistra calicem: signat cum hostia ter a labio ad labium calicis dicens.*

Through whom you continue to make all these good things, O Lord; *he signs the host and the chalice together three times, saying,* you ✠ sanctify them, ✠ fill them with life, ✠ bless them, and bestow them upon us. *He uncovers the chalice, genuflects, takes the sacrament in his right hand and holds the chalice in his left. With the host he makes the sign of the cross from lip to lip over the chalice three times, saying:*

Per ip✠sum: et cum ip✠so: et in ip✠so: *bis signat inter pectus et calicem* est tibi deo patri ✠ omnipotenti: in vnitate spiritus ✠ sancti: *eleuans parum calicem cum hostia dicit* omnis honor et gloria, *reponit hostiam cooperit calicem, genuflectit, surgit et dicit.*

Through ✠ him, and with ✠ him, and in ✠ him, *he makes the sign of the cross between his breast and the chalice,* O God, almighty Father, in the unity of the Holy Spirit, *raising the chalice with the host a little, he says,* all glory and honour is yours, *he places the host on the corporal, covers the chalice, genuflects, rises and says:*

[*The conclusion of the doxology and the Lord's Prayer that follows are given with musical notations, in the festive and the ferial tone.*]

(cont.)

Ordinarium Missę	The Ordinary of the Mass
Per omnia secula seculorum. R. Amen.	For ever and ever. R. Amen.
Iungit manus. Oremus. Pręceptis salutaribus moniti, et diuina institutione formati, audemus dicere.	*He joins his hands.* At the Saviour's command and formed by divine teaching, we dare to say:
Extendit manus. Pater noster, qui es in cęlis. Sanctificetur nomen tuum. Adueniat regnum tuum. Fiat voluntas tua, sicut in cęlo, et in terra. Panem nostrum quotidianum da nobis hodie. Et dimitte nobis debita nostra, sicut et nos dimittimus debitoribus nostris. Et ne nos inducas intentationem. R. Sed libera nos a malo.	*He extends his hands.* Our Father, who art in heaven, hallowed be thy name; thy kingdom come, thy will be done on earth as it is in heaven. Give us this day our daily bread, and forgive us our trespasses, as we forgive those who trespass against us; and lead us not into temptation. R. But deliver us from evil.
Sacerdos secrete respondit. Amen.^c	*The priest responds in a low voice*: Amen.
Deinde accipit patenam inter indicem et medium digitos, dicit. Libera nos, quęsumus, domine, ab omnibus malis, pręteritis, pręsentibus et futuris: et intercedente beata et gloriosa semper virgine dei genitrice Maria, et sanctis apostolis tuis Petro et Paulo, atque Andrea cum omnibus sanctis: *signat se cum patena a fronte ad pectus.* da propitius pacem in diebus nostris: vt ope misericordię tuę adiuti, et a peccato simus semper liberi, et ab omni perturbatione securi.	*The he takes the paten between his index and middle fingers, he says:* Deliver us, Lords, we pray, from every evil, past, present, and to come; and by the intercession of the blessed and glorious ever Virgin Mary, Mother of God, of the blessed Apostles Peter and Paul, of Andrew, and all the saints, *he signs himself with the paten from forehead to breast,* graciously grant peace in our days, that by your aid of your mercy we may be always free from sin and safe from all turmoil.
Submittit patenam hostię, discooperit calicem, genuflectit, surgit, accipit hostiam, frangit eam super calicem per medium, dicens. Per eundem dominum nostrum Iesum Christum filium tuum.	*He places the host on the paten, uncovers the chalice, genuflects, rises, takes the host, breaks it in the middle above the chalice, saying:* Through the same Jesus Christ, your Son, our Lord.
Partem quę in dextera est, ponit super patena. Deinde ex parte quę in	*He places the part of the host which he holds in his right hand on the paten.*

(*cont.*)

Ordinarium Missę	The Ordinary of the Mass
sinistra remanserat, frangit particulam dicens.	Then he breaks a particle from the part that remains in his left hand, saying:
Qui tecum viuit et regnat in vnitate spiritus sancti deus.	Who lives and reigns with You in the unity of the Holy Spirit, God.
Aliam mediam partem cum ipsa sinistra ponit super patenam, et dextera tenens particulam paruam super calice, sinistra calicem, dicit.	*He places the other half with his left hand on the paten and holding the small particle above the chalice in his right hand, and the chalice in his left, he says:*
[*The conclusion to this prayer and the following salutation with its response are given in musical notation.*]	
Per omnia secula seculorum.	For ever and ever.
R. Amen.	R. Amen.
Cum ipsa particula signat ter super calicem, dicens.	*With the same particle he signs the chalice three times, saying:*
Pax ✠ domini, sit ✠ semper vobis✠cum.	The ✠ peace of the Lord be ✠ always with ✠ you.
R. Et cum spiritu tuo.	R. And with your spirit.
Particulam ipsam imponit in calicem, dicens secrete.	*He puts the same particle into the chalice, saying in a low voice:*
Haec commixtio et consecratio corporis et sanguinis domini nostri Iesu Christi, fiat accipientibus nobis in vitam ęternam. Amen.	May this mingling and consecration of the Body and Blood of our Lord Jesus Christ avail us who receive it unto life everlasting. Amen.
Cooperit calicem, genuflectit, surgit, et inclinatus sacramento, iunctis manibus, et ter pectus percutiens dicit:	*He covers the chalice, genuflects, rises and bowing to the sacrament, with his hands joined and striking his breast three times, he says:*
Agnus dei, qui tollis peccata mundi, miserere nobis.	Lamb of God, you take away the sins of the world, have mercy on us.
Agnus dei, qui tollis peccata mundi, miserere nobis.	Lamb of God, you take away the sins of the world, have mercy on us.
Agnus dei, qui tollis peccata mundi, dona nobis pacem.	Lamb of God, you take away the sins of the world, grant us peace.
In missis pro defunctis omisso miserere nobis, dicitur, dona eis requiem: et tertio additur, sempiternam.	*In Masses for the dead, have mercy on us is omitted, it is said:* grant them rest, *and the third time is added,* everlasting.
Tunc iunctis manibus inclinatus dicit sequentes orationes.	*Then, with his hands joined and bowing he says the following prayers:*

(cont.)

Ordinarium Missę	The Ordinary of the Mass
Domine Iesu Christe, qui dixisti apostolis tuis: pacem relinquo vobis, pacem meam do vobis: ne respicias peccata mea, sed fidem ecclesię tuę; eamque secundum voluntatem tuam pacificare et coadunare digneris. Qui viuis et regnas deus: per omnia secula seculorum. Amen.	Lord Jesus Christ, who said to your Apostles: Peace I leave you, my peace I give you, look not on my sins, but on the faith of your Church, and graciously grant her peace and unity in accordance with your will. Who live and reign for ever and ever. Amen.
Si danda est pax, osculatur altare, et dans pacem dicit. Pax tecum. R. Et cum spiritu tuo.	*If the peace is to be given, he kisses the altar and giving the peace, he says:* Peace be with you. R. And with your spirit.
In missis defunctorum non datur pax, neque dicitur pręcedens oratio. Domine Iesu Christe, fili dei viui, qui ex voluntate patris, cooperante spiritu sancto, per mortem tuam mundum viuificasti: libera me per hoc sacrosanctum corpus, et sanguinem tuum, ab omnibus iniquitatibus meis, et vniuersis malis: et fac me tuis inhęrere mandatis, et a te nunquam separari permittas. Qui cum eodem deo patre et spiritu sancto viuis et regnas deus in secula seculorum. Amen.	*In Masses for the dead the peace is not given and the preceding prayer is not said.* Lord Jesus Christ, Son of the living God, who by the will of the Father, with the cooperation of the Holy Spirit, through your death gave life to the world; free me by this, your most holy Body and Blood, from all my sins and from every evil; make me always cling to your commandments, and never let me be parted from you. Who with the same God the Father and the Holy Spirit, live and reign, God, for ever and ever. Amen.
Perceptio corporis et sanguinis tui domine Iesu Christe, quod ego indignus sumere pręsumo, non mihi proueniat in iudicium et condemnationem, sed pro tua pietate prosit mihi ad tutamentum mentis et corporis, et ad medelam percipiendam. Qui viuis et regnas cum deo patre, in vnitate spiritus sancti deus: per omnia sęcula sęculorum. Amen.	May the receiving of your Body and Blood, Lord Jesus Christ, which I, though unworthy, presume to receive, not bring me to judgment and condemnation, but through your loving mercy be for me protection in mind and body, and an effective remedy. You who live and reign with God the Father, in the unity of the Holy Spirit, God, for ever and ever. Amen.
Genuflectit, surgit et dicit. Panem celestem accipiam, et nomen domini inuocabo.	*He genuflects, rises and says:* I will take the Bread of heaven, and call upon the name of the Lord.
Accipit ambas partes hostię inter pollicem et indicem sinistrę manus, et patenam inter eundem indicem et	*He takes both parts of the host between the thumb and index finger of his left hand, and the paten between the*

(*cont.*)

Ordinarium Missę	The Ordinary of the Mass
medium, et dextera percutiens pectus, dicit ter.	same index finger and the middle finger. Striking his breast with his right hand, he says three times:
Domine non sum dignus, vt intres sub tectum meum: sed tantum dic verbo, et sanabitur anima mea.	Lord, I am not worthy that you should enter under my roof, but only say the word and my soul shall be healed.
Postea dextera se signans cum hostia super patena, dicit.	*After this, signing himself with the host above the paten in his right hand, he says:*
Corpus domini nostri Iesu Christi custodiat animam meam in vitam ęternam. Amen.	May the Body of our Lord Jesus Christ preserve my soul to life everlasting. Amen.
Sumit ambas partes hostię, iungit manus, et quiescit aliquantulum. Deinde discooperit calicem, genuflectit, extergit patenam super illum, et dicit.	*He receives both parts of the host, joins his hands and pauses for a short while. Then he uncovers the chalice, genuflects, wipes the paten over it and says:*
Quid retribuam domino pro omnibus quę retribuit mihi? Calicem salutaris accipiam, et nomen domini inuocabo. Laudans inuocabo dominum, et ab inimicis meis saluus ero.	What shall I render to the Lord, for all the things he has rendered unto me? I will take the chalice of salvation, and I will call upon the name of the Lord. Praising I will call upon the Lord and I shall be saved from my enemies.
Accipit calicem, et eo se signans dicit.	*He takes the chalice and signing himself with it, he says:*
Sanguis Domini nostri Iesu Christi custodiat animam meam in vitam ęternam. Amen.	May the Blood of our Lord Jesus Christ preserve my soul to life everlasting. Amen.
Sumit totum sanguinem cum particula. Quo sumpto, si qui sunt communicandi eos communicet, antequam se purificet. Postea dicit.	*He receives all the Blood together with the particle. When he has received it, if there are communicants, he will give them communion, before he purifies himself. Afterwards he says:*
Quod ore sumpsimus Domine, pura mente capiamus: et de munere temporali fiat nobis remedium sempiternum.	What has passed our lips as food, O Lord, may we possess in purity of heart, that what has been given to us in time may be our healing for eternity.
Interim porrigit calicem ministro, qui infundit ei parum vini quo se purificat: deinde prosequitur.	*Meanwhile he holds the chalice out to the minister, who pours into it a small quantity of wine, which he purifies himself. Then he continues:*

(*cont.*)

Ordinarium Missę	The Ordinary of the Mass
Corpus tuum, domine, quod sumpsi, et sanguis quem potaui, adhęreat visceribus meis, et pręsta; vt in me non remaneat scelerum macula, quem pura et sancta refecerunt sacramenta. Qui viuis et regnas in secula seculorum. Amen.	May your Body, O Lord, which I have received, and your Blood which I have drunk, cleave to my very soul, and grant that no stain of sin may remain in me, whom these pure and holy sacraments have refreshed. You who live and reign, for ever and ever. Amen.
Sumit ablutionem, extergit et operit calicem more solito, et prosequitur missam.	*He receives the ablution, wipes and covers the chalice in the usual manner and proceeds with the Mass.*
Dicto Ite Missa est, *vel* Benedicamus domino, *inclinat se ante medium Altaris, et dicit.* Placeat tibi sancta Trinitas obsequium seruitutis męę, et pręsta; vt sacrificium quod oculis tuę maiestatis indignus obtuli, tibi sit acceptabile, mihique, et omnibus pro quibus illud obtuli, sit te miserante propitiabile. Per Christum dominum nostrum. Amen.	*When he has said,* Go, this is the dismissal, *or* Let us praise the Lord, *he bows before the altar and says:* May the tribute of my worship be pleasing to you, O Holy Trinity, and grant that the sacrifice which I, though unworthy, have offered in the presence of your Majesty, may be acceptable to you, and through your mercy obtain forgiveness for me and all for whom I have offered it. Through Christ our Lord. Amen.
Deinde benedicit populum. Benedicat vos omnipotens Deus, pa✠ter: et fi✠lius: et Spiritus ✠ sanctus.	*Then he blesses the people:* May almighty God bless you, the ✠ Father, and the ✠ Son, and the Holy ✠ Spirit.
Legit Euangelium secundum Ioannem. In principio erat verbum.	*He reads the Gospel according to John:* In the beginning was the Word.
Finito euangelio sancti Ioannis discedens, pro gratiarum actione dicit antiphonam, et quę sequuntur: quę antiphona duplicabitur in principio.	*Having finished the Gospel of Saint John, he leaves and for thanksgiving says the antiphon and what follows; the antiphon is repeated at the beginning.*
Antiphona. Trium puerorum cantemus hymnum, quem cantabant in camino ignis, benedicentes dominum.	*Antiphon.* Let us sing the hymn of the three children, which they sang in fiery furnace, praising the Lord.
Psalmus. Benedicite omnia opera domini domino.	*Psalm.* Bless the Lord, all you works of the Lord.
Psalmus. Laudate dominum in sanctis eius: *in fine.* Gloria Patri.	*Psalm.* Praise the Lord in his holy places. *At the end:* Glory be to the Father.
Deinde repetitur antiphona. Trium puerorum. *Postea dicitur* Kyrie	*Then the antiphon is repeated.* Let us sing the hymn of the three children. *Afterwards he says.* Lord, have

(*cont.*)

Ordinarium Missę	The Ordinary of the Mass
eleison. Christe eleison. Kyrie eleison. Pater noster.	mercy. Christ, have mercy. Lord, have mercy. Our Father.
V. Et ne nos inducas in tentationem.	V. And lead us not into temptation.
R. Sed libera.	R. But deliver us.
V. Confiteantur tibi domine omnia opera tua.	V. Let all your works praise you, O Lord.
R. Et sancti tui benedicant tibi.	R. And let your saints bless you.
V. Exultabunt sancti in gloria.	V. The saints shall rejoice in glory.
R. Lętabuntur in cubilibus suis.	R. They shall rejoice in their resting places.
V. Non nobis domine, non nobis.	V. Not to us, O Lord, not to us.
R. Sed nomini tuo da gloriam.	R. But to your name give glory.
V. Domine exaudi orationem meam.	V. O Lord, hear my prayer.
R. Et clamor meus ad te veniat.	R. And let my cry come to you.
V. Dominus vobiscum.	V. The Lord be with you.
R. Et cum spiritu.	R. And with your spirit.
Oremus.	Let us pray.
Oratio.	*Prayer.*
Deus, qui tribus pueris mitigasti flammas ignium, concede propitius, vt nos famulos tuos non exurat flamma vitiorum.	O God, who allayed the flames of fire for the three children, graciously grant that the flame of vices may not consume us, your servants.
Da nobis, quęsumus, domine, vitiorum nostrorum flammas extinguere, qui beato Laurentio martyri tuo, tribuisti tormentorum suorum incendia superare.	Grant us, O Lord, we pray, to extinguish the flames of our vices, as you granted to blessed Laurence to overcome the fires of his torments.
Actiones nostras, quęsumus, domine, aspirando preveni, et adiuuando prosequere, vt cuncta nostra oratio et operatio a te semper incipiat, et per te cępta finiatur. Per Christum.	Direct, O Lord, we pray, our actions by your inspiration and further them by your assistance; that our every word and work may always begin with your and be completed through you. Through Christ.
[*Then follow musical intonations for the formulas of dismissal* Ite missa est, Benedicamus domino, *and* Requiescant in pace.]	

[a] In the printed text, the words introducing the proclamation of the gospel are in red ink, which is clearly a mistake.
[b] Again the words introducing the gospel are mistakenly printed in red ink.
[c] This is the rubric for the festive tone of the Lord's Prayer. The wording of the rubric for the ferial tone is slightly different: '*Sacerdos submissa voce dicit. Amen*'.

Epilogue

The historical development I have traced in this book is marked by both change and continuity. Change is of course to be expected in a trajectory that extends for well over a millennium. From its formative period in late antiquity, the ritual shape of the Roman Mass was affected by many religious, social, cultural, political and economic transformations. It is the essential continuity that should be noticed. The celebration of the Eucharist as a liturgical act is rooted in the words and actions of Jesus at the Last Supper. The priestly and sacrificial character of this liturgical act is clear even in the early Christian period, when sources are few and far between. The Latin liturgical tradition becomes more tangible to us from the fourth century onwards, above all with the early form of the Canon of the Mass attested by Ambrose. The ritual structure of the Roman Mass was forged in the practice of the papal stational liturgy of the late ancient and early medieval periods. Many sacramentaries of the Gregorian type begin with a separate section 'How the Roman Mass is to be celebrated', which corresponds to the description of *Ordo Romanus I*. With the exception of 'soft spots' (mainly in the introductory, the offertory and the concluding rites), this Order of Mass remained stable in different forms of liturgical celebration and was ultimately standardised in the post-Tridentine reform. The further outward we move from this core structure, the more variety we find. Liturgical development always begins at the local level and the Roman Mass became dominant in the Western Church through a long process that began with the Carolingian reforms in the eighth century and reached a decisive point with the climax of the medieval papacy in the thirteenth century. At the same time, local and regional customs and traditions not only survived but were integrated into the Roman structure and thus enriched it. Most importantly, there is a considerable measure of adaptation when a normative tradition is brought to life in a liturgical celebration. The ritual shape of the Mass will depend to a significant extent on the particular building, its material resources and – above all – the persons involved.

In the course of this historical enquiry, it has become evident that some of the landmarks of liturgical scholarship need to be revisited. Three areas in particular call for renewed research: Firstly, recent scholarly contributions propose a fresh look at the Carolingian reforms and allow us to see in them an organic enrichment of the Roman tradition. Secondly, in light of the wider manuscript evidence, Bonifaas Luykx's seminal typology of the *Ordo Missae* is rife for a new treatment. This would include a reconsideration of the role of private apology prayers in the received structure of the Mass. While some of these prayers are excessive in their length and penitential emphasis, they show an interiorisation of priestly spirituality that continues to be valuable. After due pruning, these prayers were successfully integrated into the Roman Order of Mass. Thirdly, the liturgy of the later medieval period, which has sustained damning criticism from liturgical scholars, has been to some degree rehabilitated. This complex period offers not only signs of decay but also of vitality. I hope that the broader picture I have offered in this book will provide a useful starting point for further investigation.

Bibliography

Ancient and medieval sources that are cited in this book according to the standard editions listed on the abbreviations page are not included in this bibliography.

Adams, Edward, *The Earliest Christian Meeting Places: Almost Exclusively Houses?* (London: Bloomsbury, 2013).

Adams, James N., *Bilingualism and the Latin Language* (Cambridge: Cambridge University Press, 2003).

Agostini, Marco, and Giovanna Baldissin Molli, eds., *Atti del Convegno di Studi Gian Matteo Giberti (1495–1543)* (Cittadella: Biblos, 2012).

Al-Suadi, Soham, and Peter-Ben Smit, eds., *T&T Clark Handbook to Early Christian Meals in the Greco-Roman World* (London; New York: Bloomsbury T&T Clark, 2019).

Alberigo, Giuseppe et al., eds., *Conciliorum Oecumenicorum Decreta*, 3rd ed. (Bologna: Istituto per le Scienze Religiose, 1973).

Allen, David L., *Hebrews*, The New American Commentary 35 (Nashville: B&H, 2010).

Allen, Percy Stafford, Hellen Mary Allen and Heathcote William Garrod, eds., *Opus Epistolarum Des. Erasmi Roterodami*, 12 vols. (Oxford: Clarendon Press, 1906–1958).

Allison, Dale C. Jr., *Constructing Jesus: Memory, Imagination, and History* (Grand Rapids: Baker Academic, 2010).

Amiet, Andreas, 'Die liturgische Gesetzgebung der deutschen Reichskirche in der Zeit der sächsischen Kaiser 922–1023', in *Zeitschrift für schweizerische Kirchengeschichte* 70 (1976), 1–106 and 209–307.

Andrieu, Michel, *Immixtio et consecratio: La consécration par contact dans les documents liturgiques du moyen âge* (Paris: A. Picard, 1924).

Andrieu, Michel, ed., *Les Ordines Romani du haut moyen âge*, 5 vols., Spicilegium Sacrum Lovaniense 11, 23, 24, 28, 29 (Louvain: Peeters, 1931–1961).

Le pontifical romain au moyen-âge, 4 vols., Studi e testi 86–88, 99 (Vatican City: Biblioteca Apostolica Vaticana, 1938–1941).

Angenendt, Arnold, 'Missa specialis: Zugleich ein Beitrag zur Entstehung der Privatmesse', in *Frühmittelalterliche Studien* 17 (1983), 153–221.

'Keine Romanisierung der Liturgie unter Karl dem Großen? Einspruch gegen Martin Morards *'Sacramentarium immixtum' et uniformisation romaine'*, in *Archiv für Liturgiewissenschaft* 51 (2009), 96–108.

Appel, Georg, *De Romanorum Precationibus*, Religionsgeschichtliche Versuche und Vorarbeiten VII.2 (Giessen: Töpelmann, 1909).

Arbeiter, Achim, *Alt-St. Peter in Geschichte und Wissenschaft: Abfolge der Bauten, Rekonstruktion, Architekturprogramm* (Berlin: Mann, 1988).

Arnold, John H., 'Belief and the Senses for the Medieval Laity', in *Les cinq sens au Moyen Âge*, ed. Éric Palazzo (Paris: Cerf, 2016), 623–647.

Ashworth, Henry, 'The Influence of the Lombard Invasions on the Gregorian Sacramentary', in *Bulletin of the John Rylands Library, Manchester* 37 (1954), 305–327.

'The Liturgical Prayers of St Gregory the Great', in *Traditio* 15 (1959), 107–161.

Atchley, E. G. C. F., *Ordo Romanus Primus* (London: Moring, 1905).

Atkinson, Charles M., 'Zur Entstehung und Überlieferung der "Missa graeca"', in *Archiv für Musikwissenschaft* 29 (1982), 113–145.

'*Doxa in ipsistis Theo*: Its Textual and Melodic Tradition in the "Missa graeca"', in *Chant, Liturgy, and the Inheritance of Rome: Essays in Honour of Joseph Dyer*, ed. Daniel J. DiCenso, Rebecca Maloy and Henry Bradshaw Society. Subsidia 8 (London: Boydell Press, 2017), 3–32.

Auerbach, Ernst, *Literatursprache und Publikum in der lateinischen Spätantike und im Mittelalter* (Bern: Francke, 1958).

Backhaus, Knut, *Der Hebräerbrief*, Regensburger Neues Testament (Regensburg: Friedrich Pustet, 2009).

Bagatti, Bellarmino, 'L'origine gerosolimitana della preghiera Supra quae del Canone Romano', in *Bibbia e Oriente* 21 (1979), 101–108.

Baldovin, John F., *The Urban Character of Christian Worship: The Origins, Development, and Meaning of Stational Liturgy*, Orientalia Cristiana Analecta 228 (Rome: Pont. Institutum Studiorum Orientalium, 1987).

'The Fermentum at Rome in the Fifth Century: A Reconsideration', in *Worship* 79 (2005), 38–53.

Banniard, Michel, *Viva voce: Communication écrite et communication orale du IVe au IXe siècle en occident latin*, Collection des études augustiniennes. Série Moyen-âge et temps modernes 25 (Paris: Institut des études augustiniennes, 1992).

Bardy, Gustave, *La question des langues dans l'Église ancienne*, Études de Théologie Historique (Paris: Beauchesne, 1948).

Barnwell, Paul S., 'Seating in the Nave of the Pre-Reformation Parish Church', in *Pews, Benches and Chairs: Church Seating in English Parish Churches from the Fourteenth Century to the Present*, ed. Trevor Cooper and Sarah Brown (London: Ecclesiological Society, 2011), 69–86.

'How to Do without Rubrics: Experiments in Reconstructing Medieval Lay Experience', in *Late Medieval Liturgies Enacted* (2016), 235–254.

'The Nature of Late Medieval Worship: The Mass', in *Late Medieval Liturgies Enacted* (2016), 207–218.

Barthe, Claude, 'The "Mystical" Meaning of the Ceremonies of the Mass: Liturgical Exegesis in the Middle Ages', in *The Genius of the Roman Liturgy: Historical Diversity and Spiritual Reach: Proceedings of the 2006 Oxford CIEL Colloquium*, ed. Uwe Michael Lang (Chicago: Hillenbrand Books, 2010), 179–197.

Bastiaensen, Antoon A. R., 'Die Bibel in den Gebetsformeln der lateinischen Kirche', in *The Impact of Scripture in Early Christianity*, ed. Jan den Boeft and M. L. Van Poll-Van De Lisdonk, Supplements to Vigiliae Christianae 44 (Leiden; Boston; Köln: Brill, 1999), 39–57.

Bauckham, Richard, 'Sabbath and Sunday in the Post-Apostolic Church', in *From Sabbath to Lord's Day*, ed. Donald A. Carson (Grand Rapids: Zondervan, 1982), 251–298.

'Imaginative Literature', in *The Early Christian World*, ed. Philip F. Esler, vol. 2 (London: Routledge, 2000), 791–812.

Jesus and the Eyewitnesses: The Gospels as Eyewitness Testimony, 2nd ed. (Grand Rapids: Eerdmans, 2017).

Bauer, Walter, *Rechtgläubigkeit und Ketzerei im ältesten Christentum*, Beiträge zur historischen Theologie 10 (Tübingen: Mohr, 1934).

Orthodoxy and Heresy in Earliest Christianity (Philadelphia: Fortress Press, 1971).

A Greek-English Lexicon of the New Testament and Other Early Christian Literature, rev. and ed. Frederick William Danker, 3rd ed. (Chicago; London: University of Chicago Press, 2000).

Baumstark, Anton, *Geschichte der syrischen Literatur: Mit Ausschluß der christlich-palästinensischen Texte* (Bonn: A. Marcus und E. Weber, 1922).

'Das "Problem" des römischen Messkanons, eine Retractatio auf geistesgeschichtlichem Hintergrund', in *Ephemerides Liturgicae* 53 (1939), 204–243.

'Antik-römischer Gebetsstil im Messkanon', in *Miscellanea Liturgica in honorem L. C. Mohlberg*, Bibliotheca Ephemerides Liturgicae 22 (Rome: Ed. Liturgiche, 1948), vol. I, 301–331.

Liturgie comparée: Principes et méthodes pour l'étude historique des liturgies chrétiennes, Collection Irénikon, 3rd ed. (Chevetogne: Éditions de Chevetogne, 1954).

Comparative Liturgy, rev. Bernard Botte, trans. Frank Leslie Cross (Westminster: The Newman Press, 1958).

Beasley-Murray, George R., *John*, Word Biblical Commentary 36, 2nd ed. (Nashville: Thomas Nelson, 1999).

Beck, Hans-Georg, 'Die frühbyzantinische Kirche', in *Handbuch der Kirchengeschichte, Bd. II/2: Die Reichskirche nach Konstantin dem Großen – Die Kirche in Ost und West von Chalkedon bis zum Frühmittelalter 451–700*, ed. Hubert Jedin et al. (Freiburg im Breisgau: Herder, 1975), 3–92.

Bell, Catherine, *Ritual: Perspectives and Dimensions* (New York: Oxford University Press, 1997).

Belting-Ihm, Christa, *Die Programme der christlichen Apsismalerei vom 4. Jahrhundert bis zur Mitte des 8. Jahrhunderts*, Forschungen zur Kunstgeschichte und christlichen Archäologie 4, 2nd ed. (Stuttgart: Steiner, 1992).

Benini, Marco, 'Johannes Eck als achtsamer Liturgie: Sein Ingolstädter Pfarrbuch als liturgiehistorische Quelle unter besonderer Berücksichtigung der szenischen Liturgie des Osterfestkreises', in *Archiv für Liturgiewissenschaft* 57 (2015), 72–95.

Beresford-Cooke, Ernest, *The Sign of the Cross in the Western Liturgies* (London: Longmans, Green and Co., 1907).

Bergin Patrick Jr., '*Preces Speciales*: Prototype of Tridentine Musical Reform', in *The Ohio State Online Musical Journal* 2 (2009), at www.osomjournal.org/issues/2/bergin.html?.

Bernard, Philippe, 'Les *Alleluia* mélismatiques dans le chant romain: Recherches sur la genèse de l'*alleluia* de la messe romaine', in *Rivista internazionale di musica sacra* 12 (1991), 286–362.

  Du chant romain au chant grégorien (IVe–XIIIe siècle), Collection Patrimoines – Christianisme (Paris: Cerf, 1996).

Berschin, Walter, *Griechisch-lateinisches Mittelalter: Von Hieronymus zu Nikolaus von Kues* (Bern; Munich: Francke, 1980).

Berthelé, Joseph, and Marcellin Valmary, eds., 'Les instructions et constitutions de Guillaume Durand le Spéculateur, publiées d'après le manuscrit de Cessenon', *Académie des Sciences et Lettres de Montpellier: Mémoires de la Section des Lettres*, 2e Série, Tome III, 1905, 1–148.

Beumer, Johannes, 'Die ältesten Zeugnisse für die römische Eucharistiefeier bei Ambrosius von Mailand', in *Zeitschrift für katholische Theologie* 95 (1973), 311–324.

Biblia sacra iuxta Vulgatam versionem, ed. Robert Weber et al., 4th ed. (Stuttgart: Deutsche Bibelgesellschaft, 1994).

Billett, Jesse D., 'The Liturgy of the 'Roman' Office in England from the Conversion to the Conquest', in *Rome across Time and Space: Cultural Transmission and the Exchange of Ideas c. 500–1400*, ed. Claudia Bolgia, Rosamond McKitterick and John Osborne (Cambridge: Cambridge University Press, 2011), 84–110.

Bireley, Robert, *The Refashioning of Catholicism 1450–1700: A Reassessment of the Counter Reformation* (Washington, DC: The Catholic University of America Press, 1999).

Bishop, Edmund, 'The Genius of the Roman Rite', in *Liturgica Historica: Papers on the Liturgy and Religious Life of the Western Church* (Oxford: Clarendon Press, 1918), 1–19.

Blaise, Albert, *Le vocabulaire latin des principaux thèmes liturgiques*, ouvrage revu par Antoine Dumas (Turnhout: Brepols, 1966).

Blomberg, Craig, *Contagious Holiness: Jesus' Meals with Sinners* (Downer's Grove: InterVarsity Press, 2005).

Blumenthal, Uta-Renate, and Detlev Jasper, '"Licet nova consuetudo" – Gregor VII. und die Liturgie', in *Bishops, Texts and the Use of Canon Law around 1100: Studies in Honour of Martin Brett*, ed. Bruce C. Brasington and

Kathleen G. Cushing, Church, Faith and Culture in the Medieval West (Aldershot: Ashgate, 2008), 45–68.

Blunt, Anthony, *Artistic Theory in Italy, 1450–1600* (Oxford: Oxford University Press, 1962).

Böhler, Dieter, 'The Church's Eucharist, the Lord's Supper, Israel's Sacrifice: Reflections on Pope Benedict's Axiom "Without Is coherence with Its Old Testament Heritage, Christian Liturgy Simply Cannot Be understood"', in Rutherford, Janet E., and James O'Brien, eds., *Benedict XVI and the Roman Missal: Proceedings of the Fourth Fota International Liturgical Conference, 2011*, Fota Liturgy Series (Dublin; New York: Four Courts Press; Scepter, 2013), 107–123.

Bölling, Jörg, *Das Papstzeremoniell der Renaissance: Texte – Musik - Performanz*, Tradition – Reform – Innovation 12 (Frankfurt am Main: Peter Lang, 2006).

'Zur Erneuerung der Liturgie in Kurie und Kirche durch das Konzil von Trient (1545–1563). Konzeption – Diskussion – Realisation', in *Papsttum und Kirchenmusik vom Mittelalter bis zu Benedikt XVI: Positionen – Entwicklungen – Kontexte*, ed. Klaus Pietschmann, Analecta musicologica 47 (Kassel: Bärenreiter, 2012), 124–145.

Bolton, Brenda, *The Medieval Reformation*, Foundations of Medieval History (London: Edward Arnold, 1983).

Bonniwell, William R., *A History of the Dominican Liturgy 1215–1945*, 2nd ed. revised and enlarged (New York: Joseph F. Wagner, 1945).

Borromeo, Carlo, *Instructionum Fabricae et Supellectilis Ecclesiaticae Libri II*, ed. Stefano Della Torre, Monumenta Studia Instrumenta Liturgica 18 (Vatican City: Libreria Editrice Vaticana, 2000).

Bossy, John, 'The Mass as a Social Institution, 1200–1700', in *Past & Present*, no. 100 (August 1983), 29–61.

Christianity in the West, 1400–1700 (Oxford: Oxford University Press, 1985).

Botte, Bernard, 'L'Anaphore Chaldéenne des Apôtres', in *Orientalia Christiana Periodica* 15 (1949), 259–276.

'Note historique sur la concelebration dans l'Eglise ancienne', in *La Maison-Dieu* 35 (1953), 9–23.

'L'épiclèse dans les liturgies syriennes orientales', in *Sacris Erudiri* 6 (1954), 48–72.

'Problèmes de l'anamnèse', in *Journal of Ecclesiastical History* 5 (1954), 16–24.

'Problèmes de l'anaphore syrienne des Apôtres Addaï et Mari', in *L'Orient syrien* 10 (1965), 89–106.

Botte, Bernard, and Christine Mohrmann, *L'ordinaire de la messe: Texte critique, traduction et etudes*, Études liturgique 2 (Paris; Louvain: Cerf; Abbaye du Mont César, 1953).

Boughton, Lynne C., '"Being Shed for You/Many": Time-Sense and Consequences in the Synoptic Cup Citations', in *Tyndale Bulletin* 48 (1997), 249–270.

'Transubstantiation and the Latin Text of the Bible: A Problem in the *Nova Vulgata Bibliorum*', in *Gregorianum* 83 (2002), 209–224.

Bouley, Allan, *From Freedom to Formula: The Evolution of the Eucharistic Prayer from Oral Improvisation to Written Texts*, Studies in

Christian Antiquity 21 (Washington, DC: The Catholic University of America Press, 1981).

Bouyer, Louis, *Liturgy and Architecture* (Notre Dame: University of Notre Dame Press, 1967).

Eucharist: Theology and Spirituality of the Eucharistic Prayer, trans. Charles Underhill Quinn (Notre Dame; London: University of Notre Dame Press, 1968), 188–191.

Bowers, Roger, 'The Reform of the Choir of Salisbury Cathedral, *c.*1450–1549', in *Late Medieval Liturgies Enacted*, 157–176.

Bracchi, Remo, 'Il latino liturgico sulla bocca del popolo', in *Il latino e i cristiani: Un bilancio all'inizio del terzo millennio*, ed. Enrico dal Covolo and Manlio Sodi, Monumenta Studia Instrumenta Liturgica 17 (Vatican City: Libreria Editrice Vaticana, 2002), 489–507.

Bradshaw, Paul F., *The Search for the Origins of Christian Worship: Sources and Methods for the Study of the Early Liturgy*, 2nd ed. (Oxford: Oxford University Press, 2002).

'The Genius of the Roman Rite Revisited', in *Ever Directed Towards the Lord: The Love of God in the Liturgy of the Eucharist Past, Present, and Hoped For*, ed. Uwe Michael Lang (London: T&T Clark, 2007), 49–61.

Reconstructing Early Christian Worship (Collegeville: Liturgical Press, 2009).

'Did Jesus Institute the Eucharist at the Last Supper?', in *Issues in Eucharistic Praying in East and West: Essays in Liturgical and Theological Analysis*, ed. Maxwell E. Johnson (Collegeville: Liturgical Press, 2010), 1–19.

Bradshaw, Paul F., and Maxwell E. Johnson, *The Origins of Feasts, Fasts, and Seasons in Early Christianity* (Collegeville: Liturgical Press, 2011).

The Eucharistic Liturgies: Their Evolution and Interpretation, Alcuin Club Collection 87 (London: SPCK, 2012).

Bradshaw, Paul F., Maxwell E. Johnson and L. Edward Philips, *The Apostolic Tradition: A Commentary*, Hermeneia (Minneapolis: Fortress Press, 2002).

Brandenburg, Hugo, 'Altar und Grab: Zu einem Problem des Märtyrerkultes im 4. und 5. Jh.', in *Martyrium in Multidisciplinary Perspective: Memorial Louis Reekmans*, ed. Mathijs Lamberigts and Peter van Deun, Bibliotheca Ephemeridum Theologicarum Lovaniensium 117 (Leuven: Peeters, 1995), 71–98.

Ancient Churches of Rome from the Fourth to the Seventh Century: The Dawn of Christian Architecture in the West, trans. Andreas Kropp, Bibliothèque de l'Antiquité Tardive 8 (Turnhout: Brepols, 2005).

Brent, Allen, *Ignatius of Antioch: A Martyr Bishop and the Origin of Episcopacy* (London: T&T Clark Continuum, 2007).

Browe, Peter, *Die Eucharistie im Mittelalter: Liturgiehistorische Forschungen in kulturwissenschaftlicher Absicht*, ed. Hubertus Lutterbach and Thomas Flammer, Vergessene Theologen 1, 7th ed. (Münster: Lit Verlag, 2019).

'Die scholastische Theorie der eucharistischen Verwandlungswunder', in *Die Eucharistie im Mittelalter*, 251–263 (originally published in *Theologische Quartalsschrift* 110 [1929], 305–332).

'Die eucharistischen Verwandlungswunder des Mittelalters', in *Die Eucharistie im Mittelalter*, 265–289 (originally published in *Römische Quartalsschrift* 37 [1929], 137–169).

'Die Kommunion an den drei letzten Kartagen', in *Die Eucharistie im Mittelalter*, 309–324 (originally published in *Jahrbuch für Liturgiewissenschaft* 10 [1930], 56–76).

'Wann fing man an, die Kommunion außerhalb der Messe auszuteilen?', in *Die Eucharistie im Mittelalter*, 303–308 (originally published in *Theologie und Glaube* 23 [1931], 755–762).

'Die Elevation in der Messe', in *Die Eucharistie im Mittelalter*, 475–508 (originally published in *Bonner Zeitschrift für Theologie und Seelsorge* 8 [1931], 20–66).

'Der Kommunionersatz im Mittelalter', in *Die Eucharistie im Mittelalter*, 415–424 (originally published in *Ephemerides Liturgicae* 8 [1934], 534–548).

'Wann fing man an, die in einer Messe konsekrierten Hostien in einer anderen Messe auszuteilen?', in *Die Eucharistie im Mittelalter*, 383–393 (orginally published in *Theologie und Glaube* 30 [1938], 388–404).

Brown, Raymond E., *The Gospel According to John*, Anchor Bible 29–29A, 2 vols. (New York: Doubleday, 1966–1970).

Bruns, Peter, 'Kult(ur)- und Volkssprachen in der Alten Kirche', in *Forum Katholische Theologie* 29 (2012), 241–250.

Buchinger, Harald, 'Liturgy and Early Christian Apocrypha', in *The Oxford Handbook of Early Christian Apocrypha*, ed. Andrew Gregory and Christopher Tuckett (Oxford: Oxford University Press, 2015), 361–377.

Buck, Thomas Martin, *Admonitio und Praedicatio: Zur religiös-pastoralen Dimension von Kapitularien und kapitulariennahen Texten (507–814)*, Freiburger Beiträge zur mittelalterlichen Geschichte 9 (Frankfurt am Main: Peter Lang, 1997).

Budde, Achim, 'Improvisation im Eucharistiegebet: Zur Technik freien Betens in der Alten Kirche', in *Jahrbuch für Antike und Christentum* 44 (2001), 127–144.

Die ägyptische Basilios-Anaphora: Text – Kommentar – Geschichte, Jerusalemer theologisches Forum 7 (Münster: Aschendorff, 2004).

Bullough, Donald A., *Carolingian Renewal: Sources and Heritage* (Manchester: Manchester University Press, 1991).

'The Carolingian Liturgical Experience', in *Continuity and Change in Christian Worship: Papers Read at the 1997 Summer Meeting and the 1998 Winter Meeting of the Ecclesiastical History Society*, ed. Robert N. Swanson, Studies in Church History 35 (Woodbridge: Boydell Press, 1999), 29–64.

Bultmann, Rudolf, *Theology of the New Testament*, trans. Kendrick Grobel, 2 vols. (New York: Scribner, 1951–1955).

Burchard, Christoph, 'The Importance of Joseph and Aseneth for the Study of the New Testament: A General Survey and a Fresh Look at the Last Supper', in *New Testament Studies* 33 (1987), 102–134.

Burke, Peter, *The Art of Conversation* (Ithaca: Cornell University Press, 1993).

Languages and Communities in Early Modern Europe: The 2002 Wiles Lectures Given at Queen's University, Belfast (Cambridge: Cambridge University Press, 2004).

Burkert, Walter, *Klassisches Altertum und antikes Christentum. Probleme einer übergreifenden Religionswissenschaft*, Hans-Lietzmann-Vorlesungen 1 (Berlin: Walter de Gruyter, 1996).

Burton, Peter, *The Old Latin Gospels: A Study of Their Texts and Language* (Oxford: Oxford University Press, 2000).

Busse Berger, Anna Maria, *Medieval Music and the Art of Memory* (Berkeley: University of California Press, 2005).

Cabié, Robert, *La lettre du pape Innocent I à Decentius de Gubbio (19 mars 416): Texte critique, traduction e commentaire*, Bibliothèque de la Revue d'histoire ecclésiastique 58 (Louvain: Publications Universitaires, 1973).

Calkins, Robert G., 'Liturgical Sequence and Decorative Crescendo in the Drogo Sacramentary', in *Gesta* 25 (1986), 17–23.

Callam, Daniel, 'Clerical Continence in the Fourth Century: Three Papal Decretals', in *Theological Studies* 41 (1980), 3–50.

'The Frequency of Mass in the Latin Church ca. 400', in *Theological Studies* 45 (1984), 613–650.

Callewaert, Camille, *S. Léon le Grand et les textes du Léonien*, Extrait de *Sacris Erudiri* I (Bruges; La Haye: Beyart; Nijhoff, 1948).

Cameron, Alan, 'Latin Revival of the Fourth Century', in *Renaissances before the Renaissance: Cultural Revivals of Late Antiquity and the Middle Ages*, ed. Warren Treadgold (Stanford: Stanford University Press, 1984), 42–58.

Cameron, Euan, *The European Reformation*, 2nd ed. (Oxford: Oxford University Press, 2012).

Capelle, Bernard, *Travaux liturgiques de doctrine et d'histoire*, 3 vols. (Louvain: Centre Liturgique, 1955–1967).

'Le Kyrie de la messe et le pape Gélase', in *Travaux liturgiques de doctrine et d'histoire*, vol. II, 116–134 (originally published in *Révue bénédictine* 46 [1934], 126–144).

'La main de S. Grégorie dans le sacramentaire grégorien', in *Travaux liturgiques de doctrine et d'histoire*, vol. II, 161–175 (originally published in *Revue bénédictine* 49 [1937], 13–28).

'Messes du pape s. Gélase dans le sacramentaire de Vérone', in *Travaux liturgiques de doctrine et d'histoire*, vol. II, 79–105 (originally published in *Revue bénédictine* 56 [1945/1946], 12–41).

'Le texte du "Gloria in excelsis"', in *Travaux liturgiques de doctrine et d'histoire*, vol. II, 176–191 (originally published in *Revue d'histoire ecclesiastique* 44 [1949], 439–457).

'Retouches gélasiennes dans le sacramentaire de Vérone', in *Travaux liturgiques de doctrine et d'histoire*, vol. II, 106–115 (originally published in *Revue bénédictine* 61 [1951], 3–14).

'L'introduction du symbole à la messe', in *Travaux liturgiques de doctrine et d'histoire*, vol. III, 60–81 (originally published in *Mélanges Joseph de Ghellinck, S.J.*, Museum Lessianum. Section historique 13–14, 2 vols. [Gembloux: Duculot, 1951], vol. II, 1003–1028).

'L'œuvre liturgique de s. Gélase', in *Travaux liturgiques de doctrine et d'histoire*, vol. II, 146–160 (originally published in *Journal of Theological Studies* NS 2 [1951], 129–144).

'Innocent Ier e le canon de la messe', in *Travaux liturgiques de doctrine et d'histoire*, vol. II, 236–247 (originally published in *Recherches de théologie ancienne et médiévale* 19 [1952], 5–16).

'Problèmes du Communicantes de la Messe', in *Travaux liturgiques de doctrine et d'histoire*, vol. III, 269–275 (originally published in *Rivista liturgica* 40 [1953], 187–195).

Cardó, Daniel, *The Presence of the Cross and the Eucharist: A Theological and Liturgical Investigation* (Cambridge: Cambridge University Press, 2019).

'The Eucharist in the First Three Centuries', in *The Cambridge History of Ancient Christianity*, ed. Bruce Longenecker and David Wilhite (Cambridge: Cambridge University Press), forthcoming.

Carleton Paget, James, *The Epistle of Barnabas: Outlook and Background* (Tübingen: Mohr, 1994).

Carpegna Falconieri, Tommaso di, *Il clero di Roma nel medioevo: Istituzioni e politica cittadina (secoli VIII–XIII)* (Roma: Viella, 2002).

Caspari, Carl Paul, *Ungedruckte, unbeachtete und wenig beachtete Quellen zur Geschichte des Taufsymbols und der Glaubensregel*, 3 vols. (Christiania: Malling, 1866–1875).

Caspary, Hans, *Das Sakramentstabernakel in Italien bis zum Konzil von Trient: Gestalt, Ikonographie und Symbolik, kultische Funktion*, 3rd ed. (Munich: Uni-Druck, 1969).

Cattaneo, Enrico, 'Influenze veronesi nella legislazione di san Carlo Borromeo', in *Problemi di vita religiosa in Italia nel Cinquecento: Atti del convegno di storia della Chiesa in Italia (Bologna, 2–6 sett. 1985)*, Italia sacra 2 (Padua: Editrice Antenore, 1960), 122–166.

Chadwick, Anthony, 'The Roman Missal of the Council of Trent', in *T&T Clark Companion to Liturgy*, ed. Alcuin Reid (London: Bloomsbury T&T Clark, 2016), 107–131.

Chavasse, Antoine, 'Messes du pape Vigile dans le sacramentaire léonien', in *Ephemerides Liturgicae* 64 (1950), 161–213 and 66 (1952), 145–215.

Le sacramentaire gélasien (Vaticanus Reginensis 316): Sacramentaire presbytéral en usage dans les titres romains au VIIe siècle, Bibliothèque de théologie IV,1 (Tournai: Desclée, 1958).

'L'Epistolier romain du Codex de Wurtzbourg, son organisation', in *Revue Bénédictine* 91 (1981), 280–331.

'A Rome, au tournant du Ve siècle, additions et remaniements dans l'ordinaire de la messe', in *Ecclesia Orans* 5 (1988), 25–42, reprinted in *La liturgie de la ville de Rome du Ve au VIIIe siècle*, 27–45.

La liturgie de la ville de Rome du Ve au VIIIe siècle: Une liturgie conditionnée par l'organisation de la vie in urbe et extra muros, Studia Anselmiana 112, Analecta Liturgica 18 (Rome: Centro Studi San Anselmo, 1993).

Les lectionnaires romains de la messe au VIIe et au VIIe e siècle: Sources et dérivés, Spicilegii Friburgensis Subsidia 22, 2 vols. (Fribourg Suisse: Editions Universitaire, 1993).

Chavoutier, Lucien, 'Un Libellus Pseudo-Ambrosien sur le Saint-Esprit', in *Sacris Eruditi* 11 (1960), 136–192.

Chupungco, Anscar J., 'History of the Roman Liturgy until the Fifteenth Century', in *Handbook for Liturgical Studies, Vol. I: Introduction to the Liturgy*, ed. Anscar J. Chupungco (Collegeville: Liturgical Press, 1997), 131–152.

Cianca, Jenn, *Sacred Ritual, Profane Space: The Roman House as Early Christian Meeting Place*, Studies in Christianity and Judaism 1 (Montreal; Kingston: McGill-Queen's University Press, 2018).

Clark, Alan, 'The Function of the Offertory Rite in the Mass', in *Ephemerides Liturgicae* 64 (1950), 309–344.

Coebergh, Charles, 'S. Gélase Ier, auteur principal du soi-disant Sacramentaire léonien', in *Ephemerides Liturgicae* 65 (1951), 171–181.

Coleman, Ian, 'The Rubrics of Revelation: A Liturgical Reading', in *Antiphon* 21 (2017), 290–318.

Coleman, Robert, 'Vulgar Latin and the Diversity of Christian Latin', in *Actes du 1er Colloque international sur le latin vulgaire et tardif (Pécs, 2–5 septembre 1985)*, ed. József Herman (Tübingen: Niemeyer, 1987), 37–52.

Concilium Tridentinum: Diariorum, Actorum, Epistularum, Tractatuum Nova Collectio, ed. Societas Goerresiana (Freiburg: Herder, 1901–).

Connolly, Richard Hugh, 'Pope Innocent I "De nominibus recitandis"', in *Journal of Theological Studies* 20 (1919), 215–226.

Conrad, Sven, 'Renewal of the Liturgy in the Spirit of Tradition: Perspectives with a View Towards the Liturgical Development of the West', in *Antiphon* 14 (2010), 95–136.

Coutsoumpos, Panayotis, *Paul and the Lord's Supper: A Socio-Historical Investigation*, Studies in Biblical Literature 84 (Frankfurt am Main: Peter Lang, 2005), 46–51.

Cowdrey, H. E. J., *Pope Gregory VII, 1073–1085* (Oxford: Clarendon Press, 1998).

'Pope Gregory VII (1073–85) and the Liturgy', in *Journal of Theological Studies* NS 55 (2004), 55–83.

Cross, Frank Leslie, 'Pre-Leonine Elements in the Proper of the Roman Mass', in *Journal of Theological Studies* 50 (1949), 191–197.

Crossan, John D., *The Historical Jesus: The Life of a Mediterranean Jewish Peasant* (San Francisco: Harper, 1991).

Cutrone, Emmanuel J., 'Cyril's Mystagogical Catecheses and the Evolution of the Jerusalem Anaphora', in *Orientalia Christiana Periodica* 44 (1978), 52–64.

Cuva, Armando, 'Pagine di storia del ministero suddiaconale alla messa papale', in *Fons vivus – Miscellanea liturgica in memoria di don E.M. Vismara*, ed. Armando Cuva (Zurich: PaS, 1971), 287–314.

Daschner, Dominik, *Die gedruckten Meßbücher Süddeutschlands bis zur Übernahme des Missale Romanum Pius V. (1570)*, Regensburger Studien zur Theologie 47 (Frankfurt am Main: Peter Lang, 1995).

Davies, William D., *Paul and Rabbinic Judaism: Some Rabbinic Elements in Pauline Theology*, 3rd ed. (London: SPCK, 1970).

Dawson, Christopher, *The Dividing of Christendom* (San Francisco: Ignatius Press, 2009; originally published in 1965).

Day, Juliette, 'The Origins of the Anaphoral Benedictus', in *Journal of Theological Studies* NS 60 (2009), 193–211.

De Blaauw, Sible, *Cultus et decor: Liturgia e architettura nella Roma tardoantica e medievale. Basilica Salvatoris, Sanctae Mariae, Sancti Petri*, Studi e testi 355–356, 2 vols. (Vatican City: Biblioteca Apostolica Vaticana, 1994).

Met het oog op het licht: Een vergeten principe in de oriëntatie van het vroegchristelijk kerkgebouw, Nijmeegse Kunsthistorische Cahiers 2 (Nijmegen: Nijmegen University Press, 2000).

De Clerck, Paul, *La prière universelle dans le liturgies latines anciennes: temoignages patristiques et textes liturgiques*, Liturgiewissenschaftliche Quellen und Forschungen 63 (Münster: Aschendorff, 1977).

De Zan, Renato, 'How to Interpret a Collect', in *Appreciating the Collect: An Irenic Methodology*, ed. James G. Leachman and Daniel P. McCarthy, Liturgiam Aestimare: Appreciating the Liturgy 1 (Farnborough: St Michael's Abbey Press, 2008), 57–82.

Dehandschutter, Boudewijn, *Polycarpiana: Studies on Martyrdom and Persecution in Early Christianity: Collected Essays*, ed. Johan Leemans, Bibliotheca Ephemeridum theologicarum Lovaniensium 205 (Leuven: Leuven University Press, 2007).

Deighan, Gerard, 'Continuity in Sacrifice: From Old Testament to New', in *Celebrating the Eucharist: Sacrifice and Communion. Proceedings of the Fifth Fota International Liturgical Conference, 2012*, ed. Gerard Deighan, Fota Liturgy Series 5 (Wells: Smenos Publications, 2014), 87–107.

Dekkers, Eligius, *Tertullianus en de geschiedenis der liturgie*, Catholica 6,2 (Brussels; Amsterdam: De Kinkhoren; Desclée de Brouwer, 1947).

Delogu, Paolo, 'The Papacy, Rome and the Wider World in the Seventh and Eighth Centuries', in *Early Medieval Rome and the Christian West: Essays in Honour of Donald A. Bullough*, ed. Julia M. H. Smith, The Medieval Mediterranean 28 (Leiden; Boston: Brill, 2000), 197–220.

Delumeau, Jean, *Catholicism between Luther and Voltaire: A New View of the Counter-Reformation*, trans. Jeremy Moiser (London: Burns & Oates, 1977).

Denzinger, Heinrich, and Peter Hünermann, eds., *Enchiridion symbolorum definitionum et declarationum de rebus fidei et morum*, 43rd ed. (San Francisco: Ignatius Press, 2012).

Deshman, Robert, 'The Exalted Servant: The Ruler Theology of the Prayerbook of Charles the Bald', in *Viator* 11 (1980), 385–417.

Deshusses, Jean, 'The Sacramentaries: A Progress Report', in *Liturgy* 18 (1984), 13–60.

Deshusses, Jean, ed., *Le sacramentaire grégorien: Ses principales formes d'après les plus anciens manuscrits*, Vol. I: *Le sacramentaire, le supplément d'Aniane*, Spicilegium Friburgense 16, 3rd ed. (Fribourg Suisse: Édition Universitaires, 1992).

DiCenso, Daniel J., 'Revisiting the *Admonitio Generalis*', in *Chant, Liturgy, and the Inheritance of Rome: Essays in Honour of Joseph Dyer*, ed. Daniel J. DiCenso and Rebecca Maloy, Henry Bradshaw Society. Subsidia 8 (London: Boydell Press, 2017), 315–367.

Ditchfield, Simon, *Liturgy, Sanctity and History in Tridentine Italy: Pietro Maria Campi and the Preservation of the Particular*, Cambridge Studies in Italian History and Culture (Cambridge: Cambridge University Press, 1995).

'Giving Tridentine Worship Back Its History', in *Continuity and Change in Christian Worship*, ed. Robert N. Swanson, Studies in Church History 35 (Woodbridge: Boydell Press, 1999), 199–226.

Dix, Gregory, *The Shape of the Liturgy* (London: Dacre Press, 1945).

Doig, Allan, *Liturgy and Architecture from the Early Church to the Middle Ages* (Aldershot: Ashgate, 2008).

Doležalová, Klára, and Ivan Foletti, eds., *The Notion of Liminality and the Medieval Sacred Space*, Convivium Supplementum 3 (Turnhout: Brepols, 2020).

Dölger, Franz Joseph, *Sol salutis: Gebet und Gesang im christlichen Altertum mit besonderer Rücksicht auf die Ostung in Gebet und Liturgie*, Liturgiegeschichtliche Forschungen, 4/5, 2nd ed. (Münster: Aschendorff, 1925).

'Zu den Zeremonien der Meßliturgie, III: *Ite missa est* in kultur-und sprachgeschichtlicher Bedeutung', in *Antike und Christentum* 6 (1940), 81–132.

Douglas, Mary, *Natural Symbols: Explorations in Cosmology*, 2nd ed. (London; New York: Routledge, 1996).

Doval, Alexis, *Cyril of Jerusalem, Mystagogue: The Authorship of the Mystagogic Catecheses*, Patristic Monograph Series 17 (Washington, DC: The Catholic University of America Press, 2001).

Draper, Jonathan A., ed., *The Didache in Modern Research*, Arbeiten zur Geschichte des antiken Judentums und des Urchristentums 37 (Leiden; New York: Brill, 1996).

Drobner, Hubertus R., *Lehrbuch der Patrologie* (Freiburg i. Br: Herder, 1994).

Droste, Diane Lynne, *The Musical Notation and Transmission of the Music of the Sarum Use, 1225–1500* (PhD dissertation, University of Toronto, 1983).

Duchesne, Louis, ed., *Le Liber pontificalis: Texte, introduction et commentaire*, Bibliothèque des Écoles françaises d'Athènes et de Rome, 2 vols. (Paris: E. Thorin, 1886, 1892).

Duffy, Eamon, *The Stripping of the Altars: Traditional Religion in England 1400–1570*, 2nd ed. (New Haven: Yale University Press, 2005).

'Worship', in *Fields of Faith: Theology and Religious Studies for the Twenty-First Century*, ed. David F. Ford, Ben Quash and Janet Martin Soskice (Cambridge: Cambridge University Press, 2005), 119–134.

Fires of Faith: Catholic England under Mary Tudor (New Haven; London: Yale University Press, 2009).

Duval-Arnould, Louis, 'Notes sur l'édition princeps du Missel Tridentin', in *Memoriam Sanctorum Venerantes: Miscellanea in onore di Monsignor Victor Saxer*, Studi di antichità cristiana 48 (Vatican City: Pontificio Istituto di Archeologia Cristiana, 1992), 269–284.

'Nouvelles recherches sur les premières impressions du 'Missel tridentin' (1570–1571)', in *De l'histoire de la Brie à l'histoire des réformes: Mélanges offerts au chanoine Michel Veissière*, ed. Michèle Bardon et al. (Paris: Fédération des Sociétés historiques et archéologiques de Paris et de l'Ile de France, 1993), 121–137.

Dyer, Joseph, 'The Offertory Chant of the Roman Liturgy and Its Musical Form', in *Studi Musicali* 11 (1982), 3–30.

'*Tropis semper variantibus*: Compositional Strategies in the Offertories of the Old Roman Chant', in *Early Music History* 17 (1998), 1–59.

'Review of James McKinnon, *The Advent Project*', in *Early Music History* 20 (2001), 279–309.

'The Desert, the City and Psalmody in the Late Fourth Century', in *Western Plainchant in the First Millennium: Studies in the Medieval Liturgy and Its Music*, ed. Sean Gallagher, James Haar, John Nádas and Timothy Striplin (Aldershot; Burlington: Ashgate, 2003), 11–43.

'Advent and the *Antiphonale Missarum*', in *Lingua mea calamus scribae: Mélanges offerts à madame Marie-Noel Colette par ses collègues, étudiants et amis*, ed. Daniel Saulnier, Katarina Livljanic and Christelle Cazaux-Kowalski, Études grégoriennes 36 (Solesmes: Éditions de Solesmes, 2009), 101–129.

'*Psalmi ante sacrificium* and the Origin of the Introit', in *Plainsong and Medieval Music* 20 (2011), 91–121.

Dykmans, Marc, S.J., *Le cérémonial papal de la fin du Moyen-Âge à la Renaissance*, 4 vols., Bibliothèque de l'Institut Historique Belge de Rome 24–27 (Brussels; Rome: Institut Historique Belge de Rome, 1977–1985).

Edwards, Mark, *Catholicity and Heresy in the Early Church* (Farnham; Burlington: Ashgate, 2009).

Ehrman, Bart D., *The New Testament: A Historical Introduction to the Early Christian Writings* (New York: Oxford University Press, 1997).

Eizenhöfer, Leo, '*Te igitur* und *Communicantes* im römischen Meßkanon', in *Sacris Erudiri* 8 (1956), 14–75.

Canon Missae Romanae. Pars altera: Textus propinqui, Rerum Ecclesiasticarum Documenta. Series minor. Subsidia studiorum 7 (Rome: Herder, 1966).

Ellard, Gerald, 'The Odyssey of a Familiar Prayer', in *Theological Studies* 2 (1941), 221–241.

Ellebracht, Mary P., *Remarks on the Vocabulary of the Ancient Orations in the Missale Romanum*, Latinitas Christianorum Primaeva 18, 2nd ed. (Nijmegen; Utrecht: Dekker & Van de Vegt, 1966).

Elze, Reinhard, 'Gregor VII. und die römische Liturgie', in *La Riforma Gregoriana e l'Europa: Congresso internazionale, Salerno, 20–25 maggio 1985*, ed. Alfons M. Stickler et al., Studi Gregoriani 13–14, 2 vols. (Rome: LAS, 1989–1991), vol. I, 179–188.

Emerton, Ephraim, trans., *The Letters of Saint Boniface*, with a new introduction and bibliography by Thomas F. X. Noble (New York: Columbia University Press, 2000).

Emery, Gilles, 'The Ecclesial Fruit of the Eucharist in St. Thomas Aquinas', in *Nova et Vetera* (English Edition) 2 (2004), 43–60.

Engberding, Hieronymus, 'Die Kunstprosa des eucharistischen Hochgebetes der griechischen Gregoriusliturgie', in *Mullus: Festschrift Theodor Klauser*, Jahrbuch für Antike und Christentum. Ergänzungsband 1 (Münster: Aschendorff, 1964), 100–110.

Eve, Eric, *Behind the Gospels: Understanding the Oral Tradition* (London: SPCK, 2013).

Ewig, Eugen, *Trier im Merowingerreich: Civitas, Stadt, Bistum* (Trier: Paulinus-Verlag, 1954).

Fabre, Paul, and Louis Duchesne, eds., *Le Liber censuum de l'Église romaine*, 3 vols., Bibliothèque des Écoles Françaises d'Athènes et de Rome 6 (Paris: Fontemoing, 1910–1952).

Fellerer, Karl Gustav, 'Die Constitutio Docta SS. Patrum Johannes XXII.', in *Geschichte der katholischen Kirchenmusik. Bd. 1: Von den Anfängen bis zum Tridentinum*, ed. Karl Gustav Fellerer (Kassel: Bärenreiter, 1972), 379–380.

Fellerer, Karl Gustav, and Moses Hadas, 'Church Music and the Council of Trent', in *The Musical Quarterly* 39 (1953), 576–594.

Ferguson, Everett, *Church History. Volume One: From Christ to Pre-Reformation* (Grand Rapids: Zondervan, 2005).

Baptism in the Early Church: History, Theology, and Liturgy in the First Five Centuries (Grand Rapids: Eerdmans, 2009).

'Factors Leading to the Selection and Closure of the New Testament Canon: A Survey of Some Recent Studies', in *The Early Church at Work and Worship. Volume 1: Ministry, Ordination, Covenant, and Canon* (Eugene: Cascade Books, 2013), 247–279 (originally published in *The Canon Debate*, ed. Lee Martin McDonald and James A. Sanders [Peabody: Hendrickson, 2002], 295–320).

Férotin, Marius, *Le Liber Mozarabicus Sacramentorum et les manuscrits mozarabes*, Monumenta Ecclesiae Liturgica 6 (Paris: Firmin-Didot, 1912).

Feulner, Hans-Jürgen, 'Liturgy', in *Dictionary of Early Christian Literature*, ed. Siegmar Döpp and Wilhelm Geerlings (New York: Herder and Herder, 2000), 384–388.

'Zu den Editionen orientalischer Anaphoren', in *Crossroads of Cultures: Studies in Liturgy and Patristics in Honor of Gabriele Winkler*, ed. Hans-Jürgen Feulner, Elena Velkovska and Robert F. Taft (Rome: Pontificio Istituto Orientale, 2000), 251–282.

Fiey, Jean Maurice, 'Išo'yaw le Grand. Vie du catholicos nestorien Išo'yaw III d'Adiabène (580–659)', in *Orientalia Christiana Periodica* 36 (1969), 305–333, and 36 (1970), 5–46.

Fine, Steven, *This Holy Place: On the Sanctity of the Synagogue during the Greco-Roman Period*, Christianity and Judaism in Antiquity Series 11 (Notre Dame: University of Notre Dame Press, 1997).

Finke, Heinrich, ed., *Acta Concilii Constantiensis*, 4 vols. (Münster: Regensbergsche Buchhandlung, 1896–1928).

Finkelstein, Louis, 'The Birkat-Ha-Mazon', in *Jewish Quarterly Review* 19 (1928/ 29), 211–262.

Fischer, Balthasar, '"Oratio periculosa": Eine altirische Bezeichnung für die Einsetzungsworte in der Messe', in *Prex eucharistica, Volumen III: Studia, Pars prima: Ecclesia antiqua et occidentalis*, ed. Albert Gerhards, Heinzgerhard Brakmann and Martin Klöckener, Spicilegium Friburgense 42 (Fribourg: Academic Press, 2005), 237–241.

Fischer, Ludwig, ed., *Bernhardi cardinalis et Lateranensis ecclesiae prioris, Ordo officiorum ecclesiae Lateranensis*, Historische Forschungen und Quellen 2–3 (Munich; Freising: Datterer & Cie. 1916).

Fitzmeyer, Joseph A., *The Gospel According to Luke*, Anchor Bible 28–28A, 2 vols. (New York: Doubleday, (1983–1985).

First Corinthians: A New Translation with Introduction and Commentary, The Anchor Yale Bible 32 (New Haven; London: Yale University Press, 2008).

Flynn, William T., 'Approaches to Early Medieval Music and Rites', in *Understanding Medieval Liturgy: Essays in Interpretation*, ed. Helen Gittos and Sarah Hamilton (London; New York: Routledge, 2018), 57–71.

Foley, Michael P., 'The Mystic Meaning of the *Missale Romanum*', in *Antiphon* 13 (2009), 103–125.

'The Whence and Whither of the Kiss of Peace in the Roman Rite', in *The Fullness of Divine Worship: The Sacred Liturgy and Its Renewal*, ed. Uwe Michael Lang (Washington, DC: The Catholic University of America Press, 2018), 81–142 (originally published in *Antiphon* 14 [2010], 45–94).

Folsom, Cassian, 'Gestures Accompanying the Words of Consecration in the History of the *Ordo Missae*', in *The Veneration and Administration of the Eucharist: The Proceedings of the Second International Colloquium on the Roman Catholic Liturgy Organised by the Centre International d'Etudes Liturgiques* (Southampton: Saint Austin Press, 1997), 75–94.

Forrest Kelly, Thomas, *The Beneventan Chant* (Cambridge: Cambridge University Press, 1989).

Fortescue, Adrian, *The Mass: A Study of the Roman Liturgy*, 2nd ed. (London: Longmans, Green and Co, 1950).

The Early Papacy to the Synod of Chalcedon in 451, 4th ed., ed. Alcuin Reid (San Francisco: Ignatius Press, 2008).

Frank, Karl Suso, 'Maleachi 1,10ff. in der frühen Väterdeutung: Ein Beitrag zu Opferterminologie und Opferverständnis in der alten Kirche', in *Theologie und Philosophie* 53 (1978), 70–79.

Franz, Adolph, *Die Messe im deutschen Mittelalter: Beiträge zur Geschichte der Liturgie und des religiösen Volkslebens* (Freiburg im Breisgau: Herder, 1902).

Fredriksen, Paula, *Paul, the Pagans' Apostle* (New Haven: Yale University Press, 2017).

Freestone, William H., *The Sacrament Reserved: A Survey of the Practice of Reserving the Eucharist, with Special Reference to the Communion of the Sick, during the First Twelve Centuries*, Alcuin Club Collections 21 (London: Mowbray, 1917).

Frutaz, Amato Pietro, 'Contributo alla storia della riforma del Messale promulgato da san Pio V nel 1570', in *Problemi di vita religiosa in Italia nel*

Cinquecento: Atti del Convegno di storia della Chiesa in Italia (Bologna, 2–6 sett. 1958), Italia Sacra 2 (Padua: Editrice Antenore, 1960), 187–214.

Fuhrmann, Wolfgang, '"Semper reformanda": Motiv- und Argumentationstraditionen der liturgisch-musikalischen Reform', in *Papsttum und Kirchenmusik vom Mittelalter bis zu Benedikt XVI: Positionen – Entwicklungen – Kontexte*, ed. Klaus Pietschmann, Analecta musicologica 47 (Kassel: Bärenreiter, 2012), 28–56.

Gallegos, Matthew E., 'Charles Borromeo and Catholic Tradition regarding the Design of Catholic Churches', in *Sacred Architecture* 9 (2004), 14–19.

Gamber, Klaus, *Missa Romensis: Beiträge zur frühen römischen Liturgie und zu den Anfängen des Missale Romanum*, Studia Patristica et Liturgica 3 (Regensburg: Pustet, 1970).

Liturgie und Kirchenbau: Studien zur Geschichte der Meßfeier und des Gotteshauses in der Frühzeit, Studia Patristica et Liturgica 6 (Regensburg: Pustet, 1976).

Garrow, Alan J. P., *The Gospel of Matthew's Dependence on the Didache* (London: T&T Clark, 2003).

Geertz, Clifford, 'Religion as a Cultural System', in *The Interpretation of Cultures: Selected Essays* (New York: Basic Books, 1973), 87–125.

Gelston, Anthony, *The Eucharistic Prayer of Addai and Mari* (Oxford: Clarendon Press, 1992).

Gerhards, Albert, 'Crossing Borders. The Kedusha and the Sanctus: A Case Study of the convergence of Jewish and Christian Liturgy', in *Jewish and Christian Liturgy and Worship: New Insights into Its History and Interaction*, ed. Albert Gerhards and Clemens Leonhard, Jewish and Christian Perspectives Series 15 (Leiden: Brill, 2007), 27–40.

Gerhardsson, Birger, *Memory & Manuscript: Oral Tradition and Written Transmission in Rabbinic Judaism and Early Christianity, with Tradition & Transmission in Early Christianity*, with a Foreword by Jacob Neusner, The Biblical Resource Series (Grand Rapids; Livonia: Eerdmans; Dove Booksellers, 1998).

Gittos, Helen, 'Researching the History of Rites', in *Understanding Medieval Liturgy: Essays in Interpretation*, ed. Helen Gittos and Sarah Hamilton (London; New York: Routledge, 2018), 13–37.

Gittos, Helen, and Sarah Hamilton, 'Introduction', in *Understanding Medieval Liturgy*, 1–10.

Gordon, Bruce, 'Conciliarism in Late Mediaeval Europe', in *The Reformation World*, ed. Andrew Pettegree (London; New York: Routledge, 2000).

Grant, Gerard G., 'The Elevation of the Host: A Reaction to Twelfth-Century Heresy', in *Theological Studies* 1 (1940), 228–250.

Guerrini, Francesco M., ed., *Ordinarium juxta ritum Sacri Ordinis Fratrum Praedicatorum* (Rome: Collegium Angelicum, 1921).

Guidobaldi, Federico, 'L'inserimento delle chiese titolari di Roma nel tessuto urbano preesistente: osservazioni ed implicazioni', in *Quaeritur inventus colitur: Miscellanea in onore di Padre Umberto Maria Fasola*, ed. Philippe Pergola, 2 vols., Studi di antichità cristiana 40 (Vatican City: Pontificio Istituto di Archeologia Cristiana, 1989).

Gy, Pierre-Marie, 'L'office du Corpus Christi et s. Thomas d'Aquin: État d'une recherche', in *Revue des sciences philosophiques et théologiques* 64 (1980), 491–507.

Haessly, Mary Gonzaga, *Rhetoric in the Sunday Collects of the Roman Missal: with Introduction, Text, Commentary and Translation* (Cleveland: Ursuline College for Women, 1938).

Hahn, Scott, *Kinship by Covenant: A Canonical Approach to the Fulfillment of God's Saving Promises*, The Anchor Yale Bible Reference Library (New Haven; London: Yale University Press, 2009).

Consuming the Word: The New Testament and the Eucharist in the Early Church (New York: Image, 2013).

Hamilton, Sarah, 'Interpreting Diversity: Excommunication Rites in the Tenth and Eleventh Centuries', in *Understanding Medieval Liturgy: Essays in Interpretation*, ed. Helen Gittos and Sarah Hamilton (London; New York: Routledge, 2018), 125–175.

Hammerstaedt, Jürgen, and Peri Terbuyken, 'Improvisation', in *Reallexikon für Antike und Christentum* 17 (1996), 1212–1284.

Hänggi Anton, and Irmgard Pahl, eds., *Prex eucharistica. Volumen I: Textus e variis liturgiis antiquioribus selecti*, Spicilegium Friburgense 12, 3rd ed. (Freiburg; Schweiz: Universitätsverlag, 1998).

Hanssens, Jean Michel, *Institutiones liturgicae de ritibus orientalibus, Tomus II: De missa rituum orientalium, Pars prima* (Rome: Apud Aedes Pont. Universitatis Gregorianae, 1930).

'La concelebrazione sacrificale della Messa', in *Divinitas* 2 (1958), 242–267.

Hanssens, Jean Michael, ed., *Amalarii Episcopi Opera Liturgica Omnia*, 3 vols., Studi e testi 138–140 (Vatican City: Biblioteca Apostolica Vaticana, 1948–1950).

Harnack, Adolf von, *The Mission and Expansion of Christianity in the First Three Centuries*, trans. and ed. James Moffatt, 2 vols., 2nd ed. (London; New York: Williams and Norgate, 1908).

Harnack, Adolf von, ed., *Porphyrius 'Gegen die Christen', 15 Bücher. Zeugnisse, Fragmente und Referate*, Abhandlungen der königlich preussischen Akademie der Wissenschaften, Jahrgang 1916, Philosophisch-historische Klasse 1 (Berlin: Verlag der Königl. Akademie der Wissenschaften, 1916).

Harper, John, 'Enacting Late Medieval Worship: Locations, Processes and Outcomes', in *Late Medieval Liturgies Enacted*, 31–45.

Harper, Sally, Paul S. Barnwell, and Magnus Williamson, eds., *Late Medieval Liturgies Enacted: The Experience of Worship in Cathedral and Parish Church* (London; New York: Routledge, 2016).

Harting-Correa, Alice L., ed. and trans., *Walafrid Strabo, Libellus de exordiis et incrementis quarundam in observationibus ecclesiasticis rerum*, Mittellateinische Studien und Texte 19 (Leiden: Brill, 1995).

Hartzell, Karl Drew, 'Diagrams for Liturgical Ceremonies: Late 14th Century', in *Local Maps and Plans from Medieval England*, ed. Raleigh A. Skelton and Paul D. A. Harvey (Oxford: Clarendon Press, 1986), 339–341.

Haslam, Richard, 'Pellegrino Tibaldi and the Design of S. Fedele, Milan', in *Arte Lombarda* 42/43 (1975), 124–153.

Hauke, Manfred, 'Shed for Many: An Accurate Rendering of the Pro Multis in the Formula of Consecration', in *Antiphon* 14 (2010), 169–229.

'The "Basic Structure" (*Grundgestalt*) of the Eucharistic Celebration According to Joseph Ratzinger', in Rutherford, Janet E., and James O'Brien, eds., *Benedict XVI and the Roman Missal: Proceedings of the Fourth Fota International Liturgical Conference, 2011*, Fota Liturgy Series (Dublin; New York: Four Courts Press; Scepter, 2013), 70–106.

Häussling, Angelus A., *Mönchskonvent und Eucharistiefeier: Eine Studie über die Messe in der abendländischen Klosterliturgie des frühen Mittelalters und zur Geschichte der Messhäufigkeit*, Liturgiewissenschaftliche Quellen und Forschungen 58 (Münster: Aschendorff, 1973).

Hayburn, Robert F., *Papal Legislation on Sacred Music: 95 A.D. to 1977 A.D.* (Collegeville: Liturgical Press, 1979, reprinted Harrison: Roman Catholic Books, 2006).

Hayward, Robert, 'The Jewish Roots of Christian Liturgy', in *T&T Clark Companion to Liturgy*, ed. Alcuin Reid (London: Bloomsbury T&T Clark, 2016), 23–42.

Hedrick, Charles W., *History and Silence: Purge and Rehabilitation of Memory in Late Antiquity* (Austin: University of Texas Press, 2000).

Heid, Stefan, 'Gebetshaltung und Ostung in frühchristlicher Zeit', in *Rivista di Archeologia Cristiana* 82 (2006), 347–404.

'Tisch oder Altar? Hypothesen der Wissenschaft mit weitreichenden Folgen', in *Operation am lebenden Objekt: Roms Liturgiereformen von Trient bis zum Vaticanum II*, ed. Stefan Heid (Berlin: be.bra wissenschaft, 2014), 351–374.

Altar und Kirche: Prinzipien christlicher Liturgie (Regensburg: Schnell & Steiner, 2019).

Hellholm, David, and Dieter Sänger, eds., *The Eucharist – Its Origins and Contexts: Sacred Meal, Communal Meal, Table Fellowship in Late Antiquity, Early Judaism, and Early Christianity. Vol. III: Near Eastern and Graeco-Roman Traditions, Archaeology*, Wissenschaftliche Untersuchungen zum Neuen Testament 376 (Tübingen: Mohr Siebeck, 2017).

Hen, Yitzhak, *Culture and Religion in Merovingian Gaul: A.D. 481–751*, Cultures, Beliefs and Traditions 1 (New York: Brill, 1995).

The Royal Patronage of Liturgy in Frankish Gaul: To the Death of Charles the Bald (877), Henry Bradshaw Society. Subsidia 3 (London: Boydell Press, 2001).

'The Nature and Character of the Early Irish Liturgy', in *L'Irlanda e gli irlandesi nell'Alto Medioevo: Spoleto, 16–21 aprile 2009* (Spoleto: Centro italiano di studi sull'Alto Medioevo, 2010), 353–380.

'The Romanization of the Frankish Liturgy: Ideal, Reality and the Rhetoric of Reform', in *Rome across Time and Space: Cultural Transmission and the Exchange of Ideas c. 500–1400*, ed. Claudia Bolgia, Rosamond McKitterick and John Osborne (Cambridge: Cambridge University Press, 2011), 111–123.

'Key Themes in the Study of Medieval Liturgy', in *T&T Clark Companion to Liturgy*, ed. Alcuin Reid (London: Bloomsbury T&T Clark, 2016), 73–92.

Hen, Yitzhak, ed., *The Sacramentary of Echternach: (Paris Bibliothèque Nationale, MS. Lat. 9433)*, Henry Bradshaw Society 110 (London: Boydell, 1997).

Hengel, Martin, and Anna Maria Schwemer, *Jesus und das Judentum*, Geschichte des frühen Christentums 1 (Tübingen: Mohr Siebeck, 2007).

Hesbert, René-Jean, *Antiphonale Missarum Sextuplex* (Paris; Brussels: Vromant, 1935; reprinted Rome: Herder, 1967).

Hiley, David, *Western Plainchant: A Handbook* (Oxford: Clarendon Press, 1993).

Hohler, Christopher, 'Reflections on Some Manuscripts Containing 13th-Century Polyphony', in *Journal of the Plainsong & Mediaeval Music Society* 1 (1978), 2–38.

Holl, Karl, 'Kultursprache und Volkssprache in der altchristlichen Mission', in *Kirchengeschichte als Missionsgeschichte: Band I. Die Alte Kirche*, ed. Heinzgünther Frohnes and Uwe W. Knorr (Munich: Kaiser, 1974), 389–396.

Hoping, Helmut, 'Liturgy and the Triune God: Rethinking Trinitarian Theology', in *Authentic Liturgical Renewal in Contemporary Perspective: Proceedings of the Sacra Liturgia Conference held in London, 5th–8th July 2016*, ed. Uwe Michael Lang (London: Bloomsbury T&T Clark, 2017), 21–30.

My Body Given for You: History and Theology of the Eucharist, trans. Michael J. Miller (San Francisco: Ignatius Press, 2019).

Hornby, Emma, *Gregorian and Old Roman Eighth-Mode Tracts: A Case Study in the Transmission of Western Chant* (Aldershot: Ashgate, 2002; reissued London; New York: Routledge, 2009).

Hucke, Helmut, 'Graduale', in *Ephemerides Liturgicae* 69 (1955), 262–264.

'Das Dekret "Docta Sanctorum Patrum" Papst Johannes' XXII.', in *Musica Disciplina* 38 (1984), 119–131.

Hughes, Andrew, *Medieval Manuscripts for Mass and Office: A Guide to Their Organization and Terminology* (Toronto; Buffalo: University of Toronto Press, 1982).

Huglo, Michel, *Les livres de chant liturgique* (Turnhout: Brepols, 1988).

Huizinga, Johan, *The Autumn of the Middle Ages*, trans. Rodney J. Payton and Ulrich Mammitzsch (Chicago: University of Chicago Press, 1996).

Hultgren, Arland J., *The Rise of Normative Christianity* (Minneapolis: Fortress Press, 1994).

Humphreys, Colin J., *The Mystery of the Last Supper: Reconstructing the Final Days of Jesus* (Cambridge: Cambridge University Press, 2011).

Hurtado, Larry W., *Lord Jesus Christ: Devotion to Jesus in Earliest Christianity* (Grand Rapids: Eerdmans, 2005).

Huyghebaert, Nicolas, 'Une legende de fondation: le *Constitutum Constantini*', in *Le Moyen Âge* 85 (1979), 177–209.

Innes, Matthew, 'Memory, Orality and Literacy in an Early Medieval Society', in *Past & Present*, no. 158 (1998), 3–36.

Jacob, André, 'La concélébration de l'anaphore à Byzance d'après le témoignage de Léon Toscan', in *Orientalia Christiana Periodica* 35 (1969), 249–256.

Jacob, Christoph, '*Arkandisziplin*', *Allegorese, Mystagogie: Ein neuer Zugang zur Theologie des Ambrosius von Mailand*, Theophaneia 32 (Frankfurt am Main: Anton Hain, 1990).

Jacobsen, Werner, 'Organisationsformen des Sanktuariums im spätantiken und mittelalterlichen Kirchenbau: Wechselwirkungen von Altarraum und Liturgie aus kunsthistorischer Perspektive', in *Kölnische Liturgie und ihre Geschichte: Studien zur interdisziplinären Erforschung des Gottesdienstes im Erzbistum Köln*, ed. Albert Gerhards and Andreas Odenthal, Liturgiewissenschaftliche Quellen und Forschungen 87 (Münster: Aschendorff, 2000), 67–97.

Jammers, Ewald, *Musik in Byzanz, im päpstlichen Rom und im Frankenreich: Der Choral als Textaussprache*, Abhandlungen der Heidelberger Akademie der Wissenschaften, Philosophisch-historische Klasse, 1962/1 (Heidelberg: C. Winter, 1962).

Jammo, Sarhad Y. H., 'The Anaphora of the Apostles Addai and Mari: A Study of Structure and Historical Background', in *Orientalia Christiana Periodica* 68 (2002), 5–35.

Jasper, Ronald C. D., and Geoffrey J. Cuming, *Prayers of the Eucharist: Early and Reformed*, 3rd ed. (Collegeville: Liturgical Press, 1987).

Jaubert, Annie, *La date de la Cène: Calendrier biblique et liturgie chrétienne*, Études bibliques 27 (Paris: Gabalda, 1957).

  The Date of the Last Supper, trans. Isaac Rafferty (New York: Alba House, 1965).

Jeanes, Gordon, 'Early Latin Parallels to the Roman Canon? Possible References to a Eucharistic Prayer in Zeno of Verona', in *Journal of Theological Studies* N.S. 37 (1986), 427–431.

  'Eucharist', in *The Study of Liturgy and Worship: An Alcuin Guide*, ed. Juliette Day and Benjamin Gordon-Taylor (Collegeville: Liturgical Press, 2013), 135–147.

Jedin, Hubert, 'Das Konzil von Trient und die Reform des Römischen Meßbuches', in *Liturgisches Leben* 6 (1939), 30–66.

  'Das Konzil von Trient und die Reform der liturgischen Bücher', in *Ephemerides Liturgicae* 59 (1945), 5–38.

Jeffery, Peter, 'The Introduction of Psalmody into the Roman Mass by Pope Celestine I (422–432)', in *Archiv für Liturgiewissenschaft* 26 (1984), 147–165.

  'Review of James McKinnon, *The Advent Project*', in *Journal of the American Musicological Society* 56 (2003), 167–179.

Jeremias, Joachims, *Die Abendmahlsworte Jesu*, 3rd ed. (Göttingen: Vandenhoeck & Ruprecht, 1964).

  The Eucharistic Words of Jesus, trans. Norman Perrin, The New Testament Library (London: SCM Press, 1966).

Jobst, Christoph, 'Liturgia e culto dell'Eucaristia nel programma spaziale della chiesa: I tabernacoli eucaristici e la trasformazione dei presbiteri negli scritti ecclesiastici dell'epoca introno al Concilio di Trento', in *Lo spazio e il culto: Relazioni tra edificio ecclesiale e uso liturgico dal XV al XVI secolo*, ed. Jörg Stabenow (Venice: Marsilio, 2006), 91–126.

Joy, John P., 'Ratzinger and Aquinas on the Dating of the Last Supper: In Defense of the Synoptic Chronology', in *New Blackfriars* 94 (2013), 324–339.

Johnson, Lawrence J., ed., *Worship in the Early Church: An Anthology of Historical Sources*, 4 vols. (Collegeville: Liturgical Press, 2009).

Johnson, Scott F., 'The Social Presence of Greek in Eastern Christianity, 200–1200 CE', in *Languages and Cultures of Eastern Christianity: Greek*, ed. Scott F. Johnson, The Worlds of Eastern Christianity, 300–1500, vol. 6 (Farnham: Ashgate, 2015), 1–122.

Jones, Christopher A., 'The Chrism Mass in Later Anglo-Saxon England', in *The Liturgy of the Late Anglo-Saxon Church*, ed. Helen Gittos and M. Bradford Bedingfield, Henry Bradshaw Society. Subsidia 5 (London: Boydell Press, 2005), 105–142.

Jounel, Pierre, *Les rites de la Messe: Ritus servandus in celebratione Missae* (Tournai: Desclée, 1963).

Jungmann, Josef A., *The Mass of the Roman Rite: Its Origins and Development (Missarum Sollemnia)*, trans. Francis A. Brunner, 2 vols. (New York: Benziger, 1951–1955).

Missarum sollemnia: Eine genetische Erklärung der römischen Messe, 2 vols., 5th ed. (Wien: Herder, 1962).

Die Stellung Christi im liturgischen Gebet, Liturgiewissenschaftliche Quellen und Forschungen 19–20, 2nd ed. (Münster: Aschendorff, 1962).

Kavanagh, Aidan, *On Liturgical Theology: The Hale Memorial Lectures of Seabury-Western Theological Seminary, 1981* (Collegeville: Liturgical Press, 1984).

Confirmation: Origins and Reform (New York: Pueblo 1988).

Keefe, Susan, *Water and the Word: Baptism and the Education of the Clergy in the Carolingian Empire*, Publications in Medieval Studies, 2 vols. (Notre Dame: University of Notre Dame Press, 2002).

Kehr, Paul, 'Papst Gregor VIII. als Ordensgründer', in *Miscellanea Francesco Ehrle. Vol. II: Per la storia di Roma e dei papi*, Studi e testi 38 (Rome: Biblioteca Apostolica Vaticana, 1924), 248–276.

Keith, Chris, and Anthony Le Donne, eds., *Jesus, Criteria, and the Demise of Authenticity* (London; New York: T&T Clark, 2012).

Kendrick, Robert L., *Singing Jeremiah: Music and Meaning in Holy Week* (Bloomington: Indiana University Press, 2014).

Kennedy, Vincent L., 'The Pre-Gregorian Hanc Igitur', in *Ephemerides Liturgicae* 50 (1936), 349–358.

'The Franciscan *Ordo Missae* in the Thirteenth Century', in *Medieval Studies* 2 (1940), 204–222.

'For a New Edition of the Micrologus of Bernold of Constance', in *Mélanges en l'honneur de Monseigneur Michel Andrieu*, Revue des sciences réligieuses. Volume hors série (Strasbourg: Palais universitaire, 1956), 229–241.

The Saints of the Canon of the Mass, Studi di Antichità Cristiana 14, 2nd rev. ed. (Vatican City: Pontificio Istituto di Archeologia Cristiana, 1963).

Kim, Seyoon, *The 'Son of Man' as the Son of God*, Wissenschaftliche Untersuchungen zum Neuen Testament 30 (Tübingen: Mohr Siebeck, 1983).

Kirk, Alan, *Memory and the Jesus Tradition*, The Reception of Jesus in the First Three Centuries 2 (London: Bloomsbury T&T Clark, 2018).

Kirkman, Andrew, 'The Invention of the Cyclic Mass', in *Journal of the American Musicological Society* 54 (2001), 1–47.

Kittel, Gerhard, and Gerhard Friedrich, eds., *Theological Dictionary of the New Testament*, ed., trans. Geoffrey W. Bromiley, 10 vols. (Grand Rapids: Eerdmans, 1964–1976).

Klauser, Theodor, *Das römische Capitulare Evangeliorum: Texte und Untersuchungen zu seiner ältesten Geschichte*, Liturgiegeschichtliche Quellen und Forschungen 28 (Münster: Aschendorff, 1935).

'Der Übergang der römischen Kirche von der griechischen zur lateinischen Liturgiesprache', in *Miscellanea Giovanni Mercati: 1. Bibbia, letteratura cristiana antica*, Studi e testi 121 (Vatican City: Biblioteca Apostolica Vaticana, 1946), 467–482.

A Short History of the Western Liturgy: An Account and Some Reflections, trans. John Halliburton, 2nd ed. (Oxford: Oxford University Press, 1979).

Klawans, Jonathan, *Purity, Sacrifice, and the Temple: Symbolism and Supersessionism in the Study of Ancient Judaism* (Oxford: Oxford University Press, 2006).

Klein, Elizabeth, 'Perpetua, Cheese, and Martyrdom as Public Liturgy in the Passion of Perpetua and Felicity', in *Journal of Early Christian Studies* 28 (2020), 175–202.

Klöckener, Martin, 'Zeitgemäßes Beten: Meßorationen als Zeugnisse einer sich wandelnden Kultur und Spiritualität', in *Bewahren und Erneuern: Studien zur Meßliturgie. Festschrift für Hans Bernhard Meyer SJ zum 70. Geburtstag*, ed. Reinhard Meßner, Eduard Nagel und Rudolf Pacik, Innsbrucker theologische Studien 42 (Innsbruck; Wien: Tyrolia, 1995), 114–142.

'Das eucharistische Hochgebet in der nordafrikanischen Liturgie der christlichen Spätantike', in *Prex eucharistica. Volumen III: Studia. Pars prima: Ecclesia antiqua et occidentalis*, ed. Albert Gerhards, Heinzgerd Brakmann and Martin Klöckener, Spicilegium Friburgense 42 (Fribourg: Academic Press, 2005), 43–128.

Kodell, Jerome, *The Eucharist in the New Testament* (Wilmington: Michael Glazier, 1988).

Koester, Helmut, *Ancient Christian Gospels: Their History and Development* (London: SCM Press, 1990).

Kolbaba, Tia M., *The Byzantine Lists: Errors of the Latins*, Illinois Medieval Studies (Chicago: University of Illinois Press, 2000).

'Latin and Greek Christians', in *The Cambridge History of Christianity. Vol. 3: Early Medieval Christianities, c. 600–c. 1100*, ed. Thomas F. X. Noble and Julia M. H. Smith (Cambridge: Cambridge University Press, 2008), 213–229.

Kraeling, Carl H. *The Christian Building*, Excavations at Dura Europos: Final Report VIII, 2 (New Haven: Dura-Europos, 1967).

Krautheimer, Richard, 'The Carolingian Revival of Early Christian Architecture', in *The Art Bulletin* 24 (1942), 1–38.

Krautheimer, Richard with Slobodan Ćurčić, *Early Christian and Byzantine Architecture*, 4th ed. (New Haven; London: Yale University Press, 1986).

Kulp, Joshua, 'The Origins of the Seder and Haggadah', in *Currents in Biblical Research* 4 (2005), 109–134.

Kumler, Aden, '*Imitatio Rerum*: Sacred Objects in the St. Giles's Hospital Processional', in *Journal of Medieval and Early Modern Studies* 44 (2014), 469–502.

Kunze, Gerhard, *Die gottesdienstliche Schriftlesung*, Veröffentlichungen der evangelischen Gesellschaft für Liturgieforschung 1 (Göttingen: Vandenhoeck & Ruprecht, 1947).

'Die Lesungen', in *Leiturgia* 2 (1955), 87–180.

Lafferty, Maura K., 'Translating Faith from Greek to Latin: Romanitas and Christianitas in Late Fourth-Century Rome and Milan', in *Journal of Early Christian Studies* 11 (2003), 21–62.

Lampe, Peter, *Christians at Rome in the First Two Centuries: From Paul to Valentinus*, trans. Michael Steinhauser and ed. Marshall D. Johnson (London: Continuum, 2006).

Lang, Arthur P., *Leo der Grosse und die Texte des Altgelasianums mit Berücksichtigung des Sacramentarium Leonianum und des Sacramentarium Gregorianum* (Steyl: Steyler Verlagsbuchhandlung, 1957).

'Leo der Große und die Dreifaltigkeitspräfation', in *Sacris Erudiri* 9 (1957), 116–162.

'Anklänge an liturgische Texte in Epiphaniesermonen Leos des Grossen', in *Sacris Erudiri* 10 (1958), 43–126.

'Leo der Grosse und die liturgischen Texte des Oktavtages von Epiphanie', in *Sacris Erudiri* 11 (1960), 12–135.

'Anklänge an Orationen der Ostervigil in Sermonen Leos des Grossen', in *Sacris Erudiri* 13 (1962), 281–325.

'Leo der Grosse und die liturgischen Gebetstexte des Epiphaniefestes', in *Sacris Erudiri* 14 (1963), 3*–22*.

'Anklänge an Orationen der Ostervigil in Sermonen Leos des Grossen', in *Sacris Erudiri* 18 (1967–1968), 5–119.

'Anklänge an eine Heilig Geist Oration in einem Sermo Leos des Grossen auf die Fastenzeit', in *Sacris Erudiri* 23 (1978–1979), 143–170.

'Anklänge an Orationen der Ostervigil in Sermonen Leos des Grossen', in *Sacris Erudiri* 27 (1984), 129–149.

'Anklänge an Orationen der Ostervigil in Sermonen Leos des Grossen', in *Sacris Erudiri* 28 (1985), 155–381.

Lang, Uwe Michael, 'Zum Einsetzungsbericht bei ostsyrischen Liturgiekommentatoren', in *Oriens Christianus* 89 (2005), 63–76.

'Eucharist without Institution Narrative? The Anaphora of Addai and Mari Revisited', in *Die Anaphora von Addai und Mari. Studien zu Eucharistie und Einsetzungsbericht*, ed. Uwe Michael Lang (Bonn: nova & vetera, 2007), 31–65.

Turning towards the Lord: Orientation in Liturgical Prayer, 2nd ed. (San Francisco: Ignatius Press, 2009).

The Voice of the Church at Prayer: Reflections on Liturgy and Language (San Francisco: Ignatius Press, 2012).

'Votive Masses of the Holy Face of Christ in Early Printed Diocesan Missals', in *Mediaeval Studies* 79 (2017), 165–203.

'Kissing the Image of Christ in the Medieval Mass', in *Antiphon* 22 (2018), 262–272.

'Goodness of Forms: The Demand for the Artistic Quality of Music for the Liturgy', in *Antiphon* 23 (2019), 311–331.

LaVerdiere, Eugene, *Dining in the Kingdom of God: The Origin of the Eucharist according to Luke* (Chicago: Liturgical Training, 1994).

Le Goff, Jacques, 'Le christianisme médiévale en occident du concile de Nicée (325) à la Réforme (début du XVIe siècle)', in *Histoire des religions, tome II*, ed. Henri-Charles Pueh, Encyclopédie de la Pléiade (Paris: Gallimard, 1972), 749–868.

Leachman, James G., 'History of Collect Studies', in *Appreciating the Collect: An Irenic Methodology*, ed. James G. Leachman and Daniel P. McCarthy, Liturgiam Aestimare: Appreciating the Liturgy 1 (Farnborough: St Michael's Abbey Press, 2008), 1 25.

Leitmeir, Christian T., 'Catholic Music in the Diocese of Augsburg c. 1600: A Reconstructed Tricinium Anthology and its Confessional Implications', in *Early Music History* 21 (2002), 117–173.

Lemarié, Joseph, 'A propos de l'Ordo Missae du Pontifical d'Hugues de Salins (Montpellier, Bibl. Fac. de Médecine 303)', in *Didaskalia* 9 (1979), 3–9.

Leroquais, Victor, *Les sacramentaires et les missels manuscrits des bibliothèques publiques de France*, 4 vols. (Paris: s.n., 1924).

'L'ordo missae du sacramentaire d'Amiens, B.N. lat. 9432', in *Ephemerides Liturgicae* 41 (1927), 435–445.

Levy, Kenneth, 'Toledo, Rome, and the Legacy of Gaul', in *Early Music History* 4 (1984), 49–99.

Lietzmann, Hans, *Messe und Herrenmahl: Eine Studie zur Geschichte der Liturgie*, Arbeiten zur Kirchengeschichte 8 (Bonn: A. Marcus und E. Weber, 1926).

Mass and the Lord's Supper: A Study in the History of the Liturgy, trans. Dorothea H. G. Reeve (Leiden: Brill, 1979).

Lippe, Robert, ed., *Missale Romanum Mediolani, 1474*, 2 vols., Henry Bradshaw Society 17 and 33 (London: Harrison and Sons, 1899 and 1907).

Lockwood, Lewis H., 'Vincenzo Ruffo and Musical Reform after the Council of Trent', in *The Musical Quarterly* 43 (1957), 342–371.

Lohfink, Gerhard, *Gegen die Verharmlosung Jesu* (Freiburg: Herder, 2013).

Lookadoo, Jonathon, *The High Priest and the Temple: Metaphorical Depictions of Jesus in the Letters of Ignatius of Antioch*, Wissenschaftliche Untersuchungen zum Neuen Testament II/473 (Tübingen: Mohr Siebeck 2018).

Lualdi, Katharine J., 'Change and Continuity in the Liturgy of the Prône from the Fifteenth to the Seventeenth Century', in *Prédication et liturgie au Moyen Âge*, ed. Nicole Bériou and Franco Morenzoni, Bibliothèque d'histoire culturelle du Moyen Âge 5 (Turnhout: Brepols, 2008), 373–389.

Lüdemann, Gerd, *Jesus after 2000 Years: What He Really Said and Did*, trans. John Bowden (London: SCM Press, 2000).

Lunn-Rockliffe, Sophie, *Ambrosiaster's Political Theology*, Oxford Early Christian Studies (Oxford: Oxford University Press, 2007).

Luyxk, Bonifaas, *De oorsprong van het gewone der Mis, De Eredienst der kerk 3* (Utrecht; Antwerp: Spectrum, 1955).

'Der Ursprung der gleichbleibenden Teile der heiligen Messe (Ordinarium Missae)', in *Liturgie und Mönchtum* 29 (1961), 72–119.

Lynch, Joseph H., *Early Christianity: A Brief History* (Oxford; New York: Oxford University Press, 2010).

Lynch, Joseph H., and Phillip C. Adamo, *The Medieval Church: A Brief History*, 2nd ed. (London; New York: Routledge, 2014).

MacCoull, Leslie B., 'John Philoponus, On the Pasch (CPG 7267): The Egyptian Eucharist and the Armenian Connection', in *Jahrbuch der österreichischen Byzantistik* 49 (1999), 1–12 (reprinted in *Documenting Christianity in Egypt: Sixth to Fourteenth Centuries*, Variorum Collected Studies 981 [Farnham: Ashgate, 2011], no. XII).

Mack, Peter, 'Rhetoric and Liturgy', in *Language and the Worship of the Church*, ed. David Jasper and Ronald C. D. Jasper, Studies in Literature and Religion (Basingstoke: Macmillan, 1990), 82–109.

Macomber, William F., 'The Oldest Known Text of the Anaphora of the Apostles Addai and Mari', in *Orientalia Christiana Periodica* 37 (1966), 335–371.

'The Maronite and Chaldean Versions of the Anaphora of the Apostles', in *Orientalia Christiana Periodica* 39 (1971), 55–84.

'The Ancient Form of the Anaphora of the Apostles', in *East of Byzantium: Syria and Armenia in the Formative Period (Dumbarton Oaks Symposium, 1980)*, ed. Nina G. Garsoïan, Thomas F. Mathews and Robert W. Thomson (Washington, DC: Dumbarton Oaks, 1982), 73–88.

Mahrt, William, 'Toward a Revision of *Music in Catholic Worship*', in *Sacred Music* 134 (2007), 54–60.

'Gregorian Chant in the Season of Lent', in *Antiphon* 21 (2017), 93–114.

Maloy, Rebecca, *Inside the Offertory: Aspects of Chronology and Transmission* (Oxford: Oxford University Press, 2010).

Manns, Frédéric, 'Une prière judéo-chrétienne dans le Canon Romain', in *Antonianum* 54 (1979), 3–9.

'L'origine judéo-chrétienne de la prière 'Unde et memores' du Canon Romain', in *Ephemerides Liturgicae* 101 (1987), 60–68.

Mansfield, Mary C., *The Humiliation of Sinners: Public Penance in Thirteenth-Century France* (Ithaca; London: Cornell University Press, 1995).

418 *Bibliography*

Manunza, Carlo, *L'Apocalisse come 'actio liturgica' cristiana: studio esegetico-teologico di Ap 1,9–16; 3,14–22; 13,9–10; 19,1–8*, Analecta Biblica 199 (Rome: Gregorian & Biblical Press, 2012).

Marcus, Robert, *The End of Ancient Christianity* (Cambridge: Cambridge University Press, 1990).

Markschies, Christoph, 'Wer schrieb die sogenannte Traditio Apostolica? Neue Beobachtungen und Hypothesen zu einer kaum lösbaren Frage aus der altkirchlichen Literaturgeschichte', in *Tauffragen und Bekenntnis: Studien zur sogenannten 'Traditio Apostolica', zu den 'Interrogationes de fide' und zum 'Römischen Glaubensbekenntnis'*, ed. Wolfram Kinzig, Christoph Markschies and Markus Vinzent, Arbeiten zur Kirchengeschichte 74 (Berlin; New York: de Gruyter, 1999), 1–79.

Marshall, Bruce D., 'The Whole Mystery of our Salvation: Saint Thomas Aquinas on the Eucharist as Sacrifice', in *Rediscovering Aquinas and the Sacraments: Studies in Sacramental Theology*, ed. Matthew Levering and Michael Dauphinais (Chicago: Hillenbrand, 2009), 39–64.

Martimort, Aimé-Georges, 'Origine et signification de l'alleluia de la messe romaine', in *Kyriakon: Festschrift Johannes Quasten*, 2 vols. (Münster: Aschendorff, 1970), vol. II, 811–834.

'À propos du nombre des lectures à la messe', in *Revue des Sciences Religieuses* 58 (1984), 42–51.

Les lectures liturgiques et leurs livres, Typologie des sources du Moyen Age occidental 64 (Turnhout: Brepols, 1992).

Mathews, Thomas F., 'An Early Roman Chancel Arrangement', in *Rivista di Archeologia Cristiana* 38 (1962), 73–96.

Mayer, Anton L., 'Die Liturgie und der Geist der Gotik', in *Jahrbuch für Liturgiewissenschaft* 6 (1926), 68–97.

Mayer-Himmelheber, Susanne, *Bischöfliche Kunstpolitik nach dem Tridentinum: Der Secunda-Roma-Anspruch Carlo Borromeos und die mailändischen Verordnungen zu Bau und Ausstattung von Kirchen* (Munich: Tuduv, 1984).

Mazza, Enrico, *The Origins of the Eucharistic Prayer*, trans. Ronald E. Lane (Collegeville: Liturgical Press, 1995), 102–129.

McClendon, Charles B., *The Imperial Abbey of Farfa: Architectural Currents of the Early Middle Ages* (New Haven; London: Yale University Press, 1987).

McDonald, Lee Martin, and James A. Sanders, eds., *The Canon Debate* (Peabody: Hendrickson, 2002).

McGowan, Andrew B., *Ascetic Eucharists: Food and Drink in Early Christian Ritual Meals*, Oxford Early Christian Studies (Oxford: Clarendon Press, 1999).

'Rethinking Agape and Eucharist in Early North African Christianity', in *Studia Liturgica* 34 (2004), 165–176.

Ancient Christian Worship: Early Church Practices in Social, Historical and Theological Perspective (Grand Rapids: Baker Academic, 2014).

McKinnon, James, *Music in Early Christian Literature*, Cambridge Readings in the Literature of Music (Cambridge: Cambridge University Press, 1987, reprinted 1993).

The Advent Project: The Later Seventh-Century Creation of the Roman Mass Proper (Berkeley; Los Angeles; London: University of California Press, 2000).

McKitterick, Rosamond, *The Frankish Church and the Carolingian Reforms, 789–895* (London: Royal Historical Society, 1977).

'Charles the Bald (823–877) and His Library: The Patronage of Learning', in *The English Historical Review* 95 (1980), 28–47.

'Nuns' Scriptoria in England and Francia in the Eighth Century', in *Francia* 19 (1992), 1–35.

Charlemagne: The Formation of a European Identity (Cambridge: Cambridge University Press, 2008).

McLaughlin, R. Emmet, 'The Word Eclipsed? Preaching in the Early Middle Ages', in *Traditio* 46 (1991), 77–122.

McNiven, Timothy, 'Rhetorical Gesture and Response in Ancient Rome', in *Semiotica* 139 (2002), 327–330.

Meeks, Wayne A., *The First Urban Christians: The Social World of the Apostle Paul* (New Haven: Yale University Press, 1983).

Meier, John R., *A Marginal Jew: Rethinking the Historical Jesus. Volume One: The Roots of the Problem and the Person*, The Anchor Bible Reference Library (New York: Doubleday, 1991).

Mertens, Volker, 'Leisen und Rufe', in *Die Musik in Geschichte und Gegenwart*, 2nd ed., Sachteil, vol. 5 (Kassel: Bärenreiter, 1996),1075–1078.

Meßner, Reinhard, 'Grundlinien der Entwicklung des eucharistischen Gebets in der frühen Kirche', in *Prex eucharistica. Volumen III: Studia. Pars prima: Ecclesia antiqua et occidentalis*, ed. Albert Gerhards, Heinzgerd Brakmann and Martin Klöckener, Spicilegium Friburgense 42 (Fribourg: Academic Press, 2005), 3–41.

Einführung in die Liturgiewissenschaft (Paderborn: Schöningh, 2009).

Metzger, Bruce, *A Textual Commentary on the Greek New Testament: A Companion Volume to the United Bible Societies' Greek New Testament (Fourth Revised Edition)*, 2nd ed. (London; New York: United Bible Societies, 1994).

Metzger, Marcel, 'La place des liturges à l'autel', in *Revue des sciences religieuses* 45 (1971), 113–145.

'À propos des règlements ecclésiastiques et de la prétendue *Tradition apostolique*', in *Revue des sciences religieuses* 66 (1992), 249–261.

History of the Liturgy: The Major Stages, trans. Madeleine Beaumont (Collegeville: Liturgical Press, 1997).

Miquel, Pierre, ed., *Cinq mille ans de prière* (Paris: Desclée de Brouwer, 1989).

Missale Romanum: Editio Princeps (1570), Edizione anastatica, ed. Manlio Sodi and Achille Maria Triacca, Monumenta Liturgica Concilii Tridentini 2, 2nd ed. (Vatican City: Libreria Editrice Vaticana, 2012).

Mittarelli, Giovanni B., and Anselmo Costadoni, eds., *Annales Camaldulenses Ordinis Sancti Benedicti*, vol. IX (Venice: Monasterium Sancti Michaelis De Muriano, 1773).

Mohlberg, Leo Cunibert, *Radulph de Rivo: Der letzte Vertreter der altrömischen Liturgie*, 2 vols. Recueil de travaux publiés par les membres des conférences d'histoire et de philologie 29 and 42 (Louvain: Bureaux du recueil, 1911–1915).

Mohlberg, Leo Cunibert, ed., *Sacramentarium Veronense (Cod. Bibl. Capit. Veron. LXXXV[80])*, Rerum Ecclesiasticarum Documenta. Series Maior. Fontes I, 3rd ed. (Rome: Herder, 1978).

ed., *Liber Sacramentorum Romanae Aeclesiae Ordinis Anni Circuli*, Rerum Ecclesiasticarum Documenta. Series maior. Fontes IV, 3rd ed. (Rome: Herder, 1981).

Mohlbert, Leo C., and Anton Baumstark, eds., *Die älteste erreichbare Gestalt des Liber Sacramentorum anni circuli der römischen Kirche*, Liturgiegeschichtliche Quellen 11/12 (Münster: Aschendorff, 1927).

Mohrmann, Christine, *Liturgical Latin: Its Origins and Character: Three Lectures* (London: Burns & Oates, 1959).

Études sur le latin des chrétiens, 4 vols., Storia e letteratura 65, 87, 103, 143 (Rome: Edizioni di Storia e Letteratura, 1961–1977).

'Rationabilis – λογικός', in *Études sur le latin des chrétiens*, vol. I, 179–187 (originally published in *Revue internationale des droits de l'antiquité* 5 [1950], 225–234).

'Quelques observations sur l'évolution stylistique du Canon de la Messe romain', in *Études sur le latin des chrétiens*, vol. III, 227–244 (originally published in *Vigiliae Christianae* 4 [1950], 1–19).

'The New Latin Psalter: Its Diction and Style', in *Études sur le latin des chrétiens*, vol. II, 109–131 (originally published in *The American Benedictine Review* 5 [1953], 7–33).

'Problèmes stylistiques dans la littérature latine chrétienne', in *Études sur le latin des chrétiens*, vol. III, 147–170 (originally published in *Vigiliae Christianae* 9 [1955], 222–246).

'Missa', in *Études sur le latin des chrétiens*, vol. III, 351–376 (originally published in *Vigiliae Christianae* 12 [1958], 67–92).

'The Ever-Recurring Problem of Language in the Church', in *Études sur le latin des chrétiens*, vol. IV, 143–159 (originally published in *Theology of Renewal. Vol. II: Renewal of Religious Structures*, ed. Lawrence K. Shook [Montreal: Palm, 1968], 204–220).

Molin, Jean-Baptiste, 'L'*Oratio fidelium*: Ses survivances', in *Ephemerides Liturgicae* 73 (1959), 310–317.

'Le prières du prône en Italie', in *Ephemerides Liturgicae* 76 (1962), 39–42.

'L'*oratio communis fidelium* au Moyen Âge en Occident du Xᵉ au XVᵉ siècle', in *Miscellanea liturgica in onore di Sua Eminenza il Cardinale Giacomo Lercaro*, 2 vols. (Rome: Desclée, 1966–1967), vol. II, 315–468.

'Quelques textes médiévaux de la prière universelle', in *Traditio et Progressio: Studi liturgici in onore del Prof. Adrien Nocent, OSB*, ed., Giustino Farnedi, Studia Anselmiana 95, Analecta liturgica 12 (Rome: Pontificio Ateneo S. Anselmo, 1988), 338–358.

Monson, Craig A., 'The Council of Trent Revisited', in *Journal of the American Musicological Society* 55 (2002), 1–37 (reprinted in *Music and the Renaissance: Renaissance, Reformation and Counter-Reformation*, ed. Philippe Vendrix [London; New York: Routledge, 2017], 487–524).

Monti, James, *A Sense of the Sacred: Roman Catholic Worship in the Middle Ages* (San Francisco: Ignatius Press, 2012).

Moore, Gerard, 'The Vocabulary of the Collects: Retrieving a Biblical Heritage', in *Appreciating the Collect: An Irenic Methodology*, ed. James G. Leachman and Daniel P. McCarthy, Liturgiam Aestimare: Appreciating the Liturgy 1 (Farnborough: St Michael's Abbey Press, 2008), 175–195.

Morard, Martin, '"Sacramentarium immixtum" et uniformisation romaine: de l'*Hadrianum* au *Supplément* d'Aniane', in *Archiv für Liturgiewissenschaft* 46 (2004), 1–30.

'Quand liturgie épousa predication: Note sur la place de la prédication dans la liturgie romaine au moyen âge (VIIIᵉ–XIVᵉ siècle)', in *Prédication et liturgie au Moyen Âge*, ed. Nicole Bériou and Franco Morenzoni, Bibliothèque d'histoire culturelle du Moyen Âge 5 (Turnhout: Brepols, 2008), 79–126.

Moreton, Bernard, *The Eighth-Century Gelasian Sacramentary: A Study in Tradition*, Oxford Theological Monographs (Oxford: Oxford University Press, 1976).

Moreton, Michael J., 'Εἰς ἀνατολὰς βλέψατε: Orientation as a Liturgical Principle', in *Studia Patristica* 18 (1982), 575–590.

'Rethinking the Origin of the Roman Canon', in *Studia Patristica* 26 (1993), 63–66.

Morin, German, 'Le plus ancient *comes* ou lectionnaire de l'église romaine', in *Revue Bénédictine* 27 (1910), 41–74.

Morley, Neville, 'Population Size and Social Structure', in *The Cambridge Companion to Ancient Rome*, ed. Paul Erdkamp (Cambridge: Cambridge University Press, 2013), 29–44.

Morton Braund, Susanna, ed. and trans., *Juvenal and Persius*, Loeb Classical Library 91 (Cambridge, MA; London: Harvard University Press, 1969).

Mowinckel, Sigmund, *Religion und Kultus*, trans. Albrecht Schauer (Göttingen: Vandenhoeck & Ruprecht, 1953).

Mulder-Bakker, Anneke B., *Living Saints of the Thirteenth Century: The Lives of Yvette, Anchoress of Huy; Juliana of Cornillon, Author of the Corpus Christi Feast; and Margaret the Lame, Anchoress of Magdeburg* (Turnhout: Brepols, 2012).

Murphy, Amanda, Herbert L. Kessler, Marco Petoletti, Eamon Duffy and Guido Milanese, eds., *The European Fortune of the Roman Veronica in the Middle Ages*, Convivium Supplementum 2 (Turnhout: Brepols, 2017).

Murray, Paul, *Aquinas at Prayer: The Bible, Mysticism and Poetry* (London: Bloomsbury, 2013).

Nabuco, Joaquim, 'La liturgie papale et les origines du cérémonial des éveques', in *Miscellanea liturgica in honorem L. Cuniberti Mohlberg*, 2 vols., Bibliotheca Ephemerides Liturgicae 22–23 (Rome: Edizioni Liturgiche, 1948–1949), vol. I, 283–300.

Nanni, Luigi, *La parrochia studiata nei documenti lucchesi dei secoli VIII–XIII*, Analecta Gregoriana 47 (Rome: Apud aedes Universitatis Gregorianae, 1948).

Nautin, Pierre, 'Le Rite du "Fermentum" dans les Eglises Urbaines de Rome', in *Ephemerides Liturgicae* 96 (1982), 510–522.

Nebel, Johannes, *Die Entwicklung des römischen Meßritus im ersten Jahrtausend anhand der Ordines Romani: Eine synoptische Darstellung*, Pontificium Athenaeum S. Anselmi de Urbe, Pontificium Institutum Liturgicum, Thesis ad Lauream 264 (Rome, 2000).

Neidiger, Bernhard, 'Wortgottesdienst vor der Reformation: Die Stiftung eigener Predigtpfründen für Weltkleriker im späten Mittelalter', in *Rheinische Vierteljahrsblätter* 66 (2002), 142–189.

Neusner, Jacob, 'Money-Changers in the Temple: The Mishnah's Explanation', in *New Testament Studies* 35 (1989), 287–290.

Newman, John Henry, *An Essay on the Development of Christian Doctrine*, 14th impression (London: Longmans, Green, and Co., 1909).

Niederwimmer, Kurt, *Die Didache*, Kommentar zu den Apostolischen Vätern 1, 2nd ed. (Göttingen: Vandenhoeck & Ruprecht, 1993).

Nilgen, Ursula, 'Die Bilder über dem Altar: Triumph- und Apsisbogenprogramme in Rom und Mittelitalien und ihr Bezug zur Liturgie', in *Kunst und Liturgie im Mittelalter: Akten des internationalen Kongresses der Bibliotheca Hertziana und des Nederlands Instituut te Rome. Rom, 28.–30. September 1997*, ed. Nicolas Bock, Sible de Blaauw, Christoph L. Frommel and Herbert Kessler, Römisches Jahrbuch der Bibliotheca Hertziana. Beiheft zu Band 33 (1999/2000) (Munich: Hirmer, 2000), 75–89.

Noble, Thomas F. X., *The Republic of St. Peter: The Birth of the Papal State, 680–825*, The Middle Ages Series (Philadelphia: University of Pennsylvania Press, 1984).

'Kings, Clergy and Dogma: The Settlement of Doctrinal Disputes in the Carolingian World', in *Early Medieval Studies in Memory of Patrick Wormald*, ed. Stephen Baxter et al., Studies in Early Medieval Britain (Farnham: Ashgate, 2009), 237–252.

Norden, Eduard, *Die antike Kunstprosa vom VI. Jahrhundert v. Chr. bis in die Zeit der Renaissance*, 2 vols., 2nd ed. (Leipzig: Teubner, 1909).

Nordhagen, Per Jonas, 'Constantinople on the Tiber: The Byzantines in Rome and the Iconography of their Images', in *Early Medieval Rome and the Christian West: Essays in Honour of Donald A. Bullough*, ed. Julia M. H. Smith, The Medieval Mediterranean 28 (Leiden; Boston: Brill, 2000), 113–134.

Nowakowska, Natalia, 'From Strassburg to Trent: Bishops, Printing and Liturgical Reform in the Fifteenth Century', in *Past & Present*, no. 213 (November 2011), 3–39.

Nußbaum, Otto, *Kloster, Priestermönch und Privatmesse: Ihr Verhältnis im Westen von den Anfängen bis zum hohen Mittelalter*, Theophaneia 145 (Bonn: Hanstein, 1961).

Die Aufbewahrung der Eucharistie, Theophaneia 29 (Bonn: Hanstein, 1979).

O'Neill, John C., 'Bread and Wine', in *Scottish Journal of Theology* 48 (1995), 169–184.

Oakley, Francis, 'Conciliarism', in *The Oxford Encyclopedia of the Reformation*, ed. Hans J. Hillerbrand, 3 vols. (New York: Oxford University Press, 1996), vol. I, 394–397

Odenthal, Andreas, '"Ante conspectum diuinae maiestatis tuae reus assisto": Liturgie- und frömmigkeitsgeschichtliche Untersuchungen zum "Rheinischen Messordo" und dessen Beziehungen zur Fuldaer Sakramentartradition', in *Liturgie vom frühen Mittelalter zum Zeitalter der Konfessionalisierung: Studien zur Geschichte des Gottesdienstes*, Spätmittelalter, Humanismus, Reformation 61 (Tübingen: Mohr Siebeck, 2011), 16–49 (originally published in *Archiv für Liturgiewissenschaft* 49 [2007], 1–35).

Olson, Oliver K., 'Flacius Illyricus als Liturgiker', in *Jahrbuch für Liturgik und Hymnologie* 12 (1967), 45–69.

'Matthias Flacius Illyricus, 1520–1575', in *Shapers of Religious Traditions in Germany, Switzerland, and Poland, 1560–1600*, ed. Jill Raitt (New Haven: Yale University Press, 1981), 1–17.

Osborn, Eric F., *Justin Martyr*, Beiträge zur historischen Theologie 47 (Tübingen: Mohr Siebeck, 1973).

Osborne, John, 'Rome and Constantinople in the Ninth Century', in *Rome across Time and Space: Cultural Transmission and the Exchange of Ideas c. 500–1400*, ed. Claudia Bolgia, Rosamond McKitterick and John Osborne (Cambridge: Cambridge University Press, 2011), 222–236.

Ourliac, Paul, 'L'institution paroissiale dans le droit canonique du XVe siècle', in *Revue de droit canonique* 25 (1975), 93–112.

Page, Christopher, *The Christian West and Its Singers: The First Thousand Years* (New Haven; London: Yale University Press, 2010).

Palazzo, Éric, *A History of Liturgical Books from the Beginning to the Thirteenth Century*, trans. Madeleine Beaumont (Collegeville: Liturgical Press, 1993).

'Art, Liturgy and the Five Senses in the Early Middle Ages', in *Viator* 41 (2010), 25–56.

L'invention chrétienne des cinq sens dans la liturgie et l'art au Moyen Âge (Paris: Cerf, 2014).

Paléographie musicale: Les principaux manuscrits de chant grégorien, ambrosien, mozarabe, gallican, publiés en fac-similés phototypiques, par les Bénédictins de Solesmes, vol. II (Solesmes: Imprimerie Saint-Pierre, 1891).

Panofsky, Erwin, 'Renaissance and Renascences', in *The Kenyon Review* 6 (1944), 201–236.

Parkes, Henry, *The Making of Liturgy in the Ottonian Church: Books, Music and Ritual in Mainz, 950–1050*, Cambridge Studies in Medieval Life and Thought. Fourth Series 100 (Cambridge: Cambridge University Press, 2015).

'Questioning the Authority of Vogel and Elze's *Pontifical romano-germanique*', in *Understanding Medieval Liturgy: Essays in Interpretation*, ed. Helen Gittos and Sarah Hamilton (London; New York: Routledge, 2018), 75–101.

'Henry II, Liturgical Patronage and the Birth of the "Romano-German Pontifical"', in *Early Medieval Europe* 28 (2020), 104–141.

Partoens, Gert, 'Prédication, orthodoxie et liturgie: Les sermons d'Augustine prononcés à Carthage en septembre–octobre 417', in *Prédication et liturgie au Moyen Âge*, ed. Nicole Bériou and Franco Morenzoni, Bibliothèque d'histoire culturelle du Moyen Âge 5 (Turnhout: Brepols, 2008), 23–51.

Patout Burns, J. Jr., and Robin M. Jensen, *Christianity in Roman Africa: The Development of Its Practices and Beliefs* (Grand Rapids: Eerdmans, 2014).

Pecklers, Keith, *Dynamic Equivalence: The Living Language of Christian Worship*, (Collegeville: Liturgical Press, 2003).

Peri, Vittorio, '"Nichil in ecclesia sine causa": Note di vita liturgica romana nel XII secolo', in *Rivista di archeologia cristiana* 50 (1974), 249–273.

Perrin, Nicholas, *Jesus the Temple* (Grand Rapids: Bakes Academic, 2010).

Pesch, Rudolf, *Das Abendmahl und Jesu Todesverständnis*, Quaestiones disputatae 80 (Freiburg: Herder, 1978).

Peterson, Erik Frühkirche, *Judentum und Gnosis: Studien und Untersuchungen* (Freiburg: Herder, 1959).

Pfaff, Richard W., *The Liturgy in Medieval England: A History* (Cambridge: Cambridge University Press, 2009).

Pierce Joanne M., 'New Research Directions in Medieval Liturgy: The Liturgical Books of Sigebert of Minden (1022–1036)', in *Fountain of Life*, ed. Gerard Austin (Collegeville: Liturgical Press, 1986), 51–67.

'Early Medieval Prayers Addressed to the Trinity in the *Ordo Missae* of Sigebert of Minden', in *Traditio* 51 (1996), 179–200.

'The Evolution of the Ordo Missae in the Early Middle Ages', in *Medieval Liturgy: A Book of Essays*, ed. Lizette Larson-Miller, Garland Medieval Casebooks 18 (New York: Garland, 1997), 3–24.

Pierce, Joanne M., and John F. Romano, 'The *Ordo Missae* of the Roman Rite: Historical Background', in *A Commentary on the Order of Mass of the Roman Missal*, ed. Edward Foley et al. (Collegeville: Liturgical Press, 2011), 3–34.

Pietri, Charles, *Roma christiana: Recherches sur l'Eglise de Rome, son organisation, sa politique, son idéologie de Miltiade à Sixte III (311–440)*, Bibliothèque des écoles françaises d'Athènes et de Rome 224, 2 vols. (Rome: École française de Rome, 1976).

'Damase évêque de Rome', in *Saecularia Damasiana: Atti del convegno internazionale per il XVI centenario della morte di Papa Damaso I (11-12-384–10/12-12-1984)*, Studi di antichità cristiana 39 (Vatican City: Pontificio Istituto di Archeologia Cristiana, 1986), 29–58.

Pinell, Jordi, 'La grande conclusion du Canon romain', in *La Maison-Dieu* 88 (1966), 96–115.

Pitre, Brant, *Jesus and the Last Supper* (Grand Rapids: Eerdmans, 2015).

Powell, Douglas, 'Arkandisziplin', in *Theologische Realenzyklopädie* 4 (1979), 1–8.

Pristas, Lauren, 'The Orations of the Vatican II Missals: Policies for Revision', in *Communio (US)* 30 (2003), 621–653.

'The Post-Vatican II Revision of the Lenten Collects', in *Ever Directed Towards the Lord: The Love of God in the Liturgy of the Eucharist Past Present, and Hoped For*, ed. Uwe Michael Lang (London: T&T Clark [Continuum], 2007), 62–89.

Prosinger, Franz, *Das Blut des Bundes – vergossen für viele? Zur Übersetzung und Interpretation des hyper pollôn in Mk 14,24*, Quaestiones non disputatae 12 (Siegburg: Franz Schmitt, 2007).

Quoëx, Franck, 'Ritualité et chant sacré dans l'*Ordo Romanus Primus* (VII–VIIIème siècle)', in *Aevum* 76 (2002), 253–265.

'Thomas d'Aquin, mystagogue: l'*Expositio Missae* de la *Somme de théologie* (IIIa, q. 83, a. 4–5)', in *Revue Thomiste* 105 (2005), 179–225 and 435–472.

'Ritual and Sacred Chant in the *Ordo Romanus* Primus (Seventh–Eighth Century)', in *Antiphon* 22 (2018), 199–219.

Radice, Betty, trans., *Pliny: Letters, Volume II: Books 8–10. Panegyricus*, Loeb Classical Library 59 (Cambridge, MA: Harvard University Press, 1969).

Rankin, Susan, 'Carolingian Liturgical Books: Problems of Categorization', in *Gazette du livre medieval* 62 (2016), 21–33.

Rasmussen, Niels K., 'Célébration épiscopale et célébration presbytérale: un essai de typologie', in *Segni e riti nella chiesa altomedievale occidentale, 11–17 aprile 1985*, Settimane di studio del Centro italiano di studi sull'alto medioevo 33 (Spoleto: Presso la Sede del Centro, 1987), vol. II, 581–607.

Ratcliff, Edward C., 'The Institution Narrative of the Roman Canon Missae: Its Beginning and Early Background', in *Liturgical Studies*, ed. Arthur H. Couratin and David. H. Tripp (London: SPCK, 1976), 49–65 (originally published in *Studia Patristica* 2 [1957], 64–82).

Ratzinger, Joseph – Benedict XVI, *Jesus of Nazareth. Part Two: Holy Week. From the Entrance into Jerusalem to the Resurrection*, trans. Philip J. Whitmore (San Francisco: Ignatius Press, 2011).

Ratzinger, Joseph, *Theology of the Liturgy: The Sacramental Foundation of Christian Existence,* ed. Michael J. Miller, trans. John Saward, et al., Joseph Ratzinger Collected Works 11 (San Francisco: Ignatius Press, 2014).

'Form and Content of the Eucharistic Celebration', in *Theology of the Liturgy*, 299–318 (originally published in 1978).

'The Artistic Transposition of the Faith: Theological Problems of Church Music', in *Theology of the Liturgy*, 480–493 (originally published in 1978).

Regan, Patrick, 'The Collect in Context', in *Appreciating the Collect: An Irenic Methodology*, ed. James G. Leachman and Daniel P. McCarthy, Liturgiam Aestimare: Appreciating the Liturgy 1 (Farnborough: St Michael's Abbey Press, 2008), 83–103.

Reif, Stefan C., 'The Second Temple Period, Qumran Research, and Rabbinic Liturgy: Some Contextual and Linguistic Comparisons', in *Liturgical Perspectives: Prayer and Poetry in Light of the Dead Sea Scrolls*, ed. Esther G. Chazon (Leiden: Brill, 2003), 133–149.

'Prayer and Liturgy', in *The Oxford Handbook of Jewish Daily Life in Roman Palestine*, ed. Catherine Hezser (Oxford: Oxford University Press, 2010), 545–565.

Reno Smits, Edmé, *Peter Abelard: Letters IX–XIV. An Edition with Introduction* (Doctoral thesis, Rijksuniversiteit te Groningen, 1981).

Renoux Athanase, ed. and trans. *Le codex arménien Jérusalem 121*, 2 vols., Patrologia Orientalis 35.1, 36.2 (Turnhout: Brepols, 1969–1971).

Riesenfeld, Harald, 'The Gospel Tradition and Its Beginnings', in *The Gospels Reconsidered: A Selection of Papers Read at the International Congress on the Four Gospels in 1957* (Oxford: Blackwell, 1960), 131–153.

The Gospels Tradition: Essays (Oxford: Blackwell, 1970).

Righetti, Mario *Manuale di storia liturgica. Volume 1: Introduzione generale*, 3rd ed. (Milan: Editrice Ancora, 1964).

Rives, James B., *Religion and Authority in Roman Carthage from Augustus to Constantine* (Oxford: Clarendon Press, 1995).

Robinson, John A. T., *Redating the New Testament* (London: SCM Press, 1986).

Roblin, Michel, *Le terroir de Paris aux époques gallo-romaine et franque: Peuplement et défrichement dans la Civitas des Parisii (Seine, Seine-et-Oise)*, 2nd ed. (Paris: A. et J. Picard, 1971).

Roetzer, Wunibald, *Des heiligen Augustinus Schriften als liturgiegeschichtliche Quelle* (Munich: Hueber, 1930).

Roman Missal: Renewed by Decree of the Most Holy Second Ecumenical Council of the Vatican, Promulgated by Authority of Pope Paul VI and Revised at the Direction of Pope John Paul II, English translation according to the third typical edition (London: Catholic Truth Society, 2011).

Romano, John F., 'The Fates of Liturgies: Towards a History of the First Roman Ordo', in *Antiphon* 11 (2007), 43–77.

'The Ceremonies of the Roman Pontiff: Rereading Benedict's Twelfth-Century Liturgical Script', in *Viator* 41 (2010), 133–150.

Liturgy and Society in Early Medieval Rome, Church, Faith and Culture in the Medieval West (Farnham: Ashgate, 2014), 229–248.

'Innocent II and the Liturgy', in *Pope Innocent II (1130–43): The World vs the City*, ed. John Doran and Damian J. Smith, Church, Faith and Culture in the Medieval West (Abingdon; New York: Routledge, 2016), 326–351.

'Baptizing the Romans', in *Acta ad archaeologiam et artium historiam pertinentia* 31 (2019), 43–62.

Rordorf, Willy, *Der Sonntag: Geschichte des Ruhe- und Gottesdiensttages im ältesten Christentum*, Abhandlungen zur Theologie des Alten und Neuen Testaments 43 (Zurich: Zwingli Verlag, 1962).

Sabbat und Sonntag in der Alten Kirche, Traditio Christiana 2 (Zurich: Theologischer Verlag, 1972).

Rose, Els, 'Liturgical Latin in the Missale Gothicum (Vat. Reg. Lat. 317). A reconsideration of Christine Mohrmann's approach', in *Sacris Erudiri* 42 (2003), 97–121.

'Liturgical Latin in the Bobbio Missal', in *The Bobbio Missal: Liturgy and Religious Culture in Merovingian Gaul*, ed. Yitzhak Hen and Rob Meens,

Cambridge Studies in Palaeography and Codicology (Cambridge: Cambridge University Press, 2004), 67–78.

Rouillard, Philippe, 'From Human Meal to Christian Eucharist', in *Living Bread, Saving Cup: Readings on the Eucharist*, ed. R. Kevin Seasoltz (Collegeville: Liturgical Press, 1987), 126–157.

Histoire de la penitence: Des origines à nos jours (Paris: Cerf, 1996).

Rouwhorst, Gerard, 'The Reception of the Jewish Sabbath in Early Christianity', in *Christian Feast and Festival: The Dynamics of Western Liturgy and Culture*, ed. Paul Post et al., Liturgia condenda 12 (Leuven: Peeters, 2001), 223–266.

'Didache 9–10: A Litmus Test for the Research on Early Christian Eucharist', in *Matthew and the Didache: Two Documents from the Same Jewish Christian Milieu?*, ed. Huub van de Sandt (Assen; Minneapolis: Royal Van Gorcum and Fortress Press, 2005), 143–156.

Roy, Neil J., 'The Roman Canon: *Deësis* in Euchological Form', in *Benedict XVI and the Sacred Liturgy*, ed. Neil J. Roy and Janet E. Rutherford (Dublin: Four Courts Press, 2010), 181–199.

'The Development of the Roman Ritual: A Prehistory and History of the *Rituale Romanum*', in *Antiphon* 15 (2011), 4–26.

Rubin, Miri, *Corpus Christi: The Eucharist in Late Medieval Culture* (Cambridge: Cambridge University Press, 1991).

Russo, Nicholas V., 'The Validity of the Anaphora of *Addai and* Mari: Critique of the Critiques', in *Issues in Eucharistic Praying in East and West: Essays in Liturgical and Theological Analysis*, ed. Maxwell E. Johnson (Collegeville: Liturgical Press, 2010), 21–62.

Salmon, Pierre, *Analecta liturgica: Extraits des manuscrits liturgiques de la Bibliothèque vaticane. Contribution à l'histoire de la prière chrétienne*, Studi e testi 273 (Vatican City: Biblioteca Apostolica Vaticana, 1974).

'L'Ordo missae dans dix manuscrits du Xe au XVe siècle', in *Analecta liturgica* (1974), 195–221.

'Libelli Precum du VIIIe au XIIe siècle', in *Analecta liturgica* (1974), 121–194.

Salzmann, Jörg C., *Lehren und Ermahnen: zur Geschichte des christlichen Wortgottesdienstes in den ersten drei Jahrhunderten*, Wissenschaftliche Untersuchungen zum Neuen Testament II/59 (Tübingen: Mohr Siebeck, 1994).

Sanders, E. P., *Paul: The Apostle's Life, Letters, and Thought* (Minneapolis: Fortress, 2015).

Sarason, Richard S., 'Communal Prayer at Qumran and Among the Rabbis: Certainties and Uncertainties', in *Liturgical Perspectives: Prayer and Poetry in Light of the Dead Sea Scrolls*, ed. Esther G. Chazon (Leiden: Brill, 2003), 151–172.

Saulnier, Stéphane, *Calendrical Variations in Second Temple Judaism: New Perspectives on the 'Date of the Last Supper' Debate*, Supplements to the Journal for the Study of Judaism 159 (Leiden: Brill, 2012).

Saxer, Victor, 'L'utilisation de la liturgie dans l'espace urbain et suburbain: l'exemple de Rome', in *Actes du XIe congrès international d'archéologie chrétienne (Lyon-Vienne-Grenoble-Genève et Aoste, 21–28 septembre 1986)*, Collection de l'École française de Rome 123 (Rome: École française de Rome, 1989), 917–1033.

'"Figura Corporis et Sanguinis Domini": Une formule eucharistique des premiers siècles chez Tertullian, Hippolyte et Ambroise', in *Rivista di archeologia cristiana* 48 (1971), 65–89 (= *Pères saints et culte chrétien dans l'Eglise des premiers siècles*, Collected Studies Series 448 [Aldershot: Variorum, 1994], no. IV).

Schmemann, Alexander, *Eucharist: Sacrament of the Kingdom*, trans. Paul Kachur (Crestwood: St Vladimir's Seminary Press, 1987).

Schmidt, Herman A. P., *Liturgie et langue vulgaire: Le problème de la langue liturgique chez les premiers Réformateurs et au Concile de Trente*, Analecta Gregoriana 53 (Rome: Apud Aedes Unversitatis Gregorianae, 1950).

Schmitz, Josef, *Gottesdienst im altchristlichen Mailand: Eine liturgiewissenschaftliche Untersuchung über Initiation und Meßfeier während des Jahres zur Zeit des Bischofs Ambrosius († 397)*, Theophaneia 25 (Köln: Hanstein, 1975).

'Canon romanus', in *Prex eucharistica. Volumen III: Studia. Pars prima: Ecclesia antiqua et occidentalis*, ed. Albert Gerhards, Heinzgerd Brakmann and Martin Klöckener, Spicilegium Friburgense 42 (Fribourg: Academic Press, 2005), 281–310.

Schneiders, Sandra M., 'The Foot Washing (John 13:1–20): An Experiment in Hermeneutics', in *Catholic Biblical Quarterly* 43 (1981), 76–92.

Schnitzler, Theodor, 'Die erste Fronleichnamsprozession: Datum und Charakter', in *Münchener Theologische Zeitschrift* 24 (1973), 352–362.

Schöllgen, Georg, 'Hausgemeinden, ΟΙΚΟΣ-Ekklesiologie und monarchischer Episkopat', in *Jahrbuch für Antike und Christentum* 31 (1988), 74–90.

'Probleme der frühchristlichen Sozialgeschichte: Einwände gegen Peter Lampes "Buch Die stadtrömischen Christen in den ersten beiden Jahrhunderten"', in *Jahrbuch für Antike und Christentum* 32 (1989), 23–40.

Schröter, Jens, *Nehmt – esst und trinkt: Das Abendmahl verstehen und feiern* (Stuttgart: Katholisches Bibelwerk, 2010).

Schuberth, Dietrich, *Kaiserliche Liturgie: Die Einbeziehung von Musikinstrumenten, insbesondere der Orgel, in den frühmittelalterlichen Gottesdienst*, Veröffentlichungen der Evangelischen Gesellschaft für Liturgieforschung 17 (Göttingen: Vandenhoeck & Ruprecht, 1968).

Schulz, Hans-Joachim, 'Liturgie, Tagzeiten und Kirchenjahr des byzantinischen Ritus', in *Handbuch der Ostkirchenkunde Bd. II*, ed. Wilhelm Nyssen, Hans-Joachim Schulz and Paul Wiertz (Düsseldorf: Patmos, 1989), 30–100.

Die apostolische Herkunft der Evangelien: Zum Ursprung der Evangelienform in der urgemeindlichen Paschafeier, Quaestiones Disputatae 145, 3rd ed. (Freiburg: Herder, 1997).

Schürmann, Heinz, *Eine quellenkritische Untersuchung des lukanischen Abendmahlsberichtes, Lk 22, 7–38. Bd.1: Der Paschamahlbericht, Lk 22, (7–14) 15–18*, Neutestamentliche Abhandlungen 19/5, 2nd ed. (Münster: Aschendorff, 1968).

Schwiebert, Jonathan, *Knowledge and the Coming Kingdom: The Didache's Meal Ritual and Its Place in Early Christianity* (London: T&T Clark, 2008).

Senn, Frank C., *The People's Work: A Social History of the Liturgy* (Minneapolis: Fortress Press, 2006).

Serra, Dominic E., 'The Kiss of Peace: A Suggestion from Ritual Structure', in *Ecclesia Orans* 14 (1997), 79–94.

'The Greeting of Peace in the Revised Sacramentary: A New Pastoral Option', in *Liturgy for the New Millennium: A Commentary on the Revised Sacramentary*, ed. Mark R. Francis and Keith F. Pecklers (Collegeville: Liturgical Press, 2000), 97–110.

Sessa, Kristina, '*Domus Ecclesiae*: Rethinking a Category of Ante-Pacem Christian Space', in *Journal of Theological Studies* N.S. 60 (2009), 90–108.

Shepard, Jonathan, 'Western Approaches (900–1025)', in *The Cambridge History of the Byzantine Empire c.500–1492*, ed. Jonathan Shepard (Cambridge: Cambridge University Press, 2008), 537–559.

Shepherd, Massey H., 'The Liturgical Reform of Damasus I', in *Kyriakon: Festschrift Johannes Quasten*, ed. Patrick Granfield and Josef A. Jungmann, 2 vols. (Münster: Aschendorff, 1970), vol. II, 847–863.

Signori, Gabriela, 'Umstrittene Stühle: Spätmittelalterliches Kirchengestühl als soziales, politisches und religiöses Kommunikationsmedium', in *Zeitschrift für Historische Forschung* 29 (2002), 189–213.

Räume, Gesten, Andachtsformen: Geschlecht, Konflikt und religiöse Kultur im europäischen Mittelalter (Ostfildern: Jan Thorbecke Verlag, 2005).

'Einheit in der Vielfalt? Annäherungen an den "vorreformatorischen" Kirchenraum', in *Konfessionen im Kirchenraum: Dimensionen des Sakralraums in der frühen Neuzeit*, ed. Susanne Wegmann and Gabriele Wimböck, Studien zur Kunstgeschichte des Mittelalters und der frühen Neuzeit 3 (Korb: Didymos-Verlag, 2007), 215–234.

Simmons, Thomas Frederick, ed., *The Lay Folks Mass Book or the Manner of Hearing Mass: With Rubrics and Devotions for the People in Four Texts, and Offices in English According to the Use of York from Manuscripts of the Xth to the XVth century*, Early English Text Society 71 (London: Trübner, 1879).

Simperl, Matthias, 'Beobachtungen und Überlegungen zur frühen Redaktionsgeschichte des Liber pontificalis', in *Das Buch der Päpste – Liber pontificalis: Ein Schlüsseldokument europäischer Geschichte*, Römische Quartalschrift. Supplementband 67 (Freiburg i. Br.: Herder, 2020), 52–77.

'Eine Hinführung zum Umgang mit den Editionen des *Liber pontificalis*', in *Das Buch der Päpste* (2020), 458–481.

Smith, Barry D., 'The Chronology of the Last Supper', in *Westminster Theological Journal* 53 (1991), 29–45.

Smyth, Matthieu, *La liturgie oubliée: La prière eucharistique en Gaule antique et dans l'Occident non romain*, Patrimoines – Christianisme (Paris: Cerf, 2003).

'*Ante Altaria*': Les rites antiques de la messe dominicale en Gaule, en Espagne et en Italie du Nord* (Paris: Cerf, 2007).

'The Anaphora of the so-called "Apostolic Tradition" and the Roman Eucharistic Prayer', in *Issues in Eucharistic Praying in East and West: Essays in Liturgical and Theological Analysis*, ed. Maxwell E. Johnson (Collegeville: Liturgical Press, 2010), 71–97.

Soards, Marion L., *The Passion according to Luke: The Special Material of Luke 22*, Journal for the Study of the New Testament. Supplement Series 14 (Sheffield: JSOT Press, 1987).

Sodi, Manlio, ed., *Il 'Pontificalis liber' di Agostino Patrizi Piccolomini e Giovanni Burcardo (1485)*, Edizione anastatica, Monumenta Studia Instrumenta Liturgica 43 (Vatican City: Libreria Editrice Vaticana, 2006).

Souter, Alexander, *A Study of Ambrosiaster*, Texts and Studies 7.4 (Cambridge: Cambridge University Press, 1905).

Spinks, Bryan D., *Addai and Mari – The Anaphora of the Apostles: A Text for Students*, Grove Liturgical Study 24 (Bramcote: Grove Books, 1980).

'A Complete Anaphora? A Note on Strasbourg Gr. 254', in *Heythrop Journal* 35 (1984), 51–59.

The Sanctus in the Eucharistic Prayer (Cambridge: Cambridge University Press, 1991).

Do This in Remembrance of Me: The Eucharist from the Early Church to the Present Day, SCM Studies in Worship and Liturgy (London: SCM Press, 2013).

Stabenow, Jörg, 'Introduzione', in *Lo spazio e il culto: Relazioni tra edificio ecclesiale e uso liturgico dal XV al XVI secolo*, ed. Jörg Stabenow (Venice: Marsilio, 2006), 9–23.

'Auf dem Weg zum "theatrum sacrum": Bedeutungen der theatralen Analogie im Kirchenraum der Gegenreformation in Italien', in *Konfessionen im Kirchenraum: Dimensionen des Sakralraums in der frühen Neuzeit*, ed. Susanne Wegmann and Gabriele Wimböck, Studien zur Kunstgeschichte des Mittelalters und der frühen Neuzeit 3 (Korb: Didymos-Verlag, 2007), 115–136.

Standhartinger, Angela, 'Meals in *Joseph and Aseneth*', in *T&T Clark Handbook to Early Christian Meals in the Greco-Roman World*, ed., Soham Al-Suadi and Peter-Ben Smit, eds., (London; New York: Bloomsbury T&T Clark, 2019), 211–224.

Steck, Wolfgang, *Der Liturgiker Amalarius: Eine quellenkritische Untersuchung zu Leben und Werk eines Theologen der Karolingerzeit*, Münchener theologische Studien. Historische Abteilung 35 (St. Ottilien: EOS-Verlag, 2000).

Steimer, Bruno, *Vertex traditionis: Die Gattung der altchristlichen Kirchenordnungen*, Beihefte zur Zeitschrift für die neutestamentliche Wissenschaft 63 (Berlin; New York: de Gruyter, 1992).

'Apostolic Constitutions', in *Dictionary of Early Christian Literature*, ed. Siegmar Döpp and Wilhelm Geerlings (New York: Herder and Herder, 2000), 44.

Stevenson, Kenneth, *Eucharist and Offering* (New York: Pueblo, 1986).

Stroumsa, Guy G., *The End of Sacrifice: Religious Transformations in Late Antiquity*, trans. Susan Emanuel (Chicago: University of Chicago Press, 2009).

Stuiber, Alfred, 'Psalmenlesung oder Zwischengesang', in *Pietas: Festschrift für Bernhard Kötting*, ed. Ernst Dassmann and Karl Suso Frank, Jahrbuch für Antike und Christentum. Ergänzungsband 8 (Münster: Aschendorff, 1990), 393–398.

Swanson, Robert N., *Religion and Devotion in Europe, c. 1215–c. 1515*, Cambridge Medieval Textbooks (Cambridge: Cambridge University Press, 1995), 10–41.

Taft, Robert F., 'Some Notes on the Bema in the East and West Syrian Traditions', in *Orientalia Christiana Periodica* 34 (1968), 326–359.

'The Inclination Prayer Before Communion in the Byzantine Liturgy of St John Chrysostom: A Study in Comparative Liturgy', in *Ecclesia Orans* 3 (1986), 29–60.

'The Dialogue before the Anaphora in the Byzantine Eucharistic Liturgy. II: The *Sursum corda*', in *Orientalia Christiana Periodica* 54 (1988), 47–77.

'The Authenticity of the Chrysostom Anaphora Revisited: Determining the Authorship of Liturgical Texts by Computer', in *Orientalia Christiana Periodica* 56 (1990), 5–51.

'The Interpolation of the Sanctus into the Anaphora: When and Where? A Review of the Dossier: Part I', in *Orientalia Christiana Periodica* 57 (1991), 281–308.

The Byzantine Rite: A Short History, American Essays in Liturgy (Collegeville: Liturgical Press, 1992).

The Liturgy of the Hours in East and West: The Origins of the Divine Office and Its Meaning for Today, 2nd rev. ed. (Collegeville: Liturgical Press, 1993).

'The Frequency of the Celebration of the Eucharist throughout History', in *Between Memory and Hope: Readings on the Liturgical Year*, ed. Maxwell E. Johnson (Collegeville: Liturgical Press, 2000), 77–96.

A History of the Liturgy of St John Chrysostom, Vol. V: The Precommunion Rites, Orientalia Christiana Analecta 261 (Rome: Pontifical Oriental Institute 2000).

'Ex Oriente Lux? Some Reflections on Eucharistic Concelebration', in *Beyond East & West: Problems in Liturgical Understanding*, 2nd revised and enlarged edition (Rome: Edizioni Orientalia Christiana, 2001), 111–132 (revised version of an article originally published in *Worship* 54 [1980] 308–324).

'Eucharistic Concelebration Revisited: Problems of History, Practice, and Theology in East and West', in *Orientalia Christiana Periodica* 76 (2010), 277–313 and 77 (2011), 25–80.

Talley, Thomas J., *The Origins of the Liturgical Year* (New York: Pueblo, 1986).

Tambiah, Stanley J., 'A Performative Approach to Ritual', in *Proceedings of the British Academy* 65 (1979), 113–169.

Tanner, Norman, *The Church in the Later Middle Ages* (London; New York: I. B. Tauris, 2008).

Taruskin, Richard, *Music from the Earliest Notations to the Sixteenth Century*, The Oxford History of Western Music 1 (Oxford: Oxford University Press, 2006).

Taylor Jones, Claire, *Ruling the Spirit: Women, Liturgy, and Dominican Reform in Late Medieval Germany*, The Middle Ages Series (Philadelphia: University of Pennsylvania Press, 2018).

The Greek New Testament, ed. Barbara Aland et al., 4th rev. ed. (Stuttgart: Deutsche Bibelgesellschaft, 2013).

Theißen, Gerd, 'Sakralmahl und sakramentales Geschehen: Abstufungen in der Ritualdynamik des Abendmahls', in *Herrenmahl und Gruppenidentität*, ed. Martin Ebner, Quaestiones disputatae 221 (Freiburg: Herder, 2007), 166–186.

Theißen, Gerd, and Annette Merz, *The Historical Jesus: A Comprehensive Guide*, trans. John Bowden (Minneapolis: Fortress Press, 1998).

Thompson, Augustine, *Cities of God: The Religion of the Italian Communes 1125–1325* (University Park: The Pennsylvania State University Press, 2005).

Francis of Assisi: A New Biography (Ithaca: Cornell University Press, 2012).

Thomson, Francis J., 'SS. Cyril and Methodius and a Mythical Western Heresy: Trilinguism. A Contribution to the Study of Patristic and Mediaeval Theories of Sacred Languages', in *Analecta Bollandiana* 110 (1992), 67–122.

Thraede, Klaus, 'Noch einmal: Plinius d.J. und die Christen', in *Zeitschrift für die Neutestamentliche Wissenschaft* 95 (2004), 102–128.

Thümmel, Hans Georg, 'Versammlungsraum, Kirche, Tempel', in *Gemeinde ohne Tempel/Community Without Temple: Zur Substituierung und Transformation des Jerusalemer Tempels und seines Kults im Alten Testament, antiken Judentum und frühen Christentum*, ed. Beate Ego, Armin Lange and Peter Pilhofer, Wissenschaftliche Untersuchungen zum Neuen Testament 118 (Tübingen: Mohr Siebeck, 1999), 489–504.

Tichý, Radek, *Proclamation de l'Évangile dans la messe en occident: Ritualité, histoire, comparaison, théologie*, Studia Anselmiana 168 (Rome: Pontificio Ateneo S. Anselmo, 2016).

Tirot, Paul, 'Un "Ordo Missae" monastique: Cluny, Cîteaux, La Charteuse', in *Ephemerides Liturgicae* 95 (1981), 44–120 and 220–251 (also published separately in the series Biblioteca Ephemerides Liturgiae. Subsidia 21 [Rome: C.L.V. – Edizioni Liturgiche, 1981]).

'Histoire des prières d'offertoire du VIIe au XVIe siècle', in *Ephemerides Liturgicae* 98 (1984), 148–197 and 323–391 (also published separately in the series Biblioteca Ephemerides Liturgiae. Subsidia 34 [Rome: C.L.V. – Edizioni Liturgiche, 1985]).

Torevell, David, *Losing the Sacred: Ritual, Modernity and Liturgical Reform* (Edinburgh: T&T Clark, 2000).

Torrell, Jean-Pierre, *Saint Thomas Aquinas, Vol. I: The Person and His Work*, trans. Robert Royal (Washington, DC: The Catholic University of America Press, 1996).

Turner, Victor, 'Ritual, Tribal and Catholic', in *Worship* 50 (1976), 504–526.

Van Ausdall, Kristen, 'Art and Eucharist in the Late Middle Ages', in *A Companion to the Eucharist in the Middle Ages*, ed. Ian C. Levy, Gary

Macy and Kristen van Ausdall, Brill's Companions to the Christian Tradition 26 (Leiden: Brill, 2012), 541–617.

Van Bühren, Ralf, 'Kirchenbau in Renaissance und Barock: Liturgiereformen und ihre Folgen für Raumordnung, liturgische Disposition und Bildausstattung nach dem Trienter Konzil', in *Operation am lebenden Objekt: Roms Liturgiereformen von Trient bis zum Vaticanum II*, ed. Stefan Heid (Berlin: be.bra wissenschaft, 2014), 93–119.

Van de Sandt, Huub, 'Why Does the Didache Conceive of the Eucharist as a Holy Meal?', in *Vigiliae Christianae* 65 (2011), 1–20.

Van der Watt, Jan, 'The Meaning of Jesus Washing the Feet of His Disciples (John 13)', in *Neotestamentica* 51 (2017), 25–39.

Van Dijk, O. F. M., Stephen J. P., ed., *Sources of the Modern Roman Liturgy: The Ordinals by Haymo of Faversham and Related Documents, 1243–1307*, 2 vols., Studia et documenta franciscana 1–2 (Leiden: Brill, 1963).

Van Dijk, O. F. M., Stephen J. P. and Joan Hazelden Walker, *The Origins of the Modern Roman Liturgy: The Liturgy of the Papal Court and the Franciscan Order in the Thirteenth Century* (Westminster; London: The Newman Press; Darton, Longman & Todd, 1960).

Van Dijk, O. F. M., Stephen J. P. and Joan Hazelden Walker, eds., *The Ordinal of the Papal Court from Innocent III to Boniface VIII and Related Documents*, Spicilegium Friburgense 22 (Fribourg: University Press, 1975).

Van Engen, John, 'The Christian Middle Ages as an Historiographical Problem', in *The American Historical Review* 91 (1986), 519–552.

Van Gennep, Arnold, *The Rites of Passage*, trans. Monika B. Vizedom and Gabrielle L. Caffee (Chicago: University of Chicago Press, 1960).

Van Rhijn, Carine, 'The Local Church, Priests' Handbooks and Pastoral Care in the Carolingian Period', in *Chiese locali e chiese regionali nell'alto medioevo: Spoleto, 4–9 aprile 20013*, Settimane di studio del Centro italiano di studi sull'alto medioevo 61, 2 vols. (Spoleto: Centro Italiano di studi sull'alto medioevo, 2014), 689–710.

'"Et hoc considerat episcopus, ut ipsi presbyteri non sint idiothae": Carolingian Local *Correctio* and an Unknown Priests' Exam from the Early Ninth Century', in *Religious Franks: Religion and Power in the Frankish Kingdoms. Studies in Honour of Mayke de Jong*, ed. Rob Meens et al. (Manchester: Manchester University Press, 2016), 162–180.

'Carolingian Rural Priests as Local (Religious) Experts', in *Gott handhaben: Religiöses Wissen im Konflikt um Mythisierung und Rationalisierung*, ed. Steffen Patzold and Florian Bock (Berlin: Walter de Gruyter, 2016), 131–146.

'Manuscripts for Local Priests and the Carolingian Reforms', in *Men in the Middle: Local Priests in Early Medieval Europe*, ed. Carine van Rhijn and Steffen Patzold, Ergänzungsbände zum Reallexikon der Germanischen Altertumskunde 93 (Berlin: Walter de Gruyter, 2016), 177–198.

Van Slyke, Daniel G., 'The Study of Early Christian Worship', in *T&T Clark Companion to Liturgy*, ed. Alcuin Reid (London: Bloomsbury T&T Clark, 2016), 43–71.

Vanhoye, Albert, *Old Testament Priests and the New Priest: According to the New Testament*, trans. J. Bernard Orchard (Petersham: St Bede's, 1986).

Verheijen, Luc, ed., *La règle de Saint Augustin*, 2 vols. (Paris: Études Augustiniennes, 1967).

Voelker, Evelyn C., *Charles Borromeo's* Instructiones Fabricae et Supellectilis Ecclesiasticae, *1577: A Translation with Commentary and Analysis* (PhD dissertation, Syracuse University, 1977).

Vogel, Cyrille, 'Les échanges liturgiques entre Rome et les pays francs jusqu'à l'époque de Charlemagne', in *Le chiese nei regni dell'Europa occidentale e i loro rapporti con Roma sino all'800: 7–13 aprile 1959*, Settimane di studio del centro italiano di studi sull'alto Medioevo 7, 2 vols. (Spoleto: Presso la sede del Centro, 1960), 185–295.

'L'orientation vers l'Est du célébrant et des fidèles pendant la célébration eucharistique', in *L'Orient syrien* 9 (1964), 3–37.

'La réforme cultuelle sous Pépin le Bref et sous Charlemagne', in Erna Patzelt and Cyrille Vogel, *Die karolingische Renaissance: Beiträge zur Geschichte der Kultur des frühen Mittelalters*, 2nd ed. (Graz: Akademische Druck- u. Verlagsanstalt, 1965), 172–242.

'Les motifs de la romanisation du culte sous Pépin le Bref (751–768) et Charlemagne (774–814)', in *Culto cristiano, politica imperiale carolingia: 9–12 ottobre 1977*, Convegni del Centro di studi sulla spiritualità medievale 18 (Todi: Accademia tudertina, 1979), 13–41.

Medieval Liturgy: An Introduction to the Sources, rev. and trans. William G. Storey and Niels Krogh Rasmussen (Washington, DC: The Pastoral Press, 1981).

'La vie quotidienne du moine en occident à l'époque de la floraison des messe privées', in *Liturgie, spiritualité, cultures: Conférences Saint-Serge, XXIXe semaine d'études liturgiques. Paris, 29 juin – 2 juillet 1982*, ed. Achille M. Triacca et al., Bibliotheca Ephemerides Liturgicae: Subsidia 29 (Rome: C.L.V. – Edizioni Liturgiche, 1983), 341–360.

Vogel, Cyrille, and Reinhard Elze, eds., *Le Pontifical romano-germanique du dixième siècle*, 3 vols., Studi e testi 226, 227, 269 (Vatican City: Biblioteca Apostolica Vaticana, 1963–1972).

Vogüé, Adalbert de, 'Problems of the Monastic Conventual Mass', in *Downside Review* 87 (1969), 327–338.

'Eucharist and Monastic Life', in *Worship* 59 (1985), 498–510.

Von der Osten-Sacken, Peter, 'Von den jüdischen Wurzeln des christlichen Gottesdienstes', in *Liturgie als Theologie*, ed. Walter Homolka (Berlin: Frank & Timme, 2005), 130–153.

Vones, Ludwig, 'The Substitution of the Hispanic Liturgy by the Roman Rite in the Kingdoms of the Iberian Peninsula', in *Hispania Vetus: Musical-Liturgical Manuscripts: From Visigothic Origins to the Franco-Roman Transition, 9th–12th Centuries*, ed. Susana Zapke (Bilbao: Fundación BBVA, 2007), 43–59.

Wagner, Peter, *Einführung in die gregorianischen Melodien: Ein Handbuch der Choralwissenschaft. Dritter Teil: Gregorianische Formenlehre: Eine choralische Stilkunde* (Leipzig: Breitkopf & Härtel, 1925).

Walker Bynum, Caroline, *Christian Materiality: An Essay on Religion in Late Medieval Europe* (New York: Zone Books, 2011).

Walker, Rose, *Views of Transition: Liturgy and Illumination in Medieval Spain*, The British Library Studies in Medieval Culture (London; Toronto: The British Library and University of Toronto Press, 1998).

Wallace-Hadrill, David S., 'Eusebius and the Institution Narrative in the Eastern Liturgies', in *Journal of Theological Studies* N.S. 4 (1953), 41–42.

Wallraff, Martin, *Christus verus sol: Sonnenverehrung und Christentum in der Spätantike*, Jahrbuch für Antike und Christentum. Ergänzungsband 32 (Münster: Aschendorff, 2001).

Walter, Karl, ed. *Ioannis Philoponi Libellus de paschate*, Commentationes philologae Ienenses 6,2 (Leipzig: Teunber, 1899), 197–229.

Ward Perkins, John B., 'The Shrine of St. Peter and Its Twelve Spiral Columns', in *Studies in Roman and Early Christian Architecture* (London: Pindar Press, 1994), 469–488.

Ward, Anthony, and Cuthbert Johnson, eds., *The Prefaces of the Roman Missal: A Source Compendium with Concordance and Indices* (Rome: C.L.V. – Edizioni liturgiche, 1989).

Warner, George F., ed., *The Stowe Missal: Ms. D. II. 3 in the Library of the Royal Irish Academy, Dublin*, 2 vols., Henry Bradshaw Society 32 (London: Harrison and Sons, 1915).

Warren, Frederick B., ed., *The Antiphonary of Bangor: An Early Irish Manuscript in the Ambrosian Library at Milan*, 2 vols., Henry Bradshaw Society 10 (London: Harrison and Sons, 1893–1895).

Watt, James, 'The Papacy', in *The New Cambridge Medieval History: Volume 5, c.1198–c.1300*, ed. David Abulafia (Cambridge: Cambridge University Press, 1999), 107–163.

Wegman, Herman, *Christian Worship in East and West: A Study Guide to Liturgical History*, trans. Gordon W. Lathrop (New York: Pueblo Publishing Company, 1985).

Wehr, Lothar, *Arznei der Unsterblichkeit: Die Eucharistie bei Ignatius von Antiochen und im Johannesevangelium*, Neutestamentliche Abhandlungen, N.F. 18 (Münster: Aschendorff, 1987).

Welch, Anna, *Liturgy, Books and Franciscan Identity in Medieval Umbria*, Medieval Franciscans 12 (Leiden: Brill, 2015).

Wellesz, Egon, *A History of Byzantine Music and Hymnography*, 2nd ed. revised and enlarged (Oxford: Clarendon Press, 1961).

West Haddan, Arthur, and William Stubbs, eds., *Councils and Ecclesiastical Documents relating to Great Britain and Ireland*, vol. III (Oxford: Clarendon Press, 1871).

Wickham, Chris, *The Inheritance of Rome: A History of Europe from 400 to 1000* (London: Penguin Books, 2010).

Wickham Legg, John, ed., *Tracts on the Mass*, Henry Bradshaw Society 27 (London: Harrison, 1904).

Wilckens, Ulrich *Theologie des Neuen Testaments. Band 1: Geschichte der urchristlichen Theologie, Teilband 2: Jesu Tod und Auferstehung und die Entstehung der Kirche aus Juden und Heiden* (Neukirchen-Vluyn: Neukirchener Verlag, 2003).

Wilken, Robert Louis, 'Interpreting Job Allegorically: The Moralia of Gregory the Great', in *Pro Ecclesia* 10 (2001), 213–230.

Wilkinson, John, 'Orientation, Jewish and Christian', in *Palestine Exploration Quarterly* 116 (1984), 16–30.

Egeria's Travels, newly translated with supporting documents and notes, 3rd ed. (Warminster: Aris & Phillips, 1999).

Willis, Geoffrey G. Willis, *St Augustine's Lectionary*, Alcuin Club Collections 44 (London: SPCK, 1962).

'The Connection of the Prayers of the Roman Canon', in *Essays in Early Roman Liturgy*, Alcuin Club Collections 46 (London: SPCK, 1964), 121–133.

'The Variable Prayers of the Roman Mass', in *Further Essays in Early Roman Liturgy*, Alcuin Club Collections 50 (London: SPCK, 1968), 91–129.

'St Gregory the Great and the Lord's Prayer in the Roman Mass', in *Further Essays in Early Roman Liturgy* (1968), 175–188.

'The New Eucharistic Prayers: Some Comments', in *A Voice for All Time: Essays on the Liturgy of the Catholic Church since the Second Vatican Council*, ed. Christopher Francis and Martin Lynch (Bristol: Association for Latin Liturgy, 1994), 64–97 (originally published in *Heythrop Journal* 12 [1971], 5–28).

A History of Early Roman Liturgy to the Death of Pope Gregory the Great, Henry Bradshaw Society, Subsidia 1 (London: Boydell Press, 1994).

Wilmart, André, 'Le Comes de Murbach', in *Revue Bénédictine* 30 (1913), 25–69.

Wilmart, André, ed., *Analecta Reginensia: Extraits des manuscrits latins de la reine Christine conservés au Vatican*, Studi e testi 59 (Vatican City: Biblioteca Apostolica Vaticana, 1933).

Wilson, Stephen G., *Related Strangers: Jews and Christians 70–170 CE* (Minneapolis: Fortress Press, 1995).

Witczak, Michael G., 'St. Gall Mass Orders (I): MS. Sangallensis 338: Searching for the Origins of the "Rheinish Mass Order"', in *Ecclesia Orans* 16 (1999), 393–410.

'St. Gall Mass Orders (II): MS. Sangallensis 339', in *Ecclesia Orans* 22 (2005), 47–62.

'St. Gall Mass Orders (III): MS. Sangallensis 340', in *Ecclesia Orans* 24 (2007), 243–261.

Wormald, Francis, 'A Medieval Processional and Its Diagrams', in *Kunsthistorische Forschungen: Otto Pächt zu seinem 70. Geburtstag*, ed. Artur Rosenauer and Gerold Weber (Salzburg: Residenz Verlag, 1972), 129–134.

Wright, N. T., *Jesus and the Victory of God* (Minneapolis: Fortress Press, 1996).

Wright, Roger, *Late Latin and Early Romance in Spain and Carolingian France*, ARCA: Classical and medieval texts, papers, and monograph 8 (Liverpool: Francis Cairns, 1982).

A Sociophilological Study of Late Latin, Utrecht Studies in Medieval Literacy 10 (Turnhout: Brepols, 2002).

Yao, Alain-Pierre, *Les 'apologies' de l'Ordo Missae de la Liturgie Romaine: Sources – Histoire – Théologie*, Ecclesia orans. Studi e ricerche 3 (Naples: Editrice Domenicana Italiana, 2019).

Yarnold, Edward J., 'The Liturgy of the Faithful in the Fourth and Early Fifth Centuries', in *The Study of Liturgy*, ed. Cheslyn Jones et al., rev. ed. (London: SPCK, 1992), 230–244.

The Awe-Inspiring Rites of Initiation: The Origins of the R.C.I.A., 2nd ed. (Collegeville: Liturgical Press, 1994).

'Anaphoras without Institution Narratives?', in *Studia Patristica* 30 (1997), 395–410.

Yasin, Ann Marie, *Saints and Church Spaces in the Late Antique Mediterranean: Architecture, Cult, and Community*, Greek Culture in the Roman World (Cambridge: Cambridge University Press, 2009).

Yuval, Israel Jacob, 'Easter and Passover As Early Jewish-Christian Dialogue', in *Passover and Easter: Origin and History to Modern Times*, ed. Paul F. Bradshaw and Lawrence A. Hoffman (Notre Dame: University of Notre Dame Press, 2000), 98–124.

Two Nations in Your Womb: Perceptions of Jews and Christians in Late Antiquity and the Middle Ages, trans. Barbara Harshav and Jonathan Chipman (Berkeley: University of California Press, 2006).

Zawilla, Ronald, *The Biblical Sources of the Historiae Corporis Christi Attributed to Thomas Aquinas: A Theological Study to Determine Their Authenticity* (PhD dissertation, University of Toronto, 1985).

Zetterholm, Magnus, *Approaches to Paul: A Student's Guide to Recent Scholarship* (Minneapolis: Fortress, 2009).

Zheltov, Michael, 'The Anaphora and the Thanksgiving Prayer from the Barcelona Papyrus: An Underestimated Testimony to the Anaphoral History in the Fourth Century', in *Vigiliae Christianae* 62 (2008), 467–504.

Zieman, Katherine, *Singing the New Song: Literacy and Liturgy in Late Medieval England* (Philadelphia: University of Pennsylvania Press, 2008).

Index

Printed by Printforce, United Kingdom